Assessing Learners with Special Needs

An Applied Approach

SIXTH EDITION

Assessing Learners with Special Needs

An Applied Approach

Terry Overton
University of Texas–Brownsville

Merrill
is an imprint of

Upper Saddle River, New Jersey
Columbus, Ohio

Vice President and Executive Publisher: Jeffery W. Johnston
Executive Editor: Ann Castel Davis
Editorial Assistant: Penny Burleson
Senior Managing Editor: Pamela D. Bennett
Production Editor: Sheryl Glicker Langner
Production Coordination: Roxanne Klaas, S4Carlisle
Design Coordinator: Diane C. Lorenzo
Photo Coordinator: Monica Merkel
Cover Designer: Diane Y. Ernsberger
Cover art: Superstock
Production Manager: Laura Messerly
Director of Marketing: Quinn Perkson
Marketing Manager: Erica DeLuca
Marketing Coordinator: Brian Mounts

This book was set in Bookman by S4Carlisle. It was printed and bound by Edwards Brothers, Inc. The cover was printed by Phoenix Color Corp.

Chapter Opening Photo Credits: Scott Cunningham/Merrill, pp. 2, 42, 358; Lori Whitley/Merrill, p. 102; Linda Kauffman/Merrill, p. 164; Copyright © 2008 by The Riverside Publishing Company. Photograph as seen on page 14 of The Riverside Publishing Company 2008 Clinical and Special Needs Catalog reproduced with permission of the publisher. All rights reserved. p. 130; Barbara Schwartz/Merrill, p. 200; Patrick White/Merrill, p. 250; David Young–Wolff/Photo Edit Inc., p. 316; Anne Vega/Merrill, p. 404; Maria B. Vonada/Merrill, p. 453.

Pearson Education Ltd., London
Pearson Education Singapore, Pte. Ltd.
Pearson Education Canada, Inc.
Pearson Education—Japan

Pearson Education Australia PtY., Limited
Pearson Education North Asia, Ltd., Hong Kong
Pearson Educación de Mexico, S.A. de C.V.
Pearson Education Malaysia, Pte. Ltd.
Pearson Education Upper Saddle River, New Jersey

Merrill
is an imprint of

For my Family

And a special thanks to the wonderful people at the University of Texas–Brownsville

The process of monitoring and assessing students within the general education environment who have academic and behavioral challenges continues to change as a result of changes in federal regulations and discovery of evidence-based practices. The sixth edition of *Assessing Learners with Special Needs: An Applied Approach* was written to reflect these changes in the assessment process.

Like earlier editions, the primary focus of this text is to provide students with a practical approach for learning about the complex procedures of the assessment process. The sixth edition incorporates the latest revision of IDEA, the Individuals with Disabilities Education Improvement Act, or IDEA 2004 and the regulations that govern public schools. This edition includes the following changes:

- An emphasis on progress monitoring, including progress monitoring applied to the acquisition of knowledge and skills presented in this text
- Changes within the assessment process according to the regulations of IDEA 2004
- Increased number of case studies throughout the text and inclusion of exercises in the text
- Expanded chapter on special considerations including assessment of Autism Spectrum Disorders
- Increased emphasis and coverage of curriculum-based assessment
- Increased consideration of students from culturally and linguistically diverse backgrounds in the assessment process

This text presents complex concepts in a step-by-step manner and provides students with practice exercises for each step. Students also have portions of assessment instruments, protocols, and scoring tables provided as part of their practice exercises. Students will participate in the educational decision-making process using data from classroom observations, curriculum-based assessment, functional behavioral assessment, and data from norm-referenced assessment.

This text is divided into four parts. Part 1, "Introduction to Assessment," introduces students to the basic concepts in assessment and types of assessment. This part also presents the legal issues of assessment in IDEA 2004 and ethical concerns of assessment.

Part 2, "Technical Prerequisites of Understanding Assessment," addresses the topics of descriptive statistics, reliability, and validity.

Part 3, "Assessing Students," presents the mechanics of both informal and formal assessment. Students practice curriculum-based assessment, behavioral assessment, and norm-referenced assessment.

Part 4, "Interpretation of Assessment Results," discusses interpretation of data for classroom interventions, eligibility decisions, and educational planning. Numerous case studies are included in this section.

SPECIAL FEATURES OF THE SIXTH EDITION

Each chapter contains the following special features to help facilitate a better understanding of chapter content.

Key Terms and Chapter Focus: Each chapter begins with a listing of Key Terms and a Chapter Focus. These Key Terms are defined in the margin at the point in the chapter where they are presented. The Chapter Focus serves as an advance organizer for readers to better prepare them for the concepts presented in the chapter.

Check Your Understanding: These exercises provide an opportunity for readers to monitor their progress in the learning and assessment process. These activities are included in the text with answers online on the Companion Website.

Monitor Your Progress: At the end of each Part of the text, students will monitor their progress as they master the material presented. Students first complete a baseline assessment and learn how to plot their scores against an aim line.

More Practice: These activities, available on the Companion Website, provide the reader with additional opportunities to analyze and apply new knowledge to different circumstances and situations.

Read More About: Occasionally there are assessment topics on which readers may want more information. In these circumstances, additional articles and topical information are available on the Companion Website.

Chapter Summary: The summary provides an overview of the important points covered in the chapter.

Think Ahead Exercises: These end-of-chapter exercises enable readers to gauge their understanding of the chapter as a whole. Answers to these exercises are available in the Appendix or on the Companion Website.

SUPPLEMENTS

The sixth edition has an enhanced supplement support package, including a Companion Website, an Instructor's Manual with Test Items, PowerPoint slides, and a computerized test bank and assessment software (TestGen®). All of these items were developed exclusively for this text by the author.

COMPANION WEBSITE

Located at *http://www.prenhall.com/overton*, the Companion Website for this text includes a wealth of resources for both professors and students. The Syllabus Manager™ enables professors to create and maintain the class syllabus online while also allowing the student access to the syllabus at any time from any computer on the Internet. The student portion of the website helps students gauge their understanding of chapter content through the use of online chapter reviews, resources for assessment, Web links, additional activities, case studies, and interactive self-assessments.

ONLINE INSTRUCTOR'S MANUAL WITH TEST ITEMS

The Instructor's Manual (also available online at the Instructor Resource Center, described below) is organized by chapter and contains chapter lecture outlines, classroom activities, and test items (including multiple choice, true/false, short answer, and essay questions).

ONLINE POWERPOINT SLIDES

The transparencies—available in PowerPoint slide format at the Instructor Resources Center, described below, highlight key concepts, summarize content, and illustrate figures and charts from the text.

INSTRUCTOR RESOURCE CENTER

The Instructor Resource Center at *www.prenhall.com* has a variety of print and media resources available in downloadable, digital format—all in one location. As a registered faculty member, you can access and download pass-code protected resource files, course management content, and other premium online content directly to your computer.

Digital resources available for *Assessing Learners with Special Needs: An Applied Approach*, Sixth Edition, include:

- Text-specific PowerPoint® Lectures
- An online version of the Instructor's Manual

To access these items online, go to *www.prenhall.com* and click on the **Instructor Support** button and then go to the **Download Supplements** section. Here you will be able to log in or complete a one-time registration for a user name and password. If you have any questions regarding this process or the materials available online, please contact your local Pearson sales representative.

ACKNOWLEDGMENTS

I would like to express my sincere gratitude to the many students and colleagues at the University of Texas–Brownsville for your support during this project. A special thanks to Dr. Roman Garcia de Alba, Dr. Steve Chamberlain, and Dr. Mary Curtis for their encouragement during this process.

I would also like to thank the following reviewers of the sixth edition: Elaine Beason, Texas A & M University—Texarkana; Dorota Celinski, Roosevelt University; Barbara Hong, Texas A & M International University; Margaret T. McLane, The College of St. Rose; Roberta Strosnider, Towson University.

BRIEF CONTENTS

CONTENTS

Note: Every effort has been made to provide accurate and current Internet information in this book. However, the Internet and Information on it are constantly changing, so it is inevitable that some of the Internet addresses listed in this textbook will change.

Introduction to Assessment

An Introduction

testing

assessment

Individuals with Disabilities
   Education Act

No Child Left Behind Act

Individuals with Disabilities
   Education Improvement Act

disproportionality

overrepresentation

prereferral intervention
   strategies

early intervening services

response to intervention (RTI)

core academic subjects

teacher assistance team

overidentification

problem-solving model

informal assessment

curriculum-based assessment

curriculum-based measurement

criterion-related assessment

criterion-referenced tests

performance assessment

portfolio assessment

dynamic assessment

error analysis

checklists

high-stakes testing

adequate yearly progress

alternative assessments

individualized education program
   (IEP)

ecological assessment

environmental assessment

individual assessment plan

screening

*Standards for Educational and
   Psychological Testing*

norm-referenced tests

standardized tests

individualized education program
   (IEP) team

eligibility meeting

alternative planning

Individual Family Service Plan
   (IFSP)

CHAPTER FOCUS

This introductory chapter presents an overview of the assessment process in general education in today's educational environment, reflecting current emphasis on inclusion and accountability in education for all children. The evaluation of student progress in general education occurs regularly. Teachers employ a problem-solving process incorporating intervention strategies in the classroom setting as well as screening and assessment of students who, even with appropriate interventions, require additional support in their classroom setting. Various types of assessment are presented along with considerations of assessment of the child as a whole.

CEC KNOWLEDGE AND SKILLS STANDARDS

The student completing this chapter will understand the knowledge and skills included in the following CEC Knowledge and Skills Standards from Standard 8: Assessment:

CC8K1—Basic terminology used in assessment

> *CC8K2*—Legal provisions and ethical principles regarding the assessment of individuals
>
> *GC8K1*—Specialized terminology used in the assessment of individuals with disabilities
>
> *GC8K2*—Laws and policies regarding referral and placement procedures for individuals with disabilities
>
> *GC8K4*—Procedures for use with individuals who may be at risk for disabilities

ASSESSMENT: A NECESSARY PART OF TEACHING

testing A method to determine a student's ability to complete certain tasks or demonstrate mastery of a skill or knowledge of content.

assessment The process of gathering information to monitor progress and make educational decisions if necessary.

Testing is one method of evaluating progress and determining student outcomes and individual student needs. Testing, however, is only one form of assessment. **Assessment** includes many formal and informal methods of evaluating student progress and behavior.

Assessment happens every day in every classroom for the purpose of informing the teacher about needed instructional interventions. A teacher observes the behaviors of a student solving math problems. The teacher then checks the student's answers and determines the student's ability to solve that particular type of math problem. If the student made mistakes, the teacher determines the types of errors and decides what steps must be taken to correct the miscalculations. This is one type of assessment. The teacher observes behavior, gathers information about the student, and makes instructional changes according to the information obtained.

MONITOR YOUR PROGRESS

In an effort to experience progress monitoring during this course, students are encouraged to turn to the pre-test at the end of this chapter before reading any further. This pre-test will be used as a measure to determine your progress as you work through the text. You will also learn how to plot an aim line and determine if your progress is consistent with the aim line or if you need additional study interventions to maintain your progress. At the end of each part or section of this text, you will find another probe of your skill development. Each score can be plotted along the aim line to monitor your progress. Good luck!

In the routine assessment of students, behavior is observed, progress is monitored and evaluated, and interventions are planned. With effective interventions that are based on scientific research, few students will require additional assessment or special support services. Some students, however, do not respond to intensive interventions and may continue to have academic difficulties. These students may require additional assessment and evaluation for possible special education support. The very best assessment practices, however, must adhere to legal mandates, ethical standards, and basic principles of measurement. Teachers and other educational personnel have a professional responsibility to be accountable for each decision about assessment. Therefore, knowledge of the fundamentals of assessment and the various types of assessment is necessary.

Individuals with Disabilities Education Act Passed in 1990 to give new name to PL 94-142.

No Child Left Behind Act Law of 2001 that holds general education accountable for all students' academic achievement.

Individuals with Disabilities Education Improvement Act The reauthorization and amendments of IDEA.

The process of assessment plays an important role in the determination of student outcomes. The **Individuals with Disabilities Education Act** of 1997 Amendments, **No Child Left Behind Act** of 2001, and the **Individuals with Disabilities Education Improvement Act** of 2004 place more emphasis on the assessment of all students for measuring attainment of educational standards within the general curriculum (*Federal Register*, 1999; *Federal Register*, 2006; Individuals with Disabilities Education Improvement Act of 2004 Conference Committee Report, 2004 as cited in IDEA 2004; PL 107-110, 2002; Ysseldyke, Nelson, & House, 2000). The effectiveness of earlier special education programs has also been debated in the literature, and such discussions have contributed to the current inclusion movement of students with disabilities in the general education curriculum and setting (Detterman & Thompson, 1997; Detterman & Thompson, 1998; Keogh, Forness, & MacMillan, 1998; Symons & Warren, 1998). Although the percentage of students receiving special education support continues to increase, so has the percentage of students in those programs graduating with regular high school diplomas (U.S. Department of Education, 2000, 2004). The rate has increased from 43.5% of all students with disabilities graduating from high school in 1993–94 to 51.1% in 2001–2002 (U.S. Department of Education, 2004). It is concerning that even with the increasing numbers of students with special needs graduating with diplomas, nearly half of the students receiving special education support services do not. This underscores the need for more emphasis on the accountability of serving special education students and their ability to progress in the general education curriculum. Table 1.1 presents the national data on students within disability categories who graduated with a general education diploma.

Educational accountability efforts include improving education and achievement for all students, and especially improving the educational outcomes for culturally, linguistically, and ethnically diverse students, who continue to be represented in disproportionate numbers in several categories of special education (*Federal Register*, 2006; U.S. Department of Education, 1999, 2000). Federal regulations specifically target additional procedures and funding, to address the disproportionate numbers of students of various ethnic groups who are found eligible for special education, when this may be the result of other cultural factors. The regulations also address students who may be denied services due to cultural or linguistic differences. When students from various ethnic or linguistically different groups are under- or overrepresented in special education

Table 1.1   Students ages 14 and older with disabilities who graduated with a standard diploma[a]: 1993–94[b] through 2001–02[b].

Disability	1993–94	1994–95	1995–96	1996–97	1997–98	1998–99[c]	1999–2000	2000–01	2001–02
					Percent				
Specific learning disabilities	49.1	47.7	48.2	48.8	51.0	51.9	51.6	53.6	56.9
Speech/language impairments	42.9	41.7	42.2	44.8	48.1	51.2	53.2	52.3	55.7
Mental retardation	35.0	33.8	34.0	33.0	34.3	36.0	34.4	35.0	37.8
Serious emotional disturbance	27.0	26.0	25.1	25.9	27.4	29.2	28.6	28.9	32.1
Multiple disabilities	36.1	31.4	35.3	35.4	39.0	41.0	42.3	41.6	45.2
Hearing impairments	61.9	58.2	58.8	61.8	62.3	60.9	61.4	60.3	66.9
Orthopedic impairments	56.7	54.1	53.6	54.9	57.9	53.9	51.5	57.4	56.4
Other health impairments	54.6	52.6	53.0	53.1	56.8	55.0	56.5	56.1	59.2
Visual impairments	63.5	63.7	65.0	64.3	65.1	67.6	66.4	65.9	70.8
Autism	33.7	35.5	36.4	35.9	38.7	40.5	40.8	42.1	51.1
Deaf-blindness[d]	34.7	30.0	39.5	39.4	67.7	48.3	37.4	41.2	49.1
Traumatic brain injury	54.6	51.7	54.0	57.3	58.2	60.6	56.8	57.5	64.4
All disabilities	43.5	42.1	42.4	43.0	45.3	46.5	46.1	47.6	51.1

Source: U.S. Department of Education, Office of Special Education Programs, Data Analysis System (DANS). Table 4-1 in vol 2. These data are for the 50 States, DC, Puerto Rico, and the four outlying areas.

[a]The percentage of students with disabilities who exited school with a regular high school diploma and the percentage who exit school by dropping out are performance indicators used by OSEP to measure progress in improving results for students with disabilities. The appropriate method for calculating graduation and dropout rates depends on the question to be answered and is limited by the data available. For reporting under the *Government Performance and Results Act* (GPRA), OSEP calculates the graduation rate by dividing the number of students age 14 and older who graduated with a regular high school diploma by the number of students in the same age group who are known to have left school (i.e., graduated with a regular high school diploma, received a certificate-of-completion, reached the maximum age for services, died moved and are not known to be continuing in an education program or dropped out). These calculations are presented here.

[b]Data are based on a cumulative 12-month count.

[c]Two large states appear to have underreported dropouts in 1988–99. As a result, the graduation rate is somewhat inflated that year.

[d]Percentage is based on fewer than 200 students exiting school.

disproportionality
When students of a specific ethnic group are at risk for overidentification or are at risk for underrepresentation in special education.

services, it is called **disproportionality**. When too many students are found to be eligible from a specific ethnic group, it is known as **overrepresentation** of that group. For example, American Indian/Alaska Native students were 2.89 times more likely to receive special education and related services for developmental delay than any other group (U.S. Department of Education, 2006). Further explanation of disproportionality is provided in Chapter 2.

On January 8, 2002, the No Child Left Behind Act of 2001 was enacted (PL 107-110, 2002). This legislation further emphasized

overrepresentation
When the percentage of students of a culturally different group is greater than the percentage of individuals of that group in the LEA.

the accountability that educators must implement in the education of all children. Accountability in this sense means statewide assessment of all students to measure their performance against standards of achievement. Assessment of students with disabilities is based on the same principles as assessment of students in general education. Students with disabilities are required to take statewide exams or alternative exams to measure their progress within the general education curriculum. Teachers and other educational personnel must make decisions about the types of evaluations and tests and any accommodations that might be needed for statewide assessments in order to include students receiving special education support in accountability measures (*Federal Register*, 2006).

Inclusion of students with disabilities within the context of the general education classroom setting, as a mode of service delivery, has increased to more than 48% and will continue to increase due to the IDEA 2004 emphasis on general curriculum (U.S. Department of Education, 2004; *Federal Register*, 2006) and the accountability standards of No Child Left Behind (PL 107-110, 2002). This increase of students with disabilities in the general education environment results in common expectations for educational standards and common assessment (U.S. Department of Education, 1999, PL 107-110, 2002; *Federal Register*, 2006).

In November of 2004, the Individuals with Disabilities Education Improvement Act was completed by the congressional conference committee and sent to President Bush for approval. It was signed into law on December 3, 2004. This law reauthorized the original IDEA and aligned it with the No Child Left Behind Act of 2002. In the 2004 Individuals with Disabilities Improvement Act, known as IDEA 2004, additional emphasis was placed on setting high standards of achievement for students with disabilities. These high standards should reflect the general education curriculum and must be assessed by statewide assessment of all students. Like the No Child Left Behind Act, IDEA 2004 requires that school systems and state education agencies collect data to document student achievement. This most recent reauthorization of the original IDEA places higher standards of accountability on teachers and schools to ensure student achievement. The Rules and Regulations that govern state educational systems and local school systems was completed and reported in the *Federal Register* in 2006. Additional aspects of the law and the assessment requirements are presented in Chapter 2.

HISTORICAL AND CONTEMPORARY MODELS OF ASSESSMENT

Since the original public law was implemented in 1975, the typical process of assessment has included identification of specific deficits within a student that appeared to be the cause of the student's

Figure 1.1   The traditional model of assessment.

```
┌──────────────────────────────────────────────┐
│     General Education Classroom Instruction    │
│        Student Not Progressing as Expected     │
└──────────────────────────────────────────────┘
                        │
                        ▼
   ┌──────────────────────────────────────────┐
   │  Student Referred to Multidisciplinary Team │
   └──────────────────────────────────────────┘
                        │
                        ▼
        ┌──────────────────────────────────┐
        │      Team Completes Assessment      │
        └──────────────────────────────────┘
                        │
                        ▼
   ┌──────────────────────────────────────────┐
   │ Team Meeting Determines Student Found      │
   │           Eligible for Services            │
   └──────────────────────────────────────────┘
```

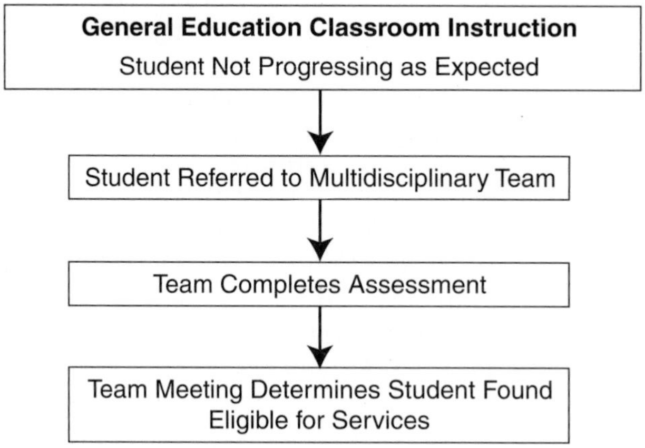

difficulty in the general education curriculum. The historical assessment model meant that when a general education teacher noticed that a student was having difficulty in the classroom, a referral was made to a multidisciplinary team. The multidisciplinary team, comprised of assessment personnel such as a school psychologist, speech clinician, and educational testing specialist, then evaluated the student. The Traditional Model of Assessment is presented in Figure 1.1. The team members and the child's parents then determined if the student met criteria for one of the categories of special education (McNamara & Hollinger, 2003). These categories are presented in Figure 1.2.

Research studies found varying referral practices and subsequently professionals in the field have recommended reform in the referral process. Research suggests referral practices in the past were inconsistent and may have been contributing to bias in the referral, assessment, and eligibility process. For example, studies found that males are referred more frequently and that students with a previous history of difficulties tend to be referred more often (Del'Homme, Kasari, Forness, & Bagley, 1996); female teachers referred students with behavioral problems more frequently than did male teachers (McIntyre, 1988); teachers referred students with learning and behavioral problems more often than those with behavioral problems alone (Soodak & Podell, 1993); and teacher referrals were global in nature and contained subjective rather than objective information in more than half the cases (Reschly, 1986; Ysseldyke, Christenson, Pianta, & Algozzine, 1983). According to research, a teacher's decision to refer may be influenced by the student's having a sibling who has had school problems as well as by the referring teacher's tolerance for certain student behaviors; the teacher with a low tolerance for particular behaviors may more readily refer students exhibiting those behaviors (Thurlow, Christenson, & Ysseldyke, 1983).

Figure 1.2 Disabilities defined in IDEA for which students are eligible for special education services.

Autism	A developmental disability significantly affecting verbal and nonverbal communication and social interaction, generally evident before age three, that adversely affects a child's educational performance. Other characteristics often associated with autism are engagement in repetitive activities and stereotyped movements, resistance change in daily routines, and unusual responses to sensory experiences. Autism does not apply if a child's educational performance is adversely affected primarily because the child has an emotional disturbance. A child who manifests the characteristics of autism after age three could be identified as having autism if other criteria are met.
Deaf-blindness	Concomitant hearing and visual impairments, the combination of which causes such severe communication and other developmental and educational needs that they cannot be accommodated in special education programs solely for children with deafness or children with blindness.
Deafness	A hearing impairment that is so severe that the child is impaired in processing linguistic information through hearing, with or without amplification that adversely affects a child's educational performance.
Emotional disturbance	A conditioning exhibiting one or more of the following characteristics over a long period of time and to a marked degree that adversely affects a child's educational performance: (A) An inability to learn that cannot be explained by intellectual, sensory, or health factors (B) An inability to build or maintain satisfactory interpersonal relationships with peers and teachers (C) Inappropriate types of behaviors or feelings under normal circumstances (D) A general pervasive mood of unhappiness or depression (E) A tendency to develop physical symptoms of fears associated with personal or school problems Emotional disturbance includes schizophrenia. The term does not apply to children who are socially maladjusted, unless it can be determined that they met other criteria for emotional disturbance.
Hearing impairment	An impairment in hearing, whether permanent or fluctuating, that adversely affects a child's educational performance but that is not included under the definition of deafness.
Mental retardation	Significantly subaverage general intellectual functioning existing concurrently with deficits in adaptive behavior and manifested during the developmental period that adversely affects educational performance.
Multiple disabilities	Concomitant impairments (such as mental retardation-blindness or mental retardation-orthopedic impairment), the combination of which causes such severe educational needs that they cannot be accommodated in special education programs solely for one of the impairments. Multiple disabilities does not include deaf-blindness.

Figure 1.2 continued.

Orthopedic impairment	Severe orhopedic impairment that adversely affects a child's educational performance. The term includes impairments caused by congenital anomaly, impairments caused by disease (e.g., poliomyelitis, bone tuberculosis) and impairments from other causes (e.g., cerebral palsy, amputations, and fractures or burns that cause contractures).
Other health impairment	Having limited strength, vitality, or alertness, including a heightened alertness to environmental stimuli, that results in limited alertness with respect to the educational environment that is due to chronic or acute health problems such as asthma, attention deficit disorder or attention deficit hyperactivity disorder, diabetes, epilepsy, a hear condition, hempophilia, lead poisoning, leukemia, nephritis, rheumatic fever, sickle cell anemia, and Tourette's syndrome, and adversely affects a child's educational performance.
Specific learning disability	A disorder in one or more of the basic psychological processes involved in understanding or using language, spoken or written, that may manifest itself in the imperfect ability to listen, speak, read, write, spell, or do mathematical calculations, including conditions such as perceptual disabilities, brain injury, minimal brain dysfunction, dyslexia, and developmental aphasia.
Speech or language impairment	A communication disorder, such as stuttering, impaired articulation, a language impairment, or a voice impairment, that adversely affects a child's educational performance.
Traumatic brain injury	An acquired injury to the brain caused by an external force, resulting in total or partial functional disability or psychosocial impairment, or both, that adversely affects a child's educational performance. Traumatic brain injury applies to open or closed head injuries resulting in impairments in one or more areas such as cognition, language, memory, attention, reasoning, abstract thinking, judgment, problem-solving, sensory, perceptual, and motor abilities; psychosocial behavior, physical functions; information processing and speech. Traumatic brain injury does not apply to brain injuries that are congenital or degenerative, or to brain injuries induced by brain trauma.
Visual impairment including blindness	An impairment in vision that, even with correction, adversely affects a child's educational performance. The term includes both partial sight and blindness.

Another study found that the characteristics of referred students may vary with student age (Harvey, 1991). Males were referred more frequently than female students at all grade levels. In the primary grade levels, younger students (for grade level) were referred more frequently than students who had birth dates farther from the school admission cutoff date (October 31). Students who were referred in the third grade or later had birth dates distributed evenly throughout the year, which suggests that students in the primary grades exhibited developmental differences rather than true learning or behavioral difficulties. Andrews, Wisnieswski, and Mulick (1997) found that students were referred at a higher rate if their height and weight were greater than average for their grade and gender. This study also found that more African-American students were referred for developmental disability services than Caucasian students and that males were referred more frequently for behavioral problems than females (Andrews et al., 1997).

Early research indicated that nationwide more than 90% of the students referred for evaluation were tested. Of those tested, 73% were subsequently found eligible for services in special education (Algozzine, Christenson, & Ysseldyke, 1982). More recently, Del'Homme et al., 1996 found that 63% of the students in their study who were referred subsequently received special education services. Students who are referred are highly likely to complete the evaluation process and receive special education services. In another study, 54% of the students referred for assessment were determined to be eligible (Fugate, Clarizio, & Phillips, 1993). Alternative practices, such as **prereferral interventions**, emerged (Graden, Casey, & Bonstrom, 1985; Graden, Casey, & Christenson, 1985). These interventions were intended to address bias in the referral process and prevent unnecessary additional assessment. By implementing intervention strategies, it was determined that the referral and evaluation rates decreased.

EARLY INTERVENING SERVICES

The inconsistent practices of the historic referral and assessment model resulted in the increasing rates of children referred for assessment and subsequently served in special education. The 2004 Individuals with Disabilities Improvement Act to IDEA began with Congressional Findings, which list areas that the Act is seeking to improve, including the use of prereferral interventions or **early intervening services**. The goal of increasing the use of early intervening services is to address the student's needs within the general education classroom and prevent additional assessment. Congress stated:

> Over 30 years of research and experience has demonstrated that the education of children with disabilities can be made more effective by providing incentives for whole school approaches and pre-referral intervention to reduce the need to label children as disabled in order to address their learning needs. (Individuals with Disabilities Education Improvement Act, 2004)

New regulations, that outline the practices expected in IDEA 2004, require school systems to provide methods of intervention for children who are at risk of having academic or behavioral difficulty. These interventions are addressed in the regulations as early intervening services. Particular emphasis is given to students in kindergarten through third grade and students who may be represented

prereferral intervention strategies Methods used by teachers and other team members to observe and modify student behaviors, learning environment, and/or teaching methods before making a formal referral.

early intervening services Evidence-based methods for addressing needs of students at risk for learning or behavioral disabilities or students who have exited from such services.

Anne Vega/Merrill

response to intervention (RTI) Application of learning or behavioral interventions and measurement of student's response to such interventions.

disproportionally; however, all students K–12 may receive these services. Early intervening services include those available to all children in the general education curriculum, such as general teaching methods, remedial instruction, and tutoring. In addition, schools are expected to use research-based methods for intervention and to document these efforts. These efforts may be included as part of the school's **response to intervention** methods, or **RTI** methods, for documenting possible learning and behavioral problems. Specific methods for data collection for response to intervention are included in the chapters on informal assessment (Chapters 6 and 7).

THREE-TIER MODEL OF INTERVENTION

core academic subjects In IDEA regulations, this includes English, reading or language arts, mathematics, science, foreign languages, civics and government, economics, arts, history, and geography.

One model that has been employed for both academic and behavioral interventions is a three-tier model. This model illustrates that the progress in **core academic subjects** of all children within the school setting should be monitored routinely. Their progress is monitored through standard methods such as statewide accountability assessment, teacher-made tests, and general educational performance in class. For students who have difficulty on these measures when compared to their peers, they are considered to be at risk of academic or behavioral problems and they then receive tier-two interventions, such as remedial assistance or tutoring. Using research-based strategies, the students receive interventions over a period of time and these efforts are documented. If these efforts fail, the teacher may request assistance through the **teacher assistance team** who recommends that the student receive intensive

teacher assistance team A team of various professionals who assist the teacher in designing interventions for students who are not making progress.

interventions, designed specifically to address the area of weakness or difficulty. If the child continues to struggle, the child may be referred for consideration of an evaluation for possible special education eligibility. The three-tier model is presented in Figure 1.3.

Functional assessment of academic performance problems has been suggested as a method of targeting difficulties and implementing specific intervention strategies (Daly, Witt, Martens, & Dool, 1997). This procedure provides hypotheses for the teacher to test through the use of classroom instructional interventions (see Figure 1.4). Once classroom teachers have documented the area of difficulty, they can systematically implement strategies for correction. Ideally, the intervention strategies will decrease referrals by resolving some students' learning or behavioral problems within the general education classroom (Nelson, Smith, Taylor, Dodd, & Reavis, 1992).

Strategies that may be selected to determine the area of academic or behavioral difficulty include observation by objective persons, informal assessment techniques, curriculum modifications, environmental (classroom) modifications, and consultation with the parents and other members of the multidisciplinary team.

Figure 1.3   A three-tier model.

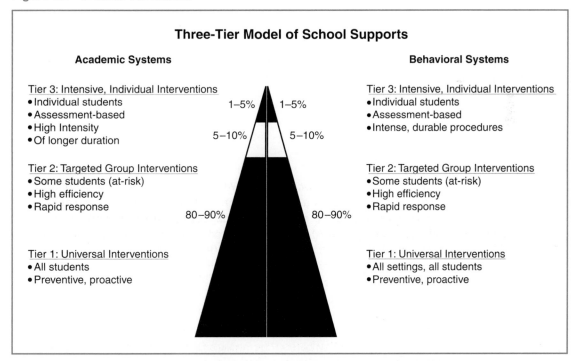

Source: Adapted from: Batsche, G. et al. (2005). *Response to intervention: Policy considerations and implementation.* Alexandria, VA: National Association of State Directors of Special Education. Retrieved from the National Association of State Directors of Special Education website *http://www.nasdse.org/documents/RtIAnAdministratorsPerspective1-06.pdf*

Figure 1.4   Academic interventions identified by the presumed function of the behavior.

Reasonable Hypotheses	Possible Interventions
The student is not motivated to respond to the instructional demands	Increase interest in curricular activities: 1. Provide incentives for using the skill 2. Teach the skill in the context of using the skill 3. Provide choices of activities
Insufficient active student responding in curricular materials	Increase active student responding: 1. Estimate current rate of active responding and increase rate during allocated time
Insufficient prompting and feedback for active responding	Increase rate of complete learning trials: 1. Response cards 2. Choral responding 3. Flash card intervention with praise/error correction 4. Peer tutoring
Student displays poor accuracy in target skill(s)	Increase modeling and error correction: 1. Reading passages to student 2. Use cover-copy-compare 3. Have student repeatedly practice correct response in context for errors
Student displays poor fluency in target skill(s)	Increase practice, drill, or incentives: 1. Have the student repeatedly read passages 2. Offer incentives for beating the last score
Student does not generalize use of the skill to the natural setting or to other materials/settings·	Instruct the student to generalize use of the skill: 1. Teach multiple examples of use of the skill 2. Teach use of the skill in the natural setting 3. "Capture" natural incentives 4. Teach self-monitoring
The instructional demands do not promote mastery of the curricular objective	Change instructional materials to match the curricular objective: 1. Specify the curricular objective and identify activities that promote use of the skill in the context in which it is generally used
Student's skill level is poorly matched to the difficulty of the instructional materials	Increase student responding using better matched instructional levels: 1. Identify student's accuracy and fluency across instructional materials and use instructional materials that promote a high rate of responding

Source: School Psychology Review, 26 (4), 558. Copyright 1997 by the National Association of School Psychologists. Reprinted by permission of the publisher.

Although effective prereferral strategies have been found to reduce the number of referrals for assessment, one study found that general education teachers had only a vague understanding of specific strategies and how to implement them (Wilson, Gutkin, Hagen, & Oats, 1998). In this study, the participating teachers viewed the prereferral process as a step in the referral process rather than an intervention to prevent assessment. Another investigation of referral practices across the United States found that state requirements varied, practices were inconsistent, and many interventions did not involve actual teaching interventions to improve academic progress (Truscott, Cohen, Sams, Sanborn, & Frank, 2005). These studies illustrate the problems encountered in the referral process and have influenced a move toward more comprehensive and detailed intervention strategies such as the evidence-based practices implemented through RTI.

overidentification
Describes the phenomenon of identifying students who seem to be eligible for special education services but who are actually not disabled.

The more frequent use of better interventions is a step forward in the prevention of unnecessary evaluation and the possibility of misdiagnosis and **overidentification** of special education students. Halgren and Clarizio (1993) found that 38% of the students in special education were either reclassified or terminated from special education. This indicates a need for more specific identification of the learning or behavioral problems through referral and initial assessment.

Valles (1998) suggested that teacher training in special and general education may be needed to prevent inappropriate referrals of minority and bilingual students. Gopaul-McNicol and Thomas-Presswood (1998) caution that teachers of students whose primary language is not English often consider bilingual education or English as a Second Language (ESL) classes as prereferral interventions. In a study of the referral and assessment practices of Asian-American students, it was found that prereferral interventions were limited and did not reflect the approaches needed that may have assisted with language development (Poon-McBrayer & Garcia, 2000). In this study, these students were referred for evaluations when language interventions may have resolved the difficulties. Teachers of students with cultural and linguistic differences should employ prereferral intervention strategies that promote language acquisition in addition to ESL or bilingual curriculum. In one study, the RTI model was applied to English Language Learners (ELL) who were at risk of reading disabilities (Linan-Thompson, Vaughn, Prater, & Cirino, 2006). In this study, students whose primary language was Spanish, received intensive interventions using evidence-based practices and made significant gains therefore avoiding the need for special education referral.

Providing consulting services to general education teachers could help resolve student problems before referral (Zins, Graden, & Ponti, 1989). Serna, Forness, and Nielsen (1998) suggest that systemic changes in referral practices are needed at the preservice level of teacher training. This type of intervention would place team members in a consulting role for a large part of their service time and decrease the time they spent testing. Fuchs (1991) found that several features need to exist in the practice of prereferral interventions. The following list is adapted from this study:

1. Prereferral intervention should be included in the job descriptions of those persons responsible for implementation. This includes both professional and paraprofessional staff.

2. A consultant or team should serve to guide the prereferral effort.

3. All staff involved should receive adequate training in the prereferral strategies.

4. The consultation effort should be efficient and exhibit desired outcomes.

5. Consultants should define the problem behavior, set goals for students and teachers, collect data, and evaluate effectiveness.

6. Interventions should be agreeable to both consultants and teachers.

7. Strategies should be implemented as designed.

8. Data should be collected at multiple intervals. (p. 263)

The prereferral team or teacher assistant team members work together to determine what strategies might be effective for specific behavioral or academic challenges. It is important that the team uses effective problem-solving as they make these decisions. One study found that the team decision-making was influenced by having more specific data collected by the teacher and that parent input was also important in the decision-making process (Etscheidt & Knesting, 2007). It was also found that the interventions were more likely to be implemented with integrity when the interventions seemed reasonable and were judged likely to be acceptable interventions.

CONTEMPORARY MODEL OF ASSESSMENT

problem-solving model Strategies for intervention that identify problem, hypothesis for intervention, and measurement of those interventions, to meet student's needs.

Difficulties with the traditional approach to referral and assessment led educators to look for more effective methods. The goal of the contemporary model of assessment is to resolve the academic or behavioral challenges experienced by the student. This **problem-solving model** emphasizes finding a solution rather than determining eligibility or finding a special education placement. The contemporary model is presented in Figure 1.5. As noted in the

Figure 1.5   The contemporary assessment model.

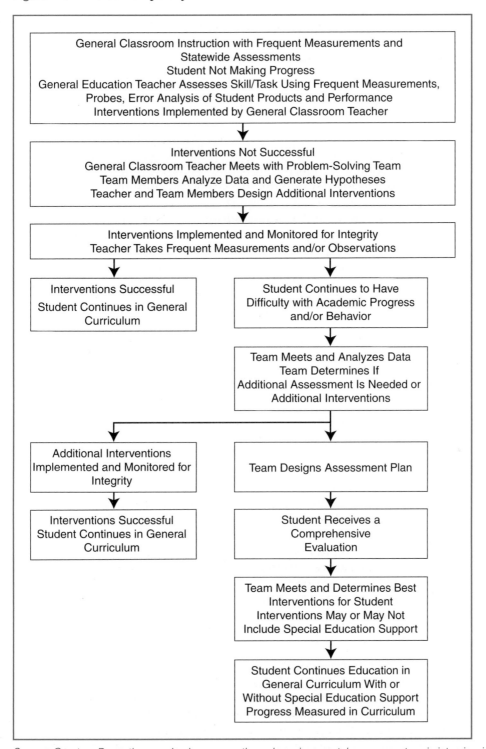

Source: Overton, Promoting academic success through environmental assessment . . . in interview in *Sch/Clinic, 39*, 149–150. Copyright 2004 by PRO–ED, Inc. Reprinted by permission of publisher.

model, several methods of assessment and intervention are employed before consideration of a referral and comprehensive evaluation. These methods include informal assessment techniques used in the general education environment. The team and the child's parents discuss the results.

Interventions are implemented and additional data are gathered to determine if the intervention was successful. When the interventions result in less improvement than had been expected, the team meets to discuss additional strategies or interventions. When a student is referred, it is only to assist in finding a solution or appropriate intervention. The intervention may or may not include special education support.

The **Check Your Understanding** exercises included with this text provide an opportunity for you to monitor your own progress in learning the assessment process. Complete the activity for Chapter 1 included here. Additional exercises are provided on the Companion Website of this text at *www.prenhall.com/overton.*

Case Study

Jaime entered kindergarten three months after his family moved into the school district. He had not attended preschool, and his mother had little time to devote to preacademic skills. Jaime lives

Check Your Understanding

Check your knowledge of the trends and foundations of assessment by completing Activity 1.1 below.

Activity 1.1

Answer the following questions.

1. According to the Traditional Assessment Model, what usually happened when a student was referred to a multidisciplinary team?

2. Research studies of the referral and assessment process found many indications of bias in the process. What are some examples of this bias?

3. Under the 2004 IDEA, the emphasis shifted from the traditional model with prereferral strategies to early intervening services. Why did the 2004 IDEA include this change?

Apply Your Knowledge

Read the case study to begin thinking about how to look for solutions for the student's difficulties. Refer to the Contemporary Assessment Model to list possible steps in the problem-solving process. _____
_____
_____

with his mother, father, and three older siblings. Jaime had experiences around other children in his extended family; however, Jaime had no experience in a structured learning environment. Within the first few weeks of school, Jaime's kindergarten teacher, Mrs. Johnson, began activities to teach phonemic awareness. Mrs. Johnson frequently measured her students' progress using curriculum-based measurement. During this assessment, Mrs. Johnson noted that Jaime was not progressing as expected.

1. According to the Contemporary Assessment Model, what steps have been taken by Mrs. Johnson?
2. List the steps that should happen before Mrs. Johnson consults with the problem-solving team.
3. What other information may be helpful in determining interventions?

For **MORE PRACTICE**, visit the Companion Website at *www.prenhall. com/overton* to analyze additional difficulties with the traditional referral process.

EVALUATING STUDENT PROGRESS IN THE CLASSROOM

informal assessment Nonstandardized methods of evaluating progress, such as interviews, observations, and teacher-made tests.

curriculum-based assessment Using the content from the currently used curriculum to assess student progress.

curriculum-based measurement Frequent measurement comparing student's actual progress with expected rate of progress.

criterion-related assessment When items of an assessment instrument are related to meeting objectives or passing skill mastery objectives.

criterion-referenced tests Tests designed to accompany and measure a set of criteria or skill-mastery criteria.

Teachers use several methods to assess student progress in the classroom. Teacher-made tests, quizzes, and other **informal assessment** are used in an attempt to discover how the student is progressing. The teacher may develop assessments directly from curriculum materials. This type of assessment is **curriculum-based assessment**. Curriculum-based assessment is commonly used to measure a student's performance within the specific classroom curriculum.

Teachers may first notice that a student is having difficulty progressing as expected by taking frequent measurements of the student's classroom performance. These frequent measurements using the curriculum that is being taught are called **curriculum-based measurements**. Research supports curriculum-based measurement as an effective method of monitoring the progress of both general and special education students (Deno, 2003; Fuchs, Deno, & Mirkin, 1984; Fuchs, Fuchs, Hamlett, Phillips, & Bentz, 1994). This method is presented in detail in Chapter 5.

When students are tested for mastery of a skill or an objective, the assessment is called **criterion-related assessment**, and tests of this type may be labeled **criterion-referenced tests**. Criterion-referenced tests compare the performance of a student to a given criterion.

Another type of assessment used in the classroom requires students to create a product that demonstrates their skills or competency; the assessment of their creation is called **performance**

performance assessment When a student is required to create a product to demonstrate knowledge.

portfolio assessment Evaluating student progress, strengths, and weaknesses using a collection of different measurements and work samples.

dynamic assessment Assessment in which the examiner prompts or interacts with the student to determine the student's potential to learn a skill.

error analysis Using a student's errors to analyze specific learning problems.

checklists Lists of skills developmentally sequenced and used to monitor student progress.

high-stakes testing Accountability assessment of state or district standards, which may be used for funding or accreditation decisions.

adequate yearly progress The criterion set for schools based upon high stakes testing results.

alternative assessments Assessment methods for students with disabilities, designed to measure progress in the general curriculum.

assessment. The assessment of a collection of various types of products or assessments collected over time that demonstrate student progress is known as **portfolio assessment**. When the assessment process includes interaction or teaching and prompting to determine a student's potential to learn a skill, the teacher has used the technique known as **dynamic assessment**. In dynamic assessment, the teacher assesses the student's ability or capacity to learn a new skill rather than testing for mastery of the skill.

Learning how the student performs tasks may also provide insight into the nature of the academic or behavioral difficulty. Observing the steps a student takes to solve a problem or complete a task can benefit the teacher as well as the student. The teacher may ask the student to verbalize the steps taken while reading a paragraph for content or while solving a math equation. The teacher can then note the types or patterns of errors the student made during the process. This type of analysis is known as **error analysis** (e.g., $7 \times 3 = 10$; the student added rather than multiplied the numbers). Teachers also develop **checklists** to identify students who have mastered skills, tasks, or developmental expectations appropriate to their grade level. Checklists can be found in some commercial materials or school curriculum guides. Placement in the specific curriculum within the general education classroom may be based on a student's performance on skills listed on these commercial checklists or on other curriculum-based assessment results.

Current reform movements in special education and general education emphasize the changing role of assessment in special education (U.S. Congress, 1993; U.S. Department of Education, 1997). The result of this trend is the encouragement of nontraditional methods of assessment and the inclusion of students with disabilities in statewide accountability and competency testing (IDEA Amendments, 1997). Including students with disabilities in district and statewide assessment, or **high-stakes testing**, is necessary to determine the effectiveness of educational programs (Ysseldyke et al., 1998). These statewide assessments are used to monitor progress of individual schools and school systems. In the No Child Left Behind Act of 2001, schools are required to show **adequate yearly progress**, or AYP, in order to demonstrate that students are mastering the curriculum in the general classroom (PL 107-110, 2002). The AYP is measured using the results of the statewide assessments. Students with disabilities who are determined unable to participate in these statewide assessments are to be tested using **alternative assessments** to measure attainment of standards. Teachers will be required to use a variety of assessment techniques to assess student competency and demonstrate mastery of educational goals and objectives.

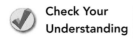

Check Your Understanding

Check your knowledge of the different types of assessment presented in the previous section by completing Activity 1.2 below.

Activity 1.2

Use the terms provided to answer the questions below.

assessment
error analysis
alternate assessments
curriculum-based assessment
performance assessment
high-stakes testing
criterion-related assessment
checklist
portfolio assessment
criterion-referenced tests
dynamic assessment

1. A teacher wants to determine why a student who can multiply single-digit numbers cannot multiply double-digit numbers. The teacher asks the student to verbally describe the steps she is using in the process of multiplying double-digit numbers. This is _____.

2. The spelling series used in one classroom contains tests that are directly tied to the spelling curriculum. When the teacher uses these tests, _____ is being used.

3. A teacher collects class work, quizzes, book reports, and writing assignments to determine the students' strengths and weaknesses in language arts. This is known as _____.

4. When a teacher assesses a student's potential to learn a new math skill by prompting or cuing the student, _____ has been used.

5. For a teacher to determine a student's understanding of the solar system, the student is required to create a project that demonstrates the Earth's position relative to designated planets. This is _____.

6. A classroom teacher along with a team of other educational professionals determined that John, who has multiple disabilities, is not able to participate in the statewide assessment. The team develops _____ to assess John's attainment of educational goals.

7. A student is not progressing as the teacher believes he should for his age expectancy. The teacher uses teacher-made tests, observation, and criterion-referenced tests to gather information about the student. This teacher is using different methods of _____ to discover why the student is not making progress.

8. To determine whether a student has mastered a specific skill or objective, the teacher uses _____.

9. A first-grade student has difficulty with fine motor skills. The teacher is concerned that the student may not have the developmental ability to learn manuscript handwriting. The handwriting series lists skills a student must master before writing letters. Using this device, the teacher has employed a _____.

10. Assessment devices in a school's language arts series provide skills and objectives for each level of English, creative writing, and literature. These are _____.

11. Each year the Mulberry Elementary School tests students to determine which students have mastered state curriculum standards. This testing is known as _____.

Apply Your Knowledge

Analyze the following sentences written by Roberto. Identify the spelling errors.

1. The yellow kat is very big.

2. The oshun has big waves.

3. The kan was bent.

Your error analysis is that Roberto. . . . _____

_____

_____

---

individualized education program (IEP) A written plan of educational interventions designed for each student who receives special education.

ecological assessment Method of assessing a student's total environment to determine what factors are contributing to learning or behavioral problems.

environmental assessment Method of assessing the student's classroom environment.

In the past, a student was referred for testing, evaluated by team members, and, if determined eligible for special education services, given an **individualized education program** (IEP) and placed in a special education setting. Although these steps were reported nationally as those most commonly followed in the evaluation process (Ysseldyke & Thurlow, 1983), they do not include the step of prereferral intervention.

A prereferral model proposed by Graden, Casey, and Christenson (1985), however, includes "identifying, defining, and clarifying the problem, analyzing the components of the classroom ecology that affect the problem, designing and implementing interventions, and evaluating intervention effectiveness" (p. 383). As Graden and colleagues have written, this type of prereferral intervention looks at many variables surrounding the student's educational performance rather than assuming first that the difficulty is with the student. This type of assessment, called **ecological assessment** or **environmental assessment**, reflects a major trend toward considering the environment and assessing students in their natural environment (Overton, 2003; Reschly, 1986). One type of environmental assessment is presented in Figure 1.6.

Figure 1.6   Assessing the academic environment.

Assessment of Academic Environment
Name of Student _____
Class: _____
Duration of observation: _____ minutes.

Check all that are observed during this observational period.
Physical Environmental Factors
_____ Seating: Individual student desks
_____ Seating: Group tables
_____ Seating: Student desks grouped in pairs or groups of four
_____ Material organized for quick student access and use
_____ Target student's materials organized
Classroom Behavioral Structure
_____ Classroom expectations (rules) posted
_____ Verbal praise for effort of students
_____ Verbal praise for target student
_____ Quiet redirection for target student when needed
_____ Inconsequential minor behaviors are ignored
_____ Transitions were smooth
_____ Time lapse to begin task less than 3 minutes (for class)
_____ Time lapse to begin task less than 3 minutes (for target student)
_____ Time lapse to begin task 5 minutes or more (for class)
_____ Time lapse to begin task 5 minutes or more (for target student)
_____ Noise level consistent with task demands
_____ Classwide behavior plan used
Classroom Teacher's Instructional Behaviors
_____ Task expectations explained verbally
_____ Task expectations explained visually (on board, etc.)
_____ Task modeled by teacher
_____ Cognitive strategies modeled by teacher first (thinking aloud)
Teacher–Students Interactions
_____ Academic behavior/responses shaped by teacher for all students
_____ Teacher used proximity as a monitoring technique for all students
_____ Teacher used proximity for reinforcement technique for all students
_____ Teacher used one-on-one instruction to clarify task for all students
Teacher–Target Student Interactions
_____ Academic behavior/responses shaped by teacher for target student
_____ Teacher used proximity as a monitoring technique for target student
_____ Teacher used proximity for reinforcement technique for target student
_____ Teacher used one-on-one instruction to clarify for target student

Figure 1.6   continued.

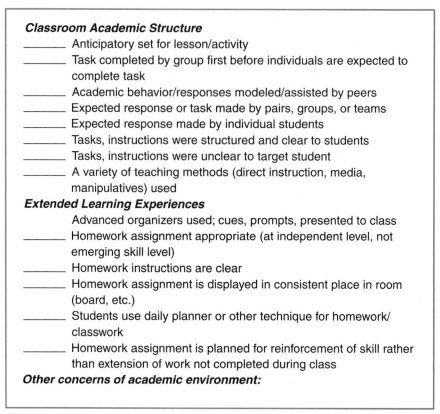

Classroom Academic Structure
_____ Anticipatory set for lesson/activity
_____ Task completed by group first before individuals are expected to complete task
_____ Academic behavior/responses modeled/assisted by peers
_____ Expected response or task made by pairs, groups, or teams
_____ Expected response made by individual students
_____ Tasks, instructions were structured and clear to students
_____ Tasks, instructions were unclear to target student
_____ A variety of teaching methods (direct instruction, media, manipulatives) used

Extended Learning Experiences
Advanced organizers used; cues, prompts, presented to class
_____ Homework assignment appropriate (at independent level, not emerging skill level)
_____ Homework instructions are clear
_____ Homework assignment is displayed in consistent place in room (board, etc.)
_____ Students use daily planner or other technique for homework/ classwork
_____ Homework assignment is planned for reinforcement of skill rather than extension of work not completed during class

Other concerns of academic environment:

Source: From "Promoting Academic Success through Environmental Assessment" by Terry Overton, *Intervention in School and Clinic* vol. *39*, no. 3, pp. 149–150. Copyright 2004 by PRO–ED, Inc. Adapted with permission.

Messick (1984) proposed a two-phase assessment strategy that emphasizes prereferral assessment of the student's learning environment. The information needed during Messick's first phase includes*

1. Evidence that the school is using programs and curricula shown to be effective not just for students in general but for the various ethnic, linguistic, and socioeconomic groups actually served by the school in question.

2. Evidence that the students in question have been adequately exposed to the curriculum by virtue of not having missed too many lessons because of absence or disciplinary

*From Assessment in context: Appraising student performance in relation to instructional quality, by S. Messick (1984). *Educational Researcher. 13*, p. 5. Copyright 1984 by American Educational Research Association. Reprinted by permission of the publisher.

exclusion from class and that the teacher has implemented the curriculum effectively.

3. Objective evidence that the child has not learned what was taught.

4. Evidence that systematic efforts were or are being made to identify the learning difficulty and to take corrective instructional action, such as introducing remedial approaches, changing the curriculum materials, or trying a new teacher.

It is no longer considered acceptable to refer students who have difficulty in the general classroom without interventions unless they appear to be experiencing severe learning or behavioral problems or are in danger of harming themselves or others. Prereferral or early intervention strategies have had positive effects. In schools where a prereferral intervention model was implemented, consultation services increased within the general education classroom, and both testing and educational placements decreased significantly (Graden, Casey, & Bonstrom, 1985). In a study by Chalfant and Psyh (1989), the inappropriate referral rate decreased to 63% and interventions were successful in approximately 88% of the cases. Recent studies have found success in preventing inappropriate referrals by employing a problem-solving model throughout the assessment process (McNamara & Hollinger, 2003; VanDerHeyden, Witt, & Naquin, 2003). The problem-solving method requires the team to determine an effecive solution for the student's academic or behavioral difficulties. As part of this problem-solving strategy, a prereferral checklist may be used by the intervention team to clarify the target areas of difficulty and generate hypotheses for interventions. An example of a prereferral checklist is presented in Figure 1.7.

DESIGNING AN ASSESSMENT PLAN

When the team members determine that a comprehensive assessment will be needed in order to determine effective interventions, an assessment plan must be constructed. Federal law mandates that evaluation measures used during the assessment process are those measures specifically designed to assess areas of concern (IDEA Amendments of 1997). (The specific laws pertaining to the education of individuals with disabilities are discussed in Chapter 2.) Through the use of appropriate early intervention strategies, the referring teacher is able to pinpoint specific areas of difficulty, and the assessment team can then design an appropriate assessment plan. The team must determine which instruments will be administered and which special education professionals are needed to complete the assessment. Federal law also requires that the instruments selected have been validated for the purpose of intended use.

Figure 1.7   A prereferral checklist to determine whether all necessary interventions have been attempted.

Prereferral Checklist

Name of Student _____

Concerned Teacher _____

Briefly describe area of difficulty:

1. Curriculum evaluation:
   _____ Material is appropriate for age and/or grade level.
   _____ Instructions are presented clearly.
   _____ Expected method of response is within the student's capability.
   _____ Readability of material is appropriate.
   _____ Prerequisite skills have been mastered.
   _____ Format of materials is easily understood by students of same age and/or grade level.
   _____ Frequent and various methods of evaluation are employed.
   _____ Tasks are appropriate in length.
   _____ Pace of material is appropriate for age and/or grade level.
2. Learning environment:
   _____ Methods of presentation are appropriate for age and/or grade levels.
   _____ Tasks are presented in appropriate sequence.
   _____ Expected level of response is appropriate for age and/or grade level.
   _____ Physical facilities are conducive to learning.
3. Social environment:
   _____ Student does not experience noticeable conflicts with peers.
   _____ Student appears to have adequate relationships with peers.
   _____ Parent conference reveals no current conflicts or concerns within the home.
   _____ Social development appears average for age expectancy.
4. Student's physical condition:
   _____ Student's height and weight appear to be within average range of expectancy for age and/or grade level.
   _____ Student has no signs of visual or hearing difficulties (asks teacher to repeat instructions, squints, holds papers close to face to read).
   _____ Student has had vision and hearing checked by school nurse or other health official.
   _____ Student has not experienced long-term illness or serious injury.

_____ School attendance is average or better.

_____ Student appears attentive and alert during instruction.

_____ Student appears to have adequate motor skills.

_____ Student appears to have adequate communication skills.

5. Intervention procedures (changes in teaching strategies that have been attempted):

_____ Consultant has observed student:

Setting	Date	Comments
1.		
2.		
3.		

_____ Educational and curriculum changes were made:

Change	Date	Comments
1.		
2.		
3.		

_____ Behavioral and social changes were made:

Change	Date	Comments
1.		
2.		
3.		

_____ Parent conferences were held:

Date	Comments
1.	
2.	
3.	

_____ Additional documentation is attached.

individual assessment plan
A plan that lists the specific tests and procedures to be used for a student who has been screened and needs further assessment.

For example, if the student has been referred for problems with reading comprehension, the appropriate assessment instrument would be one of good technical quality that has been designed to measure reading problems—specifically, reading comprehension skills. In addition to requiring selection of the appropriate tests, the law mandates that persons administering the tests be adequately trained to administer those specific tests and that more than a single instrument be used to determine eligibility for special services. To meet these mandates, the educator must design an **individual assessment plan** for each student. Maxam, Boyer-Stephens, and

screening A review
of records and
student's school
achievement to
determine what
interventions or
additional
assessment are
needed.

Alff (1986) recommended that each evaluation team follow these specific steps in preparing an assessment plan:*

1. Review all of the **screening** information in each of the seven areas (health, vision, hearing, speech and language skills, intellectual, academic, prevocational/vocational).

2. Determine what area(s) need further evaluation.

3. Determine the specific data-collection procedures to use (interviews, observation of behavior, informal or formal techniques, standardized tests).

4. Determine persons responsible for administering the selected procedures. These persons must be trained or certified if the assessment instrument calls for specific qualifications.

*Standards for
Educational and
Psychological
Testing* Professional
and ethical
standards that
suggest minimum
criteria for assessing
students.

In addition to federal mandates and recommendations from professionals in the field of special education, the professional organizations of the American Psychological Association, the American Educational Research Association, and the National Council on Measurement in Education have produced the ***Standards for Educational and Psychological Testing*** (1999), which clearly defines acceptable professional and ethical standards for individuals who test children in schools. (Several of these standards are included in later chapters of this text.) The APA *Standards* (1999) emphasize the importance of using tests for the purpose intended by the test producer and place ethical responsibility for correct use and interpretation on the person administering and scoring tests in the educational setting. Other professional organizations, such as the Council for Exceptional Children and the National Association of School Psychologists, have ethics and standards about assessment. These are presented in Chapter 2.

A student who has been referred for an initial evaluation may be found eligible for services according to the definitions of the various disabling conditions defined in federal law. (Refer to Figure 1.2.)

For **MORE PRACTICE** on distinguishing the definitions of the disability categories included in IDEA, visit the Companion Website at *www.prenhall.com/overton.*

THE COMPREHENSIVE EVALUATION

When a student has not had success in a learning environment after several prereferral strategies have been applied, a formal

*From *Assessment: A key to appropriate program placement* (Report No. CE 045 407, pp. 11–13) by S. Maxam, A. Boyer-Stephens, and M. Alff, 1986, Columbia, MO: University of Missouri, Columbia, Department of Special Education and Department of Practical Arts and Vocational-Technical Education. (ERIC Document Reproduction Service No. ED 275 835.) Copyright 1986 by the authors. Reprinted by permission.

norm-referenced tests Tests designed to compare individual students with national averages, or norms of expectancy.

standardized tests Tests developed with specific standard administration, scoring, and interpretation procedures that must be followed precisely to obtain optimum results.

referral is made. The team may then make a decision to recommend a comprehensive evaluation or perhaps a new educational intervention or alternative, such as a change in classroom teachers. If the committee recommends a comprehensive evaluation, the assessment plan is designed.

The types of assessment that may be used in a comprehensive evaluation are varied, depending upon the student's needs. Some instruments used are **norm-referenced tests** or assessment devices. These instruments have been developed to determine how a student performs on tasks when compared with students of the same age or grade level. These tests are also **standardized tests**. This means that the tests were developed with very structured and specific instructions, formats, scoring, and interpretation procedures. These specifics, written in the test manual, must be followed to ensure that the tests are used in the manner set forth by the test developers. Refer to Table 1.2 to compare the various types of tests used in assessing learners.

Table 1.2   Various types of assessment.

Type of Assessment	Purpose of Assessment	Who Administers Assessment	When Assessment Is Used
Ecological Assessment	To determine classroom environmental influences or contributions to learning	Teacher or Intervention Team member such as special education teacher	Any time students appear to have learning or behavioral difficulties
Norm-Referenced Tests	To compare a specific student's ability with that of same-age students in national sample	Group tests—by teachers, Individual tests—by teachers, school psychologists, educational diagnosticians, other members of IEP team	When achievement or ability needs to be assessed for annual, triennial, or initial evaluations
Standardized Tests	Tests given with specific instructions and procedures—often are also norm-referenced	Teachers, members of Intervention/IEP teams, such as school psychologists or educational diagnosticians	When achievement or ability need to be assessed for annual, triennial, or initial evaluations
Error Analysis	To determine a pattern of errors or specific type of errors	Teachers, other personnel working with student	Can be used daily or on any type of assessment at any time
Curriculum-Based Assessment	To determine how student is performing using actual content of curriculum	Teachers	To measure mastery of curriculum (chapter tests, etc.)

Table 1.2   continued.

Type of Assessment	Purpose of Assessment	Who Administers Assessment	When Assessment Is Used
Curriculum-Based Measurement	To measure progress of a specific skill against an aim line	Teacher	Daily or several times each week
Dynamic Assessment	To determine if student has potential to learn a new skill	Teacher, other members of Intervention or IEP team	Can be used daily, weekly, or as part of a formal evaluation
Portfolio Assessment	To evaluate progress over time in specific area	Teachers, members of Intervention or IEP team	Over a specific period of time or specific academic unit or chapters
Criterion-Referenced Tests	To assess a student's progress in skill mastery against specific standards	Teachers, members of Intervention or IEP team	To determine if student has mastered skill at end of unit or end of time period
Criterion-Related Tests	To assess student's progress on items that are similar to objectives or standards	Teachers, members of Intervention or IEP team	Same as criterion referenced tests
Checklists, Rating Scales, Observations	To determine student's skill level or behavioral functioning	Teacher, members of Intervention or IEP team	Curriculum placement determination or behavioral screening

individualized education program (IEP) team The team specified in the IDEA amendments to make decisions about special education eligibility and interventions.

eligibility meeting A conference held after a preplacement evaluation to determine if a student is eligible for services.

In addition to standardized norm-referenced tests, team members use informal methods such as classroom observations, interviews with teachers and parents, and criterion-referenced instruments. A team of designated professionals and the parents of the student make up the **individualized education program (IEP) team**. The team reviews the results from the assessments in the eligibility meeting. This meeting will determine what educational changes may be necessary to provide the best instruction for the student.

During the **eligibility meeting**, the IEP team may determine that the student is eligible for special education services based on the information collected through the evaluation process. If the student is eligible, an IEP, or individual education program, must be written for the student. If, however, the student is not eligible for special education services, **alternative planning** should be considered, including educational intervention suggestions for the student. Alternative planning may include a plan for accommodations in the general classroom setting under Section 504. This law (presented in Chapter 2) requires that students who have disabilities or needs but who are not eligible to receive services under IDEA must

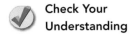
Check Your Understanding

Check your knowledge of the referral process presented in the previous section by completing Activity 1.3 below.

Activity 1.3

Using the information provided in Table 1.2, determine the type(s) of assessment that may need to be included in a comprehensive assessment plan.

1. If a teacher wants to determine the types of mistakes a student is making on written expression tasks such as sentence writing, the teacher may use _____ .

2. IEP team members are concerned that a student may be functioning within the range of mental retardation. In order to determine where the student's abilities are compared with other students his age, the team members determine that _____ should be included on the assessment plan.

3. The Teacher Assistance Team of a middle school receives a referral regarding a student who seems to have behavioral difficulty in only one of his classes during the day. In order to determine what is happening in this one classroom, the team decides that an _____ should be conducted.

4. In order to measure student progress against a standard set for all students in the same grade, _____ tests may be used.

5. When a teacher is concerned about a student's mastery of a specific math skill, the teacher may decide to use several measures, including _____ .

alternative planning A plan designed for educational intervention when a student has been found not eligible for special education services.

Individual Family Service Plan (IFSP) A plan designed for children ages 3 and younger that addresses the child's strengths and needs as well as the family's needs.

have accommodations for their needs or disabilities in the regular classroom setting. A 504 accommodation plan is designed to implement those accommodations. A sample 504 accommodation plan is presented in Figure 1.8.

When the referred child is 3 years of age or younger and eligibility for services has been determined, the law requires that an **Individual Family Service Plan (IFSP)** be developed by the team members and parents. The IFSP differs from the IEP in that the family's needs as well as the child's needs are addressed.

For **MORE PRACTICE** on distinguishing between the IEP, Section 504 Plans, and IFSPs, visit the Companion Website at *www.prenhall.com/overton.*

ASSESSING THE WHOLE CHILD: CULTURAL CONSIDERATIONS

The 1997 IDEA Amendments (presented in Chapter 2) required that state educational systems report the frequency of occurrence of disabilities and the race/ethnicity of students with disabilities. The first

Figure 1.8   Sample 504 plan.

---

504 Accommodation Plan

Name of Student _____ Date _____

1. Describe the concern for this students achievement in the classroom setting: _____

2. Describe or attach the existing documentation for the disability or concern (if documentation exists). _____

3. Describe how this affects the student's major life activities. _____ _____

4. The Child Study Team/504 Team has reviewed the case and recommends the following checked accommodations:

Physical Characteristics of Classroom or Other Environment

_____ Seat student near teacher.

_____ Teacher to stand near student when instructions are provided.

_____ Separate student from distractors (other students, air-conditioning or heating units, doorway).

Presentation of Instruction

_____ Student to work with a peer during seatwork time.

_____ Monitor instructions for understanding.

_____ Student to repeat all instructions back to teacher.

_____ Provide a peer tutor.

_____ Provide a homework helper.

_____ All written instructions require accompanying oral instructions.

_____ Teacher to check student's written work during working time to monitor for understanding.

_____ Student may use tape recorder during lessons.

---

reported results of this accounting are found in the *Twenty-Second Annual Report to Congress on the Implementation of the Individuals with Disabilities Education Act* (U.S. Department of Education, 2000). As reported in the literature for several years, particular groups of students from cultural and linguistically diverse backgrounds were found to be overrepresented in some categories of disabilities (see Table 1.3).

It has been observed that the disproportionate rate of occurrence of some students from various ethnic and cultural backgrounds happens in the disability categories that rely heavily on "clinical judgment," such as students with learning disabilities, students within the range of mild mental retardation, and students with emotional disturbances (Harry & Anderson, 1995). Fujiura

Assignments

——— Student requires reduced workload.

——— Student requires extended time for assignments.

——— Student requires reduced stimuli on page.

——— Student requires that work be completed in steps.

——— Student requires frequent breaks during work.

——— Student requires use of tape recorder for oral responses.

——— Student requires lower level reading/math problems.

——— No penalty for handwriting errors.

——— No penalty for spelling errors.

——— No penalty for grammatical errors.

Additional Accommodations for Medical Concerns (List)

_____

_____

Additional Accommodations for Behavioral Concerns (List)

_____

_____

Additional Resources for Parents (List)

_____

_____

Participating Committee Members

_____

_____

_____

_____

and Yamaki (2000) reported troubling patterns indicating that students from homes that fall in the range of poverty and that structurally include a single parent, are at increased risk for disabilities. Although there may be increased risks involved in environments that lack resources and support for single parents, the educational assessment of students from various cultural and linguistic backgrounds must be completed cautiously, fairly, and from the perspective of the child as a whole. Educators must keep the individual child's cultural, ethnic, and linguistic background in the forefront during the evaluation process.

Concern over the disproportionate rate of children from various ethnic and cultural groups being represented in special education categories resulted in directives to state educational agencies in

Table 1.3 Percentage of ethnic groups in special education.

Disability	American Indian	Asian/Pacific Islander	Black (non-Hispanic)	Hispanic	White (non-Hispanic)
Specific Learning Disabilities	1.4	1.4	18.3	15.8	63.0
Speech and Language Impairments	1.2	2.4	16.5	11.6	68.3
Mental Retardation	1.1	1.7	34.3	8.9	54.1
Emotional Disturbance	1.1	1.0	26.4	9.8	61.6
Multiple Disabilities	1.4	2.3	19.3	10.9	66.1
Hearing Impairments	1.4	4.6	16.8	16.3	66.0
Orthopedic Impairments	.8	3.0	14.6	14.4	67.2
Other Health Impairments	1.0	1.3	14.1	7.8	75.8
Visual Impairments	1.3	3.0	14.8	11.4	69.5
Autism	.7	4.7	20.9	9.4	64.4
Deaf-Blindness	1.8	11.3	11.5	12.1	63.3
Traumatic Brain Injury	1.6	2.3	15.9	10.0	70.2
Developmental Delay	.5	1.1	33.7	4.0	60.8
All Disabilities	1.3	1.7	20.2	13.2	63.6
Resident Population	1.0	3.8	14.8	14.2	66.2

Source: U.S. Department of Education (2001). *Twenty-Second Annual Report to Congress on the Implementation of the Individuals with Disabilities Education Act.* Washington, DC: Author.

IDEA 2004. The new version of IDEA includes specific mandates to states to make certain that policies and procedures are in place to prevent the disproportionate representation of ethnic groups in special education. The new requirements are discussed further in Chapter 2.

Portes (1996) posed the question, "What is it about culture and ethnicity that accounts for significant differences in response to the schooling process and its outcomes?" (p. 351). Portes further reasons that it is not fixed characteristics of students but more likely the learned behaviors and identities associated with school. An

Figure 1.9 Student progress monitoring graph.

Number Correct						Percent Correct
20	20	20	20	20	20	100%
19	19	19	19	19	19	95%
18	18	18	18	18	18	90%
17	17	17	17	17	17	85%
16	16	16	16	16	16	80%
15	15	15	15	15	15	75%
14	14	14	14	14	14	70%
13	13	13	13	13	13	65%
12	12	12	12	12	12	60%
11	11	11	11	11	11	55%
10	10	10	10	10	10	50%
9	9	9	9	9	9	45%
8	8	8	8	8	8	40%
7	7	7	7	7	7	35%
6	6	6	6	6	6	30%
5	5	5	5	5	5	25%
4	4	4	4	4	4	20%
3	3	3	3	3	3	15%
2	2	2	2	2	2	10%
1	1	1	1	1	1	5%
Your Possible Scores	**Pre-Test**	**End of Part I**	**End of Part II**	**End of Part III**	**End of Text**	

How does this graph work? Suppose you score a 10 on your pre-test or you answered 50% of the items correct. Circle that score as your baseline. If you would like to get 100% of the items correct, draw a straight line from the first score of 10 to the final % correct column score of 100%. This represents your goal line or your aim line. As you progress throughout the text, the more you study the material, the greater the chance that your scores will be along the goal line until you reach the 100% mark. See Figure 1.10 for this example. You will learn more about this process in the Curriculum-Based Measurement section of the text in Chapter 6.

example of such learned behaviors was described by Marsh and Cornell (2001), who found that minority students' experiences of school played a more important role in the likelihood of exhibiting at-risk behaviors than ethnicity. Educators must continue to strive for methods of assessment that are fair to all students. Burnette (1998) suggested the following strategies for improving accuracy in the assessment process in order to reduce disproportionate representation of minorities in special education:*

• Ensure that the staff knows requirements and criteria for referral and is kept abreast of current research affecting the process.

*Reducing the disproportionate representation of minority students in special education. ERIC/OSEP Digest E566. March 1998.

- Check that the student's general education program uses instructional strategies appropriate for the individual, has been adjusted to address the student's area of difficulty, includes ongoing communication with the student's family, and reflects a culturally responsive learning environment.
- Involve families in the decision to refer to special education in ways that are sensitive to the family's cultural background.
- Use only tests and procedures that are technically acceptable and culturally and linguistically appropriate.
- Testing personnel should have had training in conducting these particular assessments and interpreting the results in a culturally responsive manner.
- Personnel who understand how racial, ethnic, and other factors influence student performance should be included in the eligibility decision.

Figure 1.10   Example of student progress graph: Baseline score of 50, goal 100%.

Number Correct						Percent Correct
20	20	20	20	20	20	(100%)
19	19	19	19	19	19	95%
18	18	18	18	18	18	90%
17	17	17	17	17	17	85%
16	16	16	16	16	16	80%
15	15	15	15	15	15	75%
14	14	14	14	14	14	70%
13	13	13	13	13	13	65%
12	12	12	12	12	12	60%
11	11	11	11	11	11	55%
10	(10)	10	10	10	10	50%
9	9	9	9	9	9	45%
8	8	8	8	8	8	40%
7	7	7	7	7	7	35%
6	6	6	6	6	6	30%
5	5	5	5	5	5	25%
4	4	4	4	4	4	20%
3	3	3	3	3	3	15%
2	2	2	2	2	2	10%
1	1	1	1	1	1	5%
Your Possible Scores	**Pre-Test**	**End of Part I**	**End of Part II**	**End of Part III**	**End of Text**	

- When eligibility is first established, a set of firm standards for the student's progress and readiness to exit special education should be recorded.

The early writings of Vygotsky concerning special education students' development and assessment cautioned professionals to be certain that the disability was not in "the imagination of the investigators" (Vygotsky, 1993, p. 38). Vygotsky also emphasized that the qualitative aspect of assessment in determining strengths and weaknesses is important rather than the concern only for quantifiable deficits in children. Vygotsky reminded educators that children with disabilities should be viewed in light of their developmental processes in their various environments (Gindis, 1999; Vygotsky, 1993).

The way the student adapts to his or her environment, including culture and school, has a profound impact on the student's ability to have a successful school experience. Today the IDEA Amendments call for educational equity and reform as well as emphasize the use of a variety of early intervening services and assessment techniques that will be useful in educational planning rather than assessment only for determining eligibility. The remaining chapters of this text present educators with both formal and informal assessment and evaluation procedures to be used in educational planning and intervention.

To **READ MORE ABOUT** early intervention and minority overrepresentation, visit the Companion Website at *www.prenhall.com/ overton*.

CHAPTER SUMMARY

Assessment includes many types of evaluation of student progress. Assessment is necessary to monitor achievement, measure achievement of statewide curriculum standards, screen students who may require comprehensive evaluations to determine eligibility for services for disabilities, and to determine when programs need to be modified. Assessment must consider the student's cultural, linguistic, and ethnic background during the process. Assessment must view the student as a whole. The Traditional Assessment Model has been found to be problematic. Educators are now supporting a Contemporary Assessment Model that emphasizes intervention and problem solving.

THINK AHEAD

The steps of the evaluation process are structured by both federal and state laws. The federal mandates are presented in Chapter 2. Why do you think it is necessary to have laws that regulate the assessment process in education?

EXERCISES

Part I

Select the correct terms and write them in the blank spaces provided in each of the following statements:

a. assessment ✓
b. testing
c. curriculum-based assessment
d. error analysis
e. informal assessment ✓
f. prereferral intervention strategies
g. individual assessment plan
h. norm-referenced test
i. performance assessment
j. eligibility meeting

k. early intervention services
l. checklist
m. continuous assessment
n. overidentification
o. APA *Standards*
p. screening
q. IEP ✓
r. alternative planning
s. standardized tests
t. IFSP
u. dynamic assessment
v. disproportionality

_____ 1. Concerns regarding the _____ of students from diverse ethnic and cultural backgrounds emphasize the need for collecting assessment data in a variety of ways.

_____ 2. In order to assess all areas to obtain a view of the whole child, the _____ is designed for each individual student.

_____ 3. When a teacher wants to determine how a student solved a problem incorrectly, the teacher completes a(n) _____.

_____ 4. When a child from a different linguistic background is assessed by providing cues or prompts, a form of _____ has been employed.

_____ 5. As a result of the _____, an IEP or an alternative plan would be developed for a student.

_____ 6. _____ must be given in a specific manner as stated by the publisher, whereas informal tests include a variety of methods and strategies for collecting data.

_____ 7. If _____ prove to be unsuccessful, the team may conclude that the student requires additional assessment to determine if additional services are needed.

_____ 8. A test that compares a student's performance with a national sample of students of the same age or grade is known as a _____.

_____ 9. A student found to be eligible for services who is between the ages of 6 and 21 will have a personalized IEP written, whereas a(n) _____ will be designed for a student younger than school age.

_____10. Teachers who design assessment instruments from classroom materials are using _____ .

Part II

Answer the following questions:

1. One way to document that strategies have been attempted before referral is to use a

   _____

2. Why are statewide tests called high-stakes tests?

   _____

3. How might high-stakes testing improve the education of all students?

   _____

4. The 2004 Amendments to IDEA emphasize that more than 30 years of research indicates that the education of children with disabilities can be made more effective by

   _____

5. Summarize the best-practice procedures that include early intervening services and RTI and when an appropriate referral for special education may be made.

   _____

Answers to these questions can be found in the Appendix of this text or you may also complete these questions and receive immediate feedback on your answers by going to the Think Ahead module in Chapter 1 of the Companion Website.

COURSE PRE-TEST

Take this test before you read Chapter 1. You will begin to see your progress in the course when you take your next test at the end of Chapter 2. You will take a test to monitor progress at the end of each of the 4 parts of the text. Your instructor has the correct responses or you may check your responses on the Companion Website at _www. prenhall.com/overton_. After checking your responses, post on the graph at the end of the test. Each time you take a progress test, post the number of correct answers on the graph. Good Luck!

Pre-Test

Select the best answer from the terms below. Some of these terms may be used more than once.

a. dynamic assessment
b. criterion-referenced tests
c. ecological assessment
d. standard scores
e. disproportionality
f. mediation
g. negatively-skewed distribution

h. estimated true score
i. ADOS
j. measures of central tendency
k. UNIT
l. Vineland-II

m. latency recording
n. impartial due process hearing
o. overrepresentation
p. interresponse time

_____ 1. Considered the best assessment for determining students who may have a pervasive developmental disorder.

_____ 2. These include, among others, the numerical representation for the average of scores.

_____ 3. The visual representation when more scores are located above the mean.

_____ 4. A measure of intelligence that may be more fair for students who are ELL.

_____ 5. These are determined during the norming process and follow normal distribution theory.

_____ 6. Tests designed to accompany a set of skills.

_____ 7. Assessing the learning environment.

_____ 8. When students from a specific group are under- or over-represented in specific eligibility categories.

_____ 9. Assesses how a student functions across environments or settings.

_____10. Measure of time between the presentation of a stimulus and a response.

Fill in the Blanks

11. _____ is an event that occurs before the target behavior but is removed from the actual environment in which the behavior occurs.

12. The purpose of this test is to assess the cognitive abilities of children ages 3–18 applying both a theory of fluid/crystallized intelligence factors and mental processing factors.

13. When writing test reports the analysis of the comprehensive results are included in the _____ section.

14. On the UNIT, the _____ subtest uses a pencil and paper to measure reasoning and planful behavior.

15. The purpose of assessment is to _____.

16. _____ are norm-referenced measures of student achievement and retention of learned information.

17. _____ is noted by a vertical line on the student data graph.

18. _____ requires a calculation using the student's obtained score, the mean, and the reliability coefficient.

19. _____ will provide a different distribution of scores than the distribution of obtained scores.

20. The K-TEA-II provides an _____ that may be useful in determining student needs.

CHAPTER

2

Laws, Ethics, and Issues

Public Law 94-142
IDEA
IDEA Amendments of 1997
compliance
PL 99-457
IDEA 2004
due process
initial evaluation
comprehensive educational
  evaluation
informed consent
surrogate parent
consent form
parents' rights booklet
nondiscriminatory assessment
IDEA regulations
special education services

related services
grade equivalent
age equivalent
standard scores
annual goals
least restrictive environment
transition services
procedural safeguards
mediation
independent educational
  evaluation
impartial due process hearing
impartial hearing officer
Section 504 of the Rehabilitation
  Act of 1973
minority overrepresentation

CHAPTER FOCUS

This chapter includes the laws and ethical standards governing the use and interpretation of tests used in determining eligibility for special education services. The revisions in the federal regulations are a specific focus. Procedures for implementation of test results for educational interventions and issues of assessment are also included.

CEC KNOWLEDGE AND SKILLS STANDARDS

The student completing this chapter will understand the knowledge and skills included in the following CEC Knowledge and Skills Standards from Standard 8: Assessment:

CC8K1—Legal provisions and ethical principles regarding assessment of individuals

GC8K1—Specialized terminology used in the assessment of individuals with disabilities

CC8S6—Use of assessment information in making eligibility, program, and placement decisions for individuals with exceptional learning needs, including those from culturally and/or linguistically diverse backgrounds.

FROM CEC STANDARD 1: FOUNDATIONS:

CC1K4—Rights and responsibilities of students, parents, teachers and other professionals, and schools related to exceptional learning needs.

THE LAW: PUBLIC LAW 94-142 AND IDEA

Public Law 94-142 Education for All Handicapped Children Act of 1975; guarantees the right to a free and appropriate education in the least restrictive environment; renamed IDEA in 1990.

IDEA Individuals with Disabilities Education Act, passed in 1990 to give new name to PL 94-142.

IDEA Amendments of 1997 Passed in 1997, these amendments make several changes to the original law.

compliance To be operating within the federal regulations, within the confines of the law.

During the 1970s, substantial legal changes for persons with disabilities occurred. Much of the pressure for these changes came from parents and professionals. Another influential source affecting the language of the law was litigation in the civil court system. In 1975, the Education for All Handicapped Children Act, referred to as **Public Law 94-142**, was passed and two years later, the regulations were completed (Education of the Handicapped Act [EHA], 1975; *Federal Register*, 1977). In 1990, under PL 101-476, the act was renamed the Individuals with Disabilities Education Act, or **IDEA**. The regulations were written in 1992 (*Federal Register*, 1992). IDEA contains several major provisions guaranteeing the right to education for persons ages 3 to 21 with disabilities that require special services in the United States. The law grants the right to a free appropriate public education in the least restrictive environment. Many of IDEA's provisions concern the process of assessment. The law mandates that state education agencies (SEAs) ensure that proper assessment procedures are followed (*Federal Register*, 1992).

In 1997, IDEA was amended by the 105th Congress and is referred to as the **Individuals with Disabilities Education Act Amendments of 1997**. Although the original law has been in effect for two decades, professional educators must continue to monitor **compliance** with the mandates within each local education agency (LEA). Informed teachers and parents are the best safeguards for compliance in every school. Even several years after the law was enacted, one study revealed that only 28% of special educators felt they knew special education law (Silver, 1987). Congress noted continued difficulties with the implementation of the original law in the findings section of the law and stated that special education efforts should strive to ensure that students receive an appropriate education and that the rights of children and their parents are protected. The primary goals of Congress in passing the 1997 Amendments were summarized by Yell, Drasgow, and Ford (2000) and are presented in Table 2.1.

In 1999, the final regulations of the 1997 Amendments were published. The regulations governing assessment, titled Procedures for Evaluation and Determination of Eligibility (*Federal Register*, 1999), include changes to the original regulations of 1977 as well as sections that remain unchanged. The 1997 Amendments to IDEA and sections of the final regulations are incorporated in the following sections of this chapter.

Table 2.1 Congressional goals in passing IDEA 1997.

Major Goal	Explanation
Increasing parental participation	Parents must be more fully involved in the special education process through involvement in evaluation, program planning, and placement decisions.
Ensuring student access to the general curriculum	Students with disabilities have opportunity to be involved in the general curriculum and be educated with their nondisabled peers.
Decreasing inappropriate labeling	State education agencies give increased attention to racial, ethnic, and linguistic diversity to prevent inappropriate identification and mislabeling.
Using mediation to resolve disputes	Parents and educators are encouraged to work out their differences using nonadversarial means.
Improving educational results	Unnecessary paperwork requirements reduced to free teachers to focus on teaching and learning. Accountability mechanisms are incorporated in IDEA 97 (e.g., measurable annual goals).
Increasing school safety	IDEA 97 now includes disciplinary requirements.

Source: Copyright (as applicable) by the National Association of School Psychologists, Bethesda, MD. Reprinted with permission of the publisher. www.nasponline.org.

PL 99-457 IDEA amendments that extend services for special-needs children through infancy and preschool years.

In 1986 the Education for the Handicapped Act Amendments, **PL 99-457**, were passed. The final regulations, written in 1993 (*Federal Register*, 1993), were developed to promote early intervention for preschool children and infants with special needs or developmental delays. Additional changes were added in the 1997 Amendments of IDEA. Specific issues concerning PL 99-457 and the assessment of preschool children are discussed in Chapter 10.

In 2004, the Individuals with Disabilities Education Improvement Act was signed into law. This law was designed to address the portions of IDEA that needed improvement and to align this legislation with the No Child Left Behind Act of 2002. The changes included in this improvement act focused on:

- accountability of achievement by students with disabilities
- reduction of paperwork for educators and other professionals
- reduction of the noninstructional time spent by teachers (time spent completing paper work and attending meetings)
- providing additional means to resolve disagreements between schools and parents
- increasing early intervention activities and aligning this effort with No Child Left Behind

- improving teacher quality
- mandating efforts by state education agencies to decrease disproportionality of ethnic and culture representations in special education
- improvement of discipline policies of earlier legislation.

The changes in this act were based largely on the Congressional Findings listed before the actual legislation of 2004. To **READ MORE ABOUT** the Congressional Findings, visit the Companion Website at *www.prenhall.com/overton*.

Once a bill such as the Individuals with Disabilities Education Improvement Act has been signed by the president and becomes a law, the regulations are written which are the legal guidelines for implementing the law. It may take several months to two years to write the regulations. For example, when the original IDEA was passed as PL 94-142 in 1975, the regulations were not completed until 1977. More than one year after IDEA was signed into law, the final regulations were released. This chapter contains sections of the law that directly affect the assessment of children and youth of school age. The IDEA and **IDEA 2004** topics presented in this chapter are listed in Table 2.2.

IDEA 2004 Law that reauthorized and improved the 1997 Individuals with Disabilities Education Act (IDEA).

Table 2.2   IDEA topics presented in Chapter 2.

- Early intervening services
- Initial evaluations
- Parental consent
- Procedural safeguards
- Nondiscriminatory assessment
- Disproportionality of ethnic and cultural groups
- Determining needed evaluation data
- Evaluating children with specific learning disabilities
- Meeting the needs of persons with ADHD
- Multidisciplinary team evaluations
- The IEP team
- IDEA regular education teacher requirements
- Determining eligibility
- Parent participation
- Developing the IEP
- Considerations of special factors
- Transition services
- Due process
- Impartial due process hearings

IDEA AND ASSESSMENT

due process The right to a hearing to settle disputes; a protection for children with disabilities and their families.

initial evaluation A comprehensive evaluation before receiving special education services.

IDEA is a federal law containing mandates to promote fair, objective assessment practices and **due process** procedures, the foundations for legal recourse when parents or schools disagree with evaluation or placement recommendations. Teachers not only should be aware of the law but also should strive to maintain compliance in testing students, recommending placement, and developing IEPs. Teachers can help their local education agencies comply by following guidelines, meeting time lines, and correctly performing educational functions specified in the law. The first topics presented are the early intervening services that should be implemented prior to a referral for the **initial evaluation**, or the first evaluation of a student to determine if special education services are needed.

INITIAL EVALUATIONS

The provisions of IDEA as amended by the recent improvement act are presented throughout this chapter. The main section presented is Section 614 which concerns evaluations, parental consent, and reevaluations.

§614(a) Evaluations, Parental Consent, and Reevaluations—

(1) Initial Evaluations—
  (A) IN GENERAL—A State educational agency, other state agency, or local education agency shall conduct a full and individual initial evaluation in accordance with this paragraph and subsection (b) before the initial provision of special education and related services to a child with a disability under this part.
  (B) REQUEST FOR INITIAL EVALUATION—Consistent with subparagraph (D), either a parent of a child, or a State agency or local educational agency may initiate a request for an initial evaluation to determine if the child is a child with a disability.
  (C) PROCEDURES—
    (i) IN GENERAL—Such initial evaluation shall consist of procedures—
      (I) to determine whether a child is a child with a disability (as defined in section 602) within 60 days of receiving parental consent for the evaluation, or, if the State established a timeframe within which the evaluation must be conducted, within such timeframe, and
      (II) to determine the educational needs of such child.

Before a student can receive special education services in a general education classroom or in a special education setting, the members of the multidisciplinary team must complete a comprehensive

comprehensive educational evaluation A complete assessment in all areas of suspected disability.

individual evaluation of the student's needs. This evaluation should reflect consideration of the specific academic, behavioral, communicative, cognitive, motor, and sensory areas of concern. This **comprehensive educational evaluation** must be completed before eligibility can be determined. The IDEA 2004 requires that this comprehensive evaluation be completed within a specific timeframe of 60 days from the date that the parent signs a consent form for the evaluation. Additional specifications are presented in the law that address how the timeframe may be adjusted when a child transfers to a different school after the parent has signed the consent form. In addition, the law allows for flexibility of the timeframe if the parents do not produce the child for the evaluation or if the parents refuse to consent to the evaluation.

PARENTAL CONSENT

informed consent Parents are informed of rights in their native language and agree in writing to procedures for the child; consent may be revoked at any time.

The initial preplacement evaluation and subsequent reevaluations cannot take place without parental **informed consent**.

§614(a) Evaluations, Parental Consent, and Reevaluations—

(D) PARENTAL CONSENT
  (i) IN GENERAL—
    (I) CONSENT FOR INITIAL EVALUATION—The agency proposing to conduct an initial evaluation to determine if the child qualifies as a child with a disability as defined in section 602 shall obtain informed consent from the parent of such child before conducting the evaluation. Parental consent for evaluation shall not be construed as consent for placement for receipt of special education and related services.
    (II) CONSENT FOR SERVICES—An agency that is responsible for making a free appropriate public education available to a child with a disability under this part shall seek to obtain informed consent from the parent of such child before providing special education and related services to the child.
  (ii) ABSENCE OF CONSENT—
    (I) FOR INITIAL EVALUATION—If the parent of such child does not provide consent for an initial evaluation under clause (i)(I), or the parent fails to respond to a request to provide the consent, the local education agency may pursue the initial evaluation of the child by utilizing the procedures described in section 615, except to the extent inconsistent with State law relating to such parental consent.
    (II) FOR SERVICES—If the parent of such child refuses to consent to services under clause (i)(II), the local educational agency shall not provide special education and related services to the child by utilizing the procedures described in section 615.

surrogate parent Person appointed by the court system to be legally responsible for a child's education.

According to federal regulations, parental consent means that the parent, guardian, or **surrogate parent** has been fully informed of all educational activities to which he or she is being asked to consent. When a parent gives consent for an initial evaluation, for example, this means that the parent has been fully informed of the evaluation procedures and told why the school personnel believe these measures are necessary and that the parent has agreed to the evaluation.

Informed consent means that the parent has been informed in his or her native language or mode of communication. If the parent does not speak English, the information must be conveyed verbally or in writing in the parent's native language. In areas where languages other than English are prevalent, education agencies often employ bilingual personnel to translate assessment and placement information as necessary. Additionally, many state education agencies provide **consent forms** and **parents' rights booklets** in languages other than English. IDEA's statement regarding mode of communication sends a clear message that parents with visual or hearing impairments must be accommodated. The education agency must make every effort to provide sign interpreters for parents with hearing impairments who sign to communicate and large-type or Braille materials for parents with visual impairments who read in this fashion.

consent form Written permission form that grants permission for evaluation or placement.

parents' rights booklet Used to convey rights and procedural safeguards to parents.

IDEA 2004 includes provisions for allowing school systems to pursue the evaluation of a student without the parental consent if the school system follows the due process procedures within the law. In addition, this law states that parental consent for evaluation is not to be considered as consent for receiving special education services. Should parents refuse services that have been found to be necessary following the evaluation, the school system is not held responsible for the provision of such services.

The 2004 law addresses obtaining consent from parents when their child is a ward of the state in which they live. Local school systems must attempt to locate the parents and obtain consent for the evaluation and the receipt of services. However, if the parents cannot be found, the school can complete an initial evaluation without parental consent.

Parents must be notified of any action proposed by the local school regarding initial evaluations and options considered by IEP teams. These are among the many procedural safeguards provided to parents under the federal law. The law includes requirements of when parents should receive notice of their rights.

§615. Procedural Safeguards

(d) PROCEDURAL SAFEGUARDS NOTICE
   (1) IN GENERAL—
      (A) COPY TO PARENTS—A copy of the procedural safeguards available to the parents of a child with a

disability shall be given to the parents only 1 time a year, except that a copy also shall be given to the parents—

    (i)   upon initial referral or parental request for evaluation;

    (ii) upon the first occurrence of the filing of a complaint under subsection (b)(6); and

    (iii) upon request by a parent

(B) INTERNET WEBSITE—A local educational agency may place a current copy of the procedural safeguards notice on its Internet website if such a website exists.

Within the procedural safeguards information, the law requires that parents be informed of the procedures and safeguards for obtaining an initial evaluation, the requirement of prior notice before actions can be taken, information about parental informed consent, how to obtain student records and who has access to those records, and the process to follow when parents have complaints as well as the methods to resolve complaints.

Parental consent must be obtained before the school releases any student records to a third party. If, for example, the school personnel want the records to be mailed to a psychologist in private practice, the parents must consent in writing to the school to release the records and must know exactly which records are to be mailed and to whom.

Federal law requires that school personnel inform the parents before assessment and before placement that their consent is considered mandatory and may be revoked at any time. Therefore, if the parents had previously agreed to a placement for their child in a special education resource room for 1 hour per day and it is later recommended that the student receive services 3 hours per day, the parents may revoke their consent to approve special education services if they believe it to be in the best interest of their child. Should the parents revoke their consent, they are guaranteed the rights of due process. The school personnel are granted the same rights of due process and may decide to file a complaint against the parents. (Due process is discussed in more depth later in this chapter.)

The Check Your Understanding exercises included with this text provide opportunity for you to monitor your own progress in learning the assessment process. Complete this activity in Chapter 2. Additional exercises are provided on the Companion Website for this text at *www.prenhall.com/overton*.

nondiscriminatory assessment Fair and objective testing practices for students from all cultural and linguistic backgrounds.

NONDISCRIMINATORY ASSESSMENT

Many of the requirements that guide professionals in the assessment process are concerned with fair testing practice. The regulations presented on **nondiscriminatory assessment** address the issue of nondiscriminatory assessment consistent with the original

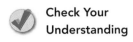 **Check Your Understanding**

Check your knowledge of procedures for initial evaluations by completing Activity 2.1 below.

Activity 2.1

Use the requirements that concern initial evaluation and informed consent to complete this activity. Choose from the phrases listed to answer the questions that follow the phrases:

> initial evaluation
> native language
> parents' rights booklet
> due process
> voluntary informed consent
> informed of activities
> mode of communication
> comprehensive evaluation
> revoke consent
> release of records
> reevaluation

1. The consent given by parents indicates that the parents have been _____ that the school personnel feel assessment procedures are necessary and in the child's best interest.

2. In compliance with IDEA, many parents are informed of their legal rights and responsibilities through the use of a _____.

3. A teacher would not be allowed to give a student's records to another interested party. Before the _____, the parents must consent in writing and receive an explanation of who would receive which records.

4. When parents decide that they no longer agree with a school placement or services for their child, they may _____, and if necessary, they may begin _____ procedures.

5. It is the responsibility of school personnel to provide information to parents in their _____ or using the _____ to comply with the federal law.

Apply Your Knowledge

Explain how the requirements regarding release of records affect the day-to-day life of a teacher (including a student teacher) working with special-needs students. _____
_____
_____

regulations. The regulations of 1999 add a statement regarding the assessment of students with limited English proficiency:

§614(b) Evaluation Procedures

(2) CONDUCT OF EVALUATION—In conducting the evaluation the local education agency shall—

(A) use a variety of assessment tools and strategies to gather relevant functional, developmental, and academic information, including information provided by the parent, that may assist in determining—

   (i) whether the child is a child with a disability; and

   (ii) the content of the child's individualized education program, including information related to enabling the child to be involved in and progress in the general education curriculum, or, for preschool children, to participate in appropriate activities;

(B) not use any single measure or assessment as the sole criterion for determining whether a child is a child with a disability or determining an appropriate educational program for the child; and

(C) use technically sound instruments that may assess the relative contribution of cognitive and behavioral factors in addition to physical or developmental factors.

This section of the law requires that multiple measures be used to obtain an accurate view of the child to determine if the child has a disability. It further states that the results of these evaluations are to be used to determine the content of the child's individualized educational program. This underscores that the purpose of the evaluation is to provide meaningful information that will assist in designing a program of intervention rather than simply evaluating a child to determine if the child is eligible for services. In addition, the law requires that the instruments used must be technically sound or, in other words, validated for such purposes.

IDEA includes the following additional requirements for evaluation of children to determine if they require special education support.

(3) ADDITIONAL REQUIREMENTS—Each local education agency shall ensure that—

(A) assessments and other evaluation materials used to assess a child under this section—

   (i) are selected and administered so as not to be discriminatory on a racial or cultural basis;

   (ii) are provided and administered in the language and form most likely to yield accurate information on what the child knows and can do academically, developmentally, and functionally, unless it is not feasible to so provide or administer;

   (iii) are used for purposes for which the assessments or measures are valid and reliable;

   (iv) are administered by trained and knowledgeable personnel; and

   (v) are administered in accordance with any instructions provided by the producer of such assessments

(B) the child is assessed in all areas of suspected disability

(C) assessment tools and strategies that provide relevant information that directly assists persons in determining the educational needs of the child are provided; and

(D) assessments of children with disabilities who transfer from 1 school district to another school district in the same academic year are coordinated with such children's prior and subsequent schools, as necessary and as expeditiously as possible, to ensure prompt completion of full evaluations

Nondiscriminatory assessment is mandated in the federal law to ensure fairness and objectivity in testing. This section requires that the instruments or techniques used in the assessment process are not racially or culturally biased. This section of the law sets forth the minimum criteria for nondiscriminatory assessment practice in special education. This section requires that the mode of communication used by the student be used in the assessment process. Like the communication standards written for parental consent, this section requires that school personnel find and use such appropriate methods as sign language or Braille if necessary to assess the individual's ability in the most fair and objective manner.

The assessment of students with limited proficiency or emerging proficiency in English is especially difficult. The law requires that assessment personnel make certain that the instruments employed in the assessment of students who have not mastered English, assess skills and abilities other than English skills.

The Act of 2004 clearly indicates that additional measures or strategies other than "tests," as well as parental input, should be considered in the evaluation process. This input should be incorporated in the eligibility decision and in educational interventions for the student. Moreover, information gathered should be for the purpose of enabling the student to participate in the general education curriculum. The assessment information is then to be used to determine if the child is eligible for special education services by meeting the criteria described in the definitions of special education (see Chapter 1). In addition, if the student is determined to be eligible for services, the assessment information gathered must be directly related to the components of the student's individualized educational program. This regulation is included as part of the emphasis that all assessment and subsequent evaluations be conducted with the goal of providing functional information that will be of benefit to the student.

In addition to using tests validated for the purpose for which they will be used, schools must ensure that tests are administered by trained personnel in the manner specified by the test producer. Much information regarding the training of personnel and administration of specific tests can be found in the individual test manuals, which the team member should study thoroughly before administration. Examples of errors made by professionals who do not comply with this section include administering tests or sections of a test to a group of students when the test was designed for individual administration, giving instructions to students in writing when the manual specifies oral presentation, or allowing 2 minutes for a test item when the test manual states that the time allowed is 90 seconds. When an examiner fails to follow directions specified by the developer of a standardized test, the results may lead to inaccurate interpretations and poor recommendations. In this regard, the testing has been unfair to the student.

The best and most consistent practice for using standardized instruments in the assessment of students for consideration of special services is to follow specific instructions provided for administration in a standardized manner. There are times, however, when the best practice for determining an *estimate* of the student's ability may require adaptation of the standardized administration. For example, it may be necessary when assessing a very young child who has a high level of anxiety or a child with limited cognitive ability to request that the parent or primary caretaker remain in the room, perhaps with the child sitting on the parent's lap. The parent in such situations may assist with some of the assessment items (such as providing translations if the young child has difficulty with articulation). In such cases, the 1999 regulations require that the modifications be explained in the written evaluation report. In such situations, an estimate of the child's ability has been obtained. This would require that additional measures, both standardized and nonstandardized, be incorporated into the assessment before making a decision about the student's eligibility.

The assessment of a student must include multiple measures designed for evaluating specific educational needs rather than using a single instrument. The law indicates that no single instrument should be used to determine eligibility. Before the passage of the original law (PL 94-142), numerous students were unfairly discriminated against because of conclusions based on a single IQ score. Often this resulted in very restrictive placement settings, such as institutions or self-contained classrooms, rather than more appropriate educational interventions. In addition to the federal mandates, court cases, such as *Larry P. v. Riles* (1984), have had a significant impact on discriminatory testing practices. This case and others are presented in Chapter 9.

Assessment can be discriminatory in other ways. The law mandates that the instruments used to assess one skill or area do not discriminate or unduly penalize a student because of an existing impairment. For example, a student with speech articulation problems who is referred for reading difficulties should not be penalized on a test that requires the student to pronounce nonsense syllables. The student in this case may have incorrectly pronounced sounds because of the speech condition, and the mispronunciations might be counted as reading errors. The reading scores obtained may be substantially lower than the student's actual reading ability because the misarticulations sounded like mispronunciations, or decoding errors, of the nonsense words.

The law also requires that students are assessed in all areas of suspected disability and that sensory, motor, and emotional areas should be included when appropriate. IDEA requires assessment personnel to consider all possible areas of need, even areas that are not typically thought to be associated or linked with the specific disability category. For example, it may not be uncommon for some students with specific learning disabilities to have difficulties in more than one academic area (e.g., spelling, writing, reading). Assessment personnel must also consider other areas that may require additional evaluation, such as emotional or motor areas. If these areas are determined to require educational interventions, these must be addressed through special education or related services (e.g., counseling or occupational therapy).

It is also required that the tests or instruments employed be psychometrically adequate. Test consumers are therefore required to have an understanding of general testing principles and the accuracy with which inferences about student's cognitive, academic, and behavioral functioning can be made using such instruments.

The law encourages the use of a variety of assessment devices and requires the participation of several professionals in the decision-making process. Using several varied assessment materials helps professionals to establish a more holistic view of the student. The professional expertise provided by a multidisciplinary team aids in promoting fair and objective assessment. It is necessary to involve many different professionals to assess all factors, such as vision, emotion, and language, that may need to be evaluated to reach the best educational decision.

These sections include the requirement to assess the student in all areas of suspected disability. In many cases, a referred student is known to have academic difficulty, but the disability might be due to many factors. The best way to determine whether the student truly has a disability, and if so, what type of disability, is to assess all of the suspected areas. For example, a referred student who demonstrated immature social skills and inappropriate behavior also demonstrated developmental and learning problems. When the referral information was submitted, background information was too limited to determine whether the student was having emotional problems or specific learning problems or possibly was subaverage in intellectual ability. In cases such as this, the law mandates that all areas be assessed to determine whether a disability exists. In this particular case, the young student was found to have a mild hearing impairment and subsequently had developed some behavioral problems. Appropriate audiological and educational interventions prevented further

Check Your Understanding

Check your knowledge of fair assessment practices by completing Activity 2.2 below.

Activity 2.2

Read the following statements to determine whether they represent fair testing practice and then circle the appropriate answer. If the statement is unfair, write a statement explaining how to correct the situation. If you think the statement is fair, explain why you think so.

1. A screening test may be used to make placement decisions about a student who was referred for special education services.

    _____ Fair _____ Unfair

    Comments: _____ .

2. Individuals who administer tests in the Woodlake local education agency are thoroughly trained to use each new instrument through school inservice sessions and graduate courses.

    _____ Fair _____ Unfair

    Comments: _____ .

3. A special education teacher is asked to test a student who speaks only Japanese. The teacher cannot find a test in that language, so he observes the student in the classroom setting and recommends that the student be placed in special education.

    _____ Fair _____ Unfair

    Comments: _____ .

4. A special education teacher is asked to give an educational test to a student from a minority culture. The test has been validated and proven to be culturally nondiscriminatory.

    _____ Fair _____ Unfair

    Comments: _____ .

5. A student is referred for an evaluation for possible eligibility for special education. The student has cerebral palsy, and the team member has no knowledge of this disorder. The team member asks the physical therapist to give advice on how to administer the test and requests that the therapist attend and assist during the evaluation. The team member also requests the assistance of the school psychologist to determine how the adaptations affect the psychometrics of the test administration. The team member documents all changes in the reevaluation report.

    _____ Fair _____ Unfair

    Comments: _____ .

6. A team decides to use the latest IQ score to make a decision regarding a change in eligibility for a student. The team agreed that no additional testing or data were necessary.

    _____ Fair _____ Unfair

    Comments: _____ .

> *Apply Your Knowledge*
>
> According to legal requirements, list the possible circumstances in which you would be required to ask for consultative guidance from other professionals during the assessment process. _____
>
> _____
>
> _____

behavioral problems from developing and helped to remediate academic skills.

Other discriminatory test practices concerned with test bias, examiner bias, for example, are presented in the section "Research and Issues Concerning IDEA" later in this chapter. The IDEA Improvement Act of 2004 includes additional specific statements regarding the initial assessment and reevaluation of students that require the consideration of additional data. These regulations concern data that may exist from previous assessments completed by the classroom teacher as well as additional data provided by the parents and other sources.

DETERMINING NEEDED EVALUATION DATA

§614(c) Additional Requirements for Evaluation and Reevaluations—

(1) REVIEW OF EXISTING EVALUATION DATA—As part of an initial evaluation (if appropriate) and as part of any reevaluation under this section, the IEP Team and other qualified professionals, as appropriate, shall—

  (A) review existing evaluation data on the child, including—

    (i) evaluations and information provided by the parents of the child:

    (ii) current classroom-based, local, or State assessments, and classroom-based observations; and

    (iii) observations by teachers and related service providers: and

  (B) on the basis of that review, and input from the child's parents, identify what additional data, if any, are needed to determine—

    (i) whether the child is a child with a disability as defined in section 602(3), and the educational needs of the child, or, in case of a reevaluation of a child, whether the child continues to have such a disability and such educational needs;

    (ii) the present levels of academic achievement and related developmental needs of the child;

    (iii) whether the child needs special education and related services, or, in the case of a reevaluation of a child, whether the child continues to need special education and related services; and

(iv) whether any additions or modifications to the special education and related services are needed to enable the child to meet the measurable annual goals set out in the individualized education program of the child and to participate, as appropriate, in the general education curriculum.

The amendments of IDEA call on professionals and parents alike to determine what data may be needed to obtain the most accurate picture of the child's current ability and educational needs. The law requires that the services are designed to assist the student in meeting the measurable goals of the IEP, and, again, the law requires that the student should participate in the general curriculum unless there is data to indicate that this would not be appropriate. For example, the student might require a specifically different test for statewide accountability of the general education curriculum and would also require a curriculum that would be different than that expected of age and grade peers.

These requirements indicate that the IEP team may review data from a variety of sources and, in the case of reevaluation, may determine that enough data exist to support continued eligibility. In such cases, the student would not be subjected to additional testing to complete the review for continued placement unless the parents request that their child be reevaluated. The student's progress is to be reviewed, although this does not necessarily involve substantial formal testing procedures. The reevaluation may consist of the testing considered to be necessary to determine the student's current educational or behavioral functioning. For example, a student who excels in math but has a specific reading disability may not require a reevaluation of math skills.

Additional regulations specify that the IEP team may conduct the review of the existing data without a meeting. Following the review, if additional data are needed, the public agency shall go about administering tests and other instruments in order to obtain the needed data. In the case of reevaluations, if additional data are not needed, the parents are to be notified by the team that no additional data are needed. Parents are also to be informed of the reasoning for the decision and that they have the right to request an assessment. Should the parents request additional assessment, the team is then required to complete the testing before determining that the child should continue receiving special education support.

EVALUATING CHILDREN WITH SPECIFIC LEARNING DISABILITIES

The federal law includes not only the definition for learning disabilities (see Chapter 1) but it also includes guidelines to assist in the determination of learning disabilities. Until the reauthorization of IDEA 2004, the law stated that a learning disability was indicated when a child had a significant discrepancy between cognitive ability and academic achievement. Using the significant discrepancy model meant that a student would likely struggle for several years during the elementary years, until a significant discrepancy could be determined. Research indicates that students could benefit from intervention during the early years and the new law reflects this research. The 2004 Amendments state:

§614(b)

(6) SPECIFIC LEARNING DISABILITIES

    (A) IN GENERAL—Notwithstanding section 607(b), when determining whether a child has a specific learning disability as defined in section 602, a local education agency shall not be required to take into consideration whether a child has a severe discrepancy between achievement and intellectual ability in oral expression, listening comprehension, written expression, basic reading skill, reading comprehension, mathematical calculation, or mathematical reasoning.

    (B) ADDITIONAL AUTHORITY—In determining whether a child has a specific learning disability, a local education agency may use a process that determines if the child responds to scientific, research-based intervention as a part of the evaluation procedures described in paragraphs (2) and (3).

According to these statements about the determination of specific learning disabilities, the IEP Team may consider data that includes formal assessments and measures of various abilities, however, it is no longer necessary to determine that a discrepancy exists between cognitive ability and achievement before a student can receive services under this category. Additionally, other assessment models, such as a response to intervention, may be used when the school employs research-based interventions as part of the assessment process. As stated in Chapter 1, in the Contemporary Assessment Model and applying early intervening services, the team may use interventions and should those interventions not result in expected progress, this may be regarded as evidence to be used in an eligibility decision. The team may then determine other data that may be needed.

MEETING THE NEEDS OF PERSONS WITH ATTENTION DISORDERS

When PL 94-142 was revised, attention disorders were studied by the U.S. Department of Education (U.S. Department of Education, 1991) for possible addition as a new disability category to IDEA. The decision was made that attention disorders (such as attention deficit disorder, or ADD) did not need a separate category because students with these disorders were already served, for the most part, in settings for students with learning or behavioral disabilities.

If the criteria for either specific learning disabilities or emotional disturbance were not met, the student could be served in an appropriate setting under the category of Other Health Impairment "in instances where the ADD is a chronic or acute health problem that results in limited alertness, which adversely affects educational performance" (U.S. Department of Education, 1991, p. 3). The terms *attention deficit disorder* and *attention deficit hyperactivity disorder* (ADHD) are included among those listed in the definition of the category of Other Health Impairment (§ 300.7(c)(9)(i), IDEA, 1997).

In cases where the attention disorder does not significantly impair the student's ability to function in the regular classroom, the student may be served within the regular classroom under the provisions of Section 504 of the Rehabilitation Act of 1973 (discussed later in this chapter). This law requires that students be given reasonable accommodations for their disability in the general education environment.

Students with attention disorders must undergo a comprehensive evaluation by a multidisciplinary team to determine whether they are eligible for services and, if so, whether they would be better served by the provisions of IDEA or of Section 504.

IEP TEAM EVALUATION

IDEA regulations
Governing document that explains IDEA in operational terms.

To decrease the possibility of subjective and discriminatory assessment, **IDEA regulations** mandate that the comprehensive evaluation be conducted by the members of a multidisciplinary IEP team. As stated in the federal requirements, each student must be assessed in a variety of areas by a team made up of professionals from various disciplines according to the individual's needs. All areas of suspected disability are assessed. If the team has determined during screening and has specified in the assessment plan that the student needs further evaluation in speech, language, reading, and social/behavioral skills, then a speech-language clinician, a special education teacher or educational diagnostician, and a school psychologist will be members of the assessment team. The team may obtain additional information from the parents, classroom teacher, school nurse, school counselor, principal, and other school personnel. Figure 2.1 describes the responsibilities of the various members who might be on the IEP team.

In compliance with the nondiscriminatory section of the law, team members employ several types of assessment and collect different types of data. Team members select instruments for their validity, technical adequacy, cultural fairness, and objectivity. Because the law requires that a variety of methods be used in

Figure 2.1   IEP Team: Who's who?

Team members include, in addition to the child's parents, the following:

Team Member	*Responsibilities*
School nurse	Initial vision and hearing screens, checks medical records, refers health problems to other medical professionals.
Special education teacher	Consultant to regular classroom teacher during prereferral process; administers educational tests, observes in other classrooms, helps with screening and recommends IEP goals, writes objectives, and suggests educational interventions.
Special education supervisor	May advise all activities of special education teacher, may provide direct services, guides placement decisions, recommends services.
Educational diagnostician	Administers norm-referenced and criterion-referenced tests, observes student in educational setting, makes suggestions for IEP goals and objectives.
School psychologist	Administers individual intelligence tests, observes student in classroom, administers projective instruments and personality inventories; may be under supervision of a doctoral-level psychologist.
Occupational therapist	Evaluates fine motor and self-help skills, recommends therapies, may provide direct services or consultant services, may help obtain equipment for student needs.
Physical therapist	Evaluates gross motor functioning and self-help skills, living skills, and job-related skills necessary for optimum achievement of student; may provide direct services or consultant services.
Behavioral consultant	Specialist in behavior management and crisis intervention; may provide direct services or consultant services.
School counselor	May serve as objective observer in prereferral stage, may provide direct group or individual counseling, may schedule students and help with planning of student school schedules.

continued.

Figure 2.1 continued.

Team Member	Responsibilities
Speech-language clinician	Evaluates speech-language development, may refer for hearing problems, may provide direct therapy or consultant services for classroom teachers.
Audiologist	Evaluates hearing for possible impairments, may refer students for medical problems, may help obtain hearing aids.
Physician's assistant	Evaluates physical condition of student and may provide physical exams for students of a local education agency, refers medical problems to physicians or appropriate therapists, school social worker, or visiting teacher.
Home-school coordinator; school social worker or visiting teacher	Works directly with family; may hold conferences, conduct interviews, and administer adaptive behavior scales based on parent interviews; may serve as case manager.
Regular education teacher	Works with the special education team, student, and parents to develop an environment that is appropriate and as much like that of general education students as possible; implements prereferral intervention strategies.

assessment, the team should make use of additional classroom observations, informal assessment measures, and parent interviews. Additional data provided by outside sources or from previous assessment should also be considered.

The IDEA amendments specify that an IEP team comprises specific individuals who reach a decision regarding the student's eligibility for services and possible interventions. Each member of the IEP team contributes carefully documented information to the decision-making process.

§ 614(d) (1) (B) Individualized Education Program Team—

The term 'individualized education program team' or 'IEP Team' means a group of individuals composed of—

   (i) the parents of a child with a disability
  (ii) not less than 1 regular education teacher of such child (if the child is, or may be participating in the regular education environment);
 (iii) not less than 1 special education teacher, or where appropriate, not less than 1 special education provider of such child;
 (iv) a representative of the local educational agency who—

(I) is qualified to provide, or supervise the provision of, specially designed instruction to meet the unique needs of children with disabilities;

(II) is knowledgeable about the general education curriculum; and

(III) is knowledgeable about the availability of resources of the local educational agency;

(v) an individual who can interpret the instructional implications of evaluation results, who may be a member of a team described in clauses (ii) through (vi)

(vi) at the discretion of the parent or the agency, other individuals who have knowledge or special expertise regarding the child, including related services personnel as appropriate; and

(vii) whenever appropriate; the child with a disability

The amendments require that at a minimum, the IEP team should include the child's parents, a general education teacher (if the child is or may be participating in the general education environment), a special education teacher, a supervisor of special education services who is knowledgeable about general curriculum and local resources, and someone who is able to interpret the instructional implications of evaluation results. In many cases, one person may fulfill more than one role on the IEP team. The school or parent may invite others as long as they have knowledge of the child or the services that will be provided. Together, the IEP team and other professionals, as appropriate, determine eligibility based on federal and state criteria.

IEP Team Member Attendance   The federal law and subsequent regulations written for IDEA required that the specific team members attend all IEP team meetings. In addition, all team members were required to attend the complete meeting even though they may not have had new information to contribute. In an effort to clarify the team members' participation and to decrease the amount of time that teachers spend away from classroom instruction, new statements were included in IDEA 2004 regarding attendance. The law includes the following statements.

§ 614(d) (1) (C) IEP Team Attendance—

(i) ATTENDANCE NOT NECESSARY—A member of the IEP Team shall not be required to attend an IEP meeting, in whole or in part, if the parent of a child with a disability and the local education agency agree that the attendance of such member is not necessary because the member's area of the curriculum or related services is not being modified or discussed in the meeting.

(ii) EXCUSAL—A member of the IEP Team may be excused from attending an IEP meeting in whole or in part when the meeting involves a modification to or discussion of the member's area of the curriculum or related services, if—

(I)　the parent and the local educational agency consent to the excusal; and

(II)　the member submits, in writing to the parent and the IEP Team, input into the development of the IEP prior to the meeting.

(iii)　WRITTEN AGREEMENT AND CONSENT REQUIRED—A parent's agreement under clause (i) and consent under (ii) shall be in writing.

These statements indicate that a member is not required to attend if there is no information being presented from that member either in written form or during the discussion by the Team. If the member is contributing to the meeting and cannot attend, with the parent's and school's consent, the member may submit the contribution in written form. As stated, the parental consent for either excusal or nonattendance must be given in writing.

These sections of the law provide guidance about how to involve general education teachers in the IEP process and encourage the child's teachers to contribute to the review and revision of the program.

DETERMINING ELIGIBILITY

IDEA 2004 Amendments include definitions and some fairly global criteria for determining eligibility for services for students with the following disabilities: autism, deaf-blindness, deafness, hearing impairment, mental retardation, multiple disabilities, orthopedic impairment, emotional disturbance, specific learning disability, speech or language impairment, traumatic brain injury, and visual impairment, including blindness. Most states have more specific criteria for determining eligibility for services, and many have different names for the conditions stated in the law. For example, some states use the term *perceptual disability* rather than *learning disability*, or *mental handicap* rather than *mental retardation.*

special education services Services not provided by regular education but necessary to enable an individual with disabilities to achieve in school.

related services Those services related to special education but not part of the educational setting, such as transporation and therapies.

During the eligibility meeting, all members should, objectively and professionally, contribute data, including informal observations. The decision to provide the student with special education services or to continue in a regular classroom without special education interventions should be based on data presented during the eligibility meeting. Parents are to be active participants in the eligibility meeting. School personnel should strive to make parents feel comfortable in the meeting and should welcome and carefully consider all of their comments and any additional data they submit. If the student has been found eligible for services, the team discusses educational interventions and specific **special education services** and **related services**. The federal requirements recommend that students are educated, as much as possible, with general education students. Related services are those determined by the IEP Team to be necessary for the child to benefit from the instructional goals of the IEP. Examples of related services include psychological services, early identification of children with disabilities, and therapeutic recreation. The 2004 regulations specifically added the related services of interpreting for students who are deaf or hard of hearing and services of the school nurse.

The improvement act of 2004 includes statements regarding when a student cannot be found eligible for services. These are stated in the following section.

§614(b)

(4) *Determination of Eligibility and Educational Need*—Upon completion of the administration of assessments and other evaluation measures:

    (A) the determination of whether the child is a child with a disability as defined in section 602(3) and the educational needs of the child shall be made by a team of qualified professionals and the parent of the child in accordance with paragraph (5); and

    (B) copy of the evaluation report and the documentation of determination of eligibility shall be given to the parent.

(5) *Special Rule for Eligibility Determination*—In making a determination of eligibility under paragraph (4)(A), a child shall not be determined to be a child with a disability if the determinant factor for such determination is—

    (A) lack of appropriate instruction in reading, including in the essential components of reading instruction (as defined in section 1208(3) of the Elementary and Secondary Education Act of 1965);

    (B) lack of instruction in math; or

    (C) limited English proficiency.

These sections state that the parent must be given a written copy of how the eligibility determination was made by the IEP Team.

This special rule for determining eligibility is aimed at preventing students from becoming eligible for special education solely on the basis of no instruction or limited instruction in reading or math. The special rule regarding appropriate instruction references the Elementary and Secondary Education Act. This reference links the Individuals with Disabilities Education Improvement Act with the No Child Left Behind Act for the definition of essential reading components. In this law, the essential components of reading are listed as:

Phonemic awareness

Phonics

Vocabulary development

Reading fluency, including oral reading skills; and

Reading comprehension strategies
[PL 107-110.§ 103(3)]

Students may not be found eligible solely on the basis of having limited English proficiency. In other words, students who have had these experiences must have other causative factors that result in the need for special education or related services. For example, a student may have had little or inappropriate instruction in math and be found eligible for services because of a reading disability if that has been documented through the evaluation.

 **Check Your Understanding**

Check your knowledge of the appropriate team member for consultation and assistance by completing Activity 2.3 below.

Activity 2.3

Determine who is the appropriate team member(s) to address the following problems and provide suggestions for interventions.

1. A student in class has been rubbing his eyes frequently, holds his books very close to his face, and seems to have difficulty seeing some printed words. You should request the assistance of   .

2. A young student in first grade has difficulty holding her pencil correctly, using scissors, and coloring in class. You notice that this student has marked difficulty when compared to the other students in class. You tried several procedures to help her learn how to use these tools, but she continues to have difficulty. You decide to refer the child to   .

3. Mr. Powers has a student in his class who seems to have difficulty staying awake. From time to time the student appears to be in a daze. Mr. Powers does not know if the child has a physical, emotional, or even drug-related problem. He asks you to help because "you know what to do with these types of problems." You advise Mr. Powers to contact   .

4. Ms. Stewart has a third grade student who just doesn't seem to be learning. She tells you she has "tried everything" including changing to an easier textbook. She feels certain that the student has a learning disability. What might be some of the suggestions you can provide for Ms. Stewart?   .

5. Miss Morales has a young male student who exhibits aggressive behaviors in class. She expresses concern that this student may harm himself or others. Your advice to Miss Morales is to   .

Apply Your Knowledge

Whom should you contact when you are not certain of the type of learning or behavioral challenge a student exhibits or if you are uncertain of who the appropriate related services personnel would be for a specific type of difficulty? _____
_____
_____

PARENT PARTICIPATION

Every effort should be made to accommodate the parents so that they may attend all conferences pertaining to their child's education. The federal requirements emphasize the importance of parental attendance.

The importance of parent involvement was underscored in the provisions of PL 99-457. The amendments require that the intervention plan, called the Individual Family Service Plan (IFSP), be designed to include the family members. As mentioned in Chapter 1, the IFSP identifies family needs relating to the child's development that, when met, will increase the likelihood of successful intervention. The legislation emphasizes the family and the child with the disability (Turnbull, 1990).

The IDEA Amendments of 1997 and the IDEA Amendments of 2004 further stressed the importance of parent participation by including the parents on the IEP team and by encouraging parents to submit additional information to be used during the eligibility and planning process. These regulations also require that the parent be given a copy of the evaluation report as well as the documentation of eligibility upon completion of the administration of tests and other evaluation materials.

grade equivalent Grade score assigned to a mean raw score of a group during norming process.

IDEA 2004 added provisions for parents to be involved in the educational planning process of their child without having to convene the whole IEP Team for changes in the educational program. This new law allows for amendments to the child's program to be made if the parent and the school personnel, such as the child's general education or special education teacher, agree.

DEVELOPING THE INDIVIDUALIZED EDUCATION PROGRAM

age equivalent Age score assigned to a mean raw score of a group during norming process.

standard scores Scores calculated during norming process of a test follow normal distribution theory.

annual goals Long-term goals for educational intervention.

Every student receiving special education services must have an individualized education program or plan (IEP) that is written in compliance with the requirements of IDEA. Current levels of educational performance may include scores such as **grade equivalents**, **age equivalents**, and/or **standard scores**. In addition, present level-of-performance information should include classroom performance measures and classroom behavior. Measurable long-term goals, or **annual goals**, must be included in the IEP. Every area in which special education services are provided must have an annual goal.

The IDEA Amendments of 2004 stated requirements for the IEP team to incorporate in the IEP. These requirements, presented in the following section, indicate what should be included in the written individual educational program, a plan for instructional intervention.

§614(d) Individualized Education Programs—

(1) DEFINITIONS—In this title:

   (A) INDIVIDUALIZED EDUCATION PROGRAM—

      (i) IN GENERAL—The term 'individualized education program' or 'IEP' means a written statement for each child with a disability that is developed, reviewed, and revised in accordance with this section and that includes—

         (I) a statement of the child's present level of academic achievement and functional performance, including—

           (aa) how the child's disability affects the child's involvement and progress in the general education curriculum;

           (bb) for preschool children, as appropriate, how the disability affects the child's participation in appropriate activities; and

           (cc) for children with disabilities who take alternate assessments aligned to alternate achievement standards, a description of benchmarks or short-term objective;

        (II) a statement of measurable annual goals, including academic and functional goals, designed to—

           (aa) meet the child's needs that result from the child's disability to enable the child to be involved in and make progress in the general education curriculum; and

           (bb) meet each of the child's other educational needs that result from the child's disability;

        (III) a description of how the child's progress toward meeting the annual goals described in subclause (II) will be

measured and when periodic reports on the progress the child is making toward meeting the annual goals (such as through the use of quarterly or other periodic reports, concurrent with the issuance of report cards) will be provided

(IV) a statement of the special education and related services and supplementary aids and services, based on peer reviewed research to the extent practicable, to be provided to the child, or on behalf of the child, and a statement of the program modifications or supports for the school personnel that will be provided for the child—

(aa) to advance appropriately toward attaining annual goals

(bb) to be involved in and make progress in the general education curriculum in accordance with subclause (I) and to participate in extracurricular and other nonacademic activities; and

(cc) to be educated and participate with other children with disabilities and nondisabled children in the activities described in this subparagraph

(V) an explanation of the extent, if any, to which the child will not participate with nondisabled children in the regular class and in the activities described in subclause (IV)(cc);

(VI) (aa) a statement of any individual appropriate accommodations that are necessary to measure the academic achievement and functional performance of the child on State and districtwide assessments consistent with section 621(a)(16)(A); and

(bb) if the IEP Team determines that the child shall take an alternate assessment on a particular State or districtwide assessment of student achievement, a statement of why—

(AA) the child cannot participate in the regular assessment and

(BB) the particular alternate assessment selected is appropriate for the child;

(VII) the projected date for the beginning of service and modifications described in subclause (IV) and the anticipated frequency, location, and duration of those services and modifications. . . .

The first requirement is that the IEP team include a statement of the student's current functioning and, most important, how the child's disability affects the child's ability to be involved with general education students. Since the 1997 Amendments it is assumed that students with disabilities will be educated with their nondisabled peers unless the IEP team provides reasons why this is not appropriate for the specific student (Huefner, 2000). The earlier regulations stated a preference for educating students in the general

least restrictive environment The environment determined to be the most like that of nondisabled peers.

education environment; however, the language included since the 1997 Amendments is stronger. These IEP requirements focus on inclusion of the student with disabilities within the mainstream environment and with general education students for education and other activities outside the educational setting. This part of IDEA is known as the provision of educational services in the **least restrictive environment** (LRE, discussed further later in the chapter).

Several court cases have resulted in interpreting the least restrictive environment requirement of the child's IEP. The movement toward inclusion as a method of providing the least restrictive environment has been found to be appropriate in some situations and not in others. Yell (1995) has offered a method that may assist IEP teams in making the determination of the appropriate educational environment that is based on the results of current interpretation within the judicial system. This method is shown in Figure 2.2.

Figure 2.2 Determination of the least restrictive environment.

School district decisions should be based on formative data collected throughout the LRE process.

1. Has the school taken steps to maintain the child in the general education classroom?
   • What supplementary aids and services were used?
   • What interventions were attempted?
   • How many interventions were attempted?
2. Benefits of placement in general education with supplementary aids and services versus special education.
   • Academic benefits
   • Nonacademic benefits
3. What are the effects of the education on other students?
   • If the student is disruptive, is the education of the other students adversely affected?
   • Does the student require an inordinate amount of attention from the teacher, thereby adversely affecting the education of others?
4. If a student is being educated in a setting other than the general education classroom, are integrated experiences available with able-bodied peers to the maximum extent possible?
   • In what academic settings is the student integrated with able-bodied peers?
   • In what nonacademic settings is the student integrated with able-bodied peers?
5. Is the entire continuum of alternative services available from which to choose an appropriate environment?

Source: From Least restrictive environment, inclusion, and students with disabilities: A legal analysis, by M. L. Yell, 1995, *Journal of Special Education, 28*, 389–404. Copyright by PRO–ED, Inc. Adapted by permission.

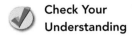

Check Your Understanding

Check your knowledge of the least restrictive environment and other requirements of IDEA by completing Activity 2.4 below.

Activity 2.4

As a special education teacher in Achievement Elementary School you are a member of the IEP team. The team is meeting to review the assessment results of a student who meets the eligibility criteria for mild mental retardation. One of the team members believes that this student should be placed in a self-contained special education setting for a majority of the school day. Explain your concerns about the environment and offer solutions.

Apply Your Knowledge

If the student in this scenario requires interventions in a special education setting, what would the team be required to include in the student's IEP? _____

_____

_____

The team must consider the extent to which the student can participate in statewide assessments. The level of participation in these assessments and any accommodations required must be stated in the IEP. It is clear that meeting the student's needs within the least restrictive environment is a goal of the Amendments of 1997 and 2004.

The 2004 Amendments add a component to the IEP that represents further alignment with the No Child Left Behind Act. In the No Child Left Behind Act, there is an emphasis on using research-based interventions and instructional methodology when addressing instruction in the early grades, especially in reading and math. In the most recent reauthorization of IDEA (2004), the IEP should include, to the extent practical, educational programming and strategies, that are based on peer-reviewed research. This represents the movement in educational reform to use instructional time wisely by incorporating teaching strategies that are supported by research in scholarly educational and psychological journals. The use of such strategies will increase the likelihood that students will make the progress expected each year. Making adequate progress in educational achievement is at the core of accountability in education. The statements regarding the IEP requirements of statewide assessment are tied to this movement of accountability in the education of students with disabilities.

The final regulations of IDEA 2004 included the definition of scientifically based research by stating that it is the same definition as that of the definition included in NCLB (also known as the Elementary and Secondary Education Act). To read more about this definition, visit the Companion Website at *www.prenhall.com/overton*.

As the Team considers the student's individual program, the 2004 Amendments require that the Team use the following guidelines to develop the IEP.

§614(d) (3) Development of the IEP—

(A) IN GENERAL—In developing each child's IEP, the IEP Team, subject to subparagraph (C), shall consider—

(i) the strengths of the child;

(ii) the concerns of the parents for enhancing the education of their child;

(iii) the results of the initial evaluation or most recent evaluation of the child; and

(iv) the academic, developmental, and functional needs of the child.

The IDEA amendments include a section of considerations for students with special factors or conditions. These considerations are presented in the following paragraphs.

§614(d) (3) (B) Consideration of Special Factors —The IEP Team shall:

(i) in the case of the child whose behavior impedes the child's learning or that of others, consider the use of positive behavioral interventions and supports, and other strategies to address that behavior;

(ii) in case of a child with limited English proficiency, consider the language needs of the child as such needs relate to the child's IEP;

(iii) in the case of the child who is blind or visually impaired, provide for instruction in Braille and the use of Braille unless the IEP Team determines, after evaluation of the child's reading and writing skills, needs, and appropriate reading and writing media (including an evaluation of the child's future needs for instruction in Braille or the use of Braille), that instruction in Braille of the use of Braille is not appropriate for the child;

(iv) consider the communication needs of the child, and in the case of a child who is deaf or hard of hearing, consider the child's language and communication needs, opportunities for direct communications with peers and professional personnel in the child's language and communication mode, academic level, and a full range of needs, including opportunities for direct instruction in the child's language and communication mode; and

(v) consider whether the child needs assistive technology devices and services.

Each of these requirements mandates the IEP team to consider specific needs of individuals, such as students with limited English proficiency and students with various disabilities. These specific needs, which have been determined through effective assessment, should be addressed in the IEP and progress monitored and reviewed, at least annually, by the IEP Team.

For **MORE PRACTICE** with IEP requirements, visit the Companion Website at *www.prenhall.com/overton.*

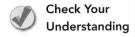 **Check Your Understanding**

Check your knowledge of comparing IDEA and Section 504 by completing Activity 2.5 below.

Activity 2.5

Refer to pages 68–70 of your text. Read the following descriptions of students and determine how their needs might best be served. Distinguish between which students fall under IDEA and which students can be served through Section 504.

1. Lorenzo was born with cerebral palsy and requires the use of a wheelchair. He is able to use a computer for word processing and completes all of his assignments using either his laptop or his computer at home. Lorenzo's most recent statewide assessments indicate that he is at or above the level expected in all academic areas. Lorenzo can be served _____.

2. Marilu has been found to have attention deficit disorder. She requires medication but her medication is time released and she does not need to take a dose at school. Marilu requires additional time to complete her assignments and performs best when she can sit near the teacher. Her report indicates that her grades are within the average range with the exception of math which is above average. Marilu can be served _____.

3. Randal has had signs of depression for the past several months. His parents decided to seek the assistance of an outside psychologist for counseling. Randal began to improve and he is now participating with his friends and playing team sports. His grades continue to decline and his reading skills are significantly below his peers. Because of his difficulty reading, his content subject grades began to fall as well. He was assessed and was found to have a significant reading disability. Randal can be served _____.

Apply Your Knowledge

A key component of a student meeting the eligibility requirements for a category of special education is that in addition to an existing condition, the condition or disability must also _____
_____
_____

TRANSITION SERVICES

In the section addressing the content of the IEP, the law addresses the needs of students who are nearing the age when they may make the transition to adult life.

§614(d) (1) (A) (i) (VIII) beginning not later than the first IEP to be in effect when the child is 16, and updated annually thereafter—

(aa) appropriate measurable postsecondary goals based upon age appropriate transition assessments related to training, education, employment, and where appropriate, independent living skills;

(bb) the transition services (including courses of study) needed to assist the child in reaching those goals; and

(cc) beginning not later than 1 year before the child reaches the age of majority under State law, a statement that the child has been informed of the child's rights under this title, if any, that will transfer to the child on reaching the age of majority under section 615(m).

transition services
Services designed to help students make the transition from high school to postsecondary education or work environment.

IDEA stressed the importance of **transition services** to prepare students 16 years or older for a work or postsecondary environment. Where appropriate in educational planning, younger students may also be eligible for such services. The law underscores the importance of early planning and decisions by all members affected, including the student. The planning for the needed transition begins by age 16 or younger, if appropriate.

The IDEA Amendments emphasized transition services to a greater extent than did other regulations. They also extended the rights to the student at the age of majority according to individual

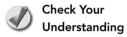 **Check Your Understanding**

Check your knowledge of the legal requirements of Individuals with Disabilities Education Improvement Act of 2004 by completing Activity 2.6 below.

Activity 2.6

After reviewing the legal requirements of IDEA 2004, complete the following.

1. IDEA 2004 requires that the IEP Team members participate in the team meetings. Under certain circumstances, some members of the IEP Team may be excused from attending the meeting. Explain when this is allowed and what must happen in order for this to be allowed.

2. Is it possible that a professional from an outside agency can determine that a child has a disability and the child should subsequently receive special education support?

3. A second-grade student recently enrolled in your school. The student is a recent immigrant from Mexico. Your school determines that the child had not previously been enrolled in school in Mexico due to his parents' lack of funds and due to a lack of transportation to school. The student's mother has recently obtained citizenship. Once the child began to attend your school, it was determined that the child could not read in English or Spanish. Can the student be referred for an evaluation for special education services?

4. Mrs. Lorenzo met with her son's teacher. They determined that her son might require an additional session of support time in the resource room which would increase the amount of time from two thirty-minute sessions per week to three thirty-minute sessions. In order to make this change to the IEP, will the Team need to be convened?

state laws. The age of majority is the age at which a child is no longer considered to be a minor (in many states, the age is 18). School personnel are responsible for communicating to the student that the rights under the law are now in the hands of the student rather than the parents. Moreover, the law requires that the student be informed of the transfer of rights a year before the student reaches the age of majority.

The 2004 Amendments add more specificity regarding the transitional assessment and appropriate annual goals. The statements stress that the postsecondary goals be measurable and that the goals should be based upon specific assessment in areas of education, employment, and daily living skills as appropriate.

DUE PROCESS

procedural safeguards Provisions of IDEA designed to protect students and parents in the special education process.

IDEA was influenced to a large degree by parent organizations and court cases involving individuals with disabilities and their right to education. When schools implement the provisions of the law, occasionally differences arise between the schools providing the service and the parents of the student with the disability. Therefore, IDEA contains provisions for parents and schools to resolve their differences. These provisions are called due process provisions.

The **procedural safeguards** are inherent throughout the portions of the law concerned with assessment. For example, parental informed consent is considered a procedural safeguard designed to prevent assessment and placement of students without parents' knowledge. Parents may withdraw their consent at any time. Other provisions promote fairness in the decision-making process. Included in these provisions are the parents' right to examine all educational records and the right to seek an independent educational evaluation as well as the right to a hearing to resolve differences.

mediation Process of settling a dispute between parents and schools without a full third-party hearing.

The IDEA Amendments of 1997 include a significant addition in the area of due process. The amendments provide new sections for promoting **mediation** as a method to resolve disagreements between parents and their local school agency. The requirements mandate local education agencies to provide mediation at no cost to the parents. The mediation process is voluntary on the part of the school and the parents. This process cannot be used by a local education agency to delay parental rights to a hearing or to deny any other rights provided in the regulations. The mediation process is to be conducted by qualified and impartial trained mediators who are included on a list maintained by each state.

IDEA 2004 adds a requirement for a resolution session to be held with the parents and the school personnel within 15 days of the filing of a complaint. This session is a step to resolve the complaint so that a formal hearing can be avoided. During this session, the school may not have an attorney present unless the parents are accompanied by their attorney. This is an opportunity for the school to resolve the issue in a timely manner. This resolution session may be waived if the parents and school personnel all agree in writing to do so. The parents may choose to waive the resolution meeting and to schedule a mediation meeting according to the 2004 Amendments.

independent educational evaluation
Comprehensive evaluation provided by a qualified independent evaluator.

The parents of a student who has been evaluated by school personnel may disagree with the results obtained during the assessment process. Should this occur, the parents have the right to obtain an independent evaluation by an outside examiner. The **independent educational evaluation** is provided by a qualified professional not employed by the local education agency. Should the independent evaluation results differ from the evaluation results obtained by school personnel, the school must pay for the evaluation. The exception to this is if the school initiates an impartial due process hearing to resolve the different results and the hearing officer finds in favor of the school. In this case, the parents would be responsible for paying for the independent evaluation. If, however, the hearing finds in favor of the parents, the school is responsible for payment.

IMPARTIAL DUE PROCESS HEARING

impartial due process hearing A hearing by an impartial officer that is held to resolve differences between a school and parents of a student with disabilities.

impartial hearing officer Person qualified to hear disputes between schools and parents; not an employee of school agency.

The parents and school are provided with procedures for filing complaints and requesting an **impartial due process hearing**. In a third-party hearing, the parents and the school may individually explain their side of the disagreement before an **impartial hearing officer**, a person qualified to hear the case. In some states, third-party hearing officers are lawyers; in other states, the hearing officers are special education professionals, such as college faculty who teach special education courses to prepare teachers.

Parents should be advised before the hearing that although counsel (an attorney) is not required for the hearing, they do have the right to secure counsel as well as experts to give testimony. After hearing each side of the complaint, the hearing officer reaches a decision. A finding in favor of the parents requires the school to comply with the ruling or appeal to a state-level hearing. In turn, if favor is found with the school, the parents must comply. If the parents do not wish to comply, they may be able to request a state-level hearing or file an appeal with a civil court.

While the school and parents are involved with due process and hearing procedures, the student remains in the classroom setting in which she was placed before the complaint was filed. This requirement has been called the stay-put provision.

SECTION 504

Section 504 of the Rehabilitation Act of 1973 A civil rights law that includes protection from discrimination and reasonable accommodations.

Section 504 of the Rehabilitation Act of 1973 includes many of the same concepts, such as procedural safeguards and evaluation, as those in IDEA. The law extends beyond the categories listed in IDEA and beyond the public school environment. This law is a civil rights law, and its purpose is to prevent discrimination against individuals with disabilities in programs receiving federal financial assistance. Students with disabilities are protected from discrimination in schools receiving federal financial assistance under Section 504, whether or not they are protected by IDEA. The law extends the educational regulations to include postsecondary environments, such as colleges and universities. It is used to address the situation of people with chronic health conditions in the public education setting who may not be addressed through IDEA, such as students with ADHD who do not need full special education support because of other significant learning disabilities.

Some notable differences exist between IDEA and Section 504 that were summarized by Yell (1997). These differences are presented in Table 2.3.

Table 2.3 Differences between IDEA and 504.

Component	IDEA	Section 504
Purpose of law	• Provides federal funding to states to assist in education of students with disabilities • Substantive requirements attached to funding	• Civil rights law • Protects persons with disabilities from discrimination in programs or services that receive federal financial assistance • Requires reasonable accommodations to ensure nondiscrimination
Who is protected?	• Categorical approach • Thirteen disability categories • Disability must adversely impact educational performance	• Functional approach • Students (a) having a mental or physical impairment that affects a major life activity, (b) with a record of such an impairment, or (c) who are regarded as having such an impairment • Protects students in general and special education
FAPE	• Special education and related services that are provided at public expense, meet state requirements, and are provided in conformity with the IEP • Substantive standard is educational benefit	• General or special education and related aids and services • Requires a written education plan • Substantive standard is equivalency

continued.

Table 2.3   continued.

Component	IDEA	Section 504
LRE	• Student must be educated with peers without disabilities to the maximum extent appropriate • Removal from integrated settings only when supplementary aids and services are not successful • Districts must have a continuum of placement available	• School must ensure that the students are educated with their peers without disabilities
Evaluation and placement	• Protection in evaluation procedures • Requires consent prior to initial evaluation and placement • Evaluation and placement decisions have to be made by a multidisciplinary team • Requires evaluation of progress toward IEP goals annually and reevaluation at least every 3 years	• Does not require consent; requires notice only • Requires periodic reevaluation • Reevaluation is required before a significant change in placement
Procedural safeguards	• Comprehensive and detailed notice requirements • Provides for independent evaluations • No grievance procedure • Impartial due process hearing	• General notice requirements • Grievance procedure • Impartial due process hearing
Funding	• Provides for federal funding to assist in the education of students with disabilities	• No federal funding
Enforcement	• U.S. Office of Special Education Programs (OSEP) (can cut off IDEA funds) • Complaints can be filed with state's department of education	• Compliance monitoring by state educational agency (SEA) • Complaint can be filed with Office of Civil Rights (OCR) (can cut off all federal funding)

Source: From *The law and special education*, by M. L. Yell, 1997, Upper Saddle River, NJ: Prentice Hall. Copyright by Prentice Hall.

For the purposes of assessment and educational planning, Section 504 seeks to meet the needs of students according to how students' conditions affect their functioning within life activities. This places the emphasis of assessment and program planning on a student's current functioning within that activity and calls for reasonable accommodations. For a college student with a specific learning disability, for example, the reasonable accommodations may include taking exams in a quiet room with extended time because of attention deficit disorder or waiving a foreign language requirement because of a specific learning disability in written language.

RESEARCH AND ISSUES CONCERNING IDEA

IDEA states that each school agency shall actively take steps to ensure that parents participate in the IEP process in several ways. First, the parents must agree by informed consent before the initial evaluation and before receiving special education services. The 1997 amendments added the provision that parents must consent prior to the reevaluation. The parents also participate in the decision-making process regarding eligibility. Following the eligibility determination, the parents are to participate in the development of the IEP. Legally, parents have the right to participate in the evaluation and IEP processes, and schools are mandated by the regulations to involve parents.

Informed consent is one of the first ways to ensure parental involvement and procedural safeguards. Informed consent is compounded by issues such as parental literacy, parental comprehension of the meaning of legal terminology, and the time professionals spend with parents explaining testing and special education. Parents' rights materials may be made more difficult to understand because of their use of highly specialized vocabulary. According to an early study involving observation and analysis of interactions in IEP conferences, parents' rights were merely "glossed over in the majority of conferences" (Goldstein, Strickland, Turnbull, & Curry, 1980, p. 283). This suggests that sufficient time may not be allotted to discussing issues of central concern to parents. Recent changes in the 1997 Amendments are designed to promote genuine parental involvement in educational assessment and planning.

Katsiyannis (1994) reviewed decisions and reports from the Office of Civil Rights (OCR) concerned with the question of procedural safeguards and parental involvement. Katsiyannis stated that the OCR found that the typical sequence of the referral/ screening process denied procedural safeguards at the prereferral stage. Furthermore, parents should be informed of procedural safeguards at the time that the student is screened to determine whether additional assessment will be conducted. Educators should keep in mind that the new regulations stress parental involvement during all stages of the assessment and planning process. These regulations provide the minimum guidelines for professionals; best practice dictates that parents should be involved throughout their child's education (Sheridan, Cowan, & Eagle, 2000).

The provision granted to parents in the IEP process is active participation in the IEP conference by contributing to the formulation of objectives and long-term goals for their children. In the past, in traditional IEP conferences, parents were found to be passive and to attend merely to receive information (Barnett, Zins, & Wise, 1984; Brantlinger, 1987; Goldstein et al., 1980; Goldstein & Turnbull, 1982; Vaughn, Bos, Harrell, & Lasky, 1988; Weber & Stoneman, 1986). Parents are now considered to be equal team members in the IEP process.

An area of additional concern involves working with parents of culturally, linguistically, or environmentally diverse backgrounds. Professionals should make certain that materials and concepts presented are at the appropriate level. Special education or legal concepts are complex for many persons who are not familiar with the vocabulary and process. For persons who do not speak English as a primary language, legal terms and specialized concepts may be difficult even though materials are presented in the individual's native language. These concepts may be different from educational concepts of their original culture. Salend and Taylor (1993) suggested that the parents' level of acculturation be considered, noting that children may become acculturated much more quickly than their parents. In addition, Salend and Taylor have reminded educators to consider the family's history of discrimination and the family structure, since these factors may have an impact on the family's interactions with school personnel. Educational professionals should make every effort to be certain that all parents are familiar with the special education process, services available, and their expected role during the assessment and IEP processes.

Parents and educators working together will benefit the student's educational program. Establishing a positive relationship with parents requires educators to work with parents in a collaborative manner. Sheridan et al. provided a list of actions that may enhance the collaborative nature of the relationship (2000). These actions are presented in Table 2.4.

ISSUES OF NONDISCRIMINATORY ASSESSMENT

minority overrepresentation
When the percentage of a culturally different group is greater in special education classes than in the local education agency.

Perhaps no other area in the field of psychoeducational assessment has received more attention than that of nondiscriminatory assessment. Much of the research and controversial issues center around the overrepresentation of minority students in special education classes. **Minority overrepresentation** is found to occur when the percentage of minority students enrolled in particular special education classes is larger than the percentage of minority students enrolled in the local education agency. In other words, if classes for mildly disabled students were made up of 28% minority students yet only 12% of the local education agency was made up of minorities, the local education agency's special education classes would have an overrepresentation of minority students.

Table 2.4 Actions reflective of collaborative relationships.

1. Listening to one another's perspective.
2. Viewing differences as a strength.
3. Remaining focused on a mutual interest (e.g., assessment and planning for student needs).
4. Sharing information about the child, the home, the school system, and problems encountered in the system.
5. Asking for ideas and opinions about the child, problems, goals, and potential solutions.
6. Respecting the skill and knowledge of each other related to the student, the disability, and contextual considerations.
7. Planning together to address parents', teachers', and students' needs.
8. Making joint decisions about the child's educational program and goals.
9. Sharing resources to work toward goal attainment.
10. Providing a common message to the student about schoolwork and behavior.
11. Demonstrating willingness to address conflict.
12. Refraining from finding fault, and committing to sharing successes.

Source: Copyright (as applicable) by the National Association of School Psychologists, Bethesda, MD. Reprinted with permission of the publisher. www.nasponline.org.

The U.S. Department of Education reported that minority over-representation in special education continues to be problematic (U.S. Department of Education, 1997). Analyzing data from the Office of Civil Rights, the U.S. Department of Education reported that although African Americans account for 16% of the total population in schools, 32% of the students in settings for persons with mild mental retardation and 29% of the students diagnosed as having moderate mental retardation are African American. In addition to these classifications, African Americans account for 24% of the students within the category of emotional disturbance and 18% of students served as having specific learning disabilities. Concerns expressed in the *Nineteenth Annual Report to Congress on the Implementation of IDEA* (U.S. Department of Education, 1997) include minority students being placed into more segregated classroom settings and restrictive curricula, which results in lower achievement.

A study examining the relationship between state financial resources and special education categories reported that states with higher numbers of children who are considered living in poverty had lower percentages of students categorized as learning disabled, and states with more financial resources had a higher percentage of students with learning disabilities (McLaughlin & Owings, 1992). Sherman concluded that risk of experiencing developmental delays, emotional disturbance, or learning disabilities increased by 2.4% if the child comes from a family experiencing poverty (Sherman, 1994).

Children experiencing poverty are more likely to have health problems, developmental problems, and low achievement, which will require special education support (U.S. Department of Education, 1997).

Much of the blame for the overrepresentation of minorities in special education has been attributed to referral and evaluation practices. The amount of attention given to the assessment process may be due in part to IDEA's emphasis on nondiscriminatory assessment. The law clearly states that educational agencies should use evaluation procedures that are not racially or culturally discriminatory. This can have many implications when assessing students who have linguistic differences and those who may come from culturally different backgrounds or deprived environments. The following list of problems of bias in assessment is adapted from Reynolds, Lowe, and Saenz (1999):

1. Inappropriate content. Students from minority populations may lack exposure to certain items on the assessment instrument.

2. Inappropriate standardization samples. Ethnic minorities were not represented in the normative sample at the time of development of the instrument.

3. Examiner and language. White, English-speaking examiners may intimidate students of color and students from different linguistic backgrounds.

4. Inequitable social consequences. Because of discriminatory assessment practices, minority students may be relegated to lower educational placements, which may ultimately result in lower-paying jobs.

5. Measurement of different constructs. White test developers designed instruments assumed to measure academic or cognitive ability for all students. When used with minority students, however, the instruments may measure only the degree to which the minority students have been able to absorb white middle-class culture.

6. Different predictive validity. Instruments designed to predict the educational or academic outcome or potential for white students might not do so for minority students.

7. Qualitatively distinct minority and majority aptitude and achievement. This suggests that persons from various ethnic groups are qualitatively different and therefore tests designed to measure aptitude in one group cannot adequately measure the aptitude of another group. (Reynolds, Lowe, & Saenz, 1999, pp. 556–557)

Additional problems in biased assessment include overinterpretation of test results. This means that an examiner may report to have assessed a trait, attribute, or characteristic that the instrument is not designed to measure (Flaugher, 1978). For example, an examiner may report a cognitive ability level or a behavioral trait based on the results of a student's academic achievement test. The assessment is inaccurate because the test was designed to measure academic achievement only.

Another problem that may arise in assessment is that of testing students whose dominant language is not English. Although some instruments are published in languages other than English, such as Spanish, the translations may result in different conceptual meanings and influence test performance and test results (Fradd & Hallman, 1983). Lopez (1995) recommended that norm-referenced instruments should not be used with bilingual students. Lopez provides several reasons for this recommendation:

1. Norms are usually limited to small samples of minority children.
2. Norming procedures routinely exclude students with limited English proficiency.
3. Test items tap information that minority children may not be familiar with due to their linguistically and culturally different backgrounds.
4. Testing formats do not allow examiners the opportunity to provide feedback or to probe into the children's quality of responses.
5. The tests' scoring systems arbitrarily decide what are the correct responses based on majority culture paradigms.
6. The standardized testing procedures assume that the children have appropriate test-taking skills (Lopez, 1995, p. 1113).

IDEA mandates that the evaluation of students for possible special education services must involve the use of tests that have been validated for the purpose for which they are used. Regardless of these legal and professional guidelines, most norm-referenced tests used in schools are not diagnostic in nature but rather measure expected academic achievement or intellectual functioning. The developmental process of many instruments gives little attention to validity studies with disabled populations. Fuchs, Fuchs, Benowitz, and Barringer (1987) called for discontinuing use of tests with no validation data on disabled populations if those tests are used for diagnosis and placement of students with disabilities. The movement toward restructuring education and the way that special education services are delivered has resulted in a call for the use of more varieties of tests that measure the student's knowledge and skills as they relate to the curriculum

(IDEA Amendments of 1997; Lipsky & Gartner, 1997; U.S. Department of Education, 1997). The use of these devices will require additional research regarding validity, reliability, and generalizability (Burger & Burger, 1994). The regulations that guide the assessment process call for careful selection of assessment instruments and state that the purpose of the assessment is to determine educational needs.

The IDEA regulations contain language requiring that at a minimum, professionals be trained in assessment and, more specifically, that training or expertise is available to enable the examiner to evaluate students with disabilities. Past research has shown that some professionals responsible for the evaluation of students with disabilities lacked competence in test selection, scoring, and interpretations (Bennett, 1981; Bennett & Shepherd, 1982; McNutt & Mandelbaum, 1980; Ysseldyke & Thurlow, 1983). Valles (1998) advocated improving teacher training at the preservice level to decrease the likelihood that minorities are inaccurately diagnosed.

Of all of the controversial areas in nondiscriminatory assessment, the most controversial area remains that of IQ testing for the purpose of determining eligibility for services under the diagnostic category of mental retardation. One professional in the field (Jackson, 1975) called for banning the use of IQ tests. Some state and local education agencies, either by litigation or voluntarily, have discontinued the use of IQ tests with minority students. Evidence indicates, however, that IQ scores continue to be the most influential test score variable in the decision-making process (Sapp, Chissom, & Horton, 1984). MacMillan and Forness (1998) argue that IQ testing may only be peripheral in placement rather than the determining factor. In their study, they concluded that the use of IQ scores may in fact prevent some students from eligibility who may truly be in need of support services. The trend in assessment to use more functional measures than traditional assessment may be the result of assessment practices viewed as biased.

IDEA and the 1997 Amendments require that other data, such as comments from parents and teachers and adaptive behavior measures, be considered in the decision-making process. In calling for a complete reconceptualization of special education and the assessment process, Lipsky and Gartner (1997) posed the following questions:

> Why must children suspected of having a disability undergo a costly, lengthy, and intrusive process in order to receive public education services similar to ones that their peers without disabilities receive without such procedures?
>
> Why must parents of children with disabilities be denied opportunities available to parents of children without disabilities to choose the neighborhood school, or "magnet" or "school of choice" programs?

Why must children be certified to enter a special education system if all children are entitled to a free and appropriate education that prepares them effectively to participate in and contribute to the society of which they are a part?

Why must parents and their children in need of special education services lose substantial free-choice opportunities to gain procedural rights?

Are the gains worth the cost? (pp. 28–29)

These questions raise important issues for consideration. In attempting to provide appropriate services that are designed to meet the individual student's needs, it seems that the system may have become cumbersome and may even be unfair for some families. Patton (1998) suggested that the current system is unfair to African-American families because of the disproportionate numbers of children from these families placed in special education because of inaccurate diagnoses. Patton further stated that the current practices are not sensitive to minority cultures and behaviors. Others have called for a redirection of special education efforts in assessment and classification, particularly in applying these procedures to students who have emotional and behavioral disorders (Ruehl, 1998; Smith, 1997). These issues need additional investigation as schools implement the IDEA Amendments, with an emphasis on education of students with special needs in the regular classroom setting.

Disproportionality The research indicating that students who are from different ethnic, cultural, or linguistic backgrounds was influential in the revisions of IDEA. One method included in the IDEA 2004 regulations is through early intervening services. Through early intervening services, students, especially students in the targeted various groups from ethnic or culturally diverse backgrounds, can receive interventions that may prevent their placement in special education.

The regulations of IDEA 2004 include specific methods that states must follow to be accountable for making efforts to reduce disproportionality. State education agencies are mandated to collect and report data on the following: types of impairments of students identified as eligible to receive services, placement or educational environments of students, the incidents of disciplinary actions, the duration of disciplinary incidents, including suspensions and expulsions of students who are served under special education. All of these data are to be reported and when specific data indicate problematic disproportionality, the state educational agency is mandated to review the data and, if necessary, revise the methods and policies for identification and placement of students in special education.

**Check Your
Understanding**

> Check your knowledge of disproportionality and other issues of IDEA
> 2004 by completing Activity 2.7.
>
> *Activity 2.7*
>
> After reviewing the research and issues of IDEA 2004, complete the
> following.
>
> 1. States are now mandated to collect data on _____ as
>   a method of determining when disproportionality may be
>   problematic.
> 2. When a student from an ethnically diverse background begins to
>   have difficulty meeting educational needs, the teacher may con-
>   tact the child study team to request _____ as a method of
>   preventing the student from a special educational referral as the
>   first plan of action to address the student's difficulties.
> 3. Traditional assessment practices may inadvertently contribute to
>   bias in assessment. What changes in the revised IDEA 2004 may
>   decrease the probability that this will occur? _____
> 4. Discuss the practices that may contribute to bias in assessment.

THE MULTIDISCIPLINARY TEAM AND THE DECISION-MAKING PROCESS

The regulations call for a variety of professionals and the parents of
the student to be involved in the assessment and IEP processes. The
decision-making process is to include all members of the IEP multidisciplinary team as another method of increasing accuracy of decisions. In a review of analogue research, Huebner (1991) determined
that often teacher perceptions disproportionately influence the
Team's decision. This results in inaccurate decision making and may
be considered a form of bias in the assessment process. School psychologists, as members of the IEP multidisciplinary team, may rely on
clinical judgment to make eligibility decisions and fail to consistently
consider information across cases; such practices, too, may lead to
errors in the decision-making process (Ward, Ward, & Clark, 1991).

   In other studies, inconsistencies in decisions about eligibility
made by teams have been found specifically in determining eligibility of mild disabilities, such as learning disabilities (Bocian, Beebe,
MacMillan, & Gresham, 1999; MacMillan, Gresham, & Bocian,
1998). These researchers concluded that various forms of evidence, such as behaviors observed by teachers, may have weighed
heavily in the decision-making process. Gresham, MacMillan, and
Bocian (1998) postulated that eligibility decisions may be based on
educational need more than actual legal criteria for students with
mild disabilities.

LEAST RESTRICTIVE ENVIRONMENT

IDEA is designed to provide special education support services in the least restrictive environment. In many cases, this means that a student will be served within the general education classroom setting. Macready (1991) proposed that when a decision is made to place a student in an environment other than the general education setting, it should be viewed conceptually as a "foster placement rather than as a placement for adoption" (p. 151). The regulations of IDEA 1997 emphasize that students with disabilities should be educated within the general education environment unless there are justifiable reasons for the student to be educated in a special education setting.

Decisions about appropriate educational environments should be made carefully. Morsink and Lenk (1992) suggested that each decision be made on an individual basis and that the teacher's training and effectiveness in instruction and all environmental factors, such as the impact on other students or limiting environmental factors, be considered. Morsink and Lenk warned that a proposed placement, seen at first as the least restrictive environment, may indeed be an inappropriate environment when these factors are not considered to be favorable.

The provision of least restrictive environment may be implemented in various ways in different states and local education agencies. One study of six states found that finances, parent advocacy, categorically based systems, and varying layers of organizational structure all influenced the way that the least restrictive environment provision was implemented (Hasazi, Johnston, Liggett, & Schattman, 1994). This study found that these variables were complex and interconnected.

The research conducted by the U.S. Department of Education indicates that there has been an increasing trend to serve students in the general education classroom environment for most of the school day (1999). Figure 2.3 illustrates this trend.

The implementation of least restrictive environment and, more specifically, inclusion has been interpreted through litigation in several state and federal courts (Kubicek, 1994; Lipsky & Gartner, 1997; Yell, 1997). In summary, the courts have interpreted that the least restrictive environment decision must first consider placement in a regular education environment with additional supplementary aids if needed. If this arrangement will be equal or better for the student than the special education setting, the student should be placed within the general education environment. The student's academic and nonacademic benefits must be considered in the decision. This includes consideration of the benefits of social interaction in nonacademic activities and environments. The IEP team must also review the effect that the student will have on the teacher in terms

Figure 2.3   Increasing trend of students with disabilities ages 6–21 served in each general education environment: 1988–89 through 1998–99.

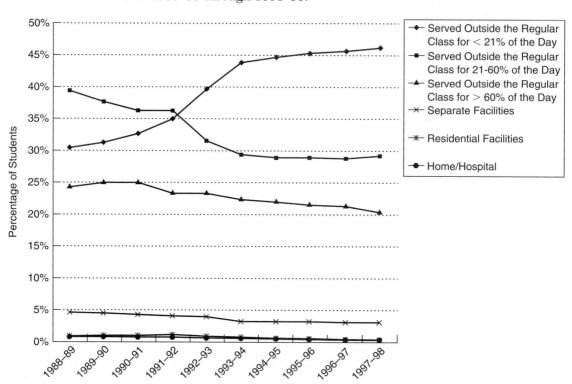

Source: U.S. Department of Education, Office of Special Education Programs, Data Analysis System [DANS], in *To assure the free appropriate public education of all children with disabilities,* 2000.

of time and attention required and the effect the student may have on the other students in the general classroom. If the educational services required for the student can be provided better and the education is considered superior in the segregated setting, the student may be placed in a special education environment. For additional review, please refer to Lipsky and Gartner (1997) and Yell (1997).

Research has produced interesting results regarding inclusion in general education settings. One study that surveyed secondary students found that more students expressed a desire for a pullout program for meeting their educational needs but enjoyed inclusion for the social aspects (Klinger, Vaughn, Schumm, Cohen, & Forgan, 1998). Some of the students in this study stated that the general education environment was simply too noisy. Bennett, Lee, and Lueke (1998) state that inclusion decisions should consider the parents' expectations. Their research found that several factors, such as the parents' view of inclusion, may have an impact on the parents' desire to have their child served in a general education setting. Another study of general education teachers' perceptions of inclusion found that more teachers were willing to include students with mild disabilities in the general education setting (Scruggs & Mastropieri, 1996). In this study, only one-third of the teachers believed that they had enough time and training to adequately serve students with disabilities in their general education classrooms. It is clear that placement decisions are complex.

IMPARTIAL HEARINGS

The procedural safeguards provided through due process seek to involve the parents in all stages of the IEP process rather than only during third-party hearings. Due process provisions specify at least 36 grounds for either schools or parents to seek a hearing (Turnbull, Turnbull, & Strickland, 1979). If abused, the process could result in chaos in the operation of school systems. The years since the law was enacted have witnessed a great deal of interpretation of uncertain issues through the judicial system (Turnbull, 1986).

Due process may be discriminatory because its cost may prohibit some families from following this procedure. The cost may involve both financial and human resources. The remaining problems are best summed up by Turnbull (1986):

> Problems remain. The greatest one seems to be the cost of due process. Cost consists of three elements: (1) the actual financial cost of the hearings; preparing for them, hiring attorneys and expert witnesses, paying for the documents required for evidence, and pursuing an appeal; (2) the emotional and psychic cost—the enormous energy and stress involved in a hearing and its appeal; and (3) the cost that consists of time spent and perhaps lost, when the child may (or may not) be receiving an appropriate education. (p. 192)

Because the financial cost may be so burdensome, educators are concerned that due process in IDEA may become yet another vehicle that increases rather than decreases discriminatory practices. Budoff and Orenstein (1981) found that upper-middle-class parents were overrepresented in due process hearings and recommended using mediation without counsel as an alternative to the expensive hearing process. The 1997 Amendments that provide specific guidelines for mediation may result in more timely and economical resolutions. Engiles, Fromme, LeResche, and Moses (1999) suggested that there are strategies that schools and personnel can implement to increase participation in mediation of parents of culturally and linguistically diverse backgrounds. These authors included strategies, at the system level as well as the practitioner level, to involve parents in mediation. Engiles et al. remind educators that some persons from various cultures do not believe that they should be involved in educational decisions, and others may not welcome the involvement of school personnel in family or personal matters. Increasing parental involvement and communication between parents and schools from the prereferral stage through the decision-making stage may decrease the need for both mediation and third-party hearings.

The difficulties with the hearing process were likely the influence in changing the 2004 Amendments to include a new resolution session. This allows the school another opportunity to resolve the issues in a more timely manner that will not require the costly and lengthy process often associated with hearings.

Should parents or schools exhaust the hearing process without satisfaction, the right remains for either party to take the case through the civil court system. IDEA continues to be interpreted through the judicial system.

ETHICS AND STANDARDS

In addition to the legal requirements of the process of assessment and planning in special and general education, ethical standards for practice have been established by professional organizations. In special education, standards of practice and policies have been set forth by the Council for Exceptional Children. The National Association of School Psychologists has established standards and ethics for professionals in the school psychology field. And the American Educational Research Association, the American Psychological Association, and the National Council on Measurement in Education have established the *Standards for Educational and Psychological Testing* (1999). These professional groups have policies regarding the education and assessment of students from culturally and linguistically diverse backgrounds.

Although professionals in the field of education and educational psychology are required by law to follow the regulations and federal mandates, the standards and ethics are established by professional groups to encourage professionalism and best practice. Sections of the standards, codes, and policies that are relevant to assessment and special education are included in the following pages.

The *Standards of Practice* set out by the Council for Exceptional Children (CEC) are similar to the federal regulations governing assessment, use of goals and objectives for planning, record keeping and confidentiality, and decision-making practices. The standards relevant to assessment are presented in Figure 2.4.

The policies of CEC for students from various ethnic groups and migrant students are designed to assist in decreasing the overrepresentation of minority students receiving special education support. These policies emphasize nondiscriminatory assessment

Figure 2.4   CEC standards for professional practice relevant to the assessment and planning process.

- Use assessment instruments and procedures that do not discriminate against persons with exceptionalities on the basis of race, color, creed, sex, national origin, age, political practices, family or social background, sexual orientation, or exceptionality.
- Base grading, promotion, graduation, and/or movement out of the program on the individual goals and objectives for individuals with exceptionalities.
- Provide accurate program data to administrators, colleagues, and parents, based on efficient and objective record keeping practices, for the purpose of decision making.
- Maintain confidentiality of information except when information is released under specific conditions of written consent and statutory confidentiality requirements.

Source: CEC policies for delivery of services: Ethnic and multicultural groups. *CEC Policy Manual*, Section Three, part 1, pp. 6, 20–21. Reprinted with permission.

practice, consideration of language dominance, and understanding of cultural heritage. The policy on migrant students calls on educational professionals to understand that the assessment and programming procedures used for stationary students are not appropriate for migrant students. It further points out that the frequent disruptions in education affect the students' lives in both educational and social areas. This CEC statement also reminds professional educators that the eligibility requirements and other special education considerations often differ from state to state. The CEC policy statements are presented in Figures 2.5 and 2.6.

In 2000, the National Association of School Psychologists revised the *Professional Conduct Manual*, which includes sections that cover all areas of practice for psychologists working within the school setting. The general principles for assessment and intervention and reporting data and conference results are presented in Figure 2.7. The principles are consistent with the legal requirements for assessment and the evaluation process.

The *Standards for Educational and Psychological Testing* also contain standards for all areas of testing and are consistent with the federal regulations. For example, the standards include language regarding using multiple measures for reaching decisions about the individual's functioning, following standardized administration procedures, and confidentiality of test results and test instruments. Selected standards are presented in Figure 2.8.

Figure 2.5 CEC policy on ethnic and multicultural groups relevant to the assessment and planning process.

Preamble

The Council believes that all policy statements previously adopted by CEC related to children with and without exceptionalities, as well as children with gifts and talents, are relevant and applicable to both minority and nonminority individuals. In order to highlight concerns of special interest to members of ethnic and multicultural groups, the following policy statements have been developed. (Chapter 08, Para. 1)

Ethnicity and Exceptionality

The Council recognizes the special and unique needs of members of ethnic and multicultural groups and pledges its full support toward promoting all efforts which will help to bring them into full and equitable participation and membership in the total society. (Chapter 08, Para. 2)

Identification, Testing, and Placement

The Council supports the following statements related to the identification, testing, and placement of children from ethnic and multicultural groups who are also exceptional.

a. Child-find procedures should identify children by ethnicity as well as type and severity of exceptionality or degree of giftedness.

b. Program service reporting procedures should identify children by ethnicity as well as exceptionality or degree of giftedness.

c. All testing and evaluation materials and methods used for the classification and placement of children from ethnic and multicultural groups should be selected and administered so as not to be racially or culturally discriminatory.

d. Children with exceptionalities who are members of ethnic and multicultural groups should be tested in their dominant language by examiners who are fluent in that language and familiar with the cultural heritage of the children being tested.

e. Communication of test results with parents of children from ethnic and multicultural groups should be done in the dominant language of those parents and conducted by persons involved in the testing or familiar with the particular exceptionality, fluent in that language, and familiar with the cultural heritage of those parents.

Source: CEC policies for delivery of services: Ethnic and multicultural groups. *CEC Policy Manual*, Section Three, part 1, pp. 6, 20–21. Reprinted with permission.

Figure 2.6 CEC policy on migrant students relevant to the assessment and planning process.

Preamble

Exceptional students who are mobile due to their parents' migrant employment, experience reduced opportunities for an appropriate education and a reduced likelihood of completing their education. Child-find and identification policies and practices, designed for a stationary population, are inadequate for children who move frequently. Incomplete, delayed, or inadequate transfer of records seriously impedes educational continuity. Interstate/provincial differences in special education eligibility requirements, programs and resources, minimum competency testing, and graduation requirements result in repetition of processing formalities, gaps in instruction, delays in the resumption of services, an inability to accumulate credits for graduation, and other serious inequities. In addition to the disruption of learning, mobility disrupts health care, training, teacher-student rapport, and personal relationships.

Source: CEC policies for delivery of services: Ethnic and multicultural groups. *CEC Policy Manual,* Section Three, part 1, pp. 6, 20–21. Reprinted with permission.

Figure 2.7 Selected principles from the National Association of School Psychologists *Professional Conduct Manual.*

C) Assessment and Intervention

1. School psychologists maintain the highest standard for educational and psychological assessment and direct and indirect interventions.
   a. In conducting psychological, educational, or behavioral evaluations or in providing therapy, counseling, or consultation services, due consideration is given to individual integrity and individual differences.
   b. School psychologists respect differences in age, gender, sexual orientation, and socioeconomic, cultural, and ethnic backgrounds. They select and use appropriate assessment or treatment procedures, techniques, and strategies. Decision-making related to assessment and subsequent interventions is primarily data-based.

2. School psychologists are knowledgeable about the validity and reliability of their instruments and techniques, choosing those that have up-to-date standardization data and are applicable and appropriate for the benefit of the child.

3. School psychologists use multiple assessment methods such as observations, background information, and information from other professionals, to reach comprehensive conclusions.

4. School psychologists use assessment techniques, counseling and therapy procedures, consultation techniques, and other direct and indirect service methods that the profession considers to be responsible, research-based practice.

---

continued.

Figure 2.7 continued.

5. School psychologists do not condone the use of psychological or educational assessment techniques, or the misuse of the information these techniques provide, by unqualified persons in any way, including teaching, sponsorship, or supervision.

6. School psychologists develop interventions that are appropriate to the presenting problems and are consistent with data collected. They modify or terminate the treatment plan when the data indicate the plan is not achieving the desired goals.

7. School psychologists use current assessment and intervention strategies that assist in the promotion of mental health in the children they serve.

D) Reporting Data and Conference Results

1. School psychologists ascertain that information about children and other clients reaches only authorized persons.
   a. School psychologists adequately interpret information so that the recipient can better help the child or other clients.
   b. School psychologists assist agency recipients to establish procedures to properly safeguard confidential material.

2. School psychologists communicate findings and recommendations in language readily understood by the intended recipient. These communications describe potential consequences associated with the proposals.

3. School psychologists prepare written reports in such form and style that the recipient of the report will be able to assist the child or other clients. Reports should emphasize recommendations and interpretations; unedited computer-generated reports, preprinted "check-off" or "fill-in-the-blank" reports, and reports that present only test scores or global statements regarding eligibility for special education without specific recommendations for intervention are seldom useful. Reports should include an appraisal of the degree of confidence that could be assigned to the information. Alterations of previously released reports should be done only by the original author.

4. School psychologists review all of their written documents for accuracy, signing them only when correct. Interns and practicum students are clearly identified as such, and their work is co-signed by the supervising school psychologist. In situations in which more than one professional participated in the data collection and reporting process, school psychologists assure that sources of data are clearly identified in the written report.

5. School psychologists comply with all laws, regulations, and policies pertaining to the adequate storage and disposal of records to maintain appropriate confidentiality of information.

Figure 2.8 Selected standards from the *Standards for Educational and Psychological Testing.*

Standard	
5.1	Test administrators should follow carefully the standardized procedures for administration and scoring specified by the test developer, unless the situation or a test taker's disability dictates that an exception should be made. (p. 63)
5.7	Test users have the responsibility of protecting the security of test materials at all times. (p. 64)
10.1	In testing individuals with disabilities, test developers, test administrators, and test users should take steps to ensure that the test score inferences accurately reflect the intended construct rather than any disabilities and their associated characteristics extraneous to the intent of the measurement. (p. 106)
10.12	In testing individuals with disabilities for diagnostic and intervention purposes, the test should not be used as the sole indicator of the test taker's functioning. Instead, multiple sources of information should be used. (p. 108)
11.3	Responsibility for test use should be assumed by or delegated only to those individuals who have the training, professional credentials, and experience necessary to handle this responsibility. Any special qualifications for test administration or interpretation specified in the test manual should be met. (p. 114)
11.20	In educational, clinical, and counseling settings, a test taker's score should not be interpreted in isolation; collateral information that may lead to alternative explanations for the examinee's test performance should be considered. (p. 117)
12.11	Professionals and others who have access to test materials and test results should ensure the confidentiality of the test results and testing materials consistent with legal and professional ethics requirements. (pp. 132–133)
13.10	Those responsible for educational testing programs should ensure that the individuals who administer and score the test(s) are proficient in the appropriate test administration procedures and scoring procedures and that they understand the importance of adhering to the directions provided by the test developer. (p. 147)
13.13	Those responsible for educational testing programs should ensure that the individuals who interpret the test results to make decisions within the school context are qualified to do so or are assisted by and consult with persons who are so qualified. (p. 148)

Source: Copyright 1999 by the American Educational Research Association, The American Psychological Association, and the National Council on Measurement in Education. Reproduced with permission of the publisher.

CHAPTER SUMMARY

For more than 25 years federal laws have been in place to provide all students having special needs with a free and appropriate education. In order to receive special education support, assessment and planning procedures, as set out in the regulations, must be completed. The laws continue to be revised and strive to provide all students with appropriate education within the general education environment. Improvements in the laws focus on increasing parental involvement and including more considerations for students from culturally and linguistically diverse backgrounds. Ethics and policies of professional organizations encourage educators and assessment personnel to consistently use best practices in assessment and planning procedures.

THINK AHEAD

The procedures used to understand the results of a student's performance on test instruments involve basic statistical methods (presented in Chapter 3). Do you think tests using the same numerical scales can easily be compared?

EXERCISES

Part I

Match the following terms with the statements below.

a. Public Law 94-142
b. IDEA
c. IDEA Amendments of 1997
d. compliance
e. PL 99-457
f. due process
g. initial evaluation
h. comprehensive educational evaluation
i. informed consent
j. surrogate parent
k. consent form
l. parents' rights booklet
m. nondiscriminatory assessment
n. special education services
o. related services
p. grade equivalent
q. standard scores

r. annual goals
s. Individuals with Disabilities Educational Improvement Act
t. least restrictive environment
u. transition services
v. procedural safeguards
w. mediation
x. independent educational evaluation
y. impartial due process hearing
z. impartial hearing officer
aa. Section 504 of the Rehabilitation Act of 1973
bb. minority overrepresentation
cc. resolution session

_____ 1. Mary, a student receiving special education services, also needs the _____ of occupational therapy and speech therapy in order to benefit from her appropriate educational plan.

_____ 2. During the screening by educational professionals, it is determined that a student has significant educational needs and is therefore referred for a(n) _____.

_____ 3. The 2004 Amendments encourage parents and educational personnel to participate in a _____ to resolve disagreements.

_____ 4. A school system that meets appropriate timelines and follows all state and federal regulations is said to be in _____.

_b,C_ 5. Parents who have a preschool-aged child with special needs may find assistance in obtaining educational services for their child through the federal regulations of _____.

_____ 6. In a specific school system, the ethnicity of the population was determined to include 17% of persons of Hispanic origin, yet more than 22% of the students receiving services for learning disabilities were of Hispanic origin. This system may have _____ of persons of Hispanic origin within the category of learning disabilities.

_____ 7. A fifth-grade student was recently assessed and was found not eligible to receive special education support. His parents decided that they disagreed with the assessment and therefore requested information to obtain a(n) _____.

_b_ 8. During a meeting of the child study team, the members determined that the prereferral intervention strategies employed with a third-grade student were not successful in remediating reading difficulties. The members must now obtain _____ in order to begin the assessment process.

_b_ 9. Initially, the federal law that mandated a free and appropriate public education for all children with disabilities was called the Education for All Handicapped Children Act. In 1990, this was renamed _____.

_____10. A major principle of IDEA is that all evaluation measures used during the assessment process should yield similar results for children regardless of their ethnicity. This principle is known as _____.

_____11. In December 2004, President Bush signed the _____.

Part II
Answer the following questions.

1. What were the sources of pressure that resulted in substantial legal changes in the 1970s?

_____

2. The Individuals with Disabilities Education Improvement Act of 2004 requires that IEPs include what type of information regarding statewide assessments?

_____

_____

_____

3. When must parents be given their due process rights according to the 2004 Amendments?

_____

_____

_____

4. List the provisions for nondiscriminatory assessment according to the federal law.

_____

_____

_____

Part III

Summarize the research findings.

1. Summarize the research findings on the IEP Team decision-making process.

_____

2. Explain how the research regarding third-party hearings may have had an impact on the changes concerning mediation and resolution sessions in the 2004 Amendments.

_____

3. Summarize the difficulties of assessing students from culturally and linguistically diverse backgrounds.

_____

_____

_____

_____

Answers to these questions can be found in the Appendix of this text or you may also complete these questions and receive immediate feedback on your answers by going to the Think Ahead module in Chapter 2 of the Companion Website.

COURSE PROGRESS MONITORING ASSESSMENT

See how you are doing in the course after the conclusion of chapters in Part I by completing the following assessment. When you are finished, check your answers with your instructor or on the

Companion Website at *www.prenhall.com/overton*. Once you have your score, return to Figure 1.9, Student Progress Monitoring Graph in Chapter 1 and plot your progress.

Progress Monitoring Assessment

Select the best answer. Some of these terms may be used more than once.

a. early intervening services	i. variance
b. RTI	j. derived score
c. norm-referenced tests	k. basal score
d. standardized tests	l. field test
e. diagnostic tests	m. KBIT
f. IDEA 2004	n. WISC-IV
g. IDEA 1997	o. phonemic synthesis
h. IDEA regulations	p. phonemic awareness

_____ 1. This federal law included strategies to closely align with the No Child Left Behind Act and specifically addresses accountability.

_____ 2. Comprehension of individual sounds that make up words.

_____ 3. The two subtests that make up this measure are Vocabulary and Matrices.

_____ 4. The initial administration of an instrument to a sample population.

_____ 5. These instruments may provide additional information used for specific academic or other weaknesses.

_____ 6. This test includes a working memory index, perceptual reasoning index, and a processing speed index as well as verbal measures.

_____ 7. One component of this federal legislation was improving teacher quality.

_____ 8. These instruments provide comparisons with students the same age across the United States.

_____ 9. These instruments are structured to ensure that all students are administered the items in the same manner so that comparisons can be made more reliably.

_____ 10. These instruments provide comparisons with groups who are representative of the student population across the United States.

Fill in the Blanks

11. In an effort to encourage parents and schools to resolve their disagreements, _____ included mediation.

12. _____ is the type of validity that indicates a measure has items that are representative across the possible items in the domain.

13. _____ validity and _____ validity are differentiated by time.

14. The formula of SD $\sqrt{1-r}$ is how to determine _____.

15. _____ is a behavioral measure that indicates how students in a class view each other.

16. _____ is a computerized assessment of a student's ability to sustain attention across time.

17. The _____ is a measure of preschool students' language development that is based on a two-dimensional language model.

18. A criterion-related measure of self-help skills, prespeech, and speech development, general knowledge, social and emotional development, reading readiness, manuscript writing, and beginning math is the _____.

19. _____ is a form that indicates that the parents understand the testing procedures and that they are granting permission to the school to assess their child.

20. _____ are included at the end of the assessment report.

Technical Prerequisites of Understanding Assessment

CHAPTER 3

Descriptive Statistics

CHAPTER 4

Reliability and Validity

CHAPTER 5

An Introduction to Norm-Referenced Assessment

Descriptive Statistics

KEY TERMS

raw score	frequency polygon
norm-referenced tests	median
nominal scale	mean
ordinal scale	standard deviation
interval scale	variability
ratio scale	measures of dispersion
derived scores	variance
standard scores	range
descriptive statistics	skewed
measures of central tendency	positively skewed
normal distribution	negatively skewed
frequency distribution	percentile ranks
mode	z scores
bimodal distribution	stanines
multimodal distribution	deciles

CHAPTER FOCUS

This chapter presents the basic statistical concepts needed to interpret information from standardized assessment.

CEC KNOWLEDGE AND SKILLS STANDARDS

The student completing this chapter will understand the knowledge and skills included in the following CEC Knowledge and Skills Standards from Standard 8: Assessment:

> *CC8K1*—Basic terminology used in assessment
>
> *CC8S5*—Interpret information from formal and informal assessments.

WHY IS MEASUREMENT IMPORTANT?

Psychoeducational assessment using standardized instruments historically has been applied in the educational decision-making process. To properly use standardized instruments, one must understand test-selection criteria, basic principles of measurement, administration techniques, and scoring procedures. Careful interpretation of test results relies on these abilities. Thus, research that questions the assessment competence of special educators and other professionals is frightening because the educational future of so many individuals is at risk.

Of concern are studies indicating typical types of mistakes made by professionals in the field: Professionals identified students as eligible for services when test scores were within the average range and relied instead on referral information to make decisions (Algozzine & Ysseldyke, 1981). Data presented during educational planning conferences played little, if any, part in the team members' decisions (Ysseldyke, Algozzine, Richey, & Graden, 1982). Professionals continued to select poor-quality instruments when better tests were available (Davis & Shepard, 1983; Ysseldyke, Algozzine, Regan, & Potter, 1980).

Research by Huebner (1988, 1989) indicated that professionals made errors in the diagnosis of learning disabilities more frequently when scores were reported in percentiles. This reflects inadequate understanding of data interpretation.

Eaves (1985) cited common errors made by professionals during the assessment process. Some of the test examiners' most common errors, adapted from Eaves's research, include:

1. Using instruments in the assessment process solely because those instruments are stipulated by school administrators.
2. Regularly using instruments for purposes other than those for which tests have been validated.
3. Taking the recommended use at face value.
4. Using the quickest instruments available even though those instruments may not assess the areas of concern.
5. Using currently popular instruments for assessment.
6. Failing to establish effective rapport with the examinee.
7. Failing to document behaviors of the examinee during assessment that may be of diagnostic value.
8. Failing to adhere to standardized administration rules, which may include
   a. Failing to follow starting rules.
   b. Failing to follow basal and ceiling rules.
   c. Omitting actual incorrect responses on the protocol, which could aid in error analysis and diagnosis.
   d. Failing to determine actual chronological age or grade placement.
9. Making various scoring errors, such as
   a. Making simple counting errors.
   b. Making simple subtraction errors.
   c. Counting items above the ceiling as correct or items below the basal as incorrect.
   d. Entering the wrong norm table, row, or column to obtain a derived score.

  e. Extensively using developmental scores when inappropriate.

  f. Showing lack of knowledge regarding alternative measures of performance.

10. Ineffectively interpreting assessment results for educational program use. (pp. 26–27)

The occurrence of such errors illustrates why educators need a basic understanding of the measurement principles used in assessment. McLoughlin (1985) advocated training special educators to the level of superior practice rather than meeting only minimum competencies of psychoeducational assessment. The *Standards for Educational and Psychological Testing* (AERA, APA, & NCME, 1999) warn that when special educators have little or no training in the basic principles of measurement, assessment instruments could be misused.

Much of the foundation of good practice in psychoeducational assessment lies in a thorough understanding of test reliability and validity as well as basic measurement principles. Borg, Worthen, and Valcarce (1986) found that most teachers believe that understanding basic principles of measurement is an important aspect of classroom teaching and evaluation. Yet research has shown that professionals who were believed to be specialists in working with students with learning problems were able to correctly answer only 50% of the items on a test of measurement principles (Bennett & Shepherd, 1982). As a result, this chapter is designed to promote the development of a basic understanding of general principles of measurement and the application of those principles.

GETTING MEANING FROM NUMBERS

raw score The first score obtained in testing; usually represents the number of items correct.

Any teacher who scores a test, either published or teacher-made, will subtract the number of items a student missed from the number of items presented to the student. This number, known as the **raw score**, is of little value to the teacher unless a frame of reference exists for that number. The frame of reference might be comparing the number of items the student answered correctly with the number the student answered correctly the previous day (e.g., Monday, 5 out of 10 responses correct; Tuesday, 6 out of 10 responses correct; etc.). The frame of reference might be a national sample of students the same age who attempted the same items in the same manner on a **norm-referenced** standardized test. In all cases, teachers must clearly understand what can and cannot be inferred from numerical data gathered on small samples of behavior known as *tests*.

norm-referenced tests Tests designed to compare an individual student's scores with national averages.

The techniques used to obtain raw scores are discussed in Chapter 5. Raw scores are used to obtain the other scores presented in this chapter.

REVIEW OF NUMERICAL SCALES

nominal scale
Numerical scale that uses numbers for the purpose of identification.

Numbers can denote different meanings from different scales. The scale that has the least meaning for educational measurement purposes is the **nominal scale**. The nominal scale consists of numbers used only for identification purposes, such as student ID numbers or the numbers on race cars. These numbers cannot be used in mathematical operations. For example, if race cars were labeled with letters of the alphabet rather than with numerals, it would make no difference in the outcome of the race. Numbers on a nominal scale function like names.

ordinal scale
Numerical scale in which numbers are used for ranking.

When numbers are used to rank the order of objects or items, those numbers are said to be on the **ordinal scale**. An ordinal scale is used to rank the order of the winners in a science fair. The winner has the first rank, or number 1, the runner-up has the second rank, or number 2, and so on. In this scale, the numbers have the quality of identification and indicate greater or lesser quality. The ordinal scale, however, does not have the quality of using equidistant units. For example, suppose the winners of a bike race were ranked as they came in, with the winner ranked as first, the runner-up as

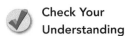 **Check Your Understanding**

Check your knowledge of the different types of numerical scales presented in the previous section by completing Activity 3.1 below.

Activity 3.1

Use the following terms to complete the sentences and answer the questions.

A. nominal scale   C. ordinal scale

B. interval scale   D. ratio scale

1. Measuring with a thermometer is an example of using numbers on the _____ scale.

2. Which scale(s) can be added and subtracted but not multiplied? _____

3. The ribbons awarded in a painting contest illustrate which scale? _____

4. Numbers pinned on the shirts of runners in a marathon are numbers used on the _____ scale.

5. The _____ scale has a true meaning of absolute zero.

Apply Your Knowledge

Which of the numerical scales is used to determine your semester GPA? _____
_____
_____

second, and the third bike rider as third. The distance between the winner and the second-place bike rider might be 9 seconds, and the difference between the second- and third-place bike riders might be 30 seconds. Although the numbers do rank the bike riders, they do not represent equidistant units.

Numbers that are used for identification that rank greater or lesser quality or amount and that are equidistant are numbers used on an **interval scale**. An example is the scale used in measuring temperature. The degrees on the thermometer can be added or subtracted—a reading of 38°F is 10° less than a reading of 48°F. The interval scale does not have an absolute-zero quality. For example, zero degrees does not indicate that there is no temperature. The numbers used on an interval scale also cannot be used in other mathematical operations, such as multiplication. Is a reading of 100°F really four times as hot as 25°F? An interval scale used in assessment is the IQ scale. IQ numbers are equidistant, but they do not possess additional numerical properties. A person with an IQ of 66 cannot be called two-thirds as smart as a person with an IQ of 99.

When numbers on a scale are equidistant from each other and have a true meaning of absolute zero, they can be used in all mathematical operations. This **ratio scale** allows for direct comparisons and mathematical manipulations.

When scoring tests and interpreting data, it is important to understand which numerical scale the numbers represent and to realize the properties and limitations of that scale. Understanding what test scores represent may decrease errors such as attributing more meaning to a particular score than should be allowed by the nature of the numerical scale.

interval scale A scale that uses numbers for ranking in which numerical units are equidistant.

ratio scale Numerical scale with quality of equidistant units and absolute zero.

DESCRIPTIVE STATISTICS

When assessing a student's behavior or performance for the purpose of educational intervention, it is often necessary to determine the amount of difference or deviance that the student exhibits in a particular area from the expected level for the age or grade. By looking at how much difference exists in samples of behavior, educational decision makers and parents can appropriately plan interventions. As previously mentioned, obtaining a raw score will not help with educational planning unless the evaluator has a frame of reference for that score. A raw score may have meaning when compared with previous student performance, or a raw score may be used to gain information from another set of scores called **derived scores**. Derived scores may be scores such as percentile ranks, **standard scores**, grade equivalents, age equivalents, or language quotients. Many derived scores obtain meaning from large sets of data or large samples of scores. By observing how a large sample of students the

derived scores Scores obtained by using a raw score and expectancy tables.

standard scores Derived scores that represent equal units; also known as *linear scores*.

same age or grade level performed on the same tasks, it becomes possible to compare a particular student with the large group to see if that student performed as well as the group, better than the group, or not as well as the group.

descriptive statistics Statistics used to organize and describe data.

Large sets of data are organized and understood through methods known as **descriptive statistics**. As the name implies, these are statistical operations that help educators understand and describe sets of data.

MEASURES OF CENTRAL TENDENCY

measures of central tendency Statistical methods for observing how data cluster around the mean.

One way to organize and describe data is to see how the data fall together, or cluster. This type of statistics is called **measures of central tendency**. Measures of central tendency are methods to determine how scores cluster—that is, how they are distributed around a numerical representation of the average score.

normal distribution A symmetrical distribution with a single numerical representation for the mean, median, and mode.

One common type of distribution used in assessment is called a **normal distribution**. A normal distribution has particular qualities that, when understood, help with the interpretation of assessment data. A normal distribution hypothetically represents the way test scores would fall if a particular test is given to every single student of the same age or grade in the population for whom the test was designed. If educators could administer an instrument in this way and obtain a normal distribution, the scores would fall in the shape of a bell curve, as shown in Figure 3.1.

In a graph of a normal distribution of scores, a very large number of the students tested are represented by all of the scores in the middle, or the "hump" part, of the curve. Because fewer students obtain extremely high or low scores, their scores are plotted or represented on the extreme ends of the curve. It is assumed that the same number of students obtained the higher scores as obtained the lower scores. The distribution is symmetric, or equal, on either side of the vertical line. The normal distribution is discussed throughout the text. One method of interpreting norm-referenced tests is to assume the principles of normal distribution theory and employ the measures of central tendency.

Figure 3.1   Normal distribution of scores, shown by the bell curve.

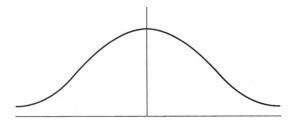

AVERAGE PERFORMANCE

Although educators are familiar with the average grade of C on a letter-grading system (interval scale), the numerical ranking of the C grade might be 70 to 79 in one school and 76 to 84 in another. If the educator does not understand the numerical meaning of *average* for a student, the letter grade of C has little value. The educator must know how the other students performed and what type of performance or score indicates average, what score is considered excellent, and what score is considered poor. To determine this, the teacher must determine what is considered average for that specific set of data.

One way to look at a set of data is to rank the scores from highest to lowest. This helps the teacher see how the group performed. After ranking the data in this fashion, it is helpful to complete a **frequency distribution** by counting how frequently each score occurred. Here is an example of 39 test scores, which the teacher ranked and then counted to record frequency:

frequency distribution Method of determining how many times each score occurs in a set of data.

DATA SET A

Score	Tally	Frequency
100	|	1
99	|	1
98	||	2
94	||	2
90	卌||	5
89	卌|| ||	7
88	卌|| 卌||	10
82	卌|| |	6
75	||	2
74	|	1
68	|	1
60	|	1

mode The most frequently occurring score in a set of scores.

By arranging the data in this order and tallying the frequency of each score, the teacher can determine a trend in the performance of the class.

Another way to look at the data is to determine the most frequently occurring score, or the **mode**. The mode can give the teacher an idea of how the group performed because it indicates the score or performance that occurred the most number of times. The mode for data set A was 88 because it occurred 10 times. In data set B (Activity 3.2), the mode was 70.

bimodal distribution A distribution that has two most frequently occurring scores.

Some sets of data have two modes or two most frequently occurring scores. This type of distribution of scores is known as a **bimodal distribution**. A distribution with three or more modes is called a **multimodal distribution**.

multimodal distribution A distribution with three or more modes.

A clear representation of the distribution of a set of data can be illustrated graphically with a **frequency polygon**. A frequency

frequency polygon A graphic representation of how often each score occurs in a set of data.

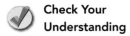

Check Your Understanding

Check your knowledge of the descriptive statistics presented in the previous section by completing Activity 3.2 below.

Activity 3.2

Refer to page 109 in your text. Place the following set of data in rank order and complete a frequency count.

Data Set B

92, 98, 100, 98, 92, 83, 73, 96, 90, 61, 70, 89, 87, 70, 85, 70, 66, 85, 62, 82

Score	Tally	Frequency	Score	Tally	Frequency
___			___		
___			___		
___			___		
___			___		
___			___		
___			___		
___			___		
___					

Apply Your Knowledge

Which of the numerical scales can be rank ordered?

_____

_____

_____

polygon is a graph with test scores represented on the horizontal axis and the number of occurrences, or frequencies, represented on the vertical axis, as shown for data set A in Figure 3.2.

The data that have been rank ordered and for which a mode or modes have been determined give the teacher some idea of how the students performed as a group. Another method of determining how the group performed is to find the middlemost score, or the **median**. After the data have been rank ordered, the teacher can merely count halfway down the list of scores; however, each score must be listed each time it occurs. For example, here is a rank-ordered set of data for which the median has been determined:

median The middle most score in a set of data.

100	79
97	79
89	79
85	68
85	62
78	60
78 median score	

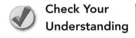

Check Your Understanding

Check your knowledge of the descriptive statistics presented in the previous section by completing Activity 3.3 below.

Activity 3.3

Refer to page 109 in your text. Rank order the following set of data, complete a frequency count, and determine the mode.

Data Set C

62, 63, 51, 42, 78, 81, 81, 63, 75, 92, 94, 77, 63, 75, 96, 88, 60, 50, 49, 74

Score	Tally	Frequency	Score	Tally	Frequency
___			___		
___			___		
___			___		
___			___		
___			___		
___			___		
___			___		

The mode is _____

Apply Your Knowledge

What do you think it would mean to the teacher if the data of three sets of exams were distributed so that the mode always occurred at the high end of the scores? _____
_____
_____

Figure 3.2 Frequency polygon for data set A.

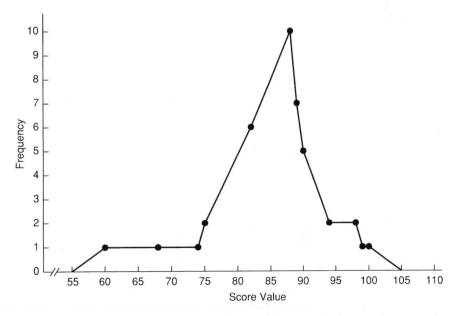

The median score has 50% of the data listed above it and 50% of the data listed below it. In this example, six of the scores are listed above 78 and six are listed below the median. Notice that although 78 is the median, it is not the mode for this set of data. In a normal distribution, which is distributed symmetrically, the median and the mode are represented by the same number.

Check Your Understanding

Check your knowledge of the descriptive statistics presented in the previous section by completing Activity 3.4 below.

Activity 3.4

Rank order the data, complete a frequency count, and make a frequency polygon.

Data Set D

50, 52, 68, 67, 51, 89, 88, 76, 76, 88, 88, 68, 90, 91, 98, 69, 89, 88, 76, 76, 82, 85, 72, 85, 88, 76, 94, 82

Score	Tally	Frequency	Score	Tally	Frequency
____			____		
____			____		
____			____		
____			____		
____			____		
____			____		
____			____		

Draw the frequency polygon here:

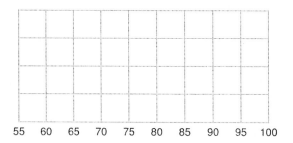

Apply Your Knowledge

What type of distribution did you plot using data set D? _____
_____
_____

In a set of data with an even number of scores, the median is the middlemost score even though the score may not actually exist in that set of data. For example,

100
96
95
90
85
83
82
80
78
77

The scores 85 and 83 occur in the middle of this distribution; therefore, the median is 84, even though 84 is not one of the scores.

Although the mode and median indicate how a group performed, these measures of central tendency do not accurately describe the

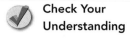

Check Your Understanding

Check your knowledge of the descriptive statistics presented in the previous section by completing Activity 3.5 below.

Activity 3.5

Find the median for the following sets of data.

Data Set E	Data Set F
100	88
99	88
96	88
88	86
84	80
83	76
82	75
79	74
76	70
75	68
70	
62	
60	

Median: _____   Median: _____

Apply Your Knowledge

Data set E has a higher median. Did the students represented by data set E perform significantly better than the students represented by data set F? Why or why not? Explain your answer. _____
_____
_____

mean Arithmetic average of a set of data.

average, or typical, performance. One of the best measures of average performance is the arithmetic average, or **mean**, of the group of scores. The mean is calculated as a simple average: Add the scores and divide by the number of scores in the set of data. For example:

90
80
75
60
70
65
80
100
80
<u>80   </u>
780 ÷ 10 = 78

The sum of the scores is 780. There are 10 scores in the set of data. Therefore, the sum, 780, is divided by the number of scores, 10. The average, or typical, score for this set of data is 78, which represents the arithmetic average.

Often teachers choose to use the mean score to represent the average score on a particular test or assignment. If this score seems to represent the typical performance on the specific test, the teacher may assign a letter grade of C to the numerical representation of the mean score. However, as discussed next, extremely high or low scores can render the mean misrepresentative of the average performance of the class.

Using measures of central tendency is one way teachers can determine which score represents an average performance for a particular group on a particular measure. This aids the teacher in monitoring student progress and knowing when a student is performing well above or well below the norm or average of the group.

The mean can be affected by an extreme score, especially if the group is composed of only a few students. A very high score can raise the mean, whereas a very low score can lower the mean. For this reason, the teacher may wish to omit an extreme score before averaging the data. If scores seem to be widely dispersed, or scattered, using measures of central tendency may not be in the students' best interests. Moreover, such scatter may suggest that the teacher needs to qualitatively evaluate the students' performance and other factors such as teaching methods.

In research and test development, it is necessary to strive for and understand the normal distribution. Because of the symmetrical quality of the normal curve, the mean, median, and mode are all

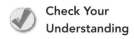
Check Your Understanding

Check your knowledge of the measures of central tendency presented in the previous section by completing Activity 3.6 below.

Activity 3.6

Find the mean, median, and mode for each set of data.

Data Set G

90, 86, 80, 87, 86, 82, 87, 92

Mean: _____   Median: _____   Mode: _____

Data Set H

41, 42, 45, 42, 46, 47, 48, 47, 41, 41

Mean: _____   Median: _____   Mode: _____

Apply Your Knowledge

Using the mean, median, and mode you obtained for data sets G and H, can you determine which group of students performed in a more similar manner as a group? Explain your answer. _____

_____

_____

---

standard deviation A unit of measurement that represents the typical amount that a score can be expected to vary from the mean in a given set of data.

variability Describes how scores vary.

represented by the same number. For example, on tests measuring intelligence, the mean IQ is 100. One hundred is also the middlemost score (median) and the most frequently occurring score (mode). In fact, more than 68% of all of the IQ scores will cluster within 1 **standard deviation**, or one determined typical unit, above and below the score of 100. The statistic known as standard deviation is very important in special education assessment when the use of tests that compare an individual student with a norm-referenced group is necessary. Finding the standard deviation is one method of calculating difference in scores, or **variability** of scores, known as dispersion.

MEASURES OF DISPERSION

measures of dispersion Statistical methods for observing how data spread from the mean.

variance Describes the total amount that a group of scores varies in a set of data.

Because special educators must determine the degree or amount of difference exhibited by individuals in behaviors, skills, or traits, they must employ methods of calculating difference from the average or expected score. Just as measures of central tendency are used to see how sets of data cluster together around an average score, **measures of dispersion** are used to calculate how scores are spread from the mean.

The way that scores in a set of data are spread apart is known as the variability of the scores, or how much the scores vary from each other. When scores fall very close together and are not widely spread apart, the data are described as not having much variability, or **variance**.

Compare the following two sets of data:

Data Set I		Data Set J	
100	75	98	75
98	75	96	75
95	75	87	75
91	72	78	75
88	70	75	72
87	69	75	72
82	68	75	72
80	67	75	72
75	51	75	72
75	50	75	72

range The distance between the highest and lowest scores in a data set.

An easy way to get an idea about the spread is to find the **range** of scores. The range is calculated by subtracting the lowest score from the highest score.

Set I	Set J
$100 - 50 = 50$	$98 - 72 = 26$

The range for set J is about half that of set I. It appears that set I has more variability than set J. Look at the sets of data again. Both sets have the same median and the same mode, yet they are very different in terms of variability. When the means are calculated, it seems that the data are very similar. Set I has a mean of 77.15, and set J has a mean of 77.05. By using only measures of central tendency, the teacher may think that the students in both of these classes performed in a very similar manner on this test. Yet one set of data has approximately twice the spread, or variability of scores. In educational testing, it is necessary to determine the deviation from the mean in order to have a clearer picture of how students in groups such as these performed. By calculating the variance and the standard deviation, the teacher can find out the typical amount of difference from the mean. By knowing these typical or standard deviations from the mean, the teacher will be able to find out which scores are a significant distance from the average score.

To find the standard deviation of a set of scores, the variance must first be calculated. The variance can be described as the degree or amount of variability or dispersion in a set of scores. Looking at data sets I and J, one could probably assume that set I would have a larger variance than J.

Four steps are involved in calculating the variance:

Step 1   To calculate the amount of distance of each score from the mean, subtract the mean for the set of data from each score.

Step 2   Find the square of each of the difference scores found in Step 1 (multiply each difference score by itself).

Step 3 Find the total of all of the squared score differences. This is called the sum of squares.

Step 4 Calculate the average of the sum of squares by dividing the total by the number of scores.

Step 1: Difference	Step 2: Multiply by Itself	Squared
$100 - 77.15 = 22.85$	$22.85 \times 22.85 =$	522.1225
$98 - 77.15 = 20.85$	$20.85 \times 20.85 =$	434.7225
$95 - 77.15 = 17.85$	$17.85 \times 17.85 =$	318.6225
$91 - 77.15 = 13.85$	$13.85 \times 13.85 =$	191.8225

Step 1: Difference	Step 2: Multiply by Itself	Squared
$88 - 77.15 = 10.85$	$10.85 \times 10.85 =$	117.7225
$87 - 77.15 = 9.85$	$9.85 \times 9.85 =$	97.0225
$82 - 77.15 = 4.85$	$4.85 \times 4.85 =$	23.5225
$80 - 77.15 = 2.85$	$2.85 \times 2.85 =$	8.1225
$75 - 77.15 = -2.15$	$-2.15 \times -2.15 =$	4.6225
$75 - 77.15 = -2.15$	$-2.15 \times -2.15 =$	4.6225
$75 - 77.15 = -2.15$	$-2.15 \times -2.15 =$	4.6225
$75 - 77.15 = -2.15$	$-2.15 \times -2.15 =$	4.6225
$75 - 77.15 = -2.15$	$-2.15 \times -2.15 =$	4.6225
$72 - 77.15 = -5.15$	$-5.15 \times -5.15 =$	26.5225
$70 - 77.15 = -7.15$	$-7.15 \times -7.15 =$	51.1225
$69 - 77.15 = -8.15$	$-8.15 \times -8.15 =$	66.4225
$68 - 77.15 = -9.15$	$-9.15 \times -9.15 =$	83.7225
$67 - 77.15 = -10.15$	$-10.15 \times -10.15 =$	103.0225
$51 - 77.15 = -26.15$	$-26.15 \times -26.15 =$	683.8225
$50 - 77.15 = -27.15$	$-27.15 \times -27.15 =$	737.1225

Step 3: Sum of Squares: 3,488.55

Step 4: Divide the Sum of Squares by the Number of Scores

$$3,488.55 \div 20 = 174.4275$$

Therefore, the variance for data set I = 174.4275.

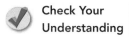

Check Your Understanding

Check your knowledge of the measures of dispersion presented in the previous section by completing Activity 3.7 below.

Activity 3.7

Calculate the variance for data set J and compare with data set I.

Data Set J	Step 1: Difference	Step 2: Multiply by Itself	Squared
98 − 77.05 =			
96 − 77.05 =			
87 − 77.05 =			
78 − 77.05 =			
75 − 77.05 =			
75 − 77.05 =			
75 − 77.05 =			
75 − 77.05 =			
75 − 77.05 =			
75 − 77.05 =			
75 − 77.05 =			
75 − 77.05 =			
75 − 77.05 =			
75 − 77.05 =			
72 − 77.05 =			
72 − 77.05 =			
72 − 77.05 =			
72 − 77.05 =			
72 − 77.05 =			
72 − 77.05 =			

Step 3: Sum of Squares: _____

Step 4: Divide the Sum of Squares by the Number of Scores. Which set of data, J or I, has the larger variance? _____

Apply Your Knowledge

Data sets I and J have means that are very similar. Why do you think there is such a large difference between the variance of I and the variance of J? _____

_____

_____

STANDARD DEVIATION

Once the variance has been calculated, only one more step is needed to calculate the standard deviation. The standard deviation helps the teacher determine how much distance from the mean is typical and how much is considered significant.

Figure 3.3   Distribution for data set I.

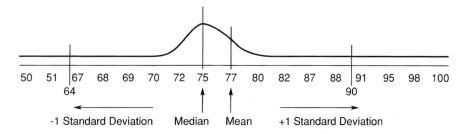

The standard deviation of a set of data is the square root of the variance.

Standard Deviation $= \sqrt{\text{Variance}}$

Because the variance for data sets I and J has already been calculated, merely enter each number on a calculator and hit the square root button. If a calculator is not available, use the square root tables located in most introductory statistics textbooks.

The square root of the variance for data set I is 13.21. Therefore, any test score that is more than 1 standard deviation above or below the mean score, either 13.21 above the mean or 13.21 below the mean, is considered significant. Look at data set I. The test scores that are more than 1 standard deviation above the mean (77.15) are 100, 98, 95, and 91. The scores that are more than 1 standard deviation below the mean are 51 and 50. These scores represent the extremes for this distribution and may well receive the extreme grades for the class: A's and F's. Figure 3.3 illustrates the distribution of scores in data set I.

Look at data set J. To locate significantly different scores, find those that are 1 or more standard deviations away from the mean of 77.05. Which scores are considered to be a significant distance from the mean?

STANDARD DEVIATION AND THE NORMAL DISTRIBUTION

In a normal distribution, the standard deviations represent the percentages of scores shown on the bell curve in Figure 3.4. More than 68% of the scores fall within 1 standard deviation above or below the mean. A normal distribution is symmetrical and has the same number representing the mean, median, and mode. Notice that approximately 95% of the scores are found within 2 standard deviations above and below the mean (Figure 3.4). To clarify the significance of standard deviation, it is helpful to remember that one criterion for the diagnosis of mental retardation is an IQ score of more than 2 standard deviations below the mean. The criterion of

Check your knowledge of the measures of dispersion presented in the previous section by completing Activity 3.8 below.

Activity 3.8

Using the following sets of data, complete a frequency count and a frequency polygon; calculate the mean, median, and mode; calculate the range, variance, and standard deviation; and list the scores that are a significant distance from the mean.

Ms. Jones's Class Data

95, 82, 76, 75, 62, 100, 32, 15, 100, 98, 99, 86, 70, 26, 21, 26, 82

Frequency count:_____

Draw the frequency polygon of the data.

15 20 25 30 35 40 45 50 55 60 65 70 75 80 85 90 95 100

Mean: _____   Median: _____   Mode:_____

Range: _____   Variance: _____   Standard deviation: _____

Test scores that are a significant distance from the mean are
_____

Mrs. Smith's Class Data

76, 75, 83, 92, 85, 69, 88, 87, 88, 88, 88, 88, 77, 78, 78, 95, 98

Frequency count:_____

Draw the frequency polygon of the data.

65 70 75 80 85 90 95 100

Mean: _____   Median: _____   Mode:_____
Range: _____   Variance: _____   Standard deviation: _____
Test scores that are a significant distance from the mean are
_____

Apply Your Knowledge

Using the information you obtained through your calculations, what can you say about the performance of the students in Ms. Jones's class compared with the performance of the students in Mrs. Smith's class?
_____
_____
_____

Figure 3.4 Percentages of population that fall within standard deviation units in a normal distribution.

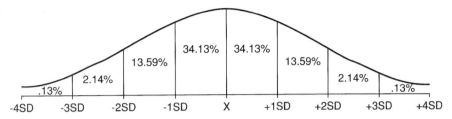

2 standard deviations above the mean is often used to determine that a student is within the gifted range. Using a standard deviation of 15 IQ points, an individual with an IQ of 70 or less and a subaverage adaptive behavior scale score might be classified as being within the range of mental retardation, whereas an individual with an IQ of 130 or more may be classified as gifted. The American Association on Mental Retardation (AAMR) classification system allows additional flexibility by adding 5 points to the minimum requirement; that is, the student within the 70–75 IQ range may also be found eligible for services under the category of mental retardation if there are additional supporting data.

MEAN DIFFERENCES

Test results such as those discussed in the preceding section should be interpreted with caution. Many tests that have been used historically to diagnose disabilities such as mental retardation have been shown to exhibit *mean differences*. A specific cultural or linguistic group may have a different mean or average score than that reported for most of the population; this is a mean difference. Accordingly, minority students should not be judged by an acceptable average for a different population. This issue is elaborated on in Chapter 9, "Measures of Intelligence and Adaptive Behavior."

SKEWED DISTRIBUTIONS

skewed Describes a distribution that has either more positively distributed scores or more negatively distributed scores.

When small samples of populations are tested or when a fairly restricted population is tested, the results may not be distributed in a normal curve. Distributions can be **skewed** in a positive or negative direction. When many of the scores are below the mean, the distribution is said to be **positively skewed** and will resemble the distribution in Figure 3.5. Notice that the most frequently occurring scores (mode) are located below the mean.

Figure 3.5   Positively skewed distribution.

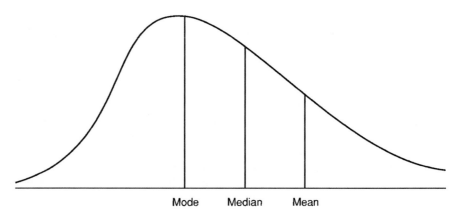

Mode   Median   Mean

Figure 3.6   Negatively skewed distribution.

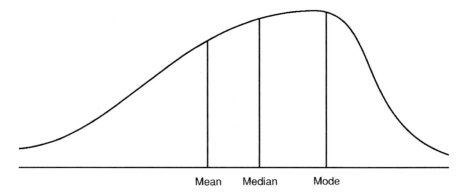

Mean   Median   Mode

positively skewed
Describes a
distribution in which
more of the scores fall
below the mean.

**negatively
skewed** Describes a
distribution in which
more of the scores fall
above the mean.

When a large number of the scores occur above the mean, the distribution is said to be **negatively skewed**, as shown in Figure 3.6. Notice that the mode and median scores are located above the mean.

Figures 3.5 and 3.6 illustrate different ways that groups of scores fall, cluster, and are dispersed. As already discussed, extreme scores can change the appearance of a set of scores. Often, when working with scores from teacher-made tests, one or two scores can be so extreme that they influence the way the data are described. That is, the scores may influence or pull the mean in one direction. Consider the following examples:

Ms. Brown	Ms. Blue
100	100
92	92
86	86
80	80

78	78
78	78
78	78
75	75
74	74
72	6
$813 \div 10 = 81.3$	$745 \div 10 = 74.5$

The sets of data are very similar except for the one extreme low score. The greater the number of scores in the class, the less influence an extreme score has on the set of data. In small classes like those often found in special education settings, the mean of the class performance is more likely to be influenced by an extreme score. If Ms. Brown and Ms. Blue each had a class objective stating that the class would pass the test with an average score of 80, Ms. Brown's class would have passed the objective, but Ms. Blue's class would not have. When the extreme score is omitted, the average for Ms. Blue's class is 82.1, which meets the class objective.

When selecting norm–referenced tests, special educators must take care to read the test manual and determine the size of the sample used in the norming process. Tests developed using larger samples are thought to result in scores that are more representative of the majority population.

TYPES OF SCORES

percentile ranks
Scores that express the percentage of students who scored as well as or lower than a given student's score.

z scores Derived scores that are expressed in standard deviation units.

Percentile ranks and **z scores** provide additional ways of looking at data. Using percentile ranks is a method of ranking each score on the continuum of the normal distribution. The extreme scores are ranked at the top and bottom, and very few people obtain scores at the extreme ends. Percentiles range from the 99.9th percentile to less than the 1st percentile. A person who scores at the extremely high end of a test may be ranked near the 99th percentile. This means that she scored as well as or better than 99% of the students the same age or grade who took the same test. A person who scores around the average, say 100 on an IQ test, would be ranked in the middle, or the 50th percentile. A person who scores in the top fourth would be above the 75th percentile; in other words, the student scored as well as or better than 75% of the students in that particular age group. The various percentile ranks and their location on a normal distribution are illustrated in Figure 3.7.

Some have argued that using a percentile rank may not convey information that is as meaningful as other types of scores, such as z scores (May & Nicewander, 1994, 1997). deGruijter (1997) argued that May and Nicewander were faulty in their reasoning regarding percentile ranks and stated that percentile ranks are not inferior indicators of ability.

Figure 3.7   Relationship of percentiles and normal distribution.

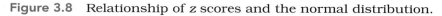

Source: From *Assessing special students* (3rd ed., p. 63) by J. McLoughlin and R. Lewis, 1990, Upper Saddle River, NJ: Merrill/Prentice Hall. Copyright 1990 by Prentice Hall. Adapted with permission.

Figure 3.8   Relationship of *z* scores and the normal distribution.

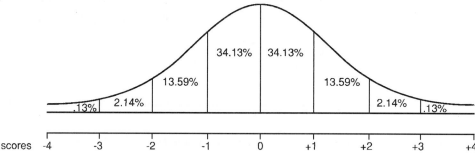

Source: From *Assessing special students* (3rd ed., p. 63) by J. McLoughlin and R. Lewis, 1990, Upper Saddle River, NJ: Merrill/Prentice Hall. Copyright 1990 by Prentice Hall. Adapted with permission.

Some tests use *T* scores to interpret test performance. *T* scores have an average or mean of 50 and standard deviation of 10. One standard deviation above the mean would be expressed as a *T* score of 60, and 40 would represent 1 standard deviation below the mean.

Another type of score used to describe the data in a normal distribution is called a *z* score. A *z* score indicates where a score is located in terms of standard deviation units. The mean is expressed as 0, 1 standard deviation above the mean is expressed as +1, 2 standard deviations above as +2, and so on, as illustrated in Figure 3.8. Standard deviation units below the mean are expressed as negative numbers. For example, a score that is 1 standard deviation below the mean is expressed using *z* scores as −1, and a score that is 2 standard deviations below is expressed as −2. Conversely, +1 is 1 standard deviation above the mean, and +2 is 2 standard deviations above the mean.

stanines A method of reporting scores that divide data into 9 groups and scores are reported as 1 through 9 with a mean of 5.

deciles A method of reporting scores that divides data into 10 groups with each group representing 10% of the obtained scores.

Stanines are used to report many group achievement test scores. Stanines divide the scores into 9 groups of scores and are reported as 1 through 9 with a mean of 5. The standard deviation unit of stanines is 2. This indicates that students who fall between the 3rd and 7th stanines are within the range expected for their age or grade group.

Deciles are scores that are reported in 10 groups ranging from a score of 10 for the lowest grouping to 100 for the highest group of scores. Each grouping represents 10% of the obtained scores.

Case Study for Score Interpretation: Percentile Ranks

Mr. Garza received a report from the school counselor regarding a student whom he had referred for an assessment of self-esteem. The student, Jorge, completed a norm-referenced questionnaire that assessed his own feelings and self-confidence about school, his peers, and his family. When the counselor met with Mr. Garza, the following scores were reported:

Self–Confidence with Peer Relationships	5th percentile rank
Self–Confidence with Family Relationships	95th percentile rank
Self–Confidence in Ability at School	12th percentile rank

In this case, self-confidence is something that is valued or consistent with better behavior and higher achievement. In other words, the more confidence a student reports, the better he may be able to function in school, with peers, and with family relationships. For Jorge, he answered in a manner that indicates he was ranked at the 5th percentile in self-confidence with peers. This means that about 95% of the students his age reported feeling more confident about their peer relationships. According to the responses made by the student, how confident is he about his ability to get along within his family? How confident is he in his ability to perform at school?

Because self-confidence is something that is valued, higher percentile ranks indicate that the student has confidence while lower percentile ranks indicate that he is not very confident about his ability.

When we assess behaviors that are impacting learning in a negative way, such as distractibility or signs of depression, for example, we want the percentile ranks to be lower. In other words, a percentile rank of 15 indicates that about 85% of the students in the sample displayed more behaviors that are consistent with distractibility or depression.

When assessing characteristics that are predictors of higher school achievement, such as IQ, we look for higher percentile ranks to indicate higher ability. A student who performed in a manner that resulted in a percentile rank of 90 indicates that the student performed better than about 90% of the students in the norm sample.

For **MORE PRACTICE** in calculating scores and applying test scores to cases, visit the Companion Website at *www.prenhall.com/overton.*

THINK AHEAD

Now that you know how to compare students' scores with each other, you will read about how to compare tests. You will learn how to determine whether tests are reliable and valid. Do you think a test must be both reliable and valid to obtain information about a student's abilities?

EXERCISES

Part I

Match these terms with the statements that follow.

a. nominal scale
b. positively skewed
c. measures of central tendency
d. frequency distribution
e. bimodal distribution
f. ordinal scale
g. multimodal
h. frequency polygon
i. measures of dispersion
j. negatively skewed

k. standard deviation
l. ratio scale
m. interval scale
n. mode
o. range
p. rank order
q. median
r. descriptive statistics
s. mean
t. normal distribution

_____ 1. In this set of data, what measures of central tendency are represented by the number 77: 65, 66, 82, 95, 77?

_____ 2. If the heights of all fifth-grade elementary students in one large city were measured, in what manner would the resulting data be displayed?

_____ 3. The following set of data is interesting because it is _____?
22, 47, 88, 62, 65, 22, 63, 89, 55, 74, 88, 99, 44, 65, 100.

_____ 4. In a university, all students are given a new student identification number upon registration. These numbers are on what scale?

_____ 5. All fourth-grade students in a Little City School were asked to participate in a reading contest to see which students could read the most books in a 3-month period. At the end of the 3 months, the winners were determined.

The 10 students who read the most books were awarded prizes. On the final day of the contest, the students anxiously looked at the list where the names were in _____ from the highest number of books read to the fewest.

_____ 6. The mean, median, and mode make up _____.

_____ 7. A seventh-grade prealgebra class completed the first test of the new school year. Here are the data resulting from the first test: 100, 99, 95, 90, 89, 85, 84, 82, 81, 80, 79, 78, 77, 76, 70, 68, 65, 62, 60, 59, 55. For this set of data, what does the number 45 represent?

_____ 8. The following set of data has what type of distribution: 88, 33, 78, 56, 44, 37, 90, 99, 76, 78, 77, 62, 90?

_____ 9. A set of data has a symmetrical distribution of scores with the mean, median, and mode represented by the number 82. This set of data represents a _____.

_____10. What term describes when a set of data has a mean that is less than the most frequently occurring scores?

Part II

Rank order the following data; complete a frequency distribution and a frequency polygon; calculate the mean, median, and mode; and find the range, variance, and standard deviation. Identify scores that are significantly above or below the mean.

Data

85, 85, 99, 63, 60, 97, 96, 95, 58, 70, 72, 92, 89, 87, 74, 74, 74, 85, 84, 78, 84, 78, 84, 78, 86, 82, 79, 81, 80, 86

_____	_____
_____	_____
_____	_____
_____	_____
_____	_____
_____	_____
_____	_____
_____	_____
_____	_____
_____	_____
_____	_____
_____	_____
_____	_____
_____	_____
_____	_____

Mean: _____   Median: _____   Mode: _____

Range: _____   Variance: _____   Standard deviation: _____

Scores that are a significant distance from the mean are

_____

Draw the frequency polygon here:

Figure 3.9 Relationships among different types of scores in a normal distribution.

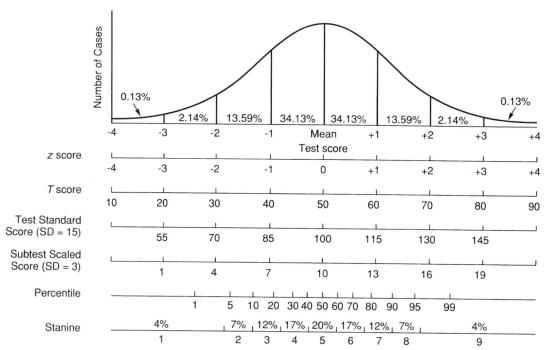

Source: From *Assessing special students* (4th ed., p. 61) by J. McLoughlin and R. Lewis, 1994, Upper Saddle River, NJ: Merrill/Prentice Hall. Copyright 1994.

Use the normal distribution shown in Figure 3.9 to answer the following questions. You may need to use a ruler or straightedge, placed on the figure vertically, to identify the answers.

1. What percentage of the scores would fall between the z scores of −2.0 and +2.0? _____

2. What percentile rank would be assigned to the z score of 0?_____

3. What percentile rank would represent a person who scored at the z score of +3.0? _____

4. Approximately what percentile rank would be assigned for the IQ score of 70? _____

5. Approximately how many people would be expected to fall in the IQ range represented by the z scores of +3.0 to +4.0? _____

Answers to these questions can be found in the Appendix of this text or you may also complete these questions and receive immediate feedback on your answers by going to the Think Ahead module in Chapter 3 of the Companion Website.

Reliability and Validity

reliability
correlation
correlation coefficient
scattergram
Pearson's r
internal consistency
test-retest reliability
equivalent forms reliability
alternate forms reliability
split-half reliability
Kuder–Richardson (K–R) 20
coefficient alpha
interrater reliability
true score

standard error of measurement
obtained score
confidence interval
estimated true score
validity
criterion-related validity
concurrent validity
predictive validity
content validity
presentation format
response mode
construct validity
validity of test use

CHAPTER FOCUS

This chapter presents reliability and validity of test instruments. You will learn the various methods of researching reliability and validity and which methods are appropriate for specific types of tests.

CEC KNOWLEDGE AND SKILLS STANDARDS

The student completing this chapter will understand the knowledge and skills included in the following CEC Knowledge and Skills Standards from Standard 8: Assessment:

CC8K1—Basic terminology used in assessment

CC8S5—Interpret information from formal and informal assessments

RELIABILITY AND VALIDITY IN ASSESSMENT

It is important for educators to feel that the assessment methods used in teaching are providing accurate information. Usually, inferences are made from test data. In each school district, these inferences and subsequent interpretations of test results may change or set the educational future of hundreds of students each school year. An understanding of the concepts of reliability and validity aids the educator in determining test accuracy and dependability as well as how much faith can be placed in the use of instruments in the decision-making process.

Reliability in assessment refers to the confidence that can be placed in an instrument to yield the same score for the same student if the test were administered more than once and to the degree with which a skill or trait is measured consistently across items of a test. Teachers administering tests of any type, formal or informal, must be aware that error will be present to some degree during test administration. Statistical methods for estimating the probable amount of error and the degree of reliability allow professionals to select instruments with the lowest estimate of error and the greatest degree of reliability. Because educators use assessment as a basis for educational intervention and placement decisions, the most technically adequate instruments are preferred.

reliability The dependability or consistency of an instrument across time or items.

CORRELATION

correlation A statistical method of observing the degree of relationship between two sets of data on two variables.

One concept important to the understanding of reliability in assessment is **correlation**. Correlation is a method of determining the degree of relationship between two variables. Reliability is determined by the degree of relationship between the administration of an instrument and some other variable (including a repeated administration of the same instrument). The greater the degree of the relationship, the more reliable the instrument.

Correlation is a statistical procedure calculated to measure the relationship between two variables. The two variables might be two administrations of the same test, administration of equivalent forms of the same test, administration of one test and school achievement, or variables such as amount of time spent studying and final exam grades. In short, correlation is a method of determining whether two variables are associated with each other and, if so, how much.

correlation coefficient The expression of a relationship between two variables.

There are three types of correlations between variables: positive, negative, and no relationship. The degree of relationship between two variables is expressed by a **correlation coefficient** (*r*). The correlation coefficient will be a number between $+1.00$ and -1.00. A -1.00 or $+1.00$ indicates a perfect degree of correlation. In reality, perfect correlations are extremely rare. A correlation coefficient of 0 indicates no relationship.

The closer to $+1.00$ the coefficient, the stronger the degree of the relationship. Hence, an *r* of .78 represents a stronger relationship than .65. When relationships are expressed by coefficients, the positive or negative sign does not indicate the strength of a relationship, but indicates the direction of the relationship. Therefore, *r* values of $-.78$ and $+.78$ are of equal strength.

POSITIVE CORRELATION

Variables that have a positive relationship are those that move in the same direction. For example, this means that when test scores representing one variable in a set are high, scores representing the other variable also are high, and when the scores on one variable are low, scores on the other variable are low. Look at the following list of scores. Students who made high scores on a reading ability test (mean = 100) also had fairly high classroom reading grades at the end of the 6-week reporting period. Therefore, the data appear to show a positive relationship between the ability measured on the reading test (variable Y) and the student's performance in the reading curriculum in the classroom (variable X).

	Scores on the Reading Ability Test (Variable Y)	Reading Grade at End of 6 Weeks (Variable X)
John	109	B+
Ralph	120	A+
Sue	88	C−
Mary	95	B+
George	116	A−
Fred	78	D−
Kristy	140	A+
Jake	135	A
Jason	138	A
Betty	95	B−
Jamie	85	C+

scattergram Graphic representation of a correlation.

To better understand this positive relationship, the scores on these two variables can be plotted on a **scattergram** (Figure 4.1). Each student is represented by a single dot on the graph. The scattergram shows clearly that as the score on one variable increased, so did the score on the other variable.

When plotting correlations on a scattergram, the closer the dots approximate a straight line, the nearer to perfect the correlation. Hence, a strong relationship will appear more linear. Figure 4.2 illustrates a perfect positive correlation (straight line) for the small set of data shown here.

	Test 1 (Variable Y)	Test 2 (Variable X)
George	100	100
Bill	95	95
Mary	87	87
Sue	76	76

Figure 4.1 Scattergram showing relationship between scores on reading ability test and reading grade for 6 weeks.

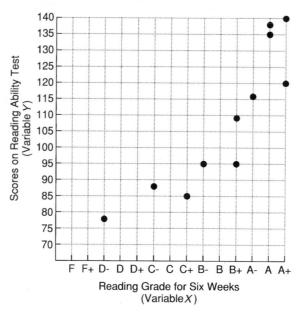

Figure 4.2 Scattergram showing a perfect positive correlation.

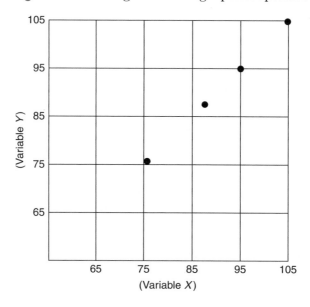

Examples of other variables that would be expected to have a positive relationship are number of days present in class and semester grade, number of chapters studied and final exam grade, and number of alcoholic drinks consumed and mistakes on a fine-motor test.

NEGATIVE CORRELATION

A negative correlation occurs when high scores on one variable are associated with low scores on the other variable. Examples of probable negative correlations are number of days absent and test grades, number of hours spent at parties and test grades, and number of hours missed from work and amount of hourly paycheck.

When the strength of a relationship is weak, the scattergram will not appear to have a distinct line. The less linear the scattergram, the weaker the correlation. Figure 4.3 illustrates scattergrams representing weak positive and weak negative relationships.

NO CORRELATION

When data from two variables are not associated or have no relationship, the $r = .00$. No correlation will be represented on a scattergram, with no linear direction either positive or negative. Figure 4.4 illustrates a scattergram of variables with no relationship.

Figure 4.3 Scattergrams showing (a) weak positive and (b) weak negative relationships.

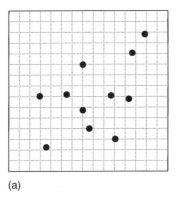
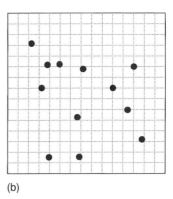

(a)   (b)

Figure 4.4 Scattergram showing no relationship.

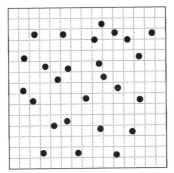

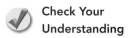 **Check Your Understanding**

Check your knowledge of positive correlation by completing Activity 4.1 below.

Activity 4.1

The following sets of data are scores on a mathematics ability test and grade-level achievement in math for fifth graders. Plot the scores on the scattergram shown here.

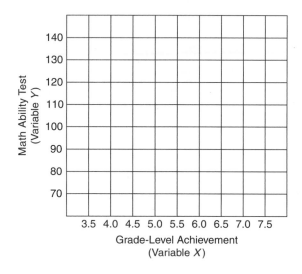

	Mathematics Ability Test Score (Variable Y)	Grade-Level Achievement (Variable X)
Wendy	115	6.5
Mary	102	5.5
Brad	141	7.4
Randy	92	4.7
Jamie	106	5.8
George	88	3.9

Apply Your Knowledge

Explain why this scattergram represents a positive correlation. _____
_____
_____

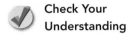

Check Your Understanding

Check your knowledge of negative correlation by completing Activity 4.2 below.

Activity 4.2

Here is an example of a negative correlation between two variables Plot the scores on the scattergram.

	Test 1 (Variable Y)	Test 2 (Variable X)
Heather	116	40
Ryan	118	38
Brent	130	20
William	125	21
Kellie	112	35
Stacy	122	19
Marsha	126	23
Lawrence	110	45
Allen	127	18
Aaron	100	55
Jeff	120	27
Sharon	122	25
Michael	112	43
James	105	50
Thomas	117	33

Test 1 (Variable *Y*)

130 — 125 — 120 — 115 — 110 — 105 — 100

15 20 25 30 35 40 45 50 55 60

Test 2 (Variable *X*)

METHODS OF MEASURING RELIABILITY

A teacher who administers a mathematics ability test to a student on a particular day and obtains a standard score of 110 (mean = 100) might feel quite confident that the student has ability in math

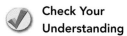

**Check Your
Understanding**

Check your ability to distinguish between positive, negative, or no correlation by completing Activity 4.3 below.

Activity 4.3

Complete the scattergrams using the following sets of data. Determine whether the scattergrams illustrate positive, negative, or no correlation.

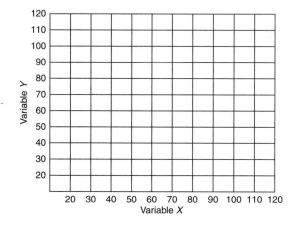

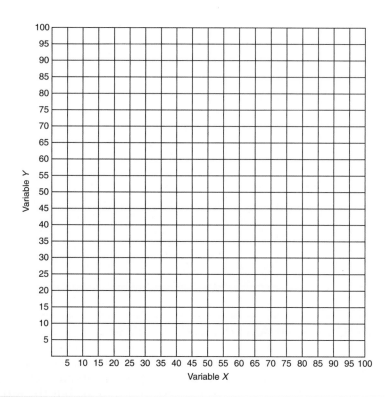

Variable **Y**	Variable **X**
100	110
96	94
86	91
67	72
77	85

Correlation appears to be

_____

Variable **Y**	Variable **X**
6	87
56	98
4	80
10	85
40	84
30	20
20	40
50	20

Correlation appears to be

_____

Apply Your Knowledge

Explain the concept of correlations: positive, negative, and no correlation.

_____

_____

_____

above expectancy for the age level. Imagine that a teacher recommended a change in the student's educational placement based on the results of that particular math test and later discovered that the math test was not reliable. Educators must be able to have confidence that test instruments used will yield similar results when administered at different times. Professionals must know the degree with which they can rely on a specific instrument.

Different methods can be used to measure the reliability of test instruments. The reliability statistics are calculated using correlational methods. One correlational method used is the Pearson's Product Moment correlation, known as **Pearson's r**. Pearson's *r* is a commonly used formula for data on an interval or a ratio scale, although other methods are used as well. The correlational studies of the reliability of tests involve checking the reliability of a test over time or the reliability of items within the

Pearson's *r*
A statistical formula for determining strength and direction of correlations.

internal consistency The consistency of the items on an instrument to measure a skill, trait, or domain.

test, known as **internal consistency**. For such studies, the procedures of test-retest, equivalent forms, split-half, and statistical methods called Kuder–Richardson formulas may be used.

TEST-RETEST RELIABILITY

test-retest reliability Study that employs the readministration of a single instrument to check for consistency across time.

One way to determine the reliability of a test is to measure the correlation of test scores obtained during one administration with the scores obtained on a repeated administration. The assumption of **test-retest reliability** is that the trait being measured is one that is stable over time. Therefore, if the trait being measured remained constant, the readministration of the instrument would result in scores very similar to the first scores, and thus the correlation between the two administrations would be positive.

Many of the traits measured in psychoeducational assessment are variable and respond to influencing factors or changes over time, such as instruction or student maturity. The readministration of an instrument for reliability studies should therefore be completed within a fairly short time period in an effort to control the influencing variables that occur naturally in the educational environment of children and youth. Typically, the longer the interval between test administrations, the more chance of variation in the obtained scores. Conversely, the shorter the interval between the two test administrations, the less likelihood that students will be influenced by time-related factors (experience, education, etc.). The difficulty with readministering the same instrument within a short period of time is that the student may remember items on the test. This *practice effect* most likely would cause the scores obtained on the second administration to be higher than the original scores, which would influence the correlation. The shorter the interval between administrations, the greater the possibility of practice effect; the longer the interval, the greater the influence of time variables.

The disadvantages of test-retest methods for checking test reliability have led to the use of other methods.

EQUIVALENT FORMS RELIABILITY

equivalent forms reliability Consistency of a test to measure some domain, traits, or skill using like forms of the same instrument.

To control for the influence of time-related and practice-effect variables of test-retest methods, test developers may choose to use **equivalent forms reliability**, also called **alternate forms reliability**. In this method, two forms of the same instrument are used. The items are matched for difficulty on each test. For example, if three items for phonetic attack of consonant blends are included on one version of a reading test, three items of the same nature must be included at the same level on the alternate form of the test. During the reliability study, each student is administered both forms, and the scores obtained on one form of the test are then paired with the

alternate forms reliability Synonymous term for equivalent forms reliability.

scores obtained on the equivalent form. The following are scores obtained on equivalent forms of a hypothetical reading test:

The Best-Ever Diagnostic Reading Test ($x = 100$)*

	Form 1	Form 2
John	82	85
Sue	76	78
Bill	89	87
Randy	54	56
Sally	106	112
Sara	115	109

*x = mean of sample.

This positive correlation indicates a fairly high reliability using equivalent forms reliability. In reality, an equivalent forms reliability study would involve a much larger sample of students. If this example had been an equivalent forms study using a large national sample, the educator could assume that both forms of the Best-Ever Reading Diagnostic Test are measuring the tested trait with some consistency.

If the test developer of the Best-Ever Reading Diagnostic Test also wanted the test to measure the stability of the trait over time, the manual would recommend that an interval of time pass between the administration of each form of the test. In using equivalent forms for measuring the stability over time, the reliability coefficient usually will not be as high as in the case of administering the same form of a test a second time. In the case of administering equivalent forms over a period of time, the influence of time-related variables will decrease the reliability coefficient as well as the practice effect that occurs in a test-retest reliability study of the same instrument.

Several published achievement and diagnostic tests that are used in special education consist of two equivalent forms. The advantage of this format is that it provides the educator with two tests of the same difficulty level that can be administered within a short time frame without the influence of practice effect. Often, local educational agencies practice a policy of administering one of the equivalent forms before writing short-term objectives for the year and administering the second form following educational interventions near the end of the school year. Educators administer the second form of the test to determine whether the educational objectives were achieved.

split-half reliability A method of checking the consistency across items by halving a test and administering two half-forms of same test.

INTERNAL CONSISTENCY MEASURES

Several methods allow a test developer to determine the reliability of the items on a single test using one administration of the test. These methods include **split-half reliability**, Kuder–Richardson (K–R) 20, and coefficient alpha.

Split-Half Reliability   Test developers rely often on the split-half method of determining reliability because of its ease of use. This method uses the items available on the instrument, splits the test in half, and correlates the two halves of the test. Because most tests have the items arranged sequentially, from the easiest items at the beginning of the test to the most difficult items at the end, the tests are typically split by pulling every other item, which in essence results in two equivalent half-forms of the test. Because this type of reliability study can be performed in a single administration of the instrument, split-half reliability studies are often completed even though other types of reliability studies are used in the test development. Although this method establishes reliability of one half of the test with the other half, it does not establish the reliability of the entire test. Because reliability tends to increase with the number of items on the test, using split-half reliability may result in a lower reliability coefficient than that calculated by another method for the entire test (Mehrens & Lehmann, 1978). In this case, the reliability may be statistically adjusted to account for the variance in length (Mehrens & Lehmann, 1978).

Kuder–Richardson 20 and Coefficient Alpha   As the name implies, internal consistency reliability methods are used to determine how much alike items are to other items on a test. An advantage of this type of reliability study is that a single test administration is required. This reflects the unidimensionality in measuring a trait rather than the multidimensionality (Walsh & Betz, 1985).

> **Kuder–Richardson (K–R) 20** A formula used to check consistency across items of an instrument with right/wrong responses.

Internal consistency is computed statistically by using either the **K–R 20** formula for items scored only right or wrong or the coefficient alpha formula for items when more than 1 point is earned for a correct response (Mehrens & Lehmann, 1978).

When a high correlation coefficient is expressed by an internal consistency formula such as K–R 20 or **coefficient alpha**, the educator can be confident that the items on the instrument measure the trait or skill with some consistency. These methods measure the consistency of the items but not the consistency or dependability of the instrument across time, as do the test-retest method or using equivalent forms in separate test administrations.

> **coefficient alpha** A formula used to check consistency across terms of an instrument with responses with varying credit.

INTERRATER RELIABILITY

Many of the educational and diagnostic tests used in special education are standardized with very specific administration, scoring, and interpretation instructions. Tests with a great deal of structure reduce the amount of influence that individual examiners may have on the results of the test. Some tests, specifically tests that allow the examiner to make judgments about student performance, have a greater possibility of influence by test examiners. In other words, there may be more of a chance that a score would vary from one examiner to another if the same student were tested by different examiners. On tests such as this, it is important to check the **interrater reliability**, or interscorer reliability. This can be accomplished by administering the test and then having an objective scorer also score the test results. The results of the tests scored by the examiner are then correlated with the results obtained by the objective scorer to determine how much variability exists between the test scores. This information is especially important when tests with a great deal of subjectivity are used in making educational decisions.

interrater reliability The consistency of a test to measure a skill, trait, or domain across examiners.

Case Study for Reliability

Mrs. Smith received a new student in her fifth-grade class. In the student's records were educational testing data. Because of difficulty in reading, the student had been assessed in her previous school using a brief screening reading test that assessed all reading levels by using a simple list of most common words. The student's scores did not indicate any reading difficulty, yet Mrs. Smith noticed that the student was struggling with the fifth-grade reader.

One aspect of technically reliable academic instruments is the number of items and the representativeness of the domain being assessed. In this case, the student was assessed with a very short instrument that did not adequately assess the domain of skills that comprise fifth-grade-level reading, such as comprehension, decoding, recognition, oral fluency, and silent reading fluency. Mrs. Smith decided to assess the student using a comprehensive reading test that measured all aspects of reading expected of a student in the fifth-grade. This administration indicated that the student was actually able to complete most reading tasks successfully at the third-grade reading level. This comprehensive reading test was more predictive of the student's actual instructional level of reading.

WHICH TYPE OF RELIABILITY IS THE BEST?

Different types of reliability studies are used to measure consistency over time, consistency of the items on a test, and consistency of the test scored by different examiners. An educator selects assessment instruments for specific purposes according to the child's educational needs. The reliability studies and information in the test manual concerning reliability of the instrument are important considerations for the educator when determining which test is best for a particular student. An educator should select the instrument that has a high degree of reliability related to the purpose of assessment. An adequate reliability coefficient would be .60 or greater, and a high degree of reliability would be above .80. For example, if the

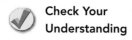

Check Your Understanding

Check your understanding of the different methods of studying reliability by completing Activity 4.4 below.

Activity 4.4

Select the appropriate reliability study for the purposes described (more than one answer may be correct).

A. split-half reliability

B. equivalent forms, separate administration times

C. K–R 20

D. interrater reliability

E. test-retest reliability

F. coefficient alpha

G. equivalent times, same administration time

_____1. Educator is concerned with item reliability, items are scored as right and wrong.

_____2. Educator wants to administer the same test twice to measure achievement objectives.

_____3. Examiner is concerned with consistency of trait over time.

_____4. Educator is concerned with item consistency, items scored with different point values for correct responses.

_____5. Examiner wants to administer a test that allows for examiner judgment.

Apply Your Knowledge

Explain the difference between internal reliability and other types of reliability. _____

_____

_____

examiner is interested in measuring a trait over time, the examiner should select an instrument in which the reliability or consistency over time had been studied. If the examiner is more concerned with the instrument's ability to determine student behavior using an instrument that allowed for a great degree of examiner judgment, the examiner should check the instrument's interrater reliability.

RELIABILITY FOR DIFFERENT GROUPS

The calculation of the reliability coefficient is a group statistic and can be influenced by the makeup of the group. The best test development and the manuals accompanying those tests will include information regarding the reliability of a test with different age or grade levels and even the reliability of a test with populations who differ on demographic variables such as cultural or linguistic backgrounds. The information in Table 4.1 illustrates how reliability may vary across different age groups.

Table 4.1 Split-half reliability coefficients, by age, for subtest, area, and total-test raw scores from the fall and spring standardization programs.

Subtest/Composite	Program (Fall/Spring)	Age 5	6	7	8	9	10
1. Numeration	F	.73	.82	.85	.90	.81	.85
	S	.51	.82	.89	.88	.89	.81
2. Rational Numbers	F	—	.24	.71	.68	.88	.89
	S	—	.27	.42	.86	.82	.86
3. Geometry	F	.63	.81	.79	.77	.82	.80
	S	.80	.81	.76	.77	.80	.75
4. Addition	F	.63	.65	.79	.84	.78	.40
	S	.58	.78	.84	.82	.84	.66
5. Subtraction	F	.25	.68	.64	.85	.89	.86
	S	.30	.70	.85	.90	.92	.85
6. Multiplication	F	.23	.41	.11	.76	.89	.90
	S	.07	.67	.68	.91	.93	.89
7. Division	F	.55	.49	.52	.51	.82	.86
	S	.18	.34	.53	.77	.80	.84
8. Mental Computation	F	—	.78	.68	.80	.85	.88
	S	—	.65	.67	.78	.78	.90
9. Measurement	F	.77	.89	.57	.77	.76	.77
	S	.92	.84	.85	.87	.84	.70
10. Time and Money	F	.50	.61	.73	.89	.87	.93
	S	.38	.70	.84	.89	.92	.86
11. Estimation	F	.44	.43	.50	.74	.86	.72
	S	.59	.50	.53	.85	.76	.84
12. Interpreting Data	F	.41	.86	.81	.80	.88	.85
	S	.32	.79	.83	.85	.88	.87
13. Problem Solving	F	.36	.60	.73	.71	.82	.86
	S	.55	.60	.77	.76	.87	.92
Basic Concepts Area[a]	F	.78	.87	.89	.91	.92	.93
	S	.82	.88	.87	.92	.92	.92
Operations Area[a]	F	.66	.86	.87	.93	.96	.96
	S	.73	.88	.92	.96	.96	.96
Applications Area[a]	F	.82	.91	.89	.94	.96	.96
	S	.88	.90	.93	.96	.96	.96
TOTAL TEST[a]	F	.90	.95	.95	.97	.98	.98
	S	.92	.95	.97	.98	.98	.98

[a]Reliability coefficients for the areas and the total test were computed by using Guilford's (1954, p. 393) formula for estimating the reliability of composite scores.
Source: From *KeyMath—Revised: A Diagnostic Inventory of Essential Mathematics, Manual. Forms A and B* (p. 67) by A. Connolly, 1988, Circle Pines, MN: American Guidance Service. Copyright 1988 by American Guidance Service. Reprinted by permission.

STANDARD ERROR OF MEASUREMENT

In all psychoeducational assessment, there is a basic underlying assumption: Error exists. Errors in testing may result from situational factors such as a poor testing environment or the health or emotions of the student, or errors may occur due to inaccuracies within the test instrument. Error should be considered when tests are administered, scored, and interpreted. Because tests are small samples of behavior observed at a given time, many variables can affect the assessment process and cause variance in test scores. This variance is called error because it influences test results. Professionals need to know that all tests contain error and that a single test score may not accurately reflect the student's **true score**. Salvia and Ysseldyke (1988a) stated, "A true score is a hypothetical value that represents a person's score when the entire domain of items is assessed at all possible times, by all appropriate testers" (p. 369). The following basic formula should be remembered when interpreting scores:

true score The student's actual score.

$$\text{Obtained score} = \text{True score} + \text{Error}$$

Conversely,

$$\text{Obtained score} - \text{True score} = \text{Error}$$

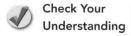

Check Your Understanding

Check your ability to interpret the data presented in Table 4.1 by answering the questions in Activity 4.5 below.

Activity 4.5

Refer to your text, Table 4.1 to answer the following questions.

1. What type of reliability is reported in Table 4.1?

2. Look at the reliability reported for age 7. Using fall statistics, compare the reliability coefficient obtained on the Numeration subtest with the reliability coefficient obtained on the Estimation subtest. On which subtest did 7-year-olds perform with more consistency?

3. Compare the reliability coefficient obtained by 9-year-olds on the Estimation subtests with the reliability coefficient obtained by 7-year-olds on the same subtest. Which age group performed with more consistency or reliability?

Apply Your Knowledge

Explain why the reliability of an instrument may vary across age groups. _____

_____

_____

standard error of measurement The amount of error determined to exist using a specific instrument, calculated using the instrument's standard deviation and reliability.

obtained score The observed score of a student on a particular test on a given day.

True score is never actually known; therefore, a range of possible scores is calculated. The error is called the **standard error of measurement**, and an instrument with a large standard error of measurement would be less desirable than an instrument with a small standard error of measurement.

To estimate the amount of error present in an individual **obtained score**, the standard error of measurement must be obtained and applied to each score. The standard deviation and the reliability coefficient of the instrument are used to calculate the standard error of measurement. The following formula will enable the educator to determine the standard error of measurement when it has not been provided by the test developer in the test manual.

$$SEM = SD \sqrt{1-r}$$

where SEM = the standard error of measurement

SD = the standard deviation of the norm group of scores obtained during development of the instrument

r = the reliability coefficient

Figure 4.5 uses this formula to calculate the standard error of measurement for an instrument with a given standard deviation of 3 and a reliability coefficient of .78. The manual for this test would probably report the SEM as 1.4. Knowing the SEM allows the teacher to calculate a range of scores for a particular student, thus providing a better estimate of the student's true ability. Using the SEM of 1.4, the teacher adds and subtracts 1.4 to the obtained score. If the obtained score is 9 (mean = 10), the teacher adds and subtracts the SEM to the obtained score of 9:

$$9 + 1.4 = 10.4$$

$$9 - 1.4 = 7.6$$

The range of possible true scores for this student is 7.6 to 10.4.

Figure 4.5 Calculating the standard error of measurement (SEM) for an instrument with a standard deviation of 3.

$$SEM = 3\sqrt{1 - .78}$$
$$SEM = 3\sqrt{.22}$$
$$SEM = 3 \times .4690415$$
$$SEM = 1.4071245$$

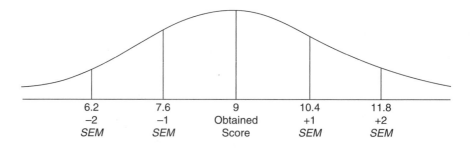

6.2	7.6	9	10.4	11.8
−2	−1	Obtained	+1	+2
SEM	SEM	Score	SEM	SEM

Thought to represent a range of deviations from an individual's obtained score, the standard error of measurement is based on the normal distribution theory. In other words, by using the standard error of measurement, one can determine the typical deviation for an individual's obtained score as if that person had been administered the same test an infinite number of times. When plotted, the scores form a bell curve, or a normal distribution, with the obtained score representing the mean, median, and mode. As with normal distributions, the range of ±1 standard error of measurement of the obtained score will occur approximately 68% of the times that the student takes the test. This is known as a **confidence interval** because the score obtained within that range can be thought to represent the true score with 68% accuracy. In the previous example, for instance, the student would score between 7.6 and 10.4 about 68% of the time.

confidence interval The range of scores for an obtained score determined by adding and subtracting standard error of measurement units.

If the teacher wanted 95% confidence that the true score was contained within a range, the band would be extended to ±2 standard errors of measurement of the obtained score. For the example, the extended range would be 6.2 to 11.8. The teacher can assume, with 95% confidence, that the student's true score is within this range.

As seen in Activity 4.6, a test with better reliability will have less error. The best tests for educational use are those with high reliability and a smaller standard error of measurement.

Applying Standard Error of Measurement   Williams and Zimmerman (1984) stated that whereas test validity remains the most important consideration in test selection, using the standard error of measurement to judge the test's quality is more important than reliability.

Williams and Zimmerman pointed out that reliability is a group statistic easily influenced by the variability of the group on whom it was calculated.

Sabers, Feldt, and Reschly (1988) observed that some, perhaps many, testing practitioners fail to consider possible test error when interpreting test results of a student being evaluated for special education services. The range of error and the range of a student's

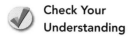

Check Your Understanding

Check your accuracy in calculating standard error of measurement by completing Activity 4.6 below.

Activity 4.6

Use the formula to determine the standard error of measurement with the given standard deviations and reliability coefficients.

$$SEM = SD \sqrt{1 - .r}$$

1. $SD = 5$ .r = .67   SEM = _____
2. $SD = 15$ .r = .82   SEM = _____
3. $SD = 7$ .r = .73   SEM = _____
4. $SD = 7$ .r = .98   SEM = _____
5. $SD = 15$ .r = .98   SEM = _____

Notice the influence of the standard deviation and the reliability coefficient on the standard error of measurement. Compare the *SEMs* in problems 3 and 4, which have the same standard deviation but different reliability coefficients. Now compare the *SEMs* in problems 4 and 5, which have the same reliability coefficient but different standard deviations.

6. What happens to the standard error of measurement as the reliability increases? _____

_____

7. What happens to the standard error of measurement as the standard deviation increases? _____

_____

Apply Your Knowledge

How might a test with a large *SEM* result in an inaccurate evaluation of a student's abilities? _____

_____

_____

score may vary substantially, which may change the interpretation of the score for placement purposes.

In addition to knowing the standard error of measurement for an assessment instrument, it is important to know that the standard error of measurement will actually vary by age or grade level and by subtests. A test may contain less error for certain age or grade groupings than for other groupings. This information will be provided in the technical section of a good test manual.

Table 4.2 is from the *KeyMath—Revised* (Connolly, 1988) technical data section of the examiner's manual. The standard errors of measurement for the individual subtests are low and fairly consistent. There are some differences, however, in the standard errors of measurement on some subtests at different levels.

Table 4.2 Standard errors of measurement, by age, for scaled scores and standard scores from the fall and spring standardization programs.

Subtest/Composite	Program (Fall/Spring)	Age							
		5	6	7	8	9	10	11	12
1. Numeration	F	1.3	1.2	1.0	1.0	1.1	1.1	1.2	1.1
	S	1.7	1.1	1.0	1.0	1.0	1.2	1.1	1.0
2. Rational Numbers	F	—	—	—	—	1.2	1.0	1.0	1.0
	S	—	—	—	1.1	1.3	1.1	1.0	0.8
3. Geometry	F	1.5	1.3	1.4	1.4	1.2	1.2	1.3	1.1
	S	1.2	1.2	1.3	1.3	1.4	1.3	1.3	1.1
4. Addition	F	1.6	1.4	1.4	1.3	1.4	1.7	1.5	1.3
	S	1.8	1.4	1.3	1.4	1.4	1.5	1.3	1.3
5. Subtraction	F	—	1.6	1.5	1.3	1.1	1.1	1.5	1.3
	S	—	1.5	1.3	1.3	1.0	1.1	1.0	1.1
6. Multiplication	F	—	—	—	1.4	1.2	0.9	1.2	1.4
	S	—	—	—	1.0	1.1	1.2	1.1	1.1
7. Division	F	—	—	1.8	1.9	1.6	1.1	1.2	1.0
	S	—	—	2.0	1.6	1.4	1.2	1.1	1.0
8. Mental Computation	F	—	—	—	1.4	1.2	1.1	1.2	1.0
	S	—	—	1.7	1.3	1.2	1.1	1.1	0.9
9. Measurement	F	1.3	1.1	1.5	1.3	1.3	1.2	1.1	1.1
	S	1.2	1.1	1.2	1.1	1.1	1.3	1.1	0.9
10. Time and Money	F	—	1.6	1.3	1.1	1.0	1.0	1.0	1.0
	S	—	1.5	1.2	1.0	0.9	1.0	0.9	0.9
11. Estimation	F	—	1.7	1.8	1.4	1.3	1.3	1.2	1.0
	S	—	1.7	1.7	1.3	1.3	1.2	1.2	1.0
12. Interpreting Data	F	—	—	1.4	1.3	1.1	1.1	1.1	1.1
	S	—	—	1.3	1.2	1.1	1.1	1.1	1.0
13. Problem Solving	F	—	—	1.8	1.6	1.3	1.1	1.2	0.9
	S	—	—	1.6	1.4	1.2	1.1	1.1	0.9
14. Basic Concepts Area	F	5.8	5.3	4.8	4.7	4.0	3.7	3.9	3.3
	S	5.5	4.8	4.8	4.0	4.2	3.9	3.7	3.0
15. Operations Area	F	7.7	5.0	4.8	4.0	3.5	3.0	3.7	3.1
	S	7.1	5.0	4.3	3.5	3.2	3.3	2.9	2.7
16. Applications Area	F	5.8	4.1	4.3	3.6	3.1	2.8	3.0	2.6
	S	5.3	4.4	3.9	3.0	2.9	2.9	2.7	2.3
TOTAL TEST	F	4.1	3.0	2.9	2.5	2.2	1.9	2.2	1.8
	S	3.8	3.0	2.7	2.1	2.1	2.0	1.8	1.6

Source: From *KeyMath—Revised: A Diagnostic Inventory of Essential Mathematics, Manual. Forms A and B* (p. 72) by A. Connolly, 1988, Circle Pines, MN: American Guidance Service. Copyright 1988 by American Guidance Service. Reprinted by permission.

Consider the standard error of measurement for the Division subtest at ages 7 and 12 in the spring (S row). The standard error of measurement for age 7 is 2.0, but for age 12 it is 1.0. The larger standard error of measurement reported for age 7 is probably due to variation in the performance of students who may or may not have been introduced to division as part of the school curriculum. Most 12-year-olds, on the other hand, have probably practiced division in class for several years, and the sample of students tested may have performed with more consistency during the test development.

Given the two standard errors of measurement for the Division subtest at these ages, if a 7-year-old obtained a scaled score (a type of standard score) of 9 on this test ($x = 10$), the examiner could determine with 68% confidence that the true score lies between 7 and 11 and with 95% confidence that the true score lies between 5 and 13. The same scaled score obtained by a 12-year-old would range between 8 and 10 for a 68% confidence interval and between 7 and 11 for 95% confidence. This smaller range of scores is due to less error at this age on this particular subtest.

Consideration of SEMs when interpreting scores for students who are referred for a special education evaluation is even more important because a student's scores on various assessments are often compared with each other to determine if significant weaknesses exist. Standard 2.3 of the *Standards for Educational and*

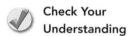

Check Your Understanding

Check your ability to use a SEM table to interpret test performance by completing Activity 4.7 below.

Activity 4.7

Use Table 4.2 to locate the standard error of measurement for the following situations.

1. The standard error of measurement for a 7-year-old who was administered the Problem Solving subtest in the fall is?_____

2. A 12-year-old's standard error of measurement for Problem-Solving if the test was administered in the fall is?_____

3. Using the standard error of measurement found in problems 1 and 2, calculate the ranges for each age level if the obtained scores were both 7. Calculate the ranges for both 68% and 95% confidence intervals._____

Apply Your Knowledge

When comparing the concepts of a normal distribution and the SEM, the SEM units are distributed around the _____ and the standard deviation units are evenly distributed around the _____.

Psychological Testing addresses the importance of considering SEMs when comparing scores:

> When test interpretation emphasizes differences between two observed scores of an individual or two averages of a group, reliability data, including standard errors, should be provided for such differences (1999, p. 32).

This is important because the differences found for one individual on two different measures may not be significant differences when the SEMs are applied. For example, historically students have been found eligible for special education services for specific learning disabilities because there were significant differences between an obtained IQ score and an academic achievement score. Look at the example below for Leonardo:

IQ score: 103

Reading Achievement Score: 88

The difference between these two scores is 15. In some school systems, the difference of 15 points may be considered significant and Leonardo could be found eligible for services for a learning disability. However, look at the range of scores when the SEMs are applied:

IQ score: 103; SEM 3 Range of Scores: 100–106

Reading Achievement Score: 88; SEM 7 Range of Scores: 81–95

In this example, basing a decision on the performance of this student on these two tests cannot be conclusive because the differences, when considering the range of scores, may not be significant. The student's true scores may actually be 100 on the IQ test and 95 on the Reading Achievement test, or a difference of only 5 points. This would indicate additional data would be needed to determine if the student required special education support. In practice, however, SEMs may not be considered when making decisions for eligibility. When the SEMs are not considered, the student may not receive accurate evaluation.

ESTIMATED TRUE SCORES

estimated true score A method of calculating the amount of error correlated with the distance of the score from the mean of the group.

Another method for approximating a student's true score is called the **estimated true score**. This calculation is founded in theory and research that the farther from a test mean a particular student's score is, the greater the chance for error within the obtained score. Chance errors are correlated with obtained scores (Salvia & Ysseldyke, 1988b). This means that as the score increases away from the mean, the chance for error increases. As scores regress toward the mean, the chance for error decreases. Therefore, if all the obtained scores are plotted on a distribution and all the values

Figure 4.6 Comparison of obtained and true scores.

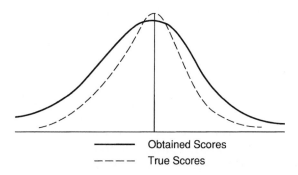

— Obtained Scores
- - - - True Scores

of error are plotted on a distribution, the comparison would appear like that in Figure 4.6. Note that the true scores are located closer to the mean with less spread, or variability. The formula for estimated true score (Nunnally, 1967, p. 220) is

Estimated true score = $M + r(X - M)$

where M = mean of group of which person is a member
   r = reliability coefficient
   X = obtained score

This formula enables the examiner to estimate a possible true score. Because of the correlation of error with obtained scores, the true score is always assumed to be nearer to the mean than the obtained score. Therefore, if the obtained score is 120 (mean = 100), the estimated true score will be less than 120. Conversely, if the obtained score is 65, the true score will be greater than 65.

Using the formula for estimated true score, the calculation for an obtained score of 115 with an r of .78 and a mean of 100 would be as follows:

Estimated true score = 100 + .78(115 − 100)

$$= 100 + .78(15)$$
$$= 100 + .11.7$$
$$= 111.7$$

In this example, 111.7 is closer to the mean of 100 than 115.

Following is an example where the obtained score is less than the estimated true score:

Obtained score = 64, Mean = 100, r = .74

Estimated true score = 100 + .74(64 − 100)

$$= 100 + .74 (-36)$$
$$= 100 - 26.64$$
$$= 73.36$$

The estimated true score can then be used to establish a range of scores by using the standard error of measurement for the estimated true score. Assume that the standard error of measurement for the estimated true score of 111.7 is 4.5. The range of scores ±1 standard error of measurement for 111.7 would be 107.2 to 116.2 for 68% confidence and 102.7 to 120.7 for 95% confidence.

The use of estimated true scores to calculate bands of confidence using standard error of measurement rather than using obtained scores has received some attention in the literature (Cahan, 1989; Feldt, Sabers, & Reschly, 1988; Sabers et al., 1988; Salvia & Ysseldyke, 1988a, 1988b). Whether using estimated true scores to calculate the range of possible scores or obtained scores to calculate the range of scores, several important points must be remembered. All test scores contain error. Error must be considered when interpreting test scores. The best practice, whether using estimated true scores or obtained scores, will employ the use of age- or grade-appropriate reliability coefficients and standard errors of measurement for the tests or subtests in question. When the norming process provides comparisons based on demographic variables, it is best to use the appropriate normative comparison.

TEST VALIDITY

To review, reliability refers to the dependability of the assessment instrument. The questions of concern for reliability are (a) Will students obtain similar scores if given the test a second time? (b) If the test is halved, will the administration of each half result in similar scores for the same student? (c) If different forms are available, will the administration of each form yield similar scores for the same student? (d) Will the administration of each item reliably measure the same trait or skill for the same student?

validity The quality of a test; the degree to which an instrument measures what it was designed to measure.

Validity is concerned not with repeated dependable results, but rather with the degree of good results for the purpose of the test. In other words, does the test actually measure what it is supposed to measure? If the educator wants to assess multiplication skills, will the test provide the educator with a valid indication of the student's math ability? Several methods can be used to determine the degree to which the instrument measures what the test developers intended the test to measure. Some methods are better than others, and some of the methods are more easily understood. When selecting assessment instruments, the educator should carefully consider the validity information.

CRITERION-RELATED VALIDITY

criterion-related validity Statistical method of comparing an instrument's ability to measure a skill, trait, or domain with an existing instrument or other criterion.

Criterion-related validity is a method for determining the validity of an instrument by comparing its scores with other criteria known to be indicators of the same trait or skill that the test developer wishes to measure. The test is compared with another criterion. The two main types of criterion-related validity are differentiated by time factors.

concurrent validity A comparison of one instrument with another within a short period of time.

Concurrent Validity **Concurrent validity** studies are conducted within a small time frame. The instrument in question is administered, and shortly thereafter an additional device is used, typically a similar test. Because the data are collected within a short time period, often the same day, this type of validity study is called concurrent validity. The data from both devices are correlated to see whether the instrument in question has significant concurrent criterion-related validity. The correlation coefficient obtained is called the *validity coefficient*. As with reliability coefficients, the nearer the coefficient is to ±1.00, the greater the strength of the relationship. Therefore, when the students in the sample obtain similar scores on both instruments, the instrument in question is said to be measuring the same trait or a degree or component of the same trait with some accuracy.

Suppose the newly developed Best in the World Math Test was administered to a sample of students, and shortly thereafter the Good Old Terrific Math Test was administered to the same sample. The validity coefficient obtained was .83. The educator selecting the Best in the World Math Test would have some confidence that it would measure, to some degree, the same traits or skills measured by the Good Old Terrific Math Test. Such studies are helpful in determining whether new tests and revised tests are measuring with some degree of accuracy the same skills as those measured by older, more researched instruments. Studies may compare other criteria as well, such as teacher ratings or motor performance of a like task. As expected, when comparing unlike instruments or criteria, these would probably not correlate highly. A test measuring creativity would probably not have a high validity coefficient with an advanced algebra test, but the algebra test would probably correlate better with a test measuring advanced trigonometry.

predictive validity A measure of how well an instrument can predict performance on some other variable.

Predictive Validity **Predictive validity** is a measure of a specific instrument's ability to predict performance on some other measure or criterion at a later date.

Common examples of tests that predict a student's ability are a screening test to predict success in first grade, a Scholastic Aptitude Test (SAT) to predict success in college, a Graduate Record Exam (GRE) to predict success in graduate school, and an academic potential or academic aptitude test to predict success in school. Much of psychoeducational assessment conducted in schools concerns using test results to predict future success or failure in a particular educational setting. Therefore, when this type of testing is carried out, it is important that the educator selects an instrument with good predictive validity research. Using a test to predict which students should enroll in basic math and which should enroll in advanced algebra will not be in the students' best interests if the predictive validity of the instrument is poor.

CONTENT VALIDITY

content validity
Occurs when the items contained within the test are representative of the content purported to be measured.

Professionals may assume that instruments reflecting a particular content in the name of the test or subtest have **content validity**. In many cases, this is not true. For example, on the Wide Range Achievement Test—Revision 3 (Wilkinson, 1993), the subtest Reading does not actually measure reading ability. It measures only one aspect of reading: word recognition. A teacher might use the score obtained on the subtest to place a student, believing that the student will be able to comprehend reading material at a particular level. In fact, the student may be able to recognize only a few words from that reading level. This subtest has inadequate content validity for measuring overall reading ability.

For a test to have good content validity, it must contain the content in a representative fashion. For example, a math achievement test that has only 10 addition and subtraction problems and no other math operations has not adequately represented the content of the domain of math. A good representation of content will include several items from each domain, level, and skill being measured.

Some of the variables of content validity may influence the manner in which results are obtained and can contribute to bias in testing. These variables may conflict with the nondiscriminatory test practice regulations of IDEA and the APA *Standards* (1985). These variables include **presentation format** and **response mode**.

presentation format The method by which items of an instrument are presented to a student.

1. *Presentation format.* Are the items presented in the best manner to assess the skill or trait? Requiring a student to silently read math problems and supply a verbal response could result in test bias if the student is unable to read at the level presented. The content being assessed may be math applications or reasoning, but the reading required to complete the task has reduced the instrument's ability to assess math skills for this particular student. Therefore, the content validity has been threatened, and the results obtained may unduly discriminate against the student.

response mode The method required for the examinee to answer items of an instrument.

2. *Response mode.* Like presentation format, the response mode may interfere with the test's ability to assess skills that are unrelated to the response mode. If the test was

designed to assess reading ability but required the student to respond in writing, the test would discriminate against a student who had a motor impairment that made writing difficult or impossible. Unless the response mode is adapted, the targeted skill—reading ability—will not be fairly or adequately measured.

Content validity is a primary concern in the development of new instruments. The test developers may adjust, omit, or add items during the field-testing stage. These changes are incorporated into a developmental version of the test that is administered to samples of students.

CONSTRUCT VALIDITY

construct validity
The ability of an instrument to measure psychological constructs.

Establishing **construct validity** for a new instrument may be more difficult than establishing content validity. *Construct*, in psychoeducational assessment, is a term used to describe a psychological trait, personality trait, psychological concept, attribute, or theoretical characteristic. To establish construct validity, the construct must be clearly defined. Constructs are usually abstract concepts, such as intelligence and creativity, that can be observed and measured by some type of instrument. Construct validity may be more difficult to measure than content because constructs are hypothetical and even seem invisible. Creativity is not seen, but the products of that trait may be observed, such as in writing or painting.

In establishing the construct validity of an instrument, the validity study may involve another measure that has been researched previously and has been shown to be a good indicator of the construct or of some degree or component of the construct. This is, of course, comparing the instrument to some other criterion, which is criterion-related validity. (Don't get confused!) Often in test development, the validity studies may involve several types of criterion-related validity to establish different types of validity. Anastasi (1988) listed the following types of studies that are considered when establishing a test's construct validity:

1. *Developmental changes.* Instruments that measure traits that are expected to change with development should have these changes reflected in the scores if the changeable trait is being measured (such as academic achievement).

2. *Correlations with other tests.* New tests are compared with existing instruments that have been found valid for the construct being measured.

3. *Factor analysis.* This statistical method determines how much particular test items cluster, which illustrates measurement of like constructs.

4. *Internal consistency.* Statistical methods can determine the degree with which individual items appear to be measuring the same constructs in the same manner or direction.

5. *Convergent and discriminant validation.* Tests should correlate highly with other instruments measuring the same construct but should not correlate with instruments measuring very different constructs.

6. *Experimental interventions.* Tests designed to measure traits, skills, or constructs that can be influenced by interventions (such as teaching) should have the intervention reflected by changes in pretest and posttest scores. (pp. 153–159)

Table 4.3 illustrates how construct validity is applied.

VALIDITY OF TESTS VERSUS VALIDITY OF TEST USE

validity of test use The appropriate use of a specific instrument.

Professionals in special education and in the judicial system have understood for quite some time that test validity and **validity of test use** for a particular instrument are two separate issues (Cole, 1981). Tests may be used inappropriately even though

Table 4.3   The Gray Oral Reading Tests. Applying construct validity to a reading instrument.

1. Because reading ability is developmental in nature, performance on the GORT-4 should be strongly correlated to chronological age.

2. Because the GORT-4 subtests measure various aspects of oral reading ability, they should correlate with each other.

3. Because reading is a type of language, the GORT-4 should correlate significantly with spoken language abilities.

4. Because reading is the receptive form of written language, the GORT-4 should correlate with tests that measure expressive written language.

5. Because reading is a cognitive ability, the GORT-4 should correlate with measures of intelligence or aptitude.

6. Because the GORT-4 measures reading, it should correlate with measures of automatized naming.

7. Because the GORT-4 measures reading, the results should differentiate between groups of people known to be average and those known to be low average or below average in reading ability.

8. Because the GORT-4 measures reading, changes in scores should occur over time due to reading instruction.

9. Because the items of a particular subtest measure similar traits, the items of each subtest should be highly correlated with the total score of that subtest.

Source: From *Gray Oral Reading Tests—4: Examiner's Manual.* By J. L. Wiederholt & B. R. Bryant, 2001. Copyright: Pro-Ed., Austin, Texas. Reprinted with permission.

they are valid instruments (Cole, 1981). The results obtained in testing may also be used in an invalid manner by placing children inappropriately or inaccurately predicting educational futures (Heller, Holtzman, & Messick, 1982).

Some validity-related issues contribute to bias in the assessment process and subsequently to the invalid use of the test instruments. Content, even though it may validly represent the domain of skills or traits being assessed, may discriminate against different groups. *Item bias*, a term used when an item is answered incorrectly a disproportionate number of times by one group compared to another group, may exist even though the test appears to represent the content domain. An examiner who continues to use an instrument found to contain bias may be practicing discriminatory assessment, which is failure to comply with IDEA.

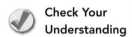

Check Your Understanding

Check your ability to understand the concepts of reliability and validity applied to actual research data on a specific achievement test by completing Activity 4.8 below.

Activity 4.8

The Best Achievement Test ever was recently completed and is now on sale. You are trying to determine if the test would be appropriate for elementary age students. The tables below are samples of what is provided in the test manual. Review the tables and answer the questions below.

Grade	Standard Error of Measurement	Test-Retest Score Reliability	Concurrent Criterion-Related Validity	Split-Half Reliability Coefficients
Grade K	6.27	.71	.65	.67
Grade 1	5.276	.79	.83	.75
Grade 2	4.98	.80	.82	.80
Grade 3	4.82	.81	.84	.81
Grade 4	4.80	.80	.83	.82
Grade 5	4.82	.81	.82	.83

1. Based on this information, in which grades would you feel that the test would yield more reliable results? Why? _____
2. Would you consider purchasing this instrument? _____
3. Explain how the concurrent criterion-related validity would have been determined? _____
   _____

Predictive validity may contribute to test bias by predicting accurately for one group and not another. Educators should select and administer instruments only after careful study of the reliability and validity research contained in test manuals.

RELIABILITY VERSUS VALIDITY

A test may be reliable; that is, it may measure a trait with about the same degree of accuracy time after time. The reliability does not guarantee that the trait is measured in a valid or accurate manner. A test may be consistent and reliable but not valid. It is important that a test has had thorough research studies in both reliability and validity.

THINK AHEAD

The concepts presented in this chapter will be applied in the remaining chapters of the text. How do you think these concepts help professionals evaluate instruments?

EXERCISES

Part I

Match the following terms with the correct definitions.

a. reliability
b. validity
c. internal consistency
d. correlation coefficient
e. coefficient alpha
f. scattergram
g. estimated true score
h. Pearson's *r*
i. interrater reliability
j. test-retest reliability
k. equivalent forms reliability

l. true score
m. predictive validity
n. criterion-related validity
o. positive correlation
p. K–R 20
q. validity of test use
r. negative correlation
s. confidence interval
t. split-half reliability
u. standard error of measurement

_____ 1. A new academic achievement test assesses elementary-age students' math ability. The test developers found, however, that students in the research group who took the test two times had scores that were quite different upon the second test administration, which was conducted 2 weeks after the initial administration. It was determined that the test did not have acceptable _____.

_____ 2. A new test was designed to measure the self-concept of students at middle-school age. The test required students to use essay-type responses to answer three questions regarding their feelings about their own self-concept. Two assessment professionals were comparing the students' responses and how these responses were scored by the professionals. On this type of instrument, it is important that the _____ is acceptable.

_____ 3. In studying the relationship between the scores of the administration of one test administration with the second administration of the test, the number .89 represents the _____.

_____ 4. One would expect that the number of classes a college student attends in a specific course and the final exam grade in that course would have a _____.

_____ 5. In order to have a better understanding of a student's true abilities, the concept of _____ must be understood and applied to obtained scores.

_____ 6. The number of times a student moves during elementary school may likely have a _____ to the student's achievement scores in elementary school.

_____ 7. A test instrument may have good reliability; however, that does not guarantee that the test has _____.

_____ 8. On a teacher-made test of math, the following items were included: two single-digit addition problems, one single-digit subtraction problem, four problems of multiplication of fractions, and one problem of converting decimals to fractions. This test does not appear to have good _____.

_____ 9. A college student failed the first test of the new semester. The student hoped that the first test did not have strong _____ about performance on the final exam.

_____10. No matter how many times a student may be tested, the student's _____ may never be determined.

Part II

Complete the following sentences and solve the problem.

1. The score obtained during the assessment of a student may not be the score, because all testing situations are subject to chance _____.

2. A closer estimation of the student's best performance can be calculated by using the _____ score.

3. A range of possible scores can then be determined by using the _____ for the specific test.

4. The smaller the standard error of measurement, the more _____ the test.

5. When calculating the range of possible scores, it is best to use the appropriate standard error of measurement for the student's _____ provided in the test manual.

6. The larger the standard error of measurement, the less _____ the test.

7. Use the following set of data to determine the mean, median, mode, range, variance, standard deviation, standard error of measurement, and possible range for each score assuming 68% confidence. The reliability coefficient is .85.

Data: 50, 75, 31, 77, 65, 81, 90, 92, 76, 74, 88

Mean: _____   Median: _____   Mode: _____

Range: _____   Variance: _____   Standard deviation: _____

Standard error of measurement: _____

Obtained Score:	**Range of True Scores:**
a. 50	From ____ to ____
b. 75	From ____ to ____
c. 31	From ____ to ____
d. 77	From ____ to ____
e. 65	From ____ to ____
f. 81	From ____ to ____
g. 90	From ____ to ____
h. 92	From ____ to ____
i. 76	From ____ to ____
j. 74	From ____ to ____
k. 88	From ____ to ____

Companion
Website

Answers to these questions can be found in the Appendix of this text or you may also complete these questions and receive immediate feedback on your answers by going to the Think Ahead module in Chapter 4 of the Companion Website.

CHAPTER

5

An Introduction to Norm-Referenced Assessment

domain	chronological age
item pool	test manual
developmental version	protocol
field test	raw score
norm-referenced test	basal
sample	ceiling
norm group	accommodations
interpolation	assistive technology

CHAPTER FOCUS

This chapter presents the basic mechanics of test design and test administration that the examiner needs to know before administering norm-referenced tests. Following a description of test construction, various techniques for completing test protocols and administering instruments are explained. Both individual norm-referenced testing and statewide high-stakes accountability assessment are discussed.

Norm-referenced assessment is the method that compares a student with the age or grade-level expectancies of a norm group. It is the standard method used in placement and classification decisions. The degree or amount of deviance from the expected norm is an important factor in determining whether a student meets the eligibility requirements necessary to receive special education services (Shapiro, 1996).

CEC KNOWLEDGE AND SKILLS STANDARDS

The student completing this chapter will understand the knowledge and skills included in the following CEC Knowledge and Skills Standards from Standard 8: Assessment:

CC8K1—Basic terminology used in assessment

CC8K4—Use and limitations of assessment instruments

CC8K5—National, state, or provincial, and local accommodations and modifications

CC8S9—Develop or modify individual assessment strategies

CC8S5—Interpret information from formal and informal assessments

GC8S3—Select, adapt, and modify assessments to accommodate the unique abilities and needs of individual with disabilities

GC8S4—Assess reliable methods of response of individuals who lack typical communication and performance

HOW NORM-REFERENCED TESTS ARE CONSTRUCTED

domain An area of cognitive development or ability thought to be evidenced by certain behaviors or skills.

item pool A large collection of test items thought to effectively represent a particular domain or content area.

developmental version The experimental edition of a test that is field-tested and revised before publication.

field test The procedure of trying out a test by administering it to a sample population.

norm-referenced test A test designed to yield average performance scores, which may be used for comparing individual student performances.

sample A small group of people thought to represent the population for whom the test was designed.

norm group A large number of people who are administered a test to establish comparative data of average performances.

Test developers who wish to develop an instrument to assess an educational **domain**, behavioral trait, cognitive ability, motor ability, or language ability, to name a few areas, will establish an item pool of test items. An **item pool** is a representation of items believed to thoroughly assess the given area. The items are gathered from several sources. For example, developers may use published educational materials, information from educational experts in the field, published curriculum guides, and information from educational research to collect items for the initial item pool for an educational domain. These items are carefully scrutinized for appropriateness, wording, content, mode of response required, and developmental level. The items are sequentially arranged according to difficulty. The developers consult with professionals with expertise in the test's content area and, after thorough analysis of the items, administer a **developmental version** to a small group as a **field test**. During the field-testing stage, the test is administered by professionals in the appropriate discipline (education, psychology, speech-language, etc.). The professionals involved in the study critique the test items, presentation format, response mode requirements, administration procedures, and the actual test materials. At this time, revisions may be made, and the developmental version is then ready to be administered to a large sample of the population for whom it was designed. The steps of test construction are illustrated in Figure 5.1.

A **norm-referenced test** is designed to provide the teacher with the capability of comparing the performance of one student with the average performance of other students in the country who are of the same age or grade level. Since it is not practical or possible to test every student of that same age or grade level, a **sample** of students is selected as the comparison group, or **norm group**. In the norming process, the test is administered to a representative sample of students from across the country. A good representation will include a large number of students, usually a few thousand students, who represent diverse groups. Ideally, samples of students from all cultures and linguistic backgrounds who represent the diverse students for whom the test was developed will be included in the norming process. The norming process should also include students with various disabilities.

The development of a norm-referenced test and the establishment of comparison performances usually occur in the following manner. The items of the test, which are sequentially arranged in the order of difficulty, are administered to the sample population. The performance of each age group and each grade group is analyzed. The average performance of the 6-year-olds, 7-year-olds,

Figure 5.1 Steps in test development.

1. Domain, theoretical basis of test defined. This includes support for construct as well as defining what the domain is not.
2. Exploration of item pool. Experts in the field and other sources of possible items are used to begin collecting items.
3. Developmental version of test or subtests.
4. Field-based research using developmental version of test or subtests.
5. Research on developmental versions analyzed.
6. Changes made to developmental versions based on results of analyses.
7. Standardization version prepared.
8. Sampling procedures to establish how and where persons in sample will be recruited.
9. Testing coordinators located at relevant testing sites representing preferred norm sample.
10. Standardization research begins. Tests are administered at testing sites.
11. Data collected and returned to test developer.
12. Data analyzed for establishing norms, reliability, validity.
13. Test prepared for final version, packaging, protocols, manual.
14. Test available for purchase.

8-year-olds, and so on is determined. The test results are analyzed by grade groups as well, determining the average performance of first graders, second graders, and so on. The analysis of the test results might resemble Table 5.1.

The average number correct in Table 5.1 represents the arithmetic average number of items successfully answered by the age or grade group of students who made up the norming sample. Because these figures will later be used to compare other students' performances on the same instrument, it is imperative that the sample of students be representative of the students who will later be assessed. Comparing a student to a norm sample of students who are very different from the student will not be an objective or fair comparison. Factors such as socioeconomic, cultural, or linguistic background; existing disabilities; and emotional environment are variables that may influence a student's performance. The student should be compared with other students with similar backgrounds and of the same age or grade level.

The data displayed in Table 5.1 illustrate the mean performance of students in a particular age or grade group. Although the data represent an average score for each age or grade group, test developers often analyze the data further. For example, the average

Table 5.1   Analysis of results from the Absolutely Wonderful Academic Achievement Test.

Grade	Average Number of Items Correct	Age	Average Number of Items Correct
K	11	5	9
1	14	6	13
2	20	7	21
3	28	8	27
4	38	9	40
5	51	10	49
6	65	11	65
7	78	12	79
8	87	13	88
9	98	14	97
10	112	15	111
11	129	16	130
12	135	17	137

interpolation The process of dividing existing data into smaller units for establishing tables of developmental scores.

performance of typical students at various times throughout the school year may be determined. To provide this information, the most accurate norming process would include nine additional administrations of the test, one for each month of the school year. This is usually not practical or possible in most instances of test development. Therefore, to obtain an average expected score for each month of the school year, the test developer usually calculates the scores using data obtained in the original administration through a process known as **interpolation**, or further dividing the existing data (Anastasi & Urbina, 1998).

Suppose that the test developer of the Absolutely Wonderful Academic Achievement Test actually administered the test to the sample group during the middle of the school year. To determine the average performance of students throughout the school year, from the first month of the school year through the last month, the test developer further divides the correct items of each group. In the data in Table 5.1, the average performance of second graders in the sample group is 20, the average performance of third graders is 28, and the average performance of fourth graders is 38. These scores might be further divided and listed in the test manual on a table similar to Table 5.2.

chronological age The numerical representation of a student's age, expressed in years, months, and days.

The obtained scores also might be further divided by age groups so that each month of a **chronological age** is represented. The scores for age 11 might be displayed in a table similar to Table 5.3.

It is important to notice that age scores are written with a dash or hyphen, whereas grade scores are expressed with a decimal.

Table 5.2   Interpolated grade equivalents for corresponding raw scores.

Number of Items Correct	Grade
17	2.0
17	2.1
18	2.2
18	2.3
19	2.4
20	2.5
20	2.6
21	2.7
22	2.8
23	2.9
24	3.0
25	3.1
26	3.2
27	3.3
27	3.4
28	3.5
29	3.6
30	3.7
31	3.8
32	3.9
33	4.0
34	4.1
35	4.2
36	4.3
37	4.4
38	4.5
39	4.6
40	4.7
42	4.8
43	4.9

Table 5.3   Interpolated age equivalents for corresponding raw scores.

Average Number of Items Correct	Age Equivalents
57	11–0
58	11–1
60	11–2
61	11–3
62	11–4
63	11–5
65	11–6
66	11–7
68	11–8
69	11–9
70	11–10
71	11–11
72	12–0

This is because grade scores are based on a 10-month school year and can be expressed by using decimals, whereas age scores are based on a 12-month calendar year and therefore should not be expressed using decimals. For example, 11–4 represents an age of 11 years and 4 months, but 11.4 represents the grade score of the 4th month of the 11th grade. If the scores are expressed incorrectly, a difference of about 6 grades or 5 years could be incorrectly interpreted.

BASIC STEPS IN TEST ADMINISTRATION

test manual
A manual that accompanies a test instrument and contains instructions for administration and norm tables.

When administering a norm-referenced standardized test, it is important to remember that the test developer specified the instructions for the examiner and the examinee. The **test manual** contains much information, which the examiner must read thoroughly and understand before administering the test. The examiner should practice administering all sections of the test many times before using the test with a student. The first few attempts of practice administration should be supervised by someone who has had experience with the instrument. Legally, according to IDEA, any individual test administration should be completed in the manner set forth by the test developer and should be administered by trained personnel. Both legal regulations and standards and codes of ethics hold testing personnel responsible for accurate and fair assessment.

protocol The response sheet or record form used by the examiner to record the student's answers.

The examiner should carefully carry out the mechanics of test administration. The first few steps are simple, although careless errors can occur and may make a difference in the decisions made regarding a student's educational future. The **protocol** of a standardized test is the form used during the test administration and for scoring and interpreting test results.

BEGINNING TESTING

The following suggestions will help you, the examiner, establish a positive testing environment and increase the probability that the student will feel comfortable and therefore perform better in the testing situation.

1. Establish familiarity with the student before the first day of testing. Several meetings in different situations with relaxed verbal exchange are recommended. You may wish to participate in an activity with the student and informally observe behavior and language skills.

2. When the student meets with you on test day, spend several minutes in friendly conversation before beginning the test. Do not begin testing until the student seems to feel at ease with you.

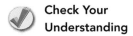

Check Your Understanding

Check your ability to use developmental score tables by completing Activity 5.1 below.

Activity 5.1

Refer to the tables in your text and answer the following questions.

1. In Table 5.1, what was the average score of the sample group of students in grade 7? _____

2. According to Table 5.1, what was the average number of correct items of the sample group of students who were 16 years of age? _____

3. What was the average number of correct items of the sample group of students who were 6 years of age? _____

4. Why did students who were in first grade have an average number of 14 correct responses while students in grade 6 had an average of 65 correct responses? _____

5. According to the information provided in Table 5.2, what was the average number of correct responses for students in the third month of grade 3? _____

6. Were students in the sample tested during the third month of the third grade? _____ By what means was the average for each month of the school year determined? _____

7. According to the information provided in Table 5.3, what was the average number of correct responses for students of the chronological age 11–2? _____

8. Write the meaning of these expressions:

   4.1 means _____
   4–1 means _____
   3.3 means _____
   6–7 means _____
   10.8 means _____

Apply Your Knowledge

Write an explanation for a parent that clarifies the difference between a grade-equivalent score and the grade level of academic functioning. _____
_____
_____

3. Explain why the testing has been suggested at the level of understanding that is appropriate for the student's age and developmental level. It is important that the student understand that the testing session is important, although the child should not feel threatened by the test. Examples of explanations include the following:
   • To see how you work (solve) math problems.
   • To see how we can help you achieve in school.

- To help you make better progress in school.
- [Or if the student has revealed specific weaknesses] To see how we can help you with your spelling [or English, or science, etc.] skills.

4. Give a brief introduction about the test, such as: "Today we will complete some activities that are like your other school work. There are some math problems and reading passages like you have in class," or, "This will help us learn how you think in school," or "This will show us the best ways for you to . . . (learn, read, work math problems)."

5. Begin testing in a calm manner. Be certain that all instructions are followed carefully.

During test administration, the student may ask questions or give answers that are very close to the correct response. On many tests, clear instructions are given that tell the examiner when to prompt for an answer or when to query for a response. Some items on certain tests may not be repeated. Some items are timed. The best guarantee for accurate assessment techniques is for the examiner to become very familiar with the test manual. General guidelines for test administration, suggested by McLoughlin and Lewis (2001), are presented in Figure 5.2.

Figure 5.2 General guidelines for test administration.

Test administration is a skill, and testers must learn how to react to typical student comments and questions. The following general guidelines apply to the majority of standardized tests.

STUDENT REQUESTS FOR REPETITION OF TEST ITEMS

Students often ask the tester to repeat a question. This is usually permissible as long as the item is repeated verbatim and in its entirety. However, repetition of memory items measuring the student's ability to recall information is not allowed.

ASKING STUDENTS TO REPEAT RESPONSES

Sometimes the tester must ask the student to repeat a response. Perhaps the tester did not hear what the student said, or the student's speech is difficult to understand. However, the tester should make every effort to see or hear the student's first answer. The student may refuse to repeat a response or, thinking that the request for repetition means the first response was unsatisfactory, answer differently.

STUDENT MODIFICATION OF RESPONSES

When students give one response, then change their minds and give a different one, the tester should accept the last response, even if the modification comes after the tester has moved to another item. However, some tests specify that only the first response may be accepted for scoring.

CONFIRMING AND CORRECTING STUDENT RESPONSES

The tester may not in any way—verbal or nonverbal—inform a student whether a response is correct. Correct responses may not be confirmed; wrong responses may not be corrected. This rule is critical for professionals who both teach and test, because their first inclination is to reinforce correct answers.

Figure 5.2   continued.

REINFORCING STUDENT WORK BEHAVIOR

Although testers cannot praise students for their performance on specific test items, good work behavior can and should be rewarded. Appropriate comments are "You're working hard" and "I like the way you're trying to answer every question." Students should be praised between test items or subtests to ensure that reinforcement is not linked to specific responses.

ENCOURAGING STUDENTS TO RESPOND

When students fail to respond to a test item, the tester can encourage them to give an answer. Students sometimes say nothing when presented with a difficult item, or they may comment, "I don't know" or "I can't do that one." The tester should repeat the item and say, "Give it a try" or "You can take a guess." The aim is to encourage the student to attempt all test items.

QUESTIONING STUDENTS

Questioning is permitted on many tests. If in the judgment of the tester the response given by the student is neither correct nor incorrect, the tester repeats the student's answer in a questioning tone and says, "Tell me more about that." This prompts the student to explain so that the response can be scored. However, clearly wrong answers should not be questioned.

COACHING

Coaching differs from encouragement and questioning in that it helps a student arrive at an answer. The tester must *never* coach the student. Coaching invalidates the student's response; test norms are based on the assumption that students will respond without examiner assistance. Testers must be very careful to avoid coaching.

ADMINISTRATION OF TIMED ITEMS

Some tests include timed items; the student must reply within a certain period to receive credit. In general, the time period begins when the tester finishes presentation of the item. A watch or clock should be used to time student performance.

Source: From *Assessing Special Students* (5th ed., p. 87 by J. McLoughlin and R. Lewis, 2001, Upper Saddle River, NJ: Merrill/Prentice Hall. Copyright by Prentice Hall. Reprinted by permission).

As stated in professional ethics and IDEA, tests must be given in the manner set forth by the test developer and adapting tests must be done by professionals with expertise in the specific area being assessed who are cognizant of the psychometric changes that will result.

CALCULATING CHRONOLOGICAL AGE

Many tests have protocols that provide space for calculating the student's chronological age on the day that the test is administered. It is imperative that this calculation is correct because the chronological age may be used to determine the correct norm tables used for interpreting the test results.

The chronological age is calculated by writing the test date first and then subtracting the date of birth. The dates are written in the

Figure 5.3   Calculation of chronological age for a student who is 8 years, 6 months old.

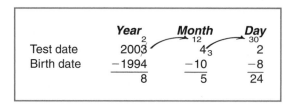

order of year, month, and day. In performing the calculation, remember that each of the columns represents a different numerical system, and if the number that is subtracted is larger than the number from which the difference is to be found, the numbers must be converted appropriately. This means that the years are based on 12 months and the months are based on 30 days. An example is shown in Figure 5.3.

Notice in Figure 5.3 that when subtracting the days, the number 30 is added to 2 to find the difference. When subtraction of days requires borrowing, a whole month, or 30 days, must be used. When borrowing to subtract months, the number 12 is added, because a whole year must be borrowed.

When determining the chronological age for testing, the days are rounded to the nearest month. Days are rounded up if there are 15 or more days by adding a month. The days are rounded down by dropping the days and using the month found through the subtraction process. Here are some examples:

	Years	Months	Days	
Chronological age:	7–	4–	17	rounded up to 7–5
Chronological age:	9–	10–	6	rounded down to 9–10
Chronological age:	11–	11–	15	rounded up to 12–0

Case Study for Determining Chronological Age

Mrs. Luke believed that Sandra was excelling in math ability and needed to be placed in a higher-level class. Mrs. Luke decided to administer a norm-referenced math test to find out how Sandra's math skills compared to a national sample. Once she had administered and scored the test, she discovered that the results were lower than she had expected. Mrs. Luke was confused because she knew that Sandra performed better than her grade peers. Mrs. Luke took another look at the test protocol and discovered these errors in her calculation. Can you identify the errors?

Date of Test:	2005	6	15
Date of Birth	1996	7	17
Chronological Age	9	9	28

The correct chronological age should be

8 years   10 months   18 days

The incorrect calculation meant that Mrs. Luke compared Sandra with students who were nearly 10 years of age (9 years–10 months) when she should have compared Sandra with 8-year-old students. This error resulted in standard scores that placed Sandra in the low average range. When the error was corrected and Sandra was compared with the correct age group, her scores were within the high average range.

Check Your Understanding

Check your ability to calculate chronological age by completing Activity 5.2 below.

Activity 5.2

Calculate the chronological ages using the following birth dates and test dates.

	Year	**Month**	**Day**
1. Birth date: 3-2-1991			
Test date: 5-4-2001			
Date of test: _____	_____	_____	_____
Date of birth: _____	_____	_____	_____
Chronological age: _____	_____	_____	_____

1. Birth date: 3-2-1991   Date of test: _____ _____ _____
   Test date: 5-4-2001   Date of birth: _____ _____ _____
                               Chronological
                                       age: _____ _____ _____

2. Birth date: 7-5-1996   Date of test: _____ _____ _____
   Test date: 11-22-2004   Date of birth: _____ _____ _____
                               Chronological
                                       age: _____ _____ _____

3. Birth date: 10-31-1997   Date of test: _____ _____ _____
   Test date: 06-20-2000   Date of birth: _____ _____ _____
                               Chronological
                                       age: _____ _____ _____

Round the following chronological ages to years and months.

	Year	**Month**	**Day**	**Rounded to**
4.	7–	10–	23	_____
5.	11–	7–	14	_____
6.	14–	11–	29	_____

Apply Your Knowledge

Why do you think it is so important to have the exact chronological age of a student before you administer and score a test? _____
_____
_____

Figure 5.4   Calculation for student who began with item 1 and correctly answered 8 of 15 attempted items.

```
1.  __1__          11. __0__
2.  __1__          12. __1__
3.  __1__          13. __0__
4.  __1__          14. __0__
5.  __0__          15. __0__
6.  __0__          16. _____
7.  __1__          17. _____
8.  __1__          18. _____
9.  __0__          19. _____
10. __1__          20. _____

Raw Score:  __8__
```

CALCULATING RAW SCORES

raw score The first score obtained in test administration; usually the number of items counted as correct.

The first score obtained in the administration of a test is the **raw score**. On most educational instruments, the raw score is simply the number of items the student answers correctly. Figure 5.4 shows the calculation of a raw score for one student. The student's correct responses are marked with a 1, incorrect responses with a 0. The number of items answered correctly on this test was 8, which is expressed as a raw score. The raw score will be entered into a table in the test manual to determine the derived scores, which are norm-referenced scores expressed in different ways. The administration of this test was stopped when the student missed three consecutive items because the test manual stated to stop testing when this occurred.

DETERMINING BASALS AND CEILINGS

The student whose scores are shown in Figure 5.4 began with item 1 and stopped after making three consecutive errors. The starting and stopping points of a test must be determined so that unnecessary items are not administered. Some tests contain hundreds of items, many of which may not be developmentally appropriate for all students.

Most educational tests contain starting rules in the manual, protocol, or actual test instrument. These rules are guides that can help the examiner begin testing with an item at the appropriate level. These guides may be given as age recommendations—for example, 6-year-olds begin with item 10—or as grade-level recommendations—for example, fourth-grade students begin with item 25. These starting points are meant to represent a level at which the student could answer all previous items correctly and are most accurate for students who are functioning close to age or grade expectancy.

Often, students referred for special education testing function below grade- and age-level expectancies. Therefore, the guides or starting points suggested by the test developers may be inappropriate. It is necessary to determine the **basal** level for the student, or the level at which the student could correctly answer all easier items, those items located at lower levels. Once the basal has been established, the examiner can proceed with testing the student. If the student fails to obtain a basal level, the test may be considered too difficult, and another instrument should be selected.

basal Thought to represent the level of skills below which the student would correctly answer all test items.

The rules for establishing a basal level are given in the test manuals, and many tests contain the information on the protocol. The basal rule may be the same as a ceiling rule, such as three consecutively correct responses and three consecutively incorrect responses. The basal rule may also be expressed as correctly completing an entire level. No matter what the rule, the objective is the same: to establish a level that is thought to represent a foundation and at which all easier items would be assumed correct.

The examples shown in Figure 5.5 illustrate a basal rule of three consecutive correct responses on Test I and a basal of all items answered correctly on an entire level of the test on Test II.

It may be difficult to select the correct item to begin with when testing a special education student. The student's social ability may seem to be age appropriate but academic ability may be significantly

Figure 5.5 Basal level established for test I for three consecutive correct responses; basal level for test II established when all items in one level (grade 1) are answered correctly.

TEST I		TEST II		
1. _____		**Level K**	1. _____	
2. _____			2. _____	
3. _____			3. _____	
4. _____			4. _____	
5. _____		**Grade 1**	5. __1__	
6. __1__			6. __1__	
7. __1__			7. __1__	
8. __1__			8. __1__	
9. __0__				
10. __1__		**Grade 2**	9. __0__	
			10. __1__	
			11. __0__	
			12. __1__	

below expectancy for the age and grade placement. The examiner may begin with an item that is too easy or too difficult. Although it is not desirable to administer too many items that are beneath the student's academic level, it is better to begin the testing session with the positive reinforcement of answering items correctly than with the negative reinforcement of answering several items incorrectly and experiencing a sense of failure or frustration. The examiner should obtain a basal by selecting an item believed to be a little below the student's academic level.

Even when the examiner chooses a starting item believed to be easy for a student, sometimes the student will miss items before the basal is established. In this case, most test manuals contain instructions for determining the basal. Some manuals instruct the examiner to test backward in the same sequence until a basal can be established. After the basal is determined, the examiner proceeds from the point where the backward sequence was begun. Other test manuals instruct the examiner to drop back an entire grade level or to drop back the number of items required to establish a basal. For example, if five consecutive correct responses are required for a basal, the examiner is instructed to drop back five items and begin administration. If the examiner is not familiar with the student's ability in a certain area, the basal may be even more difficult to establish. The examiner in this case may have to drop back several times. For this reason, the examiner should circle the number of the first item administered. This information can be used later in the test interpretation.

Students may establish two or more basals; that is, using the five-consecutive-correct rule, a student may answer five correct, miss an item, then answer five consecutive correct again. The test manual may address this specifically, or it may not be mentioned. Unless the test manual states that the examiner may use the second or highest basal, it is best to use the first basal established.

When calculating the raw score, all items that appear before the established basal are counted as correct. This is because the basal is thought to represent the level at which all easier items would be passed. Therefore, when counting correct responses, count items below the basal as correct even though they were not administered.

Just as the basal is thought to represent the level at which all easier items would be passed, the **ceiling** is thought to represent the level at which more difficult items would not be passed. The ceiling rule may be three consecutive incorrect or even five items out of seven items answered incorrectly. Occasionally, an item is administered above the ceiling level by mistake, and the student may answer correctly. Because the ceiling level is thought to represent the level at which more difficult items would not be passed, these items usually are not counted. Unless the test manual states

ceiling Thought to represent the level of skills above which all test items would be answered incorrectly; the examiner discontinues testing at this level.

that the examiner is to count items above the ceiling, it is best not to do so.

USING INFORMATION ON PROTOCOLS

The protocol, or response form, for each test contains valuable information that can aid in test administration. Detailed instructions regarding the basal and ceiling rules for individual subtests of an educational test may be found on most protocols for educational tests.

Many tests have ceiling rules that are the same as the basal rules; for example, five consecutive incorrect responses are counted as the ceiling, and five consecutive correct responses establish the basal.

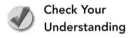
Check Your Understanding

Check your ability to calculate basals by completing Activity 5.3 below.

Activity 5.3

Using the following basal rules, identify basals for these students.

Test I **(Basal: 5 consecutive correct)**	**Test II** **(Basal: 7 consecutive correct)**	
1. _____	Grade 4	25. _____
2. _____		26. _____
3. _____		27. _____
4. _____		28. _____
5. _____		29. _____
6. __1__		30. _____
7. __1__	Grade 5	31. __1__
8. __1__		32. __1__
9. __1__		33. __1__
10. __1__		34. __1__
11. __0__		35. __1__
12. __1__	Grade 6	36. __1__
13. __0__		37. __1__
14. __1__		38. __0__
		39. __1__
		40. __0__
Basal items are:_____		Basal items are:_____

The instructions given in the test manual state that if a student fails to establish a basal with 5 consecutive correct items, the examiner must drop back 5 items from the first attempted item and begin testing. Which item would the examiner begin with in the following examples? _____

Example 1

22. _____
23. _____
24. _____
25. _____
26. _____
27. _____
28. _____
29. __1__
30. __0__
31. _____
32. _____

Drop to item: _____

Example 2

116. _____
117. _____
118. _____
119. _____
120. _____
121. __1__
122. __1__
123. __0__
124. _____
125. _____
126. _____

Drop to item: _____

Apply Your Knowledge

What is the meaning of basal level, and how does it relate to a student's ability? _____

_____

_____

Since some tests have different basal and ceiling rules, it is necessary to read instructions carefully. If the protocol does not provide the basal and ceiling rules, the examiner is wise to note this at the top of the pages of the protocol for the sections to be administered.

The protocols for each test are arranged specifically for that test. Some forms contain several subtests that may be arranged in more than one order. On very lengthy tests, the manual may provide information about selecting only certain subtests rather than administering the entire test. Other tests have age- or grade-appropriate subtests, which must be selected according to the student's level. Some instruments use the raw score on the first subtest to determine the starting point on all other subtests. And finally, some subtests require the examiner to begin with item 1 regardless of the age or grade level of the student. Specific instructions for individual subtests may be provided on the protocol as well as in the test manual.

Educational tests often provide training exercises at the beginning of subtests. These training exercises help the examiner explain the task to the student and better ensure that the student understands the task before answering the first scored item. The student may be allowed to attempt the training tasks more than once, or the examiner may be instructed to correct wrong answers and explain the correct responses. These items are not scored, however, and a subtest may be skipped if the student does not understand the task. The use of training exercises varies.

ADMINISTERING TESTS: FOR BEST RESULTS

Students tend to respond more and perform better in testing situations with examiners who are familiar with them (Fuchs, Zern, & Fuchs, 1983). As suggested previously, the examiner should spend some time with the student before the actual evaluation. The student's regular classroom setting is a good place to begin. The examiner should talk with the student in a warm manner and repeat visits to the classroom before the evaluation. It may also be helpful for the student to visit the testing site to become familiar with the environment. The examiner may want to tell the student that they will work together later in the week or month. The testing session should not be the first time the examiner and student meet. Classroom observations and visits may aid the examiner in determining which tests to administer. Chances for successful testing sessions will increase if the student is not overtested. Although it is imperative that all areas of suspected disability be assessed, multiple tests that measure the same skill or ability are not necessary.

For **MORE PRACTICE** in the mechanics of determining chronological age, basals, ceilings, and raw scores, visit the Companion Website at *www.prenhall.com/overton*.

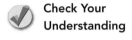

Check Your Understanding

Check your ability to calculate basal and ceiling scores by completing Activity 5.4 below.

Activity 5.4

Calculate the raw scores for the following protocol sections. Follow the given basal and ceiling rules.

Protocol 1	Protocol 2
(Basal: 5 consecutive correct; Ceiling: 5 consecutive incorrect)	**(Basal: 3 consecutive correct; Ceiling: 3 consecutive incorrect)**

Protocol 1	Protocol 2
223. _____	10. _____
224. _____	11. __1__
225. _____	12. __1__
226. _____	13. __1__
227. __1__	14. __1__
228. __1__	15. __1__
229. __1__	16. __1__
230. __1__	17. __1__
231. __1__	18. __1__
232. __0__	19. __0__
233. __1__	20. __1__
234. __1__	21. __1__

235. __0__   22. __1__
236. __0__   23. __0__
237. __0__   24. __0__
238. __0__   25. __0__
239. __0__   26. _____

Raw score: ———   Raw score: ———

1. Which protocol had more than one basal? _____
2. What were the basal items on protocol 1? _____
3. What were the ceiling items on protocol 1? _____
4. What were the basal items on protocol 2? _____
5. What were the ceiling items on protocol 2? _____

Apply Your Knowledge

What is the meaning of ceiling level, and how does it relate to the student's ability? _____

_____

_____

Check Your Understanding

Check your ability to calculate a raw score by completing Activity 5.5 below.

Activity 5.5

Using the protocol and the responses in Figure 5.6, determine the basal and ceiling items for this student.

1. How many trials are allowed for the training exercises on this subtest? _____
2. According to the responses shown, what items are included in the student's basal level? _____
3. What instructions are provided about establishing the basal? _____
4. According to the responses shown, what items are included in the student's ceiling level? _____

Apply Your Knowledge

What information are you able to learn from this page of the protocol?

_____

_____

_____

Figure 5.6   Basal and ceiling rules and response items for a subtest from the Peabody Individual Achievement Test—Revised.

SUBTEST 2
Reading Recognition

Training Exercises

	Trial 1	Trial 2	Trial 3
Exercise A.	(1) _____	(1) _____	(1) _____
Exercise B.	(3) _____	(3) _____	(3) _____
Exercise C.	(2) _____	(2) _____	(2) _____

Basal and Ceiling Rules
Basal: *highest* 5 consecutive correct responses
Ceiling: *lowest* 7 consecutive responses containing 5 errors

Starting Point
The item number that corresponds to the subject's raw score on General Information.

43. ledge	1	
44. escape	1	
45. northern	1	
46. towel	1	
47. kneel	1	
48. height	0	
49. exercise	1	
50. observe	1	
51. ruin	0	
52. license	1	
53. uniforms	0	
54. pigeon	1	
55. moisture	0	
56. artificial	1	**READING RECOGNITION**
57. issues	0	Ceiling Item _____
58. quench	0	minus Errors _____
59. hustle	0	equals RAW SCORE
60. thigh	0	

Source: From *Peabody Individual Achievement Test–Revised*, subtest 2, Reading Recognition, by F. C. Markwardt, 1989, Circle Pines, MN: American Guidance Service. Copyright 1989 by American Guidance Service. Reprinted by permission.

After the examiner and student are in the testing room, the examiner should attempt to make the student feel at ease. The examiner should convey the importance of the testing situation without making the student feel anxious. As suggested by McLoughlin and Lewis (2001), the examiner should encourage the student to work hard and should reinforce the student's attempts and efforts, not correct responses. Responses that reinforce the efforts of the student may include statements such as "You are working so hard today," or "You like math work," or "I will be sure to tell your teacher [or mother or father, etc.] how hard you worked." If the student asks about performance on specific items ("Did I get that one right?"), the examiner should again try to reinforce effort.

Young students may enjoy a tangible reinforcer upon the completion of the testing session. The examiner may tell the student near the end of the session to work just a few more items for a treat or surprise. Reinforcement with tangibles is not recommended during the assessment, because the student may lose interest in the test or no longer pay attention.

During the administration of the test, the examiner must be sure to follow all instructions in the manual. As stated in professional standards and IDEA, tests must be given in the manner set forth by the test developer, and adapting tests must be done by professionals with expertise in the specific area being assessed who are cognizant of the psychometric changes that will result.

Cole, D'Alonzo, Gallegos, Giordano, and Stile (1992) suggested that examiners consider several additional factors to decrease bias in the assessment process. The following considerations, adapted from Cole et al. (1992), can help the examiner determine whether the test can be administered in a fair way:

1. Do sensory or communicative impairments make portions of the test inaccessible?

2. Do sensory or communicative impairments limit students from responding to questions?

3. Do test materials or method of responding limit students from responding?

4. Do background experiences limit the student's ability to respond?

5. Does the content of classroom instruction limit students from responding?

6. Is the examiner familiar to the student?

7. Are instructions explained in a familiar fashion?

8. Is the recording technique required of the student on the test familiar? (p. 219)

OBTAINING DERIVED SCORES

The raw scores obtained during the test administration are used to locate other derived scores from norm tables included in the examiner's manuals for the specific test. The derived scores may include percentile ranks, grade equivalents, standard scores with a mean of 100 or 50, and other standardized scores, such as z scores.

There are advantages and disadvantages to using the different types of derived scores. Of particular concern is the correct use and interpretation of grade equivalents and percentile ranks. These two types of derived scores are used frequently because the basic theoretical concepts are thought to be understood; however, these two types of scores are misunderstood and misinterpreted by professionals (Huebner, 1988, 1989; Wilson, 1987). The reasons for this misinterpretation are the lack of understanding of the numerical scale used and the method used in establishing grade-level equivalents.

Percentile ranks are used often because they can be easily explained to parents. The concept, for example, of 75% of the peer group scoring at the same level or below a particular student is one that parents and professionals can understand. The difficulty in interpreting percentile ranks is that they do not represent a numerical scale with equal intervals. For example, the standard scores between the 50th and 60th percentiles are quite different from the standard scores between the 80th and 90th percentile ranks.

The development of grade equivalents needs to be considered when using these derived scores. Grade equivalents represent the average number of items answered correctly by the students in the standardization sample of a particular grade. These equivalents may not represent the actual skill level of particular items or of a particular student's performance on a test. Many of the skills tested on academic achievement tests are taught at various grade levels. The grade level of presentation of these skills depends on the curriculum used. The grade equivalents obtained therefore may not be representative of the skills necessary to pass that grade level in a specific curriculum.

TYPES OF SCORES

The concepts of standard scores, percentile ranks, and age and grade equivalents have been introduced. Standard scores and percentile ranks are scores used to compare an individual student with the larger norm group to determine relative standing in the areas assessed, such as mathematics skills or IQ. Standard scores include those scores with an average or mean of 100 as well as other scores such as T scores, which have an average of 50, or z scores, which convey the student's standing in terms of standard deviation units. Refer to Figure 3.9 to locate scores. For example, a z score of -1.0 indicates that the student is 1 standard deviation below average and if this score is converted to a standard score with a mean of 100, the standard score of this student is 85. If the student's z score is converted to T scores, the student's T score is 40 (T score average is 50; SD of 10).

Other scores that may be used to compare the student's standing to the norm group are stanine scores. Stanine scores, like percentile ranks, are not equidistant. Stanines are based on a system of dividing the distribution into 9 segments with an average or mean of 5 and a standard deviation of 2. This means that the previously presented student score of 85 and a z score of –1.0 would have a stanine score of 3. The data or student scores within the stanine sections represent large segments of ability and therefore do not convey very precise indications of a student's performance or ability.

GROUP TESTING: HIGH-STAKES ASSESSMENT

The protocol examples and basal and ceiling exercises presented thus far in the chapter are typical of individualized norm-referenced instruments. Other instruments commonly used in schools are norm-referenced standardized group achievement tests. These instruments are administered to classroom-size groups to assess achievement levels. Group achievement tests are increasingly used to assess accountability of individual students and school systems. These instruments are also known as high-stakes tests because the results of such tests often have serious implications of accountability, accreditation, and funding for school systems. States and districts use such instruments to be certain that students are meeting expected academic standards for their grade placement. In addition, at least 26 states use the results of statewide assessment to determine if students are allowed to graduate, and 6 states use such assessment for grade promotion (U.S. Department of Education, 2000).

Principles to guide the assessment of students for accountability have been proposed by Elliott, Braden, and White (2001), who suggest that school systems keep in mind that assessment should be logical and serve the purpose for which it is intended. They state that systems should set their standards or goals first before developing assessments. In addition, they remind school personnel that high-stakes testing should measure educational achievement rather than try to create achievement. As with individual assessment, these authors state, no single instrument has the capability to answer all achievement questions and multiple measures should be used. And finally, as with other educational instruments, high-stakes assessments should be reliable and valid for their specific purpose.

Brigham, Tochterman, and Brigham (2000) point out that in order for high-stakes assessment to be beneficial for students with special needs, such tests should provide useful information for planning. Such information would inform the teacher about what areas students have mastered, what areas are at the level of instruction, and the areas to which students have not been exposed. These authors further state that the information provided to teachers in high-stakes assessment is often not provided in a timely manner so that instructional interventions can occur. In addition, high-stakes

Barbara Schwartz/Merrill

assessment may not be completed annually but rather biannually, so that the results have little if any impact on the student's actual educational planning.

The 1997 IDEA Amendments require that students with disabilities be included in statewide and districtwide assessments. For some students, the assessments are completed with **accommodations** for their specific disabilities. The Amendments require that students who are unable to complete these assessments should be administered alternate assessments. When the 1997 Amendments required that students with disabilities be included in statewide accountability assessment, most states did not have such accountability systems in place for students eligible under IDEA (Thurlow, Elliott, & Ysseldyke, 1998). The Amendments required educators to decide and include in the IEP process which students would take statewide assessments, which students would require accommodations for the statewide assessments, and which students would require alternate assessment for accountability.

This decision-making process has proved to be complicated and should be reached by the IEP team. Educators must also address the issue of statewide assessment for students being served under Section 504, and the decisions should be included in the student's Section 504 plan (Office of Special Education and Rehabilitative Services, 2000). Thurlow et al. have proposed a decision-making form to assist educators in determining which students should be included in statewide assessment or require accommodations or alternate assessment.

According to Thurlow et al., the questions that should be considered when determining which students should be administered

accommodations
Necessary changes in format, response mode, setting, or scheduling that will enable a student with disabilities to complete the general curriculum or test.

statewide assessment, which students require accommodations, and which students should be provided alternate assessment, focus on the standards that the students are expected to master. If students are expected to master the standards expected of all general education students, the students should be administered the statewide assessment. For students who are given accommodations in the general education classroom in order to participate in the curriculum, accommodations should be included in the administration of statewide assessments. Finally, for students who are expected to meet general education standards, even with accommodations, these students should be administered an alternate assessment.

For students with disabilities who require accommodations for participation in statewide assessment, the accommodations must not alter what the test is measuring. Accommodations include possible changes in the format of the assessment, the manner in which the student responds, the setting of the assessment, or in scheduling (Office of Special Education and Rehabilitative Services, 2000). The team members determine the accommodations needed in order for the student to participate in the assessment and include such modifications in the student's IEP.

Students from culturally and linguistically diverse backgrounds who are considered to be English-language learners (limited English proficiency) may require accommodations to ensure that academic skills and knowledge are being assessed rather than English skills. As with assessment to determine eligibility, students must be assessed in specific areas of content or ability rather than for their English reading or communication skills. If required, accommodations may be included for the student's language differences (Office of Special Education and Rehabilitative Services, 2000).

The team determines to use an alternate assessment method when the student will not be able to participate, even with accommodations, in the statewide or districtwide assessments. Alternate assessments are to be designed that include the same areas or domains as the statewide assessments. The test content should reflect the appropriate knowledge and skills and should be considered a reliable and valid measure of the content.

ACCOMMODATIONS IN HIGH-STAKES TESTING

assistive technology Necessary technology that enables the student to participate in a free, appropriate public education.

Students who participate in the general education curriculum with limited difficulty most likely will not require accommodations for high-stakes testing. Students who require accommodations in the general education or special education setting—such as extended time for task completion, or use of **assistive technology** (speech synthesizer, electronic reader, communication board)—to participate in the general curriculum will most likely require accommodations to participate in high-stakes testing. The purpose of accommodations during the assessment is to prevent measuring the student's disability and to allow a more accurate assessment of the student's progress in the general curriculum.

The determination of need for accommodations should be made during the IEP process. The types of accommodations needed must be documented on the IEP. Following the statewide or districtwide assessment, teachers should rate the accommodations that proved to be helpful for each specific student (Elliott, Kratochwill, & Schulte, 1998). The following adapted list of accommodations has been suggested by these authors:

1. Motivation—Some students may work best with extrinsic motivators such as verbal praise.

2. Providing assistance prior to administering the test—To familiarize the student with test format, test-related behavior or procedures that will be required.

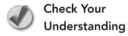

Check Your Understanding

Complete the questions of high-stakes assessment in Activity 5.6 below.

Activity 5.6

Match these terms to the statements that follow.

a. alternate assessment

b. statewide assessment

c. high-stakes assessment

d. accommodations

_____ 1. Juan is receiving special education support in the general classroom setting. Although he reads the same textbooks as other students, he must use a word processor to complete his writing assignments. His IEP team has determined that he will require _____ for his standardized statewide assessment.

_____ 2. When assessment determines promotion to the next grade in secondary school, the assessment is called _____.

_____ 3. Allowing students to complete assessment in a small group in a separate room is considered a type of _____.

_____ 4. The IEP team must include statements that address _____.

_____ 5. Lupitina has been receiving her education within a self-contained special education environment since she entered school. Her development is 5 years below the level of her peers. The IEP team must determine if Lupitina should have accommodations for her assessment, or if she will require _____.

3. Scheduling—Extra time or testing over several days.

4. Setting—Includes location, lighting, acoustics, specialized equipment.

5. Providing assistance during the assessment—To assist a student with turning pages, recording response, or allowing the child's special education teacher to administer the test.

6. Using aids—Any specialized equipment or technology the child requires.

7. Changes in test format—Braille edition or audiotaped questions.

Source: From "The Assessment Accommodations Checklist" by S. N. Elliott, T. R. Kratochwill, and A. G. Schulte, 1998, *Teaching Exceptional Children,* Nov./Dec. pp.10–14.

In the *Accommodations Manual* of the Council of Chief State School Officers (Thompson, Morse, Sharpe, & Hall, 2005), the following adapted list of accommodation categories are described for use in statewide assessment:

Presentation accommodations—An example might be a student with a significant reading disability may be provided the content through a means other than reading.

Response accommodations—An example of this type of accommodation would be a student who cannot respond in writing would be allowed to respond in another format such as use of a communication board or other technology.

Setting accommodations—This type of accommodation would be used when it is necessary to provide the assessment in a different location for reasons such as accessibility or when a student cannot process information in a distracting environment.

Timing and scheduling accommodations—students who require extended time or students who require frequent breaks to sustain attention would benefit from these accommodations.

ALTERNATE ASSESSMENT

Students who are not able to participate in the regular statewide assessment, or in the statewide assessment with accommodations, are required to complete an alternate assessment. The alternate assessment should be designed to reflect progress in the general education curriculum at the appropriate level. The intent of the alternate assessment is to measure the student's progress along the continuum of general education expectations.

States participating in statewide assessments determine individually how the state will provide alternate assessments for students who are not able to complete the assessments with accommodations. A state may use a statewide curriculum with set expectations for each grade level. These skills and expectations exist on a continuum, and this may be used as a basis for the alternate assessment. The skill level measured on the alternate assessment may actually be at a level below the expectations for students in school. For example, a young student with a significant cognitive disability may not be able to master the skills expected of a first- or second-grade student. The skills that may be measured for progress may be the preacademic skills necessary to progress toward the first- and second-grade skills.

The type and level of the assessment may be determined individually for each student requiring alternate assessments. Portfolio assessment, performance-based assessment, authentic assessment, and observations are methods used by states as alternate assessment for high-stakes testing. Many states are continuing to develop both acceptable accommodations and alternate tests (Elliott et al., 1998; Thurlow et al., 1998; Ysseldyke, Nelson, & House, 2000).

ISSUES IN HIGH-STAKES TESTING

Typically in the field of special education assessment new concepts and regulations in the assessment of students with special needs have been met with questions and issues that must be considered. The mandate in the 1997 Amendments to include all students in high-stakes assessment was added to the law as a measure of accountability. Student progress must be measured to determine if programs are effective. This mandate continues in IDEA 2004.

As this mandate has been implemented in schools, there have been problems and concerns. Ysseldyke, Thurlow, Kozleski, and Reschly (1998) identified 16 critical issues. Some of these issues include concerns about the inconsistency of definitions, federal law requirements, variability among states and districts, differences in standards of expectations for students with disabilities, lack of participation of students with disabilities in test development and standardization of instruments, and lack of consistency regarding decisions for accommodations and alternate assessment.

Other issues involve the conceptual understanding of the purpose and nature of the assessment. Gronna, Jenkins, and Chin-Chance (1998) state that students with disabilities have typically been excluded from national norming procedures, yet these students are now to be compared with these national samples to determine how much progress they have made. These authors raise the question of how to compare students with disabilities with the national norms when the students with disabilities, by definition, are expected to differ from the established norms. This is an area of continued research and debate in the field of special education. Nichols and Berliner (2007) argue that mandatory statewide assessments have resulted in damaging the American education system for all students and that alternate assessments may not be the best way to measure progress. Yeh (2006) found that some teachers reported that high-stakes assessment helped teachers target and individualize instruction, and that their students who disliked reading or had difficulties with academics felt more in control of their own learning. Yovanoff and Tindal (2007) suggest that performance task-based reading alternate tests can be scaled to statewide assessments, although determining the validity and reliability may be difficult. Perner (2007) states that the development of alternate assessments is difficult and that states require more time to develop appropriate measures.

In response to the difficulties often encountered by educators who must design alternative assessments or provide accommodations for assessments, there has been an interest in designing all assessments to be more fair and user friendly for all learners from the beginning rather than attempting to fit a test to a student's needs after it has been developed. This concept, known as Universal Design, has been gaining attention in both instructional methods and assessments. The Principles of Universal Design are presented in Table 5.4.

Table 5.4   Principles of Universal Design.

Principle One: Equitable Use: The design is useful and marketable to people with diverse abilities.

1a. Provide the same means of use for all users: identical whenever possible; equivalent when not.
1b. Avoid segregating or stigmatizing any users.
1c. Provisions for privacy, security, and safety should be equally available to all users.
1d. Make the design appealing to all users.

Principle Two: Flexibility in Use: The design accommodates a wide range of individual preferences and abilities.

2a. Provide choice in methods of use.
2b. Accommodate right- or left-handed access and use.
2c. Facilitate the user's accuracy and precision.
2d. Provide adaptability to the user's pace.

Principle Three: Simple and Intuitive Use: Use of the design is easy to understand, regardless of the user's experience, knowledge, language skills, or current concentration level.

3a. Eliminate unnecessary complexity.
3b. Be consistent with user expectations and intuition.
3c. Accommodate a wide range of literacy and language skills.
3d. Arrange information consistent with its importance.
3e. Provide effective prompting and feedback during and after task completion.

Table 5.4   continued.

Principle Four: Perceptible Information: The design communicates necessary information effectively to the user, regardless of ambient conditions or the user's sensory abilities.

4a. Use different modes (pictorial, verbal, tactile) for redundant presentation of essential information.

4b. Provide adequate contrast between essential information and its surroundings.

4c. Maximize "legibility" of essential information.

4d. Differentiate elements in ways that can be described (i.e., make it easy to give instructions or directions).

4e. Provide compatibility with a variety of techniques or devices used by people with sensory limitations.

Principle Five: Tolerance for Error: The design minimizes hazards and the adverse consequences of accidental or unintended actions.

5a. Arrange elements to minimize hazards and errors: most used elements, most accessible; hazardous elements eliminated, isolated, or shielded.

5b. Provide warnings of hazards and errors.

5c. Provide fail safe features.

5d. Discourage unconscious action in tasks that require vigilance.

Principle Six: Low Physical Effort: The design can be used efficiently and comfortably and with a minimum of fatigue.

6a. Allow user to maintain a neutral body position.

6b. Use reasonable operating forces.

6c. Minimize repetitive actions.

6d. Minimize sustained physical effort.

Principle Seven: Size and Space for Approach and Use: Appropriate size and space is provided for approach, reach, manipulation, and use regardless of user's body size, posture, or mobility.

7a. Provide a clear line of sight to important elements for any seated or standing user.

7b. Make reach to all components comfortable for any seated or standing user.

7c. Accommodate variations in hand and grip size.

7d. Provide adequate space for the use of assistive devices or personal assistance.

Source: The Center for Universal Design, North Carolina State University, 1997.

CHAPTER SUMMARY

This chapter provided information about norm-referenced instruments used in individual and group settings. Both types of instruments are used to measure academic achievement in schools. Group measures include statewide mandated achievement measures that may need to be adapted for students with disabilities.

THINK AHEAD

The most frequently used tests in education are achievement tests. In the next chapter, you will use portions of commonly used instruments to learn about achievement tests and how they are scored.

EXERCISES

Part I

Match the following terms with the correct definitions.

a. domain	i. grade equivalent
b. norm-referenced tests	j. norm group
c. item pool	k. interpolated
d. test manual	l. chronological age
e. accommodations	m. stanines
f. ceiling	n. basal
g. raw score	o. field test
h. developmental version	p. protocol

_____ 1. When a test is being developed, the test developer attempts to have this represent the population for whom the test is designed.

_____ 2. This step is completed using the developmental version to determine what changes are needed prior to the completion of the published test.

_____ 3. This represents the level of items that the student would most probably answer correctly, although they may not all be administered to the student.

_____ 4. When a teacher scores a classroom test including 10 items and determines that a student correctly answered 7, the number 7 represents a _____.

_____ 5. Information regarding how a test was developed is usually contained in the _____.

_____ 6. A student's standard score that compares the student with age peers is found by using the student's raw score and the student's _____ and the norm tables.

_____ 7. A teacher discovers that although only second, third, and fifth graders were included in the norm sample of a test, scores were presented for fourth grade. The fourth-grade scores were _____.

_____ 8. A student's actual skill level is not represented by the _____.

_____ 9. Both individual and group assessments may be _____ that compare students with age or grade expectations.

_____10. Students with disabilities who have IEPs and students who are served under Section 504 may need _____ for statewide assessments.

_____11. A student score that is reported to be exactly average with a score of 5 is reporting using _____ scores.

Part II

Select the type of accommodation and match with the following statements.

a. setting

b. scheduling

c. response mode

d. assessment format

_____ 1. Lorenzo, who participates in the general curriculum, requires Braille for all reading material. He will require changes in _____.

_____ 2. Lorenzo also requires the use of a stylus for writing or answers questions orally. He will also require changes in _____ .

_____ 3. When Susie is in the general classroom setting, she often is distracted and requires additional time to complete her assignments. On her Section 504 plan, the team members should include accommodations of _____.

_____ 4. George is a student with a specific reading disability. In his general education classroom, George's teacher and the classroom aide must read all instructions to him and often must read questions and multisyllabic words to him. On his IEP, the team has included a statement of accommodation of _____ .

Part III

Discuss the issues and concerns of the statewide assessment of students with disabilities.

Part IV

Using the portions from the *KeyMath—Revised* (Connolly, 1988) protocol in Figure 5.7, determine the following:

1. Chronological age: _____

2. Domain scores: _____

3. Raw score: _____

4. Basal item: _____

5. Ceiling item: _____

Figure 5.7 Chronological age portion and Numeration subtest from the *KeyMath—Revised* protocol.

	YEAR	MONTH	DAY
Test date	91	10	5
Birth date	84	11	10
Chronological age	___	___	___

1 NUMERATION

General Directions:

Read Chapter 3 in the *Manual* carefully before administering and scoring the test. The correct procedures for establishing the subtest basal and ceiling are detailed in the chapter. Briefly, the criteria are as follows: *The basal is the 3 consecutive correct responses immediately preceding the easiest item missed; the ceiling is 3 consecutive errors.*

Begin administration at the Numeration item designated as the starting item for the student's grade level. Score items by penciling a 1 (correct) or 0 (incorrect) in the box. Continue administration until a basal and a ceiling have been established for the Numeration subtest. Use the Numeration basal item (the first item of the Numeration basal) to determine the starting points for the remaining subtests; for example, if the student's Numeration basal item is 18, begin the Rational Numbers subtest at item 2, begin the Geometry subtest at item 13, and so on.

The item-score boxes are positioned in columns indicating which domain each item belongs to. When totaling the scores in a domain column, count as *correct* the *unadministered* items in that column that *precede* the easiest item administered. The resulting total for the column is the domain score. The sum of the domain scores is the subtest raw score.

GRADE	Item		Numbers 0-9	Numbers 0-99	Numbers 0-999	Multi-digit numbers
K,1 ▶	1. how many deer		1			
	2. as many fingers		1			
	3. read 5, 2, 7		1			
	4. read in order 5, 2, 7		1			
	5. how many people		0			
2,3 ▶	6. fourth person		1			
	7. ____ 20 ____			0		
	8. read in order 36 15 70 32			1		
	9. how many rods			0		
4 ▶	10. how many dots			0		
	11. order 643 618 305 648				1	
5-7 ▶	12. blue dot			0		
	13. 729 739 749 ____ ____				0	
	14. order 3,649 3,581 3,643					0
	15. how many small cubes					
8,9 ▶	16. round to nearest hundred					
	17. how many pencils					
	18. four-digit number					
	19. read 6,019,304					
	20. number in blue box					
	21. how many small cubes					
	22. three-digit number					
	23. less than positive four					
	24. what does 10^4 represent					
____ CEILING ITEM	DOMAIN SCORES					

SUBTEST RAW SCORE (Sum of domain scores) [ ]

Answers to these questions can be found in the Appendix of this text or you may also complete these questions and receive immediate feedback on your answers by going to the Think Ahead module in Chapter 5 of the Companion Website.

COURSE PROGRESS MONITORING ASSESSMENT

See how you are doing in the course after the conclusion of PART II by completing the following assessment. When you are finished, check your answers with your instructor or on the Companion Website *www.prenhall.com/overton*. Once you have your score, return to Figure 1.9, Student Progress Monitoring Graph in Chapter 1 and plot your progress.

Progress Monitoring Assessment

Select the best answer. Some of these terms may be used more than once.

A. Academic achievement tests
B. Curriculum-based measurement
C. Curriculum-based assessment
D. Behavior rating profile–2
E. Child behavior checklist
F. Estimated true score
G. Standard error of measurement

H. Content validity
I. Construct validity
J. Section 504
K. Age equivalent
L. High-stakes tests
M. FBA
N. Arena assessment
O. Reliability
P. Coefficient

_____ 1. The indicator of common variance of two variables.

_____ 2. This type of curriculum-based instrument does not have diagnostic capability unless an error analysis is completed on the student's work.

_____ 3. A developmental score that may not be very useful to interpret.

_____ 4. These measures are often used when assessing very young children.

_____ 5. This type of validity looks at difficult-to-measure concepts.

_____ 6. This behavior rating scale includes a classroom observation instrument.

_____ 7. This measure indicates how much error may be on a test based on the score's distance from the mean.

_____ 8. This curriculum-based measure assesses the student's performance to see if it is aligned with the goal or aim line.

_____ 9. This method of measuring error on a test uses the standard deviation in the computation.

_____10. This measurement of error is usually used to calculate confidence intervals.

Fill in the Blanks

11. Both _____ and _____ require that students be instructed using research-based interventions.

12. The _____ is a behavior rating system that includes forms for teachers, parents, and the student as well as a developmental interview for the parent.

13. The _____ includes a measure of the student's attitude toward math.

14. The _____ case resulted in more careful assessment for the determination of mental retardation.

15. The Stanford–Binet V categorizes scores within the 120–129 range as _____.

16. Regulatory disturbances might be assessed when the assessment involves _____.

17. The blending of isolated sounds into a whole word is called _____.

18. For each student served in special education, a _____ must be in place to plan the instruction.

19. Story starters might be useful in the informal assessment of _____.

20. As part of the process of the testing _____, previous educational experiences should be considered.

PART

3

Assessing Students

Curriculum-Based Assessment and Other Informal Measures

curriculum-based assessment

curriculum-based measurement

formative assessment

summative assessment

correct letter sequence

probes

oral reading fluency

maze

baseline score

aimline

performance assessment

criterion-referenced tests

direct measurement

subskill

task analysis

subtask

error analysis

checklists

questionnaires

work samples

permanent products

authentic assessment

portfolio assessment

CHAPTER FOCUS

curriculum-based assessment Using content from the currently used curriculum to assess student progress.

Student academic performance in school is best measured using the actual curriculum materials that the student is expected to master. These assessment methods are collectively called **curriculum-based assessment**. This chapter introduces the various methods used in the classroom to assess student performance. These methods, also generally known as informal methods of assessment, provide valuable information to assist with planning and effective interventions.

CEC KNOWLEDGE AND SKILLS STANDARDS

The student completing this chapter will understand the knowledge and skills included in the following CEC Knowledge and Skills Standards from Standard 8: Assessment:

CC8K1—Basic terminology used in assessment

CC8K3—Screening, prereferral, referral, and classification procedures

GC8K4—Procedures for early identification of young children who may be at risk for disabilities

CC8S2—Administer nonbiased formal and informal assessments

CURRICULUM–BASED MEASUREMENT

In Chapter 1 you learned that the Traditional Assessment Model largely employs the use of norm-referenced tests with the goal of determining a student's eligibility for special education support. With the reforms in education and special education, the emphasis is now on prevention strategies. Prevention and early intervention strategies are the focus of the Contemporary Assessment Model (see Chapter 1 page 17).

Early intervention methods prevent students from slipping behind their peers in expected levels of academic achievement. One way that teachers can prevent students from falling behind their peers is to closely monitor their progress so that mistakes can be noticed early and interventions, such as a change in teaching strategies, can be implemented. **Curriculum-based measurement**, or CBM, is a method of monitoring instruction regularly. The student's CBM is based on the achievement goal for the school year (Fuchs, 2004). For example, if the goal is to comprehend fourth-grade-level reading material, the CBMs are based on fourth-grade-level reading passages even though at the beginning of the year the student reads at the third-grade level. The monitoring of progress lets the teacher know if the child is making adequate progress under the current educational conditions. This close monitoring, for the purpose of making instructional decisions in the classroom, has been found to result in better academic achievement (Fuchs & Fuchs, 1986; Fuchs, Butterworth, & Fuchs, 1989; Fuchs, Fuchs, Hamlett, & Stecker, 1991).

One reason that curriculum-based measurement is considered the optimal assessment technique for monitoring progress is that it is a **formative** type of evaluation. An evaluation is considered formative when the student is measured during the instructional period for acquisition of skills and goals. This formative evaluation allows the teacher to make observations and decisions about the student's academic performance in a timely manner. Curriculum-based measurement may also be called progress monitoring because it is a formative type of evaluation. An evaluation is considered **summative** if it is a measurement taken at the end of the instructional period. For example, end-of-chapter tests or end-of-year tests are summative.

To compare curriculum-based measurement, curriculum-based assessment, and commercially produced norm-referenced achievement tests, see Table 6.1.

HOW TO CONSTRUCT AND ADMINISTER CURRICULUM-BASED MEASUREMENTS

In the 1970s, research efforts by the University of Minnesota resulted in the initial development of curriculum-based measures

curriculum-based measurement Frequent measurement comparing student's actual progress with expected rate of progress.

formative assessment Ongoing assessment that is completed during the acquisition of a skill.

summative assessment Assessment that is completed at the conclusion of an instructional period to determine level of acquisition or mastery.

Table 6.1 Comparisons of curriculum-based measurement, curriculum-based assessment, and commercial academic achievement tests.

Curriculum-Based Measurements	Curriculum-Based Assessments	Commercial Academic Achievement Tests
1. Repeated measures of same academic skill level based on end-of-year goal (formative)	1. Usually given at end of instructional period (summative)	1. Given to students to determine possible eligibility for special education support
2. Administered one or two times per week during academic period (school year)	2. Each test represents new material	2. Many instruments do not have alternate forms and cannot be repeated frequently for valid results
3. Are standardized and have adequate reliability	3. May be teacher-made and not standardized	3. Have adequate reliability and construct validity but content may not be relevant for specific students
4. Have content validity	4. May not have adequate reliability and validity	4. Are summative measures
5. May be a more fair measure of academic progress for ethnically and linguistically diverse students	5. May or may not be considered more fair for ethnically and linguistically diverse students	5. May be more prone to bias
6. May be administered to group (spelling and math)	6. May be administered to groups	6. Individual administration (for purposes of determining eligibility)
7. Research supports use in early skills acquisition for elementary and middle grades; some support for use in secondary grades	7. Teacher-made instruments used for summative evaluation; have not been researched	7. Instruments designed to assess all grade levels from pre-academic through adulthood
8. Specific skills assessed for reading fluency, spelling letter sequences, and math skills	8. Assesses mastery of specific content or skill taught during academic period	8. Assesses the broad domain of academic skills and achievement
9. May be used diagnostically for specific skills assessed and rate of learning	9. No true diagnostic capability unless error analysis is completed	9. May have diagnostic capability for a variety of skills
10. Compares student with his or her own performance on skill measured; may be compared to peers in class, compared with local norms, or compared with norms of researched groups	10. Compares student against a standard of mastery (student must pass 80% of items at end of chapter)	10. Compares student with national norm group or with self for diagnostic analysis (strengths and weaknesses across domain)
11. May be part of data collected for eligibility consideration	11. May be part of data collected for eligibility consideration	11. May be part of data collected for eligibility consideration

(Deno, 1985; Deno, Marston, & Mirkin, 1982; Deno, Marston, Shinn, & Tindal, 1983). The result of the research and continuing work in the field of curriculum-based measurement was the identification of measures that have consistently been found to have reliability and validity for the measurement of progress in reading, spelling, writing, and mathematics. Deno stated that these measurements met specific design criteria in order to be considered CBMs. In brief, these criteria are

1. The measures must have sufficient reliability and validity so that they could be used confidently by classroom teachers to make educational decisions.

2. These measures must be easy to use and understand so that teachers could employ them easily and teach others how to use them.

3. The results found by using the CBMs would need to be easy to explain to others, such as parents and other school personnel.

4. Because these measures would be used frequently throughout the school year, they have to be inexpensive (Deno, 1985).

Significant research indicates that there are simple measures that can assist teachers with monitoring progress for the purpose of making data-based educational decisions. According to Shinn, Nolet, and Knutson (1990), most curriculum-based measures should include the following tasks:

1. In reading, students read aloud from basal readers for 1 minute. The number of words read correctly per minute constitutes the basic decision-making metric.

2. In spelling, students write words that are dictated at specific intervals (either 5, 7, or 10 seconds) for 2 minutes. The number of **correct letter sequences** and words spelled correctly are counted.

correct letter sequence The sequence of letters in a specific word.

3. In written expression, students write a story for 3 minutes after being given a story starter (e.g., "Pretend you are playing on the playground and a spaceship lands. A little green person comes out and calls your name and. . ."). The number of words written, spelled correctly, and/or correct word sequences are counted.

probes Tests used for in-depth assessment of the mastery of a specific skill or subskill.

4. In mathematics, students write answers to computational problems via 2-minute **probes**. The number of correctly written digits is counted. (p. 290)

oral reading fluency The number of words the student is able to read aloud in a specified period of time.

In the next sections you will learn how to construct CBMs for **oral reading fluency**, spelling, and mathematical operations.

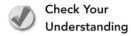 **Check Your Understanding**

Check your ability to recall the terms and concepts presented thus far in Chapter 6 by completing Activity 6.1 below.

Activity 6.1

Read each description below and determine if it illustrates **summative** or **formative evaluation**.

1. A classroom teacher administers a quiz following the introduction of each new concept in geometry. _____

2. The special education teacher requires her students to read oral passages twice a week to determine their rate of fluency and accuracy of reading. _____

3. In science, the teacher administers a unit test and uses the score as part of the end of term grade. _____

4. A third-grade language arts teacher uses curriculum based measurement twice each week to determine if students are correctly sequencing the letters in the spelling words. _____

5. Your assessment instructor administers a final exam to determine your mastery of assessment skills. _____

6. In this text, the pre-test and Part I, II, III, and IV tests are examples of _____ .

These methods are adapted from Fuchs and Fuchs (1992), Hosp and Hosp (2003), Marston (1989), and Scott and Weishaar (2003).

Constructing CBMs for Reading   In order to assess reading for a specific grade level, the teacher will need to have a sufficient number of passages to use for two types of activities at least two times per week. In addition to students reading the words orally so that the correct words can be counted for oral fluency, the **Maze** method has been found to provide valid results for comprehension. The Maze method requires that the student read a passage with missing words and select the correct word from three choices. Instructions for both of these types of assessment are presented next.

Maze A measure of reading comprehension that requires the student to supply a missing word in a passage.

Oral Reading Fluency Measure   For this measure, you will select three passages to be used to determine the baseline data for each student. For the repeated measures for the school year, you will need two passages per week. For example, if the instructional period is 25 weeks, you will need 50 passages plus the 3 passages for the baseline data. Select a total of 53 passages for oral reading fluency measures for each student reading at that grade level. It is important that the students not be exposed to these passages until the passages are used for the measurement. These passages can be taken from the basal reader or other books of the same readability level. If you are not certain of the readability level, the passage may be typed into a word processing program, such as Microsoft Word, that contains a readability calculator. Other methods for determining readability may also be used, such as the readability formulas found in reading textbooks. Research by Hintze and Christ (2004) supports closely controlling readability level for increased reliability of the reading measures. In their study, controlled readability was defined by carefully selecting passages that represented the middle 5 months of the grade-level readability level. This means that all passages for the third grade, for example, ranged from 3.3 to 3.7 in readability level.

For each passage used there will be one copy for the teacher and one for the student. The teacher's copy will have a cumlative sum of the number of words for each line. See Figure 6.1 for an example of a teacher passage. As the student reads each passage orally for the period of 1 minute, errors are scored on the teacher's copy and the number of words read correctly are totaled. The types of errors recorded are presented in Table 6.2.

baseline score The beginning score against which student progress is measured.

In order to determine the student's **baseline score**, the student reads three passages orally. The teacher notes the errors and sums the correct words. The scores for the three passages can be averaged for a baseline score or the median score can be selected as the baseline score. Because the data include only three scores, taking the median score may be more representative of the student's current oral reading ability.

The literature includes expected levels of progress for the tasks of oral reading fluency, spelling, written language, and mathematics operations (Deno, Fuchs, Marston, & Shin, 2001; Fuchs, Fuchs, & Hamlett, 1993). The expectations for reading are presented in Table 6.3.

aimline The goal line against which progress is measured in curriculum-based measurement.

Once the baseline number has been determined, the teacher can estimate the goal or number of words expected to be read by the end of the year and then plot an **aimline** to monitor progress. For example, a second-grade student who obtains a baseline of 55 correctly read words per minute can be expected to increase oral reading by approximately 38 words by the end of the year. This would result in a total of 93 correctly read words per minute. This is calculated in the following manner:

Baseline = 55

Weekly increase in number of words expected for 2nd grade = 1.5 per week

Figure 6.1 Example of teacher's passage of a CBM for oral reading fluency.

CBM #4/Grade 1

Student:	Teacher:	
School:	Date:	
Grade:	Examiner:	
# attempted	# of errors	# read correctly

Instructions

You are going to read this story title <u>Taking Pictures</u> out loud. This story is about when Fox has his picture taken with different friends (place the reading passage in front of the student, face down). Try to read each word. You can use your finger to keep your place. If you come to a word you don't know, I'll tell it to you. You will read for one minute. Be sure to do your best reading. Do you have any questions? (Turn the passage right side up.) Put your finger on the first word. Begin.

Taking Pictures

On Monday Fox and <u>Millie</u> went to the fair.	7
"Let's have our picture taken," said Fox.	14
"Oh, yes, let's do," said <u>Millie</u>.	19
"Click," went the camera. And out came the pictures.	28
"Sweet," said <u>Millie</u>.	30
"One for you and one for me," said Fox.	39
On Tuesday Fox and <u>Rose</u> went to the fair.	46
"How about some pictures?" said Fox.	52
"Tee-hee," said <u>Rose</u>.	55
"Click," went the camera and out came the pictures.	64
"Tee-hee," said <u>Rose</u>.	67
"I'll keep mine always," said Fox.	73
On Wednesday Fox and <u>Lola</u> went to the fair.	80
"I don't have a picture of us," said Fox.	89
"Follow me," said <u>Lola</u>.	92
"Click," went the camera. And out came the pictures.	101
"What fun!" said Lola. "I'll carry mine everywhere."	108
"Me too," said Fox.	112

Source: Project AIM Staff, University of Maryland, 1999–2000 which was funded by the Department of Education, Office of Special Education. Deborah Speece, Lisa Pericola Case, and Dawn Eddy Molloy, Principle Investigators. Available from http://www.glue.umd.edu/%7Edlspeece/cbmreading/examinermat/grade1/pass4.pdf.

Number of weeks of instruction following baseline period = 25

$$1.5 \times 25 = 38 + 55 = 93$$

In order to plot the aimline, the teacher would begin at the baseline score (55 words) and draw a line to the goal (93 words), as shown in Figure 6.2. To monitor the instruction, the data are plotted two

Table 6.2 Oral reading errors for CBMs.

Type of Error	Example of Passage Text	Actual Student Response
Teacher-supplied word	The girl swam in the race.	The girl. . .in the race (teacher supplies "swam").
Student passes on word	The girl swam in the race.	The girl. . .pass, in the race.
Student mispronounces word	The girl swam in the race.	The girl swarm in the race.
Student omits word	The girl swam in the race.	The swam in the race.
Student reads words out of order	The girl swam in the race.	The girl swam the in race.
Student substitutes a word	The girl swam in the race.	The girl swam in the pool.

Source: Adapted from "Curriculum-based measurement for reading progress" by Scott, V. G., & Weishaar, M. K. (2003), *Intervention in School and Clinic, 38*(3), 153–159.

Table 6.3 Weekly growth rates for reading.

Grade	Realistic Growth Rate	Special Education Students	General Education Students	Ambitious Growth Rates
1	2 words	.83 word	1.8 words	3 words
2	1.5 words	.57 word	1.66 words	2 words
3	1 word	.58 word	1.18 words	1.5 words
4	.85 word	.58 word	1.01 words	1.1 words
5	.5 word	.58 word	.58 word	.8 word
6	.3 word	.62 word	.66 word	.65 word

Source: Copyright (as applicable) by the National Association of School Psychologists, Bethesda, MD. Reprinted with permission of the publisher. www.nasponline.org.

Figure 6.2 Oral reading fluency goal.

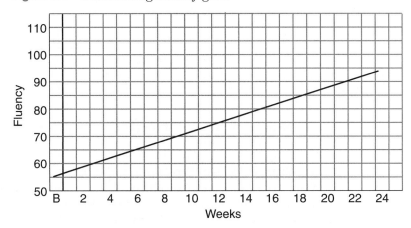

Figure 6.3 Curriculum-based measurement data for two interventions used with one student.

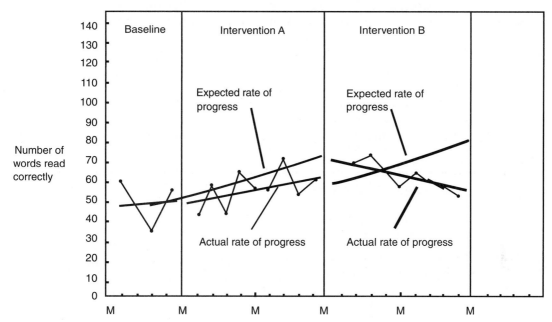

Source: Copyright (as applicable) by the National Association of School Psychologists, Bethesda, MD. Reprinted with permission of the publisher. www.nasponline.org.

times per week. When a student falls below the aimline for three consecutive measures, the instruction should be adjusted. When the student excels above the aimline for three consecutive measures, the instruction should be made more challenging.

Figure 6.3 presents an example of how curriculum-based measurement is used to determine when an instructional change is indicated. The student in Figure 6.3 failed to make the projected progress and therefore needs an educational change to progress within the curriculum.

Maze Reading Method One global measure of general reading ability is the Maze task. To construct CBMs to assess this aspect of reading ability, select passages in a manner similar to the oral reading passages. These passages must be passages new to the student, however, and they should represent the student's reading grade level. The first sentence in each passage is presented exactly as it is printed in the grade-level textbook. Following the first sentence, you delete one word from the next sentence and insert a blank. The student will have three word choices for each blank from which to select the correct word based on the meaning of the text. To complete the construction of these passage probes, you delete each *n*th word. For example, in the second sentence you delete the sixth word and every sixth word thereafter. In order to make certain that the task adequately assesses the comprehension aspect of reading, Fuchs and Fuchs (1992) used the following criteria to select distracters for the items. The distracters should not

> make contextual sense;
> rhyme with the correct choice;
> sound or look like the correct choice;
> be a nonsense word;
> require the student to read ahead to eliminate;
> be too high in vocabulary.

In addition, the distracters should be of approximately the same length as the correct word.

CAUTION ABOUT USING EXPECTED GROWTH RATES IN READING

In a study of more than 6,000 students, Silberglitt and Hintze (2007) found that not all student performance was consistent with expected growth rates when using averages of aggregated data. The results of this study suggest that teachers should employ other methods when establishing goals or aimlines that might be more representative of an individual student's ability to respond to interventions in reading. For example, these researchers suggested that the goal can be set using expected growth rates for the student's decile group (such as students who are ranked within the lowest decile group be compared with the expected growth rate of that decile group). Another alternative suggestion was for the teacher to establish a criterion-referenced goal rather than comparing students to the average of the aggregated data. These researchers state that adapting the expected goal for students based on where they are within the group (rather than comparing the students with the average of the group) may offer a method of monitoring progress effectively without the need for interventions to be provided through special education services. This method appears to be a more fair way to measure progress following interventions in reading for students who may be within the lower achievement group; however, they do not fall within the group of students who require special education services.

Constructing CBMs for Spelling   To assess spelling ability, both the number of correct letter sequences and the number of correctly spelled words can be plotted. The measures are constructed from grade-level spelling words and should include approximately 12 words for grades 1–3 and 18 words for grades 4–8 (Shinn, 1989). In order to score correct letter sequences, a point is given for each

Check Your Understanding

Determine a baseline reading score and the aimline for a first-grade student by completing Activity 6.2 below.

Activity 6.2

Determine the baseline and the aimline for this first-grade student.

1. A first-grade teacher asked each student to read 3 passages aloud. Matt's scores were:

   10, 15, 13

   What is the baseline score? _____

2. Following the determination of the baseline score, the aimline should be determined. Refer to Table 6.3 in your text to determine the number of words a first-grade student is expected to increase each week. If there are 27 weeks remaining in the academic year, what is the goal? Draw the aimline.

3. What should teachers remember when establishing goals in reading using expected growth rates? _____

two letters that are in the correct sequence. For the correct beginning and ending letters, 1 point is given for each. For example, the number of correct letter sequences for the correctly spelled word *time* is 5. One point is scored for the *t*, one point for the correct sequence of *ti*, another point for *im*, another for *me*, and another for the correct ending letter of *e*.

For spelling, a baseline is taken in the same manner as for reading fluency and the aimline is plotted in the same manner, based on the weekly number of correct letter sequences expected. For the expected growth rate, see Table 6.4. An example of a CBM spelling measure is presented in Figure 6.4.

Constructing CBMs for Mathematics For a math CBM, the problems should be operational (addition, subtraction, multiplication, division). The two-minute math probes should be constructed of at least 25 math problems each (Fuchs & Fuchs, 1991). Select or generate 25 grade-level computational problems per probe and construct three math sheets or probes for the baseline score and two probes for each week during the academic period. Students

Table 6.4 Expected weekly growth rates for spelling: Correct letter sequences.

Grade	Realistic Growth Rate	Ambitious Growth Rate
2	1 letter sequence	1.5 letter sequences
3	.65 letter sequence	1 letter sequence
4	.45 letter sequence	.85 letter sequence
5	.3 letter sequence	.65 letter sequence
6	.3 letter sequence	.65 letter sequence

Source: Copyright (as applicable) by the National Association of School Psychologists, Bethesda, MD. Reprinted with permission of the publisher. www.nasponline.org.

Figure 6.4 Analysis of a spelling test.

complete as many problems as they can for the two-minute period. The teacher then counts the number of correct digits and plots the number on the student's graph. The weekly expected rate of growth for math is presented in Table 6.5.

REVIEW OF RESEARCH ON CURRICULUM-BASED MEASUREMENT

Curriculum-based measurement of progress has been found to noticeably affect academic achievement when the results are used to modify instructional planning. A brief review of many years of research studies supports the use of curriculum-based measurement, for several reasons.

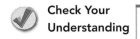

Check Your Understanding

Determine a baseline spelling score and the aimline for a second-grade student by completing Activity 6.3 below.

Activity 6.3

1. Look at the student's performance on the following CBM in spelling. Determine the correct letter sequence score. If you convert this to the percentage of letter sequences correct, what is the percent? What is the spelling score on the test based simply on the number of words spelled correctly?

Word	Student's Spelling of Word
bat	bat
cat	cat
sat	sat
fat	fat
look	lok
book	book
took	took
cook	cook
seek	seek
meek	mek

2. The other two scores obtained to determine the baseline were 40 and 44. What is the baseline score? _____

3. Refer to Table 6.4 in your text. For a realistic growth rate, how many correct letter sequences is the student expected to increase each week in the 2nd grade? _____

4. There are 25 weeks remaining in the school year. What is the goal for this student? _____

5. Construct the aimline.

Table 6.5   Expected weekly growth rates for math: Number of correct digits.

Grade	Realistic Growth Rate	Ambitious Growth Rate
1	.3 correct digit	.5 correct digit
2	.3 correct digit	.5 correct digit
3	.3 correct digit	.5 correct digit
4	.70 correct digit	1.15 correct digits
5	.75 correct digit	1.20 correct digits
6	.45 correct digit	1 correct digit

Source: Copyright (as applicable) by the National Association of School Psychologists, Bethesda, MD. Reprinted with permission of the publisher. www.nasponline.org.

When curriculum-based measurement was used for instructional programming, students were found to have somewhat greater gains than when it was used for testing purposes alone (Fuchs, Fuchs, & Hamlett, 1989). The more effective teachers were sensitive to the results of the assessment and used them to adapt or modify instruction rather than merely using curriculum-based measurement as a measurement device, such as grading or establishing a working level for IEP objectives.

The use of curriculum-based measurement has been linked to better understanding, by students, of the expectancies of their academic performance (Fuchs, Butterworth, & Fuchs, 1989). Students in this study indicated that they received more feedback than students not receiving curriculum-based measurement. Research has also indicated that teachers using curriculum-based measurement tended to set goals with higher expectations than did teachers who were not using these methods (Fuchs et al., 1989). Use of curriculum-based measurement along with providing instructional intervention strategies to general education teachers were promising in increasing the achievement of low-achieving students and students in general education classes with learning disabilities (Fuchs, Fuchs, Hamlett, Phillips, & Bentz, 1994). One study applied curriculum-based measurement in the general education classroom as part of a functional behavioral analysis (Roberts, Marshall, Nelson, & Albers, 2001). In this study, the use of curriculum-based measurement to determine appropriate instructional levels resulted in decreased off-task behaviors. When applied in this manner, curriculum-based measurement allowed instruction to be tailored; it may therefore be viewed as a prereferral strategy.

Curriculum-based measurement has been found effective for use in universal screening of students for early reading acquisition skills (Ardoin, Witt, Suldo, Connell, Koenig, Restar, Slider, & Williams, 2004; Marchand-Martella, Ruby, & Martella, 2007). In this study, the use of one reading probe was found to be sufficient for predicting overall reading achievement. Another study by Clarke and Shinn (2004) found that math CBMs for early math skills were reliable when used with first-grade students to identify students who may be at risk in mathematics. In a review of the use of CBMs in mathematics, Foegen, Jiban, and Deno (2007) found that there was adequate evidence for use of CBMs in the elementary grades for monitoring the acquisition of problem-solving and basic math facts. CBMs have also been found to predict future performance of students on high-stakes state achievement assessment (McGlinchey & Hixson, 2004).

In a study of curriculum-based measurement as one method of determining special education eligibility (Marston, Mirkin, & Deno, 1984), it was found to be an accurate screening measure for referral for special education and was less influenced by teacher variables.

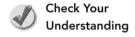

Check Your Understanding

Determine a baseline math score and the aimline for a first-grade student by completing Activity 6.4 below.

Activity 6.4

1. A student was administered 3 math probes to determine the baseline score. Based on the scores below, what is the baseline score?
   _____
   17, 14, 16

2. Refer to Table 6.5 to determine the realistic expected growth rate for a first-grade student. There are 28 weeks remaining in the academic year. Determine the goal for this student. _____

3. Construct the aimline.

Its use appeared to result in less bias, as evidenced by more equity in the male–female ratio of referrals (Marston et al., 1984). Canter (1991) supported using curriculum-based measurement to determine eligibility for special education services by comparing the student's progress in the classroom curriculum to the expectations within the average range for the grade level. The student's actual progress may indicate the need for special education intervention.

Curriculum-based measurement has been found useful when the school employs a problem-solving model as the process for interventions (Deno, 1995; Marston, Muyskens, Lau, & Canter, 2003; Shinn, 2002). For this reason, CBM naturally fits within the Contemporary Assessment Model and is consistent with the movement for assessing learning difficulties by employing response-to-intervention strategies.

Curriculum-based measurement has been studied as a possible method of identifying students in special education placements who are ready to move back into the general education setting (Shinn, Habedank, Rodden-Nord, & Knutson, 1993). Using this method may help general education teachers smoothly integrate students from special education environments by providing data to assess progress and use in planning interventions. One study has also suggested that curriculum-based measures might be beneficial in measuring the effects of medication on students with attention disorders (Stoner, Carey, Ikeda, & Shinn, 1994). In this study, Stoner and colleagues (1994) replicated another study and found evidence suggesting that CBM may be one measure of determining the effect of methylphenidate on academic performance. Additional research in this area may add insight to the emerging field of effective treatment of students with attention deficit disorder.

One study found that when CBM was combined with peer tutoring, students in a general classroom setting made significantly greater achievement gains (Phillips, Hamlett, Fuchs, & Fuchs, 1993). Another study found substantial overall gains in reading fluency, although at-risk students did not progress at the same rate as their grade peers (Greenwood, Tapia, Abbott, & Walton, 2003). Meherns and Clarizio (1993) assert that CBM is helpful in determining when instruction should be adapted, but it does not necessarily provide information about what to change or how to provide the instruction. They advocate using CBM with other diagnostic assessment.

Baker and Good (1995) found that CBM used in assessing reading was as reliable and valid when used with bilingual students as when used with English-only students. They also found that CBM was a sensitive measurement of the reading progress made by bilingual students. Kamps et al. (2007) found that the use of progress monitoring of intensive interventions for students who are English-language learners offers effective tier two interventions. This study suggested that these methods were as effective with ELL students as they were with English-only students. Haager (2007) had inconsistent results when using RTI with ELL students and suggested that students receiving interventions in the first grade may require additional time for reading acquisition skills before they can be expected to meet the reading criteria set for the second grade.

performance assessment Assessment that requires the student to create an answer or product to demonstrate knowledge.

In their sample of fourth-grade students, Fuchs and Fuchs (1996) found that curriculum-based measurement combined with **performance assessment** provides teachers more in-depth assessment, which results in better instructional decisions. Another study found that general education teachers who employed CBM designed better instructional programs and had students who experienced greater gains in achievement than did teachers who did not use CBM (Fuchs et al., 1994). Allinder (1995) found that teachers who used CBM and had high teacher efficacy, set high student goals, and their students had significantly greater growth. In the Allinder study, special education teachers using CBM who had greater teaching efficacy set more goals for their students.

Teachers who were asked to compare CBM with norm-referenced assessments rated CBM as a more acceptable method of assessment (Eckert, Shapiro, & Lutz, 1995). Another study suggested that students enjoy participating in CBM and that their active participation in this process may increase their feelings of responsibility for learning (Davis, Fuchs, Fuchs, & Whinnery, 1995).

CAUTIONS

Several researchers have issued statements of caution about employing curriculum-based measurement. Like other types of assessment, curriculum-based measurement may be more useful in some situations and less useful in others. Heshusius (1991) cautions that curriculum-based assessment may not allow for measurement of some important constructs in education, such as creativity, areas of interest, and original ideas. Hintze, Shapiro, and Lutz (1994) found that CBM was more sensitive in measuring progress when used with traditional basal readers rather than literature samples, indicating that the materials contribute to difficulty in accurate measurement. Meherns and Clarizio (1993) suggest that CBM should be used as part of comprehensive assessment with other measures because of continuing concerns about the reliability and validity of CBM. Silberglitt and Hintze (2007) caution against using average aggregated growth rate expectations to establish reading goals.

When using data from CBMs to make educational decisions, teachers should keep in mind that time of day, presentation format of instruction, and other conditions should be considered (Parette, Peterson-Karlan, Wojcok, & Bardi, 2007). Stecker (2007) reminds educators that there are many variables of student performance and success that are not measured within CBMs, and that these variables, such as environment and family concerns, should be considered when using CBMs in the decision-making process.

 **Check Your Understanding**

To review your understanding of the CBM literature, complete Activity 6.5 below.

Activity 6.5

Answer the following questions about curriculum-based assessment.

1. What did students report about using CBMs in classroom instruction according to Fuchs, Butterworth, and Fuchs? _____

2. One study reported the decrease in off-task behaviors when CBMs were employed. Why would this impact behavior? _____

3. One study by Marston, Mirkin, and Deno found that the use of CBMs was an effective measure to be used in the special education eligibility process. Why? _____

4. What did Baker and Good find in their research using CBMs with bilingual students? _____

CRITERION-REFERENCED ASSESSMENT

criterion-referenced tests Tests designed to accompany and measure a set of criteria or skill-mastery criteria.

Criterion-referenced tests compare the performance of a student to a given criterion. This criterion can be an established objective within the curriculum, an IEP criterion, or a criterion or standard of a published test instrument. The instrument designed to assess the student's ability to master the criterion is composed of many items across a very narrow band of skills. For example, a criterion-referenced test may be designed to assess a student's ability to read passages from the fifth-grade-level reading series and answer comprehension questions with 85% accuracy. For this student, the criterion is an IEP objective. The assessment is made up of several passages and subsequent comprehension questions for each passage, all at the fifth-grade reading level. No other curriculum materials or content items are included. The purpose is to determine if the student can answer the comprehension questions with 85% accuracy. Criterion-related assessment that uses curriculum materials is only one type of curriculum-based assessment.

Although many criterion-referenced instruments are nonstandardized or perhaps designed by the teacher, a few criterion-referenced instruments are standardized. Some norm-referenced instruments yield criterion-related objectives or the possibility of adding criterion-related objectives with little difficulty. Examples of these instruments are the KeyMath–Revised (Connolly, 1988), K-TEA–II (Kaufman & Kaufman, 2004), and the WRMT–R (Woodcock, 1987). (See Chapter 5 for norm-referenced tests.)

Adapting standardized norm-referenced instruments to represent criterion-referenced testing is accomplished by writing educational objectives for the skills tested. To be certain that the skill or task has been adequately sampled, however, the educator may need to prepare additional academic *probes* to measure the student's skills. Objectives may represent long-term learning goals rather than short-term gains, determined by the amount of the material or the scope of the task tested by the norm-referenced test. Figure 6.5 illustrates how an item from the WRMT–R might be expanded to represent criterion-referenced testing.

In addition to adapting published norm-referenced instruments for criterion-related assessment, educators may use published criterion-referenced test batteries, such as the Brigance Inventories, that present specific criteria and objectives. Teachers may also create their own criterion-referenced tests.

THE BRIGANCE INVENTORIES

The Brigance Inventories (Brigance, 2004, 1999, 1977, 1981, 1991) are a standardized assessment system that provides criterion-referenced assessment at various skill levels. Norms are available

Figure 6.5 Examples of criterion-referenced testing.

Items missed	On the Word Attack subtest: the long a–e pattern in nonsense words—*gaked, straced;* the long i–e pattern in nonsense word—*quiles*
Deficit-skill	Decoding words with the long vowel-consonant-silent-*e* pattern
Probe	Decoding words orally to teacher: *cake, make, snake, rake, rate, lake, fake, like, bike, kite*
Criterion	Decode 10/10 words for mastery. Decode 8/10 words to 6/10 words for instructional level. Decode 5/10 words or fewer for failure level; assess pre - requisite skill level: discrimination of long/short vowels (vowels: *a, i*).

for some levels of the Brigance (Glascoe, 1999, 2004). Each battery contains numerous subtests, and each item is referenced by objectives that may be used in developing IEPs. The Brigance system includes three criterion-referenced instruments for the various age groups served in special education. These instruments include the Brigance Diagnostic Inventory of Early Development, the Brigance Diagnostic Comprehensive Inventory of Basic Skills–Revised, and the Brigance Diagnostic Inventory of Essential Skills. In each system, the educator should select only the areas and items of interest that identify specific strengths and weaknesses.

In addition to the three criterion-referenced instruments for the assessment of skills, a Brigance Diagnostic Life Skills Inventory and a Brigance Diagnostic Employability Skills Inventory are also available for secondary students in special education and vocational education programs. The Basic Skills Inventory is available in English and Spanish. The Brigance instruments should not be administered in their entirety.

Instruments   The Brigance Diagnostic Inventory of Early Development–Second Edition (Brigance, 2004) is an inventory within the system that was designed to assess the skills and development of children from birth to age 6 years and 11 months. Many of the subtests concern developmental areas of motor development. This test provides criterion-related measurement for self-help skills, prespeech and speech development, general knowledge, social and emotional development, reading readiness, manuscript writing, and beginning math. This instrument may be used along with additional data to support decisions regarding educational programming decisions as well as instructional decisions for the student's individual education program (IEP). This instrument has been norm-referenced, and raw scores can be

Patrick White/Merrill

converted to developmental scores (age equivalents), percentile ranks, and standard scores (Glascoe, 2004).

The Comprehensive Inventory of Basic-Skills–Revised is designed for use with elementary-aged students (Brigance, 1999). Table 6.6 presents the list of skills assessed on this inventory. A set of specific skills is listed within each of the skill areas assessed. The

Table 6.6   Skills assessed on the Brigance Diagnostic Comprehensive Inventory of Basic Skills–Revised.

Readiness	Math
Speech	Numbers
Listening	Number facts
Word recognition	Computation of whole numbers
Oral reading	Fractions and mixed numbers
Reading comprehension	Decimals
Word analysis	Percents
Functional word recognition	Time
Spelling	Money
Writing	U.S. customary measurement
Reference skills	Metrics
Graphs and maps	

Table 6.7 Functional word recognition.

Alphabetical Listing of Basic Sight Vocabulary	Assessments for Basic Skills
H-1 o	Basic Sight Vocabulary
H-2 o	Direction Words
H-3 o	Number words
❖H-4 o	Warning and Safety Signs
H-5 o	Informational Signs
H-6 o	Warning Labels
H-7 o	Food Labels
Supplemental and Related Lists/Skill Sequences	
H-1Sa	Contractions
H-1Sb	Abbreviations
H-2Sa	Direction Words for Writing Activities
H-2Sb	Direction Words for Speaking Activities
H-2Sc	Direction Words for Study Activities
H-2Sd	Direction Words for Physical Activities
H-4S	Warning and Safety Signs
H-5S	Informational Signs
H-6S	Warning Labels
H-7S	Labels on Packaged Foods

Source: Brigance Diagnostic Comprehensive Inventory of Basic Skills-Revised. (1999). A. H. Brigance. Curriculum Associates, North Billerica, MA. Reprinted with permission.

specific skills for the area of functional word recognition are presented in Table 6.7. A sample of one skill assessed, informational signs (H-5), is presented in Figure 6.6. Selected subtests have been norm-referenced, and developmental scores, percentiles, and standard scores exist for those specific subtests.

The Brigance system comprises large, multiple-ring notebook binders that contain both student and examiner pages. The pages may be turned to resemble an easel format, or the pages to be administered may be removed from the binder. A warning included in the test cautions the examiner to select the necessary subtests and avoid overtesting.

TEACHER-MADE CRITERION-REFERENCED TESTS

Instead of relying on published instruments, classroom teachers may develop their own criterion-referenced tests. This type of

Figure 6.6   Brigance Diagnostic Inventory of Basic Skills examiner page.

SKILL: Reads informational signs.

STUDENT RECORD BOOK: Page 23.

CLASS RECORD BOOK: Page 25.

ASSESSMENT METHOD: Individual oral response.

MATERIALS: S-240, S-241, and S-242.

DISCONTINUE: Your discretion, or after three consecutive errors.

TIME: Your discretion, or see **INDIVIDUALIZING THE TIME LIMIT**, on page 226.

ACCURACY: Give credit for each correct response.

NOTES: (See **NOTES** on pages 240–41.)

STUDENT-PAGE FORMAT FOR S-242

DIRECTIONS

This assessment is made by asking the student to read aloud the informational signs on S-240 through S-242.

Point to the informational signs on S-242, and

Say: **These are words we often see on signs. Look at each word carefully and read it aloud. Begin here.** Point to the word with which you want the student to begin.

If the student mispronounces a word,

Say: **Try it again.** Point to the word.

OBJECTIVE

By _____(date)_____, when shown a list of fifty-eight informational signs, (student's name) will read (quantity) of the signs.

41. **Ticket Office**	46. KEEP TO RIGHT	51. *THIS WAY OUT*	56. WILL RETURN AT 1:00 P.M.
42. U.S. MAIL	47. *LOST and FOUND*	52. **Please Pay When Served**	57. NO PERSON UNDER 18 YEARS OF AGE ALLOWED
43. **Waiting Room**	48. **OPEN COME IN**	53. HELP KEEP OUR PARK CLEAN	
44. WALK IN	49. Ring for Service	54. Not for Deposit of MAIL	58. *ADMISSION* Adults...................$6.00 Children 5–14 ....$4.00 Children UNDER 5 ..Free
45. HANDLE WITH CARE	50. **THIS SIDE UP**	55. PLEASE WAIT TO BE SEATED	

Source: Brigance Diagnostic Comprehensive Inventory of Basic Skills-Revised. (1999). A. H. Brigance. Curriculum Associates, North Billerica, MA. Reprinted with permission.

assessment allows the teacher to directly link the assessment to the currently used curriculum. By writing the criterion to be used as the basis for determining when the student has reached or passed the objective, the teacher has created a criterion-referenced test. When the test is linked directly to the curriculum, it also becomes a curriculum-based assessment device and may be referred to as **direct measurement**. For example, the teacher may use the scope and sequence chart from the reading series or math text to write the objectives that will be used in the criterion-related assessment.

direct measurement Measuring progress by using the same instructional materials or tasks that are used in the classroom.

Research supports the use of criterion-referenced assessment in the classroom and other settings (Glaser, 1963; Hart & Scuitto, 1996; McCauley, 1996). The first questions regarding the use of criterion-referenced assessment were raised in the literature in 1963 by Glaser. The issues Glaser raised seemed to be current issues in the debate about better measurement techniques to accurately determine student progress. Glaser stated that the knowledge educators attempt to provide to students exists on a continuum ranging from no acquisition to mastery. He stated that the criterion can be established at any level where the teacher wishes to assess the student's mastery or acquisition. This type of measurement is used to determine the student's position along the continuum of acquisition or mastery.

Hart and Scuitto (1996) concluded that using criterion-referenced assessment is practical, has social validity, and may assist with educational accountability. This type of assessment can be adapted to other areas, such as a child's speech and language development (McCauley, 1996). Criterion-referenced assessment has been shown to be useful in screening entering kindergarten and first-grade students for school readiness (Campbell, Schellinger, & Beer, 1991) and has also been used to determine appropriate adaptations for vocational assessments to assist in planning realistic job accommodations (Lusting & Saura, 1996). In a review of criterion-referenced assessment during the past 30 years, Millman (1994) concluded that to represent a true understanding of the student's ability, this type of assessment requires "item density." He suggests that to accurately assess whether a student has mastered a domain or area, the assessments need to have many items per domain. Teachers who construct their own criterion-referenced assessments should be certain that enough items are required of the student that they can determine accurately the level of mastery of the domain.

One difficulty that teachers may have in constructing criterion-referenced tests is establishing the exact criterion for whether the student has passed the objective or criterion. Shapiro (1989) suggested that one quantitative method of determining mastery would be to use a normative comparison of the performance, such as using a specific task that 80% of the peers in the class or grade have mastered. The teacher may wish to use a criterion that is associated with a standard set by the school grading policy. For example, answering 75% of the items correctly might indicate that the student needs improvement; 85% correct might be an average performance; and 95% correct might represent mastery. Or, the teacher might decide to use a criterion that the student can easily understand and chart. For example, getting 5 out of 7 items correct indicates the student could continue with the same objective or skill; getting 7 out of 7 items correct indicates the student is ready to move up to the next skill level. Often, the teacher sets the criterion using logical reasoning rather than a quantitative measurement (Shapiro, 1989).

Evans and Evans (1986) have suggested other considerations for establishing criteria for mastery:

> Does passing the test mean that the student is proficient and will maintain the skills?
>> Is the student ready to progress to the next level in the curriculum?
>> Will the student be able to generalize and apply the skills outside the classroom?
>> Would the student pass the mastery test if it were given at a later date? (p. 10)

The teacher may wish to use the following measures for criterion-referenced tests:

More than 95% = mastery of objective
90 to 95% = instructional level
76 to 89% = difficult level
Less than 76% = failure level

Similar standards may be set by the individual teacher, who may wish to adjust objectives when the student performs with 76 to 89% accuracy and when the student performs with more than 95% accuracy. It is important to remember that students with learning difficulties should experience a high ratio of success during instruction to increase the possibility of positive reinforcement during the learning process. Therefore, it may be better to design objectives that promote higher success rates. Figure 6.7 illustrates a criterion-referenced test written by a teacher for addition facts with sums of 10 or less. The objective, or criterion, is included at the top of the test.

Using criterion-referenced assessment may provide better information about student achievement levels and mastery of academic objectives; however, the criterion-referenced test may not always adequately represent growth within a given curriculum. To more effectively measure student progress within a curriculum, teachers should rely on measures that use that curriculum, such as curriculum-based assessment and direct measurement.

Figure 6.7   Teacher-made criterion-referenced test.

OBJECTIVE

John will correctly answer 9 out of 10 addition problems with sums of 10 or less.

5	3	8	9	4	6	7	2	4	1
+2	+2	+2	+1	+5	+2	+3	+4	+3	+6

Performance: _____

Objective passed: _____   Continue on current objective: _____

Check Your Understanding

subskill A small part of a skill, used in task analysis.

In Activity 6.6, you will determine whether the student responses illustrated indicate mastery of the **subskill** assessed by the *Basic Skills* test. Complete Activity 6.6 below.

Activity 6.6

1. Look at the student responses on the following teacher-made criterion-referenced test. Determine if the student met the criterion stated as the objective.

   Objective

   John will correctly answer 9 out of 10 addition problems with sums of 10 or less.

5	3	8	9	4	6	7	2	4	1
+2	+2	+2	+1	+5	+2	+3	+4	+3	+6
7	5	10	10	8	4	10	6	7	7

2. Can you describe the types of errors that John made?

   _____

Apply Your Knowledge

Using the suggested mastery level, instructional level, difficulty level, and failure level provided in your text, where does this student fall on this particular skill according to this criterion-referenced test?

_____

_____

_____

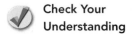

Check Your Understanding

The skills included in Activity 6.7 resemble those that would be included at the beginning level of a reading series. In this activity, you will select the information from one skill to write an objective and construct a short criterion-referenced test. The test should measure the student's mastery of the objective. Complete Activity 6.7 below.

Activity 6.7

Read the following list of skills necessary to complete level P1 of the Best in the Country Reading Series, adopted by all school systems in the country. Answer the questions that follow.

P1 Skills

- Associates pictures with story content.
- Follows sequence of story by turning pages at appropriate times.
- Associates the following letters with their sounds: b, d, c, g, h, j, k, l, m, n, p, q, r, s, t.
- Can match letters (from above) to pictures of objects that begin with the same sounds.
- Can correctly sequence the following stories:

  "A School Day": Mary gets on the bus, goes to school. George brings a rabbit to class; the rabbit gets out of the cage. Mary helps George catch the rabbit.

  "The Field Trip": Ralph invites the class to visit his farm. Sue, John, Mary, and George go on the trip. The animals are (a) a chicken, (b) a goat, (c) a cow, and (d) a horse. The goat follows the class; the goat tries to eat Ralph's shirt.

- Can name all characters in preceding stories.
- Can summarize stories and answer short comprehension questions.

Answer the Following

1. Select one P1 skill and write a behaviorally stated objective that includes the criterion acceptable for passing the objective. _____

2. Design a short criterion-referenced test to measure the skill objective written in number 1 of P1-level reading series. _____

Apply Your Knowledge

Write a behaviorally stated objective for students reading this chapter. _____
_____
_____

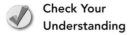 **Check Your Understanding**

Check your ability to complete a task analysis in Ac'

Activity 6.8

Answer the following questions.

1. Look at the following task analysis. Can you identify other sma. steps, or subskills, that should be included? Write the additional steps in the spaces provided.

   Skill: Adding numbers greater than 10

   Adds numbers 0–10 with sums greater than 10.

   Adds number facts 1–9 with sums greater than 10.

   Adds number facts 1–9 with sums less than 10.

   Adds number facts 1–8 with sums less than 10.

   Identifies numbers 1–10.

   Can count objects 1–10.

   Additional subskills: _____

2. Write a task analysis for the following skills.

   Skill: Recognizes initial consonant sounds and their association with the consonant letters of the alphabet.

   Necessary subskills: _____

Apply Your Knowledge

Select one of the subskills and write an idea or strategy for instruction.

_____

_____

_____

TASK ANALYSIS AND ERROR ANALYSIS

task analysis Breaking task down into parts to determine which part is causing difficulty for student.

subtask Small units of a task used to complete a task analysis.

Teachers often use task and error analyses without realizing that an analysis of student progress has been completed. **Task analysis** involves breaking down a task into the smallest steps necessary to complete the task. The steps actually reflect subskills, or **subtask**, which the student must complete before finishing a task. In academic work, many of these subskills and tasks form a hierarchy of skills that build throughout the school years. As students master skills and tasks, they face new, more advanced curricular tasks that depend on the earlier skills. In mathematics, for example, understanding of numerals and one-to-one correspondence must precede understanding of basic addition facts. A student must conquer addition and subtraction before tackling multiplication and division. Therefore, a thorough task analysis of skill deficits, followed by an informal assessment, may provide the teacher with information about what the student has or has not mastered.

Error analysis is an assessment method that a teacher can use with formal, informal, and direct measures, such as classwork. This is a method of discovering patterns of errors. A teacher may notice that a student who understands difficult multiplication facts, such as those of 11s, 12s, and 13s, continues to miss computation problems of those facts. With a careful error analysis of responses on a teacher-made test, the teacher determines that the student has incorrectly lined up the multiplicands. The student understands the math fact but has made a mistake in the mechanics of the operation.

One way that teachers can perform error analyses is to become familiar with the scope and sequence of the classroom curriculum materials. The teacher guides that accompany classroom materials are a good starting place to develop a thorough understanding of the materials and how to perform an error analysis of the students' responses. For example, a basal reading series may provide a sequence chart of the sounds presented in a given book at a specific level. Using this sequence chart, the teacher can first determine which

error analysis Analyzing a student's learning problems by determining error patterns.

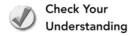

Check Your Understanding

Practice analyzing errors by completing Activity 6.9 below.

Activity 6.9

Look carefully at the student's responses in the following work sample from a language class. Analyze the errors the student made. Write your analysis in the space provided.

> *Items missed*—On a spelling test, the following words were missed by the student: break (spelled brak), dream (spelled dreem), and waist (spelled wast).

1. What is the deficit skill? _____

2. What words might be included in a probe written by the teacher to address this deficit skill? _____

> *Probe*—Decoding words orally to teacher:
> *Criterion*—Decode 10/10 words for mastery
> Decode 9/10 words for instructional level
> Decode 8/10 words or fewer indicates failure level

Apply Your Knowledge

Design a criterion-referenced probe for this skill and select the criterion necessary for mastery of the skill. _____
_____
_____

Check Your Understanding

Check your ability to recall the terms introduced thus far in the chapter by completing Activity 6.10 below.

Activity 6.10

Use the terms discussed in the chapter to complete the following sentences.

1. Using material from the curriculum content in test items is called _____.

2. Using informal assessment composed of actual classwork curriculum materials is called _____.

3. A teacher who adds behavioral objectives following the analysis of test items on a standardized norm-referenced test has adapted the instrument to reflect _____ testing.

4. When a student has not mastered a specific skill, the teacher may wish to test the student more thoroughly on the one skill by developing a _____.

5. When a teacher assesses daily from the curriculum content, the assessment is called _____.

6. Assessing the subskills, or substeps, within a task is referred to as _____.

7. Analyzing the types of errors made on a test or on student work samples is called _____.

8. Teacher-made quizzes, curriculum-based assessment, criterion-referenced assessment, class assignments, and tests are all types of _____ assessment.

Apply Your Knowledge

Why would teachers prefer informal tests for measuring progress rather than commercial tests? _____
_____
_____

errors the student has made and then analyze the possible reason for the errors. Perhaps the student's errors are all errors in words with vowel combinations (such as ea, ie, ee, oa). The teacher can next perform a task analysis of the prerequisite skills the child needs to master those sounds and be able to decode words with those sounds.

Task analysis is a breaking down of the actual task or response expected to determine which prerequisite skills are lacking or have not been mastered. Error analysis often precedes task analysis because the teacher may need to look for a pattern of errors to determine exactly which task needs additional analysis.

TEACHER-MADE TESTS

Many of the types of informal assessment described in this chapter are measures that can be designed by teachers. A study by Marso and Pigge (1991) found that teachers made several types of errors in test construction and tended to test items only at the knowledge level. This study also found that the number of years of experience teaching did not make a significant difference in the number and type of errors made in test construction. The types of items developed by teachers in this study included short response, matching, completion, true-false, and multiple choice, with essay items used infrequently. In constructing tests, these teachers made the most errors in matching items, followed by completion, essay, and true-false. Teachers may write test items using different levels of learning, although many teachers use items at the knowledge level because they are easier to write. Such items require the student to merely recall, recognize, or match the material. Higher-order thinking skills are needed to assess a student's ability to sequence, apply information, analyze, synthesize, infer, or deduct. These items may be more difficult and time-consuming to construct.

Case Study for Teacher-Made Tests

Mr. Smithers was a first-year teacher of fourth-grade-level students. One of the tasks he had difficulty with was constructing tests. He had several commercially produced tests for many of the books he was using with his students, but he often taught additional material and wanted to write his own items. He noticed that when he constructed his own tests, students almost always made very high grades. Although this was exciting for the students, he was not certain that he was accurately measuring their ability.

Mr. Smithers decided to ask his mentor teacher, Mrs. Roberts, to assist him. He showed Mrs. Roberts some examples of the items he had written to assess the student's understanding of the concept of division.

1. $4 \div 2 =$
2. $8 \div 2 =$
3. $6 \div 2 =$

Mrs. Roberts pointed out that the items were assessing the basic division facts that students in the fourth grade would be able to learn by simple rote memory. In other words, this was at the simple skill level rather than at the conceptual level. Mrs. Roberts suggested that Mr. Smithers look over the scope-and-sequence chart in the curriculum guide to determine the range of possible concepts in the fourth-grade math curriculum. She noted that Mr. Smithers might want to design some of his problems to assess more critical or higher-level thinking and problem solving. She also encouraged him to try to write some story or word problems to determine if his students knew when the process of division would be used rather than other operations such as addition or subtraction.

Mr. Smithers returned to his classroom and constructed the following problems to assess the conceptual understanding of division facts.

1. You and four of your friends decide to order two large 10-slice pizzas. You are all hungry and want to be sure everyone gets the same number of slices. How many pieces will each one get?

2. In your art class there are two long tables. Your art teacher tells you that you must all sit around the two tables. Since there are 16 students in the class, how many students will be at each table?

3. Your dog has been sick and your dad took him to the veterinarian. When he returns with your dog, he tells you that the veterinarian gave your dog a pill and said that he needs to take three more pills evenly spaced over the next 12 hours. How often will you need to give your dog a pill?

checklists Lists of academic or behavioral skills that must be mastered by the student.

For **MORE PRACTICE** constructing a teacher-made test, visit the Companion Website at *www.prenhall.com/overton.*

questionnaires Questions about a student's behavior or academic concerns that may be answered by the student or by the parent or teacher.

In addition to being aware of the level of difficulty of test items, teachers must be aware of types of errors made in constructing items, and how the items are associated on a test. Some of the most common types of errors made in Marso and Pigge's study are presented in Figure 6.8.

OTHER INFORMAL METHODS OF ACADEMIC ASSESSMENT

work samples Samples of a student's work; one type of permanent product.

Teachers employ many informal assessment methods to monitor the academic progress of students. Some of these methods combine the techniques of error analysis, task analysis, direct measurement, curriculum-based assessment, probes, and criterion-related assessment. These methods include making **checklists** and **questionnaires** and evaluating student **work samples** and **permanent products**.

permanent products Products made by the student that may be analyzed for academic or behavioral interventions.

Teacher-made checklists may be constructed by following an error analysis, identifying the problem area, and completing a task analysis. For each subskill that is problematic for the student, the teacher may construct a probe or a more in-depth assessment instrument. Probes may appear as short quizzes and may be timed to determine content mastery. For example, a teacher may give 10 subtraction facts for students to complete in 2 minutes. If the teacher

Figure 6.8 Most common test format construction errors.

Matching Items

Columns not titled

"Once, more than once, or not at all" not used in directions to prevent elimination

Response column not ordered

Directions do not specify basis for match

Answering procedures not specified

Elimination due to equal numbers

Columns exceed 10 items

Multiple-Choice Items

Alternatives not in columns or rows

Incomplete stems

Negative words not emphasized or avoided

"All or none of above" not appropriately used

Needless repetitions of alternatives

Presence of specific determiners in alternatives

Verbal associations between alternative and stem

Essay Exercises

Response expectations unclear

Scoring points not realistically limited

Optional questions provided

Restricted question not provided

Ambiguous words used

Opinion or feelings requested

Problem Exercises

Items not sampling understanding of content

No range of easy to difficult problems

Degree of accuracy not requested

Nonindependent items

Use of objective items when calculation preferable

Completion Items

Not complete interrogative sentence

Blanks in statement, "puzzle"

Textbook statements with words left out

More than a single idea or answer called for

Question allows more than a single answer

Requests trivia versus significant data

True-False Items

Required to write response, time waste

Statements contain more than a single idea

Negative statements used

Presence of a specific determiner

Statement is not question, give-away item

Needless phrases present, too lengthy

Interpretive Exercises

Objective response form not used

Can be answered without data present

Errors present in response items

Data presented unclear

Test Format

Absence of directions

Answering procedures unclear

Items not consecutively numbered

Inadequate margins

Answer space not provided

No space between items

Source: Adapted with permission from Ronald Marso and Fred Pigge, 1991, An analysis of teacher-made tests: Item types, cognitive demands, and item construction errors, *Contemporary Educational Psychology, 16,* pp. 284–285. Copyright 1991 by Academic Press.

uses items from the curriculum to develop the probe, the probe will be a curriculum-based assessment. The teacher may also establish a criterion for mastery of each probe or in-depth teacher-made test. This added dimension creates a criterion-referenced assessment device. The criterion may be 9 out of 10 problems added correctly. To effectively monitor the growth of the student, the teacher may set criteria for mastery each day as direct measurement techniques are employed. As the student meets the mastery criterion established for an objective, the teacher checks off the subskill on the checklist and progresses to the next most difficult item on the list of subskills.

Other informal methods that have been designed by teachers include interviews and checklists. These can be used to assess a variety of areas. Wiener (1986) suggested that teachers can construct interviews and questionnaires to assess report writing and test taking. For example, a teacher may wish to find out additional information about how students best can complete assignments such as reports or projects. A questionnaire may be designed to ask about student preferences for

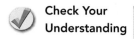

**Check Your
Understanding**

Check your ability to correct errors in the items of a teacher-made test by completing Activity 6.11 below.

Activity 6.11

Use the information presented in Figure 6.8 to determine the errors made in the following examples of teacher-made test items. Write a corrected item for each of the following items.

True-False Items

T F 1. It is not true that curriculum-based assessment can be developed by the classroom teacher.

T F 2. Compared to norm-referenced assessment and other types of assessment used in general and special education to assess the classroom performance of students, curriculum-based assessment may be more sensitive to assessing the current classroom performance of students.

Multiple-Choice Items

1. In the assessment of students to determine the individual needs of learners, what types of assessment may be used?
     a. norm-referenced tests, curriculum-based assessment, teacher-made instruments
     b. norm-referenced instruments, curriculum-based assessment, teacher-made tests, classroom observations, probes
     c. any of the above
     d. only a and b
     e. only a and d
     f. none of the above

2. The results of assessment may assist the team in making an:
     a. goal
     b. IEP
     c. objectives
     d. decision

Apply Your Knowledge

Use the information in Figure 6.8 to write matching test items for the terms: curriculum-based assessment, direct assessment, and teacher-made tests. _____

_____

_____

teacher instructions, previous experiences with these types of tasks, and how assignments should be evaluated. A teacher may want to determine how students plan or think about their projects and what steps they have found useful in the past to complete these tasks.

Interviews and questionnaires can be written to determine students' study habits. These types of questions may include the type of environment the student prefers, what subjects are easier for the student to study independently, and which subjects are more problematic.

Teachers can also gather helpful information by informally reviewing students' work samples—actual samples of work completed by the student. Samples can include daily work, homework, tests, and quizzes. Work samples are one kind of permanent product. Other permanent products evaluated by the teacher include projects, posters, and art.

INFORMAL ASSESSMENT OF READING

Comprehension, decoding, and fluency are the broad areas of reading that teachers assess using informal methods. Comprehension is the ability to derive meaning from written language, whereas decoding is the ability to associate sounds and symbols. Fluency is the rate and ease with which a student reads orally.

Howell and Morehead (1987) presented several methods to informally assess comprehension. For example, students may be asked to answer comprehension questions about the sequence of the story and details of events in the story. Other techniques might include asking the students to paraphrase or tell the story or events in their own words, answering vocabulary items, or completing cloze or maze tasks.

A study by Fuchs and Fuchs (1992) found that the cloze and story retelling methods were not technically adequate and sensitive enough to measure the reading progress of students over time. The Maze method, however, was determined to be useful for monitoring student growth. This seems to suggest that the story retelling and the cloze methods may be best used for diagnostic information or as instructional strategies rather than as a means to monitor progress within a curriculum.

Barnes (1986) suggested using an error analysis approach when listening to students read passages aloud. With this approach, the teacher notes the errors made as the student reads and analyzes the errors to determine whether they change the meaning of the passage. The teacher then notes whether the substituted words look or sound like the original words.

Decoding skills used in reading can also be assessed informally. The teacher may design tests to measure the student's ability to

Orally read isolated letters, blends, syllables, and real words

Orally read nonsense words that contain various combinations of vowel sounds and patterns, consonant blends, and digraphs

Orally read sentences that contain new words. The teacher may sample the reader used by the student to develop a list of words to decode, if one has not been provided by the publisher. A sample may be obtained by selecting every 10th word, selecting every 25th word, or, for higher-level readers, randomly selecting stories from which random words will be taken. Proper nouns and words already mastered by the student may be excluded (e.g., *a*, *the*, *me*, *I*).

Fluency is assessed to determine the reading rate and accuracy of a student using a particular reading selection. Reading fluency will be affected by the student's ability to decode new words and by the student's ability to read phrase by phrase rather than word by word. The teacher may assess oral reading fluency of new material and previously read material. Howell and Morehead (1987) suggested that the teacher listen to the student read a passage, mark the location reached at the end of 1 minute, and then ask the student to read again as quickly as possible. The teacher may note the difference between the two rates as well as errors.

Another assessment device used by teachers to measure reading skills is informal reading inventories, which assess a variety of reading skills. Inventories may be teacher-made instruments that use the actual curriculum used in instruction or commercially

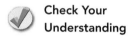

Check Your Understanding

Check your ability to write informal reading items by completing Activity 6.12 below.

Activity 6.12

Use the following passage to design brief informal assessment instruments in the spaces provided.

Elaine sat on the balcony overlooking the mountains. The mountains were very high and appeared blue in color. The trees swayed in the breeze. The valley below was covered by a patch of fog. It was a cool, beautiful fall day.

1. Write an informal test using the cloze method. Remember to leave the first and last sentences intact. _____

2. Write an informal test using the Maze method. Remember to leave three word choices beneath each blank provided for the missing words. _____

3. Select a sentence from the passage and write an informal test using the sentence verification method. Write three sentences, one of which has the same meaning as the original sentence.
_____

Apply Your Knowledge

Which of these methods was easiest for you to write? Why? _____
_____
_____

prepared devices. Commercially prepared instruments contain passages and word lists and diagnostic information that enable the teacher to analyze errors. One such instrument has been designed by Burns and Roe (1989).

Considerations When Using Informal Reading Inventories The cautions about grade levels and curriculum verification stated in the previous section should be considered when using any commercially prepared informal reading inventory. Gillis and Olson (1987) advised teachers and diagnosticians to consider the following guidelines when selecting commercially prepared informal reading inventories:

1. If possible, select inventories that have mostly narrative selections and mostly expository selections for placing elementary students in basal materials.

2. If possible, select inventories in which most of the selections are well organized.

3. When a passage on the form you are using is poorly organized or not of the appropriate text type for your purpose, use a passage at the same level from an alternate form. If an appropriate passage is not available, rewrite a passage from the inventory or write an appropriate passage.

4. When a student's comprehension scores are erratic from level to level, examine the passages to see whether the variability could be due to shifts between types of text or between well and poorly organized passages.

5. Finally, remember that the instructional level you find is just an estimate. Confirm it by observing the student's performance with classroom materials. Adjust placement if necessary. (pp. 36–44)

INFORMAL ASSESSMENT OF MATHEMATICS

The teacher may use curriculum-based assessment to measure all areas of mathematics. The assessment should be combined with both task analysis and error analysis to determine specific problem areas. These problem areas should be further assessed by using probes to determine the specific difficulty. In addition to using these methods, Liedtke (1988) suggested using an interview technique to locate deficits in accuracy and strategies. Liedtke included such techniques as asking the student to create a word problem to illustrate a computation, redirecting the original computation to obtain additional math concept information (e.g., asking the student to compare two of his answers to see which is greater), and asking the student to solve a problem and explain the steps used in the process.

Howell and Morehead (1987) suggested several methods for assessing specific math skills. Their techniques provide assessment of accuracy and fluency of basic facts, recall, basic concepts, operations, problem-solving concepts, content knowledge, tool and unit knowledge, and skill integration.

These authors suggest other techniques for checking recall and handwriting. For example, they suggest asking the student to orally respond to basic operations facts rather than responding in writing. The responses should be scored as correct or incorrect and can then be compared with the established criterion for mastery (such as 90% correct). When a student responds to written tasks such as copying numbers or writing digits, the student's ability to write the digits can be evaluated and compared with the student's oral mastery of math facts. In this way, the teacher may determine if the student's ability to write digits has an impact on responding to written math problems.

INFORMAL ASSESSMENT OF SPELLING

A common type of informal spelling assessment is a spelling test of standard format. The teacher states the word, uses the word in a sentence, and repeats the word. Most elementary spelling texts provide this type of direct curriculum-based assessment. The teacher may wish to assign different words or may be teaching at the secondary level, where typical spelling texts are not used. The teacher may also need to assess the spelling of content-related words in areas such as science or social studies. Or, the teacher may use written samples by the student to analyze spelling errors. One method of analyzing spelling errors, proposed by Guerin and Maier (1983), is shown in Table 6.8.

INFORMAL ASSESSMENT OF WRITTEN LANGUAGE

A student's written language ability may be assessed informally by collecting and analyzing written work samples. Written samples may be analyzed for spelling, punctuation, correct grammar and usage, vocabulary, creative ability, story theme, sequence, and plot. If the objective of instruction is to promote creativity, actual spelling, punctuation, and other mechanical errors should not be scored against the student on the written sample. These errors, however, should be noted by the teacher and used in educational planning for English and spelling lessons. One informal assessment technique for written language skills proposed by Shapiro (1996) includes the following steps:

1. A series of "story starters" should be constructed that can be used to give initial ideas for students to write about. These starters should contain items that most children will find of sufficient interest to generate a written story.

Table 6.8   Analysis of spelling errors used in informal assessment.

	Definitions	Example Heard	Example Written
Phonetic Ability			
PS	Substitutions: placing another sound or syllable in place of the sound in the word	match nation	mach nashun
PO	Omissions: leaving out a sound or syllable from the word	grateful temperature	graful tempature
PA	Additions: adding a sound or syllable to the original	purchase importance	purchasing importantance
PSe	Sequencing: putting sounds or syllables in the wrong order	animal elephant	aminal elelant
Visualization			
VS	Substitutions: substitution of a vowel or consonant for those in the given word	him chapel	hin chaple
VO	Omissions: leaving out a vowel, or consonant, or syllable from those in the given word	allow beginning	alow begining
Phonetic Ability			
VA	Additions: adding a vowel, consonant, or syllable to those in the given word	welcome fragrant	wellcome fragerant
VSe	Sequencing: putting letters or syllables in the wrong order	guardian pilot	guardain pliot
Linguistic Performance			
LS	Substitution: substitution of a word for another having somewhat the same meaning	ring house	bell home
	Substitution: substituting another word because of different language structure (teacher judgment)	came ate	come et
	Substitution: substitution of a completely different word	pear polish	pair collage
LO	Omissions: omitting word endings, prefixes suffixes	pushed unhelpful	pusht helpful
LA	Additions: adding endings, prefixes, suffixes	cry forget	crys forgetting
LSe	Sequencing: reversing syllables	discussed disappoint	discusted dispapoint

Source: From *Informal Assessment in Education* (pp. 218–219) by G. R. Guerin and A. S. Maier, 1983, Palo Alto, CA: Mayfield Publishing. Copyright 1983 by Mayfield Publishing. Reprinted by permission.

2. The evaluator should give the child a copy of the story starter and read the starter to him or her. The evaluator then tells the student that he or she will be asked to write a story using the starter as the first sentence. The student should be given a minute to think about a story before he or she is asked to begin writing.

3. After 1 minute, the evaluator should tell the child to begin writing, start the stopwatch, and time for 3 minutes. If the child stops writing before the 3 minutes are up, he or she should be encouraged to keep writing until time is up.

4. The evaluator should count the number of words that are correctly written. "Correct" means that a word can be recognized (even if it is misspelled). Capitalization and punctuation are ignored. The rate of the correct and incorrect words per 3 minutes is calculated. If the child stops writing before the 3 minutes are up, the number of words correct should be multiplied by 180 for the number of words correct per 3 minutes. (p. 125)

Shapiro also suggested creating local norms to compare students. The number of words correct may be used as a basis for writing short-term objectives. This informal method may be linked directly to classroom curricula and may be repeated frequently as a direct measure of student writing ability. Writing samples may also be used to analyze handwriting. The teacher uses error analysis to evaluate the sample, write short-term objectives, and plan educational strategies. One such error analysis of handwriting skills is shown in Figure 6.9.

PERFORMANCE ASSESSMENT AND AUTHENTIC ASSESSMENT

Performance testing is designed so that the student creates a response from the student's existing knowledge base. The U.S. Office of Technology Assessment defines performance assessment as "testing methods that require students to create an answer product that demonstrates their knowledge or skills" (1992, p. 16). The teacher may use a variety of formats in performance assessment, including products that the student constructs. Harris and Graham (1994) state that performance assessment stresses the student's active construction in demonstrating knowledge.

The types of tasks that teachers may require a student to complete in performance assessment may include the student's explanation of process as well as the student's perception of the task and the material learned. This type of assessment may involve several levels of cognitive processing and reasoning and may allow educators to tap into areas not assessed by more traditional types of

Figure 6.9 One method of handwriting analysis.

Directions: Analysis of handwriting should be made on a sample of the student's written work, not from a carefully produced sample. Evaluate each task and mark in the appropriate column. Score each task "satisfactory" (1) or "unsatisfactory" (2).

I. Letter formation

A. Capitals (score each letter 1 or 2)

A _____	G _____	M _____	S _____	Y _____
B _____	H _____	N _____	T _____	Z _____
C _____	I _____	O _____	U _____	
D _____	J _____	P _____	V _____	
E _____	K _____	Q _____	W _____	
F _____	L _____	R _____	X _____	

Total _____

Score
(1 or 2)

B. Lowercase (score by groups)

  1. Round letters
    a. Counterclockwise
      a, c, d, g, o, q   _____
    b. Clockwise
      k, p   _____
  2. Looped letters
    a. Above line
      b, d, e, f, h, k, l   _____
    b. Below line
      f, g, j, p, q, y   _____
  3. Retraced letters
    i, u, t, w, y   _____
  4. Humped letters
    h, m, n, v, x, z   _____
  5. Others
    r, s, b   _____

C. Numerals (score each number 1 or 2)

1 _____	4 _____	7 _____	10–20 _____
2 _____	5 _____	8 _____	21–99 _____
3 _____	6 _____	9 _____	100–1,000 _____

Total _____

continued.

Figure 6.9   continued.

II. Spatial relationships

                                                                              Score
                                                                              (1 or 2)

    A. Alignment (letters on line)   _____
    B. Uniform slant   _____
    C. Size of letters
        1. To each other   _____
        2. To available space   _____
    D. Space between letters   _____
    E. Space between words   _____
    F. Anticipation of end of line (hyphenates, moves to next line)   _____
                                                                   Total _____

III. Rate of writing (letters per minute)

                                                                              Score
                                                                              (1 or 2)

Grade 1:20
     2:30
     3:35
     4:45
     5:55
     6:65
     7 and above: 75   _____

Scoring	*Satisfactory*	*Questionable*	*Poor*
I. *Letter formation*			
A. Capitals	26	39	40
B. Lowercase	7	10	11
C. Numerals	12	18	19
II. *Spatial relationships*	7	10	11
III. *Rate of writing*	1	2	6

Source: From *Informal Assessment in Education* (p. 228) by G. R. Guerin and A. S. Maier, 1983, Palo Alto, CA: Mayfield Publishing. Copyright 1983 by Mayfield Publishing. Reprinted by permission.

authentic assessment
Assessment that requires the student to apply knowledge in the real world.

assessment. When considering performance assessment as an alternative for making educational placement decisions, Elliott and Fuchs (1997) caution that performance assessment should be used in conjunction with other types of assessment because of insufficient knowledge regarding psychometric evidence and the lack of professionals who are trained to use this type of assessment reliably. Glatthorn suggested criteria for educators to use in the evaluation of performance tasks (1998). These criteria are presented in Table 6.9.

Authentic assessment differs from performance assessment in that students must apply knowledge in a manner consistent with

Table 6.9 Criteria for evaluating performance tasks.

Does the performance task

- Correspond closely and comprehensively with the standard and benchmarks it is designed to assess?
- Require the student to access prior knowledge in completing the task?
- Require the use of higher order thought processes including creative thinking?
- Seem real and purposeful, embedded in a meaningful context that seems authentic?
- Engage students' interest?
- Require the students to communicate to classmates and others the processes they used and the results they obtained, using multiple response modes?
- Require sustained effort over a significant period of time?
- Provide the student with options?
- Seem feasible in the context of schools and classrooms, not requiring inordinate resources or creating undue controversy?
- Convey a sense of fairness to all, being free of basis?
- Challenge the students without frustrating them?
- Include criteria and rubrics for evaluating student performance?
- Provide both group and individual work, with appropriate accountability?

Source: Performance Assessment and Standard-Based Curricula: The Achievement Cycle by A. A. Glatthorn (1998). Copyright by Eye on Education. Larchmont, NY.

generalizing into a real-world setting, or students may complete the task in the real world. Archbald (1991) states that authentic assessment requires a disciplined production of knowledge using techniques that are within the field in which the student is being assessed. The student's tasks are instrumental and may require a substantial amount of time to complete. The student may be required to use a variety of materials and resources that may include working in collaboration with other students.

PORTFOLIO ASSESSMENT

portfolio assessment
Evaluating student progress, strengths, and weaknesses using a collection of different measurements and work samples.

One method of assessing a student's current level of academic functioning is through **portfolio assessment**. A portfolio is a collection of student work that provides a holistic view of the student's strengths and weaknesses. The portfolio collection contains various work samples, permanent products, and test results from a variety of instruments and methods. For example, a portfolio of reading might include a student's test scores on teacher-made tests, including curriculum-based assessments, work samples from daily work and homework assignments, error analyses on work and test samples, and the results of an informal reading inventory with miscues noted and analyzed. The assessment of the student's progress would assess decoding skills, comprehension skills, fluency, and so on. These measures would be collected over a period of time. This type of assessment may be useful in describing the current progress of the student to his parents (Taylor, 1993).

The essential elements of effective portfolio assessment were listed by Shaklee, Barbour, Ambrose, and Hansford (1997), who included the following assessment elements:

> Assessment should:
> be authentic and valid.
> encompass the whole child.
> involve repeated observations of various patterns of behavior.
> be continuous over time.
> use a variety of methods for gathering evidence of student performance.
> provide a means for systematic feedback to be used in the improvement of instruction and student performance.
> provide an opportunity for joint conversations and explanations between students and teachers, teachers and parents, and students and parents. (p. 10)

Ruddell (1995) provides the following list of possible products that could be included in a portfolio for assessing literacy in the middle grades:

> samples of student writing
> story maps
> reading log or dated list of books student has read
> vocabulary journal
> artwork, project papers, photographs, and other products of work completed
> group work, papers, projects, and products
> daily journal
> writing ideas
> reading response log, learning log, or double-entry journal or writing from assigned reading during the year
> letters to pen pals, letters exchanged with teacher
> out-of-school writing and artwork
> unit and lesson tests collected over the grading period or academic year (p. 191)

Paratore (1995) reports that establishing common standards for assessing literacy through the use of portfolio assessment provides a useful alternative in the evaluation of students' reading and writing skills. Hobbs (1993) found portfolio assessment useful in providing supplemental information for eligibility consideration that included samples of the quality of work that was not evident in standardized assessment.

Portfolio data were also found to provide information to teachers that was more informative and led to different decisions for instructional planning (Rueda & Garcia, 1997). This study found that the recommendations were more specific and that student strengths were more easily identifiable using this form of assessment.

INFORMAL AND FORMAL ASSESSMENT METHODS

In Chapter 7 you will be introduced to norm-referenced testing. These tests are useful in assessing factors that cannot be reliably or validly assessed using informal measures. There are some difficulties with using norm-referenced tests, however, and this has led to the shift to the response-to-intervention method, problem-solving method, and the increased use of informal measures, such as CBMs, to collect data.

Some of the difficulties with the use of norm-referenced assessment are presented in the next section.

PROBLEMS OF NORM-REFERENCED ASSESSMENT

The weaknesses attributed to norm-referenced assessment include problems specific to the various instruments and problems with test administration and interpretation. Norm-referenced tests may not adequately represent material actually taught in a specific curriculum (Shapiro, 1996). In other words, items on norm-referenced tests may include content or skill areas not included in the student's curriculum. Salvia and Hughes (1990) wrote:

> The fundamental problem with using published tests is the test's content. If the content of the test—even content prepared by experts—does not match the content that is taught, the test is useless for evaluating what the student has learned from school instruction. (p. 8)

Good and Salvia (1988) studied the representation of reading curricula in norm-referenced tests and concluded that a deficient score on a norm-referenced reading test could actually represent the selection of a test with inadequate content validity for the current curriculum. Hultquist and Metzke (1993) determined that curriculum bias existed when using standardized achievement tests to measure the reading of survival words and reading and spelling skills in general.

In addition, the frequent use of norm-referenced instruments may result in bias because limited numbers of alternate forms exist, creating the possibility of test wiseness among students (Fuchs, Tindal, & Deno, 1984; Shapiro, 1996). Another study revealed that norm-referenced instruments are not as sensitive to academic growth as other instruments that are linked more directly to the actual classroom curriculum (Marston, Fuchs, & Deno, 1986). This means that norm-referenced tests may not measure small gains made in the classroom from week to week.

According to Reynolds (1982), the psychometric assessment of students using traditional norm-referenced methods is fraught with many problems of bias, including cultural bias, which may result in test scores that reflect intimidation or communication problems rather than ability level. These difficulties in using norm-referenced testing for special education planning have led to the emergence of alternative methods of assessment.

THINK AHEAD

When a student has academic difficulty and does not respond to the intensive interventions employed in a general education setting, a referral to special education may result. In order to make this determination, additional data, such as academic achievement and diagnostic data, may be required. Chapter 7 presents an overview of the assessment of academic achievement using norm-referenced methods.

EXERCISES

Part I

Match the terms with the correct definitions.

a. criterion-referenced assessment
b. curriculum-based measurement
c. task analysis
d. error analysis
e. informal assessment
f. questionnaire

g. formative
h. summative
i. probes
j. checklist
k. portfolio
l. aimline
m. authentic assessment
n. performance assessment

_____ 1. A teacher reviews the information provided in a student's norm-referenced achievement scores. She determines that the student has a weakness in the area of multiplication with regrouping, but she is not certain exactly how the student is completing the process. In order to determine this, the teacher decides to use _____.

_____ 2. A teacher who works with students in the range of mild mental retardation would like to assess the students' ability to return the correct amount of change when given a $10.00 bill to pay for an item that costs $2.85. How might the teacher decide to assess this skill? _____

_____ 3. To determine the specific skills applied in completing double-digit addition problems, the teacher can complete a _____.

_____ 4. In a daily living skills class, a teacher can assess the student's ability to make a complete meal by using _____.

_____ 5. A teacher assesses students' knowledge of the science unit by each student's book report, test grade, written classroom assignments, lab experiences, and journal. This group of science products demonstrates one example of _____.

_____ 6. Error analysis, checklists, direct measurement, authentic assessment, portfolio assessment, probes, and curriculum-based assessment are examples of _____.

_____ 7. A teacher sets a standard of reaching 90% mastery on the test assessing basic reading decoding skills of second-grade-level words. This test is an example of _____.

_____ 8. Asking the parent of a child to complete a survey about the specific behaviors observed during homework time is an example of using _____ as part of the assessment.

_____ 9. A teacher decides to evaluate the progress of her students following the conclusion of a science unit. This type of assessment is known as _____.

_____10. By adding the number of correct letter sequences found in the baseline to the number of weekly expected CLSs for the year, the teacher can then plot the _____.

Part II

Use the terms in Part I to select a method of informal assessment for the following situations. Write the reason for your selection.

1. Standardized test results you received on a new student indicate that she is performing two grade levels below expectancy. You want to determine which reading book to place her in.

   Method of assessment: _____

   Reason: _____

2. A student who understands division problems when presented in class failed a teacher-made test. You want to determine the reason for the failure.

   Method of assessment: _____

   Reason: _____

3. Following a screening test of fifth-grade level spelling, you determine that a student performs inconsistently when spelling words with short vowel sounds:

   Method of assessment: _____

   Reason: _____

4. A student seems to be performing at a different level than indicated by norm-referenced math test data. You think you

should meet with his parents and discuss actual progress in the classroom.

Method of assessment: _____

Reason: _____

5. A teacher wants to monitor the progress of students who are acquiring the basic addition computation skills. In order to determine if students are progressing toward the end-of-the-year goal, the teacher can employ:

Method of assessment: _____

Reason: _____

Answers to these questions can be found in the Appendix of this text or you may also complete these questions and receive immediate feedback on your answers by going to the Think Ahead module in Chapter 6 of the Companion Website.

Academic Assessment

achievement tests

screening tests

aptitude tests

diagnostic tests

adaptive behavior scales

norm-referenced tests

curriculum-based assessment

diagnostic instruments

domain

language assessment

receptive language

expressive language

written language

CHAPTER FOCUS

This chapter includes several commonly used norm-referenced individual achievement tests. Information is presented that will enable you to understand how the basic methods of studying reliability and validity are applied to these instruments. You will learn some basic scoring methods that will allow you to generalize these skills to other instruments.

Professionals working with students who require special services are concerned with how students perform on educational measures. One way to measure educational performance is to use norm-referenced achievement tests. Of all standardized tests, individually administered achievement tests are the most numerous (Anastasi & Urbina, 1998).

CEC KNOWLEDGE AND SKILLS STANDARDS

The student completing this chapter will understand the knowledge and skills included in the following CEC Knowledge and Skills Standards from Standard 8: Assessment:

CC8K4—Use and limitations of assessment instruments

CC8S2—Administer nonbiased formal and informal assessments

CC8S5—Interpret information from formal and informal assessments

ACHIEVEMENT TESTS

achievement tests Tests used to measure academic progress, what the student has retained in curriculum.

screening tests Brief tests that sample a few items across skills or domains.

aptitude tests Tests designed to measure strength, talent, or ability in a particular area or domain.

diagnostic tests Individually administered tests designed to determine specific academic problems or deficit areas.

adaptive behavior scales Instruments that assess a student's ability to adapt to the world in different situations.

norm-referenced tests Tests designed to compare individual students with national averages, or norms of expectancy.

curriculum-based assessment Using content from the currently used curriculum to assess student progress.

Used in virtually every school, **achievement tests** are designed to measure what the student has learned. These tests may be developed to measure a specific area of the educational curriculum, such as written language, or to measure across several areas of the curriculum, such as math, reading, spelling, and science. Brief tests containing items that survey a range of skill levels, domains, or content areas are known as **screening tests.** Screening tests assess no one area in depth. Screening tests provide the educator with a method to determine weak areas that need additional assessment in order to determine specific skill mastery or weaknesses.

Aptitude tests contain items that measure what a student has retained but also are designed to indicate how much the student will learn in the future. Aptitude tests are thought to indicate current areas of strength as well as future potential. These tests are used in educational planning and include both group and individually administered tests. **Diagnostic tests** are those used to measure a specific ability, such as fine-motor ability. **Adaptive behavior scales** measure how well students adapt to different environments.

STANDARDIZED NORM-REFERENCED TESTS VERSUS CURRICULUM-BASED ASSESSMENT

The use of **norm-referenced tests** to measure academic achievement helps educators make both placement and eligibility decisions. When selected and administered carefully, these tests yield fairly reliable and valid information. As discussed in the previous chapter, norm-referenced instruments are researched and constructed in a systematic way and provide educators with a method of comparing a student with a peer group evaluated during the standardization process of the test development. Comparing a student to a norm reference group allows the educator to determine whether the student is performing as expected for the age or grade. If the student appears to be significantly behind peers developmentally, special services may be recommended.

Curriculum-based assessment tests students on the very curriculum used for instruction. In this method of determining mastery of skills or specific curriculum, the student may be compared with past performance on similar items or tasks. Curriculum-based testing, which is very useful and necessary in special education, is discussed further in Chapter 6.

REVIEW OF ACHIEVEMENT TESTS

This text is designed to involve the reader in the learning process and to help the reader develop skills in administering and interpreting tests. Rather than include numerous tests, many of which the future teacher may not use, this chapter presents achievement tests selected because of their frequent use in schools or because of their technical adequacy. The following are individually administered screening achievement tests used frequently by educators:

1. *Woodcock–Johnson III.* This revised edition of the Woodcock–Johnson–Revised Psychoeducational Battery includes two forms, A and B. It contains cognitive and achievement tests, each of which includes standard and extended batteries. The same sample was assessed using all components of the battery to establish the normative data. Using the same sample enhances the diagnostic capability for determining domain-specific skills and their associated cognitive abilities as well as discrepancies between ability and achievement (McGrew & Woodcock, 2001).

2. *Peabody Individual Achievement Test–4.* This test was listed as one of the most frequently used by professionals in Child Service Demonstration Centers (Thurlow & Ysseldyke, 1979), by school psychologists (LaGrow & Prochnow-LaGrow, 1982), by special education teachers who listed this as one of the most useful tests (Connelly, 1985), and by teachers who are in both self-contained and resource classrooms for students with learning disabilities (German, Johnson, & Schneider, 1985).

3. *Kaufman Test of Educational Achievement (K-TEA-II).* The K-TEA-II is a recent revision of the original K-TEA. It was conormed with the K-ABC.

4. *Wechsler Individual Achievement Test, Second Edition.* This revised instrument was designed to be used in conjunction with the Wechsler Intelligence Scales or other measures of cognitive ability and assesses the academic areas specified in special education regulations.

5. *Wide Range Achievement Test.* This test was listed as useful by teachers of students with emotional disabilities, learning disabilities, and mental retardation (Connelly, 1985); by teachers in self-contained and resource rooms for students with learning disabilities (German, Johnson, & Schneider, 1985); by school psychologists (LaGrow & Prochnow-LaGrow, 1982; Reschly, 1988); and by teachers in Child Service Demonstration Centers (Thurlow & Ysseldyke, 1979). This text describes the third edition of the Wide Range Achievement Test (Wilkinson, 1993).

6. *Mini-Battery of Achievement.* This is included as a fairly new screening achievement battery (Woodcock, McGrew, & Werder, 1994). This test has a format similar to the Woodcock–Johnson Tests of Achievement–Revised. It is presented as an alternative to the WRAT3.

These tests, which represent several academic areas, are discussed in the following sections. Their reliability and validity are presented in an effort to encourage future teachers to be wise consumers of assessment devices.

WOODCOCK-JOHNSON III TESTS OF ACHIEVEMENT (WJ III)

This new edition of the Woodcock-Johnson (Woodcock, McGrew, & Mather, 2001), presented in an easel type of format, comprises two parallel achievement batteries that allow the examiner to retest the same student within a short amount of time with less practice effect. The battery of subtests allows the examiner to select the specific clusters of subtests needed for a particular student. This achievement battery has standard tests and extended tests. An Examiner Training Workbook is included that will assist examiners in learning how to administer the subtests, understand basal and ceiling rules, and learn how to complete the scoring included on the protocol (Wendling & Mather, 2001). A checklist is provided in the manual for each subtest of the WJ III Achievement Tests. Each of the checklists states the specific skills and steps the examiner must follow in order to complete standardized administration of the instrument.

Some features of the WJ III Tests of Achievement include the following:

1. Basal and ceiling levels are specified by individual subtests. For many of the subtests, when the student answers six consecutive items correctly, the basal is established; and when the student answers six consecutive items incorrectly, the ceiling is established. Other subtests have basal levels of four consecutive correct and ceilings of four consecutive incorrect. Additional basal and ceiling rules include specific starting points and time limits for stopping the subtest administration. Examiners should study the basal and ceiling rules and refer to the protocol and the examiner's manual for specific rules.

2. Derived scores can be obtained for each individual subtest for estimations of age and grade equivalents only. Other standard scores are available using the computer scoring program.

3. The norm group ranged in age from 2 to 90 years and older and included students at the college/university level through graduate school.

4. The use of extended age scores provides a more comprehensive analysis of children and adults who are not functioning at a school grade level.

5. The WJ III Tests of Achievement include subtests that require the student to use paper and pencil as well as subtests that are administered using a tape player. The protocol contains icons to denote when the test response booklet or the tape player is needed as well as which subtests are timed.

6. The examiner's manual includes suggested guidelines for using the WJ III with individuals who are English language learners, individuals with reading and/or learning disabilities, individuals with attentional and behavioral difficulties, individuals with hearing or visual impairments, and individuals with physical impairments.

7. The computer scoring program includes an option for determining the individual's cognitive-academic language proficiency level.

8. A Test Session Observation Checklist is located on the front of the protocol for the examiner to note the individual student's behavior during the assessment sessions.

9. Transparent scoring templates are provided for reading and math fluency subtests.

The Woodcock-Johnson Tests of Achievement are organized into subtests and clusters. The subtests are grouped into broad clusters to aid in the interpretation of scores. The examiner may select the specific clusters needed to screen a student's achievement level and combine the administration of selected cognitive clusters to determine a pattern of strengths and weaknesses. For example, a student who is suspected of having difficulties with math reasoning would be administered the subtests of quantitative concepts and applied problems. A student who has had difficulty with beginning reading skills might be given the cluster to assess phoneme/grapheme knowledge which includes the subtests of word attack and spelling of sounds.

Standard Battery   The following paragraphs describe the subtests in the Standard Battery.

Letter-Word Identification. The student is presented with a picture, letter, or word and asked to identify it orally. The basal and ceiling levels are, respectively, six lowest consecutive items correct and the six highest items incorrect.

Reading Fluency. This timed subtest presents statements for the student to read and determine if the statements are true or not true. It assesses how quickly the student reads the sentences, makes decisions about the statement validity, and circles the correct response. The time limit is 3 minutes.

Story Recall. All items are presented using the audio recording provided. The student listens to the short stories and then tells the story to the examiner. Instructions for continuing and stopping the administration of the subtest are provided in the protocol and are based on the number of points the student earns.

Understanding Directions. This subtest requires the stimulus pictures on the easel and oral instructions by the examiner. As the student looks at the pictures, the examiner provides instructions such as "First point to the dog then the bird if the dog is brown." Specific instructions are provided in the protocol regarding when the student discontinues the subtest based on the number of points earned.

Calculation. Math problems are presented in a paper-and-pencil format. The problems include number writing on the early items and range from addition to calculus operations on the more advanced items. The basal and ceiling levels are, respectively, the six lowest consecutive items correct and the six highest consecutive items incorrect.

Math Fluency. This subtest is included in the student's response booklet. The student is required to complete problems of basic operations of addition, subtraction, multiplication, and division. This subtest is timed and the student solves as many problems as possible within 3 minutes.

Spelling. This subtest assesses the individual's ability to write words that are presented orally by the examiner. The early items include tracing lines and letters, and the more advanced items include multisyllabic words with unpredictable spellings. The basal and ceiling levels are, respectively, six consecutive correct and incorrect items.

Writing Fluency. This paper-and-pencil subtest consists of pictures paired with three words. The examiner instructs the student to write sentences about each picture using the words. The student is allowed to write for 7 minutes. Correct responses are complete sentences that include the three words presented.

Passage Comprehension. The examiner shows the student a passage with a missing word, and the student must orally supply the word. The basal and ceiling levels are, respectively, the six lowest consecutive items correct and the six highest incorrect items.

Applied Problems. The examiner reads a story math problem, and the student must answer orally. Picture cues are provided at the lower levels. The basal and ceiling levels are determined in the same manner as for the Calculation subtest.

Writing Samples. This subtest requires the student to construct age-appropriate sentences meeting specific criteria (for syntax, content, etc.). The items are scored as 2, 1, or 0 based on the quality of the responses. The examiner's manual provides a comprehensive scoring guide.

Story Recall—Delayed. On this subtest, the student is asked to recall the stories presented in a previous subtest, Story Recall. The delayed subtest can be presented from 30 minutes to 8 days following the initial administration of Story Recall.

Extended Battery   The subtests included in the Extended Battery are described in the following paragraphs.

Word Attack. The student is asked to read nonsense words aloud. This subtest measures the student's ability to decode and pronounce new words. The basal is established when a student answers six consecutive items correctly, and the ceiling is six consecutive incorrect responses.

Picture Vocabulary. The items in this subtest require the student to express the names of objects presented in pictures on the easel. The basal and ceiling levels are, respectively, the six lowest consecutive correct and six highest incorrect items.

Oral Comprehension. These items are presented on the audiotape and require that the student complete the missing word in the presented items. The items range from simple associations to more complex sentences. The basal and ceiling levels are, respectively, the six lowest consecutive correct and six highest incorrect items.

Editing. This subtest requires the student to proofread sentences and passages and determine the errors of punctuation, capitalization, usage, or spelling. The student is asked to correct errors in written passages shown on the easel page. The basal and ceiling levels are, respectively, the six lowest consecutive correct and six highest incorrect items.

Reading Vocabulary. This subtest contains three sections: Part A, Synonyms; Part B, Antonyms; and Part C, Analogies. All three sections must be completed in order to obtain a score for the subtest. The student is asked to say a word that means the same as a given word in Part A and to say a word that has the opposite meaning of a word in Part B. In Part C, the student must complete analogies. Only one-word responses are acceptable for the subtest items. The examiner obtains a raw score by adding the number of items correct in the two subtests. The basal and ceiling levels are, respectively, the four lowest consecutive items correct and four highest incorrect responses.

Quantitative Concepts. This subtest includes two parts: Part A, Concepts; and Part B, Number Series. Both sections must be completed in order to obtain a score for the subtest. Items cover math vocabulary, concepts, and the completion of missing numbers presented in various types of series. The examiner's manual states that no mathematical decisions are made in response to these test items. Picture cues are given for some items in the lower levels. The basal and ceiling instructions are different for each part and are contained in the protocol.

Academic Knowledge. This subtest contains three parts: Part A, Science; Part B, Social Studies; and Part C, Humanities. For the Science section, the examiner orally presents open-ended questions covering scientific content. The basal and ceiling levels are, respectively, the three lowest consecutive correct and three highest incorrect items. Picture cues are given at the lower and upper levels. The Social Studies section orally presents open-ended questions covering topics about society and government. The basal and ceiling levels are the same as for the Science section. Picture cues are given at the lower level. The questions in the Humanities section cover topics the student may have learned from the cultural environment. The basal and ceiling levels are the same as for the Science and Social Studies sections.

Spelling of Sounds. The examiner presents the first few items of this subtest orally and the remaining items are presented using the audiotape. The individual is asked to write the spellings of nonsense words. This requires that the student be able to associate the sounds heard with the written letter. The basal and ceiling levels are, respectively, the four lowest consecutive items correct and the highest four items incorrect.

Sound Awareness. This subtest contains four sections: Part A, Sound Awareness—Rhyming; Part B, Sound Awareness—Deletion; Part C, Sound Awareness—Substitution; and Part D, Sound Awareness—Reversal. The items for Part A require the student to determine and generate words that rhyme. Part B requires the student to say parts of the original stimulus provided on the audiotape. Part C requires that the individual change a specified part of the stimulus word. Part D requires the student to perform two tasks. First, the student is asked to reverse compound words. Then the student is required to reverse the sounds of letters to create new words. This subtest is arranged so that each part is more difficult than the previous part. Within each part, items are also sequenced from easier to more difficult items. The basal is one item correct for each of the sections, and the ceilings vary for each section.

Punctuation and Capitalization. This subtest includes items that require the student to write the correct punctuation for specific stimuli presented by the examiner and in the response booklet. For example, a sentence in the response booklet may

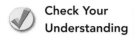

Check Your Understanding

Check your understanding of the Woodcock–Johnson III Tests of Achievement by completing Activity 7.1 below.

Activity 7.1

1. How many parallel forms are included in the third edition of the Woodcock–Johnson Tests of Achievement? What is the advantage of having different forms of the same instrument?_____

2. What is the age range of the WJ III?_____

3. What populations were included in the norming process of the third edition?_____

4. What new school level is included in the WJ III? Why?_____

Apply Your Knowledge

Refer to the WJ III subtest descriptions in your text. Which subtests would not be appropriate for a student to complete in the standard fashion if the student had a severe fine-motor disability and could not use a pencil or keyboard? What adaptations would be appropriate? Explain the ethical considerations that should be addressed by making such adaptations. _____

_____

_____

need quotation marks or a capital letter. The individual writes the needed punctuation or capitalization in the response booklet. The basal and ceiling levels are, respectively, the six lowest consecutive correct and the six highest incorrect items.

PEABODY INDIVIDUAL ACHIEVEMENT TEST–REVISED (PIAT–R)

The PIAT–R (Markwardt, 1989) is contained in four easels, called Volumes I, II, III, and IV. For this revision, the number of items has been increased on the existing subtests. The subtests are General Information, Reading Recognition, Reading Comprehension, Mathematics, Spelling, and Written Expression.

Subtests

General Information. Questions in this subtest are presented in an open-ended format. The student gives oral responses to questions that range in topic from science to sports. The examiner records all responses. A key for acceptable responses is given throughout the examiner's pages of the subtest and provides suggestions for further questioning.

Reading Recognition. The items at the beginning level of this subtest are visual recognition and discrimination items that require the student to match a picture, letter, or word. The student must select the response from a choice of four items. The more difficult items require the student to pronounce a list of words that range from single-syllable consonant-vowel-consonant words to multisyllable words with unpredictable pronunciations.

Reading Comprehension. This subtest is administered to students who earn a raw score of 19 or better on the Reading Recognition subtest. The items are presented in a two-page format. The examiner asks the student to read a passage silently on the first page of each item. On the second page, the student must select from four choices the one picture that best illustrates the passage. The more difficult-to-read items also have pictures that are more difficult to discriminate.

Mathematics. Math questions are presented in a forced-choice format. The student is orally asked a question and must select the correct response from four choices. Questions range from numeral recognition to trigonometry.

Spelling. This subtest begins with visual discrimination tasks of pictures, symbols, and letters. The spelling items are presented in a forced-choice format. The student is asked to select the correct spelling of the word from four choices.

Written Expression. This subtest allows for written responses by the student; level 1 is presented to students who are functioning at the kindergarten or first-grade level, level II to students functioning in the second- to twelfth-grade levels. The basal and ceiling levels do not apply.

Scoring The examiner uses the raw score on the first PIAT–R subtest, General Information, to determine a starting point on the following subtest, Reading Recognition. The raw score from the Reading Recognition subtest then provides a starting point for the Reading Comprehension subtest, and so on throughout the test. The basal and ceiling levels are consistent across subtests. A basal level is established when five consecutive items have been answered correctly. The ceiling level is determined when the student answers five of seven items incorrectly. Because the Written Expression subtest requires written responses by the student, the basal and ceiling levels do not apply.

The PIAT–R yields standard scores, grade equivalents, age equivalents, and percentile ranks for individual subtests and for a Total Reading and a Total Test score. The manual provides for standard error of measurement for obtained and derived scores. The raw score from the Written Expression subtest can be used with the raw score from the Spelling subtest to obtain a written language composite. Scoring procedures are detailed in Appendix I of the PIAT–R examiner's manual.

KAUFMAN TEST OF EDUCATIONAL ACHIEVEMENT, 2ND EDITION (K-TEA-II)

The K-TEA-II (Kaufman & Kaufman, 2004) is an individually administered achievement battery for children ages 4 years and 6 months to 25 years. This instrument provides subtests to assess children of preschool age through young adults in college. There are two forms of this comprehensive achievement measure, Form A and Form B. Having equivalent forms allows for repeated testing of constructs and items of equivalent difficulty and content while possibly decreasing the influence of the practice effect. The K-TEA-II was conormed with the Kaufman Assessment Battery for Children, Second Edition (K-ABC-II; Kaufman & Kaufman, 2004). Using both forms of this instrument permits a more valid comparison of cognitive and academic ability across instruments.

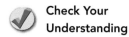

Check Your Understanding

Check your understanding of the PIAT–R protocol by completing Activity 7.2 below.

Activity 7.2

Refer to your text and Figure 7.1 to complete this exercise.

1. How is the starting point for the Reading Recognition subtest determined?_____
2. How is the Reading Comprehension start point determined? _____
3. What response mode is used on many of the items on this test?_____
4. How does this response mode impact scores?_____
5. Using the information provided on the portion of the PIAT–R protocol shown on page 262, determine the Total Reading Raw Score. Add the Reading Recognition and the Reading Comprehension raw scores. To determine the Total Test raw score, add all subtest raw scores. Write the sums in the appropriate spaces.
6. Using the raw score data, look up the standard scores on the following table and write the scores in the appropriate spaces on the protocol sheet._____

Apply Your Knowledge

Make a general statement regarding the student's academic functioning based on the standard scores you determined on the PIAT–R. Does the student have any academic strengths or weaknesses according to these scores?_____
_____
_____

The complete K-TEA-II, the Comprehensive Form and additional reading-related areas, includes the following composites, which are comprised of the respective subtests:

Reading—Letter & Word Identification; Reading Comprehension
Math—Math Concepts and Applications; Math Computation
Written Language—Written Expression; Spelling
Oral Language—Listening Comprehension; Oral Expression
Sound-Symbol—Phonological Awareness; Nonsense Word Decoding; Letter and Word Recognition
Decoding—Letter & Word Decoding; Nonsense Word Decoding

Figure 7.1 Basal and ceiling rules and response items for a subtest from the Peabody Individual Achievement Test–Revised.

SUBTEST 2
Reading Recognition

Training Exercises

	Trial 1	Trial 2	Trial 3
Exercise A.	(1) _____	(1) _____	(1) _____
Exercise B.	(3) _____	(3) _____	(3) _____
Exercise C.	(2) _____	(2) _____	(2) _____

Basal and Ceiling Rules
Basal: *highest* 5 consecutive correct responses
Ceiling: *lowest* 7 consecutive responses containing 5 errors

Starting Point
The item number that corresponds to the subject's raw score on General Information.

43. ledge _____ 1
44. escape _____ 1
45. northern _____ 1
46. towel _____ 1
47. kneel _____ 1
48. height _____ 0
49. exercise _____ 1
50. observe _____ 1
51. ruin _____ 0
52. license _____ 1
53. uniforms _____ 0
54. pigeon _____ 1
55. moisture _____ 0
56. artificial _____ 1
57. issues _____ 0
58. quench _____ 0
59. hustle _____ 0
60. thigh _____ 0

READING RECOGNITION
Ceiling Item _____
minus Errors _____
equals RAW SCORE _____

Oral Fluency—Associational Fluency; Naming Facility
Reading Fluency—Word Recognition Fluency; Decoding Fluency
(Kaufman & Kaufman, 2004, pp 2–3)

A description of each subtest, including the stimuli and the task demands, is presented in Table 7.1.

The K-TEA-II has increased the comprehensive and diagnostic capability of the original K-TEA. The teacher will be able to determine more specifically the strengths and weaknesses of the student's performance due to the increased coverage of error analyses by subtest and within-item performance. For example, the teacher can not only determine that the student has difficulty with fractions but also that

Table 7.1   Brief description of K-TEA-II Comprehensive Form subtests.

Subtest	Range	Description
Letter & Word Recognition	Ages 4:6–25:11	The student identifies letters and pronounces words of gradually increasing difficulty. Most words are irregular to ensure that the subject measures word recognition (reading vocabulary) more than decoding ability.
Reading Comprehension	Grade 1–Age 25:11	For the easiest items, the student reads a word and points to its corresponding picture. In following items, the student reads a simple instruction and responds by performing the action. In later items, the student reads passages of increasing difficulty and answers literal or inferential questions about them. Finally, the student rearranges five sentences into a coherent paragraph, and then answers questions about the paragraph.
Math Concepts & Applications	Ages 4:6–25:11	The student responds orally to test items that focus on the application of mathematical principles to real-life situations. Skill categories include number concepts, operation concepts, time and money, measurement, geometry, data investigation, and higher math concepts.
Math Computation	Grade K–Age 25:11	The student writes solutions to math problems printed in the Student Response Booklet. Skills assessed include addition, subtraction, multiplication, and division operations; fractions and decimals; square roots, exponents, signed number, and algebra.
Written Expression	Ages 4:6–25:11	Kindergarten and pre-kindergarten children trace and copy letters and write letters from dictation. At Grades 1 and higher, the student completes writing tasks in the context of an age-appropriate storybook format. Tasks at those levels include writing sentences from dictation, adding punctuation and capitalization filling in missing words, completing sentences, combining sentences, writing compound and complex sentences and, starting at Spring of Grade 1, writing an essay based on the story the student helped complete.

continued.

Table 7.1   continued.

Subtest	Range	Description
Spelling	Grade 1–Age 25:11	The student writes words dictated by the examiner from a steeply graded word list. Early items require students to write single letters that represent sounds. The remaining items require students to spell regular and irregular words of increasing complexity.
Listening Comprehension	Ages 4:6–25:11	The student listens to passages played on a CD and then responds orally to questions asked by the examiner. Questions measure literal and inferential comprehension.
Oral Expression	Ages 4:6–25:11	The student performs specific speaking tasks in the context of a real-life scenario. Tasks assess pragmatics, syntax, semantics, and grammar.
Phonological Awareness	Grades K–6	The student responds orally to items that require manipulation of sounds. Tasks include rhyming, matching sounds, blending sounds, segmenting sounds, and deleting sounds.
Nonsense Word Decoding	Grade 1–Age 25:11	The student applies phonics and structural analysis skills to decode invented words of increasing difficulty.
Word Recognition Fluency	Grade 3–Age 25:11	The student reads isolated words as quickly as possible for 1 minute.
Decoding Fluency	Grade 3–Age 25:11	The student pronounces as many nonsense words as possible in 1 minute.
Associational Fluency	Ages 4:6–25:11	The student says as many words as possible in 30 seconds that belong to a semantic category or have a specified beginning sound.
Naming Facility (RAN)	Ages 4:6–25:11	The student names objects, colors, and letters as quickly as possible.

Source: From *Kaufman Test of Educational Achievement, 2nd Edition: Comprehensive Form Manual.* (2004). Kaufman, A. S. and Kaufman, N. L., p. 4. Circle Pines, MN: AGS Publishing.

the student has not mastered the skills of adding or subtracting numerators or denominators or performing operations with equivalent fractions or determining common denominators. This information can then be used to write specific objectives, design teaching strategies, or create curriculum-based measures of mathematical operations.

The K-TEA-II includes four timed subtests that assess how quickly a student can retrieve or express specific information related to reading skills. When administering these subtests, particular care should be taken to the standardized requirements for administering and scoring because these are not all calculated in the same manner. For example, while some subtests are based on the student's actual performance within a specific time period, the

Naming Facility subtest score is based on the conversion of the student's performance to a point score (Kaufman & Kaufman, 2004).

The subtests on the K-TEA-II also have varying rules for the establishment of basal and ceiling levels. The examiner should carefully read and adhere to the specific administration procedures. Some of the subtests require that a student miss four consecutive items in order to establish a ceiling, another subtest may require four of five responses as incorrect in order to establish a ceiling, yet another may require five of six responses for the ceiling level. Some subtests follow different discontinue rules and others require that the examiner encourage the student to complete all of the items for a specific level. It is imperative that the examiner follow all of the standardized instructions during the administration in order to obtain a valid representation of the student's academic ability.

Scoring the Comprehensive Form of the K-TEA-II Most items on the K-TEA-II are scored as 1 for correct response and 0 for incorrect. There are some exceptions to this scoring. The timed items are scored based on performance or a conversion score based on performance. The Written Expression subtest and the Oral Expression subtest include items that have multiple criteria for scoring. In addition to determining the raw scores and the error patterns, the K-TEA-II provides norm tables for converting the raw score data to standard scores for the subtests and composites. Norm tables for percentile ranks, confidence intervals, and developmental scores, such as age equivalents, are provided. An example of a scored protocol is presented in Figure 7.2.

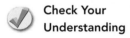

Check Your Understanding

Complete Activity 7.3 below to determine your general understanding of the K-TEA-II.

Activity 7.3

1. You are concerned about a student who is having difficulty answering questions about reading passages. In addition to assessing the student's ability with curriculum materials, you decide to assess the student's skills using a norm-referenced test. Which subtest of the K-TEA-II assesses a student's ability to answer literal and inferential questions?_____

2. Most of your kindergarten students have been making adequate progress in their ability to match sounds, blend sounds, segment sounds, and delete sounds. The data you collected using CBMs indicates that one student has not made adequate progress. You decided to assess this student using the K-TEA-II. Which subtests would you decide to use?_____

3. What is the difference between an item level error analysis and a within item error analysis?_____

Figure 7.2 Figure from page 18 of K-TEA-II manual.

KTEA·II

Kaufman Test of Educational Achievement, Second Education
]Alan S. Kaufman & Nadeen L. Kaufman

Comprehensive Form
Form A

Name: _Robyn Harris_   Sex: _F_ ID: _____
School: _____   Grade: _2_
Teacher: _____ Examiner: _____
Medications: _____

	Year	Month	Day
Test Date	2004	5	26
Birth Date	1996	9	14
Age	7	6	12

Norms Used:
☐ Age
☐ Grade: Fall
☒ Grade: Spring

	Subtest Raw Score	Standard Score Subtest	Standard Score Composite	CAC Subtests PreK–K	CAC Subtests GR. 1–12⁺	Confidence Interval Band	Confidence Interval Interval	%ile Rank	Grade Equiv.	Age Other
2 Letter & Word Recognition	47	99			99	± 4	(95 – 103)	47	2.6	___
6 Reading Comprehension	25	98			98	± 5	(93 – 103)	45	2.6	___
Reading			Sum 197 → 98			± 3	(95 – 101)	45		___
3 Math Concepts & Applications	53	130			130	± 8	(122 – 138)	98	4.11	___
5 Math Computation	21	123			123	± 8	(115 – 131)	94	3.8	___
Math			Sum 253 → 129			± 6	(123 – 135)	97		___
7 Written Expression	159	73			73	± 12	(61 – 85)	4	1.2	___
8 Spelling	18	85				± 6	(79 – 91)	16	1.6	___
Written Language			Sum 158 → 77			± 7	(70 – 84)	6		___
9 Listening Comprehension	30	103			103	± 10	(93 – 113)	58	3.0	___
10 Oral Expression	65	105				± 10	(95 – 115)	63	3.4	___
Oral Language			Sum 208 → 104			± 8	(96 – 112)	61		___

Comprehensive Achievement Composite (CAC)   Sum 626 ↓   Std. Score 105   ± 4 (101 – 109) 63   ___

Reading-Related Subtests	Raw Score	Standard Score				
1 Phonological Awareness	20	99	± 9	(90 – 108)	47	2.6
4 Nonsense Word Decoding	16	103	± 7	(96 – 110)	58	3.0
11 Word Recognition Fluency	___		± ___	(___ – ___)	___	___
12 Decoding Fluency	___		± ___	(___ – ___)	___	___
13 Associational Fluency	19	93	± 13	(80 – 106)	32	1.9
14 Naming Facility (RAN)	11	96	± 8	(88 – 104)	39	2.2

AGS PUBLISHING
© 2004 AGS Publishing
4201 Woodland Road,
Circle Pines, MN 55014-1796
800-328-2560 www.agsnet.com

Product Number: 32215-RF
A 0 9 8 7 6 5 4 3 2 1

Source: Kaufman Test of Educational Achievement (2nd ed.), (2004), page 18 of the Examiner's Manual. Circle Pines, MN: AGS publishers. Reprinted with permission.

Comparisons Within the K-TEA-II Once the selected subtests or the entire K-TEA-II have been administered and scored, the examiner can compare subtests and composites of the student's scores in order to identify academic strengths and weaknesses. A completed portion of the protocol in which the subtest scores and the composite scores are compared is illustrated in Figure 7.3.

Remember that the level of significance selected indicates the amount of chance occurrence of the difference. In other words, if a level of significance of .05 is selected, this indicates that the difference between the two scores occurs by chance only 5 times out of 100. Also, if the .01 level of significance is selected, the amount of difference would occur only 1 time out of 100. In other words, there is a 99% chance that the difference is a truly significant difference.

Once it is determined that a difference is significant, the examiner also needs to find out how frequently the difference occurred in the norm sample. A difference can be significant statistically but that difference may also occur frequently within the general population. If it is a common occurrence, it may not require educational intervention. This is especially true if the difference is significant because one score is average and the other score is an even higher score. This may indicate a significant strength in a specific academic area. Tables are provided within the K-TEA-II manual to locate the frequency of occurrence and level of significance for comparisons between subtests, between composites, and between the K-ABC-II and the K-TEA-II.

Figure 7.3 K-TEA-II subset and composites comparisons.

Composite Comparisons If difference is significant, circle composite with higher standard score.

	Standard Score	Diff.	Standard Score		Significance		Frequency of Occurrence		
Reading	98	31	129	(Math)	<.05	(<.01)	<15%	<10%	(<5%)
(Reading)	98	21	77	Written Language	<.05	(<.01)	<15%	<10%	(<5%)
Reading	98	6	104	Oral Language	<.05	<.01	<15%	<10%	<5%
(Math)	129	52	77	Written Language	<.05	(<.01)	<15%	<10%	(<5%)
(Math)	129	25	104	Oral Language	<.05	(<.01)	(<15%)	<10%	<5%
Written Language	77	27	104	(Oral Language)	<.05	(<.01)	<15%	(<10%)	<5%
Reading	98	4	102	Decoding	<.05	<.01	<15%	<10%	<5%
					<.05	<.01	<15%	<10%	<5%

Circle if significant or infrequent (refer to Appendix 1).

Subtest Comparisons If difference is significant, circle subtest with higher standard score.

	Standard Score	Diff.	Standard Score		Significance		Frequency of Occurrence		
Reading Comprehension	98	5	103	Listening Comprehension	<.05	<.01	<15%	<10%	<5%
Written Expression	73	32	105	(Oral Expression)	<.05	(<.01)	<15%	(<10%)	<5%
Oral Expression	105	2	103	Listening Comprehension	<.05	<.01	<15%	<10%	<5%
					<.05	<.01	<15%	<10%	<5%
					<.05	<.01	<15%	<10%	<5%

Circle if significant or infrequent (refer to Appendix 1).

**Check Your
Understanding**

To experience scoring a math achievement test, complete Activity 7.4 below.

Activity 7.4

A third-grade boy age 8-7 answered the items on a math calculation subtest in the following manner:

1.	11.	21. 1	31. 1
2.	12.	22. 1	32. 0
3.	13.	23. 1	33. 0
4.	14.	24. 0	34. 0
5.	15. 1	25. 1	35. 0
6.	16. 1	26. 1	36. 0
7.	17. 1	27. 0	37.
8.	18. 1	28. 0	38.
9.	19. 1	29. 0	39.
10.	20. 0	30. 0	40.

1. The basal for this subtest is 5 consecutive items correct and the ceiling is 5 consecutive items incorrect. What is the raw score?

   _____

2. The Daily Math Skills subtest has already been scored. The obtained raw score for the Daily Math Skills subtest was 38. Write the appropriate scores in the spaces provided on the sample protocol.

Math Composite

	Raw Score	Standard Score	Percentile Rank
Math Calculation			
Daily Math Skils			
Math Composite			

3. Add the raw scores and place the sum in the raw score box for the math composite score. Look at the norm table below. Locate the standard scores and percentile ranks for this student. Write the scores in the appropriate spaces.

Math Calculation

Raw Scores	Standard Score	Percentile Rank
23	83	13
24	82	12
25	80	10
26	79	9
27	78	8

Daily Math Skills

Raw Score	Standard Score	Percentile Rank
36	100	50
37	101	53
38	102	55
39	103	58
40	104	61

Math Composite Scores

Raw Score	Standard Score	Percentile Rank
62	89	24
61	90	26
62	91	28
63	92	30

Apply Your Knowledge

With the average standard score of 100 and the median percentile rank of 50, in what area(s) does this third-grade student appear to need intervention? _____

_____
_____

Determining Educational Needs Using the K-TEA-II The K-TEA-II provides several scores that can be used to determine educational needs of the individual student. The performance of the student can be analyzed for patterns of errors by comparing the types of items answered correctly and the types of items answered incorrectly. In addition, the within-items comparison for some subtests

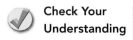

Check Your Understanding

Check your ability to calculate and determine significant differences in comparing composites of an achievement test by completing Activity 7.5 below.

Activity 7.5

On the test presented in Activity 7.4, an examiner can determine if there are any significant differences between composite scores. Look at the composite scores listed below. Subtract the scores to determine the amount of difference between the composite scores.

Math Composite	92
Written Language Composite	87
Reading Composite	72

On the following table, write the differences in the appropriate spaces. Look at the table and determine if any of the differences between composite scores are significant.

Composite Comparisons

Composites	Difference	Significant at the .05 Level	Significant at the .01 Level
Math-Written Language		17	20
Written Language-Reading		18	22
Math-Reading		16	19

Apply Your Knowledge

How would you explain the significant difference concept to the parents of this child? How might this significant difference impact educational interventions? _____

_____

_____

allows further analysis that can be used to determine educational needs. An example of a student's responses on the Nonsense Word Decoding subtest protocol is presented in Figure 7.4. The student's responses have been scored as pass or fail (a 0 or 1), and the specific pronunciations have been noted by the examiner. The raw score is determined and the errors are then analyzed on a separate form that allows the examiner to complete a within-item error analysis. The results of the error analysis within the items can be used to determine the educational needs of the student. These needs are the basis for writing educational objectives, designing teaching strategies, and identifying which specific skills will be

Figure 7.4 Portion of the Nonsense Word Decoding protocol, p.10, Form A.

#	Word	Score	Single/Double Consonant	Initial Blend	Medical Final Blend	Consonant Digraph	Wrong Vowel	Short Vowel	Long Vowel	Vowel Team/Diphthong	R-controlled Vowel	Silent Letter	Prefix/Word Beginning & Suffix/Inflection	Hard/Soft CGS	Initial/Final Sound	Insertion/Omission	Misordered Sounds	Whole Word Error
35	disenquoyment	0 (1)		qu						oy			dis en ment					
36	bortioned	0 (1) b	r							o		tion ed					
37	guarnal	0 (1) g	r n						ua			al					
38	cheigh	(0) 1			ch				ei		gh							
39	gemnissent	0 (1) g m n ss					e i					ent		✓			MPA
40	norpesious	(0) 1 n r p s					e			o		ious					
41	dovign	(0) 1 d v n					o (i)				g						
42	quintabulent	0 (1) b	i qu	nt			i a (u)					ent				✓	
43	slield	0 (1)	sl	ld					le								
44	wredgiest	(0) 1 r	g				e				w d	iest					
45	sydalogue	(0) 1 s d l g				(y) a o					ue						
46	panpaudiatory	(0) 1 p	d				a	i	au			pan tory					UN
47	cyctarious	(0) 1 c c t t					y			(a)		ious					
48	shresplenescent	(0) 1 (n) s	shr	spl			e e(e)					ent	c			✓	
49	pnoutiest	0 1 n	t						ou			iest	p				
50	squertious	0 1	r	squ						e		tious					
	Total Errors by Category		2	2	0	0	1	3	2	1	1	1	1	1	2	4	1	4

CONSONANTS | *VOWELS* | *OTHER*

Source: Kaufman, A. S. and Kaufman, N. L., (2004). K-TEA-II Comprehensive Form A. Circle Pines, MN: AGS Publishing.

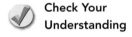

Check Your Understanding

Complete a within-item error analysis of the Nonsense Word Decoding subtest. Use the section of the protocol presented in Figure 7.4 to complete Activity 7.6.

Activity 7.6

Refer to Figure 7.4 of your text to answer the following questions.

1. The portion of this error analysis includes the student's performance on items 35–50. Based on this section of the error analysis, which short vowel sounds seem to be problematic?_____

2. In which categories did the student have no errors?_____

3. How many errors were made that were considered entire word mistakes?_____

4. How many types of vowel errors were made by this student? _____

5. What is meant by the term "misorderd sounds"?_____

Apply Your Knowledge

Give examples of words with insertion and omission errors._____

_____

_____

monitored through other classroom assessment methods, such as curriculum-based assessment.

Kaufman Test of Educational Achievement– II–Brief Form   The KTEA-II Brief Form is an instrument designed for screening students when an estimate of achievement is needed. For example, a student may be screened to determine if additional data are needed for a re-evaluation. This measure includes only three subtests: Reading, Math, and Written Expression. The Reading subtest includes reading recognition items and reading comprehension items. For example, a student is presented short paragraphs with comprehension questions and single words or letters for recognition. On the Math subtest, items include math computation as well as math application problems. The Written Expression items include both spelling and written language. This short assessment is presented in an easel format like the comprehensive battery, and the test publisher estimates administration time ranges from 10 to 40 minutes depending on the age of the child. This instrument was designed for children from 4 and ½ years of age to adults 90 years of age.

WECHSLER INDIVIDUAL ACHIEVEMENT TEST, SECOND EDITION (WIAT-II)

The WIAT-II (Psychological Corporation, 2001) is an individually administered achievement test made up of nine subtests. Students ages 4-0 to 19-11 or in grades PreK (age 5) through college may be administered this instrument. The administration of this instrument to college students and adults can be completed using the WIAT-II Supplement for College Students and Adults. This revised edition of the WIAT contains changes in individual items, subtests, and scoring. The revised edition expanded several subtests and added the new subtest, Pseudoword Decoding. The WIAT was designed to help educators in determining discrepancies between measured intellectual ability and academic achievement. The revised test format includes easels, paper-and-pencil tasks, and separate reading cards. Starting points and ceiling rules, which vary by subtests, are presented in the manual and on the protocol form. Some items are timed and cues are provided to the examiner in the test stimulus booklets and in the protocol. Examiners are also provided rules for reverse administration in the examiner's manual and on the protocol if the student does not establish a basal. A parent report form is included within the protocol.

The WIAT includes subtests in the areas of oral expression and listening comprehension. These areas are not typically included in other academic achievement tests and may offer the educator useful information for intervention. This test provides skill information on the protocol of the math subtests that can easily be adapted to write educational objectives. The protocol includes qualitative observation items that the examiner may simply check following the administration of each subtest. Additional information regarding each subtest follows.

Subtests

Word Reading. This subtest was called Basic Reading in the original version of the WIAT. This revised subtest has been expanded and includes items at the PreK level. The early items include visual memory and visual discrimination of letters. Items of letter recognition or letter naming are presented next, followed by items in which the student is asked to discriminate rhyming words. Students are then asked to generate rhyming words to specific stimuli. Then students are asked to determine two of three words that begin with the same sound followed by words with the same ending sounds. Students are then asked to discriminate the letters that make specific sounds; this includes isolated vowels, consonants, and consonant blends. On more difficult items, the student is presented with words on a card and asked to read the words aloud.

Numerical Operations. Items for PreK students include number recognition, number sequencing (1–10), dictation of specific numbers, and counting. Additional items require the student to respond in writing to solve calculation problems. More difficult items are problems that involve geometry, percent, decimals, and simple algebraic equations.

Reading Comprehension. In this subtest, the first-grade student is asked to point to the picture that matches the word. Simple sentence items follow with specific target words that are scored by the examiner. Beginning with second-grade items, the student reads written passages and then responds to questions asked by the examiner. In addition to passage items, sentences are also presented for oral reading accuracy. Beginning with the third-grade items, student reading speed is timed. Specific starting and stopping points are used rather than ceiling levels.

Spelling. The student responds in writing to letters, sounds, or words dictated by the examiner. Homonyms are presented in bold in the protocol.

Pseudoword Decoding. This subtest is presented on a reading card and is administered to students in grades 1 and above. The examiner should listen to the audiotape and become familiar with the correct pronunciation prior to the initial administration of the test. The student's responses are recorded exactly using correct pronunciation or phonetic symbols.

Math Reasoning. This subtest requires the student to solve math problems that require reasoning. The student is presented with items on the easel and may use pencil and paper if needed.

The PreK items include counting pictures and distinguishing pictures with more objects. Other early-level items include recognizing shapes and interpreting simple picture graphs. More difficult items include answering story-type problems and interpreting complex graphs.

Written Expression. This subtest contains the following five sections: alphabet writing, word fluency, sentences, paragraph, and essay. This subtest requires the student to respond in writing to various prompts. Written-expression paragraphs and essays are scored for mechanics, organization, and vocabulary.

Listening Comprehension. This subtest was revised to include receptive vocabulary items, sentence comprehension, and expressive vocabulary. Following orally presented items, the student responds to questions asked by the examiner. The items include picture cues, and the lower levels require the student to point to the answer.

Oral Expression. This subtest was revised to include the following four sections: sentence repetition (for the early grades only), word fluency, visual passage retell, and giving directions. Sentence repetition requires the student to repeat sentences. The word fluency subtest is timed. Other items assess the student's ability to use words to describe picture cues, give directions, or provide explanations. The student responds orally. The examiner must write the student's responses or use a tape recorder to tape the responses.

Scoring   The scoring of the revised edition of the WIAT is more complex than the original version. Items on the Word Reading, Mathematics Reasoning, Spelling, Numerical Operations, Pseudoword Reading, and Listening Comprehension subtests receive a 1 when answered correctly and 0 when incorrect. Scoring for the Reading Comprehension and Written Expression subtests is slightly more complicated; the manual includes instructions and practice exercises. Raw scores are used to obtain derived scores that may be based on either grade- or age-normative data. Grade norm tables are presented for fall, winter, and spring. The correct table is determined by the date of testing according to the following guidelines: fall for August–November, winter for December–February, and spring for March–July. Standard scores—with a mean of 100, percentile ranks, age equivalents, and grade equivalents—are available for both subtests and composites. Supplemental scores, in quartiles and deciles, are available. Tables are provided to determine significant differences between individual subtest scores and composite scores. To assist in decisions regarding significant discrepancies between ability and achievement, tables are provided that display differences between scores on the WIAT-II and the Wechsler

Check Your Understanding

Check your understanding of the WIAT-II by completing Activity 7.7 below.

Activity 7.7

Answer the following questions about the WIAT-II.

1. Which subtest includes items that assess phonemic awareness and early reading skills?_____

2. Which subtest includes expressive vocabulary and sentence comprehension?_____

3. A student who scored significantly below the levels expected on the subtests of word reading, reading comprehension, spelling, and pseudoword decoding but was within the range expected on other subtests might have been referred to determine if a _____exists.

4. A student in your class seems to take longer to respond in writing on tasks he is asked to do during class time. He also writes much shorter responses and often writes very short and simple words. His reading level is at the range expected, however, he may have difficulty with _____.

Apply Your Knowledge

Which subtests of the WIAT-II would you analyze closely for a student in your class who is struggling in math?_____

_____

_____

Intelligence Scale for Children, Third Edition, between the WIAT-II and the Wechsler Adult Intelligence Scale, Third Edition, and between the WIAT-II and the Wechsler Preschool and Primary Scale of Intelligence. Tables are provided with levels of statistical significance for differences between predicted and actual subtest scores and composite scores for using the predicted-achievement method.

WIDE RANGE ACHIEVEMENT TEST–REVISION 3 (WRAT3)

The WRAT3 is a screening achievement test that was designed to "measure the codes which are needed to learn the basic skills of reading, spelling, and arithmetic" (Wilkinson, 1993, p. 10). This test is composed of three subtests that may be administered in any order and may be given to persons ages 5 through 75. Because it is a screening instrument, the WRAT3 should be used not to diagnose learning problems but rather to determine whether additional testing is necessary. This third revision, unlike the WRAT–R, may be given to any person within the age range of 5–75 and is no longer divided by age levels. The test includes alternate forms, the Blue Test and Tan Test, which may be administered alone or together for a combined score. Students who are not administered the items for ages 5–7 are given credit for those items. The Spelling and Reading subtests use a 5/10 rule for the basal and ceiling. This means that individuals age 8 and above must be presented with the beginning items if they do not correctly answer the first 5 items presented, and that testing stops when students miss 10 consecutive items. The Arithmetic subtest uses a 5/15-minute criterion: Students age 8 and above must answer at least 5 items correctly or be given the beginning oral items, and testing stops at the 15-minute time limit.

Subtests

Reading. This subtest contains a plastic card with a small sample of letters and words that the student reads aloud to the examiner. The naming of letters is considered a prereading task. The student is allowed 10 seconds to recognize each word. The examiner scores the subtest by crossing out the first letter of incorrect words and by circling the item number for correct responses. Each correct item is worth 1 point. This subtest does not measure word attack or any form of reading comprehension.

Spelling. This subtest begins with name writing and letter writing for students ages 5 through 7. Students are asked to write their name and then to write letters spoken by the examiner. The student is then asked to spell words presented orally. The examiner pronounces a word, gives a sentence that includes the word, and then repeats the word; the student responds in writing on the protocol.

Arithmetic. This subtest contains a few counting items and oral response items, but the remainder of the subtest is a paper-and-pencil task of computation. Students may first solve a small sample of math problems presented on the protocol. Students ages 5 through 7 begin this subtest with the oral problems and progress to the calculation items. This subtest has a 15-minute time limit.

Scoring

The raw scores on the WRAT3 may be used to obtain standard scores, grade scores, and absolute scores. Absolute scores have a mean of 500 and were determined by using the Rasch analysis to determine item difficulty. The absolute scores allow for a person to be compared with the entire continuum of the domain or areas without using age or grade comparisons. Item analyses using the absolute scores are provided in the WRAT3 examiner's manual.

WOODCOCK–MCGREW–WERDER MINI-BATTERY OF ACHIEVEMENT

This instrument is an individually administered easel test designed to screen academic achievement across several areas.

Subtests The test is structured to include the following subtests.

Reading. Reading is assessed using three subtests: reading identification, reading vocabulary, and reading comprehension. The reading identification subtest includes a list of letters and words that the student reads aloud. The reading vocabulary subtest assesses a student's ability to provide antonyms for given words. The reading comprehension subtest includes short passages with a word missing that the student must provide. The easier items present pictures and words. The student must find the picture that best represents the words.

Writing. A student's writing skills are screened by assessing writing mechanics such as spelling, punctuation, and grammar or usage. The subtests include dictation, which measures the student's ability to provide responses independently, and proofing, which requires the student to identify writing errors when presented with visual stimuli. This test does not include items that measure written expression but rather measures writing mechanics.

Mathematics. These skills are screened by assessing basic calculation using a pencil-and-paper format and by assessing math reasoning and concepts. The reasoning and concepts subtest includes visual stimuli in easel format as well as verbal cues.

Factual Knowledge. This is assessed through the use of questions presented orally. Information included on these items is information students learn through their environment and educational experiences.

Scoring Items are scored as 1 or 0 for all subtests. Raw scores are entered into a computer scoring program that yields a one-page report of standard scores (mean of 100 and standard deviation of 15), percentile ranks, and age/grade equivalent for each subtest.

SELECTING ACADEMIC ACHIEVEMENT TESTS

The tests reviewed in this chapter represent the more commonly used instruments in public school assessment. One instrument may be particularly better to use in the situation than in another. The strengths and weaknesses are presented in Table 7.2 to provide some guidance in selecting instruments.

Table 7.2 Academic achievement tests.

Name of Instrument	Purpose of Test	Constructs Measured	Standardization Information	Reliability Information	Validity Information
Woodcock–Johnson Tests of Achievement, Third Edition	Comprehensive assessment of academic areas	Reading, oral language, math, written language, academic fluency, academic applications	More than 8,000 persons ages 2 to more than 90 years. Variables included race, sex, Hispanic/non-Hispanic, occupation, level of education, and community size.	Test-retest, interrater reliability, alternate forms reliability, and internal consistency. Most reliability coefficients for internal reliability in the .90s.	Concurrent validity research with other measures such as the K-TEA and the WIAT. Validity coefficients ranged from .79 to 65.
Kaufman Test of Educational Achievement, Second Edition	Comprehensive assessment of academic areas	Reading, reading-related composites, math, written language, oral language	Sample of 2,400 students in grades K–12. Variables included ethnicity, education level of parents, geographic region, sex.	Internal consistency reliability for subtests and composites; most in the .90s, alternate forms reliability, interrater reliability.	Construct validity, concurrent validity studies with the WJ-III, PIAT-R/NU, confirmatory factor analysis.
Wechsler Individual Achievement Test, Second Edition	Assessment of academic achievement	Reading, written expression, math, listening comprehension, oral expression	Included 3,600 students in grades PreK through 12 and ages 4–19. Variables included race/ethnicity, sex, geographic area, parents education level. Fall and spring testing periods.	Reliability research included internal consistency measures, test-retest, and interscorer reliability. Coefficients ranged from .81 to .99.	Construct validity, content validity, and criterion-related validity research included in manual.

Name of Instrument	Purpose of Test	Constructs Measured	Standardization Information	Reliability Information	Validity Information
Wide Range Achievement Test	Screening for three basic academic skills	Reading recognition, spelling, and math operations	More than 4,000 persons included in sample with consideration of age, sex, geographic region, race, and socioeconomic level.	Test-retest reliability, alternate forms reliability, and internal consistency research using coefficient alpha are included in manual.	Content and criterion-related validity studies included in the manual. Construct validity information included.
Mini-Battery of Achievement	Screening across several academic areas	Reading identification, comprehension, and vocabulary; writing mechanics and spelling; math calculation and reasoning; factual knowledge	The sample included more than 6,000 persons ranging in age from 4 to 95. Adequate demographic and geographic representation in norm sample.	Test-retest and split-half reliability research included, with coefficients ranging from .70 to .98. Greatest inconsistency noted in children younger than 6 years of age.	Concurrent validity research indicated coefficients ranging between .70s to upper .80s.

DIAGNOSTIC TESTING

diagnostic tests Tests used to obtain futher information about specific skills.

Teachers often need additional information to make the correct decisions for educational interventions. Instruments that can yield more detailed information for making such decisions are known as **diagnostic tests.**

REVIEW OF DIAGNOSTIC TESTS

The tests presented here represent those commonly used by teachers; they have also been selected because of existing research. The assessment of the basic skill areas of reading, mathematics, spelling, and written language is presented in this chapter. The uses of diagnostic tests are shown in Figure 7.5.

KEYMATH–3 DIAGNOSTIC ASSESSMENT (KEYMATH–3 DA)

The KeyMath–3 DA (Connolly, 2007) is presented in an easel format and consists of two equivalent forms, A and B. The KeyMath–3 is aligned with the Standards of the National Council of Teachers of Mathematics (NCTM, 2000) and the matrix reflecting this alignment is included in the appendix of the test manual. The alternate forms may be administered every three months to monitor progress of the student in mathematics. The third edition of this diagnostic mathematics battery includes computer scoring software and progress monitoring capability. The software program will provide a functional analysis of the student's responses on the instrument and will yield the specific items that require intervention. The functional analysis provides behavioral objectives that may be used to drive the math intervention process. The instrument may be administered to students who are 4 years and 6 months of age to students who are 21 years of age who are within the skill levels provided by the instrument. The estimated administration time ranges from 30–90 minutes.

On the KeyMath–3 DA, many of the items are presented orally by the examiner. The computation items for the basic math operations of addition, subtraction, multiplication, and division, are presented as paper-and-pencil tasks. This test includes subtests that are grouped into three areas: Basic Concepts, Operations, and Applications. Table 7.3 presents the areas, **domains**, and content of the revised KeyMath–3 DA.

domain Area of cognitive development or ability thought to be evidenced by certain behaviors or skills.

Subtests and Content Areas

Basic Concepts. In this content area, items are presented to assess the conceptual understanding of numeration, algebra, geometry, measurement, and data analysis and interpretation.

Table 7.3 Content specification of KeyMath–3 DA: Subtests and content of domains.

Areas	Basic Concepts	Operations	Applications
Strands and Domains	**Numeration** Early number awareness Place value and number sense Magnitude of numbers Fractions Decimals Percentages Exponents, integers, multiples, and factors **Algebra** Early algebraic awareness Algebraic uses of numbers and geometry Symbolic representation Ratio and proportion Coordinate graphing **Geometry** Early geometric awareness Two-dimensional shapes Three-dimensional shapes Lines and angles Formulas Grids and coordinate planes **Measurement** Early awareness of measurement Standard units Time Money Data analysis and probability Early awareness of data and probability Charts, tables, and graphs Graphical representation Statistics Probability	**Mental Computation and Estimation** Early awareness of mental computation Mental computation chains Mental computation with whole numbers Mental computation with rational numbers Estimation and whole numbers Estimation and rational numbers **Addition and Subtraction** Algorithms to add and subtract whole numbers Algorithms to add and subtract rational numbers Integers Algebra **Multiplication and Division** Algorithms to multiply and divide rational numbers Integers Algebra	**Foundations of Problem Solving** Analysis of problems Word problems **Applied Problem Solving** Numerations Algebra Geometry Measurement Data analysis and probability

Source: Adapted from *KeyMath–3 DA* (Appendix E pp.341–345) by A. J. Connolly, 2007, NCS Pearson, Inc. Minneapolis, MN: Pearson Assessments. Reprinted by permission.

Figure 7.5   Appropriate uses of diagnostic tests.

Initial assessment process	To assess areas in which questions remain regarding a student's ability in an academic skill—such as reading—or subskill—such as phonological awareness
Reevaluation	To assess specific areas that the team determines necessary in order to make a decision regarding continued eligibility for services or interventions
Assessment of progress	Classroom teacher uses to measure progress toward objectives in specific academic area
Additional data for classroom interventions	Classroom teacher needs additional information to adjust interventions or planning or to obtain in-depth information about student's mastery of a specific skill

Numeration. These items sample the student's ability to understand the number system and the functional application of that system. Items include tasks such as counting, identifying numbers, identifying missing numbers in a sequence, understanding concepts of more and less, and reading multidigit numbers.

Algebra. This subtest measures understanding of the concepts and skills used in pre-algebraic problems and includes items such as number sentences, functions, and equations.

Measurement. Items range from recognition and identification of units of measurement to problems that involve application and changing of the various units of measurement, and includes items of time and money.

Geometry. These items range from understanding spatial concepts and recognizing shapes to interpreting angles and three-dimensional figures.

Operations. This content area includes computation problems using paper and pencil and mental computation items that are presented in the easel format.

Mental Computation. This orally administered subtest includes math operations problems and more difficult problems that require several steps and operations to complete.

Addition and Subtraction. This subtest assesses the student's ability to perform addition and subtraction computation problems.

Multiplication and Division. This subtest is presented in the same format as the addition and subtraction subtests and includes simple grouping problems (sets) and more difficult multiplication of mixed numbers and fractions. The items cover a range of difficulty levels and contain some multistep, or "long" division, computations, addition and subtraction of fractions, and beginning algebraic computations.

Application. This content area includes problems that are representative of how mathematics is used in everyday life.

Foundations of Problem Solving. These items assess a student's early ability or "readiness" to complete application problems.

Applied Problem Solving. On these items, the student is presented with math problems of daily living such as calculating sales tax or categorization of objects.

Scoring   Grade level starting points are provided on the protocol. The basal is established when a student responds correctly to at least three items in the set before missing an item. If the student incorrectly responds to an item, the items are presented in reverse order until the student successfully answers three consecutive items correctly. The basal level is the three items prior to the first incorrect response. The ceiling is established when a student incorrectly answers four consecutive items. Once the raw scores for each subtest are calculated, they are used to locate the standard scores in the examiner manual.

The KeyMath–3 DA provides scale scores for the individual subtests. These scores have a mean of 10 and a standard deviation of 3. Each of the three areas and the total test score are presented as standard scores with a mean of 100 and a standard deviation of 15 for all age and grade groups. Norm tables are included for fall and spring for standard scores and percentile ranks. Age and grade equivalent developmental scores are also provided. Areas can be compared so that it may be determined if a student is significantly strong or weak in a specific math area.

Tables provide information regarding a student's functional range according to the subtest raw scores. There are tables that indicate which items are focus items that the student missed and yet the items fall below the student's functional range. These items may be in particular need of intervention. Information on a subsequent table indicates the items that the student answered correctly that were above the student's functional level.

Another score is provided to assist with measurement of ongoing progress. This is called the growth scale value or GSV. An example of the graphing of the GSV is presented in Figure 7.6.

Figure 7.6   Graphical display of the KeyMath–3 DA Progress Report.

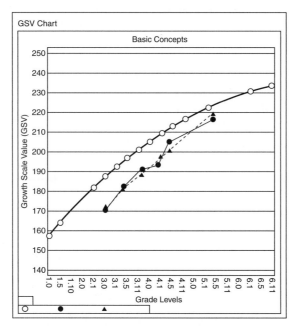

Source: KeyMath–DA, by J. A. Connolly, 2007. Page 32 of the Examiner's Manual,
NCS Pearson, Inc. Minneapolis, MN. Reprinted with permission.

The examiner uses the raw scores to locate scaled scores for each subtest and then sums the raw scores of the subtests for the area raw score. The area raw scores are used to determine area standard scores, percentile ranks, and age or grade equivalents.

Comparing Area Standard Scores for Significance   The examiner compares the standard scores obtained on the three areas in the section of the protocol titled "Area Comparisons," shown in Figure 7.7. The examiner writes the standard scores in the appropriate spaces and writes or >, <, = on each of the lines between the boxes. The standard score differences are determined by subtracting the scores. To determine significance level, the examiner refers to a table in the manual that lists the differences that are considered significant. If the difference is listed as significant at the .05 level, this means that the chances are 95 out of 100 that a true difference exists and there are only 5 chances out of 100 that the difference is by error or chance. The level of .01 means that the difference exists with only 1 possibility of 100 that the difference is by error or chance.

In addition to an indication of the chance occurrence of such a difference, it is recommended that the frequency of such a difference be determined. For example, how often would a student have such a difference between areas happen? To determine this, the examiner refers to a table in the examiner's manual.

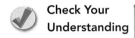

Check Your Understanding

Check your ability to score a portion of the KeyMath–3 DA by completing Activity 7.8 below.

Activity 7.8

Complete the following problems.

1. One student's responses for the Addition and Subtraction subtest are shown on the KeyMath–3 DA protocol in Figure A below. Calculate the raw score and then write your answer on the protocol.

Figure A

Addition and Subtraction

Note: Skip this subtest if the examinee's Numeration ceiling item is 6 or below.
See Chapter 2 in the KeyMath–3 DA manual for details.

OPERATIONS

Numeration Ceiling Item	Item	Score		Description	Correct Response
4–19 ▶	1.	①	0	1 + 2	3
	2.	①	0	0 + 5	5
	3.	①	0	6 − 0	6
20, 21 ▶	4.	①	0	7 + 2	9
	5.	①	0	4 − 2	2
	6.	1	⓪	8 − 8	0
22–25 ▶	7.	①	0	9 + 5	14
	8.	1	⓪	14 − 7	7
	9.	1	⓪	21 + 7	28
26–29 ▶	10.	1	⓪	14 + 6	20
	11.	1	⓪	56 − 5	51
	12.	1	0	13 + 47	60
30–34 ▶	13.	1	0	50 − 9	41
	14.	1	0	45 + 59	104
	15.	1	0	305 + 97	402

Ceiling Item	Errors	Raw Score*
☐	— ☐	= ☐

*Read the scoring instructions on page 10 of this record form before calculating the subtest raw score.

Source: p. 3 of KeyMath Protocol Copyright 1971, 1976, 1988, 1998, 2007 NCS Pearson, Inc. KeyMath is a trademark of NCS Pearson, Inc.

2. This student's other raw scores for the Operations subtests have been entered in Figure B. Write the raw score calculated in problem 1 in the appropriate space in Figure B below.

Figure B

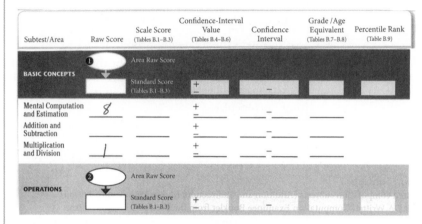

Source: KeyMath 3-Protocol Front Page KeyMath Protocol Copyright 1971, 1976, 1988, 1998, 2007. NCS Pearson, Inc. KeyMath is a trademark of NCS Pearson, Inc. Reprinted with permission.

Figure C

Mental Computation and Estimation	Addition and Subtraction	Multiplication and Division	Foundation of Problem Solving	Applied Problem Solving	Scale Score
37–40	30–35	22–31	26–27	32–35	19
35–36	29	21	25	30–31	18
33–34	—	20	—	29	17
31–32	28	18–19	24	27–28	16
29–30	27	17	23	26	15
27–28	26	15–16	21–22	24–25	14
24–26	25	14	20	23	13
22–23	24	13	19	21–22	12
21	23	11–12	17–18	20	11
19–20	22	—	15–16	18–19	10
17–18	20–21	9–10	14	16–17	9
15–16	18–19	8	12–13	14–15	8
12–14	16–17	7	11	12–13	7
10–11	14–15	5–6	9–10	10–11	6
7–9	12–13	4	7–8	8–9	5
5–6	9–11	2–3	5–6	6–7	4
3–4	6–8	1	4	5	3
2	4–5	0	3	3–4	2
0–1	0–3	—	0–2	0–2	1
1.0	1.4	0.9	1.2	1.2	68% CI

Source: From KeyMath-3 Examiner's Manual p. 237 Protocol Copyright 1971, 1976, 1988, 1998, 2007. NCS Pearson, Inc. KeyMath is a trademark of NCS Pearson, Inc. Reprinted with permission.

Figure D

From KeyMath–3 Examiner's Manual p. 237

Standard Score	Basic Concepts	Operations	Applications	Total Test
85	77	39	24	140–142
84	75–76	38	—	137–139
83	73–74	37	23	133–136
82	71–72	36	22	129–132
81	70	35	—	126–128
80	68–69	34	21	123–125
79	67	32–33	20	120–122
78	65–66	31	—	116–119
77	63–64	30	19	112–115
76	61–62	28–29	18	109–111
75	60	27	17	105–108
74	58–59	25–26	16	101–104
73	56–57	24	—	97–100
72	54–55	23	15	93–36
71	52–53	22	—	89–92
70	50–51	20–21	14	84–88
69	47–49	19	13	80–83
68	45–46	18	12	76–79
67	42–44	17	11	73–75
66	40–41	16	—	68–72
65	37–39	14–15	10	64–67
64	34–36	13	9	60–63
63	31–33	12	—	56–59
62	29–30	11	8	52–55
61	26–28	10	7	48–51
60	24–25	9	—	45–47
59	22–23	8	6	42–44
58	20–21	7	—	39–41
57	19	—	5	36–38
56	18	6	—	33–35
55	0–17	0–5	0–4	0–32
90% CI	5	7	8	4

Source: From KeyMath-3 Examiner's Manual p. 237 Protocol Copyright 1971, 1976, 1988, 1998, 2007, NCS Pearson, INC KeyMath is a trademark of NCS Pearson, Inc. Reprinted by permission.

Add the subtest raw scores to determine the area raw score and then write this score in the figure. Use the portions of the tables (Figures C and D) to locate scale scores and standard scores. Write these in the appropriate spaces.

Apply Your Knowledge

How would you interpret this student's standard scores for his parents? Write your explanation._____

_____

_____

The KeyMath–3 DA was normed on 3,630 people ages 4 years and 6 months through 21 years and 11 months of age. Persons who participated in the norming process were English proficient. The norm sample was representative of the population of the United

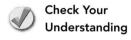

Check Your Understanding

Check your ability to determine if differences between scores are significant by completing Activity 7.9 below.

Activity 7.9

Complete the following problems.

1. A third-grade student obtained the KeyMath–3DA area standard scores shown at the bottom of Figure B. Write the standard scores in the appropriate spaces in Figure 7.7a. Indicate whether the comparisons are <, >, or = and determine the differences.

2. Using the information provided in Figures 7.7b and 7.7c, determine whether the differences found in problem 1 are significant. Write the significance level and write the frequency of occurrence in Figure 7.7a.

Apply Your Knowledge

Identify this student's strengths and weaknesses according to the information obtained regarding significant differences. How would you explain this to the student's parents? Write your explanation. _____

_____

_____

Figure 7.7a   KeyMath Protocol

Area	>, <, =	Area	Standard Score Difference	Significance Level	Frequency of Occurrence
75 **BASIC CONCEPTS**	___	**OPERATIONS**	___	___	___
7 5 **BASIC CONCEPTS**	___	82 **APPLICATIONS**	___	___	___
___ **OPERATIONS**	___	8 2 **APPLICATIONS**	___	___	___

Source: p. 9 KeyMath Protocol Copyright 1971, 1976, 1988, 2007 NCS Pearson, Inc. KeyMath is a trademark of NCS Pearson, Inc.

Figure 7.7b   KeyMath Examiners Manual p. 320.

Significance Levels Corresponding to Area Standard Score Differences

Grade	Signification Level	Basic Concepts vs. Operations	Basic Concepts vs. Applications	Operations vs. Applications
K	NS	0–12	0–13	0–13
K	<.05	13–16	14–17	14–17
K	<.01	17+	18+	18+
1	NS	0–9	0–9	0–7
1	<.05	10–12	10–13	8–10
1	<.01	13+	14+	11+
2	NS	0–10	0–10	0–10
2	<.05	11–13	11–13	11–14
2	<.01	14+	14+	15+
3	NS	0–8	0–9	0–10
3	<.05	9–11	10–12	11–13
3	<.01	12+	13+	14+
4	NS	0–7	0–8	0–9
4	<.05	8–10	9–10	10–12
4	<.01	11+	11+	13+

Source: p. 320 KeyMath Protocol Copyright 1971, 1976, 1988, 2007, NCS Pearson, Inc. KeyMath is a trademark of NCS Pearson, Inc.

Figure 7.7c   KeyMath Examiner's Manual p. 320.

Frequencies of Occurrence Corresponding to Area Standard Score Differences

Grade	Frequency of Occurrence	Basic Concepts vs. Operations	Basic Concepts vs. Applications	Operations vs. Applications
K	>10%	0–20	0–12	0–21
K	6–10%	21–28	13–17	22–29
K	1–5%	29–34	18–24	30–44
K	<1%	35+	25+	45+
1	>10%	0–16	0–14	0–16
1	6–10%	17	15	17–19
1	1–5%	18–24	16–26	20–26
1	<1%	25+	27+	27+
2	>10%	0–14	0–13	0–15
2	6–10%	15–18	14–15	16–18
2	1–5%	19–21	16–17	19–25
2	<1%	22+	18+	26+
3	>10%	0–13	0–13	0–18
3	6–10%	14–15	14–15	19–21
3	1–5%	16–19	16–19	22–24
3	<1%	20+	20+	25+
4	>10%	0–12	0–11	0–14
4	6–10%	13–14	12–14	15–16
4	1–5%	15–19	15–17	17–20
4	<1%	20+	18+	21+

Source: p. 320 KeyMath Protocol Copyright 1971, 1976, 1988, 2007, NCS Pearson, Inc. KeyMath is a trademark of NCS Pearson, Inc.

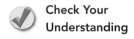

Check Your
Understanding

Check your ability to determine a student's profile on the KeyMath–3 DA by completing Activity 7.10 below.

Activity 7.10

This student's scale scores and confidence intervals have been entered below on the score profile sheet. Complete the sheet by shading in the profile in Figure 7.8. Complete the profile of the area scores at the bottom of the profile. How would you interpret these scores for parents? _____
What would be the areas and skills of concern? _____

States in race/ethnicity, sex, parent's education level, and geographic location. The norm sample reflected the U.S. population based on the 2004 survey of the U.S. Bureau of Census.

The examiner's manual provides evidence of internal reliability including split-half reliability for subtests, area, and total test scores. Additional reliability information is provided for alternate forms and test-retest reliability. Validity information includes construct validity, content validity, and concurrent criterion related validity. Studies with clinical samples with the KeyMath included samples of children with attention-deficit hyperactivity disorder, learning disabilities in reading, in math, and in reading and math, and students with mild intellectual disabilities. A study with a sample of gifted students provided evidence of discrimnant validity with that sample of students who, on average, earned points that were consistently one-standard deviation above the mean of the instrument on both scale scores and standard scores.

Test of Mathematical Abilities–2 (TOMA–2)   The TOMA (Brown, Cronin, & McEntire, 1994) was designed to assess some areas of math that may not be addressed by other instruments. This test, now in its second edition, was developed to be used with students who range in age from 8-0 to 18-11. The test authors present the following questions, not answered by other instruments, as their rationale for developing the TOMA:

1. What are the student's expressed attitudes toward mathematics?
2. What is the student's general vocabulary level when that vocabulary is used in a mathematical sense?

Figure 7.8 KeyMath–3 Protocol p.8 Form B.

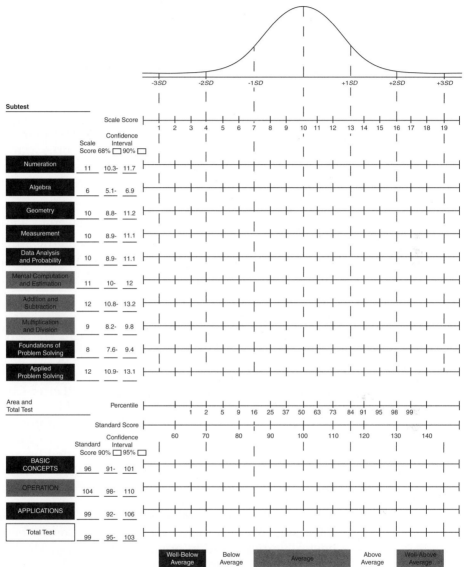

Source: page 8, KeyMath Protocol, Copyright 1971, 1976, 1988, 2007 NCS Pearson, Inc. KeyMath is a trademark of NCS Pearson, Inc.

3. How knowledgeable is the student (or group of students) regarding the functional use of mathematics facts and concepts in our general culture?

4. How do a student's attitudes, vocabulary, and general math information compare with the basic skills shown in the areas of computation and story problems?

5. Do the student's attitudes, vocabulary, and level of general math information differ markedly from those of a group of age peers? (Brown, Cronin, & McEntire, 1994, p. 1)

This instrument was developed to help the teacher find the answers to these questions. The TOMA–2 consists of five subtests, with the fifth subtest, Attitude Toward Math, considered supplemental. The remaining subtests are Vocabulary, Computation, General Information, and Story Problems. The subtests yield standard scores with a mean of 10, a math quotient with a mean of 100, age equivalents, and percentile ranks. The manual gives precautions against misinterpretation of test scores and encourages further diagnostic assessment if a math disability is suspected.

The test authors list three diagnostic questions that the TOMA–2 may help educators answer:

1. Where should the student be placed in a curriculum?
2. What specific skills or content has the student mastered?
3. How does this student's overall performance compare with that of age or grade peers? (Brown, Cronin, & McEntire, 1994, p. 1)

WOODCOCK READING MASTERY TESTS–REVISED (WRMT–R)

The WRMT–R (Woodcock, 1987) consists of two forms that are not exactly equivalent. One form, G, contains two additional reading-readiness subtests and a supplementary Letter Checklist. For this reason, Form G is the version that should be used with younger or lower-level readers. The other form, H, contains subtests equivalent to the four other subtests contained in Form G. A general screening of reading ability can be obtained by administering the Short Scale, which includes only the Word Identification and the Passage Comprehension subtests.

Subtests For this revision of the WRMT, the subtests of Word Identification, Word Attack, and Passage Comprehension remained basically unchanged in presentation format. The Word Attack subtest contains an error analysis inventory, but the presentation format remains the same. Substantial changes have been made in some of the subtests, and these changes affect their presentation. A new subtest, Visual-Auditory Learning, has been added.

Visual-Auditory Learning. In this subtest, the examiner visually presents a picture or rebus type of symbol while orally presenting a word. After seeing four symbols and hearing their accompanying words, the student must use the newly learned symbols to "read" sentences presented on the subsequent easel page. The student then sees four new symbols and is asked to "read" sentences that include both the first symbols and the new symbols. This process continues throughout the subtest unless the student reaches a ceiling by making a specific number of errors. If the student reaches a ceiling, the cutoff score based on total errors is used to determine the raw score. If the student does not make the number of errors used to stop the testing but rather completes all of the stories on the subtest, the number of total errors is subtracted from the number 134 to determine the raw score. This subtest is found only on Form G of the WRMT–R.

Letter Identification and Supplementary Letter Checklist. These two subtests are contained only on Form G of the revised WRMT. The Letter Identification subtest does provide norm scores; however, the Supplementary Letter Checklist is used for error analysis only. The examiner has the option of presenting the task to measure the student's ability to name the letters or the sounds of the letters.

Word Identification. This subtest measures the student's ability to orally read the visually presented words. The words at the easiest level represent sight words and other words selected from several basal reading series. The more difficult words were selected from various sources. This subtest attempts to measure identification of the word. The student must say the word aloud; comprehension of the word is not measured.

Word Attack. This subtest visually presents nonsense words, which the student must decode orally. This test measures the student's ability to use phonetic attack and structural analysis in reading new words aloud. An error analysis page included in the protocol assists the examiner in identifying specific phonetic errors that need educational remediation.

Word Comprehension. This subtest samples the student's ability to provide missing words for analogies, synonyms, and antonyms. This subtest actually comprises three smaller subtests, which can be analyzed by categories for understanding vocabulary. The examiner calculates three raw scores and locates the *W* score on the protocol rather than from norm tables.

Passage Comprehension. This subtest presents a sentence or passage with a missing word. The student orally provides the missing word after silently reading the passage. The lower-level items contain picture cues, and most of the difficult items are fairly content specific. The most difficult items were taken from textbooks, newspaper articles, and the like.

Scoring On most of the WRMT–R subtests, the student establishes the basal after answering six consecutive items correctly and the ceiling after answering six consecutive responses incorrectly. The

Visual-Auditory Learning subtest, however, contains a cutoff score chart to determine when the student has reached a ceiling level.

Scoring the WRMT–R will result in comprehensive information about the student's individual reading ability. In addition to an error analysis for the Word Attack subtest and qualitative scoring of the Supplementary Letter Checklist, this battery can provide the examiner with the following information:

1. Standard error of measurement is provided for each W score, and confidence bands may be calculated for each subtest.

2. Space on the protocol for error responses helps the examiner complete an error analysis of reading ability.

3. Several diagnostic profiles may be plotted according to the student's performance based on percentile ranks, grade equivalents, and relative performance index scores.

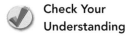

Check Your Understanding

Check your ability to obtain a raw score for a portion of the WRMT–R by completing Activity 7.11 below.

Activity 7.11

Complete the following problems.

1. A student taking the WRMT–R Visual-Auditory Learning subtest completed stories 1 through 4 and made 46 errors. In Figure H, find the row that contains stories 1–4, because the student completed four stories. Locate the number 46, and then locate the total error estimate beneath in the total errors row (stories 1–7). Write the total error estimate in the appropriate space in Figure H _____.

2. Subtract the total error estimate from 134 to obtain the raw score for this subtest. Write the score on Figure H _____.

Apply Your Knowledge

What is the purpose of using the cutoff score table?_____
_____
_____

Figure H

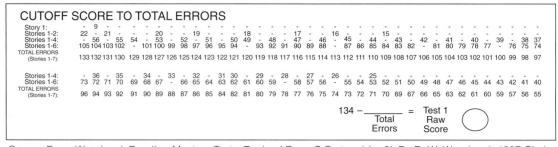

Source: From *Woodcock Reading Mastery Tests–Revised Form G Protocol (p. 3).* By R. W. Woodcock 1987 Circle Pines, MN. American Guidance Service. Copyright 1976 by American Guidance Service.

Once having mastered the scoring, the examiner obtains a comprehensive evaluation of reading. The examiner uses raw scores to enter tables to obtain the derived scores of W scores, grade and age equivalents, and standard error of measurement for W scores. The examiner compares the student's obtained W scores with reference scores for age or grade-level comparisons.

The table that contains the reference scores also contains column numbers. The column numbers are used to find percentile ranks and standard scores on another table. Two column numbers are given for each reference score. After making the comparison by subtracting the reference score from the obtained W score, the examiner selects the correct column number and enters the relative performance index table, a portion of which is shown in Figure 7.9.

The examiner determines the correct column by the following criteria: If the difference between the W and the reference score is less than 100, the column number on the left is used to enter the table; if the difference is greater than 100, the column number on the right is used to enter the table. The column numbers may be different for the scores obtained in the standard error of measurement confidence bands. When the standard error of measurement is added to the difference score, the new score may be greater than 100 when the original difference score was less than 100. This means that the column number on the right would be used to determine the relative performance index and percentile rank for the confidence band scores. When the standard error of measurement is subtracted from the difference score, the new score may be less than 100 when the original score was not. Again, the new score found by using the standard error of measurement would require a different column number for the relative performance index table.

The WRMT–R presents cluster scores for reading as well as individual subtest scores. The clusters are Readiness (Form G only), Basic Skills, and Reading Comprehension. The Readiness cluster includes the Visual-Auditory and Letter Identification subtests. Word Identification and Word Attack subtests make up the Basic Skills cluster. The Reading Comprehension cluster is made up of the Word Comprehension and Passage Comprehension subtests. The cluster W scores are obtained by finding the average of the two subtest W scores in each cluster. A Total Reading cluster score is found by averaging the four subtests contained on both forms of the test: Word Identification, Word Attack, Word Comprehension, and Passage Comprehension.

PROCESS ASSESSMENT OF THE LEARNER: TEST BATTERY FOR READING AND WRITING (PAL–RW)

The PAL–RW is designed to assess the processes used in initial and emerging reading and writing skills as well as the skills expected

Figure 7.9   Table G all forms, columns 25 to 30, difference scores 115 to 144.

Table G. Relative Performance Indexes, Percentile Ranks, and Standard Scores (mean = 100, *SD* = 15)

Column						
25	**26**	**27**	**28**	**29**	**30**	
PR/Std	PR/Std	PR/Std	PR/Std	PR/Std	PR/Std	DIFF
98 132	98 130	97 129	96 126	93 122	90 119	144
98 131	98 129	97 128	95 125	93 122	90 119	143
98 130	97 129	97 127	95 125	92 121	89 119	142
98 129	97 128	96 127	95 124	92 121	89 118	141
97 129	97 127	96 126	94 124	91 120	88 118	140
97 128	96 127	96 125	94 123	91 120	87 117	139
97 127	96 126	95 125	93 122	90 119	87 117	138
96 127	95 125	95 124	93 122	90 119	86 116	137
96 126	95 125	94 123	92 121	89 118	86 116	136
95 125	95 124	94 123	92 121	88 118	85 115	135
95 124	94 123	93 122	91 120	88 117	84 115	134
94 124	93 123	92 122	90 119	87 117	83 115	133
94 123	93 122	92 121	90 119	86 116	83 114	132
93 122	92 121	91 120	89 118	85 116	82 114	131
92 122	91 121	90 120	88 118	85 115	81 113	130
92 121	91 120	90 119	87 117	84 115	80 113	129
91 120	90 119	89 118	86 117	83 114	79 112	128
90 119	89 118	88 118	86 116	82 114	79 112	127
89 119	88 118	87 117	85 115	81 113	78 111	126
89 118	87 117	86 116	84 115	80 113	77 111	125
87 117	86 116	85 116	83 114	79 112	76 111	124
86 117	85 116	84 115	82 114	78 112	75 110	123
85 116	84 115	83 114	81 113	77 111	74 110	122
84 115	83 114	82 114	80 112	76 111	73 109	121
83 114	82 114	81 113	78 112	75 110	72 109	120
82 114	81 113	80 112	77 111	74 110	71 108	119
81 113	79 112	78 112	76 111	73 109	70 108	118
79 112	78 112	77 111	75 110	72 109	69 108	117
78 111	77 111	76 110	74 109	71 108	68 107	116
76 111	75 110	74 110	72 109	70 108	67 107	115

Source: From *Woodcock Reading Mastery Tests–Revised Examiner's Manual* (p. 172) by R. W. Woodcock, 1987. Circle Pines, MN: American Guidance Service. Copyright 1987 by American Guidance Service. Reprinted by permission.

during the intermediate grades in school (through grade 6). This battery can be used for students ranging in age from 5 years to 13 years of age. It assesses the prerequisite and requisite skills needed to read, write, and take notes in school. Several skill areas are assessed. A brief description of each subtest is presented in the following section.

Alphabetic Writing. This subtest requires the student to write as many letters of the alphabet as possible under a timed format.

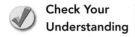

**Check Your
Understanding**

Check your ability to score a portion of the WRMT–R by completing Activity 7.12 below.

Activity 7.12

Complete the problems and answer the questions that follow.

1. Use the information shown in Figure I to determine the difference between the obtained *W* score and the reference score for the Word Identification subtest. Choose from the figure the column number that will be used to find the relative performance index and the percentile rank for the obtained *W* score._____

2. Using the obtained difference score from problem 1, complete the confidence bands (Figure I) by adding and subtracting the standard error of measurement given in the figure. Write the answers in the appropriate spaces on the portion of the protocol in Figure I. Choose from the figure the column number that will be used to find the relative performance index and percentile ranks for the confidence band scores._____

3. The relative performance index for this student is 99/90. Write 99 in the appropriate spaces in Figure I. Use the previous table to find the standard score and percentile rank for the obtained difference score found in problem 1 for the Word Identification subtest. Write your answer in the appropriate spaces in Figure I._____

4. Use the table to obtain the standard scores and percentile ranks for the confidence bands. Write your answer in the appropriate spaces in Figure I._____

5. What do the confidence band scores represent?_____

Figure I Protocol section for WRMT—R Word Identification subtest.

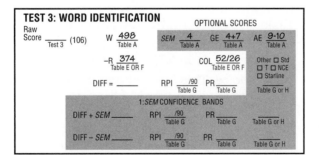

Source: From *Woodcock Reading Mastery Tests—Revised, Protocol* (p. 12) by R. W. Woodcock, 1987. Circle Pines, MN: American Guidance Service. Copyright 1987 by American Guidance Service. Reprinted by permission.

This assesses the child's memory of the alphabet as well as the child's ability to graphically represent the letters. Fluency or automaticity of this ability is considered due to the subtest time limit of 5 minutes. Qualitative analysis is included as part of the scoring, with omissions, reversals, inversions, sequencing errors, case confusions (upper and lower case), and cursive letters noted by the examiner. The test is administered to students in grades K–6.

Receptive Coding. The child is asked to match or discriminate letters within words. Letter sequencing is also assessed. These tasks tap into the child's visual memory of letters and sequences of letters. This subtest is administered to children in grades K–6.

Expressive Coding. Similar tasks as in receptive coding, however the student is required to write responses in a response booklet. The sequencing tasks require the child to understand concepts such as first or fifth to identify and correctly write the specific letter or letters. Children in grades 4–6 are administered this subtest.

Rapid Automatic Naming (RAN). Because automaticity or fluency is essential for mastery of reading and writing, there are several RAN subtests included on the PAL–RW. Qualitative analyses and quantitative analyses can be completed for each of the subtests of RAN–Letters (grades K–6), RAN–Words (grades 1–6), RAN–Digits (grades K–6), RAN–Digits and Words (grades 1–6).

Note Taking. There are two tasks for assessing the note-taking skills of students in grades 4–6. These tasks are scored both qualitatively and quantitatively. Students listen and take notes for a passage read by the examiner.

Rhyming. Two tasks assess the prereading skills of rhyming discrimination and rhyming fluency. This subtest is administered to students in kindergarten.

Syllables. Students in grades K–6 are administered this subtest. The task requires students to understand and manipulate the deletion of syllables they hear and say.

Phonemes. This subtest is administered to students in grades K–6, who must delete sounds of words and nonsense words. Tasks are differentiated by grade level.

Rimes. Students in grades 1–6 must hear, manipulate, and then say words in which they delete a sound.

Word Choice. This subtest assesses the student's ability to discriminate between words with correct written spellings and incorrect written spellings. The discriminations become more difficult according to the grade placement of the student, with students in grades 4–6 being required to discriminate more complex and unpredictable words. Visual memory and memory for visual sequencing of letters are required for this subtest.

Pseudoword Decoding. This subtest is for students in grades 1–6. Students are asked to read nonsense words.

Story Retell. This subtest is administered to students in kindergarten. Students are asked to listen to a story, answer specific questions about the story, and then retell the story. Scoring criteria for responses are provided.

Finger Sense. This subtest is administered to students in grades K–6. Students must physically respond to finger sequencing tasks and respond to tasks that require them to have adequate sensation within their fingers. Students are also required to determine specific letters that are "written" on their fingers by the examiner.

Sentence Sense. Students are required to read and discriminate which sentence, in sets of three sentences, make sense. Silent reading fluency and comprehension are necessary due to the timed format.

Copying. On these tasks, students are required to copy written sentences in a timed format. Both copying fluency and accuracy of writing is important, and scoring criteria are provided. Students in kindergarten complete Task A and students in grades 1–6 complete Task B.

This fairly new assessment instrument offers a variety of subtests that tap into the individual skills needed to read and write in school successfully. This test is not a comprehensive assessment of reading comprehension, but it offers a format in which to assess other skills needed, such as memory, sequencing, association, and fluency of the visual, aural, and motor abilities required for reading and written language skills. These skills are the skills that should be developmentally in place for students in kindergarten through grade 6 and therefore expand beyond the skills of phonemic awareness.

The scores available for this instrument are decile scores that are used to form a profile of the student's ability. Figure 7.10 illustrates a completed scored protocol with the decile profile.

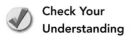

Check Your Understanding

Complete Activity 7.13 below.

Activity 7.13

Answer the following questions about the skills assessed on the PAL Test Battery for Reading and Writing.

1. One of the subtests of the PAL tests the student's ability to repeat sequences with their fingers. What is the name of this subtest?
   _____

2. Which subtest assesses a student's ability to select the correct spellings of words?_____

3. On which subtests are phonemic awareness and early prereading skills assessed?_____

4. Which complex subtest requires the student to be able to understand concepts such as position placement in a sequence of letters in order to respond to the task of the subtest?_____

Figure 7.10   Example of a completed score-profile page of the record form of the process assessment of the learner from the *PAL Test Battery for Reading and Writing Administration and Scoring Manual*, p. 24.

Subtest/Content	Raw Score	Decile Score	Profile									
Alphabet Writing Score	3	≤40	10	20	30	(40)	50	60	70	80	90	100
Receptive Coding Total Score	34	≤30	10	20	(30)	40	50	60	70	80	90	100
Expressive Coding Total Score			10	20	30	40	50	60	70	80	90	100
RAN												
Letters Total Time	89	≤20	10	(20)	30	40	50	60	70	80	90	100
Words Time	47	≤20	10	(20)	30	40	50	60	70	80	90	100
Digits Total Time	92	≤20	10	(20)	30	40	50	60	70	80	90	100
Words & Digits Time	93	≤10	(10)	20	30	40	50	60	70	80	90	100
Note-Taking Task A Score			10	20	30	40	50	60	70	80	90	100
Rhyming Total Score			10	20	30	40	50	60	70	80	90	100
Syllables Total Score	10	≤100	10	20	30	40	50	60	70	80	90	(100)
Phonemes Total Score	30	≤100	10	20	30	40	50	60	70	80	90	(100)
Rimes Total Score	6	≤70	10	20	30	40	50	60	(70)	80	90	100
Word Choice Total Score	1	≤10	(10)	20	30	40	50	60	70	80	90	100
Pseudoword Decoding Total Score	15	≤40	10	20	30	(40)	50	60	70	80	90	100
Story Retell Total Score			10	20	30	40	50	60	70	80	90	100
Finger Sense												
Repetition Item 1 Time	9	≤30	10	20	(30)	40	50	60	70	80	90	100
Repetition Item 2 Time	9	≤30	10	20	(30)	40	50	60	70	80	90	100
Succession Item 1 Time	14	≤50	10	20	30	40	(50)	60	70	80	90	100
Succession Item 2 Time	10	≤80	10	20	30	40	50	60	70	(80)	90	100
Localization Score	10	≤100	10	20	30	40	50	60	70	80	90	(100)
Recognition Score	10	≤100	10	20	30	40	50	60	70	80	90	(100)
Fingertip Writing Score	7	≤80	10	20	30	40	50	60	70	(80)	90	100
Sentence Sense Total Score	5	≤40	10	20	30	(40)	50	60	70	80	90	100
Copying												
Task A Score	27	≤100	10	20	30	40	50	60	70	80	90	(100)
Task B Score	60	≤100	10	20	30	40	50	60	70	80	90	(100)
Note-Taking Task B Score			10	20	30	40	50	60	70	80	90	100

Source: V. W. Beringer (2001). San Antonio, TX: The Psychological Corporation.

The PAL–RW manual contains a chapter on how the results of the assessment can be used for interventions. The appendices include criterion-referenced measures that may be reproduced for instructional purposes.

OTHER DIAGNOSTIC TESTS

The remainder of this chapter summarizes several other tests frequently used in the classroom. Some of these tests will not require the lengthy test administration time required by tests presented in the first section of the chapter. Some of these tests may be administered, in part or in their entirety, to groups of students. These tests are included here because they provide useful information to the educator for diagnosing deficits in specific academic areas and aid in educational planning.

GRAY ORAL READING TESTS–FOURTH EDITION (GORT–4)

The GORT–4 provides the teacher with a method of analyzing oral reading skills. This instrument is a norm-referenced test that may be administered to students ages 7-0 through 18-11. The GORT–4 has equivalent forms so that students may be reassessed using the same instrument. This newest version of the GORT has an additional story for the lowest level on both forms of the instrument to allow for better exploration of the emerging reading skills of young students. On this instrument, the student reads stories aloud to the teacher, who scores rate, accuracy, fluency, comprehension, and overall reading ability. The comprehension score is derived from answers to questions asked by the teacher following each story. The oral reading miscues may be analyzed in the following areas: meaning similarity, function similarity, graphic/phonemic similarity, multiple sources (of errors), and self-correction. The authors state that the purposes of the GORT–4 are to identify students with problems, determine strengths and weaknesses, document progress, and to conduct research using the GORT–4 (Wiederholt & Bryant, 2001, pp. 4–5).

TEST OF READING COMPREHENSION–THIRD EDITION (TORC–3)

The TORC–3 was designed to assess reading comprehension using eight subtests. The instrument includes four subtests in the reading comprehension core: general vocabulary, syntactic similarities, paragraph reading, and sentence sequencing. These skills are assessed using a variety of task formats, such as multiple-choice items for general vocabulary and discrimination of sentences for syntactic similarities. The diagnostic supplements include the following subtests: mathematics vocabulary, social skills vocabulary, science vocabulary, and reading the directions of schoolwork. The test manual includes suggestions for additional assessment methods.

TEST OF WRITTEN LANGUAGE–3 (TOWL–3)

The third edition of the TOWL includes two alternate forms test booklets (A and B) and is organized into three composites: Overall Written Language, Contrived Writing, and Spontaneous Writing (Hammill & Larsen, 1996). TOWL–3 contains eight subtests, of which three are calculated from the spontaneously written story. The student completes all test items in the student response booklet. This instrument may be administered in small groups, although for optimal monitoring of written responses, individual administration appears to be best. A description of each subtest follows:

1. Vocabulary—The student is provided a stimulus word and required to use the word in a sentence.
2. Spelling—The student is required to spell dictated words.
3. Style—The student writes dictated sentences and must punctuate sentences and capitalize properly.
4. Logical Sentences—The student is provided an illogical sentence and is required to edit it so that it is more logical.
5. Sentence Combining—The student is presented two or more sentences per item and must combine them into one meaningful and grammatically correct sentence.

   For subtests 6, 7, and 8, the student is asked to write a story when shown a stimulus picture. The requirements for each subtest are:
6. Contextual Conventions—The student's story response is scored for punctuation, capitalization, spelling, and other conventional rules of writing.
7. Contextual Language—The student's story response is scored for sentence construction, quality of vocabulary, and grammar.
8. The student's story response is scored for the following: plot, prose, development of characters, interest, and additional aspects of composition (Hammill & Larsen, 1996).

TEST OF WRITTEN SPELLING–4 (TWS–4)

A standardized spelling test, the TWS–4 (Larsen, Hammill, & Moats, 1999) consists of two alternate forms that can be administered to individual students or to groups of students ages 6-0 to 18-11. Instructions for starting points and basal and ceiling levels are presented in the examiner's manual. During administration of this test, the student begins at the appropriate entry level and continues until the ceiling has been reached. The ceiling is established when the student misses five words consecutively. Once the ceiling has been reached, the examiner checks to see that the basal of five consecutive items answered correctly was obtained. For students who did not establish a basal, the examiner administers items in reverse order until five consecutive items are spelled correctly, or until the student reaches item 1. All items below the established basal are scored as correct. Raw scores are used to enter tables for standard scores with a mean of 100, percentile ranks, age equivalents, and grade equivalents.

This revision of the TWS includes more elaboration for examiners regarding the theoretical bases of the test and a discussion of the skills of spelling in English. The authors also provide a useful chapter on additional assessment methods of spelling and other related skills, such as the assessment of phoneme awareness. These additional assessment methods offer the use of this instrument as part of a total evaluation effort in which teachers would use additional methods and may use an alternate form of the TWS for measuring gains following interventions.

ASSESSING OTHER LANGUAGE AREAS

language assessment Measuring verbal concepts and verbal understanding.

The ability to understand and express ideas using correct language is fundamental for school achievement. **Language assessment**, through tests that measure a student's understanding and use of language, is presented in this section. Tests administered by speech clinicians in an effort to diagnose and remediate speech disorders (articulation, voice, or fluency disorders) are beyond the scope of this text. Effective remediation of language disorders is considered a shared responsibility of the clinician, teacher, and parent, who each must be familiar with the tests to diagnose and monitor these skills. These tests assess a student's **receptive language** vocabulary, oral **expressive language**, and **written language** skills. In addition to actual test instruments, informal assessment of written language is conducted in the classroom as well and is presented in Chapter 6.

receptive language Inner language concepts applied to what is heard.

expressive language Language skills used in speaking or writing.

PEABODY PICTURE VOCABULARY TEST–4 (PPVT–4)

written language Understanding language concepts and using them in writing.

The PPVT–4 (Dunn & Dunn, 2007) measures the student's verbal comprehension skills by presenting a series of four visual stimuli and requesting the student to discriminate the stimulus that best represents the orally stated word. An example of this format is illustrated in Figure 7.11. Two equivalent forms of this individually

Figure 7.11 Example of visual stimuli presented to measure verbal comprehension skills in the PPVT–4.

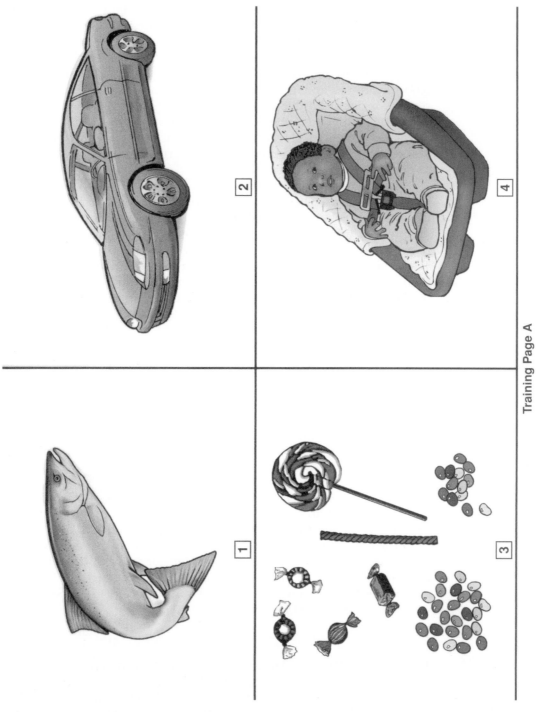

Source: From *Peabody Picture Vocabulary Test–4* (training plate D) by L. M. Dunn and L. M. Dunn, 2006. Reprinted by permission.

administered language test, form A and form B, allow retesting to monitor progress. This test includes an easel test, examiner's manual, norms booklet, and protocol. Derived scores include standard scores, percentile ranks, normal curve equivalents, stanines, age equivalents, and GSV or growth scale values. Scoring is fairly easy, and the basal level is determined when the student correctly answers all of the items in a set or misses only one item in the set. The ceiling is determined when the student incorrectly answers at least eight items in the set. The examiner's manual provides easy examples and cases to illustrate scoring and interpretation of raw scores. The examiner's manual also includes an analysis worksheet to determine if the student has more difficulty with the receptive vocabulary of nouns, verbs, or attributes. This may assist with planning interventions for promoting language development.

The examiner is cautioned to use this instrument with children who are English speakers because the PPVT–4 was normed on students who were proficient in English. The examiner's manual provides evidence of internal consistency, alternate forms reliability, test-retest reliability, content validity, concurrent criterion related validty, and discriminant validity comparing clinical groups with nonclinical groups. The PPVT–4 was conormed with the Expressive Vocabulary Test–2.

EXPRESSIVE VOCABULARY TEST–2

This instrument was conormed with the receptive language measure, the PPVT–4. This instrument was normed with persons ages 2 years and 6 months of age to those over 90 years of age. There are two forms of this measure, Forms A and B. The student's expressive vocabulary is assessed by asking the student to name a picture or to provide a synonym for a picture. Specific instructions with acceptable prompts are provided in the examiner's manual. Children are not penalized on this measure for mispronunciations or articulation errors if the work is recognizable. The examiner's manual includes worksheets that will assist the examiner in determining if the child has weaknesses in expressive vocabulary used at home or at school. An additional worksheet is provided for an analysis of parts of speech for each item of the instrument. Therefore, it can be determined that the student has a strength in nouns but has difficulty with verbs or attributes. These analyses may provide useful information to assist with language development interventions.

TEST OF LANGUAGE DEVELOPMENT–PRIMARY: THIRD EDITION (TOLD–P:3)

The Primary edition of the TOLD–P:3 (Newcomer & Hammill, 1997) was designed for use with students ranging in age from 4-0 to 8-11. The theoretical structure is based on a two-dimensional language model, described in the manual. TOLD–P:3 contains the following subtests: Picture Vocabulary, Relational Vocabulary, Oral Vocabulary, Grammatic Understanding, Sentence Imitation, Grammatic Completion, Word Discrimination, Phonemic Analysis, and Word Articulation. The standard scores on these subtests may be used to obtain quotients for the following composites: spoken language, listening, organizing, speaking, semantics, and syntax. Derived scores include standard scores (mean = 10), quotients (mean = 100), and percentile ranks. Age equivalents are available. The format of response includes both forced-choice and open-ended responses. The student is also asked to repeat sentences on the Sentence Imitation subtest and fill in missing words for the Grammatic Completion subtest. In the Word Discrimination subtest, the student must discriminate between same and different items, which the examiner states orally. The student must name pictured items and correctly pronounce the names in the Word Articulation subtest. Table 7.4 lists the skills measured by the subtests; understanding the skills enables the teacher to interpret results and use the interpretations to develop educational plans.

Table 7.4   Content within subtests of the TOLD–P:3.

I. *Picture Vocabulary* measures the ability to understand the meaning of individual words when spoken.

II. *Relational Vocabulary* measures the ability to organize incoming language into categories that permit the perception of relationships.

III. *Oral Vocabulary* measures the ability to define individual stimulus words precisely.

IV. *Grammatic Understanding* measures the ability to comprehend sentences having differing syntactic structures.

V. *Sentence Imitation* measures the ability to repeat complex sentences accurately.

VI. *Grammatic Completion* measures the ability to complete a partially formed sentence by supplying a final word that has a proper morphological form.

VII. *Word Discrimination* measures the ability to discern subtle phonological differences between two words spoken in isolation.

VIII. *Phonemic Analysis* measures the ability to segment spoken words into smaller phonemic units by remembering and uttering the component of a word that remains after a portion is removed from the original stimulus word.

IX. *Word Articulation* measures the ability to say (i.e., articulate) a series of single words properly.

Source: Examiner's Manual for Test of Language Development–Primary: Third Edition (p. 44). Austin, TX: Pro–Ed. 1997.

TEST OF LANGUAGE DEVELOPMENT–INTERMEDIATE: THIRD EDITION (TOLD–I:3)

The Intermediate edition of the TOLD–I:3 (Hammill & Newcomer, 1997) was constructed to aid in the diagnosis of students with language problems. The theoretical structure of the TOLD–I:3 is similar to the two-dimensional model of the TOLD–P:3. The following subtests are used to assess language skills for students aged 8-0 through 12-11: Sentence Combining, Picture Vocabulary, Word Ordering, Generals, Grammatic Comprehension, and Malapropisms. The examiner presents all subtests orally; items include forced-choice and open-ended questions. Derived scores of the TOLD–I:3 are standard scores (mean = 10), quotients (mean =100), and percentile ranks by age norms. Age equivalents are available.

SELECTING DIAGNOSTIC INSTRUMENTS

The instruments presented in this chapter are among those most used by educators to determine academic difficulties. Some instruments are recommended for specific academic areas or skills. Thus, an examiner may appropriately select one instrument because it contains subtests that will yield information necessary for academic planning and intervention. Table 7.5 presents a summary of the instruments in Chapter 7.

For **MORE PRACTICE** in deciding when to use achievement and diagnostic tests, visit the Companion Website at *www.prenhall. com/overton*.

RESEARCH AND ISSUES

Research is emerging on the newly revised versions of the tests presented in this chapter but is scant on the newly developed instruments, such as the KeyMath–3 DA. Selected research of the existing research and reviews of the instruments, and issues of academic assessment, are summarized here.

In a review of strengths and weaknesses of the WJ III Tests of Achievement, Mather, Wendling, and Woodcock (2001) noted that the inclusion of timed subtests may not be important in some settings and that students' performance on timed substests may be influenced by their culture. Moreover, these authors expressed concern that the complexity of some subtests, such as Understanding Directions and Story Recall, may result in responses that are difficult to interpret and score. They also stated that writing tasks on this instrument are limited to one-sentence responses.

Table 7.5   Diagnostic standardized academic tests.

Name of Test	Purpose of Test	Constructs Measured	Standardization Information	Reliability Information	Validity Information
KeyMath–3 DA	Comprehensive and diagnostic assessment of math skills	Basic math concepts, math operations, math applications	Sample included 3,630 persons ages 4 years 6 months–21 years 11 months Variables included geographic region, ethnicity, socioeconomic status, parental education level.	Alternate forms reliability coefficients .96–A .97–B for Total Test split-half reliability.	A variety of research supporting evidence for content validity, construct validity, concurrent criterion-related validity in manual.
Test of Mathematical Abilities–Second Edition	Assesses other aspects of math not found on other measures	Math vocabulary, attitude toward math, general math information	More than 2,000 students from 26 states. Variables included race, community, disability status.	Internal consistency coefficients and group coefficients ranged from .73 to .98; test-retest ranged from .66 to .93.	Concurrent criterion-related validity ranged from low to adequate; construct validity was supported.
Process Assessment of the Learner: Test Battery for Reading and Writing	Assessing the processes involved in reading and writing	Pre-reading and writing processes such as receptive and expressive coding, alphabetic writing, phonemic awareness skills, acquisition of written symbols, short-term memory of visual and oral symbols and sounds associated with reading, fluency of recall or rapid automatic naming	There were 868 students in the standardization sample ages 5–13 years. Variables considered include race/ethnicity, geographic region, and parent education level. Test developers sought to approximate the 1998 U.S. Census representation.	The manual includes reliability studies of internal consistency of alpha coefficients, test-retest reliability, and interscorer reliability. Coefficients ranged from adequate to high.	Evidence of content and construct validity provided. Concurrent criterion-related validity information provided with other diagnostic and reading/writing measures. Strong support for clinical discriminant validity provided.

Test	Purpose	Areas Assessed	Sample	Reliability	Validity
Woodcock Reading Mastery Tests–Revised	Assesses the skills of reading	Reading decoding skills, reading comprehension skills	More than 6,000 persons in sample from K to adult; variables include age, sex, race, geographic region.	Split-half reliability coefficients in the 90s.	Content and construct validity studies. Coefficients ranged from .48 to .91.
Gray Oral Reading Tests–Fourth Edition	Assesses oral reading skills	Accuracy, fluency, comprehension, and overall oral reading ability	More than 1,600 persons from four geographic regions. Variables included race, ethnicity, family income and educational status, age.	Alternative forms reliability, interscorer reliability, and test-retest reliability with coefficients ranging from .85 to .99	Content validity, differential item functioning, criterion-related validity research supports test validity.
Test of Reading Comprehension–Third Edition	Assesses reading comprehension skills	Reading comprehension, vocabulary from content-related areas	The sample included more that 1,900 students. Variables considered were age, sex, race, ethnicity, and geographic region.	Internal consistency, interscorer, content and time sampling were considered with reliability coefficients ranging from .79 to .98.	Information provided for content, construct, and criterion-related validity. Information provided for discriminant validity for specific groups.
Test of Written Language–Third Edition	Assessment of various written language skills	Written language, spelling skills, vocabulary	More than 2,000 students were included in the sample. Variables considered were sex, race and ethnicity, community type, disability, and geographic region.	Interscorer, coefficient alpha, split-half reliability, and test-retest reliability information ranged from adequate to high.	Concurrent criterion-related validity, factor analysis information provided and considered adequate.
Test of Language Development–Primary: Third Edition	Various aspects of language development of young children	Vocabulary, grammatical and syntactic understanding, articulation of words and phonemic analysis	The sample included 1,000 students ages 4-0 to 8-11. Variables considered were sex, community size, race, ethnicity, educational level of parents, family income and geographic region.	Reliability coefficients ranged from .77 to .99 for content sampling, internal consistency measures, time sampling, and interscorer reliability studies.	Content validity, construct validity, and criterion-related validity studies included in the manual, with coefficients ranging from .52 to .97.

Table 7.5 continued.

Name of Test	Purpose of Test	Constructs Measured	Standardization Information	Reliability Information	Validity Information
Test of Language Development–Intermediate: Third Edition	Assessment of general language skills of children ages 8-0 through 12-11	Vocabulary, grammatical comprehension	A portion of the sample was included from previous studies with a sample size of 779. Variables considered include sex, community size, race, ethnicity, parent occupation, and geographic area.	Internal consistency using coefficient alpha, content sampling, and interscorer reliability presented in the manual, with coefficients ranging from .83 to .97.	Criterion-related validity, construct validity, item validity, and factor analysis information included in the manual.
Test of Written Spelling–Fourth Edition	Assessment of spelling skills	Spelling skills	Over 4,000 students were included in the standardization of the TWS–2 and TWS–3 combined, with no new cases added for TWS–4. The sample considered the variables of race, sex, ethnicity, and geographic region.	Internal reliability coefficients were high, ranging from .93 to .99. Test-retest reliability studies were adequate although the sample sizes of the studies for reliability were small.	Content, criterion-related validity information, and construct validity research included and based on developmental gains.
Peabody Picture Vocabulary Test–Third Edition Expressive Vocabulary Text–2	Assessment of vocabulary skills through equivalent forms Assesses expressive vocabulary	Receptive vocabulary expressive vocabulary ability to name pictures and provide synonyms	Sample included 3,540 persons ranging in age from 2 years to 90+. Variables included sex, ethnicity, age, education level of person or parents, and geographic region. Representation based on 2004 U.S. Census survey data. Conormed with the PPVT–4, see above for standarization sample	Internal consistency studies included split-half and alternate forms. Test-retest information included. All coefficients ranged from the .83 to .90s for both forms Split-half reliability ranged from .88–.97	Examiner's manual provides various research studies providing evidence. of coustract, Criterion related and content validity. Evidence provided for clinical discriminant validity. with clinical samples

Litchenberger and Smith (2005) pointed out some of the weaknesses of the WAIT–II. These authors report that the WIAT–II has a limited ceiling on some of the subtests and that this may cause difficulty in determining the functioning of students who are gifted. In addition, variability in standard errors of measurement across ages, indicates a weakness with reliability. For teachers who often interpret testing results and relate these results to instruction, it is also problematic that quartile and decile scores are unfamiliar. The WIAT–II also has limited items representing some skills that are found on the Skills Analysis.

The publishers of some achievement tests have renormed or updated the normative information available for the achievement batteries, for example, the PIAT–R–NU. When these tests undergo a normative update, there may be differences in between the groups of students who participate in one domain or on specific subtests. This may result in some variability between subtests on the same instrument (Johnson, 1999).

Berninger (2006) suggests that instruments such as the Process Assessment of the Learner and the WIAT–II should be used in combination with intensive interventions for reading and written language for students who are at risk for developing written language disabilities. This may offer an advantage over using CBM type progress monitoring alone since the student would be assessed and compared with age norms.

The K-TEA-II has weaknesses in the ceiling level and floor level when the test is administered to very young or old students on some subtests (Litchenberger & Smith, 2005). For example, on some subtests a young student with a raw score of 0 may earn a standard score between the low 60s and 80s. These authors also noted some weaknesses in the standard error of measurements for some specific age groups on specific subtests.

In a review by Cascella (2006), it was noted that some language assessments provide normative data on students with intellectual disabilities. This may be helpful when trying to determine if a student should receive additional speech and language therapy in the school setting. In this review, it was noted that the TOAL–3, the TOLD–I:3, the TOLD–P:3, the PPVT–3, and the EVT provided such norms.

In older reviews of the PIAT–R (Allinder & Fuchs, 1992), the authors cautioned that the format of the test instrument, including multiple choice on some subtests, may encourage guessing. These reviewers also cautioned that information obtained from multiple-choice items is diagnostically different from information obtained when a response must be produced independently by the student. They reminded consumers that this instrument was designed as a wide-range screening instrument and should therefore not be used in educational decision making involving placement, eligibility, or planning. Another study found that changing the visual stimuli associated with the PIAT–R Written Expression subtest resulted in significantly higher scores for structure (Cole, Muenz, Ouchi, Kaufman, & Kaufman, 1997).

Slate (1996) compared several measures frequently used in assessing students with learning disabilities. In this study, the WIAT, KeyMath–R, Woodcock–Reading Mastery–Revised, and the PIAT–R were compared. While many of the subtests were positively correlated, there remained significant variance and mean differences. In other words, although reading subtests may share common constructs and similar items, students may perform quite differently across such subtests of different achievement batteries. Therefore, what may be perceived as a true difference in abilities may really be the result of differences in the tests, not the student.

THINK AHEAD

How do you think student behaviors influence a student's ability to make successful progress in school? In the next chapter, you will learn a variety of methods used to study and assess behavior in a school setting.

EXERCISES

Part I

Match the following terms with the correct definitions.

a. individual achievement test
b. screening test
c. group achievement tests
d. diagnostic tests
e. composite scores
f. achievement tests
g. aptitude tests
h. receptive coding

i. expressive coding
j. norm-referenced tests
k. subtests
l. curriculum-based assessment
m. curriculum-based measurement
n. level of significance

_____ 1. This indicates the amount of chance occurrence of the difference between two scores _____.

_____ 2. Statewide assessment instruments are one form of _____.

_____ 3. The reading passages from the basal text are used to assess the students' levels at the end of each chapter. This is a form of _____.

_____ 4. When one student is compared with a national sample of students of the same age, it is called _____.

_____ 5. Reading decoding and reading comprehension of a test will yield an overall reading score for students. In this example, reading decoding and reading comprehension are _____.

_____ 6. The K-TEA-II and the PIAT–R are individually administered _____.

_____ 7. A broad-based instrument that samples a few items across the domains of a curriculum is called _____.

_____ 8. A student was administered a norm-referenced reading test and found to have inconsistent performance. The teacher was not certain that he had determined the difficulty using classroom informal methods. In order to obtain more in-depth information about reading, he decided to use different _____ for more specific skill assessment.

_____ 9. When informal methods and classroom interventions do not seem to have effective results, a teacher may need additional assessment information. One method is using _____ to compare the student to national average performance.

_____10. These instruments are designed to measure strength, talent, or ability in a particular domain or area.

Part II

Match the following tests with the statements below.

a. Woodcock–Johnson Tests of Achievement–III
b. KeyMath–3
c. Kaufman Test of Educational Achievement–II
d. Peabody Individual Achievement Test–R
e. Wide Range Achievement Test–3
f. Wechsler Individual Achievement Test–II
g. Woodcock–McGrew–Werder Mini-Battery of Achievement
h. Test of Mathematical Ability
i. Process Assessment of the Learner
j. Test of Written Spelling–4
k. PPVT–4
l. EVT–2

_____ 1. This diagnostic test is normed for students through the grade skill levels of 12th grade in mathematics.

_____ 2. This test, which includes a factual knowledge subtest, is a more comprehensive screening test than the WRAT3.

_____ 3. This test has standard and supplemental batteries.

_____ 4. This diagnostic test may be used in the very early grades to assess the cognitive abilities and functions required for reading.

_____ 5. This diagnostic test would not be used to assess complex calculus skills or other college level math.

_____ 6. This test provides cluster scores and individual subtest scores.

_____ 7. These academic achievement instruments were conormed with their cognitive assessment instruments.

_____ 8. This achievement test includes a Language Composite that measures both expressive language and receptive listening skills.

_____ 9. This academic achievement test includes many multiple-choice items that may encourage guessing.

_____10. This test includes measures for rapid naming.

_____11. This vocabulary assessment asks the student to name pictures or provide synonyms.

_____12. This vocabulary test was conormed with the PPVT–4.

Companion Website

Answers to these questions can be found in the Appendix of this text or you may also complete these questions and receive immediate feedback on your answers by going to the Think Ahead module in Chapter 7 of the Companion Website.

Assessment of Behavior

academic engaged time
schoolwide positive behavioral
   support
manifestation determination
behavioral intervention plan
functional behavioral assessment
replacement behaviors
functional behavioral analysis
direct observation
event recording
interval recording
anecdotal recording
duration recording
latency recording
interresponse time
functional assessment interview

target behaviors
baseline
antecedent
setting events
establishing operation
frequency counting
time sampling
checklists
questionnaires
interviews
sociograms
ecological assessment
projective techniques
sentence completion tests
drawing tests
apperception tests

CHAPTER FOCUS

**academic engaged
time** The time when
the student is
actively involved in
the learning process.

This chapter addresses the assessment of behaviors that decrease **academic engaged time** and interfere with learning, such as externalizing (acting out) behaviors (including those attributed to attention deficit disorders), and the assessment of emotional and social difficulties of students. The 1997 IDEA Amendments included new mandates for the assessment of behaviors that may impede student academic success. These legal regulations for behavior remained in the 2004 IDEA. A discussion of tier one behavioral management is presented briefly at the beginning of this chapter. Methods used for functional behavioral assessment are discussed, followed by published instruments used to measure behavioral and emotional difficulties. Specific requirements for determining emotional disturbance are presented at the end of the chapter.

CEC KNOWLEDGE AND SKILLS STANDARDS

The student completing this chapter will understand the knowledge and skills included in the following CEC Knowledge and Skills Standards from Standard 8: Assessment:

CC8K1—Basic terminology used in assessment

CC8K2—Legal provisions and ethical principles regarding assessment of individuals

CCK83—Screening, prereferral, referral, and classification procedures

CG8K2—Laws and policies regarding referral and placement procedures for individuals with disabilities

CC8K5—Interpret information from formal and informal procedures

GC8S1—Implement procedures for assessing and reporting both appropriate and problematic social behaviors of individuals with disabilities

TIER ONE BEHAVIORAL INTERVENTIONS

schoolwide positive behavioral support Proactive strategies defined by school staff and based on behavioral principles.

Behavioral challenges, like educational challenges, are to be addressed within the three-tier structure in the school setting. This means that prior to a student receiving a referral for special education, teachers and staff should indicate the interventions that have been implemented and document that these interventions were not successful. As with educational interventions, these behavioral interventions are to be implemented consistently and with integrity. A well-known strategy to address the three-tier model is **schoolwide positive behavioral support systems**. These systems are structured by the local school and provide consistent schoolwide positive behavioral expectations. All adults consistently implement all school rewards, rules, and consequences. The implementation of such programs is most successful when all teachers and staff believe in and support the school's goals for improving behavior. This is considered a tier one intervention. The behavioral tiers are presented in Figure 8.1

Figure 8.1   Three tiers for behavioral interventions.

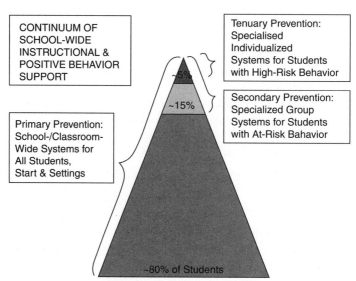

Source: From: *OSEP Technical Assistance Center on Positive Behavior Interventions and Supports.* www.pbis.org/schoolwide.htm. Reprinted with permission.

Tier two behavioral interventions include small group interventions and some specific intensive efforts for students at risk. Examples of these interventions include mentoring, classroom opportunities for the at risk student to be successful and be rewarded, and discussion with the student about expectations and rewards and consequences. When students fail to respond to these interventions, data may be collected through techniques such as functional behavioral assessments, behavioral analysis or frequency counts to determine baselines of behavior, attempt interventions, and observe increases in positive behavior or increases in negative behavior. These techniques are presented following the discussion of legal requirements.

REQUIREMENTS OF THE 1997 IDEA AMENDMENTS

manifestation determination A hearing to determine if a student's behavior is the result of the student's disability.

behavioral intervention plan A plan designed to increase positive behaviors and decrease negative behaviors before these become problematic.

functional behavioral assessment A multi-component assessment to determine the purpose of target behaviors.

The behavioral assessment and behavioral planning mandates of the 1997 IDEA Amendments were included as a method of ensuring procedural safeguards for students with behaviors that interfere with educational success. Prior to the Amendments, the application of discipline procedures for students with disabilities and students without disabilities was inconsistent (Yell, Drasgow, & Ford, 2000). Special education students who were repeatedly suspended from school for several days each time or who were expelled from school were no longer receiving a free appropriate education. In addition, these punitive types of disciplinary procedures often resulted in more harm to the student or caused the negative behaviors to escalate (Kubick, Bard, & Perry, 2000).

Congress also sought to make schools safe for all learners and therefore provided educators with the means to discipline students fairly (Drasgow & Yell, 2001). To ensure that students requiring special education support were assisted with their behavioral needs rather than merely punished for behaviors, the 1997 IDEA Amendments and 2004 Amendments required schools to determine if the behaviors were the result of or manifested by the student's existing disability. This is referred to as a **manifestation determination**, which is a procedure required before a student receiving special education services can be suspended for more than 10 school days.

The manifestation determination is required to be completed as quickly as possible and must meet federal regulations. Part of the requirements of manifestation determinations include confirming that the student's IEP was appropriately written and followed. The IEP must include the present levels of educational performance and behavioral functioning. In addition, the student exhibiting the behaviors should have a **behavioral intervention plan** in place that is based on a **functional behavioral assessment**.

replacement behaviors Appropriate behaviors that are incompatible with the negative behaviors they replace.

The student's present levels of behavioral functioning are to be based on information obtained in the functional behavioral assessment and should be written in clear, understandable language (Drasgow, Yell, Bradley, & Shriner, 1999). The regulations required that the behavioral intervention plan include strategies for positive behavioral support and interventions that provide the student with acceptable **replacement behaviors** to be used by the student rather than the problematic behaviors.

Functional behavioral assessments are measures to determine the function or purpose of a child's behavior. Functional behavioral assessment does not aim to label or name the type of behavior or disorder, such as hitting or depression, respectively, but rather seeks to answer the question of why. Why is the student using the behavior? Once this has been determined, interventions can be developed to promote positive acceptable replacement behaviors. A functional behavioral assessment should define the target behavior, determine when the behavior occurs and when it does not occur, and generate hypotheses about the possible function of the behavior. Once these have been determined, the hypotheses are tested or tried so that the exact function can be found (O'Neill, Horner, Albin, Sprague, Storey, & Newton, 1997). The testing out of hypotheses is also called **functional behavioral analysis**. Personnel who are responsible for this phase of the functional behavioral assessment should receive additional training in the procedures due to the possibility that manipulating the student's environment may result in more negative behaviors being exhibited (O'Neill et al., 1997). Drasgow and Yell summarized when functional behavioral assessments should be conducted and when they must be conducted. This information is presented in Figure 8.2.

functional behavioral analysis An analysis of the exploration of behaviors that occur when variables such as antecedents or consequences are manipulated.

Figure 8.2   IDEA '97 Requirements Regarding FBAs.

When an FBA *Should* Be Conducted	When an FBA *Must* Be Conducted
• When a student's problem behavior impedes his or her learning or the learning of others.	• When suspensions or placements in an alternative setting exceed 10 consecutive days or amount to a change in placement.
• When a student's behavior presents a danger to himself or herself or others.	• When a student is placed in an interim alternative educational setting for 45 days when his or her misconduct involves weapons or drugs.
• When a student's suspension or placement in an interim alternative educational setting approaches 10 cumulative days.	• When a due process hearing officer places a student in an interim alternative educational setting for behavior that is dangerous to himself or herself or others.

Source: Functional behavioral assessments: Legal requirements and challenges by Erik Drasgow and Mitchell Yell. In *School Psychology Review, 30*(2), 239–251, 243. Copyright 2001 by the National Association of School Psychologists. Reprinted by permission of the publisher.

direct observation
Observations of student behaviors in the environment in which the behaviors occur.

event recording
Recording the frequency of a target behavior; also called frequency counting.

interval recording
Sampling a behavior intermittently for very brief periods of time; used to observe frequently occurring behaviors.

Federal regulations require that both special education personnel and general education personnel participate in the functional behavioral assessment along with the student's parents (Conroy, Clark, Gable, & Fox, 1999). Initial efforts to apply functional behavioral assessments may have resulted in schools treating the requirements as merely a compliance issue (Gable, Hendrickson, & Smith, 1999). In other words, schools may not have completed extensive functional behavioral assessments but rather completed the minimal amount of paperwork needed to comply with the mandates. This resulted in numerous due process hearings brought by parents who believed that their children were not appropriately served or assessed prior to suspensions or other disciplinary actions (Drasgow & Yell, 2001). Most of these hearings found in favor of the parents due to inadequate or nonexistent functional behavioral assessments. It is necessary to fully understand the functional behavioral assessment process in order to fully comply with the law.

FUNCTIONAL BEHAVIORAL ASSESSMENTS

anecdotal recording
Observations of behavior in which the teacher notes all behaviors and interactions that occur during a given period of time.

duration recording
Observations that involve the length of time a behavior occurs.

latency recording
Observations involving the amount of time that elapses from the presentation of a stimulus until the response occurs.

interresponse time
The amount of time between target behaviors.

Information to determine why a student displays a specific behavior can be obtained through three broad methods of assessment (O'Neill et al., 1997; Witt, Daly, & Noell, 2000). The first method of assessment is the indirect method. It includes techniques such as interviewing the classroom teacher and parents, reviewing data in the school records, completing behavioral rating scales, checklists, and so on. These methods are presented later in the chapter. Another method used in functional behavioral assessment is called the **direct observation** or descriptive observational method. This requires that the student be observed in the environment in which the behaviors are occurring. During this part of the assessment, several techniques may be employed, such as **event recording**, **interval recording**, **anecdotal recording**, **duration recording**, **latency recording**, and **interresponse time**. These terms are presented in the following section of the chapter. Finally, the third broad method of assessment is the functional behavioral analysis method. During both the indirect assessment and the direct observation phases of the assessment, hypotheses are generated regarding the purpose or function of the behavior. In the functional behavioral analysis portion of the assessment, the variables believed to be triggering the behavior and the possible consequences following the behavior are manipulated. By this manipulation, it can be determined exactly why the student is using the behavior. For example, following the initial phases of the functional behavioral assessment, it is hypothesized that the reason a student is calling out in class is to receive peer attention. During the functional behavioral analysis, the hypothesis of peer attention is tested. Students in the class are instructed to ignore the calling-out behavior, and the calling out decreases. When students react to the calling-out behavior, such as by turning to look at the target student when calling out occurs, the calling out increases. Thus, the function of the calling out is to receive peer attention. Following the functional behavioral analysis and additional assessment, the students in the class are instructed to ignore all calling-out behavior and to reinforce appropriate hand raising by paying attention to the target student. This manipulation of the consequence (peer attention) resulted in decreasing the calling out and in an appropriate replacement behavior (raising hand).

Educational personnel may also need to use **functional assessment interviews** with teachers, parents, and the target student (Gresham, Watson, & Skinner, 2001). During these interviews, the goal is to obtain information that will assist in formulating a hypothesis about the function of the target behavior. These interviews will provide information concerning how the student functions in various environments. When interviewed, the student can share feelings and concerns about school and other areas of life.

DIRECT OBSERVATION TECHNIQUES

The first step in the intervention of behavioral problems is the identification of **target behaviors**. Once the exact behavior or behaviors have been identified, direct observations can begin. Direct observation enables the teacher to note how often a behavior occurs and to establish a **baseline**, which will be used to monitor the student's progress following intervention. Direct observation also enables the teacher to note the possible **antecedent** events that may trigger the target behavior or that may increase the likelihood that it will occur.

Behavioral observations can be completed by the teacher or by another objective professional or trained paraprofessional. Behaviors may be observed for frequency, duration, intensity, or for the length of time between responses, or interresponse time (Gresham et al., 2001). The observer should remember two important guidelines for effective behavioral observation: Be objective and be specific. The observer should be fair and nonjudgmental and should precisely pinpoint or identify problem behaviors. The identified behaviors should be stated exactly so that two observers would be able to agree about whether the behavior is or is not occurring.

ANTECEDENTS

Antecedents may be actual events that increase the probability of target behaviors occurring. Antecedents may also be events that occur in another setting prior to the actual target behavior. These are called **setting events**. For example, a setting event may be that a

functional assessment interviews The interview component of the functional behavioral assessment (FBA) that provides information about possible purposes of target behaviors.

target behaviors Specific behaviors that require intervention by the teacher to promote optimal academic or social learning.

baseline The frequency, duration, or latency of a behavior determined before behavioral intervention.

antecedent An event that occurs prior to the target behavior and increases or decreases the probability of the target behavior.

setting event A specific event that occurs before the target behavior but is removed from the actual environment in which the behavior occurs.

student has an argument at home with an older sibling before coming to school. This antecedent may increase the probability that the student will exhibit externalizing target behaviors within the school environment. Other events that may increase the probability of a target behavior may be the events that make a consequence more attractive. For example, a student may be more anxious to receive an edible reward as a consequence when the student is hungry. This may increase the probability that a student will behave in a specific way, such as stealing another student's lunch. This type of an event is known as an **establishing operation**, or EO (Michael, 2000).

establishing operation Events occurring before the target behavior that alter the receptivity of the consequence and increase or decrease the probability of occurrence of the target behavior.

ANECDOTAL RECORDING

Behavioral intervention strategies are based on a clear understanding of why a behavior occurs. Behavioristic principle is founded in the theory that behaviors are maintained or increased by the reinforcing events that follow the event or behavior. Events that happen prior to the target behavior may increase the likelihood that the behavior will be exhibited. These conditions occurring prior to the exhibited behavior are known as antecedents. The teacher may recognize when a behavior occurs but not be able to identify the reinforcing event or the antecedent event. One behavioral observation technique that will enable the teacher to hypothesize about the exact antecedent event and reinforcing event, or consequence, is called anecdotal recording.

In the anecdotal recording method, the teacher observes the student and writes down everything that occurs in the situation. The teacher or other educational or behavioral professional observes the student for a specific time period, usually when the behavior seems to occur most frequently. The teacher may wish to observe during a particular academic subject time, such as math class, or during a nonacademic time when the behavior occurs, such as lunch or recess.

An anecdotal recording might look like this:

Name: Mary
Observation Time:

9:30 a.m.	Language Arts—Mary enters the classroom and walks around the room twice, then sits in her chair. Mary looks out of the window.
9:32 a.m.	Mary speaks out: Teacher, can I go to the office? Response: Mary, get your workbook out and turn to page 56.
9:33 a.m.	Mary gets workbook out and begins to look at the pictures on several of the pages. Continues for quite some time.
9:45 a.m.	Mary speaks out: What page, teacher? Teacher responds: Page 56.
9:47 a.m.	Mary speaks out: Teacher, can I use a pencil? Response: Here is a pencil, Mary.

Using the anecdotal format for observation provides a basis for analyzing the antecedent, behavior, and consequence. The antecedent is the event preceding the behavior, and the consequence is the event following the behavior. The antecedent may actually trigger the behavior, whereas the consequence is thought to maintain or reinforce the behavior. In the preceding example, the antecedent, behavior, and consequence analysis, or A-B-C, might look like this:

A	B	C
Mary enters room sits in chair and	walks around	allowed to walk freely
looks at the teacher	talks out	teacher responds
looks at pages in workbook, then looks at teacher	talks out	teacher responds
looks at the teacher	talks out	teacher responds

This analysis provides information that will help the teacher plan a behavioral intervention strategy. It appears that the reinforcing event for Mary's talking out is the teacher responding to Mary. It also seems that the teacher has not provided an organizational intervention plan that will convey to Mary the behaviors expected of her when beginning academic work or instruction. Through this observation, two behaviors have been targeted for intervention: organizational behavior (ready for work) and talking out. The organizational behaviors expected can be broken down into specific behaviors for intervention: student in chair, pencils ready, books out, paper ready.

EVENT RECORDING

Event recording assesses the frequency with which behaviors occur. The teacher marks or tallies the number of times specific behaviors occur. This information, the initial recording of data, creates a baseline for the teacher to use as a comparison following intervention. This type of recording is useful for observing easily detectable behaviors for short periods of time. Examples of this type of behavior include time on task, talking out, and hitting. One illustration of **frequency counting**, another name for event recording, is shown in Figure 8.3.

Observations using event recording are typically completed for an entire class period or continuously for a specified time period. Other methods for observing behaviors intermittently or for short periods of time are **time sampling** and interval recording.

frequency counting Counting the occurrence of a specific behavior; same as event recording.

time sampling When the behavioral observation samples behavior through the day or class period.

Figure 8.3   An example of event recording (frequency counting).

Name ___Joe_____

Target behavior: __Out of seat_____

	Mon.	Tues.	Wed.
9:00 – 10:00	ⅢⅢ ⅢⅢ	ⅢⅢ ⅢⅢ Ⅱ	ⅢⅢ ⅢⅢ Ⅰ
10:00 – 11:00	Ⅱ	Ⅰ	Ⅲ
11:00 – 12:00	Ⅰ	Ⅲ	Ⅱ

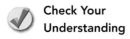

Check Your Understanding

Check your ability to analyze an anecdotal recording and a functional assessment interview by completing Activity 8.1 below.

Activity 8.1

Read the following anecdotal recording, which covers 2 days of class, and then answer the questions.

Name: John

Monday

John enters classroom.

Teacher (T): Let's get ready for math class.

   John (J): Can we go on the field trip Thursday?

      T: Yes, John. We will go on Thursday.

      J: I can't find my math book.

      T: Look in your desk, John. Now, let's work problems 1 to 10 on page 284.

      J: [Throws pencil on the floor. Picks pencil up.]

      T: John, let's get to work.

      J: [Crumbles paper up, throws on floor. Throws book on floor.]

      T: That's it, John! Go to the office.

      J: [Smiles. Leaves the room.]

Tuesday

John enters classroom.

T: Now class, let's get our math books out.

 J: [Out of seat. Goes to pencil sharpener.]

T: John, when do we sharpen our pencils?

J: [No response.]

T: Pencil time is after lunch. Now, get your math book out. Turn to page 286. Let's check our homework.

J: [Slams book on desk. Groans.]

T: Today we will continue the division problems. John, get your book open.

J: [Throws book on floor.]

T: Okay! To the office!

J: [Smiles, leaves the room.]

Analyze the observations of John's behavior for antecedent, behavior, and consequence.

A	B	C
_____	_____	_____
_____	_____	_____
_____	_____	_____
_____	_____	_____
_____	_____	_____
_____	_____	_____

Functional Assessment Interview

During the functional assessment interview, John describes how he feels about his behavior. He reports that he is not happy in class and that the tasks have become too difficult. He states that he has not been able to keep up with the assignments the teacher gives each day for homework. Additional questioning about his homework routine reveals that John's parents work different shifts and that he often is responsible for younger siblings in the evenings until his father returns. He adds that due to child care difficulties, his mother wakes the children at 4:30 a.m. each day so that they may be at an aunt's house by 5:00, where he then sleeps for another hour before getting ready to come to school. He believes that he is too tired on some days to concentrate on his schoolwork. When asked if he has discussed these issues with his teachers, he states that it is too hard for him to talk about these concerns with other students in the classroom.

What additional important information was obtained in the functional interview? _____

Apply Your Knowledge

Based on your analysis of the antecedents, behaviors, and consequences, what purpose is the behavior serving for John? What would you recommend for an intervention plan? _____

_____

_____

Figure 8.4   Sample chart for time sampling of on-task and nontask behaviors.

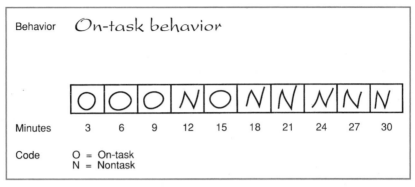

Source: From *Teaching Strategies for Children in Conflict* (2nd ed., p. 84) by H. L. Swanson and H. R. Reinert, 1984, New York: Times Mirror/Mosby College Publishing. Copyright 1984 by Times Mirror/Mosby College Publishing. Reprinted by permission.

TIME SAMPLING

Time sampling uses frequency counting or event recording techniques for various times throughout the day or class period. The teacher identifies the target behaviors and records student activity for a time period, such as 2 or 5 minutes, throughout the period or day. The teacher is sampling the behavior to get an idea of how often the behavior occurs, without observing continuously. This enables the teacher to observe more than one student or more than one behavior throughout the day. An example of a time-sampling observation is shown in Figure 8.4.

INTERVAL RECORDING

Interval recording is used when the teacher wants to observe several students or behaviors at one time, record intermittently throughout the day or class period, and record behaviors that occur too frequently to record each event, such as stereotypical behaviors (Kerr & Nelson, 2002). During interval recording, the teacher notes whether the behavior is occurring or not occurring. The time intervals may be very short throughout the day. The observation might be for a very brief period of time, such as 2 minutes, during which the teacher notes every 30 seconds whether or not the behavior is occurring. An example of interval recording is shown in Figure 8.5.

DURATION RECORDING

The duration recording technique is used when the length of the behavior is the target variable of the behavior. For example, a student may need to increase the amount of time spent on task. The

Figure 8.5 Sample interval recording form.

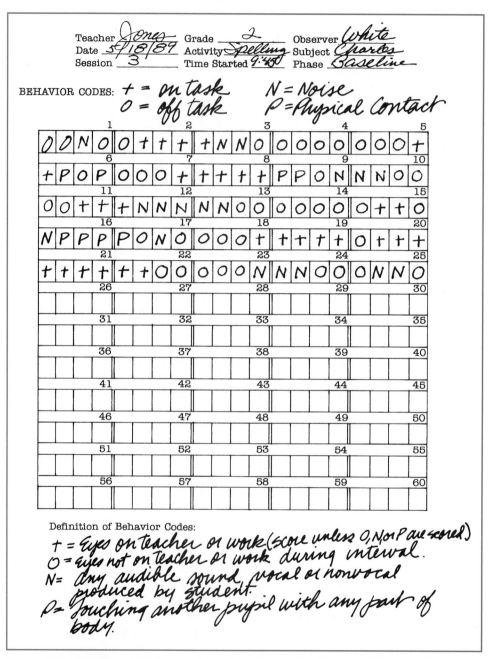

Teacher _Jones_ Grade _2_ Observer _White_
Date _5/18/89_ Activity _Spelling_ Subject _Charles_
Session _3_ Time Started _9:45_ Phase _Baseline_

BEHAVIOR CODES: + = on task   N = Noise
　　　　　　　　O = off task   P = Physical Contact

1				2				3				4				5
O	O	N	O	O	+	+	+	+	N	N	O	O	O	O	O	O	O	O	+
6				7				8				9				10
+	P	O	P	O	O	O	+	+	+	+	+	P	P	O	N	N	N	O	O
11				12				13				14				15
O	O	+	+	+	N	N	N	N	N	O	O	O	O	O	O	O	+	+	O
16				17				18				19				20
N	P	P	P	P	O	N	O	O	O	O	+	+	+	+	O	+	+	+	
21				22				23				24				25
+	+	+	+	+	+	O	O	O	O	O	N	N	N	O	O	O	N	N	O
26				27				28				29				30
31				32				33				34				35
36				37				38				39				40
41				42				43				44				45
46				47				48				49				50
51				52				53				54				55
56				57				58				59				60

Definition of Behavior Codes:

+ = Eyes on teacher or work (score unless O, N or P are scored)
O = eyes not on teacher or work during interval.
N = Any audible sound, vocal or nonvocal produced by student.
P = Touching another pupil with any part of body.

Source: From *Strategies for Addressing Behavior Problems in the Classroom* (4th ed., p. 97) by M. M. Kerr and C. M. Nelson, 1989. Upper Saddle River, NJ: Merrill/Prentice Hall. Copyright 2002 by Prentice Hall. Reprinted by permission.

teacher will record how long the student remains on task following the directive to do so. The duration recording might look like this:

Name *Ralph*
Task *writing assignment*

On Task	Off Task
2 min	60 s
60 s	2 min
60 s	60 s

On-task/off-task ratio is 4:8 min = 50% on task

This brief duration recording revealed that Ralph is on task only 50% of the expected time. Following intervention by the teacher, such as a prompting signal or behavioral contract or other strategy, it is hoped that the student's on-task time would increase, while off-task time would decrease. Reinforcement for on-task time would increase the probability that Ralph would remain on task longer. A duration recording of on-task time during the intervention or treatment should be compared with the baseline data of 50% to note the effectiveness of the intervention strategies.

LATENCY RECORDING

The latency recording method of observation also involves the element of time. This is an observation in which the time is recorded from the moment a stimulus (such as a command) is given until the response occurs. The element of elapsed time is recorded. For example, the time is recorded from the moment the teacher gives spelling instructions until the student begins the assignment. If the student must be prompted several times during the completion of the task, the latency is recorded each time the student is prompted (Evans, Evans, & Schmid, 1989).

INTERRESPONSE TIME

Latency recording measures the amount of time elapsed between the specific stimulus and the actual response. Interresponse time assesses the length of time between the behaviors or responses (Gresham et al., 2001). For example, a student may be distracted or off task every 2 minutes between the observation period of 2:00 to 3:00 P.M., but become distracted only every 20 minutes during the observation period of 10:00 to 11:00 A.M. This assessment would then pose additional questions—such as, is the subject matter more interesting or easier in the morning observation, are there more hands-on activities, is the student tired in the afternoons, or has the student been prescribed a medication for distractibility that is administered only in the morning?

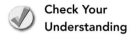

Check Your
Understanding

Check your ability to complete a behavioral analysis for a fifth-grade student by completing Activity 8.2 below.

Activity 8.2

Use the following information to analyze the behavior of a fifth-grade student named Amber.

Day 1
Anecdotal recording:
Amber was presented with her arithmetic worksheet following the direct instruction lesson with her group. After several minutes, she began to work on the first problem. During the time period of receiving the work and beginning the work, she was observed looking through her desk to find the necessary materials. When she located her pencil and paper, she dropped the assignment page on the floor. She picked the paper up and placed it on her desk. She sharpened her pencil and began to work. During the period that she was seated at her desk working, approximately 10 minutes, she was observed looking around the room and watching other students. When a sound occurred outside the room, she would look in the hallway or out the window. When papers were collected, she had completed the first 2 of 15 problems. One problem was correct, but the second problem was not calculated correctly because of a careless error.

Day 2
Latency recording: Time elapsed from assignment to working behavior: 5 minutes.

Interval recording: Observations during work time:

+ = **On task**   0 = **Off task**

0	0	0	0	0	+	+	0	0	+
Minutes 1	2	3	4	5	6	7	8	9	10

1. Analyze the anecdotal recording. What are the antecedents, behaviors, and consequences? _____

         A   **B**   **C**

2. Analyze the latency recording information. _____
3. Analyze the interval recording data. How often is the student on task? _____

Apply Your Knowledge

Based on the information provided, why do you think Amber is having difficulty with this task? What recommendations would you suggest for Amber? _____

_____

_____

STRUCTURED CLASSROOM OBSERVATIONS

Observation methods discussed so far in this chapter may be teacher-made, informal instruments that can be used for prereferral, assessment, and intervention of behavioral problems. A structured classroom observation form called the Direct Observation Form (Achenbach, 1986) is one part of the Child Behavior Checklist (CBCL) system, a multiaxial system for assessment of behavioral and emotional problems. Other forms in this system are described throughout the chapter in the appropriate topical sections.

CHILD BEHAVIOR CHECKLIST: DIRECT OBSERVATION FORM, REVISED EDITION

The Direct Observation Form (Achenbach, 1986) is four pages in length, including general instructions and guidelines. The first page consists of the student's identifying information (name, date of birth, observation settings, and so on) and the general administration instructions. The inside pages of the form comprise three parts: an observation rating scale on which to mark observed behaviors and rate their intensity or severity, a space for anecdotal recording of all events during the observation period, and an interval recording form. The observer makes several observations of the target student across several different settings. The observer compares the target student with two grade and gender peers. When comparing the target student, the observer ascertains whether the student is significantly different from the two control students in on-task behavior. This method is often used to assess behavioral disorders such as attention deficit disorder. Often, the criterion for indicating possible attention problems is that the target student's off-task behavior score is 1.5 or 2 standard deviations above the control students' scores. The observer marks the items on the rating scale if the target child exhibits the behaviors during the observation. Figure 8.6 illustrates the types of items represented on the Direct Observation Form. These items are then scored, as are the other rating scales and interviews of the multiaxial CBCL system, for significant behavior problems. The behaviors are defined on two broad bands: (1) externalizing (acting out); and (2) internalizing (turning inward), which includes problems such as anxiety or withdrawal. In addition, the system notes the occurrence of several clinical behavioral syndromes, such as social problems, somatic complaints, aggressive behavior, and attention problems. The other components of the CBCL are scored along the same broad and narrow bands of behavior and emotional functioning.

Figure 8.6   Behavioral checklist.

	Yes	No
1. Student is prepared for work each period.	_____	_____
2. Student begins assignment on request.	_____	_____
3. Student stays on task with no distractions.	_____	_____
4. Student completes tasks.	_____	_____
5. Student stays on task but is sometimes distracted.	_____	_____
6. Student complies with teacher requests.	_____	_____
7. Student raises hand to speak.	_____	_____
8. Student talks out inappropriately.	_____	_____
9. Student completes homework.	_____	_____
10. Student is aggressive toward peers.	_____	_____
11. Student is disruptive during class.	_____	_____
12. Student talks out of turn.	_____	_____
13. Student is verbally aggressive.	_____	_____
14. Student has damaged property belonging to others.	_____	_____

OTHER TECHNIQUES FOR ASSESSING BEHAVIOR

checklists Lists of academic or behavioral skills that must be mastered by the student.

questionnaires Questions about a student's behavior or academic concerns that may be answered by the student or by the parent or teacher; also called interviews.

interviews Formal or informal questions asked orally by the examiner.

sociograms Graphic representation of the social dynamics within a group.

ecological assessment Analysis of the student's total learning environment.

Some techniques for assessing behavior do not involve direct observation of behavior. These techniques include **checklists**, **questionnaires**, **interviews**, **sociograms**, and **ecological assessment**. These methods rely on input from others, such as parents, teachers, or peers, rather than on direct observation of behavior. When these indirect methods are used with direct observation, the teacher can plan effective behavioral intervention strategies.

CHECKLISTS AND RATING SCALES

A checklist is a list of questions that the respondent completes by checking the appropriate responses. The respondent may answer yes or no or may check off the statements that apply to the student. The teacher, the parents, or both may complete the checklist. An example of a behavioral checklist was given earlier, in Figure 8.6.

A rating questionnaire may be similar in content to a checklist, although the respondent rates the answer. For example, the format of the checklist in Figure 8.6 would change so that the respondent would rate student behaviors as never, almost never, sometimes, somewhat often, frequently, or almost always. This format allows for interpretation of the extremes. The student behavior might be rated as almost never completing assignments, but frequently being verbally aggressive and sometimes damaging property. This information helps the teacher pinpoint areas that need observation and further evaluation.

Elliot, Busse, and Gresham (1993) suggested that the following issues be considered when using rating scales:

1. Ratings are summaries of observations of the relative frequency of specific behaviors.

2. Ratings of social behavior are judgments affected by one's environment and rater's standards for behavior.

3. The social validity of the behaviors one assesses and eventually treats should be understood.

4. Multiple assessors of the same child's behavior may agree only moderately.

5. Many characteristics of a student may influence social behavior; however, the student's sex is a particularly salient variable.

Several rating forms are commonly used in the assessment of behavior problems. Many of these include forms for teachers and parents. Common examples include the Teacher Report Form (Achenbach, 1991b) and the Child Behavior Checklist (Achenbach, 1991a), the Behavior Rating Profile-2 (Brown & Hammill, 1990), and the Conners Teacher Rating Scales and Conners Parent Rating Scales (1997). These forms and scoring systems ask a variety of questions about the student, and the parent or teacher rates the student on each item.

ASEBA—ACHENBACH SYSTEM OF EMPIRICALLY BASED BEHAVIOR ASSESSMENT (ASEBA) PARENT, TEACHER, AND YOUTH REPORT FORMS

The Achenbach System of Empirically Based Behavior Assessment (ASEBA), also known as the Child Behavior Checklist, (Achenbach, 1991a; Achenbach & Rescorla, 2001), includes a Parent Report Form, and companion forms such as the Teacher Report Form (Achenbach, 1991b, Achenbach & Rescorla, 2001) and the Youth Self-Report (Achenbach, 1991c). (The system's Direct Observation Form and interview form are discussed in other sections of this chapter.) This system also includes a preschool version with an informal language survey (Achenbach & Rescorla, 2000).

The Achenbach system allows for the student to be rated on both positive, or adaptive, behaviors and behavioral syndromes. In 1991, the author revised the system to allow the profiles to be scored consistently across the parent, teacher, and youth scales (McConaughy & Achenbach, 1993). The parent form includes, in addition to the rating scales, some open-ended questions, such as "What concerns you most about your child?"

The two ASEBA forms are available for parents: one for children aged $1\frac{1}{2}$–5 years and another for students aged 6–18 years. The

Teacher Report Form is for students aged 6–18. Items on these instruments are closely related so that both parents and teachers are rating the student on similar dimensions. An example of a Teacher Report Form profile is shown in Figure 8.7.

In addition to the teacher and parent forms, a self-rating form is available for students aged 11–18. The Youth Self-Report (Achenbach, 1991c, Achenbach & Rescorla, 2001) covers many of the same topics as the teacher and parent forms. This instrument can be evaluated qualitatively to determine the student's perceptions of himself. The student also answers items concerning current academic achievement and rates himself on social dimensions, such as getting along with family members.

Figure 8.7 CBCL. Teacher Report Form showing sample profile for female student.

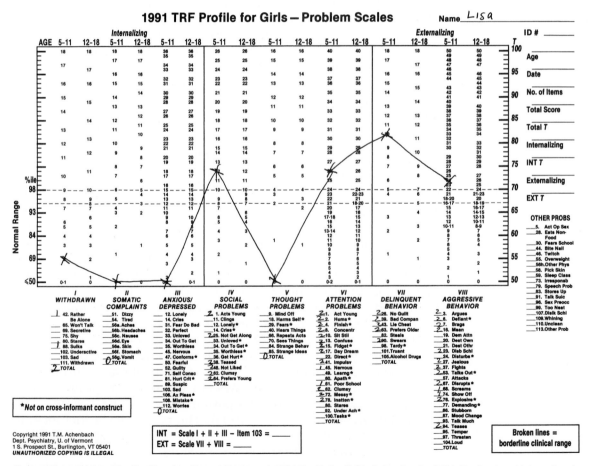

Source: From *Manual for the Teacher Report Form and 1991 Profile* by T. M. Achenbach, 1991, Burlington: University of Vermont Department of Psychiatry. Copyright 1991 by T. M. Achenbach. Reprinted by permission.

Examiner manuals address the issues of validity and reliability for each of the individual parts of the multiaxial ASEBA system by Achenbach (1991a, 1991b, 1991c, Achenbach & Recorla, 2000, 2001). The examiner is provided with detailed information about content and criterion-related validity and the discriminant validity of using cutoff scores to identify students with specific behavioral problems. Test-retest, testing across time, and reliability of raters are presented, and the technical quality of the systems appears to be adequate or above on all measures.

BEHAVIOR ASSESSMENT SYSTEM FOR CHILDREN, SECOND EDITION (BASC–2)

This assessment system includes rating scales for parents to complete, rating scales for teachers to complete, a developmental history form for parents, and self-reports for students ages 8–25 years. This system includes an observation form for recording observations within the classroom environment. The BASC–2 system was developed to be used with students ages 2 to 25 years of age. The system provides a method for distinguishing students with attention deficit disorder, depression, other behavioral concerns, and social maladjustments. Scores indicate students who are within a clinical range of significance; at risk for having difficulties; and average, low, and very low. The BASC–2 also indicates how well students are adapting in a positive manner. Scores on the adaptive scales are noted to be very high, high, average, at risk, and clinically significant. The BASC–2 includes an audiotape provided for students who have difficulty reading the self-report form in English but who understand spoken English. The student self-report form is presented in a true-false format. The instrument may be hand scored and computer scoring provides additional information such as the validity of the specific test administration. The BASC–2 provides a means of comparing the student with both the norm sample and clinical samples. This may be more helpful in determining the severity of behavioral difficulties.

The examiner's manual provides information regarding the standardization and norm samples for all components of the BASC–2. The total number of students and parents for the norm samples was 4,650 for the Teacher Rating Scale; 4,800 for the Parent Rating Scale; and 3,400 for the Self-Report of Personality. The samples were representative geographically, and gender and race/ethnicity were also considered and approximated U.S. population estimates.

The manual presents reliability and validity information for all scales. Ample technical data for internal consistency, test-retest reliability, interrater reliability, standard error of measurement, factor structure of scales, and concurrent validity data are presented.

Behavior Rating Profile–2   The Behavior Rating Profile–2 (Brown & Hammill, 1990) includes forms for the student, parent, and teacher. The student completes the rating by marking that items are true or false about herself. The teacher and parents rate the student by marking that the items are very much like the student, not like the student, like the student, or not at all like the student. This system allows the examiner to compare how the student, teacher, and parent perceive the student. It also categorizes the student's perceptions into the various environments of the student's life: school, home, and peer relationships. This enables the examiner to determine whether the student has more positive feelings about school, relationships with peers, or relationships with parents. The instrument is scored using a standard score with a mean of 10 and a standard deviation of 3. The examiner can plot a profile that presents a view of how the student, parent, and teacher perceive the student.

The manual provides reliability and validity information that includes studies conducted with relatively small samples. The internal consistency and test-retest coefficients seem to be adequate, with many reported to be in the .80s. Validity studies include criterion-related research, with reported coefficients ranging from below acceptable levels to adequate. The authors provide discussion of content and construct validity.

Conners Rating Scales–Revised   The Conners system (Conners, 1997) includes the following scales:

Conners Parent Rating Scale–Revised: Long Version

Conners Parent Rating Scale–Revised: Short Version

Conners Teacher Rating Scale–Revised: Long Version

Conners Teacher Rating Scale–Revised: Short Version

Conners-Wells' Adolescent Self-Report Scale: Long Version

Conners-Wells' Adolescent Self-Report Scale: Short Version

Auxiliary Scales

Conners Global Index–Parent

Conners Global Index–Teacher

Conners ADHD/DSM-IV Scales–Parent

Conners ADHD/DSM-IV Scales–Adolescent

The revised version of this instrument includes several substantial changes. The author states that the revised version provides multidimensional scales that assess ADHD and other disorders that may exist with the attention disorders. The new version includes additional methods for assisting mental health professionals in making *DSM-IV diagnoses* (*Diagnostic and Statistical Manual*, 4th Edition, American Psychiatric Association, 1994). The former edition of the Conners included a Hyperactivity Index, which is now called the Conners' Global Index.

The Conners Rating Scales–Revised was developed with a large standardization sample (more than 8,000) with representative samples in the United States and Canada. In addition to representative norms, several studies are included in the manual that compare ethnic differences in samples of the following groups: African American/Black, Asian, Caucasian, Hispanic, Native American, and Other. These studies are presented in adequate detail in the manual, with main-effect differences by ethnic group provided for each scale. Consumers of this instrument are encouraged to read this section of the manual carefully when using the instrument for diagnostic purposes with the mentioned ethnic groups.

The dimensions of the Conners Rating Scales include oppositional, cognitive problems/inattention, hyperactivity, anxious-shy, perfectionism, social problems, and psychosomatic. The special "Quick Score" paper included with the rating scales enables the teacher or other member of the multidisciplinary team to score the short form in minutes. The long versions of the various rating scales involve much more effort to score, and hand scoring using the profile sheets is difficult because of the large number of columns included on the page. Computer scoring is available.

Reliability studies included internal reliability. Internal consistency for the various scales ranged from .72 to .95. Some variability exists on some scales with different age groups. For example, teacher ratings were more consistent for the younger and older age groups than for other age groups.

Validity studies in the Conners examiner's manual address factorial validity, convergent validity, divergent validity, discriminant validity, and concurrent validity. Information concerning this research is much more extensive than the previous edition and seems to range from below acceptable levels to adequate. Many of the studies included small samples. The author states that research in this area is continuing.

QUESTIONNAIRES AND INTERVIEWS

The questions found on questionnaires are similar to the items on checklists, but the respondent is encouraged to describe the behaviors or situations where the behavior occurs. The respondent answers with narrative statements. For example, the questions might appear as follows:

1. How is the student prepared for class each day?
2. Describe how the student begins assignments during class.
3. How does the student perform during distractions?
4. How often does the student complete homework assignments?
5. How does the student respond during class discussions?

Figure 8.8   Interview questions adapted for both parent and student.

Parent Interview	Student Interview
1. How do you think your child feels about school this year?	1. Tell me how you feel about school this year.
2. Tell me how your child completes homework assignments.	2. Describe how you go about finishing your homework.
3. Describe the responsibilities your child has at home.	3. What type of things are you expected to do at home? Do you think you complete those things most of the time?

The respondent should be encouraged to provide objective responses that describe as many variables of the behavior as possible. Interviews are completed using questions similar to those used on questionnaires. The evaluator verbally asks the respondent the questions and encourages objective, detailed information. The interview format may also be used with the student to obtain information about the student's feelings and perceptions about the target behaviors. Figure 8.8 illustrates how an interview could be adapted so that both parents and the student could provide answers.

Child Behavior Checklist: Semistructured Clinical Interview   Interviews may be conducted by different members of the multidisciplinary team. Often, these interviews are unstructured and informal. Achenbach and McConaughy (1989, 1990) developed a semistructured interview and observation form to be used with students aged 5–11. This interview assesses the student's feelings about school, family, and peers as well as affect or emotional functioning. The examiner is provided with, in addition to the interview, an observation form to rate behaviors of and comments by the student observed during the interview. The student is asked open-ended questions and guided through the interview process. This interview can be useful in determining the current social and emotional issues concerning the student.

SOCIOGRAMS

The sociogram method enables the teacher to obtain information about the group dynamics and structure within the classroom. This information can be interpreted to determine which students are well liked by their peers, which students are considered to be the leaders in the group, and which students are believed to be successful in school.

A sociogram is constructed by designing questions that all members of the class will be asked to answer. The questions might include, "Whom would you select to be in your group for the science project?" or "Whom would you invite to the movies?" The answers are then collected and interpreted by the teacher. The diagram in Figure 8.9a illustrates a sociogram; Figure 8.9b lists questions asked of a class of fourth-grade students.

The data are analyzed to determine who the class members perceive as being the class stars, the social isolates, and so on. The teacher also can determine where mutual choices exist (where two students share the same feelings about each other) and can identify cliques and persons who are neglected. The teacher can then use this information to intervene and structure social and academic situations that would promote fair social skills. Role plays, class projects, and school social activities could be used to increase the interpersonal interaction opportunities for social isolates and neglectees.

ECOLOGICAL ASSESSMENT

Ecological assessment analyzes the student's total learning environment. This analysis includes the student's interactions with others (peers, teachers, paraprofessionals, parents, and other persons who are directly involved with the student's learning process); the teacher's interactions with other students in the classroom; the methods of presentation of materials; materials used in the classroom; the physical environment; and the student's interactions with others in different settings, such as the playground or lunchroom. All of the informal behavioral assessment methods presented thus far may be used as a part of ecological assessment.

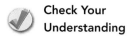

Check Your Understanding

Check your ability to analyze a sociogram of a classroom by completing Activity 8.3 below.

Activity 8.3

Use Figure 8.9a to analyze the social dynamics of this classroom.
1. Which students have made mutual choices? _____
2. Which students seem to be isolated from their peers? _____
3. Which students appear to be in cliques or groups? _____
4. Which students seem to be the most socially popular? _____
5. Who are the academic stars? _____

Apply Your Knowledge

List other questions that you may find useful in a sociogram: _____
_____
_____

Figure 8.9 Sociogram (a) and sociogram questions (b).

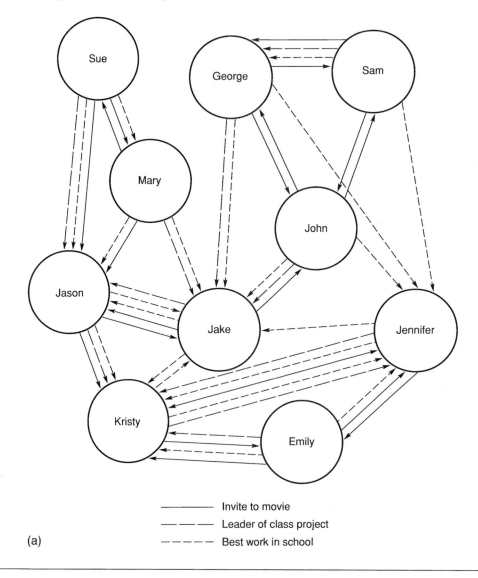

——————— Invite to movie
— — — — Leader of class project
— — — — Best work in school

(a)

Sociogram questions.

1. Name two students in our class whom you would most like to invite to a movie (or other activity).
   a. _____
   b. _____

2. In our class, whom would you like to be the leader of our class project? _____

3. Name two students in our class who do the best work in school.
   a. _____
   b. _____

(b)

MORE PRACTICE-ANALYSIS OF BEHAVIORAL CASE

Mrs. Soto taught in a 7th grade resource setting. She was a new teacher and by November she began to feel that she was settling into her routine for lesson planning and instructional delivery. During the first week of December, she was notified that a new student would be transferring into her classroom from another city by the beginning of the second week of December. Following the appropriate meeting and review of the student's records by the IEP team, the new student, named Don, began attending her resource room each day for 1 hour. Don was receiving special education support services for mathematics. By Don's second week, Mrs. Soto noticed that Don had some organizational difficulties. She assisted him with strategies for organizing his books and papers. Don seemed to understand the expectations of the class and the school. Following the winter break in December, Don once again seemed to be disorganized. Mrs. Soto reviewed the organizational strategies and Don seemed to remember how the class was organized and what he was expected to do. Within a week, Mrs. Soto noticed that Don was coming to class without his materials. These were the observations she made:

Don—Preparation for work in resource room.

	Tardy	**Without Materials**
Monday	5 mins.	yes—another student brought materials to Don
Tuesday	7 mins.	yes—another student brought materials to Don
Wednesday	5 mins.	yes—another student brought materials to Don
Thursday	6 mins.	yes—Mrs. Soto sent Don for materials
Friday	7 mins.	yes—Don asked to go get materials

With this documentation, Mrs. Soto discussed the matter with Don. Don apologized and told Mrs. Soto he would be on time to class and try to improve.

The following week, Don was on time 3 of 5 days however, he continued to come to class without materials.

1. What questions would you ask Don?
2. What strategies would you use to change this behavior?
3. Write a behavioral objective for the strategies you would use and the behaviors you expect.

Once you have written the answers to these questions, read the next section.

Mrs. Soto investigated and determined that Don enjoyed talking with a student who worked in the office as a student assistant during the time period that he was in the resource room. Don would stop by and talk to this student and leave his books so that the friend could bring them to his class or he could return to visit with his friend again. How could you use this information in your behavior planning strategy?

The teacher variable is one area that can be assessed by direct observation and other techniques such as questionnaires. Guerin and Maier suggested surveying teachers to determine their level of teacher competency. This would include assessing areas such as level of instruction, teaching strategies, types of instruction, media used in the classroom, and general communication and interaction with students and parents. These types of questionnaires can be designed to be completed by the teacher or by an objective observer. The student's educational materials should be evaluated for their appropriateness for the individual student. The level of difficulty, format, and mode of presentation and response are important considerations. The following variables should be evaluated when assessing materials:

Analyzing Instructional Materials

1. Are the objectives of the materials appropriate for the student?
2. Do the ability/readability levels match the current instructional level of the student?
3. Is the interest level appropriate for the student?
4. Does the method of presentation match the student's strength for learning?
5. Are prerequisite steps needed before the student can attempt the task?
6. Does the format of the material contain extraneous stimuli that can confuse or distract the student?
7. Does the material contain information not necessary for task completion?
8. Are too many tasks contained on one page?
9. Is the student capable of completing the task in the amount of time allowed?
10. Does the task need to be broken down into smaller tasks?
11. Is the student capable of responding with relative ease in the manner required by the materials?
12. Can the criterion level for success be reduced?
13. Does the material allow the student to self-check or self-correct?
14. Does the material allow the student to observe progress? (Overton 1987, pp. 111–115)

Case Study for Behavior Analysis

Mr. Blackburn noticed that one of his students in his second-grade class, Gracelyn, was enthusiastic during the morning classes but had been having difficulty in the afternoon. She disturbed other students and generally seemed to be unhappy in class. Sometimes Gracelyn would say things to her peers that would result in an argument and she would be asked to leave the classroom. Mr. Blackburn collected the following data for afternoon classes:

	Off-Task Behaviors	**Negative Remarks to Peers**
Monday	5	2
Tuesday	6	3
Wednesday	1	0
Thursday	6	3
Friday	7	3

After he collected the data, he noticed that Wednesday Gracelyn's behavior was markedly better than the other days of the week. He began to analyze all the variables within the environment such as academic tasks, lunchroom behavior, seating arrangements, and other environmental factors. He concluded that the only variable that was different on Wednesday was that another student, Joyce, a student who came into the class in the afternoons, was absent on Wednesday. He decided the next step would be to discuss this with Gracelyn. When Mr. Blackburn talked to her, she reported that she and Joyce had been friends last year but now Joyce had a new best friend and she was afraid that she did not like her anymore. After the data analysis and the discussion with Gracelyn, Mr. Blackburn was able to intervene and assist Gracelyn with the social skills she needed to resolve this issue.

For **MORE PRACTICE** in the analysis of behavioral cases, visit the Companion Website at *www.prenhall.com/overton.*

PROJECTIVE ASSESSMENT TECHNIQUES

projective techniques
Techniques used to analyze a student's feelings by what the student projects into the story card or other stimulus.

The measures presented in this section are measures that are scored more subjectively; they are often referred to as **projective techniques**. These measures include sentence completion tests, drawing tests, and apperception tests, which require the student to tell a story about some stimulus, such as picture cards. These instruments are most likely administered by the school psychologist, school counselor, or other professional, such as a clinical psychologist, who has the training and experience required to administer such instruments. Teachers and other members of the multidisciplinary team may be required to make eligibility and planning decisions based on the results of these instruments. It is beneficial to teachers, therefore, to understand the nature of the instruments and how they might be used in the assessment process.

SENTENCE COMPLETION TESTS

sentence completion tests Stems of sentences that the student completes; analyzed for themes.

Sentence completion tests provide stems or beginnings of sentences that the student is required to finish. The stems have been selected to elicit comments from the student on such topics as relationships with parents and friends and feelings about oneself. The examiner analyzes the comments written by the student for themes rather than analyzing each sentence independently. The Rotter Incomplete Sentence Blank (Rotter & Rafferty, 1950) is an example of this type of instrument. Figure 8.10 presents stems similar to those on sentence completion tests.

DRAWING TESTS

drawing tests Tests in which student draws figures, houses, trees, or families; scored developmentally and projectively.

Drawing tests attempt to screen the student's feelings about self, home, and family. Each of these instruments follows a simple format. The student is presented with a form or a piece of plain paper and is asked to draw a picture of himself; of a house, a tree, and a person; or of his family doing something together. These tests are commonly known as the Draw-a-Person, Human-Figure Drawing, House-Tree-Person, and Kinetic Family Drawings. The drawings may be scored subjectively by an examiner who has had training and experience in this type of assessment. More empirically based scoring systems are also available: the Kinetic Family Drawing System for Family and School (Knoff & Prout, 1985), the Draw-a-Person: Screening Procedure for Emotional Disturbance (Naglieri, McNeish, & Bardos, 1991), and the Human-Figure Drawing Test (Koppitz, 1968). The Draw-a-Person can be scored developmentally using a system like that by Naglieri (1988) or Harris (1963).

The newer versions of scoring systems include standardization information and developmental information. The Kinetic Family Drawing System for Family and School includes questions that the examiner asks the student about the drawings. For example, one question is "What does this person need most?" (Knoff & Prout, 1985, p. 5). The scoring booklet provides various characteristics that the student may have included in the drawings. The examiner checks to see whether a characteristic, such as the omission of

Figure 8.10   Sample items from a sentence completion test.

1. Sometimes I wish _____ .
2. I wish my mother would _____ .
3. I feel sad when _____ .
4. My friends always _____ .
5. My father _____ .

body parts, is present in the student's drawing. Guidelines for interpreting these characteristics are provided in the manual through a listing of relevant research on drawing analysis. The examiner analyzes themes that exist within the drawing on such dimensions as figure characteristics and actions between figures. Several case studies are provided for the examiner to use as guidelines for learning how to interpret the drawings.

The scoring system of the Draw-a-Person: Screening Procedure for Emotional Disturbance uses scoring templates and a norm-referenced method of scoring the drawings. The instrument is to be used as a screening device to determine whether the student needs further emotional or behavioral assessment. The manual provides examples of using the templates and scoring exercises using case studies for learning the system. Derived scores include T scores with a mean of 50 and a standard deviation of 10 and percentile ranks. The scores are interpreted as follows (Naglieri et al., 1991):

Less than 55	Further evaluation is not indicated
55 to 64	Further evaluation is indicated
65 and above	Further evaluation is strongly indicated (p. 63)

An example of the template scoring system from the manual is presented in Figure 8.11.

Figure 8.11   Example of the Naglieri et al. template scoring system for the Draw-a-Person test.

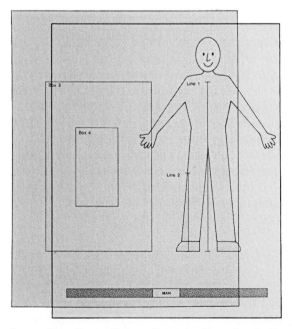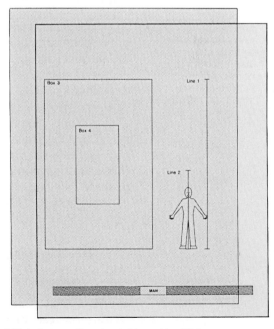

The standardization information and technical data provided in the Naglieri et al. (1991) manual is fairly extensive and impressive for a projective drawing instrument. The sample included 2,260 students, ages 6 to 17 years. Approximately 200 students were represented in each age group. Consideration was given for age, sex, geographic region, population of community, ethnicity, race, parent occupation, and socioeconomic status. Internal consistency was researched using the coefficient alpha, and coefficients were adequate, ranging from .67 to .78. The standard error of measurement is approximately 5 for all ages. The test-retest information gives a coefficient of .67, although the sample for this study was fairly small (n = 67). Both intrarater and interrater agreement was studied and resulted in coefficients of .83 and .84, respectively. This study was also small, using 54 cases and 2 raters.

Descriptive statistics are included for validity studies that used the scoring system to compare students who had been clinically diagnosed with emotional or behavioral problems to students without such problems. The scoring system did discriminate between the groups, at least at the .05 significance level. Construct validity is supported by discriminant validity studies of intelligence testing and the Naglieri et al. Draw-a-Person scoring system. The research presented indicates that two separate areas are assessed by the Draw-a-Person and intelligence tests.

APPERCEPTION TESTS

apperception tests Student's feelings about what she perceives to be happening in a picture or other stimulus; influenced by personal experiences.

Apperception tests consist of a set of picture or story cards that have been designed to elicit responses about emotional issues. These instruments may be administered and interpreted only by professionals with the training and experience required by the test developers. Most of these projective techniques require that the examiner possess advanced graduate-level training in psychological assessment. Because apperception tests may contribute information used by the multidisciplinary team to determine educational and behavioral interventions, teachers should understand what these instruments attempt to measure and how they are interpreted. Two commonly used instruments are the Children's Apperception Test (Bellak & Bellak, 1949, 1952; Bellak & Hurvich, 1965) and the Roberts Apperception Test for Children (Roberts, 1982).

Children's Apperception Test (CAT)   The CAT comprises two tests and a supplement for special situations (Bellak & Bellak, 1949, 1952; Bellak & Hurvich, 1965). The original test (animal figures) consists of 10 picture cards that depict animals engaged in human situations. The authors developed the instrument as an apperception method, which they define as "a method of investigating personality by studying the dynamic meaningfulness of the individual differences in perception of standard stimuli" (Bellak & Bellak, 1949, p. 1). The examiner evaluates a student's verbal responses to the picture cards in an effort to better understand how the student feels about herself and her relationships with family members.

The authors originally believed that younger children would identify more readily with animal figures and that these figures were more cultural and gender free. Figure 8.12 presents a picture-story card from the animal figures of the CAT. They later developed the CAT human figures as an answer to research studies that indicated the value of human-figure picture cards (Bellak & Hurvich, 1965). These picture-story cards maintain many of the same story themes and emotionally charged situations as in the animal figures; but the figures are now human, with some remaining fairly gender neutral.

The supplement to the CAT (Bellak & Bellak, 1952) contains various pictures depicting unusual situations using animal figures. Examples include a picture of a pregnant "mother" type of animal, an animal in a doctor's office, and an animal walking with crutches. Any of these specific cards may be selected by the examiner and used with the animal or human figures.

The CAT is scored subjectively along psychoanalytic themes such as regression, fear, anxiety, and denial; the manuals provide

Figure 8.12   Picture card 8 of the Children's Apperception Test.

Source: From *Children's Apperception Test (Animal Figures)* by L. Bellak and S.S. Bellak, 1999, Larchmont, NY: C.P.S. Copyright 1991 by C.P.S., Inc. Reprinted by permission of C.P.S., Inc., Box 83, Larchmont, NY 10538.

guidelines for scoring the instrument. Technical data provided in the manuals do not meet the standards set forth by many test developers in terms of reliability and validity.

Roberts–2   The second edition of the Roberts (Roberts & Gruber, 2005), like its original version, the Roberts Apperception Test for Children (McArthur & Roberts, 1982), presents story-picture cards of human figures engaged in situations with family members and peers. The second edition may be used with students ranging in age from 6 through 18 years. Of 27 stimulus cards, the student responds to 11 cards that are specific to the student's gender, as well as to 5 gender-neutral cards. This instrument has Hispanic cards and cards representing African American children as well as the set for Caucasian children. The cards were designed to elicit comments about the student's feelings about fear, parental relationships, dependency, peer and racial interaction, and so on. The examiner instructs the student to tell a story about what happened before, during, and after each scene pictured and to tell what the characters are doing, saying, and thinking. The examiner scores responses according to guidelines set forth in the manual, which gives information on adaptive indicators, clinical problems such as aggression or anxiety, and measures such as social cognitive functioning.

The manual includes information about the standardization of the instrument as well as studies comparing students within the normal range of emotional functioning with several different clinical samples. Reliability information includes interrater reliability and test-retest reliability studies. Median interrater reliability correlations ranged from .43 to 1.00. The validity information included in the manual presents several studies of the factors measured, as well as the instrument's ability to discriminate clinical from nonclinical groups. Generally, the information presented appears to be adequate for this type of behavior instrument.

COMPUTERIZED ASSESSMENT OF ATTENTION DISORDERS

Instruments have been developed for the assessment of sustained focused attention and impulsive responding patterns. Difficulty with these behaviors is believed to be characteristic of students with attention deficit disorders. This type of difficulty may be manifested as distractibility, impulsivity, and overactivity in classroom situations. These instruments should not be used as a single measure of attention problems, but rather should be used in combination with other measures, particularly classroom observations. Two such computerized systems currently used in clinical practice and research are the Continuous Performance Test (Gordon, 1983) and the Conners Continuous Performance Test (Conners, 1993). All tests of this general type are known as CPTs.

CONTINUOUS PERFORMANCE TEST

In Gordon's (1983) Continuous Performance Test, the student must discriminate between visual stimuli presented for a period of 9 minutes. The stimuli are numbers that appear at the rate of 1 per second. Scores are computed for the number of correct responses, omissions, and commissions. This instrument has been widely researched, and the author reports reliability coefficients ranging from .66 to .80.

CONNERS CONTINUOUS PERFORMANCE TEST

The Conners Continuous Performance Test is presented in much the same manner as Gordon's version (Conners, 1993; Conners, 1997). This CPT, however, lasts for 14 minutes, and the visual stimuli—letters—appear at varying rates throughout the administration. The student must maintain focused sustained attention, and the number of targets hit is calculated to determine impulsivity and loss of attention. Interpretive, computer-generated reports give derived scores for hit rate, reaction time, pattern for standard error or variability, omissions, commissions, attentiveness, and response tendencies such as risk taking. Data included in the manual and from computer reports compare the student with age and gender peers in a clinical group of students with attention deficit disorders.

DETERMINING EMOTIONAL DISTURBANCE

According to federal regulations, students may be found to be eligible for interventions under the category of emotional disturbance if they meet one the following criteria:

> An inability to learn that cannot be explained by other factors (such as a sensory or learning disorder)
> Difficulty in establishing and maintaining relationships with peers and adults
> Behaviors that are inappropriate for the circumstances
> A persistent mood of unhappiness or depression
> And
> Physical symptoms manifested as the result of fears or concerns about school or other problems.

It is important to note that a student may have some difficulties with emotion, such as a student who has depression, and not be eligible for services. For example, a student may be depressed; however, if there is no educational need for special education support, the student would not be found eligible for services. Students who manifest only mild behavioral problems without a coexisting emotional disorder, will also not likely be served under special education. For many students with such behavioral issues, it is simply a matter of poor learning or social maladjustment. It is also noteworthy that most students with attention deficit disorders or other physiologically based disorders such as Tourette's syndrome, will be served under the category of Other Health Impaired. The reasoning for this distinction is that although these disorders have behavioral manifestations, these disorders are not the result of an emotional disorder. This distinctions may be difficult for teachers to distinguish without additional assessment data from the school psychologist.

One instrument that may be used to assist in making such determinations, in combination with other behavioral and developmental data from parents and teachers, is the Scale for Assessing Emotional Disturbance (Epstein & Cullinan, 1998). The measures on this instrument are consistent with the five requirements of the federal regulations. The classroom teacher and other educators working with the student may be asked to complete a variety of questionnaires and checklists to assist in the determination. Students who are found to have emotional disturbance must manifest these behaviors across environments and in social interactions with a variety of peers and adults. The use of multiple checklists provides information about these multiple settings and social encounters.

RESEARCH AND ISSUES

The assessment of emotional and behavioral problems is by nature more ambiguous than other types of assessment, such as assessment of intellectual or academic achievement ability. The techniques range from systematic observations and computer assessment to projective techniques, such as telling stories about picture cards. The research on each of these methods has existed in volumes in the literature for many years. The research summarized in the following list represents some of the recent studies using the instruments often employed in settings that serve children and youth. Other measures, such as the Rorschach inkblot test (Rorschach, 1921, 1942), are more often used in clinical settings and therefore were not included in this text.

1. In a review of literature about functional behavioral assessment (FBA), it was found that FBA has largely studied high-rate behaviors in students with low-incidence disabilities, such as self-injurious behaviors in children with mental retardation (Ervin, Radford, Bertsch, Piper, Ehrhardt, & Poling, 2001). Additional research is needed on low-rate

behaviors (such as aggressive acts) in students with high-incidence disabilities, such as learning disabilities.

2. Northup and Gulley reviewed research that applied functional behavioral assessment in samples of students with attention deficit hyperactivity disorder and found that it is a useful technique to use in determining the interaction and effectiveness of medication with various environmental stimuli (2001).

3. Curriculum-based assessment used as part of a functional behavioral assessment was found to be an effective strategy in identifying escape-motivated behaviors of students within a general education classroom (Roberts, Marshall, Nelson, & Albers, 2001).

4. Information gained from functional behavioral assessments in preschool students at risk for attention deficit hyperactivity disorder was found to be an effective method of identifying specific strategies that decreased the problematic behaviors (Boyajian, DuPaul, Handler, Eckert, & McGoey, 2001).

5. In a review of the Behavior Rating Profile, Second Edition, the instrument's strengths include high criterion-related, concurrent, and construct validity, a sociogram, and the ability for assessment of behavioral, social, emotional, and interpersonal areas (Javorsky, 1998–1999). The weaknesses cited included the lack of students with behavioral/emotional difficulties in the norming group, lack of interrater reliability, lack of the ability to discriminate between different diagnostic categories of behavioral/emotional problems, limited use with younger students, and no information regarding intervention strategies.

6. In a study using school-referred males comparing the Teacher Report Form and the Child Behavior Checklist to the Youth Self-Report, it was found that the youth and the teacher and parent forms did not have high agreement, especially when the students rated themselves on externalizing behaviors (Lee, Elliott, & Barbour, 1994). The study found a somewhat higher agreement between parents and teachers in rating students. These findings seem to suggest that youth tend to underrate themselves on problem behaviors, which emphasizes the need for multimethod and multiinformant assessment.

7. An extensive review of the use of rating scales in different cultures resulted in noticeable differences related to culture (Reid, 1995). Because of the reliance of subjective interpretation by the rater, Reid suggests that use of rating scales in

other cultures may not be appropriate for use in diagnosing attention deficit disorder. He cautions that some symptoms may be influenced by variables related to culture, such as low socioeconomic status (SES) or other stressors.

8. In a study by Weine, Phillips, and Achenbach (1995) comparing results of the Child Behavior Checklist, differences were found in Chinese and American children. The Chinese children were found to be rated higher by their teachers for delinquent behavior, for being anxious/depressed, and on the internalizing scale. American children were rated higher on the Child Behavior Checklist on aggressive behavior. American children were rated higher by their teachers in attention problems.

9. A study comparing teacher responses on a teacher rating scale for Caucasian and African-American students found that teachers rated African-American students higher on all symptoms (Reid, DuPaul, Power, Anastopoulos, Rogers-Adkinson, Nell, & Ricco, 1998). Reid et al. caution that other measures should be used for diagnosis of attention deficit disorder for African Americans rather than relying on just teacher rating scales.

10. In a review by Walker of the Behavior Assessment System for Children, the BASC was stated to be fairly easy to administer and score, and it also had good evidence of interrater reliability (1998–1999). Walker stated that the weaknesses of the BASC were that no definitions were provided in the test manual, and students with disabilities were underrepresented in the normative sample, as well as students who are culturally, linguistically, and ethnically diverse. Walker noted that the instrument should be used only for screening purposes.

11. Oesterheld and Haber (1997) found that the items on the Conners test and the Child Behavior Checklist were difficult for Native-American parents to understand. The Native Americans often did not have similar words or concepts in their language or feared that their responses would be misinterpreted by the dominant culture.

12. Stanford and Hynd (1994) studied the difference between students with attention deficit disorder with and without hyperactivity and students with learning disabilities. Parents and teachers of students with hyperactivity endorsed more externalizing types of items on the Child Behavior Checklist. Parents and teachers of students who had attention deficit disorder without hyperactivity and students with learning disabilities endorsed fewer externalizing items.

13. The Child Behavior Checklist, Teacher Report Form, and Semistructured Clinical Interview for Children were found to have discriminant validity when comparing children with behavior disorders and nonreferred children (McConaughy & Achenbach, 1996). The discriminant validity was not as high when comparing children with behavior disorders and children with learning disabilities.

14. A study in a public school setting focused on interrater reliability among teachers using the Conners Teacher Rating Scale. Both certified teachers of students with emotional problems and their teacher aides were consistent in their ratings (Mattison, Bagnato, Mayes, & Felix, 1990). The strongest interrater correlations were on the scale's hyperactivity and conduct disorders factors. This seems to suggest that the Conners Teacher Rating Scale has adequate interrater reliability and may be an appropriate instrument in conjunction with other assessment techniques for screening for acting-out or externalizing behaviors.

15. Research of family drawings by students with divorced parents and those without divorced parents indicated differences around themes of interpersonal relationships (Spigelman, Spigelman, & Englesson, 1992). Students from homes with divorce seemed to have more omissions of family members and indications of conflict within relationships with siblings.

16. A study of human figure drawings with 5-year-old students found no significant differences between the drawings of aggressive and nonaggressive students (Norford & Barakat, 1990). It appears that this type of technique is not developmentally appropriate for use with students younger than 6.

17. Research using chronically ill children found that the Roberts Apperception Test for Children was able to differentiate children with adaptive coping styles from children with maladaptive coping styles (Palomares, Crowley, Worchel, Olson, & Rae, 1991).

18. Kroon, Goudena, and Rispens (1998) reviewed the Roberts Apperception Test for Children and stated that the psychometrics of the instrument appeared adequate, although the research presented in the manual is quite limited.

19. A study of students with and without attention deficit disorder identified both false positives and false negatives during use of a Continuous Performance Test (Trommer, Hoeppner, Lorber, & Armstrong, 1988). In addition, differences in these groups on other measures suggest that CPTs

may involve some higher-level cognitive tasks rather than pure attentive ability. Thus, CPTs should be interpreted with caution and always should be analyzed with data from multiple sources.

20. Research comparing CPT performance of students with learning disabilities and a matched control group indicated that students with learning disabilities made more omission errors but did not differ on the number of commission errors (Eliason & Richman, 1987). The authors suggest that the constructs of attention and memory are highly interrelated and may result in students with learning disabilities making more omission errors on this type of measure.

21. Research using a CPT determined favorable decreases in the number of errors made in a sample of students with attention deficit disorder following treatment with methylphenidate—Ritalin (Forness, Swanson, Cantwell, Guthrie, & Sena, 1992). This suggests that CPTs may be sensitive to measurement of the treatment of students with stimulant medication.

22. In a review of research, Loiser, McGrath, and Klein (1996) found that children with ADHD made a higher number of omission and commission errors than did non-ADHD children. They also found that children treated with methylphenidate made significantly fewer errors on the CPT than those who were not treated.

23. On a CPT, students with attention deficit disorder with hyperactivity made almost twice the number of errors of commission as did students with attention deficit disorder without hyperactivity (Barkley, DuPaul, & McMurray, 1990). This same study determined that students with attention deficit disorder and hyperactivity scored significantly worse on the ASEBA aggressive and delinquent scales than did students with attention deficit disorder without hyperactivity, students with learning disabilities, and the control sample of students.

24. Although the Children's Apperception Test has been revised, it continues to be criticized by professional reviewers due to the lack of adequate psychometric quality (Knoff, 1998; Reinehr, 1998).

25. Mueller, Brozovich, and Johnson reviewed the Conners Rating Scales–Revised (1998–1999). These reviewers noted the difficulty in scoring the Conners; they also noted that the readability level for the parent form was ninth grade. These reviewers questioned whether the readability level might be too high for some parents.

It is evident from the small sample of research reviewed in this chapter that many factors are to be considered in the assessment of students exhibiting behavioral and emotional problems. It is important that multiple measures and multiple informants be used and that the individual student's environment be assessed as well (Clarizio & Higgins, 1989). In a review of relevant research on assessment of attention and behavioral disorders, Schaughency and Rothlind (1991) stressed the need for a variety of methods, such as interviews, teacher ratings, observations, and peer nominations. These techniques may aid in determining whether the difficulties are reactions to the environment or reactions to current stress within the student's world. As with all assessment, a holistic view of the complete student and his environment is necessary.

THINK AHEAD

Cognitive abilities and the assessment of intelligence remain a part of the assessment process in determining the need for special education intervention. Chapter 9 presents the most commonly used measures of intelligence and adaptive behavior.

EXERCISES

Part I

Match the following terms with the statements.

a. checklist
b. direct observation
c. permanent product recording
d. setting event
e. anecdotal recording
f. interresponse time
g. functional behavior assessment
h. time sampling
i. projective techniques
j. target behavior
k. an apperception test
l. work samples
m. CPT
n. establishing operation
o. event recording
p. latency
q. interval recording
r. drawing tests
s. baseline

_____ 1. A teacher wants to determine the exact number of times a student inappropriately leaves his seat. The teacher needs this information before an intervention begins. This initial data collection technique about the student's behavior is referred to as the _____.

_____ 2. Although information can be obtained by questioning persons who work with a specific student, in order to determine what behavior occurs in a specific environment, the method of _____ will need to be used over multiple sessions.

_____ 3. By writing down information about a student's behavior that can later be analyzed for antecedent, behavior, and consequence, the teacher has used _____ as part of the functional behavioral assessment.

_____ 4. A teacher notices that one specific student has not been able to complete class work in the amount of time allotted. He notices that all other students in the class usually finish within the time frame expected. This specific student seems to take some time getting prepared to begin assignments. To establish a baseline about this specific behavior, the teacher will need to record the _____ time between the time the assignment is presented and the time the student begins to work.

_____ 5. A teacher and additional objective educational personnel have observed a student's off-task behavior in several settings. During the assessment process, the school psychologist may administer a _____ to measure distractibility and sustained focused attention on a computerized assessment.

_____ 6. A test that requires the psychologist to analyze story responses a student gives when shown specific picture cards is called _____.

_____ 7. Although much information can be obtained from norm-referenced standardized assessments, in order to analyze a student's progress and productivity in a curriculum, _____ should be collected and evaluated.

_____ 8. The evaluation of the information collected in question 7 is called _____.

_____ 9. An elementary teacher questions a third-grade student following a fight on the playground. The student is quite upset and relays to the teacher that his parents were fighting that morning before school and he witnessed his father shoving his mother. This incident may be referred to as the _____ of the child's behavior on the playground.

_____10. Assessment techniques such as completing sentence stems and drawing pictures of a house or person are called _____.

_____11. An assessment reveals that a child's continued calling out during class time is a method used by the child to gain the teacher's attention. This assessment, that identifies the reason for the student's calling out, is known as _____ .

_____12. Students display many varieties of behaviors during a school day. When specific behaviors are identified as problematic behaviors that require interventions, they are referred to as _____ .

Part II

Read the following scenario. Complete an analysis of the scenario and identify the **highlighted** phrases or words behaviorally.

A middle-school student has begun **arguing** and **getting into fights** during **unstructured times** during the school day. You observe that nobody seems to provoke the student, but rather the student becomes argumentative **whenever another student jokingly touches** or **comes near** the target student. The result of the student's problematic behaviors is that the student who was jokingly touching or coming near the target student **backs away** and **leaves the target student alone.** The target student seems to be happier during structured times during adult supervision. Upon questioning the target student, you learn that his older brother **has been hitting the target** student when **the parents are not at home.**

Provide your analysis below: _____

_____

_____

Anwers to these questions can be found in the Appendix of this text or you may also complete these questions and receive immediate feedback on your answers by going to the Think Ahead module in Chapter 8 of the Companion Website.

Measures of Intelligence and Adaptive Behavior

intelligence	acculturation
adaptive behavior	cross-battery assessment
IQ	simultaneous processing
innate potential	sequential processing
environmental influence	

CHAPTER FOCUS

Chapter 9 presents common assessment measures of cognitive ability and adaptive behavior. Teachers may be required to complete adaptive behavior measures and should also have an understanding of the use of intelligence tests.

CEC KNOWLEDGE AND SKILLS STANDARDS

The student completing this chapter will understand the knowledge and skills included in the following CEC Knowledge and Skills Standards from Standard 8: Assessment:

CC8K1—Basic terminology used in assessment.

CC8K2—Legal provisions and ethical principles regarding assessment of individuals.

CC8K4—Use and limitations of assessment instruments.

CC8K3—Screening, prereferral, referral, and classification procedures.

CC8S2—Administer nonbiased formal and informal assessments.

CC8S5—Interpret information from formal and informal assessments.

MEASURING INTELLIGENCE

intelligence A general concept of an individual's ability to function effectively within various settings; usually assessed by intelligence tests.

The measurement of **intelligence** has been a controversial issue in educational and psychological assessment for the past several years. Even though professionals in the field disagree to some extent about the definition of intelligence and about the fairness and importance of intelligence testing, the assessment of intellectual ability is mandated by IDEA for the diagnosis of many disabilities.

adaptive behavior One's ability to function in various environments.

This federal law also requires the assessment of **adaptive behavior**, or how a student functions within the environment, for the diagnosis of mental retardation.

This chapter presents a review of individual measures of intelligence and adaptive behavior that commonly are used in schools to diagnose students with learning or emotional disabilities. Group intelligence tests may be administered in school systems to students in the regular education curriculum; for special education diagnostic purposes, however, group IQ tests are not appropriate. Tests constructed to be administered in an individual setting are commonly used to measure cognitive abilities. Although teachers will not be responsible for administering intelligence tests, special education teachers should possess an understanding of the interpretation of intelligence test results and their possible implications for educational planning. A general discussion of intelligence testing and the court cases that have influenced current practice are presented before the review of intelligence tests.

THE MEANING OF INTELLIGENCE TESTING

IQ Intelligence quotient; expressed as a standard score, usually with a mean of 100.

The results of intelligence tests are usually reported in the form of a standardized **IQ** (intelligence quotient) score. The IQ score is a quotient that is derived in the following manner:

$$IQ = MA + CA \times 100$$

In this calculation, MA means the mental age of the student and CA is the chronological age of the student. Using this formula, a child with a mental age of 9 and a chronological age of 11 would have an IQ of around 82. A student with a mental age of 14 and a chronological age of 10 would have an IQ of 140. It is important for the special education professional to understand what an IQ score is and is not. To possess a basic understanding of IQ scores, the professional educator should consider what is measured by IQ tests, that is, the content and presentation of the items on an IQ test and what the items represent. It is a commonly held myth that IQ scores are measurements of potential that is innate in a person. The following statements illustrate some current views about intelligence and intelligence testing expressed in the literature:

> The IQ does not reflect a global summation of the brain's capabilities and is certainly not an index of genetic potential, but it does predict school achievement effectively. (Kaufman, 1979, p. 9)
>
>   Ultimately, intelligence is not a kind of ability at all, certainly not in the same sense that reasoning, memory, verbal fluency, etc., are so regarded. Rather it is something that is inferred from the way these abilities are manifested under different conditions and circumstances. (Wechsler, 1974, p. 5)

> Intelligence—unlike height and weight, but like all psychological constructs—must be measured indirectly; it must be inferred from intelligent behavior, past and present. (Hopkins, Stanley, & Hopkins, 1990, p. 374)

> Measurement of current intellectual performance has become confused with measurement of innate potential. Intelligence tests do not assess potential; they sample behaviors already learned in an attempt to predict future learning. (McLoughlin & Lewis, 1990, p. 187)

> Child-standardized intelligence performance provides a quantitative index of developmental status, but does not provide information on those functions that have not developed nor on the route by which the child arrived at his or her current developmental state. (Swanson & Watson, 1989, p. 93)

> Historically, intelligence has been an enigmatic concept. It is a much valued construct or quality that is extremely difficult to define. Is intelligence the same as verbal ability? Analytical thinking? Academic aptitude? Strategic thinking? The ability to cope? Different theorists might argue for each, or a combination of these abilities. Similarly, they might ask whether intelligence is, or should be, defined in the same way for individuals of different cultural, ethnic, or social backgrounds. (Taylor, 1989, pp. 185–186).

Wasserman and Tulsky (2005) note that, "Over 100 years of debate have failed to lead to a consensus definition of this core psychological construct" (p. 14). The theories upon which these tests are based influence their use and interpretation. As the development of intelligence tests continue, and that development is based on researched theories, the measurement and interpretation of intelligence test results will continue to be more meaningful for interventions (Kamphaus, Winsor, Rowe, & Kim, 2005).

Even more controversial than the meaning of intelligence is the apparent bias that may occur by using individual IQ tests to classify and place students in special education (Reschly, 1981). Taylor (1989) questioned using the same definition of intelligence for individuals of all cultures, which reflects the concern that minority students are overrepresented in special education classrooms (Heller, Holtzman, & Messick, 1982). Specifically, African American students have been overrepresented in classrooms for students with mental retardation (Heller et al., 1982; Tucker, 1980), and Hispanic students have been increasingly found in classrooms for the learning disabled (Mick, 1985; Tucker, 1980). With the new regulations focused on decreasing disproportionality, it is even more important to make certain that formal assessment measures are free from ethnic, cultural, and linguistic bias.

Salvia and Ysseldyke (1988) underscored the importance that culture and background have on intellectual assessment:

> Acculturation is the single most important characteristic in evaluating a child's performance on intelligence tests.... The culture in which a child lives and the length of time that the child has lived in that

culture effectively determine the psychological demands a test item presents. (p. 149)

Taylor and Richards (1991) noted that persons obtaining similar scores on IQ tests manifest differences in their pattern of responding. These authors found that while white students scored higher on the Wechsler Scales than black and Hispanic students, different patterns were evident, with black students showing verbal strength and Hispanic students showing strength in perceptual ability.

innate potential Thought to be one's ability from birth.

The issues of **innate potential**, learned behaviors, **environmental influence**, and **acculturation**, and their influence on intelligence testing, have fueled the fire of many professional debates (Herrnstein & Murray, 1994). Intelligence testing, however, like all testing in education, is simply the way that a student responds to a set of stimuli at a specific point in time. Reynolds (1982) reviewed and summarized the general problems with bias in assessment; these are presented, as adapted, in Figure 9.1. Some of the problems of intelligence testing stem from content validity, construct validity, predictive validity (Messick, 1980), and the mean differences obtained by groups of different cultural or ethnic backgrounds (Reschly, 1981), as well as problems that affect all types of standardized testing, such as examiner familiarity (Fuchs & Fuchs, 1989).

environmental influence The impact of the environment on the student's learning ability.

acculturation The influence of one culture on another culture.

ALTERNATIVE VIEWS OF INTELLECTUAL ASSESSMENT

The use of traditional intelligence tests in schools has been criticized for producing different results for different groups (Canter, 1997). The movement toward change in special education assessment, accountability, and educational reform in schools has also had an influence on the use of traditional assessment methods. Due to these trends, it is likely that assessment personnel along with researchers will seek alternative types of assessment models and methods of determining intellectual ability. Canter stated that "intelligence testing as we practice it today seems increasingly out-of-step with the needs of tomorrow's schools" (1997, p. 256). Dissatisfaction with the traditional psychometric approach has stimulated research and theoretical exploration of additional definitions and techniques used to assess intellectual ability. For example, Gardner (1993) presents a model with seven intelligences:

> But there is an alternative vision that I would like to present—one based on a radically different view of the mind and one that yields a very different view of the school. It is a pluralistic view of mind, recognizing many different and discrete facets of cognition, acknowledging that people have different cognitive strengths and contrasting cognitive styles. ... One such approach I have called my "theory of multiple intelligences." (1993, pp. 6–7)

Figure 9.1   Indicators of possible bias in assessment.

1. *Inappropriate content.* Black or other minority children have not been exposed to the material involved in the test questions or other stimulus materials. The tests are geared primarily toward white middle-class homes and values.

2. *Inappropriate standardization samples.* Ethnic minorities are underrepresented in the collection of normative reference group data.

3. *Examiner language bias.* Since most psychologists are white and speak primarily only standard English, they intimidate black and other ethnic minorities. They are also unable to accurately communicate with minority children. Lower test scores for minorities then are said to reflect only this intimidation and difficulty in the communication process and not lowered ability levels.

4. *Inequitable social consequences.* As a result of bias in educational and psychological tests, minority group members, who are already at a disadvantage in the educational and vocational markets because of past discrimination, are disproportionately relegated to dead-end educational tracts and are thought unable to learn. Labelling effects also fall under this category.

5. *Measurement of different constructs.* Related to (1) above, this position asserts that the tests are measuring significantly different attributes when used with children from other than the white middle-class culture.

6. *Differential predictive validity.* While tests may accurately predict a variety of outcomes for white middle-class children, they fail to predict at an acceptable level any relevant criteria for minority group members. Corollary to this objection is a variety of competing positions regarding the selection of an appropriate, common criterion against which to validate tests across cultural groupings. Scholastic or academic attainment levels are considered by a variety of black psychologists to be biased as criteria.

7. *Qualitatively distinct minority and majority aptitude and personality.* The idea here is that majority and minority cultures are so different that they result in substantial influences on personality and aptitude development. Due to these influences, different tests are required to accurately measure personality and aptitude.

Source: Adapted from "The Problem of Bias in Psychological Assessment" by C. R. Reynolds, P. A. Lowe, & A. L. Saenz; in C. R. Reynolds and T. B. Gutkin (Eds.), *The Handbook of School Psychology,* 3rd ed., 1999 (pp. 556–557), New York: John Wiley & Sons. Copyright 1999 by John Wiley & Sons. Adapted by permission.

The seven types of intellectual ability proposed by Gardner include linguistic intelligence, logical-mathematical intelligence, spatial intelligence, musical intelligence, bodily-kinesthetic intelligence, interpersonal intelligence, and intrapersonal intelligence. Gardner stresses the need for fair intellectual assessment that would assess all areas rather than only the linguistic and logical-mathematical assessment included in traditional intellectual assessment instruments.

Carroll had proposed a theory of intelligence that is based on three levels or stratums (Carroll, 2005). In this theory, a general or overarching intelligence influences the skills and abilities included within the other two levels or stratums. Level two includes more specific skills and abilities than the *g* or general factor of intelligence, and level three includes very specific abilities and skills.

The concept of dynamic assessment is another area of current research in the quest for alternate assessment models. This model uses the assessment experience to measure the precise task of learning. The tasks used in dynamic assessment are those in which the learner is presented with interventions to determine how the learner responds to those strategies or interventions. The learner begins a task and is assisted by the examiner rather than merely observed by the examiner. Lidz (1997) points out the differences between traditional and dynamic assessment:

> Most of our (traditional) procedures provide information only about the learner's independent level of performance and infer future from previous functioning.... Dynamic assessment begins where traditional psychometric assessment ends. Instead of terminating the procedure with the establishment of a ceiling, the dynamic assessor views the ceiling as an area of functioning that warrants assessment. (1997, pp. 281–282)

Others caution against the rapid adoption of alternative measures of intelligence without scientific basis for the changes (Lopez, 1997). While additional researchers call for the use of cross-battery assessment of cognitive abilities, noting that the use of multiple measures of cognitive skills and abilities can better account for the variety of abilities that must be measured (Flanagan & Ortiz, 2001). Brown, Reynolds, and Whitaker (1999) state that although many alternate assessment measures of IQ have been proposed, professionals should rely on research-based methods, including traditional standardized assessment instruments. Therefore, in most states, traditional IQ tests continue to be used as a part of the assessment process. Based on the individual student's measured performance on tasks on the IQ tests, the team members infer the student's intellectual ability (Turnbull, Turnbull, Shank, Smith, & Leal, 2002).

Even though IQ testing has received much criticism, MacMillan and Forness remind assessment personnel that traditional IQ scores derived from traditional methods serve a function in schools today (1998). As these authors point out,

> What IQ tells us is that if nothing is done and the child remains in general education with no adjustment to instructional strategies, the child with a low score is likely to experience failure—the lower the score, the greater the probability and the greater the degree of failure that the child will encounter. (1998, p. 251)

The most important consideration for school personnel using or interpreting IQ assessment data is that the data obtained from these assessments are only a small part of the information employed in the decision-making process (Prifitera, Saklofske, Weiss, & Rolfhus, 2005). Therefore, it is most important to select measures that will provide useful information and assist in making educational and behavioral interventions.

LITIGATION AND INTELLIGENCE TESTING

The issues of intelligence testing and the overrepresentation of minorities in special education classrooms led to litigation that has affected current practice in the field, including the decreased use of intelligence tests by some state and local education agencies for the diagnosis of disabling conditions (Bersoff, 1981). Major court cases that have involved the assessment of intellectual ability are *Larry P. v. Riles* (1984) and *PASE v. Hannon* (1980). Other cases have involved assessment and placement procedures: *Diana v. State Board of Education* and *Lora v. New York City Board of Education*. These cases are summarized in Figure 9.2.

Figure 9.2   Summary of court cases involving IQ assessment.

Larry P. v. Riles (1984). This case resulted in the court's finding that schools could no longer use standardized but unvalidated IQ tests for the purpose of identifying and placing black children into segregated special education classes for children designated as educable mentally retarded (EMR) (Turnbull, 1990, p. 92).

PASE v. Hannon (1980). Although PASE (Parents in Action on Special Education) found that some of the items in the tests were discriminatory, the court upheld that the tests were generally nondiscriminatory. More important, it found that the tests were not the sole basis for classification and that the school district therefore was complying with the Education of the Handicapped Act, EHA, which requires multifaceted testing (Turnbull, 1990, p. 95).

Diana v. State Board of Education (1970). In this case, the state board of education of California agreed to test students in their native language, to omit unfair test items of a verbal nature, to construct tests that would reflect the culture of Mexican American students, and to provide tests that would be standardized for Mexican Americans (Ysseldyke & Algozzine, 1982).

Lora v. New York City Board of Education (1984). This case required that the school system use objective and improved referral and assessment methods and multidisciplinary evaluations to reach decisions for diagnosis of students with emotional disturbance. The court found that the method previously in use was racially discriminatory and ruled that the school system could no longer consider school monetary problems or availability of services as reasons to place or not to place students in special education (Wood, Johnson, & Jenkins, 1990).

Due to the recent litigation involving the testing of intelligence as well as the information included in the assessment sections of IDEA, a movement toward more objective testing practices is currently under way in the assessment field. In addition, professionals are reminded to follow the *Code of Fair Testing Practices in Education* (see Chapter 2) by the Joint Committee on Testing Practices and the standards set forth by the AERA (1999).

For **MORE PRACTICE** on understanding what IQ tests measure, visit the Companion Website at *www.prenhall.com/overton.*

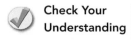

Check Your Understanding

Complete Activity 9.1 below to assess your knowledge of content on legal considerations and concepts of intelligence.

Activity 9.1

Match the following terms to the descriptions.

A. *PASE v. Hannon*

B. *Diana v. State Board of Education*

C. inappropriate content

D. inequitable social consequences

E. inappropriate standardization sample

F. differential predictive validity

G. *Lora v. New York City Board of Education*

H. *Larry P. v. Riles*

I. examiner language bias

J. measurement of different constructs

K. IQ score

L. intelligence testing

_____ 1. Case involving administering tests in a language other than the child's native language.

_____ 2. Case concerning students who were placed in a school for students with emotional disturbance without the benefit of nondiscriminatory assessment.

_____ 3. Standardized norm-referenced assessment of cognitive abilities; the indirect measurement of the construct of intelligence.

_____ 4. When, as the result of discriminatory assessment, minority students are placed in dead-end educational or vocational tracts.

_____ 5. When a test measures different constructs for people of different groups.

_____ 6. A test may accurately predict for one group of students but not as accurately for another group, which results in this.

_____ 7. A numerical representation of intellectual ability.

_____ 8. When the examiner does not possess skill in communicating in the student's native language, it may result in this.

_____ 9. Case finding that the use of IQ tests to place black students in classes for persons with mental retardation was a discriminatory practice.

_____ 10. Case finding the same IQ tests to be nondiscriminatory even though a few items were found to be biased.

Apply Your Knowledge

Summarize how court cases have influenced the use of intelligence tests. _____

_____

_____

USE OF INTELLIGENCE TESTS

The use of intelligence tests remains controversial in part because of inappropriate use in the past. Revised instruments, alternative testing practices, and understanding of the ethnic or cultural differences that may occur are promising improvements in the assessment of intelligence. Intelligence testing is likely to remain a substantial part of the assessment process because of the known correlation between performance on IQ tests and school achievement (Reschly & Grimes, 1995). Kaufman (1994) states that intelligence tests should be used "as a helping agent rather than an instrument for placement, labeling, or other types of academic oppression" (p. 1). Kaufman has long advocated for the intelligent use of intelligence tests. McGrew and Flanagan (1998) state that to have a complete picture of a person's true intellectual ability, a cross battery or multiple measures of intelligence tests should be used. Given that IQ tests will continue to be used, educators must promote fair and appropriate use of intelligence measures. Reschly and Grimes (1995) set forth the following guidelines for appropriate use of IQ tests:

1. Appropriate use requires a context that emphasizes prevention and early intervention rather than eligibility determination as the initial phase in services to students with learning and behavior problems.

2. Intellectual assessment should be used when the results are directly relevant to well-defined referral questions and other available information does not address those questions.

3. Mandatory use of intellectual measures for all referrals, multifactored evaluations, or reevaluations is not consistent with best practices.

4. Intellectual assessment must be part of a multifactored approach, individualized to a child's characteristics and the referral problems.

5. Intellectual assessment procedures must be carefully matched to characteristics of children and youth.

6. Score reporting and interpretation must reflect known limitations of tests, including technical adequacy, inherent error in measurement, and general categories of performance.

7. Interpretation of performance and decisions concerning classification must reflect consideration of overall strengths and weaknesses in intellectual performance, performance on other relevant dimensions of behavior, age, family characteristics, and cultural background.

8. Users should implement assertive procedures to protect students from misconceptions and misuses of intellectual test results. (pp. 436–437)

Special education professionals can obtain meaningful information from IQ test results if they understand the types of behavior that are assessed by individual subtests and items. Readers should take notice of the possible areas of testing bias as well as previous court decisions as they study the tests reviewed in this chapter.

REVIEW OF INTELLIGENCE TESTS

This chapter reviews some of the tests most commonly used by schools to measure cognitive ability or intelligence. Perhaps the best-known intelligence measures are the Wechsler Scales, three separate tests designed to assess intellectual functioning at different age levels. The Wechsler Preschool and Primary Scale of Intelligence–Revised (WPPSI–III) was developed for use with children aged 2–6 to 7–3; it is reviewed in Chapter 10, "Special Considerations of Assessment in Early Childhood and Transition." The Wechsler Adult Intelligence Scale–Third Edition (WAIS–III) (discussed later) is used with youth 16 years of age through adulthood. The Wechsler Intelligence Scale for Children–Fourth Edition assesses school-aged children ranging in age from 6 through 16–11.

A newly revised Kaufman Assessment Battery for Children, Second Edition (K-ABC-II) has an even stronger theoretical base than the original version (Kufman & Kaufman, 2004). It allows the examiner to score the test based on one of two theoretical viewpoints, with one theoretical framework yielding a composite score that is not as heavily influenced by language or linguistic differences. This instrument will no doubt receive attention in those schools where an increasingly larger percentage of students whose primary language is not English are currently enrolled.

Other measures of intelligence are commonly used with school-aged children. The following are reviewed briefly in this chapter: the Woodcock-Johnson–Tests of Cognitive Ability, Third Edition, Stanford–Binet Intelligence Scale–Fifth Edition, Detroit Tests of Learning Aptitude–4, and the Kaufman Adolescent and Adult Intelligence Test. As with the Wechsler Scales and the K-ABC-II, these tests may not be administered by the teacher; however, test results provided by the psychologist or diagnostician may be useful to the teacher.

WECHSLER INTELLIGENCE SCALE FOR CHILDREN–FOURTH EDITION

The WISC–IV (Wechsler, 2003a) is designed to assess the global intellectual ability and processing ability of children ages 6–0 through 16–11. Unlike the earlier editions, this test does not provide verbal and performance IQ scores. The structure of the scoring system is based on the supported factor structure of the test. Therefore, the test results are presented with a Full Scale IQ score as well as index or processing scores. The test developers report that the basal and ceiling levels of the instrument have been expanded so that a more accurate assessment of intellectual ability can be obtained for very young students (6 years of age) as well as students in the older age group (aged 16 years). This provides more accuracy in measurement of ability for children who have cognitive limitations at the younger end and who have superior cognitive functioning at the upper end.

The constructs that are assessed on this instrument are presented in Figure 9.3. The subtests are included within each index cluster. The subtests presented in italics are the supplemental subtests or the subtests that can be used if a particular subtest is spoiled during the administration. A discussion of each subtest is presented in the following section.

Subtests of the WISC–IV   The following subtests are grouped by index scores. For example, the Similarities, Vocabulary, Comprehension, Information, and Word Reasoning subtests all support the factor structure of the Verbal Comprehension Index score. This means that research using the scores obtained during the standardization process indicates that these subtests all contribute to the Verbal Comprehension Index. In other words, a student who scores high on these subtests is likely to have strength in the area of verbal comprehension. We would anticipate that students with strength in this area would be able to score consistently across the subtests. When a student scores very low on one or two subtests,

Figure 9.3   From the *WISC–IV Technical and Interpretive Manual,* p. 6.

VCI

Similarities
Vocabulary
Comprehension
Information
Word Reasoning

PRI

Block Design
Picture Concepts
Matrix Reasoning
Picture Completion

FSIQ

WMI

Digit Span
Letter–Number
Sequencing
Arithmetic

PSI

Coding
Symbol Search
Cancellation

Note: Supplemental subtests are shown in italics

VCI—Verbal Comprehension Index
PRI—Perceptual Reasoning Index
WMI—Working Memory Index
PSI—Processing Speed Index

Source: David Wechsler, 2003, *Wechsler Intelligence Scale for Children,* 4th ed. San Antonio, TX: The Psychological Corporation.

the psychologist may give additional instruments to determine if this is a true weakness. The psychologist may also complete additional assessment or collect additional data when a student scores lower on one index than other indicates. This type of assessment is called **cross-battery assessment**.

cross-battery assessment Administering subtests from two or more tests to determine if a weakness exists in a particular skill or ability.

Verbal Comprehension Subtests   The following subtests support the construct of verbal comprehension. These subtests have been found to be heavily weighted in the understanding of language concepts.

Similarities. On this subtest students are required to compare two words read by the examiner to determine how the two words are alike. The responses may be scored as a 0, 1, or 2.

Vocabulary. The student is asked to define common words. For the younger child, pictures serve as the stimulus for the item. For children aged 9 to 16 years, the written form of the words are presented as the item stimulus.

Comprehension. The items on this subtest assess the child's knowledge of common concepts learned incidentally or from experiences or the environment. For example, some questions tap into understanding of social issues, such as keeping your word to a friend; other items assess information for everyday functioning such as paying bills or maintaining good health. These items may therefore be influenced by the child's experiences or environment, whether that environment is limited or enriched.

Information. These items assess information that may also be obtained from experiences or education. Items may include questions similar to the number of legs a cat has or the number of weeks in a month. In other words, this information is likely to have been learned prior to test administration and the child is simply using recall to respond to the question. This is a supplemental subtest of the Verbal Comprehension Index.

Word Reasoning. This subtest presents clues that the child must use to respond with a specific word for a common object. A series of clues are presented and the student is given a chance with each clue to respond with the correct answer. This is a supplemental subtest of the Verbal Comprehension Index.

Perceptual Reasoning Subtests. Perceptual reasoning means that a person is able to look at visual stimuli and tap into reasoning skills to solve novel problems. In other words, these types of items may not be as heavily influenced by previous education experiences, but rather require the student to see a stimulus, process that visual concept mentally, and respond with a solution.

Block Design. On this subtest, students are required to manipulate and copy a pattern of red and white blocks. This is a timed subtest and students are awarded additional points when the pattern is copied quickly and accurately. The task requires that students use visual-motor responses and that they have the visual-perceptual ability to understand and reproduce the stimulus.

Picture concepts. The student is presented with one picture and several rows of pictures. The student must select pictures from the rows of pictures to form a common concept. This task requires the child to use abstract verbal reasoning skills.

Matrix Reasoning. This subtest presents visual stimuli that represent incomplete matrices. The child is asked to select the representation that would complete the matrix. There are four types of matrices on this subtest, including pattern completions, classifications, and analogical and serial reasoning (Wechsler, 2003b).

Picture Completion. The child is required to scan pictures and either name or point to a missing part. This task may be influenced by previous experiences because many of the pictures are common objects in the environment. This is a supplemental subtest of the Perceptual Reasoning Index.

Working Memory Subtests When an item is presented that requires the student to hold on to the stimuli for a period of time in order to solve the task, it is referred to as a working memory item. These items may require visual or auditory working memory.

Digit Span. On this subtest, the examiner says a series of numbers to the child that the child must repeat as a series. The series become increasingly longer. The series of numbers are presented forward and backward.

Letter-Number Sequencing. On this subtest, the student hears a series of letters with numbers and is required to recall the numbers in ascending order and also the letters in alphabetical order. Children 6 and 7 years old perform the simpler tasks of counting and reciting part of the alphabet.

Arithmetic. This is a supplemental subtest of the Working Memory Index. On this subtest, the child is presented with math problems that must be solved mentally. This subtest requires working memory and some knowledge of math operations and reasoning.

Processing Speed Subtests The subtests included in this index score assess how quickly a person can complete a task. The subtests included in the index require visual-motor processing and fine-motor skills required to respond to the items. All subtests in this index are timed.

Coding. On this subtest, the student is required to copy visual symbols that correspond to visually presented numbers.

Symbol Search. The student is presented with an initial symbol or with two symbols at the beginning of each row of symbols. The child must scan the row of symbols and determine if one or the initial symbols is present in that row. The task requires visual discrimination and memory.

Cancellation. On this subtest the student is presented with a page of small pictures and asked to mark all animals on the page of pictures. The subtest has two formats of presentation, random and organized. This is a supplemental subtest on the Processing Speed Index.

Scores Obtained on the WISC–IV Subtests are scored by using the raw scores to obtain the derived scaled scores. The scaled scores have a mean of 10. A score is obtained for each of the indices along with the Full Scale Intelligence Quotient. The index scores and the FSIQ score are based on the standard score with a mean of 100 and a standard deviation of 15. Additional process scores may be obtained; however, these are obtained from data collected by the administration of the existing subtests and are used primarily for diagnostic purposes. For example, data collected during the administration of the Digit Span subtest can be used to obtain the Digit Span Forward and Digit Span Backward scaled scores.

Figure 9.4 illustrates a portion of the completed protocol of the WISC–IV. This illustration shows the student's scaled scores, composite scores, percentile ranks, confidence intervals, FSIQ, and the score profiles. The composite scores, which are based on the mean

Figure 9.4   Example of completed summary page.

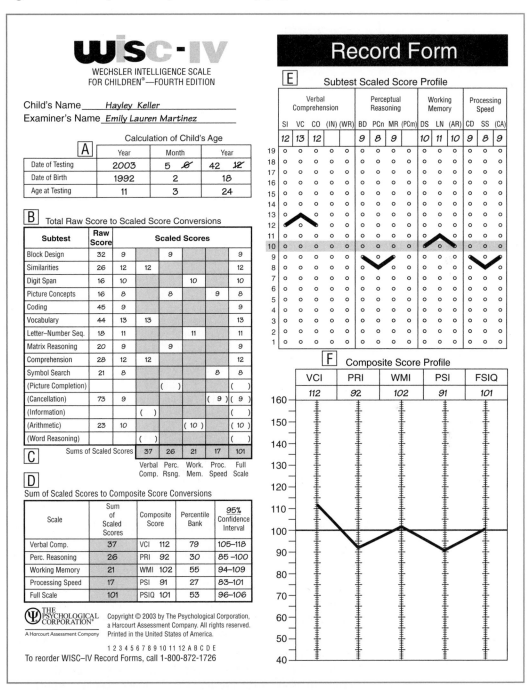

Source: From *Wisc-IV Scoring and Administration Manual,* p. 46. David Wechsler, 2003, *Wechsler Intelligence Scale for Children,* 4th ed. San Antonio, TX: The Psychological Corporation.

Figure 9.5   Portion of WISC–IV Protocol.

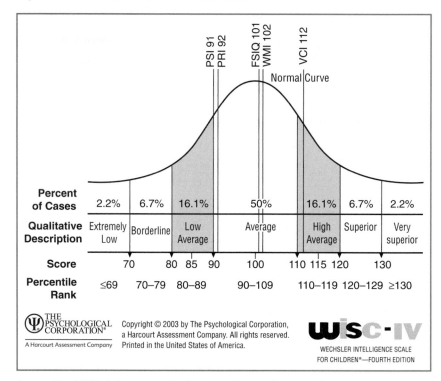

Source: David Wechsler, 2003, *Wechsler Intelligence Scale for Children,* 4th ed. San Antonio, TX: The Psychological Corporation.

of 100, can be related to the normal distribution. On one page of the protocol, the scores may be plotted on a bell curve. This curve also includes the descriptive terms or categories often used when the WISC–IV is interpreted. This portion of the protocol is represented in Figure 9.5.

WECHSLER ADULT INTELLIGENCE SCALE–THIRD EDITION

The Wechsler Adult Intelligence Scale–Third Edition (WAIS–III) was published in 1997. Many of the same subtests of the children's version are included on the scales for adults.

Subtests   Examples of the subtests included on the WAIS–III are:

Letter-Number Sequencing. This additional verbal subtest presents a mixed series of numbers and letters that the examinee must repeat back to the examiner, with the numbers in ascending order and the letters in alphabetical order. This subtest assesses short-term auditory memory as well as the ability to mentally manipulate stimuli according to specific parameters and to respond orally. This subtest is optional and is not required to determine IQ scores.

Matrix Reasoning. This additional performance subtest presents visual stimuli that the examinee must evaluate to determine which of the stimuli will complete the visual pattern. This subtest assesses visual analytical and abstract reasoning.

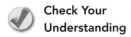

Check Your Understanding

Check your knowledge of the terms presented in association with the Wechsler Scales by completing Activity 9.2 below.

Activity 9.2

Match the following terms with the correct descriptions.

A. WAIS–III

B. WPPSI–R

C. WISC–IV

D. Verbal Comprehension Index

E. Perceptual Reasoning Index

F. Full-scale IQ

G. Digit span

H. Coding

I. K-ABC-II

J. Similarities

K. Block design

L. Information

M. Picture completion

N. Working Memory Index

O. Vocabulary

P. Processing Speed Index

Q. Word reasoning

R. Processing Speed Index

S. Comprehension

T. Arithmetic

U. Matrix reasoning

_____ 1. This edition has four index scores: perceptual reasoning, verbal comprehension, working memory, and processing speed.

_____ 2. This Wechsler test is designed to be used through adulthood.

_____ 3. This subtest presents math story problems, and performance can be influenced by attention span and concentration or working memory.

_____ 4. On this subtest, the examiner asks the student how two things are alike.

_____ 5. This index score represents the student's ability to attend and process infomation and complete tasks with this information.

_____ 6. On this subtest, the examiner provides clues and the student uses the clues to provide a specific word.

_____ 7. The subtests on this index represent the student's ability to quickly respond on fine motor tasks.

_____ 8. This instrument includes subtests that assess tasks believed to measure one's simultaneous and successive processing ability on cognitive tasks.

_____ 9. This subtest contains red and white cubes and measures perceptual organization, spatial ability, synthesis, and re-production of models.

_____10. Performance on this Verbal Comprehension subtest can be influenced by the student's conscience or moral sense.

_____11. This subtest is divided into two parts, forward and back-ward, and measures auditory short-term memory and free-dom from distractibility.

_____12. This IQ score reflects the performance of the student on all four indexes.

_____13. This Wechsler test was designed to be used with children from the ages of 2 years and 6 months to 7 years and 3 months.

_____14. Which of the cognitive assessment instruments can be ad-ministered to school age students ages 6–16 ?

Apply Your Knowledge

Which of the subtests described for the Wechsler Scales can be influenced by weakness in the visual-motor areas? _____

_____

_____

The third edition provides additional items on the lower end and additional practice items on some of the subtests. This instrument is clinically more user friendly for examinees who are functioning significantly below the average. These additional items may allow examinees at the lower end to respond to more items before reach-ing a ceiling, providing the clinician with a better picture of an examinee's ability.

This edition eliminated several items of the WAIS–R that proved to be biased or outdated (Wechsler, 1997). The third edition moved Object Assembly to optional status rather than keep it as a manda-tory subtest. In general, the materials are more attractive, sturdier, and easier to handle. The sequence of administration is also im-proved and is easier to administer.

KAUFMAN ASSESSMENT BATTERY FOR CHILDREN, SECOND EDITION

The Kaufman Assessment Battery for Children, Second Edition (K-ABC-II) assesses the cognitive ability of children aged 3-0 to 18-11. This newly revised instrument includes a revised method of scoring and interpretation. Although this instrument will not be administered by teachers, an understanding of the theoretical bases of the scoring will assist the teacher in interpreting the results and considering the results for interventions.

Before the test is administered, the psychologist must decide which theoretical base will be used to administer and score the instrument. A brief explanation of each theoretical base follows.

One theoretical base, Luria's neurological processing theory, is quite extensive; however, one of the major premises of the theory is that the brain functions using two modes of processing: **simultaneous** and **sequential processing**. The K-ABC-II includes subtests that assess a student's ability to perceive and process information that is presented sequentially. This means that each stimulus that the child processes is linked to the previous stimulus and must be processed sequentially in order to perform the task or solve the problem. Other subtests include items that must be processed simultaneously, that is, the stimuli must be processed and integrated at the same time in order to perform the task.

The scoring of the K-ABC-II using the Luria model will yield Scale Index scores for Sequential processing, Simultaneous processing, Learning, Planning, and the Mental Processing Index for the general measure of cognitive ability.

The other theoretical base for scoring is based on the Cattell-Horn-Carol theory of intelligence. This theory is founded on three levels or stratums of intellectual ability. The first level is general intellectual functioning, commonly called the *g* factor. The next level is comprised of broad cognitive abilities, and the final level is made up of narrow abilities of cognitive functioning. The CHC theory is sometimes described as broad fluid and crystallized abilities. On the K-ABC-II, scoring according to the CHC theory will provide a Fluid Crystallized Index score for the global cognitive score.

Additional Scale Indexes include Gsm for short-term memory, Gv for visual processing, Glr for learning, Gf for fluid reasoning, and Gc for crystallized ability. Tasks that assess the Gsm processing include those that require short-term and working memory. Tasks that assess Gv are those that require for example, visual memory, spatial relations, spatial screening, and visualization. Tasks that measure Glr require long-term memory and recall. The assessment of the Gf scale requires fluid reasoning or adapting and solving novel problems or figuring out how to do something one has not been exposed to in the past. The Gc scale assesses general information learned from the environment or previous experiences.

Another index that is available for scoring on the K-ABC-II is the Nonverbal Index. This index includes subtests that do not rely heavily on language skills or learned verbal concepts. For example, students may be asked to solve problems that require copying visual patterns using manipulatives or to imitate hand movements. This scale is

simultaneous processing
Presenting one stimulus at a time that is processed in sequence and linked to previous stimulus.

sequential processing
Presenting stimuli at the same time to be processed and integrated.

especially appropriate for students who may not have mastery of the English language or may have other language difficulties. It can be used to provide an estimate of cognitive functioning without using subtests that are heavily weighted in language or verbal concepts.

For very young children, only a general cognitive score is available. Either the Fluid Crystallized Index or the Mental Processing Index scores may be obtained.

STANFORD–BINET, FIFTH EDITION

The fifth edition of the Stanford-Binet may be administered to persons ages 2–85+ years (Roid, 2003b). This instrument consists of 10 subtests and can yield a Full Scale IQ score, a Nonverbal IQ score, and a Verbal IQ score. The factors assessed on this instrument include Fluid Reasoning, Knowledge, Quantitative Reasoning, Visual-Spatial Reasoning, and Working Memory. Within each factor or area, a variety of activities are administered to obtain the score for the factors. The activities included within the factors are presented in Figure 9.6, which provides a brief description of the tasks and the performance requirements for them. For example, you will note that the Visual-Spatial Processing factor is assessed verbally and nonverbally. For the nonverbal task requirement, the student works puzzles that are solved using visual-perceptual motor skills. For the verbal task requirement, of the Visual-Spatial Processing factor, the student must respond to questions and problems verbally. The

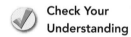

Check Your Understanding

Complete Activity 9.3 below.

Activity 9.3

Answer the following questions about the K-ABC-II.

1. What is the term that means a student processes each bit of information, one bit at a time, and that each new piece of information is linked to the previous bit of information? _____

2. What two broad cognitive abilities are included in the CHC theory of intelligence? _____

3. Which index may be particularly useful when assessing a student who has Spanish as a primary language? _____

4. For very young students, what type of scores are available? _____

Apply Your Knowledge

What type of information is represented on a test that assesses crystallized intelligence? _____
_____
_____

Figure 9.6   Organization of the Stanford-Binet V.

Factors		Domains	
		Nonverbal (NV)	**Verbal (V)**
	Fluid Reasoning (FR)	**Nonverbal Fluid Reasoning*** Activities: Object Series/ Matrices (Routing)	**Verbal Fluid Reasoning** Activities: Early Reasoning (2–3), Verbal Absurdities (4), Verbal Analogies (5–6)
	Knowledge (KN)	**Nonverbal Knowledge** Activities: Procedural Knowledge (2–3), Picture Absurdities (4–6)	**Verbal Knowledge*** Activities: Vocabulary (Routing)
	Quantitative Reasoning (OR)	**Nonverbal Quantitative Reasoning** Activities: Quantitative Reasoning (2–6)	**Verbal Quantitative Reasoning** Activities: Quantitative Reasoning (2–6)
	Visual-Spatial Processing (VS)	**Nonverbal Visual-Spatial Processing** Activities: Form Board (1–2), Form Patterns (3–6)	**Verbal Visual-Spatial Processing** Activities: Position and Direction (2–6)
	Working Memory (WM)	**Nonverbal Working Memory** Activities: Delayed Response (1), Block Span (2–6)	**Verbal Working Memory** Activities: Memory for Sentences (2–3), Last Word (4–6)

Note: Names of the 10 subtests are in **bold italic**. Activities include the levels at which they appear.
* = Routing subtests

Organization of the SB5.

Source: Roid, G. H. (2003) Stanford Binet Intelligence Scales, Fifth Edition, Examiner's Manual, p.24. Itasca, IL. Riverside Publishing. Reprinted with permission.

problems for this task involve directional terms or prepositional words for correct responses. Yet both the verbal and nonverbal tasks are concerned with Visual-Spatial Processing.

The categories of IQ scores on the Binet–V are the following:

145–160	Very gifted or highly advanced
130–144	Gifted or highly advanced
120–129	Superior
110–119	High Average
90–109	Average
80–89	Low Average
70–79	Borderline impaired or delayed
55–69	Mildly impaired or delayed
40–54	Moderately impaired or delayed

(Roid, 2003c, p.150)

WOODCOCK–JOHNSON III TESTS OF COGNITIVE ABILITIES

The Woodcock-Johnson III Tests of Achievement are interpreted for general academic areas such as reading, math, and written language. Students may also be assessed in areas such as oral language, academic skills, academic fluency, and phoneme/ grapheme knowledge. The Woodcock-Johnson III Tests of Cognitive Abilities include assessment of areas such as general intellectual ability, cognitive factors like visual-spatial thinking and auditory processing, and clinical clusters such as working memory and phonemic awareness. These two batteries together can provide a comprehensive assessment of cognitive abilities and academic skills.

The cognitive tests, like the achievement measures, are divided into the standard battery and the extended battery. The subtests

 **Check Your Understanding**

Use the information provided in Figure 9.6 to apply the test results of the Stanford–Binet-V to a case with classroom implications in Activity 9.4 below.

Activity 9.4

Case study using SB–V

The following scores were obtained by a 4th grade student who was referred for learning difficulties following several interventions. After reading the scores below, answer the questions about the student's performance. Refer to your text as needed for information about the SB–V.

	Domains	
	Nonverbal	**Verbal**
Fluid Reasoning	11	9
Knowledge	9	9
Quantitative Reasoning	12	8
Visual-Spatial Processing	14	10
Working Memory	7	7

Composite Profile

Nonverbal	IQ	108
Verbal	IQ	93
Full Scale	IQ	101
Fluid Reasoning		100
Knowledge		92
Quantitative Reasoning		99
Visual-Spatial Reasoning		109
Working Memory		80

---

1. What areas appear to represent strengths in cognitive processing? _____

2. What areas represent the areas of concern? _____

3. As a teacher, what areas would be of concern to you when thinking about instruction? _____

4. As you look at the domain scores, in what way was the student able to process math best? _____

Apply Your Knowledge

What recommendations would you make to parents about homework assignments that need to be completed at home? _____

_____

_____

---

included on the standard battery are verbal comprehension, visual-auditory learning, spatial relations, sound blending, concept formation, visual matching, numbers reversed, incomplete words, auditory working memory, and visual-auditory learning-delayed.

The WJ III Tests of Cognitive Abilities, like the achievement tests, are computer scored. The scoring program is easy to use, and comparative data for age and grade norms, confidence intervals, standard scores, and percentile ranks are available.

DETROIT TESTS OF LEARNING APTITUDE–4 (DTLA–4)

The DTLA–4 contains 10 subtests, which are grouped into a variety of composites. These composites include the General Mental Ability Composite, the Optimal Composite, the Domain Composites, and the Theoretical Composites. The General Mental Ability Composite is made up of the scores of all 10 of the subtests. The Optimal Composite is found by using the four highest scores obtained on the individual subtests in an effort to find the "best estimate of a person's overall 'potential'" (Hammill, 1998, p. 20). The Domain Composites include the following four domains: Linguistic Domain, Cognitive Domain, Attentional Domain, and Motoric Domain. The Theoretical Composites comprise a variety of combinations of subtests that the author believes represent assessment of abilities according to theoretical models such as those set forth by Cattell and Horn, Das, Jensen, and Wechsler.

The author presents additional research in this fourth edition of the DTLA in an effort to support the validity of test constructs and theoretical foundation. The research presented is an improvement over previous editions, although the studies do not appear to have been carried out with the same rigor expected of other well-known tests that measure intelligence and abilities.

As suggested by the subtest and composite titles, some of the subtests are verbal, some are presented visually and require fine-motor responses such as reproducing line drawings, and still others require short-term auditory memory and the ability to follow oral directions. This instrument may be used, along with other measures, to document the possibility of distractibility or visual-motor difficulties. This instrument may provide insight into a student's abilities in some areas, although it seems to lack adequate research to stand alone as a measure of intelligence for the purposes of placement and intervention decisions.

KAUFMAN BRIEF INTELLIGENCE TEST (KBIT)

Designed as a screening instrument, the KBIT (Kaufman & Kaufman, 1990) should not be used as part of a comprehensive evaluation to determine eligibility or placement. According to the manual, the test serves to screen students who may be at risk for developing educational problems and who then should receive a comprehensive evaluation. The test takes about 15–30 minutes to administer and consists of two subtests: Vocabulary and Matrices. The Vocabulary subtest has two parts: Expressive and Definitions. These two subtests are designed to measure crystallized intelligence (Vocabulary) and fluid intelligence (Matrices).

NONVERBAL INTELLIGENCE TESTS

Three commonly used measures—the Universal Test of Nonverbal Intelligence, the Comprehensive Test of Nonverbal Intelligence, and

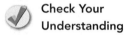

Check Your Understanding

Check your ability to answer questions about measures of cognitive ability by completing Activity 9.5 below.

Activity 9.5

Answer the following questions about the measures of cognitive ability.

1. _____ has a strong theoretical base that includes different ways to interpret the test based on those theories.
2. _____ is the Wechsler Scale that assesses adults.
3. The _____ includes both verbal and nonverbal domains.
4. Which test includes an attentional domain? _____

Apply Your Knowledge

When would a school psychologist give more than one measure of cognitive evaluation for an inital evaluation? _____
_____
_____

the Nonverbal Test of Intelligence, Third Edition, are reviewed here to provide examples of this type of assessment.

UNIVERSAL NONVERBAL INTELLIGENCE TEST

The Universal Nonverbal Intelligence Test (UNIT) is an intellectual assessment measure for children ages 5 years through 17 years 11 months. It includes six subtests and may be given as a standard battery, abbreviated battery, or extended battery (Bracken & McCallum, 1998). The most typical administrations are the standard battery, which includes four subtests, and the extended battery, which includes all subtests. The abbreviated battery of two subtests is given for screening rather than diagnostic purposes. The test measures reasoning and memory skills through the nonverbal presentation of the subtests. The subtest descriptions are presented in Figure 9.7.

The test developers designed this instrument to be a fair measure of intellectual ability for children and adolescents for whom it may be difficult to obtain an accurate estimate of ability on tests that are heavily weighted with verbal items and content. For example, children and adolescents who have hearing impairments, who are from culturally or linguistically diverse environments, or who have not mastered the English language. This assessment instrument may also be a more fair estimate of intellectual ability for students with mental retardation and for students with other disorders that impact verbal communication, such as autism.

In order to present a nonverbal assessment in a manner that does not require spoken language, several gestures for communication during the administration are provided in the manual. For example, palm rolling conveys a message to the student to continue, keep going, or take your turn now. These gestures are illustrated in the manual; the gesture called palm rolling is presented in Figure 9.8.

The possible test scores that can be obtained on the UNIT include scores for the various subtests, scale scores, and a full scale IQ score. The scale scores are for the four scales of memory, reasoning, and symbolic and nonsymbolic concepts. The memory scale assesses not only the storing of information but also the skills and abilities needed for memory, such as attending, encoding, and organization. The reasoning subtest taps into problem-solving ability. The symbolic scale assesses abilities that are believed to be precursors to understanding and using language, and the nonsymbolic scale assesses processing, perception, and integration of information. The symbolic and nonsymbolic scales both assess mediation, or what one does cognitively with the material as it is processed, associated, and retained or used to solve problems.

Figure 9.7   Descriptions of the UNIT subtests.

Overview of the UNIT

| Table 1.1 | **Descriptions of the UNIT Subtests** |

Symbolic Memory

The examinee views a sequence of universal symbols for a period of 5 seconds. After the stimulus is removed, the examinee re-creates the sequence using the Symbolic Memory Response Cards. Each item is a series of universal symbols for *baby*, *girl*, *boy*, *woman*, and *man*, depicted in green or black. Symbolic Memory is primarily a measure of short-term visual memory and complex sequential memory for meaningful material.

Cube Design

Cube Design involves the presentation and direct reproduction of two-color, abstract, geometric designs. While viewing the stimulus design, the examinee reconstructs the design directly on the stimulus book or response mat, using green-and-white one-inch cubes. Cube Design is primarily a measure of visual–spatial reasoning.

Spatial Memory

The examinee views a random pattern of green, black, or green and black dots on a 3×3 or 4×4 grid for a period of 5 seconds. After the stimulus is removed, the examinee re-creates the spatial pattern with green and black circular chips on the blank response grid. Spatial Memory is primarily a measure of short-term visual memory for abstract material.

Analogic Reasoning

Analogic Reasoning presents incomplete conceptual or geometric analogies in a matrix format and requires only a pointing response. The items feature either common objects or novel geometric figures. The examinee completes the matrix analogies by selecting from four response options. Analogic Reasoning is primarily a measure of symbolic reasoning.

Object Memory

The examinee is presented a random pictorial array of common objects for 5 seconds. After the stimulus is removed, a second pictorial array is presented, containing all of the previously presented objects and additional objects to serve as foils. The examinee recognizes and identifies the objects presented in the first pictorial array by placing response chips on the appropriate pictures. Object Memory is primarily a measure of short-term recognition and recall of meaningful symbolic material.

Mazes

The examinee uses paper and pencil to navigate and exit mazes by tracing a path from the center starting point of each maze to the correct exit, without making incorrect decisions en route. Increasingly complex mazes are presented. Mazes is primarily a measure of reasoning and planful behavior.

Source: From *The Universal Nonverbal Intelligence Test: Examiner's Manual,* p. 3, by B. A. Bracken and R. S. McCallum, 1998. Itasca, IL: Riverside Publishing Company.

384

Figure 9.8 Palm rolling.

Palm Rolling
With one or both hands held out and
with palms up and fingers together,
the wrists are rotated toward the
body so that the hands inscribe small
circles in the air.
This gesture communicates
"Go ahead" or "You try it now."

Palm Rolling

Source: From *The Universal Nonverbal Intelligence Test: Examiner's Manual,* p. 49.
B. A. Bracken and R. S. McCallum, 1998. Itasca, IL: Riverside Publishing Company.

The subtest scores have a mean of 10 and the scales have quotients with a mean of 100. The standard scores are interpreted using the following guidelines:

Very superior	>130
Superior	120–130
High average	110–120
Average	90–110
Low average	80–90
Delayed	70–80
Very delayed	>70

Case Study for Intellectual Assessment

Read the following background information about a second-grade student named Lupita.

Name: Lupita Garcia
Date of Birth: 2-1-1996
Date of Evaluation: 4-6-2004
Age: 8-2
Grade Placement: 2.8

BACKGROUND AND REFERRAL INFORMATION

Lupita is currently enrolled in the second grade at Wonderful Elementary School. She has been attending this school since October of the current school year. There was a delay in receiving her school records from another state and, therefore, it was not known for several months that Lupita had been in the referral process at her previous school. School records from her previous school indicate that she has attended three schools since she entered kindergarten about 3 years ago.

Lupita lives with her mother and father, who until recently were migrant farm workers. Her parents now have full-time employment in the city and plan to make this community their home. Lupita has two older sisters.

Information provided through a home study reveals that all family members speak both English and Spanish. Lupita's mother, who was born in the United States, reported that she learned English while growing up because in school she was not allowed to speak Spanish as her parents did at home. Lupita's father was raised in Mexico, where he attended school until he was 12 years of age. At that time, he stopped going to school in order to work the field with his parents. Mr. Garcia reported that his English is not as good as his wife's, and therefore she helps Lupita with all of her homework assignments.

Mrs. Garcia said that she has taught her children to speak English first because she knew that would be important for school. Although she has emphasized English in the home, Mr. Garcia usually speaks to the children in Spanish. Mr. Garcia is very proud of his daughter's ability to use English so well because he often must rely on his daughters to translate for him when they are in the community.

Lupita's reason for referral is due to academic difficulties in learning to read. The child study team met four times to plan and implement strategies for intervention in an attempt to assist Lupita. Lupita has been receiving additional assistance from the school system's bilingual program. As part of the referral process, Mrs. Garcia completed a home language assessment. The results of that assessment indicate that while both languages are spoken in the home, English is the primary language and is used in approximately 75% of communication within the home. Despite these findings, the team members were not certain about Lupita's mastery of English, particularly at the level required for academic learning and especially in the area of reading.

Following the last meeting of the team, the members agreed, at the urging of Mrs. Garcia, to complete a comprehensive evaluation.

Given the background information about Lupita, the team members decided that the K-ABC-II nonverbal index and the UNIT would yield the most fair estimate of Lupita's intellectual ability.

COMPREHENSIVE TEST OF NONVERBAL INTELLIGENCE (CTONI)

This instrument includes six subtests that may be used with persons ages 6-0 to 89-11 years of age (Hammill, Pearson, & Wiederholt, 1996).

Figure 9.9 Examples of pictorial categories and geometric categories.

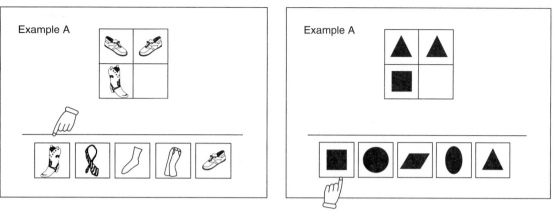

Source: From *Comprehensive Test of Nonverbal Intelligence, Examiner's Manual,* p. 11. *Examiner's Manual for the Comprehensive Test of Nonverbal Intelligence,* by D. D. Hammill, N. A. Pearson, & J. L. Wiederholt, 1997. Austin, Tx: Pro–ED. Reprinted by permission.

The six subtests include: pictorial analogies, geometric analogies, pictorial categories, geometric categories, pictorial sequences, and geometric sequences. Examples of the pictorial and geometric categories are shown in Figure 9.9. The administration of all subtests will yield a nonverbal intelligence composite, the administration of the pictorial subtests will provide a pictorial nonverbal composite, and administration of the geometric subtests will provide a geometric nonverbal intelligence component.

The CTONI has three principal uses according to the authors. It can be used with persons for whom other instruments assessing intelligence would be inappropriate or biased; to make comparisons between verbal measures and nonverbal intelligence; and for research. The authors report that the instrument was developed using multiple theoretical bases rather than a single theory.

This test may be administered by using oral instructions or by presenting the instructions through pantomime. The instrument should be administered through pantomime for all persons who are hearing impaired and for persons who speak a language other than English.

TEST OF NONVERBAL INTELLIGENCE–THIRD EDITION (TONI–3)

This instrument was designed to assess a single cognitive process of solving novel abstract problems (Brown, Sherbenou, & Johnsen, 1997). The authors state that the TONI–3 is a language- and motor-reduced instrument that also reduces cultural influence. It may be used with students ages 6-0 to 89-11. This test includes two equivalent forms, A and B. The instructions are presented to the examinee using pantomime. The authors state that the administration time is approximately 45 minutes.

RESEARCH ON INTELLIGENCE MEASURES

Many of the most popular intelligence measures have recently been revised, and research continues to emerge in the literature. Some research studies on earlier editions and test reviews are summarized here.

1. After an extensive review of evidence in the literature and other sources, Schrank and Flanagan conclude that the WJ–III Tests of Cognitive Ability are well grounded in the CHC theory, or Three Stratum Theory, proposed by Carroll (2003).

2. Miller (2007) reports that the theoretical structure of the WJ–III Tests of Cognitive Ability make this instrument useful in assessing persons referred for school neuropsychological assessment. The abilities assessed on this instrument fall within an assessment model employed in the field of school neuropsychology.

3. Schrank, et al. (2002) noted that the WJ–III Tests of Cognitive Achievement needed additional research to support the use with various clinical groups.

4. Prewett (1992) found that the KBIT's correlation with the WISC–III supports its use as a screening instrument. Prewett and McCaffery (1993) found that the KBIT should be interpreted as only a rough estimate of the IQ that can be obtained on the Stanford–Binet. Kaufman and Wang (1992) found that the differences in means obtained by blacks, Hispanics, and whites on the KBIT are in agreement with mean differences found on the WISC–R. Canivez (1996) found high levels of agreement between the KBIT and the WISC—III in the identification of students with learning disabilities using discrepancies between these measures and the WJ–R.

5. Differences in scores were found between Asian and white children on the K-ABC (Mardell-Czudnowski, 1995). In this study, the Asian children scored higher on the sequential processing scale but showed no differences on the mental processing scales. The achievement scale scores were

higher for children who had previously lived in the United States for at least 4 years.

6. Valencia, Rankin, and Livingston (1995) found evidence of content bias in the items of the K-ABC. In this study, 14% of the items on the Mental Processing scale and 63% of the items on the Achievement scale were determined to be biased against the Mexican American children who participated in the research. These authors suggest that the opportunity to learn specific test content may be the contributing reason for the bias of these items.

7. On the K-ABC, an analysis of data from the standardization sample indicated that the construct validity was similar for both African American and white children (Fan, Wilson, & Reynolds, 1995). This research included four statistical analyses of existing data. An analysis of the data by Keith et al. (1995) determined a similar conclusion.

8. Kaufman, Litchenberger, Fletcher-Janzen, and Kaufman (2005) note that the KABC–II provides limited assessment of expressive language skills and that some clinical comparisons are not possible due to age limitations on specific subtests such as Story Completion and Rover.

9. Several researchers have questioned the factor structure of the WISC–III indicating that there is evidence for the first two factors of verbal comprehension and performance; however, the freedom from distractibility and processing speed factors appear to be weak and perhaps misnamed (Carroll, 1997; Keith & Witta, 1997; Kranzler, 1997; Kush, 1996; Ricco, Cohen, Hall, & Ross, 1997).

10. In one study using the Stanford–Binet IV, students in a general education classroom were found to have more variability in their scores than students already receiving special education services. This may be due in part to the greater degree of homogeneity of the group of students receiving services. Gridley and McIntosh (1991) found that the scores of children aged 2 to 6 years and 7 to 11 years did not support the factor theory purported by the test authors.

11. In a study by Roid and Pomplin (2005), it was found that using the scores for assistance in differential diagnosis between clinical groups, such as distinguishing between students with mental retardation and students with low-functioning autism, could not be done without additional assessment measures. The use of the scores from the Binet IV alone did not differentiate between some clinical groups.

12. In a concurrent validity study, Canivez (1995) found similarities in the WISC–III and KBIT scores. However, he suggested that the KBIT be used only for screening and more comprehensive measures should be used for detailed interpretations of ability. Other researchers have found that the KBIT may be suitable for screening but it is not suitable for determining other comprehensive information (Parker, 1993; Prewett & McCaffery, 1993).

13. Vig and Jedrysek (1996) researched the performance of children with language impairments on the Stanford-Binet and found that the Stanford–Binet IV may be inappropriate for use with 4- and 5-year-olds because of the minimal expectations of this age group on the Binet.

14. In a review of the CTONI, Nicholson warned examiners to use additional assessment instruments when using the CTONI (1998–1999). Nicholson noted that the CTONI does not provide a comprehensive measure of intelligence or nonverbal intelligence.

15. Smith reviewed the KBIT and noted that use of the instrument with persons of different cultural backgrounds may be measuring acculturation rather than ability, especially on the vocabulary subtest (1998–1999). The review also pointed out the strong psychometric characteristics of this screening instrument.

ASSESSING ADAPTIVE BEHAVIOR

Adaptive behavior is a term used to describe how well a student adapts to the environment. The importance of this concept was underscored by the passage of PL 94-142, which contained the requirement of nondiscriminatory assessment-specifically, the mandate to use more than one instrument yielding a single IQ score for diagnosis (*Federal Register*, 1977). The measurement of adaptive behavior must be considered before a person meets the criteria for mental retardation. A student who functions within the subaverage range of intelligence as measured on an IQ test but who exhibits age-appropriate behaviors outside the classroom should not be placed in a setting designed for students with mental retardation.

Adaptive behavior measurement is also emphasized as one possible method of promoting nonbiased assessment of culturally different students (Mercer, 1979; Reschly, 1982). Use of adaptive behavior scales in the assessment of students with learning problems can add another perspective that may be useful in planning educational interventions (Bruininks, Thurlow, & Gilman, 1987; Horn & Fuchs, 1987). Other researchers have found the assessment of adaptive behavior useful in educational interventions for learning-disabled students (Bender & Golden, 1988; Weller, Strawser, & Buchanan, 1985). Adaptive behavior scales are instruments that usually are designed to be answered by a parent or teacher or some other person familiar with the student's functioning in the everyday world. The questions are constructed to obtain information about the student's independent functioning level in and out of school. Many of the items measure self-reliance and daily living skills at home and in the community.

Reschly (1982) reviewed the literature on adaptive behavior and determined that several common features were presented. The measuring of adaptive behavior had the common concepts of (a) developmental appropriateness, (b) cultural context, (c) situational or generalized behaviors, and (d) domains. Reschly found that definitions of adaptive behavior and the measurement of that behavior were based on expectations of a particular age, within the person's culture, and in given or general situations and that the behaviors measured were classified into domains.

Harrison (1987) reviewed research on adaptive behavior and drew the following conclusions:[*]

1. There is a moderate relationship between adaptive behavior and intelligence.
2. Correlational studies indicate that adaptive behavior has a low relationship with school achievement, but the effect of adaptive behavior on achievement may be greater than the correlations indicate and adaptive behavior in school may have a greater relationship with achievement than adaptive behavior outside school.
3. There is typically a moderate to a moderately high relationship between different measures of adaptive behavior.
4. Adaptive behavior is predictive of certain aspects of future vocational performance.
5. There is a possibility that the use of adaptive behavior scales could result in the declassification of mentally retarded individuals, but no evidence was located to indicate that this is actually happening.
6. There are few race and ethnic group differences on adaptive behavior scales.
7. There are differences between parents' and teachers' ratings on adaptive behavior scales.

[*]From "Research with Adaptive Behavior Scales" by P. Harrison, 1987, *The Journal of Special Education, 21,* pp. 60–61. Copyright 1987 by PRO–ED, Inc. Reprinted by permission.

8. Adaptive behavior scales differentiate among different classification groups such as normal, mentally retarded, slow learner, learning disabled, and emotionally disturbed.

9. Adaptive behavior scales differentiate among mentally retarded people in different residential and vocational settings.

10. Adaptive behavior is multidimensional.

11. Adaptive behavior can be increased through placement in settings which focus on training adaptive behavior skills.

12. Adaptive behavior scales exhibit adequate stability and interrater reliability.

Although earlier research found that there were differences between parent and teacher ratings on adaptive behavior, Foster-Gaitskell and Pratt (1989) found that when the method of administration and familiarity with the adaptive behavior instrument were controlled, differences between parent and teacher ratings were not significant.

The formal measurement of adaptive behavior began with the development of the Vineland Social Maturity Scale (Doll, 1935). The assessment of adaptive behavior as a common practice in the diagnosis of students, however, did not occur until litigation found fault with school systems for the placement of minority students based only on IQ results (Witt & Martens, 1984). Some researchers feel that the assessment of adaptive behavior in students being evaluated for special education eligibility should not be mandated until further research on adaptive behavior instruments has occurred (Kamphaus, 1987; Witt & Martens, 1984). After reviewing several of the newer adaptive behavior scales, Evans and Bradley-Johnson (1988) cautioned examiners to select instruments carefully because of the low reliability and validity of the instruments. These authors issued the following considerations for professionals using adaptive behavior instruments:[*]

a. Scales must be selected that were standardized using the type of informant to be employed in the assessment (e.g., ABI [Adaptive Behavior Inventory] with teachers and Vineland Survey Form or SIB [Scales of Independent Behavior] with caregivers).

b. If valid information is to be obtained, the response format of the scale must be readily understood by the informant, i.e., not be confusing.

[*]From "A Review of Recently Developed Measures of Adaptive Behavior" by L. Evans and S. Bradley-Johnson, 1988, *Psychology in the Schools, 25,* p. 286. Copyright 1988 by Psychology in the Schools. Reprinted by permission.

    c. In some cases it will be helpful to select a scale with both normative data on both a nonretarded and a retarded group.

    d. If information on maladaptive behavior is desired, only ABS:SE [Adaptive Behavior Scale, School Edition], the SIB, and the Vineland Survey Form address this area.

    e. The number of items on subtests of interest should be considered in interpretation to insure that an adequate sample of behavior has been obtained.

    f. For eligibility decisions, total test results, rather than subtest scores, should be used. Total test results are based upon a larger sample of behavior and are much more reliable and valid.

    g. If different scales are used for the same student, quite different results may be obtained due to many factors, including different response formats, content, and technical adequacy.

    h. Different informants (teacher vs. parent) may perceive a student's performance differently due to personal biases and the different demands of the settings.

    i. Validity of results must be evaluated in each case based upon problems inherent to rating scales (e.g., informant bias, avoidance of extreme choices).

The examiner should remember these considerations when selecting an adaptive behavior scale and choose the instrument that best suits the needs of the student.

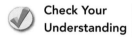

Check Your Understanding

Check your ability to answer questions about adaptive behavior by completing Activity 9.6 below.

Activity 9.6

1. Adaptive behavior is the ability one has to _____.
2. Assessments of adaptive behavior may be used to _____.
3. According to Reschly (1982), what are the four concepts of the assessment of adaptive behavior? _____

Apply Your Knowledge

What are some of the findings summarized by Harrison (1987) about the research of adaptive behavior? _____

_____

_____

REVIEW OF ADAPTIVE BEHAVIOR SCALES

The adaptive behavior scales reviewed in this chapter are the Vineland Adaptive Behavior Scales (Survey Form, Expanded Form, and Classroom Edition), the AAMR Adaptive Behavior Scale—School, Second Edition, the Adaptive Behavior Inventory (ABI and ABI Short Form), and the Adaptive Behavior Inventory for Children. As stated previously, examiners should be cautious in selecting the scale appropriate for the student's needs. Some scales have been normed using special populations only, some scales have been normed using both special and normal populations, and some scales contain items for assessing maladaptive behavior as well as adaptive behavior. The size of the samples used during standardization and the reliability and validity information should be considered.

VINELAND–II: VINELAND ADAPTIVE BEHAVIOR SCALES, SECOND EDITION

A revision of the original Vineland Social Maturity Scale (Doll, 1935), and the Vineland Adaptive Behavior Scales (Sparrow, Balla, & Cicchetti, 1984), this edition of these adaptive behavior scales contain additional items at the lower levels and is consistent with the recommendations of the American Association on Mental Deficiency (Sparrow, Cicchetti, & Balla, 2005). The scales include the Survey Interview Form, the Parent/Caregiver Form, and the Teacher Rating Form. The Parent Form is available in Spanish. The Interview Form and the Parent Rating Form assess the same skills; however, the Parent Form is in a rating scale format.

The Survey and Parent Forms may be used to obtain information about individuals who range in age from 0 to 90 years. The Teacher Form was designed for students ages 3 to 21 years and 11 months. The areas assessed include communication, daily living skills, socialization, motor skills, and an optional maladaptive behavior scale. Computer scoring is available. Scores that are provided using the Vineland–II include scale scores, percentile ranks, standard scores, age equivalents, and domain and adaptive behavior composite scores.

AAMR ADAPTIVE BEHAVIOR SCALE–SCHOOL, SECOND EDITION (ABS–S2)

Test developers constructed the ABS–S2 (Lambert, Nihira, & Leland, 1993) as one method to determine whether persons meet the criteria for the diagnosis of mental retardation. The ABS–S2 is divided into two parts based on (a) independent living skills and (b) social behavior. The domains assessed in each are listed in Figure 9.10.

Figure 9.10   Areas assessed by the AAMR Adaptive Behavior Scale–School, Second Edition.

Part I: Independent Living Domains	Part II: Social Behavior Domains
Independent Functioning	Social Behavior
Physical Development	Conformity
Economic Activity	Trustworthiness
Language Development	Stereotyped and Hyperactive Behavior
Numbers and Time	Self-Abusive Behavior
Prevocational/Vocational Activity	Social Engagement
Self-Direction	Disturbing Interpersonal Behavior
Responsibility	
Socialization	

The person most familiar with the student may administer the scale by completing the items, or a professional who is familiar with the child may complete the items. The information is plotted on a profile sheet to represent the student's adaptive behavior functioning. Standard scores, percentile ranks, and age equivalents are provided in the manual.

INTELLIGENCE AND ADAPTIVE BEHAVIOR: CONCLUDING REMARKS

Intelligence tests for diagnosis of learning problems should be applied with caution. Refer to Tables 9.1 and 9.2 for a summary of the instruments presented in Chapter 9. In addition to the many problems and issues surrounding the use of intelligence tests, the interpretation of test results is largely dependent on the training of the individual examiner. Some professionals believe that appropriate classification can occur only after numerous formal and informal assessments and observations. Others rely on only quantitative test data. Some professionals may use a factor analysis approach to determine learning disabilities, whereas others use informal and curriculum-based achievement measures.

The determination of the classification of mild mental retardation or educational disability is complicated by many social and legal issues. In a review of the problems and practices in the field for the past 20 years, Reschly (1988) advocated the need for a change of focus in the diagnosis and classification of students with mental retardation.

Table 9.1 Instruments for assessment of IQ.

Name of Instrument	Purpose of Test	Constructs Measured	Standardization Information	Reliability Information	Validity Information
Wechsler Intelligence Scale for Children–IV	Assess overall intellectual ability for children ages 6-0 to 16-11	Verbal Comprehension, Perceptual Reasoning, Working Memory, Processing Speed, Full Scale IQ	Sample based on U.S. Census of 2000. Variables include geographic region, ethnicity, gender, age, parental education level.	Adequate to high evidence of split-half reliability, test-retest reliability SEMs, inter-scorer reliability.	Evidence supports validity based on content validity, construct validity, confirmatory factor analysis.
Kaufman Assessment Battery for Children–II	Assess processing and cognitive abilities of children ages 3–18	Fluid/ Crystalized intelligence factors and Mental Processing factors	Total sample of 3,025 children ages 3–18. Variables include sex, age, ethnicity, parental education level, and geographic region.	Evidence of test-retest reliability, internal consistency, SEMs, reliability of nonstandard administration, differences by ethnicity, sex, and parental education level.	Evidence of construct validity, factor analytic data, concurrent criterion-related validity data
Stanford–Binet V	General and specific cognitive and processing abilities	Fluid reasoning, knowledge quantitative reasoning, visual-spatial processing, working memory	Total sample of 4,800 persons in norming and standardization process. Variables considered include sex, age, community size, ethnicity, socioeconomic status, and geographic region.	Internal consistency SEM, test-retest reliability, and interscorer reliability research supports consistency of instrument.	Validity research includes content and construct validity and concurrent criterion-related validity. Factor analytic studies also support validity.

Test	Purpose/Description	What It Measures	Sample/Norms	Reliability	Validity
Woodcock-Johnson III Tests of Cognitive Ability	Measures cognitive factors, clinical clusters, intracognitive discrepancies. Instrument designed to be used with the WJ III tests of Achievement	Global cognitive ability, specific processing clusters, predicted academic achievement	More than 8,000 persons included in the sample. Variables included ethnicity, community size, geographic region. Adult sample includes educational and occupational variables.	Information regarding test-retest reliability, interrater reliability, alternate forms reliability, and internal consistency reliability included. Most reliability coefficients for internal consistency are reported to be in the .90s.	Concurrent criterion-related validity research included. Evidence of construct and content validity included.
Detroit Tests of Learning Aptitude	General mental processing composites of cognitive skills	General mental composite, linguistic, attention, and motor domains	1,350 students in 37 states were included. Demographic variables considered were gender, rural or urban community, race (white, black, other); ethnicity (African American, Hispanic, Native American, or other), and geographic region. Family income, educational attainment of parents, disability status, and age (6 years to 17 years of age) were also considered.	Internal consistency coefficients were calculated using coefficient alpha and ranged from .71 to .97. Test-retest reliability yielded coefficients ranging from .71 to .99 when compared across the various age groups.	Content validity, criterion-related validity, and construct validity information are presented in the manual.

continued.

Table 9.1 continued.

Name of Instrument	Purpose of Test	Constructs Measured	Standardization Information	Reliability Information	Validity Information
Universal Nonverbal Intelligence Test	Assesses nonverbal reasoning and cognitive abilities	Memory, reasoning, symbolic mediation, nonsymbolic mediation	The standardization sample included more than 2,000 students, with the variables of sex, age, race, Hispanic origin, region, parental educational level, and general or special education placement.	A sample of 1,765 children participated in the reliability and validity studies. Evidence of internal consistency in general, clinical, and special samples, test-retest reliability.	A sample of 1,765 children participated in the reliability and validity studies. Evidence of content validity, confirmatory factor analysis, concurrent criterion-related validity.
Comprehensive Test of Nonverbal Intelligence	Assesses various nonverbal cognitive abilities	Nonverbal analogies, categories, and sequences	The norm sample of the CTONI included 2,901 persons in 30 states. The characteristics of geographic area, gender, race (white, black, other) urban/rural residence, ethnicity (Native American, Hispanic, Asian, African American, other), family income, and parents' educational level were considered in the norm sample.	Reliability information was provided for internal consistency, standard error of measurement, test-retest reliability, and interrater reliability. All coefficients were within the adequate to high range.	Validity information for content validity including analyses of the content validity of other measures of nonverbal intelligence, relationship to theories of intelligence, item analysis, and differential item functioning analysis.

| Test of Nonverbal Intelligence—Third Edition | Brief measure of nonverbal cognitive ability | Abstract problem-solving skills of nonverbal items | A total of 3,451 persons representing 28 states were included in the norming sample. The demographic considerations in the norming process were based on the 1997 *Statistical Abstracts of the United States* (U.S. Bureau of the Census, 1997). These factors included geographic region, gender, race (white, black, other), residence (urban/rural), ethnicity (Native American, Hispanic, Asian, African American, and other), disability status (no disability, learning disability, speech-language disorder, mental retardation, other disability). In addition, the family income of parents, educational level of parents, and educational level of adult subjects were considered. | Evidence of reliability includes internal consistency measures using coefficient alpha and standard error of measurement, alternate forms reliability, test-retest reliability, and interrater reliability. All reliability coefficients presented in the manual were within the .90s. | Adequate evidence of content validity, criterion-related validity, and some evidence of construct validity. |

Table 9.2 Adaptive behavior instruments.

Name of Instrument	Purpose of Test	Constructs Measured	Standardization Information	Reliability Information	Validity Information
Vineland–II	Assesses adaptive behavior for persons ranging in age from 0 to 90	Communication, daily living skills, socialization, motor skills, and maladaptive behavior	The standardization sample for the Vineland included 3,695 persons ranging in age from birth to 18-11 years. Variables considered in the sample were sex, geographic region, parental educational level, race or ethnic group, community size, educational placement and age. Additional clinical groups who were also in norm group included students with ADHD, emotional disturbance, learning disabilities, mental retardation, noncategorical developmentally delayed, speech and/or language impaired, and other (such as OHI, multiple disabilities)	Evidence of split-half, test-retest, and interrater reliability. Reliability coefficients range from adequate to high.	Information included construct validity, content validity, and criterion-related validity studies. Construct validity was based on developmental progression and factor analysis of domains and subdomains. Content validity information also provided.

Vineland Adaptive Behavior–Expanded Form	Expanded form of adaptive behavior assessment	More detailed assessment of communication, daily living skills, socialization, motor skills, and maladaptive behavior.	The same norming sample used for the expanded form	The manual reports on reliability studies using split-half, test-retest, and interrater reliability measures. Split-half reliability coefficients were in the .80s for the standardization sample, and in the .80s and .90s for supplementary norms. Information for the test-retest and interrater reliability is based on the Survey Form information.	Information given includes construct validity, content validity, and criterion-related validity. Studies were based on the Survey Form, and discussion of estimating coefficients for the Expanded Form is included.
AAMR–Adaptive Behavior Scale-2	Assessment of adaptive behavior	Independent living skills and social skills	The ABS–S2 was normed on a sample of 2,074 persons with mental retardation and 1,254 persons who were nondisabled. The variables of race, gender, ethnicity, urban and rural residence, geographic region, and age (3–18) were considered in the sample.	Information on interrater reliability, internal consistency, and test-retest reliability is presented in the manual. All coefficients presented range from adequate to high.	The examiner's manual addresses construct and item validity for students with and without mental retardation.

The classification system reforms advocated would place more emphasis on three dimensions: (1) severe, chronic achievement deficits; (2) significantly deficient achievement across most if not all achievement areas; and (3) learning problems largely resistant to regular interventions. The students meeting these criteria will be virtually the same as the current population with MMR; however, their classification will not carry the stigma of comprehensive incompetence based on biological anomaly that is permanent. (p. 298)

For **MORE PRACTICE** in understanding intellectual and adaptive behavior assessment, visit the Companion Website at *www. prenhall.com/overton.*

THINK AHEAD

This text has been concerned primarily with the assessment of students within school age, typically from about age 6 to 18. Students who require the assistance of special education services as part of their educational intervention often require services during preschool years and have additional needs for postsecondary years. The assessment of students in the years of early childhood and in the years requiring special considerations for transition to adulthood are presented in Chapter 10.

EXERCISES

Part I
Select the terms to complete the statements that follow.

a. intelligence
b. adaptive behavior
c. IQ
d. achievement
e. bidialectal
f. traditional measures of IQ

g. nonverbal
h. acculturation
i. multiple intelligences
j. environmental influence
k. dynamic assessment

_____ 1. Because many of the instruments used to assess intelligence and achievement include numerous items of a verbal nature, the assessment of students whose primary language is not English should be given a _____ measure _____ in addition to other measures.

_____ 2. IDEA includes statements of determining eligibility that require the team to exclude _____ as the primary reason for a disability before determining a student as eligible for special education services.

_____ 3. Minority students who may appear to be within the range of mental retardation on measures developed for use with students from the majority culture may not be within the range of mental retardation on _____ measures.

_____ 4. Students who have a dominant language other than English are often referred to as being bilingual, and students whose primary language is English and nonstandard English are referred to as _____.

_____ 5. Bilingual students may have difficulty with both the language items on standardized assessments and the level of _____ required to perform well on the items.

_____ 6. Once the standardized assessment has been completed, an examiner may use the method of _____, incorporating teaching, to determine the student's potential to learn the failed items.

_____ 7. The measure of this is actually a ratio comparing a student's mental age and chronological age.

Answers to these questions can be found in the Appendix of this text or you may also complete these questions and receive immediate feedback on your answers by going to the Think Ahead module in Chapter 9 of the Companion Website.

CHAPTER

10

Special Considerations of Assessment in Early Childhood and Transition

Public Law 99-457
developmental delay
at risk for developmental delay
biological risk factors
environmental risk factors
Individual Family Service Plan
family-centered program
family-focused program
expressive language disorders
receptive language disorders
play evaluations
arena assessment

interactive strategies
observations
situational questionnaires
ecobehavioral interviews
phonemic awareness
phonemic synthesis
phonemic analysis
autism spectrum disorders
assistive technology
assistive technology evaluation
transition planning
supported employment

CHAPTER FOCUS

The assessment process included thus far in the text concerns primarily the assessment of students of school age. This chapter includes the issues and procedures needed to assess very young children and older students with transition needs. The assessment of infants and young children involves different procedures and methods from assessment of school-aged children. Federal regulations require that much of the assessment process include extensive interviews with parents and that the family needs be considered. Federal regulations also require additional procedures to assist students and parents with the transition from school to adulthood. These methods and issues are presented in this chapter.

CEC KNOWLEDGE AND SKILLS STANDARDS

The student completing this chapter will understand the knowledge and skills included in the following CEC Knowledge and Skills Standards from Standard 8: Assessment:

GCK8K2—Laws and policies regarding referral and placement procedures for individuals with disabilities

GCK8K3—Types and importance of information concerning individuals with disabilities available from families and public agencies

GCK84—Procedures for early identification of young children who may be at risk for disabilities

CC8S1—Gather relevant background information

GC8S2—Use exceptionality specific assessment instruments with individuals with disabilities

LEGAL GUIDELINES OF EARLY CHILDHOOD EDUCATION

Public Law 99-457
IDEA amendments
that extend services
for special-needs
children through
infancy and
preschool years;
mandates services
for children ages 3–5
with disabilities.

Public Law 99-457 is the law that set forth many of the guidelines and provisions of serving infants and toddlers. Many of the guidelines were incorporated into the 1997 amendments. The assessment of infants and young children presents several issues and concerns not found in the assessment of school-age children. Many of these issues are related to the young age of the child. For example, these young children present unique challenges in assessment because they must be evaluated in domains and areas that are not based on school-related competencies such as academic achievement. These children are evaluated in other areas such as physical challenges, developmental motor skills, functional communication skills, behaviors in specific situations, and developmental competence. The assessment of young children and infants also includes the unique component of family needs and a family plan for appropriate intervention.

IDEA provides for educational intervention for children beginning at age 3. Part C of the IDEA Amendments of 1997 authorizes funding to states for intervention for special-needs infants and toddlers. The aspects of IDEA that pertain to the assessment of infants, toddlers, and preschool children are presented in the following section.

INFANTS, TODDLERS, AND YOUNG CHILDREN

Federal regulations define the population of children eligible to be served, define the methods of assessment, provide procedural safeguards, and outline procedures to be used for intervention based on the family's needs.

**developmental
delay** When an
infant or child
experiences delay in
physical, cognitive,
communicative,
social, emotional, or
adaptive
development.

**at risk for
developmental
delay** When a child
is believed to be at
risk for delay in one
or more areas if
interventions are not
provided.

ELIGIBILITY

Infants and toddlers from birth to age 2 who are experiencing **developmental delays** in one or more of the following areas are eligible for services: cognitive development, physical development (includes vision and hearing), communication development, social or emotional development, and adaptive development. Infants and toddlers may also be eligible for services if they have a diagnosed physical or mental condition that is likely to result in developmental delay. The law gives the individual states discretion to determine the lead agency to provide services for infants and toddlers with special needs. The states also have the option to provide services for children 3 years of age and younger considered to be **at risk for developmental delay** unless the child has appropriate interventions.

Children eligible for early childhood services are those with the same disabilities defined for school-aged children: autism, deaf-blindness, deafness, hearing impairment, mental retardation, multiple disabilities, orthopedic impairment, other health impairment, serious emotional disturbance, specific learning disability, speech or language impairment, traumatic brain injury, and visual impairment. Infants and toddlers who have a diagnosed physical or mental condition that is known to have a high probability of resulting in developmental delay are also eligible (IDEA Amendments, 1997).

Although not all states choose to serve infants and toddlers who are at risk for developmental delays, many states have responded to this category of infants and toddlers and provide intervention services. Katz (1989) lists as **biological risk factors** "prematurity associated with low birth weight, evidence of central nervous system involvement (intraventricular hemorrhage, neonatal seizures), prolonged respiratory difficulties, prenatal maternal substance use or abuse" (p. 100). These risk factors may not always result in an early diagnosed physical condition but may prove problematic as the child develops.

In addition to biological risk factors, **environmental risk factors** often exist. The most often cited environmental risk factors found by Graham and Scott (1988) are poor infant/child interaction patterns, low maternal educational level, young maternal age, disorganization or dysfunction of the family, and few family support networks. Suggestions for assessing infants at risk are given later in this chapter.

biological risk factors Health factors, such as birth trauma, that place a child at risk for developmental disabilities.

environmental risk factors Environmental influences, such as the mother's young age, that place a child at risk for developmental disabilities.

EVALUATION AND ASSESSMENT PROCEDURES

The 1997 IDEA Amendments define evaluation as the ongoing procedures used by qualified personnel to determine the child's eligibility and continued eligibility while the child is served under this law. The amendments state that

§ 636
a. ...the state shall provide, at a minimum for each infant or toddler with a disability, and the infant's or toddler's family, to receive—
   1. a multidisciplinary assessment of the unique strengths and needs of the infant or toddler and the identification of services appropriate to meet such needs;
   2. a family-directed assessment of the resources, priorities, and concerns of the family and the identification of the supports and services necessary to enhance the family's capacity to meet the developmental needs of the infant or toddler. (IDEA Amendments of 1997, p. 62)

Individual Family Service Plan (IFSP) Plan required by PL 99-457 that includes the related needs of the family of the child with disabilities.

The regulations require that an IFSP, or **Individual Family Service Plan**, be developed for each infant or toddler and its family. This family service plan shall include

1. a statement of the infant's or toddler's present levels of physical development, cognitive development, communication development, social or emotional development, and adaptive development, based on objective criteria;
2. a statement of the family's resources, priorities, and concerns relating to enhancing the development of the family's infant or toddler with a disability;
3. a statement of the major outcomes expected to be achieved for the infant or toddler and the family, and the criteria, procedures, and timelines used to determine the degree to which progress toward achieving the outcomes is being made and whether modifications or revisions of the outcomes or services are necessary;

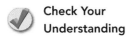

Check Your Understanding

Check your ability to define terms used in the discussion of serving infants and toddlers by completing Activity 10.1.

Activity 10.1

Complete the sentences using the following terms.

> developmental delay
> at risk for developmental delay
> family's
> 6 months
> IFSP

1. Family assessment includes determining the _____ priorities and concerns related to enhancing the development of the child.
2. A child with _____ may be measured by the appropriate instruments and found in one or more of the following areas: cognitive development, physical development, communication development, social or emotional development, adaptive development.
3. _____ must incorporate the family's description of its resources, priorities, and concerns related to the development of the child.
4. The time set for a review of the IFSP of infants and young children is _____.

Apply Your Knowledge

Explain why the family involvement is emphasized in both the assessment stage and the development and implementation of the IFSP.

_____

_____

_____

4. a statement of specific early intervention services necessary to meet the unique needs of the infant or toddler and the family, including the frequency, intensity, and method of delivering services. (IDEA Amendments of 1997, pp. 62–63)

In addition, this plan must include a statement detailing how the services will be provided within the child's natural environment and to what extent any services will not be provided in the child's natural environment. The plan must also include the anticipated dates for the services to begin and a statement about the expected duration of the services. The coordinator of the services must be named, and the steps that will be taken to transition the child to preschool or other services must be outlined (IDEA Amendments, 1997).

The amendments require that the IFSP be reviewed every 6 months (or more frequently as appropriate) and the family given the review of the plan. The IFSP must be evaluated at least once a year.

The assessment of infants and young children must also follow IDEA's regulations concerning nondiscriminatory assessment, parental consent, confidentiality, and due process procedural safeguards. The law requires annual evaluation of progress but notes that because of the rapid development during this period of a child's life, some evaluation procedures may need to be repeated before the annual review.

ISSUES AND QUESTIONS ABOUT SERVING INFANTS AND TODDLERS

A goal of PL 99-457 was to incorporate family members as partners in the assessment of and planning for the infant or child with developmental disabilities. Since the law's passage in 1986, many concerns have been raised by clinical practitioners working with these regulations. Of chief concern is the role of the parents in the assessment and planning process (Dunst, Johanson, Trivette, & Hamby, 1991; Goodman & Hover, 1992; Katz, 1989; Minke & Scott, 1993).

The issues raised by Goodman and Hover include confusion with the interpretation and implementation of the family assessment component. The regulations may be misunderstood as requiring mandatory assessment of family members rather than voluntary participation by the parents. The family's strengths and needs as they relate to the child, not the parents themselves, are the objects of the assessment. Furthermore, these authors contended that a relationship based on equal standing between parents and professionals may not result in a greater degree of cooperation and respect than the traditional client-professional relationship. When the parents and professionals are viewed as equal partners, the professional surrenders the role of expert. Goodman and Hover suggested that the relationship be viewed as reciprocal rather than egalitarian. An assessment process directed by the parents may not be in the child's best interest, because the parents retain the right to restrict professional inquiry.

Katz (1989) observed that the family's view of the child's most important needs takes precedence over the priorities perceived by the professional team members. In some instances, parents and professionals must negotiate to agree on the goals for the child. The family will be more motivated to achieve the goals that they believe are important.

The law clearly states that the IFSP be developed with parent participation. This is true whether or not the family participates in the assessment process. In practice, parent participation varies, according to a study of the development of IFSPs in three early-childhood intervention programs (Minke & Scott, 1993). This study found that parents do not always participate in goal setting for their children, play a listening role without soliciting input from professionals, appear to need better explanations by professionals, and may become better child advocates with early participation. These issues are similar to issues associated with parent participation during eligibility meetings for school-aged children (refer to Chapter 2).

Differences in the implementation of PL 99-457 may be the result of state-determined policies and procedures. One area of difference seems to be in the interpretation of how families should be involved in the early intervention process. Dunst et al. (1991) described the **family-centered program** and the **family-focused program** as paradigms representing two such interpretations. In the family-centered program paradigm, family concerns and needs drive the assessment, anything written on the IFSP must have the family's permission, and the family's needs determine the actual roles played by case managers. The family-focused program paradigm restricts assessment to the family's needs only as they relate to the child's development, the goals are agreed on mutually by professionals and parents, and the case manager's role is to encourage and promote the family's use of professional services. It seems clear that the interpretation and implementation of PL 99-457 differ from state to state and may yet be problematic.

Another type of assessment of young children and their families, called Intervention-Based Multifactored Evaluation, has been proposed (Barnett, Bell, Gilkey, Lentz, Graden, Stone, Smith, & Macmann, 1999). These authors suggest that the assessment and eligibility process should be directly linked to the level of interventions required for instruction. Further, these authors believe that a child should be found eligible for services only when there are notable discrepancies between the child's ability and the peers within the environment. For example, the target child may have discrepancies between the level of assistance required and the rate of

family-centered program Program in which the assessment and goals are driven by the family's needs and priorities.

family-focused program Program in which the family's needs are considered but goals and plans are reached through mutual agreement between the family and education professionals.

learning, the level of caregiver monitoring, or the adaptations of the curriculum, when compared to age peers. When these differences require more time or adaptation than can be accomplished within the general educational environment, special education support services are required. These authors propose a data collection method across tasks and behaviors, similar to the assessment methods used in curriculum-based measurement and in functional behavioral assessments. This method of assessment would be within the spirit of the federal regulations, which require that assessment results be linked directly to interventions.

In addition to involvement of the family in the assessment process, the Division of Early Childhood, or DEC, of the Council for Exceptional Children (CEC) recommends that all assessment be developmentally appropriate, include familiar environments and people, and be functional (Sandall, Hemmeter, Smith, & McLean, 2005). An assessment is considered functional when data is collected

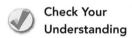

Check Your Understanding

Check your ability to answer questions about IFSPs and serving infants and toddlers by completing Activity 10.2 below.

Activity 10.2

Answer the questions and complete the sentences.

1. What five areas of child development must the IFSP address? _____

2. The IFSP must include the expected _____ of the interventions and the degree to which _____ toward achieving them is being made.

3. In which of the program paradigms does the parent play a more active role in the assessment and planning process? _____

4. According to Minke and Scott (1993), parents may need better _____ from professionals.

5. Katz (1989) stated that in some instances, parents and professionals must _____ on goals for the child.

6. According to Goodman and Hover (1992), when assessment is directed by the parents, what problems may occur? _____

7. What are the assessment recommendations of the Division of Early Childhood? _____

Apply Your Knowledge

Discuss how the IFSP must balance the parents' and child's needs.
_____
_____
_____

in situations that are common in the child's daily routine. This type of assessment will result in more reliable and valid information.

An issue in the implementation of services for infants and toddlers is the identification of young children. A study by Snyder, Bailey, and Auer (1994) found that when children were identified, they may be identified differently than school-aged children. Snyder et al. found that 72% of the states used determination systems that included combinations or noncategorical systems.

METHODS OF EARLY-CHILDHOOD ASSESSMENT

As previously noted, many states serve children who are considered at risk for developmental disabilities. The discussion of assessment methods presented in this text applies to children with existing developmental disabilities as well as to those who may be at risk for developmental disabilities if they do not receive early childhood intervention.

Regulations require that qualified personnel assess children in many developmental areas; for example, assessments of vision, hearing, speech, and medical status are part of a multifactored evaluation. Detailed assessment in these areas is beyond the scope of this text. Measures presented include behavior questionnaires, observations, interviews, checklists, and measures of cognitive and language functioning. Techniques used in the assessment process are also presented.

ASSESSMENT OF INFANTS

Documenting developmental milestones and health history is primarily the responsibility of health professionals. Infants may be suspected of having developmental delays or of being at risk for developmental delays if there are clinical indications of concern. Mayes (1991) cited the following indications of need for an infant assessment:

1. Regulatory disturbances—Sleep disturbances, excessive crying or irritability, eating difficulties, low frustration tolerance, self-stimulatory or unusual movements.

2. Social/environmental disturbances—Failure to discriminate mother, apathetic, withdrawn, no expression of affect or interest in social interaction, excessive negativism, no interest in objects or play, abuse, neglect, or multiple placements, repeated or prolonged separations.

3. Psychophysiological disturbances—Nonorganic failure to thrive, recurrent vomiting or chronic diarrhea, recurrent dermatitis, recurrent wheezing.

4. Developmental delays—Specific delays (gross motor, speech delays). General delays or arrested development. (p. 445)

The prenatal, birth, and early neonatal health history is an important component of the evaluation of infants and is required by PL 99-457. Following the careful history taking of the infant's health factors, Greenspan (1992) organizes the infant/toddler/young child assessment using the following factors:

1. Prenatal and perinatal variables.
2. Parent, family, and environmental variables.
3. Primary caregiver and caregiver/infant-child relationship.
4. Infant variables: Physical, neurologic, physiologic, and cognitive.
5. Infant variables: Formation and elaboration of emotional patterns and human relationships. (pp. 316–317)

Of particular concern in assessing the infant are regulatory patterns, or how the infant reacts to stimuli in the environment and processes sensory information (Greenspan, 1992; Mayes, 1991). This includes how the infant interacts with and reacts to caregivers, the infant's sleeping habits, level of irritability, and so on. This type of assessment relies on observations using checklists and parent interviews or questionnaires. One commonly used observation assessment instrument for newborn infants is the Neonatal Behavioral Assessment Scale (Brazelton, 1984), which includes both reflex items and behavioral observation items. Use of this scale to determine control states (such as sleeping, alert) underscores the importance of this aspect of infant behavior to more complex functions, such as attention (Mayes, 1991). This scale can be used with infants up to 1 month of age.

The Uzgiris-Hunt Ordinal Scales of Psychological Development (Uzgiris & Hunt, 1975) present a Piagetian developmental perspective for assessment during the first 2 years of the infant's life. These six scales include assessment for such skills as visual pursuit, object permanence, manipulation of and interaction with factors in the environment, development of vocal and gestural imitation, and development of schemes for relating to the environment. This instrument requires the use of several objects and solicitation of reactions and responses of the infant. This system, a comprehensive assessment based on the Piagetian model, has been criticized for being developed using primarily infants from middle-class families (Mayes, 1991).

Another instrument used to assess young children and toddlers (ages 1–42 months) is the Bayley Scales of Infant Development-II

(Bayley, 1993). This revised formal instrument now includes in the manual improved statistical research regarding reliability and validity. Like most infant/toddler instruments, the Bayley requires the examiner to manipulate objects and observe the reactions and behavior of the infant. The scale assesses mental functions such as memory, problem solving, verbal ability, and motor functions such as coordination and control; it also includes a behavioral rating scale. In addition to the standardization sample, clinical samples were included in the development of this revision. The clinical samples included infants and young children who were premature, HIV positive, exposed prenatally to drugs, or asphyxiated at birth, and those who had Down syndrome, autism, developmental delays, or otitis media.

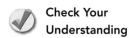

Check Your Understanding

Check your knowledge of assessment instruments used in serving infants and toddlers by completing Activity 10.3 below.

Activity 10.3

Match the following terms with the correct descriptions.

A. Uzgiris-Hunt Ordinal Scales of Psychological Development
B. Bayley Scales of Infant Development–II
C. Neonatal Behavioral Assessment Scale
D. regulatory disturbances
E. infant variables
F. developmental delays

1. This measure of infant assessment is used to determine the possible risk of developmental disabilities of infants from birth to 1 month of age _____.
2. These include physical, neurological, and emotional factors that influence the child's development _____.
3. This instrument is based on Piagetian developmental theory and is used for infants through 2 years of age _____.
4. These include sleep disturbances, irritability, and unusual movements _____.
5. This revised instrument includes research on several clinical samples and is used for children aged 1 to 42 months _____.

Apply Your Knowledge

How do you think regulatory disturbances might influence a child's ability to learn? _____
_____
_____

ASSESSMENT OF TODDLERS AND YOUNG CHILDREN

Many of the instruments discussed in earlier chapters contain basal-level items for toddlers and young children, including the K-ABC-II, WJ III Tests of Achievement, Vineland Adaptive Behavior Scales, Achenbach's Child Behavior Checklist, and Stanford-Binet V. Following is a brief survey of some of the most commonly used and newest instruments that are specifically designed to assess the development and behavior of young children. Instruments that assess general developmental ability of toddlers and young children can also be used to collect additional data to determine the likelihood of disorders in language. For example, young children may appear to have global developmental delays; however, assessment of general development may indicate development is progressing as expected with the exception of language disorders, such as **expressive** or **receptive language disorders**.

expressive language disorders
Significant difficulty with oral expression.

receptive language disorders
Significant difficulty understanding spoken language.

MULLEN SCALES OF EARLY LEARNING: AGS EDITION

This instrument assesses the cognitive functioning of children ages birth through 68 months (Mullen, 1995) and is to be used by assessment personnel with experience in the evaluation of infants and young children. The test author estimates the test administration time to range from 15 minutes to 60 minutes depending on the age of the child. The instrument uses many common manipulative objects to assess the child's gross motor, visual, fine-motor, and receptive and expressive language abilities.

The theoretical basis of the test design is included in the manual and is presented in developmental stages. The expectations of a given developmental stage are listed, followed by the tasks used to assess each of the expected developmental indicators. For example, at stage 2–4 months 0 days to 6 months 30 days—a child's vision is refined and visual reception is assessed using the following items: stares at hand, localizes on objects and people, looks for an object in response to a visual stimulus followed by an auditory stimulus.

Technical Data

Norming Process The manual provides information regarding the standardization process, which included 1,849 children. The standardization process was completed over an 8–year time span and was conducted within the south, northeast, west, north, and south-central regions. The variables of gender, ethnicity, race, age, and community size were considered in construction of the sample.

Reliability The reliability studies contained in the manual were split-half reliability for internal consistency, test-retest reliability, and interscorer reliability. The reliability coefficients ranged from adequate and low/adequate to high. This may in part reflect the instability of developmental scores at the very early ages. Several of the sample sizes used in the reliability studies for some ages were small (38 for test-retest of the gross motor scale for ages 1 to 24 months).

Validity Evidence of construct validity, concurrent validity, and exploratory factor analyses is presented in the examiner's manual. The research regarding developmental progression to support the constructs being measured suggests validity of the scales as developmental indicators.

THE WECHSLER PRESCHOOL AND PRIMARY SCALE OF INTELLIGENCE, 3RD EDITION

The Wechsler Preschool and Primary Scale of Intelligence, 3rd Edition (WPPSI-III) was developed for use with children ages 2 years and 6 months of age to age 7 years and 3 months. This test provides three composite scores of intellectual ability: Verbal Intelligence Quotient, Performance Intelligence Quotient, and Full Scale Intelligence Quotient.

Test developers note that the recent revision of this instrument focused on five major goals. These goals were to:

- update theoretical foundations
- increase developmental appropriateness
- enhance clinical utility
- improve psychometric properties, and
- increase user-friendliness (Wechsler, 2002, p. 10).

In an effort to meet these goals, the revised instrument has items for younger children and increased the number of items for the younger and older age groups. This instrument now has more comprehensive measures of fluid reasoning than the previous edition. The instructions for both the child and the examiner have been improved by including easier to understand instructions for the child and more clear instructions for the examiner. Moreover, this revised edition includes additional items for teaching and expanded and additional queries.

The WPPSI-III has separate subtests for the major age divisions. The age divisions include children ages 2 years 6 months to 3 years 11 months and children ages 4 years to 7 years and 3 months. The third edition of the WPPSI is organized in the following manner:

For ages 2 years and 6 months to 3 years and 11 months—Children are administered the following Core Subtests and may be administered the following Supplemental subtest:

Core Subtests   For the Verbal IQ:

Receptive Vocabulary   On this subtest the child is presented 4 pictures and asked to identify 1 of those pictures. This subtest may be influenced by auditory and visual memory.

Information   This subtest assesses the child's previously learned factual information. The child's responses may be influenced by experiences and environment.
For the Performance IQ:

Block Design   This subtest requires the child to copy a visual pattern and assesses the child's ability to use visual motor skills and visual organizational skills. This subtest is a core subtest for all age groups.

Object Assembly   This is a timed subtest that is a core subtest for the younger age group and a supplemental subtest for the older age group. Children are required to complete a series of puzzles. This task may be influenced by visual perceptual, visual spatial, and visual motor organizational skills. This taps into the child's ability to analyze pieces of a whole and to construct the whole object.

Supplemental Subtest

Picture Naming   This is a supplemental subtest for the younger age group and an optional subtest for the older age group. On this subtest, the child is presented with pictures and is asked to name the picture. This subtest may be influenced by visual and auditory long term memory, word knowledge, and expressive language skills.

For ages 4 years to 7 years and 3 months—Children are administered the following Core Subtests and may be administered the following Supplemental subtests and optional subtests:

Core Subtests   For the Verbal IQ:

Information   This subtest assesses the child's previously learned factual information. The child's responses may be influenced by experiences and environment. This is a required core subtest for all age divisions.

Vocabulary   This subtest requires the student to respond to items assessing basic word knowledge and may be influenced by the child's previous experience and environment. These items are a measure of long term memory for verbal information.

Word Reasoning   This subtest assesses verbal knowledge and reasoning skills.

For the Performance IQ:

Block Design   This subtest requires the child to copy a visual pattern and assesses the child's ability to use visual motor skills and visual organization skills. This subtest is a core subtest for all age groups.

Matrix Reasoning   The skills visual processing and abstract reasoning may influence the child's ability to successfully complete these tasks. This subtest presents visual stimuli consisting of an incomplete matrix. The child is asked to scan several choices and select the missing piece from those choices.

Picture Concepts   The child is shown rows of pictures and then asked to select another picture with the same characteristics. The child's performance on this subtest may be influenced by visual reasoning and visual conceptual memory.

Coding   The Coding Subtest contributes to a Full Scale IQ but not to the Verbal or Performance IQ.

Supplemental Subtests

Comprehension   This subtest is largely influenced by verbal concepts learned from previous experiences and also requires practical knowledge and the ability to reason or analyze specific situations.

Picture Completion   This subtest assesses the child's ability to scan pictures and determine what essential detail is missing.

Similarities   This subtest uses a sentence completion format to assess the child's ability to analyze how 2 things are alike.

Object Assembly   Children are required to complete a series of puzzles. This task may be influenced by visual perceptual, visual spatial, and visual motor organizational skills. This taps into the child's ability to analyze pieces of a whole and construct the whole object.

Additional optional subtests are included for the older age division. These subtests are:

Receptive Vocabulary   This is a core subtest for the younger age division and presents the same task demands for the older age group as the younger age group.

Picture Naming   On this subtest, the child is presented with pictures and is asked to name the picture. This subtest may be influenced by visual and auditory long-term memory, word knowledge, and expressive language skills.

Technical Data   Norming Process—During the development of this revision, children from the general population and special clinical groups were assessed. The standardization sample included 1,700 children in stratified age groups from age 2 years 6 months to 7 years and 3 months. The variables considered in the norm group included age, sex, race/ethnicity (white, African American, Hispanic, Asian, other), parental education level, and geographic region. The standardization sample was selected to correspond with the 2000 U.S. Census.

The special groups studied during the development of the test include the following groups: intellectually gifted, mental retardation, developmental delay, at risk, developmental risk factors, autistic disorder, expressive language delay, mixed expressive-receptive language delay, limited English proficiency, attention deficit/hyperactivity disorder, and motor impairment.

Reliability   The manual provides evidence of adequate internal consistency as measured by split-half reliability for both age divisions and the overall standardization sample. The manual includes evidence of small standard errors of measurement across age groups. Test-retest stability and interrater reliability are adequate.

Validity   Evidence of validity is presented in the manual and includes measures of criterion-related validity, confirmatory factor analysis, and validity of use with special groups. The evidence presented indicates that the WPPSI-III successfully discriminates between the special groups and the norm sample. The manual presents a discussion of the study of content validity.

AGS EARLY SCREENING PROFILES

The AGS Early Screening Profiles (Harrison et al., 1990) present a comprehensive screening for children aged 2 to 6-11 years. The battery contains items that are administered directly to the child and surveys that are completed by parents, teachers, or both. The components, shown in Figure 10.1, are described in the following paragraphs.

Components

Cognitive/Language Profile   The child demonstrates verbal abilities by pointing to objects named or described by the examiner,

Figure 10.1   Components of the AGS Early Screening Profiles.

PROFILES

Cognitive/Language Profile

Source: direct testing of child
Time: 5 to 15 minutes

Cognitive Subscale
Visual Discrimination Subtest (14 items)

Logical Relations Subtest (14 items)
Language Subscale
Verbal Concepts Subtest (25 items)
Basic School Skills Subtest (25 items)

Motor Profile

Source: direct testing of child
Time: 5 to 15 minutes

Gross-Motor Subtest (5 items)
Fine-Motor Subtest (3 items)

Self-Help/Social Profile

Source: parent, teacher questionnaires
Time: 5 to 10 minutes

Communication Domain (15 items)
Daily Living Skills Domain
    (15 items)
Socialization Domain (15 items)
Motor Skills Domain (15 items)

SURVEYS

Articulation Survey

Source: direct testing of child
Time: 2 to 3 minutes

Articulation of Single Words
    (20 items)
Intelligibility During
    Continuous Speech (1 rating)

Home Survey

Source: parent questionnaire
Time: 5 minutes

(12 items)

Health History Survey

Source: parent questionnaire
Time: 5 minutes

(12 items)

Behavior Survey

Source: examiner questionnaire
Time: 2 to 3 minutes

Cognitive/Language
    Observations (9 items)
Motor Observations
    (13 items)

Source: From *Screening Profiles* by Patti Harrison, Alan Kaufman, Nadeen Kaufman, Robert Bruininks, John Rynders, Steven Ilmer, Sara Sparrow & Domenic Cicchetti. © 1990 American Guidance Service, Inc., 4201 Woodland Road, Circle Pines, MN 55014-1796. Reproduced with permission of the Publisher. All rights reserved.

discriminates pictures and selects those that are the same as the stimulus, solves visual analogies by pointing to the correct picture, and demonstrates basic school skills such as number and quantity concepts and the recognition of numbers, letters, and words. Items are presented in an easel format, and sample items are included to teach the tasks.

Motor Profile   These items assess both gross-motor and fine-motor developmental skills. Gross-motor skills measured include imitating movements, walking on a line, standing on one foot, walking heel-to-toe, and performing a standing broad jump. Fine-motor tasks include stringing beads, drawing lines and shapes, and completing mazes.

Self-Help/Social Profile   Questionnaires completed by teachers and parents measure the child's understanding of oral and written language, daily self-care skills such as dressing and eating, ability to do chores, and community skills such as telephone manners. Social skills that assess how well the child gets along with others and questions measuring the child's fine- and gross-motor skills are included in this section of the instrument.

Articulation Survey   In this easel-format task, the examiner asks the child to say words that sample the child's ability to articulate sounds in the initial, medial, and final position.

Home Survey and Health History Survey   These questionnaires completed by the parents assess parent-child interactions; types of play; frequency of parent reading to the child; health problems of the mother's pregnancy, labor, and delivery; and health history of the child, such as immunization schedule.

Behavior Survey   An observation form is used to rate the child's behavior in several categories such as attention, independence, activity level, and cooperativeness.

Technical Data

Norming Process   The test manual provides detailed descriptions of the development of test items and questions included on parent and teacher questionnaires. The following variables, representative of the 1986 U.S. Census data, were considered in the national standardization sample: age, gender, geographic region, parental educational level, and race or ethnic group.

Reliability   Reliability research presented in the manual includes coefficient alpha for internal consistency and immediate test-retest and delayed test-retest research. Coefficients are adequate to moderately high for all measures.

Validity   Validity studies presented in the manual include content validity, construct validity, part-total correlations, and concurrent validity research with cognitive measures used with early childhood students. Many of the validity coefficients are low to adequate.

KAUFMAN SURVEY OF EARLY ACADEMIC AND LANGUAGE SKILLS (K-SEALS)

The K-SEALS (Kaufman & Kaufman, 1993) was developed as an expanded version of the language measure of the AGS Early Screening Profiles. Normed for children aged 3-0 to 6-11, the instrument includes three subtests: Vocabulary; Numbers, Letters, and Words; and Articulation Survey. Scores for expressive and receptive language skills may be obtained from the administration of the Vocabulary and Numbers, Letters, and Words subtests. Scores for early academic skills, such as number skills and letter and word skills, may be computed for children aged 5-0 to 6-11. Items are presented in an easel format with visual and verbal stimuli and are similar to the items on the AGS Early Screening Profiles. Half of the items from the Vocabulary and Numbers, Letters, and Words subtests are identical to those on the AGS Early Screening Profiles. The Articulation Survey from the AGS test is repeated in its entirety on the K-SEALS, but the error analysis is expanded on the K-SEALS.

Scoring   The manual includes norm tables for converting raw scores into percentile ranks and cutoff scores for the categories of "potential delay" or "OK."

Technical Data   The K-SEALS was standardized as part of the standardization of the AGS Early Screening Profiles. The same variables were considered to promote representativeness in the sample. Reliability and validity information for the K-SEALS includes split-half reliability, test-retest reliability, intercorrelations, construct validity, content validity, concurrent validity, and predictive validity. Individual subtest coefficients for reliability and validity studies ranged from low to adequate, but total test coefficients appear adequate for most studies cited.

BRIGANCE SCREENS

The Brigance Screens (Brigance, 1997, 1998a, 1998b; Glascoe, 1998) are a system of assessment instruments designed to screen for both development risk and potential advanced development. The screens are designed for the ages of 1-9 to 7-6 and are arranged in easel format for administration. Parent and teacher ratings are included.

The domains assessed in the Brigance Screens include visual/fine/and graphmotor, gross motor, quantitative concepts, personal information, receptive vocabulary, prereading/reading skills, expressive vocabulary, and articulation/verbal fluency/syntax. These domains are assessed using the criterion-referenced approach. The instrument was designed to be administered in approximately 15 minutes.

Scoring   Norm tables are provided for age-equivalent scores for motor development, communication development, and cognitive development. Percentile ranks are presented for total scores.

Technical Data   The standardization sample for the 1995 re-standardization included a total of 408 students. Demographic information is provided in the technical manual, which includes tables for the following characteristics: geographic sites, educational level of child, gender, racial and ethnic background, educational level of parents, family income (participation in free lunch program), parents' marital status, and ages. The technical manual also presents information regarding the performance of the sample by demographic characteristics (such as participation in free lunch program).

Reliability   The technical manual presents information for internal consistency, test-retest reliability, and interrater reliability. Total internal reliability coefficients are in the .90s for 2-year-olds to first graders. The end-of-first-grade reliability coefficient was .52. Test-retest reliability coefficients ranged from the mid-.50s to the upper-.90s. Interrater reliability coefficients were reported to be in the mid- to upper-.90s.

Validity   The technical manual reports information on content validity, construct validity, concurrent validity, predictive validity, and discriminant validity. Coefficients ranged widely from low to adequate.

DEVELOPMENTAL INDICATORS FOR THE ASSESSMENT OF LEARNING–THIRD EDITION (DIAL–3)

This instrument was developed in an effort to screen young children who may be at risk for future learning difficulties (Mardell-Czudnowski & Goldenberg, 1998). The test authors state that the purpose of this instrument is to "identify young children in need of further diagnostic assessment" (Mardell-Czudnowski & Goldenberg, 1998, p. 1). The test may be used to assess children ages 3 years through 6-11. The test assesses the areas mandated by IDEA 1997, including motor skills, concepts, language, self-help, and social skills. The motor, concepts, and language skills are assessed through performance items presented to the child. The self-help or adaptive skills and social skills areas are assessed through parent questionnaires. Instructions are also presented for the examiner to assess social adjustment through observations obtained during the assessment session. A fairly detailed theoretical basis for the development of the test and research pertaining to specific areas assessed are presented in the manual.

The DIAL–3 has been developed in both English and Spanish, although there are no separate Spanish norms. Using item response theory (Rasch one-parameter model), the Spanish and English versions were equated so that the performance of the Spanish-speaking children could be compared with the performance of the English-speaking children (Mardell-Czudnowski & Goldenberg, 1998, p. 75). The test includes several concrete manipulative items, including three dials to be used as stimuli for items in the concepts, motor, and language areas. Pictures, blocks, and a color chart are among the other items included.

Components

Motor   This component of the DIAL–3 includes both fine- and gross-motor tasks. The child is requested to complete such items as jumping, cutting, and writing his name (as appropriate).

Concepts   This component assesses the child's ability to identify colors and parts of the body as well as concepts such as biggest, cold, and longest. The child is also assessed in counting skills and ability to sort by shape and name shapes.

Language   This component assesses the child's ability to provide some personal information, such as name and age, identify pictures of objects, and name letters. In addition, the child's articulation is assessed for developmental risk.

Parent Questionnaire   Composed of several parts, this questionnaire is used to assess developmental history and self-help skills on a 15-item rating scale. It includes a social skills rating scale, a rating scale for areas of parental concern, and a section for rating the screening program using the DIAL–3.

Technical Data   The standardization sample included 1,560 children who ranged in age from 3 to 6-11. The sample matched the 1994 Census data. The following variables were considered in selecting the sample: age, gender, geographic region, race/ethnicity, and parent educational level. Information is also provided in the manual regarding the children in the sample who were receiving special services.

Reliability   Internal reliability was researched using coefficient alpha. The coefficients ranged from .66 to .87 (for median coefficients). The total DIAL–3 test-retest reliability coefficients for two age groups were .88 and .84.

Validity   Extensive information is provided in the manual about the development of the items in both the English and the Spanish versions. Information is presented concerning the reviews of items for content and potential bias as well as the rationale for selection of specific items. Concurrent validity studies were conducted with the DIAL–R, the Early Screening Profiles, the Battell, the Bracken Screening Test, the Brigance Preschool Screen, the PPVT–III, and the Social Skills Rating System. Corrected coefficients were scattered considerably, from extremely low to adequate.

TECHNIQUES AND TRENDS IN INFANT AND EARLY-CHILDHOOD ASSESSMENT

The assessment methods presented in this chapter are formal methods of assessment. Current literature suggests that alternative methods of assessment be used with or in place of traditional assessment of infants and young children (Cohen & Spenciner, 1994; Fewell, 1991; Paget, 1990; Sinclair, Del'Homme, & Gonzalez, 1993). Among the alternative methods suggested by various studies are play evaluations, arena assessment, interactive strategies, observations, situational questionnaires, and ecobehavioral interviews.

play evaluations
Observational informal assessment in a natural play environment.

Play evaluations can yield useful information about how the child interacts with people and objects and can be completed in a naturalistic environment. They can be useful in determining the child's activity level, reaction to novel stimuli, and affect. The characteristics of play listed by Bailey and Wolery (1989) are presented in Table 10.1. Using these characteristics as guidelines, the examiner can assess many behaviors of the child in a naturalistic environment for developmental progress in social skills, activity level, motor skills, frustration tolerance, communication skills with the examiner or caretaker while playing, and so on.

arena assessment
Technique that places the child and facilitator in the center of the multidisciplinary team members during the evaluation.

Arena assessment can be arranged for any method of assessment defined in this chapter, except perhaps for formal cognitive assessment on standardized instruments. Arena assessment is a technique in which all members of the multidisciplinary team surround the child and examiner or facilitator and observe as they interact in multiple situations. Play evaluations, formal play or preacademic tasks,

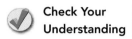

Check Your Understanding

Check your ability to answer questions about assessment instruments used with young children by completing Activity 10.4 below.

Activity 10.4

Answer the following questions about the assessment instruments used with young children.

1. Which instrument for younger ages includes many of the same subtests as the WISC–IV? _____

2. Which instrument was standardized at the same time as the AGS Early Screening Profiles? _____

3. What instrument provides scores for expressive and receptive language skills as well as early academic skills for children aged 5 and 6 years? _____

4. Which instrument includes an articulation survey but does not have the expanded error analysis included in the K-SEALS? _____

5. Which instrument includes both direct assessment and questionnaires/ratings to be completed by caretakers? _____

Apply Your Knowledge

Language development is consistently evaluated in preschool evaluations. What other areas of development does language development influence? _____

_____

_____

Table 10.1   Characteristics of play.

Characteristic	Description
Intrinsic motivation	Play is not motivated by biological drives (e.g., hunger) but comes from within the child and not from the stimulus properties of the play objects.
Spontaneous and voluntary	Play involves free choice; children engage in play because they want to, not because someone assigns it to them.
Self-generated	Play involves the child actively generating the activities.
Active engagement	Play involves active attention to the activities of play.
Positive affect	Play involves pleasurable or enjoyable activities or results in pleasurable or enjoyable consequences.
Nonliterality	Play involves activities that are carried out in a pretend or "as-if" nature—less serious or real.
Flexibility	Play involves variability in form or context and can be done in a variety of ways or situations.
Means more than ends	Play involves emphasis on the activity itself rather than on the goal of the activity.

Source: From *Assessing Infants and Preschoolers with Handicaps* (p. 432) by D. B. Bailey and M. Wolery, 1989, Upper Saddle River, NJ: Merrill/Prentice Hall. Reprinted by permission.

Figure 10.2   Team members conducting an arena assessment.

Source: From *Assessment of Young Children* by Libby G. Cohen and Loraine Spenciner. Copyright © 1992 by Longman Publishers. Reprinted with permission.

communication items, and so on may all be presented in this format. All members of the team record the child's responses throughout the evaluation session. This might be a more effective method of assessment of infants and young children because it may reduce the number of assessment sessions (Cohen & Spenciner, 1994). Figure 10.2 illustrates the arena assessment model.

interactive strategies Strategies used by the examiner that encourage the child to use communication to solve problems.

Interactive strategies can be useful in the assessment of young children. These strategies assess the child's abilities to solve problems through interpersonal interactions with the examiner (Paget, 1990). The examiner may alter the problems presented to observe the child's responses to frustration, humor, or different types or objects of play. The strategies are aimed at encouraging the child to communicate with the examiner to solve the problem.

observations An informal assessment method of activities, language, and interactions in various settings.

Observations can be used in a variety of settings and across a variety of tasks. The child may be observed in the home or preschool classroom environment with peers, siblings, and caretakers. All areas of assessment in early childhood can be enhanced through observations. The child's behavior, social skills, communication skills, cognitive level, speech, motor skills, motor planning, adaptive behaviors, activity level, frustration tolerance level, attention span, and self-help skills can be assessed through multiple observations. When observations are combined with information from parent questionnaires and more formal assessment measures, the examiner can gain a holistic view of the child's developmental progress.

situational questionnaires Questionnaires that assess the child's behavior in various situations.

Situational questionnaires are useful when comparing the child's behavior in specific situations. Examples of these are the

Home Situations Questionnaire and the School Situations Questionnaire (Barkley, 1990). The parents and teachers rate the child's behavior, activity level, and attention span in a variety of situations, such as when the parents talk on the telephone, when visitors are in the home, and when the child is interacting with peers. These questionnaires allow for more direct analysis and intervention for problematic behaviors.

ecobehavioral interviews
Interviews of parents and teachers that assess behavior in different settings and routines.

In **ecobehavioral interviews**, parents and teachers describe a child's behaviors in everyday situations, such as during daily routines, bedtimes, class activities, and transitions from one activity to the next (Barnett, Macmann, & Carey, 1992). These responses are analyzed to determine problem behaviors that occur across settings or situations. Behavioral interventions are then targeted to remediate the behaviors in the situations described by the parents and teachers.

OTHER CONSIDERATIONS IN ASSESSING VERY YOUNG CHILDREN

The best practice of assessment across all ages of children involves multiple measures, multiple examiners, and multiple situations or environments. This is especially important for infants, toddlers, and young children because of the influence that temperament, physical health, and current physical state (alertness or sleepiness) may have during an evaluation period. A holistic view of the child's developmental level can be gained by observing the child in many different settings, using both formal and informal assessment, and analyzing the observed behaviors.

Because of the very rapid pace of development of young children, assessment and monitoring of progress should be ongoing, as stated in PL 99-457 (*Federal Register*, 1993). This rapid progress contributes to the instability of scores obtained at very young ages. The variability of the educational and home environments can also contribute to the instability of scores.

Analysis of formal early-childhood assessment instruments indicates that the reliability and validity of the subtests are moderately adequate to below acceptable levels. The coefficients tend to be more acceptable for total test or total instrument scores. Barnett et al. (1992) cautioned against using profile analysis of individual subtests at young ages and suggested that only global scores be used. Katz (1989) warned of the dangers that could occur when very young children are falsely identified through assessment. That is, the child's scores might indicate developmental difficulties, but in reality, the child is not disabled. This false identification may result in changes in parent-child interactions and diminished expectations held for the child.

At the other end of the identification process are the children who need services but remain unidentified. In a study by Sinclair et al. (1993), students who were previously undiagnosed were referred for assessment of behavioral disorders. This study involved a three-stage, multiple-gating system that was used to screen preschool children for behavioral disorders. In this study, 5% of the sample who had not previously been identified as having behavioral difficulties were referred for a comprehensive evaluation.

Review of the literature on the assessment of infants and young children indicates that new trends are emerging. It is hoped that these trends will remedy some of the difficulties of assessing children at very young ages.

Table 10.2 summarizes the strengths and weaknesses of the instruments presented in this chapter.

Table 10.2   Summary of instruments of early childhood assessment.

Instrument	Strengths	Weaknesses
Neonatal Behavioral Assessment Scale	Useful for infants through 1 month of age Assesses behavior and reflex actions	Not typically used in educational setting Requires specific training for use
Uzgiris-Hunt Ordinal Scales of Psychological Development	For children up to 2 years of age Good theoretical basis	Lengthy administration time Norm sample not representative
Bayley Scales of Infant Development-II	Manual has improved statistical data Standardization included clinical samples Assess many areas of development	Lengthy administration time Specific training necessary
Mullen Scales of Early Learning: AGS Edition	Integration of developmental concepts and theoretical foundations included in manual Includes ages birth–68 months	Small sample sizes for reliability, validity data
Wechsler Preschool and Primary Scales of Intelligence, 3rd Edition	Subtests are like those in other Wechsler Scales Appropriate for ages 2-6 to 7-3	Reliability and validity improved in 3rd edition, motor-performance subtests continue to have lower ability
AGS Early Screening Profiles	Include both direct and indirect assessment across multiple situations and skills	Low to adequate reliability and validity coefficients
Kaufman Survey of Early Academic and Language Skills	Expands the language sections of the AGS Early Screening Profiles Offers expanded analysis of articulation errors	Subtest coefficients low to adequate

continued.

Table 10.2 continued.

Instrument	Strengths	Weaknesses
Brigance Screens	Assesses across various ages; criterion-referenced; provides parent and teacher rating system	Norms could be expanded
Developmental Indicators for the Assessment of Learning	Spanish and English versions; parent questionnaire included; fairly comprehensive	Does not provide age-equivalent scores

PHONEMIC AWARENESS

phonemic awareness
Comprehension of individual sounds that make up words.

phonemic synthesis
The blending of isolated sounds into a whole word.

phonemic analysis
The breaking up of a word into isolated sounds.

Legal regulations require that the child's level of functioning in the areas of physical development, cognitive development, communication development, social or emotional development, and adaptive development be addressed during the assessment process. Assessment in these areas provides information for educational personnel about how to implement interventions necessary for childhood development and future educational success. One skill area that may assist assessment personnel in understanding the preschool child's readiness for academic tasks is the area of **phonemic awareness**. A child with this skill is able to determine the separate sounds in spoken words. This awareness is a conscious awareness that words are made up of phonemes or sounds (Snider, 1995).

The skills involved in being able to distinguish the sounds of words are important in learning to read (Turnbull, Turnbull, Shank, Smith, & Leal, 2002). A comprehensive review of the literature regarding the effects of instruction in phonemic awareness on reading skills indicated that both word reading skills and reading comprehension improved with phonemic awareness (Ehri, Nunes, Willows, Schuster, Yaghoub-Zadeh, & Shanahan, 2001). Research also suggests that early interventions that promote phonemic awareness may reduce the number of young students referred for special education services (Lennon & Slesinski, 1999).

Phonemic awareness is composed of subskills and tasks that can be assessed by informal methods. For example, the skills of **phonemic synthesis** or blending of sounds, **phonemic analysis** or breaking the words into sounds, rhyming, and substitution, are some of the phonemic awareness skills that may be evaluated by educators (Snider, 1995). Assessment of subskills in preschool, such as rhyming, have been found to be significant predictors of later reading skills in first grade readers (Missall, Reschly, Betts,

McConnell, Heistad, et al 2007). Specific tasks used to assess phonemic awareness listed by Ehri et al. (2001) include

1. Phonemic isolation, which requires recognizing individual sounds in words; for example, "Tell me the first sound in paste." (/p/)
2. Phoneme identity, which requires recognizing the common sound in different words; for example; "Tell me the sound that is the same in bike, boy, and bell." (/b/)
3. Phoneme categorization, which requires recognizing the word with the odd sound in a sequence of three or four words, for example, "Which word does not belong? bus, bun, rug." (rug)
4. Phoneme blending, which requires listening to a sequence of separately spoken sounds and combining them to form a recognizable word; for example, "What word is /s//k//u//l/?" (school)
5. Phoneme segmentation, which requires breaking the word into its sounds by tapping out or counting the sounds or by pronouncing and positioning a marker for each sound; for example, "How many phonemes in sip?" (3:/s//i//p/)
6. Phoneme deletion, which requires recognizing what word remains when a specified phoneme is removed; for example, "What is smile without /s/?" (mile) (Ehri et al., 2001, p. 252)

An informal assessment instrument for assessing phonemic awareness was constructed by Snider (1997). This instrument, along with other published instruments to assess emerging reading skills, may be used to assess phonemic awareness in kindergarten students. Figure 10.3 presents sample items for the Test of Phonemic Awareness.

In addition to using informal assessment instruments designed by teachers, preacademic reading skills, such as identifying the sounds of letters or rhyming, may be assessed using many of the instruments previously presented in this text, such as the Woodcock Reading Mastery Test–Revised and instruments designed for use with preschool children, such as the Developmental Indicators for the Assessment of Learning, 3rd ed. (DIAL–3), and the Kaufman Brief Survey of Early Academic and Language Skills. The Woodcock–Johnson III Tests of Achievement include the subtest called Sound Awareness that contains rhyming, deletion, and substitution sections. The Wechsler Individual Achievement Test II includes items that assess rhyming and ability to determine words with the same initial and ending sounds. These instruments may assist with determining how a student compares to a norm sample population as well as determining the specific skills mastered.

In the following activity, you will construct a teacher-made instrument to measure phonemic awareness. Use the information presented in Figure 10.4 to develop your items.

Figure 10.3　Sample items from Test of Phonemic Awareness.

Phoneme Segmentation

Model: Today we're going to play a word game. I'm going to say a word and I want you to break the word apart. You are going to tell me each sound in order. For example, if I say cat, you say /c/ /a/ /t/. Let's try a few more words.

Directions: Say the sounds in _____.

Practice Items: to, dog

Test Items:

1. she

2. red

3. lay

Strip Initial Consonant

Model: Listen to the word task. If I take away the sound /t/, ask is left. What word is left? Let's try some more.

Directions: Listen to the word _____. If you take away the // sound, what word is left?

Practice items: ball, pink

Test Items:

1. told

2. hill

3. nice

Source: From "The relationship between phonemic awareness and later reading achievement, Test of Phonemic Awareness," by Vicki Snider. In *Journal of Educational Research* (Mar/Apr/97) *90*(4), pp. 203–212. Reprinted with permission of the Helen Dwight Reid Educational Foundation. Published by Heldref Publications, 1319 Eighteenth St., NW, Washington, DC 20036-1802. Copyright 1997.

ASSESSMENT OF CHILDREN REFERRED FOR AUTISM SPECTRUM DISORDERS

autism spectrum disorders A group of pervasive disorders that are characterized by significant difficulties in capacity for social reciprocity, communication delays, and repetitive behavior patterns.

The number of children with autism and **autism spectrum disorders** has been increasing in recent years. The Center for Disease Control and Prevention(CDC) estimates that approximately 1 in every 150 children who have an autism spectrum disorder (CDC, 2007). These disorders are under the category of Pervasive Developmental Disorders that include three primary areas of potential impairment (American Psychiatric Association, 2000). The areas of impairment include communication delays or abnormalities,

Figure 10.4   Sample Words for teaching letter sounds and phonemic awareness.

Lesson	New Letter Sound	Review	Rhyming [onset][rime]	Blending/ Segmenting
1	/a/		[s,f,m,r] {at} [z,l,r,sh] {ip}	am, an, if, at
2	/m/	a,m	[f,m,r,v] {an} [f,m,n,s] {eat}	am, me, up, mat
3	/t/	a,m,t	[s,v,m,n] {et} [l,r,s] {ock}	mat, miss, at, Sam, mit
4	/s/	a,m,t	[s,l,th,k] {ick} [l,r,s,p] {ay}	sat, fat, fit, sit, am, mad
5		a,m,t,s	[m,s,b,t] {ee} [f,n,g,s] {ame}	it, am, mat, fit, Sam, Sid
6	/i/	a,m,t,s	[f,c,v,p] {an} [b,f,r,h] {ed}	at, sit, if, fit, sad, mat
7		a,m,t s,i	[b,n,s,r] {ag} [k,l,p,th] {ick}	sat, it, am, fat, fit, miss
8	/f/	a,m,t s,i	[b,c,f,t] {all} [b,s,f,sh] {ell}	mad, Sid, fit, rat, dad, at
9		a,m,t s,i,f	[d,f,m,sh] {ine} [b,j,qu,t] {ack}	rad, fit, sad, add, rat, mit
10		a,m,t s,i,f	[b,h,l,s] {and} [b,d,j,l] {ump}	rag, sad, did, fit, at, mad

difficulties with social reciprocity or interactions with people, and patterns of unusual or repetitive behaviors. This disorder is typically manifested by the age of three but may not be recognized or diagnosed until later ages due to a variety of complicating issues (Overton, Fielding, Garcia de Alba, 2007).

Early indications that a child may have an autism spectrum disorder are that the child fails to have the social communication skills expected of a youngster (Filipek, 1999). These skills are expected to develop during the early toddler years and therefore children who do not begin to develop these skills may be referred for assessments during this developmental period. Although children may be assessed prior to their third birthday, generally, the

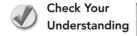

**Check Your
Understanding**

Check your ability to construct a teacher-made test of phonemic awareness by completing Activity 10.5 below.

Activity 10.5

Construction of a Teacher-Made Test of Phonemic Awareness

Look at the letter sounds and tasks presented in Figure 10.3 and Figure 10.4. Use these to construct a teacher-made test on phonemic awareness. For example, the first sound to assess is /a/. In order to make a rhyming item, provide an example of a rhyming word that uses the sounds /a//t/ or at. The words that may be formed using at and the other consonants provided are: sat, fat, mat, and rat.

Model: Listen to this word "at." I know some words that rhyme with "at": "mat and fat."

Next sound to be assessed is /i/.

Directions: Now listen to this word: zip. Tell me a word that rhymes with zip. (Acceptable responses might be lip, rip, ship).

Continue with the construction of the test for the following items:

Blending/segmenting of am, an, if, at. To blend, you ask the student to say sounds together that you first say in isolation. When the sounds are said together, they form a word (/a//m/ together is am). To make segmenting items, you provide an example of how a word sounds, then how it sounds when each sound is pronounced (am then /a//m/).

1. Model (blending):

2. Directions:

3. Model (segmenting):

4. Directions:

Substitution Items. These items make new words when one sound is replaced with another sound. (fat/rat). Use any of the words presented in Figure 10.4 for the items.

5. Model (substitution):

6. Directions:

Apply Your Knowledge

Use the information provided in Figure 10.3 and Figure 10.4 to complete an additional phonemic awareness item. This time, construct an item (model and directions) for the task of phoneme categorization. For this task, the student must tell you which word does not belong to a list of words.

Model:

Directions:

younger the child, the less reliable the assessment results. This lack of reliability at younger ages reflects the differences in development that occur during the early years.

The assessment of autism spectrum disorders, like other types of assessment for potential disabilities, involves observations and data collection from a variety of sources and environments. Moreover, the assessment of children referred for autism spectrum disorders should be developmentally appropriate as suggested by DEC (Sandall et al, 2005). Data should be collected from parents, early childhood caregivers, teachers, and most importantly, from direct assessment of the child. These methods should include rating scales, interviews, observations in the natural environment (home or early childhood classroom or daycare setting), and age appropriate assessment with specific diagnostic instruments for children referred for autism spectrum disorders. Selected screening and diagnostic instruments are presented below.

GILLIAM AUTISM RATING SCALE-2 (GARS-2)

The GARS-2 is a rating scale that can be used as a first step screening assessment for children who are suspected of having characteristics of an autism spectrum disorder. Children between the ages of 3 years to 22 years can be screened with this instrument. The GARS-2 may be completed by parents, teachers, or other educators or professionals who know the child. This brief screener requires approximately 10 minutes to complete. The three core areas of autism spectrum disorders, communication, social interactions, and stereotyped behaviors, are included within the items of this assessment. More than 1,100 children were included in the norming of this instrument and the sample was modeled on the U.S. 2000 Census data. This rating scale should be used for screening purposes only and children who appear to have characteristics within the three areas assessed should be referred for additional assessments.

CHILDHOOD AUTISM RATING SCALE (CARS)

The CARS is a rating scale that should be used as part of the screening for possible autism spectrum disorders. This is a very brief, fifteen item, rating scale that the examiner completes after observing the child. The items provide a means of rating the child on indicators such as adaptation to change, relating to people, and imitation. On each item, the child is rated as apropriate for the specific behavior, mildly abnormal, moderately abnormal, and severely abnormal. The child's total score falls within three diagnostic categories: Nonautistic, Autistic (mild to moderate autism), and Autistic (severe autism).

The examiner's manual includes data on the clinical sample of children upon which the instrument was developed. The results of assessment of more than 1,600 children were used to develop the instrument over a period of fourteen years. The ages of the children included in the initial development of the instrument range from 0 to 11 + years. The sample included 75% males and 25% females. Ethinic groups included in the manual were described as Black, White, and Other. IQ ranges presented for the sample were 0-69, 70-84, and 85 and older. Reliability information included internal consistency reliability research, interrater reliability information and test-retest reliability information. Validity information included criterion-related validity information. The manual is very short and contains guidance on the scoring criteria. This instrument, due to the limited number of items, is best used for screening purposes. Children who were initially assessed with this instrument and who appear to have the characteristics of an autism spectrum disorder, should be evaluated with additional direct assessment instruments and multiple observations in natural settings.

THE AUTISM DIAGNOSTIC OBSERVATION SCHEDULE (ADOS)

The ADOS has been referred to as the "gold standard" in the assessment of autism spectrum disorders. This instrument provides a method for direct assessment of children and adults who manifest the characteristics of autism. The ADOS assesses all behavioral areas of autism; however, cut-off scores are provided only for abnormalities in communication and abnormalities in reciprocal social interactions (Lord, Rutter, DiLavore, Risi, 2002). In order to assess repetitive stereotyped behaviors, additional assessments, such as the Autism Diagnostic Interview—Revised (Rutter, LeCourteur, & Lord, 2002), should be administered. The ADOS has four levels or modules of administration. The appropriate level for administration for a specific child is determined by their level of language development. For example, children who are nonverbal are administered Module 1 and adults who are verbal are administered Module 4.

The ADOS is difficult to learn and complex to score and it is recommended that a team of professionals administer the instrument and discuss the behavioral score for each item following the administration. It is also recommended that the administration of the instrument be video recorded so that the behaviors in question can be reviewed during the scoring process.

The instrument was developed using the results obtained employing earlier versions of the instrument, the PL-ADOS (pre-linguistice Autism Diagnostic Obsevation Schedule, DiLavore, Lord, & Rutter, 1995), and the 1989 version of the ADOS (Lord et al, 1989). The current ADOS includes items from these earlier versions and additional items developed to assess older and more verbal individuals (Lord et al, 2002).

The ADOS was developed primarily by using results of samples of children who were referred for evaluations for potential developmental disorders (Lord et al, 2002). Results from clinical centers were combined and the final sample upon which the ADOS was validated included all English speaking children and adults. The ethnicity was 80% Caucasion, 11% African American, 4% Hispanic, 2% Asian American, and 2% other or mixed ethnic groups. Information provided in the manual includes summary statistics for all four modules for autistic, PDD-NOS, and Non-Spectrum children and adults. Consistency was researched on the instrument by analysis of test-retest, interrater reliability, and internal consistency across all groups for the four modules. Even though this instrument is considered to be the highest standard for assessment of autism spectrum disorders, it is nonetheless a fairly new technique and research continues in the investigation of sensitivity and specificity (Gotham, Risi, Pickles, & Lord, 2007; Overton, Fielding, Garcia de Alba, 2007; Overton, Fielding, Garcia de Alba, in press).

THE AUTISM DIAGNOSTIC INTERVIEW-REVISED (ADI-R)

The ADI-R (Rutter et al, 2002), is an extensive clinical interview that should be completed by a professional trained in conducting interviews. In the school setting, the person most likely to conduct this type of interview would be the school psychologist, counselor, or clinical social worker. The interview may take up to 2 and 1/2 hours. The results of the interview can assist the clinical team in determining if the referred child has an autistic spectrum disorder and can assist the team in knowing what additional data may need to be collected. The ADI-R includes questions about early behaviors that may be characteristic of an autistic spectrum disorder. For example, there are several questions about regression of language skills and questions about repetitive behavior patterns. These items are not accounted for in the scoring of the ADOS and, therefore, it is recommended that both the ADOS and the ADI-R be used in the evaluation. These instruments, when used together along with other assessment techniques, are helpful in determining the specific disorder that may be manifest if it is not an autism spectrum disorder and can provide data to determine if more than one disorder is present (Overton, Fielding, Garcia de Alba, 2007). For example, children with autism may also exhibit symptoms of anxiety or depression. The team should employ a variety of methods to determine if the child has more than one area of concern.

ASSISTIVE TECHNOLOGY AND ASSESSMENT

assistive technology Any assistive device that enables persons with disabilities to function better in their environments.

Assistive technology is a term that is used to designate any device that a student requires to function within the academic environment. Such devices range from a specially designed spoon for eating to computer software that can transfer spoken language to written language. Assistive technology may also include computer

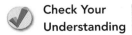

Check Your Understanding

Check your understanding of assessment for children who are referred for possible autism spectrum disorders by completing Activity 10.6 below.

Activity 10.6

Select the correct term for each statement below.

A. autism spectrum disorders   F. CARS
B. expressive language disor-   G. GARS-2
   ders   H. communication
C. receptive language disorders   I. repetitive patterns of behavior
D. ADOS   J. reciprocal social Interaction
E. ADI-R

_____ 1. The _____ is an instrument that a parent, teacher, or other professional uses to rate observations for children referred for autism spectrum disorders.

_____ 2. The _____ should be administered by a professional with training in clinical interviewing techniques.

_____ 3. A child who does not have oral language but may be average in other skills may have a(n) _____.

_____ 4. This instrument is considered the standard for direct assessment of autism spectrum disorders.

Apply Your Knowledge

What is the difference between the direct assessment methods and indirect assessment methods for assessing children referred for autism spectrum disorders? _____

_____

_____

software programs that are necessary for instructional purposes due to the specific type of disability manifested by the child.

In order to determine if any assistive technology devices may be required for a student with special needs, an **assistive technology evaluation** is conducted. This evaluation should be conducted by professionals who are knowledgeable about such techniques and equipment, and how to implement their use. The evaluation should include assessing the student's method of mobility, fine and gross motor needs, visual and auditory perceptual needs, accessibility needs to function within the environment, computer technology needs, communication needs, and any other area in which the child may require assistive devices.

Before the actual devices are selected, the student's general cognitive ability should be considered so that developmentally

assistive technology evaluation An assessment to determine what devices are needed to promote successful functioning within the school educational environment.

appropriate techniques and devices are employed. Once the student's assistive technology needs are determined, the evaluation must consider how the actual devices will be used within the environment. In addition to acquiring such devices, the student may need accommodations in order to use the devices. It is important that all devices be tested with the student so that it can be determined that selected devices fit the student's needs. All of these considerations will promote the student's ability to have access to the general educational curriculum as much as possible. The techniques and equipment that are required for a successful education should be documented in the student's IEP. It is imperative that the team monitor the student's use and success with any assistive technology deemed necessary for the student's education. As pointed out by Bryant (1998), part of the follow-up should include assessing the teacher's understanding and skill in using the assistive technology in the school setting.

TRANSITION AND POSTSECONDARY CONSIDERATIONS

transition planning
Planning for meeting students' needs following high school.

The legal requirements stated in the IDEA 2004 Amendments were presented in Chapter 2. The important components for educators include the inclusion within the IEP of the transitional needs of students from the beginning age of 16. The statement addressing these needs in the IEP must be updated each year and include the specific **transition planning** needed, as well as the areas of study required to meet those needs. By the time the student reaches 16, or sooner if determined necessary for the transition goals set out by the IEP team, the IEP must include information regarding other agencies and the responsibilities of stated agencies.

The other component that educators must remember is that one year before the student reaches the age of majority expressed in state law, the student must be informed of his or her rights that will be transferred to the student as the student reaches the age of majority. This is to be acknowledged in a statement of the IEP.

The emphasis on transitional services that assist students in their movement from school to adult life is a reflection of the data indicating negative outcomes for students with disabilities (Levinson, 1995; U.S. Department of Education, 1999; U.S. Department of Education, 2000). The number of students graduating from high school with a standard diploma has increased to 47.6% (U.S. Department of Education, 2004). The remaining 52.4% of students with disabilities who leave high school receive a certificate of completion, reach the maximum age for services, or simply drop out of school. Students with disabilities who are least likely to receive a high school diploma are students with emotional disturbance, mental retardation, multiple disabilities, and autism. Some of the disability groups for low incidence disorders had very few students included in the analysis (deafblindness). The graduate rates by disability are presented in Table 10.3.

One factor that may influence the number of students with disabilities who graduate from high school is the requirement by some states of exit examinations as criteria for graduation. Research indicates that students with disabilities are less likely to graduate if they are required to pass a high school exit examination. This finding was consistent regardless of the disability category; however, it

Table 10.3 Students ages 14 and older with disabilities who graduated with a standard diploma[a]: 1993–94[b] through 2001–02[b].

Disability	1993–94	1994–95	1995–96	1996–97	1997–98	1998–99[c]	1999–2000	2000–01	2001–02
					Percent				
Specific learning disabilities	49.1	47.7	48.2	48.8	51.0	51.9	51.6	53.6	56.9
Speech/language impairments	42.9	41.7	42.2	44.8	48.1	51.2	53.2	52.3	55.7
Mental retardation	35.0	33.8	34.0	33.0	34.3	36.0	34.4	35.0	37.8
Serious emotional disturbance	27.0	26.0	25.1	25.9	27.4	29.2	28.6	28.9	32.1
Multiple disabilities	36.1	31.4	35.3	35.4	39.0	41.0	42.3	41.6	45.2
Hearing impairments	61.9	58.2	58.8	61.8	62.3	60.9	61.4	60.3	66.9
Orthopedic impairments	56.7	54.1	53.6	54.9	57.9	53.9	51.5	57.4	56.4
Other health impairments	54.6	52.6	53.0	53.1	56.8	55.0	56.5	56.1	59.2
Visual impairments	63.5	63.7	65.0	64.3	65.1	67.6	66.4	65.9	70.8
Autism	33.7	35.5	36.4	35.9	38.7	40.5	40.8	42.1	51.1
Deaf-blindness[d]	34.7	30.0	39.5	39.4	67.7	48.3	37.4	41.2	49.1
Traumatic brain injury	54.6	51.7	54.0	57.3	58.2	60.6	56.8	57.5	64.4
All disabilities	43.5	42.1	42.4	43.0	45.3	46.5	46.1	47.6	51.1

Source: U.S. Department of Education, Office of Special Education Programs, Data Analysis System (DANS). Table 4-1 in vol 2. These data are for the 50 States, DC, Puerto Rico, and the four outlying areas.

[a]The percentage of students with disabilities who exited school with a regular high school diploma and the percentage who exit school by dropping out are performance indicators used by OSEP to measure progress in improving results for students with disabilities. The appropriate method for calculating graduation and dropout rates depends on the question to be answered and is limited by the data available. For reporting under the *Government Performance and Results Act* (GPRA), OSEP calculates the graduation rate by dividing the number of students age 14 and older who graduated with a regular high school diploma by the number of students in the same age group who are known to have left school (i.e., graduated with a regular high school diploma, received a certificate-of-completion, reached the maximum age for services, died, moved and are not known to be continuing in an education program or dropped out). These calculations are presented here.

[b]Data are based on a cumulative 12-month count.

[c]Two large states appear to have underreported dropouts in 1988–99. As a result, the graduation rate is somewhat inflated that year.

[d]Percentage is based on fewer than 200 students exiting school.

proved to be most significant for students with mental retardation and speech and language impairments (Thurlow, Ysseldyke, & Anderson, 1995). This may continue to have an impact on the numbers of students with disabilities who are able to graduate due to the assessment requirements of the IDEA 1997 Amendments. Recall that the 1997 Amendments mandate that the assessments for students with disabilities be consistent with the assessment of students without disabilities.

Individuals with disabilities who leave the school environment are less likely to be employed than persons without disabilities, and those who are employed are more likely to earn less than persons without disabilities (Kaye, 1998; Levinson, 1995). Persons with disabilities are likely to live at home with their parents or have other nonindependent arrangements (Levinson, 1995; U.S. Department of Education, 1995). Persons with disabilities who are able to live in the community are more likely to live alone with little social participation (Kaye, 1998). As Levinson states,

> There is little doubt that, given the high unemployment and underemployment rates among persons with disabilities, the high percentage who continue to live at home following the completion of high school, and the elevated dropout rate among students with disabilities, efforts in the area of special education have not resulted in their successful integration into society. (Levinson, 1995, p. 910)

The research findings and requirements of the federal regulations result in additional assessment responsibilities of educational personnel to meet students' needs as they exit the educational system. The assessment process should begin before the student reaches age 14 and needs to continue until the student has exited from the educational system.

ASSESSMENT OF TRANSITION NEEDS

The focus of the assessment process of students nearing their teen years should change to reflect postsecondary school needs. The student's functioning and needs should be determined in the areas of educational or instructional needs, vocational training or employment needs such as **supported employment**, community experiences, and adult daily living skills. The goals and objectives must include consideration of future plans to enter the adult world as independently as possible.

supported employment
Employing a person with a disability with persons without disabilities. Arrangement is for at least minimum wage and may include a job coach or other supports.

Research regarding best practice for transition assessment and planning has shown that the most successful transition plans with more successful outcomes result from involvement of both students and parents in the assessment and planning process (Brotherson & Berdine, 1993; Thoma, Rogan, & Baker, 2001). Student participation includes teaching students how to advocate for their needs or use the skills of self-determination (Lindsey, Whemeyer, Guy, & Martin,

2001). Self-determination has been defined as "a combination of skills, knowledge, and beliefs that enable a person to engage in goal directed, self-regulated, autonomous behavior" (Field, Martin, Miller, Ward, & Wehmeyer, 1998, p. 2). In order to assist students with their transition needs, educators must assess the student's ability to advocate for their own needs.

Assessment for transition planning incorporates both standardized assessment methods to determine educational achievement, cognitive functioning, behavioral functioning, and other areas as needed. For example, assessment measures such as the Wechsler Intelligence Scales for Children, Fourth Edition; the Wechsler Intelligence Scales for Adults, Third Edition, the Stanford-Binet V, the Woodcock-Johnson III Tests of Achievement and Tests of Cognitive Abilities, and the Wechsler Individual Achievement Tests II may be used throughout the school and transitional periods to assess intelligence and achievement.

Assessment for transition also includes assessing the career and vocational interests, skills, life skills, and social and leisure skills. Clark offered several suggestions for assessment to plan for transition (Clark, 1996, pp. 89–90). The following list is adapted from Clark:

1. Select assessment instruments and procedures on the basis of how to answer key questions in a student's individual transition planning: Who am I? What do I want in life, now and in the future? What are some of life's demands that I can meet now?

2. Make assessment ongoing starting as early as possible, but no later than age 14, and continuing through life.

3. Use multiple types and levels of assessment.

4. Make 3-year reevaluations for all secondary students—useful for their next placement or environment.

5. Assessment procedures should be efficient and effective.

6. Organize assessment data for easy access for IEP planning and instructional planning.

7. Arrange for one person to be responsible for coordinating the assessment process.

8. Develop a transition assessment approach that is not only cultural/language fair, but also culture/language enhanced–questions should be posed in culturally appropriate ways rather than reflecting only majority culture/language values.

Methods of determining the transitional needs of students include conducting a needs interview or using a commercially published instrument to determine such transition needs. One such instrument is the Transition Planning Inventory (Clark & Patton, 1997).

TRANSITION PLANNING INVENTORY: UPDATED VERSION (TPI-UV)

This inventory contains four inventory forms: Student Form, Home Form, School Form, and Further Assessment Recommendations Form (Clark & Patton, 2006). The forms contain items on which the student, parent, and educational personnel rate the student's current functioning. The Home Form is available in the following languages: Spanish, Chinese, Japenese, and Korean. The items survey the domains of employment, further education and training, daily living, leisure activities, community participation, health, self-determination, communication, and interpersonal relationships. The student form also includes questions of career awareness, future plans for living and working, community participation, and leisure and hobby interests. The forms are easy to administer. This instrument allows for multiple informants to participate in assessing transition needs for the student. The authors state that this instrument may be used to determine the future transition needs of any student. The updated edition of the TPI includes the additional resource publication, Informal Assessments for Transition Planning (Clark, Patton, and Moulton, 2000). Another publication is available that incorporated the TPI, Case Studies in Assessment for Transition Planning (Trainor, Patton, & Clark, 2005).

Technical Data

Instrument Construction Because the TPI is not a norm-referenced instrument, the information included in the test manual focuses on test development and on the reliability and validity of the inventory. The authors indicate that the 46 transition planning statements reflect the domains used across various states. The instrument may be administered in alternative ways for students with special needs. An explanation of the expected student behaviors for each item is included in the manual. For example, for an education/training item of "Knows how to gain entry to an appropriate post-school community employment training program," the explanation provided is: "Student knows how to find and get into an on-the-job training program of interest to the student" (Clark & Patton, 2006).

Reliability The internal reliability was studied using coefficient alpha, and the reliability coefficients ranged between .70 and .95. Test-retest reliability coefficients ranged from .70 to .98.

Validity Information for evidence of content and criterion-related validity is included in the manual. Evidence suggests that the TPI was viewed as including necessary content for transition planning.

ASSESSING FUNCTIONAL ACADEMICS

As previously stated, the standardized assessment instruments as well as informal methods may be used to assess the current level of academic functioning of students with transition needs. The informal methods presented in Chapter 8 are very appropriate for determining the level of academic functioning as it applies to everyday living situations.

In addition to previously mentioned methods and tests, the Kaufman Functional Academic Skills Test (K-FAST) may be used (Kaufman & Kaufman, 1994). It is presented in the following section.

KAUFMAN FUNCTIONAL ASSESSMENT SKILLS TEST (K-FAST)

The K-FAST was designed to be administered individually to adolescent and adult students (Kaufman & Kaufman, 1994). This instrument assesses the skills needed for the math and reading skills required in everyday life situations. The authors state that this test was not designed to replace other existing achievement batteries, but rather to add information regarding a student's competency for functioning outside the school environment. The instrument

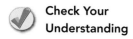

Check Your Understanding

Check your ability to determine the transition needs of a student by completing Activity 10.7 below.

Activity 10.7

Use the student profile from the Transition Planning Inventory to determine the transition needs for Jimmy.
    List possible needs below:

1. Employment needs:

2. Further education/training:

3. Daily living:

4. Leisure activities:

5. Community participation:

6. Health:

7. Self-determination:

8. Communication:

9. Interpersonal relationships:

Apply Your Knowledge

Use the information obtained from the TPI to write a behavioral objective for Jimmy's self-determination needs. _____
_____
_____

presents the items in an easel format with oral instructions by the examiner. The math items include such content as the value of money, telling time, reading graphs, and more difficult items covering percentages and calculating the area of a room. The reading items include reading signs, symbols, recipes, and want ads. The test may be administered to persons ranging from age 15 to age 75 and older. The scores provided include standard scores, percentile ranks, and descriptive categories.

Technical Data

Norming Process   The development of the K-FAST included developmental versions and tryout exams. The total representative standardization sample included 1,424 people from 27 states. The variables were age, gender, geographic region, socioeconomic status of parents or of examinees, and race/ethnic groups. The sample reflected the U.S. population in terms of characteristics and distribution of abilities when compared with the theoretical normal distribution.

Reliability   Two measures of reliability were obtained for the K-FAST, including split-half reliability for internal consistency and test-retest reliability for consistency across time. Internal reliability coefficients ranged from .83 to .97. The test-retest coefficients ranged from .84 to .91.

Validity   The validity was studied using factor analytic studies for construct validity, developmental changes as support for construct validity, and concurrent criterion-related validity with general intellectual measures. The validity coefficients varied on the comparisons with tests of general intelligence; however, validity appears to range from adequate to high.

Case Study on Transition Planning

Eric's parents met with his teacher and the school counselor for a conference about Eric's future plans. His parents reported that Eric gets along very well with all family members and with the other children in the neighborhood. They stated that they are allowing Eric to participate in the driver's education course at school. They have not decided if Eric will be able to take his driver's test and stated they are waiting to hear from the instructor regarding Eric's ability to drive. Eric's father said that he has taken Eric out for some practice runs in a neighborhood parking lot on Sundays when there is no traffic in the area.

Eric's parents expressed concern about Eric's independence and were especially eager to learn ways to assist Eric in learning independent living skills. His mother reported that she has made attempts to engage Eric in learning how to cook but that he is not really interested. She said that he would live on pizza if the choice were left to him. Eric's parents said that they envision Eric living in his own apartment someday and marrying. They hope that he will be able to have a steady job and be able to support a family. They also stated that Eric currently has a crush on a neighborhood girl who lives on their block, but that she is not very interested in Eric.

This has been a little difficult for Eric to understand, but his father reported that Eric seems to be feeling better about this issue. Mr. and Mrs. Parks are interested in Eric continuing with a vocational training program as long as possible. They also reported that they will assist Eric financially, if needed, to complete enough training so that he can maintain a job. They were interested in learning of outside community agencies where they could go for assistance after Eric leaves the public school setting.

Transitional Planning Inventory

Areas of Need Indicated by Student (Completed with assistance of teacher)

Employment

How to get a job

General job skills and work attitude

Further Education and Training

How to gain entry into a community employment training program

Daily Living

How to locate a place to live

How to set up living arrangements

How to manage money

Community Participation

Understanding basic legal rights

How to make legal decisions

How to locate community resources

How to use community resources

How to obtain financial assistance

PARENT INTERVIEW

Eric's parents agreed with the areas of need identified by Eric and added the following concerns:

Self-Determination

How to recognize and accept his own strengths and limitations

How to express his ideas and feelings appropriately

How to set personal goals

Interpersonal Relationships

How to get along with supervisor

INTERVIEW WITH ERIC

Eric was excited to come into the office for his interview. He said that his parents had told him about their interview the day before and now it was his turn to talk about getting a job and an apartment someday. Eric said that his favorite part of school is when he goes to the vocational training center in the afternoons. He likes learning about the mechanical aspects of cars. He also reported that the last activity of the day is his driver's education class. He hopes to be able to pass his driving test by the end of the school year but remarked that he may not be able to do that until next year.

Eric stated that he wants to get an apartment someday when he is older, "like when I am about 40." He said that he enjoys living with his parents and he enjoys living in his neighborhood. He stated that even if he moved into an apartment, he wanted to remain in the area where he currently lives. He said that he knows his way around and wants to live close to his friends.

Eric reported that he wants to learn more about how to get a job so that when his training is completed, he can start to work right away. He said he would like to save his money to buy a car. He said that he is not really anxious to live by himself and that he doesn't know much about buying groceries or doing laundry. He said his mother usually helps him with these chores.

With this information, Eric's teacher was able to complete task analyses on the target skills. Following this analysis, Eric's teacher and parents designed specific objectives and interventions to assist Eric with his transition needs. To monitor the progress of Eric as this instruction was implemented, his teacher used curriculum-based measurement to determine if Eric was making adequate progress.

RESEARCH AND ISSUES RELATED TO TRANSITION PLANNING AND ASSESSMENT

The outcomes for students with disabilities continue to be problematic. Research indicates, for example, that young women with learning disabilities tend to be at risk for early-age pregnancy and for single motherhood (Levine & Nourse, 1998).

Although self-determination has been cited as best practice for the development of effective transition planning, research indicates that students are not participating in a manner reflecting self-determination in the transition/IEP process (Thoma et al., 2001). These researchers found that students with cognitive disabilities attended meetings but were not active during the meetings. Moreover, teachers and parents tended to discuss issues about the students rather than engaging the students in the discussion.

Postsecondary research assessing the admission process and accommodations for students continuing their education in 2- and 4-year schools indicates that accommodations are applied inconsistently (Vogel, Leonard, Scales, Hayeslip, Hermansen, & Donnells, 1998). Differences were found in where and how services were delivered to students with disabilities.

Even though students are to be told their rights in the education process that will transfer to them upon reaching the age of majority, individuals with cognitive disabilities are often assumed to lack the competence to assert their opinions about their own education (Lindsey et al., 2001). This appears to be the case even though most students have not legally been declared as incompetent under state law.

Even when students are included in the formal planning process, there are a number of areas that should be evaluated to assist in determining the student's ability to transition well after the secondary school years. For example, students should be evaluated to determine their strengths and weakness in problem-solving, self-evaluation, self-monitoring, and communication skills (Hong, Ivy, Gonzalez, & Ehrensberger, 2007). These skills, along with self-determination, may increase the likelihood of post-secondary success.

In a study analyzing how parenting and family patterns influence post-secondary outcomes for students with disabilities, it was determined that students from families in which the parents exposed their children to employment and career activities fared better after high school (Lindstrom, Doren, Metheny, Johnson, & Zane, 2007). It was also noted that students whose parents acted as advocates tended to have better employment adjustments than students whose parents were protective and better than students whose parents were disengaged from the post-secondary process. This may suggest that these parents modeled more deterministic behavior and that their children were more engaged themselves in the post-secondary planning and outcomes.

Think Ahead

Once the student has been administered a battery of tests, the teacher must be able to interpret the results and make educational recommendations. The next chapter includes the steps for test interpretation.

EXERCISES

Part I

Match the correct terms with the statements that follow.

a. PL 99-457
b. developmental delays
c. phonemic synthesis
d. biological risk factors
e. environmental risk factors
f. IFSP
g. family-centered program
h. family-focused program
i. arena assessment
j. phoneme awareness
k. situational questionnaire
l. ecobehavioral interview
m. play evaluations
n. phonemic analysis

_____ 1. This technique used in the assessment of infants and toddlers may decrease the time spent in assessment.

_____ 2. Once the family's needs and the young child's needs are determined, the information is used to complete _____ .

_____ 3. When a child is asked to sound out each isolated sound in a whole word, the teacher is requiring the child to use

_____ .

_____ 4. Among the possible reasons for _____ are physical development behind that of age peers and cognitive functioning below the levels expected.

_____ 5. The transition needs of students age 16 years and older are required to be included in a student's IEP by the 1997 Amendments of IDEA; _____ mandate services for children aged 3 to 5 with disabilities.

_____ 6. When a child appears to behave and function differently in specific situations, a _____ may be used to assess these behaviors or abilities.

_____ 7. When a child is able to hear and say isolated sounds, recognize that sounds make up words, discriminate between sounds, provide rhyming words to target words, substitute sounds upon request, and identify words with specific sounds, the child is demonstrating evidence of _____ .

Part II

Answer the following questions.

1. What are some criticisms and issues of family involvement as specified in early-childhood assessment?

_____

_____

2. What are the clinical indications that an infant may need a full evaluation according to Mayes (1991)?

_____

_____

3. What areas are assessed when infants are evaluated? Describe these areas in your answer.

_____

_____

4. What are some general considerations and problems of assessing infants, toddlers, and young children?

_____

_____

Part III

List and discuss some of the
ment and planning.

452

1. _____
   _____

2. _____
   _____

3. _____
   _____

4. _____
   _____

Answers to these questions can be found in th
text or you may also complete these questions and
ate feedback on your answers by going to the Think A
in Chapter 10 of the Companion Website.

COURSE PROGRESS MONITORING ASSESSMENT

See how you are doing in the course after the conclusion of PART
chapters by completing the following assessment. When you are
finished, check your answers with your instructor or on the Companion Website *www.prenhall.com/overton*. Once you know your
score, return to Figure 1.8, Student Progress Monitoring Graph in
Chapter 1 and plot your progress.

Progress Monitoring Assessment

Select the best answer. Some of these terms may be used more than
once.

a. Standardized tests   h. ADI-R
b. Age Equivalent   i. IDEA 2004
c. Reliability coefficient   j. Estimated true score
d. Negatively skewed   k. Disproportionality
e. RTI   l. Progress Monitoring
f. WISC-IV   m. TPI-UV
g. FBA   n. NCLB

_____ 1. The indicator of common variance of two variables.

_____ 2. A developmental score that may not be very useful to
           interpret.

_____ 3. The visual representation when more scores are located
           above the mean.

_____ 4. This is an extensive clinical developmental interview that
           is used to make a determination of an autism spectrum
           disorder.

_____ 5. One component of this legislation was to improve teacher quality.

_____ 6. This test includes a working memory index, perceptual reasoning index, and a processing speed index as well as verbal measures.

_____ 7. This measure indicates how much error may be on a test based on the score's distance from the mean.

_____ 8. When students from a specific group are over/under represented in specific eligibility categories.

_____ 9. These instruments are structured to ensure that all students are administered the items in the same manner so that comparisons can be made more reliably.

_____10. This will assist teachers in determining the function of problematic behaviors.

Fill in the Blanks

_____11. Both _____ and _____ require that students be instructed using research-based interventions.

_____12. The _____ includes a measure of the student's attitude toward math.

_____13. The square root of $1 - .r$ is one variable used to determine the _____.

_____14. On the UNIT, the _____ subtest uses a pencil and paper to measure reasoning and planful behavior.

_____15. _____ is noted by a vertical line on the student data graph.

_____16. The blending of isolated sounds into a whole word is called _____.

_____17. The _____ is a measure of preschool students' language development that is based on a two-dimensional language model.

_____18. In order to determine if a student is within the range of mental retardation, cognitive ability and _____ are assessed.

_____19. IDEA requires that _____ is obtained prior to assessment.

_____20. _____ are a group of disorders that are characterized by abnormalities in communication, social interactions, and repetitive patterns of behavior.

Interpretation of
Assessment Results

CHAPTER 11
Interpreting Assessment for Educational Intervention

Interpreting Assessment for Educational Intervention

educational planning
eligibility decisions
behaviorally stated short-term
    objectives
benchmarks

long-term goals
interindividual interpretation
intra-individual interpretation
cross-battery assessment

CHAPTER FOCUS

When students have not responded to interventions made by teachers and other professionals, the student may then be referred for a more comprehensive assessment as part of the problem-solving process. Following the assessment, the meeting with the team is conducted to determine if a student requires special education support in order to make educational progress. In some cases, these students will be determined eligible for services through special education. The team must then use the test data to design educational goals and objectives.

This chapter provides suggestions for interpreting test results and designing educational goals for appropriate interventions. You will be presented with a complete case that includes test scores, interpretations, goals, and objectives. Test results help educators make decisions about educational interventions, planning, and possible eligibility for special education services. After the professional interprets a student's test results from norm-referenced tests, classroom observations, informal assessment, and parental input, the team members use the results as part of the data to make a decision concerning eligibility, interventions, and if age appropriate, long-term transition plans. The teacher then uses curriculum-based assessment, teacher-made tests, and direct measurement techniques to monitor progress and adapt instruction.

CEC KNOWLEDGE AND SKILLS STANDARDS

The student completing this chapter will understand the knowledge and skills included in the following CEC Knowledge and Skills Standards from Standard 8: Assessment:

CC8S5—Interpret information from formal and informal assessments.

CC8S6—Use assessment information in making eligibility, program, and placement decisions for individuals with exceptional learning needs, including those from culturally and/or linguistically diverse backgrounds.

CC8S7—Report assessment results to all stakeholders using effective communication skills.

Test results are most useful when interpreted and presented in a clear format with specific information relating to educational and behavioral strategies. The regulations of the 1997 Amendments to IDEA require that assessment data be interpreted and used to develop educational and behavioral interventions that will be of benefit to the student. Hoy and Retish (1984) determined that test reports generally lacked the characteristics necessary for ease of **educational planning**. In this chapter, a model of interpreting test results to assist with **eligibility decisions** and plan program interventions is presented. The second part of the chapter illustrates how to use test results to write effective **behaviorally stated short-term objectives**, **benchmarks**, and **long-term goals** and how to continue to monitor student progress through direct assessment.

When interpreting the results of standardized tests, classroom observations, student interviews, parent interviews, questionnaires, surveys, and other methods of assessment, it is important to remember the holistic view of the child or adolescent as well as the environment from which the child comes. Tharinger and Lambert (1990) offered the following guidelines for the assessment and interpretive process*:

1. A child is dependent on the environment to fulfill basic physiological and psychological needs.
2. A child's family is the most active shaper of her or his environment.
3. A child is also an active participant in shaping her or his environment.
4. A child's functioning is multiply and transactionally determined.
5. A child strives to adapt to her or his environment regardless of the health of the environment.
6. A child's motivations for her or his behavior may not be conscious.
7. A child's attachment, separations, and losses are very significant factors in her or his psychological development.
8. A child's current functioning must be evaluated in light of her or his past functioning.
9. A child's behavior can only be understood in relation to current context and the influence of past contexts.
10. As a child develops, conflicts, tensions, and problems are inevitable and necessary. The important factor for assessment is how the child and significant others respond to these conflicts.

educational planning Interventions and strategies used to promote educational success.

eligibility decisions The determination of whether a student will receive special education services.

behaviorally stated short-term objectives Observable and measurable objectives that provide evidence of a student's progress toward annual goals.

benchmarks The major markers that provide evidence of a student's progress toward annual goals.

long-term goals Statements of anticipated progress that a student will make in one year upon which the short-term objectives and benchmarks are based.

11. If the child's thoughts, behaviors, or feelings appear atypical, it is important to consider where, under what circumstances, and at what developmental level this thought pattern, behavior, or emotional expression would make sense.

12. Both the child and her significant environments (i.e., school and home) need to be assessed. (p. 95)

INTERPRETING TEST RESULTS FOR EDUCATIONAL DECISIONS

One purpose of the assessment process is to consider test results to determine if a student requires interventions provided through special education services. Eligibility is determined by using set criteria stated in IDEA. These criteria may vary from state to state for the different types of disabilities but must remain within the IDEA guidelines. This means that the definitions and criteria may be written by the state; however, students who would be found eligible according to the federal law must not be excluded by the state criteria. The scope of this text focuses primarily on mild to moderate disabilities. The most common types of mild to moderate disabilities are learning disabilities, mental retardation, speech/language impairment, and emotional or behavioral disturbances. Students with attention disorders are also often served by educators who teach students with mild to moderate disabilities. These students may be served in the general education environment under the provisions of Section 504 of the Rehabilitation Act of 1973 (refer to Chapter 2) or under the IDEA category of "other health impaired" if the attention problem does not coexist with another disability, such as a learning disability.

The criteria for the qualification of a specific category and eligibility for special education services as stated in IDEA are used as a basis for interpreting test results. Table 11.1 lists the criteria for mild to moderate disabilities as well as the common characteristics of students with attention deficit disorders.

THE ART OF INTERPRETING TEST RESULTS

Most of this text has focused on quantitative measurement, informal data collection, and information from multiple informants about student abilities. A teacher or diagnostician may know how to effectively administer test items, score tests, and collect data; however, the art of interpreting meaning from all of the data and information must also be mastered. Accurate interpretation involves

Table 11.1 Key diagnostic criteria of IDEA for attention disorders and mild/moderate disabilities.

Disability	Key Criteria	Assessment Devices
Mental retardation	Subaverage intellectual, academic, and adaptive behavior (2 or more standard deviations below expectancy for age and according to generally accepted guidelines)	Standardized IQ tests, academic achievement and diagnostic tests, adaptive behavior scales, parent interviews, classroom observations
Learning disability	Average or above in intelligence; specific deficits in academics, cognitive language, or perceptual processing weaknesses may be used. Discrepancy between cognitive ability and achievement NOT required. Response to evidence-based or research-based interventions and performance on academic work should be considered in the decision-making process.	Standardized IQ test, academic achievement and diagnostic tests, classroom observations, permanent products, informal measures, parent interviews, perceptual-motor tests, curriculum-based measurement
Emotional disturbance	Behavioral or emotional difficulties that interfere with academic or developmental progress: unexplained physical problems, pervasive unhappiness, withdrawal, and so on	Standardized IQ tests, academic achievement and diagnostic tests, clinical interviews, parent interviews, classroom observations, projective tests, personality or behavioral inventories, DSM-IV criteria
Speech/language impairment	Communication difficulty that interferes with academic progress, ability to speak, or normal developmental progress	Speech or language diagnostic tests, classroom observations, parent interviews, academic achievement tests
Attention deficit disorders		
1. With hyperactivity	Externalizing behaviors, talking out, talking too much, impulsive actions, activity level beyond developmental expectations, poor schoolwork, incomplete or missing assignments	DSM–IV evaluation, behavioral ratings by different persons and in different environments, Continuous Performance Tests, cognitive and achievement tests, multiple direct classroom observations
2. Inattentive type	Poor schoolwork, incomplete or missing assignments, confusion, excessive daydreaming, self-distracting behavior, difficulty following directions and following through	Same as for hyperactive type

Disability	Key Criteria	Assessment Devices
3. Combined (hyperactivity and inattention)	Combination of characteristics found in hyperactive and inattentive ADD	Same as for hyperactive type
4. Autism spectrum disorders	Significant deficits in the capacity for social reciprocity, abnormalities in communication, repetitive, restrictive, stereotyped patterns of behavior	Indirect assessment using rating scales, observations in natural environment, direct assessment of child (ADOS for example) developmental clinical interview with caregivers

interindividual interpretation
Comparing a student to a peer norm group.

intra-individual interpretation
Comparing a student with his or her own performance.

both **interindividual** and **intra-individual interpretation** of test results. Interindividual interpretation involves comparing the student with other students in the norm group to determine how different the student is from that group. Intra-individual interpretation may be even more important than interindividual interpretation. For intra-individual interpretation, the teacher uses the test results and other data collected to compare the student's own performances in determining strengths and weaknesses. These strengths and weaknesses are then used in effective educational and behavioral planning.

Generally, all possible areas of suspected disability are assessed according to the recommended tests and evaluation measures given in Table 11.1. The following procedures are suggested for evaluating the student and interpreting test results.

1. *Parental permission.* The professional must secure parental permission before conducting an individual assessment or making a referral.

2. *Screening for sensory impairments or physical problems.* Before a psychoeducational evaluation is recommended, the student's vision, hearing, and general physical health should be screened. When these areas are found to be normal or corrections for vision/hearing impairments are made, the evaluation procedure can continue.

3. *Parent interview.* The professional should question the parent regarding the student's progress, development, developmental history, family structure, relationships with family and peers, and independent adaptive behavior functioning.

4. *Intellectual and academic assessment.* The team members should administer an intelligence measure and academic

Check Your Understanding

To check your understanding of the mild/moderate criteria, complete Activity 11.1 below.

Activity 11.1

Answer the following questions.

1. What are the general criteria used to determine if a student is functioning within the range of mental retardation? _____

2. Which term listed in Table 11.1 is used when the student has communication problems affecting developmental progress? _____

3. Which term listed in Table 11.1 indicates that a student has discrepancies between ability and academic performance? _____

4. In determining _____, behavioral observations, clinical interviews, information from multiple informants, and projective tests may be used. _____

5. Which tests are typically administered to assess for the possibility of learning disabilities? _____

6. For what categories of disabilities are classroom observations recommended as part of the assessment process? _____

7. What are the key components for the assessment of autism spectrum disorders? _____

Apply Your Knowledge

How are the characteristics of students with attention disorders with hyperactivity and the characteristics of students with attention disorders, inattentive type, similar? How are they different?
_____
_____
_____

achievement or diagnostic instrument, conduct classroom observations, and complete an informal evaluation.

5. *Behavioral assessment.* If the assessment and the information from the parents and teacher indicate behavioral, emotional, or attention problems, the student should also be assessed by a school or clinical psychologist to obtain behavioral, emotional, and personality information.

6. *Test interpretation.* Several members of the evaluation team may interpret test results. The team members may write separate or combined reports. In interpreting results, the assessment team should accomplish the following:

a. Rule out any sensory acuity problems and refer to or consult with medical personnel if physical problems are suspected.

b. Determine whether any home conflicts are present and refer to school psychologist or school counselor if they are suspected or indicated.

c. If appropriate, consideration of previous educational experiences and how these experiences may have influenced student's achievement (such as frequent moves, migrant student experiences, period of time student has lived in the United States, parents' educational experiences and views on the education process, and frequent absences).

d. If appropriate, consideration should be given and assessment should be conducted of any language factors (assessment to determine primary language should be completed during the referral/assessment process, interviews to determine language spoken in the home, and for bilingual students, determination of proficiency level in both languages).

e. Determine whether learning or school problems are exhibited in a particular school environment (unstructured play or lunchroom) or are associated with one subject area or a particular teacher, peer, or adult.

f. Compare ability on intellectual, academic, or adaptive behavior measures. Are there apparent discrepancies in functioning? Do perceptual or motor deficits appear to influence ability in specific academic areas? Is the student functioning higher in one area than in others? Is the student functioning significantly below expectancy in one or more areas? How do the formal test results compare with classroom assessments?

g. Determine whether emotional/behavioral problems exist. Does the student appear to be progressing slowly because of behavioral or emotional difficulties? Does the student adapt well in various situations? Does the student have good relationships with peers and adults? Is attention or activity level interfering with academic and social progress? Does a functional behavioral assessment need to be completed?

h. Determine whether speech/language problems are present. Is the student having difficulty understanding language or following oral lectures or directions? Does the student make articulation errors that are not age appropriate?

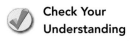

To check your understanding of the procedures for evaluation, complete Activity 11.2 below.

Activity 11.2

Complete the following sentences.

1. Before a decision is made that involves educational or intellectual ability, screening for _____ should be completed.

2. If there appears to be a conflict in the home or emotional or behavioral problems are suspected, the student should be referred for _____.

3. If a student has average or above intellectual functioning, average emotional/behavioral functioning, and average adaptive behavior skills but has significant difficulty in academic areas and specific fine-motor ability, he may be determined to have _____.

4. A student who is below expectancy in all academic areas, is subaverage in intellectual functioning, and has below-average adaptive behavior may be found to be functioning within the range of _____.

5. A student who has a communication problem that is affecting her relationships with peers and her ability to progress in school may have a _____.

6. A student who has impulsive behavior, acts out, has difficulty completing schoolwork, exhibits too much activity when observed, and whose parents and teachers rate as having these types of behavioral problems may be found to have _____.

Apply Your Knowledge

The initial stage of the assessment process should be concerned with _____
_____
_____

As these questions are answered, the diagnostician or special education teacher begins to form a picture of how the student processes information and how the strengths and weaknesses noted during test performance and observations may affect learning and behavior. From these interpretations, the teacher can make recommendations that will provide educational intervention and support to benefit the student and promote academic progress. The psychoeducational report or reports are then written to facilitate appropriate intervention strategies.

INTELLIGENCE AND ADAPTIVE BEHAVIOR TEST RESULTS

Cognitive or intellectual measures are generally administered by school psychologists, clinical psychologists, or educational diagnosticians. The results from these tests should be interpreted and used to plan educational interventions. Interindividual interpretations may indicate that the student is within the range of mental retardation or, has a specific learning disability, emotional disturbance, developmental immaturity, or average or above-average intellectual functioning. Intra-individual interpretations should be provided by the person who administered the tests. These interpretations may pinpoint specific demonstrated strengths as well as problems with distractibility, attention deficits, auditory short-term memory, visual retention, verbal comprehension, abstract visual reasoning, visual memory difficulties, and so on. Interpretation of the cognitive measures may refer to patterns of functioning noticed. Patterns of functioning may be explained as significant differences between verbal areas of functioning and visual-motor abilities, spatial reasoning or functioning, or perceptual-organization abilities. These patterns may be indicated by significant weaknesses in particular areas or by more global scores, such as significant differences between verbal and performance IQ scores (e.g., a verbal IQ of 108 and a performance IQ of 71). These weaknesses or discrepancies may be linked to particular learning difficulties. The examiner's descriptions of the student's performance may help the team plan effective educational strategies.

cross-battery assessment
Comparing a student's performance in specific areas of processing or skills across more than one instrument.

A more in depth analysis of cognitive processing scores across several instruments may be included in the interpretation of results by the school psychologist, school neuropsychologist, or a clinical psychologist. This type of analysis, in which a student's skills and abilities are analyzed across several instruments is known as **cross-battery assessment** (Flanagan & Harrison, 2005; Flanagan & Ortiz, 2001). Specifically, this type of interpretation has a theoretical basis in the CHC theory of cognitive ability. This type of analysis is often used to evaluate the abilities of students who are referred for learning disabilities, traumatic brain injury, neurodevelopmental disorders, or other types of disabilities that originate from frank organic brain abnormalities (Miller, 2007).

EDUCATIONAL ACHIEVEMENT AND DIAGNOSTIC TEST RESULTS

The educator may be responsible for administering norm-referenced educational achievement and other diagnostic tests. Scoring these instruments may be somewhat mechanical, although great care should be taken when scoring tests and interpreting the results. The first method of interpretation involves interindividual interpretation: Compare the student with age/grade expectations.

Data provided on norm tables will enable the examiner to determine how a student compares with age/grade peers. Is the student significantly above expectations (in the 90th percentile, for example)? Is the student average (in the 50th percentile range) on some measures but significantly below peers (below the 10th percentile) on other measures? The examiner must plot a profile of how the student performs when compared to these expectations.

Intra-individual interpretation means that the examiner will identify specific strengths and weaknesses in academic achievement, other abilities, and behavioral areas. Because the areas of strength and weakness should be defined as specifically as possible, tests that provide error analysis are most helpful. This analysis can be broken down further by task and used to develop teacher-made tests or informal probes if more information is needed.

WRITING TEST RESULTS

Interpreting and writing test results so that meaningful information is available for the persons responsible for the delivery of educational service is the most important concern when preparing reports. Bagnato (1980) suggested the following guidelines for making psychoeducational reports easy to use in the development of IEPs:

1. Be organized by multiple developmental or functional domains rather than only by tests given.
2. Describe specific areas of strength and skill deficits in clear behavioral terms.
3. Emphasize process variables and qualitative features regarding the child's learning strategies.
4. Highlight lists of developmental ceilings, functional levels, skill sequences, and instructional needs upon which assessment/ curriculum linkages can be constructed to form the IEP.
5. Detail efficient suggestions regarding behavioral and instructional management strategies. (p. 555)

Although psychoeducational reports may differ in format, they include the same general content. Typically, the identifying information is presented first: student name, date of birth, parents' names, address, grade placement, date(s) of evaluation, methods of evaluation, and the name of the examiner. Presented next is the background and referral information, which may include sociological information such as the size of family, student's relationship with family members, other schools attended, and any previous academic, behavioral, developmental, or health problems.

Following the preliminary information are the test results. An interpretation is presented, and recommendations for interventions, further evaluations, or changes in placement are then suggested. The following is an outline of a psychoeducational report.

I. Identifying Data
II. Background and Referral Information
    A. Background
    B. Referral
    C. Classroom Observation
    D. Parent Information
III. Test Results
IV. Test Interpretations
V. Summary and Conclusions
    A. Summary
    B. Recommendations for Educational Interventions
    C. Recommendations for Further Assessment

Writing style is also important in writing test results. Words should be selected carefully to convey an objective assessment. Goff (2002) suggested specific guidelines for educators to follow in report preparation when normative tests are used. These guidelines, presented in Table 11.2, include samples of educators' reports and suggested improvements.

Table 11.2   Guidelines for writing objective reports.

Background Information

- Make sure that all statements are attributed. The statement *Jack's mother is very supportive, which contributes to his academic success* is not attributed. Jack's father may strongly disagree if there is a custody battle. This statement could easily be rewritten to attribute the comment to its source: *Ms. Jones, Jack's teacher, reported that Jack's mother has been very supportive and that this support has contributed to Jack's academic success.*

- Do not ask the reader to make assumptions. The statement *Her teacher reports a noticeable difference in Jill's attention span when she does not take her medication* requires the reader to make an assumption. Some students will perform better when not on medication because they become more diligent in monitoring their own behavior to prove they do not need it.

Classroom Observations and Test Observations

- Make sure that you provide observations, not interpretations of behavior. The statement *James really liked the lesson* is an interpretation. This could be rewritten as *James stated, "I really like this work."* NOTE: This is not an interpretation because you are directly quoting Jack. The statement *The work he was given was too hard for James* is also an interpretation and could be rewritten as *James did not complete the more difficult items successfully.*

Test Results

- Make a standard comment about the mean and standard deviation of the test used. For example: *The standard scores for the WJ—III have a mean of 100 and a standard deviation of 15.*

- Report standard scores, percentile ranks, and standard errors of measure. Report both subtest scores and composite or broad area scores. A table in the body of the report or at the end is usually the clearest way to communicate this information.

continued.

Table 11.2 continued.

Test Interpretation

- Discuss clear strengths and weaknesses in performance only if variation in scores reaches statistical significance (usually to the .05 level). Otherwise, the variation should be considered to be normal variability.

Summary and Conclusions

- Tie a review of the Background Information, Observations, Test Results, and Test Interpretation together in summary form. Your summary should pull everything together.
- Your strongest conclusions will be based on concerns supported by Background Information, Observations, and Test Interpretation.

  Observations and evaluation data support the parents' and teacher's concern that Billy has a reading deficit. In addition, he scored well below average on assessments of written language. This supports a recommendation of remediation services in language arts.

- If a student does better in one part of a domain than another, note this difference. *Tonya performed at an average level on a subtest that assesses reading comprehension, but scored well below average on a subtest that assesses word identification skills.* This supports a recommendation that, while remediating word attack skills, the student could continue to be presented with age-appropriate content.
- If the testing data do not support a claim of weakness, look first to differences in task demands of the testing situation and the classroom when hypothesizing a reason for the difference.
- *Although weaknesses in mathematics were noted as a concern by his teacher, Billy scored in the average range on assessments of mathematics skills. These tests required Billy to perform calculations and to solve word problems that were read aloud to him. It was noted that he often paused for 10 seconds or more before starting pencil-and-paper tasks in mathematics.*
- This supports a recommendation that the teacher attempt to redirect him to task frequently and to avoid the assumption that a long pause means that Billy is unable to solve a problem.
- If the testing data indicate a weakness that was not identified as a concern, give first priority to explaining the discrepancy to the limitations with the testing.
- *Billy's teacher stated that he does well in spelling. However, he scored well below average on a subtest of spelling skills. Billy appeared to be bored while taking the spelling test so a lack of vigilance in his effort may have depressed his score. Also, the spelling tests he takes in school use words he has been practicing for a week. The lower score on the Spelling subtest of this assessment may indicate that he is maintaining the correct spelling of words in long-term memory.*
- Do not use definitive statements of the "real" child when reporting assessment results. A 45-minute test does not give you definitive knowledge of the student. The statement *The results of this screening show that Jack has strength in language arts and is weak in mathematics could be rewritten as Based on the results of this screening, Jack's language arts skills were assessed to be an area of strength while his mathematics skills were assessed to be an area of weakness.*

Recommendations

- Be careful of using "should" in your recommendations. It means that you are directing another professional on how to do his or her job even though that other professional may have a much more comprehensive knowledge of the child than you.
- Do not make placement recommendations based solely on the results of an achievement test. Make academic recommendations only if your full assessment provides adequate information to make these recommendations with confidence. Remember, specific recommendations can only be made by someone with thorough knowledge of the curriculum and the domain being assessed.

Source: Guideline for Writing Reports. Reprinted with permission of author: W. H. Goff (2002).

The following case study presents test results and interpretations. Read the results and notice interpretations and how they are implemented in the educational recommendations. For instructional purposes, the reasons for the recommendations are given with each recommendation. The reasons for recommendations are not typically included in reports.

Case Study 1: Sue

Name: Sue Smith

Date of Birth: 6-8-94

Dates of Evaluation: 11-20-04, 11-28-04

Age: 10-6

Current Grade Placement: 3.3

Examiner: Hazel Competent

Instruments: Wechsler Intelligence Scale for Children–Fourth Edition

Woodcock-Johnson III Tests of Achievement: Standard and Extended Battery

Test of Auditory Perceptual Skills

Teacher Report Form (Achenbach)

Work sample analysis

Classroom observations

Conference with parents

BACKGROUND INFORMATION AND REFERRAL

Sue was referred for testing by her parents for the possible consideration of special education services. Sociological information reported normal developmental progress and a warm, caring home environment. Sue's parents reported that they felt education was important and wanted Sue's progress to improve. Sue appears to have good relationships with both parents and her two older brothers.

Sue repeated kindergarten and received low grades during her first- and second-grade years. Sue is currently enrolled in third grade, and the teacher reported that Sue has difficulty with phonics and reading words that "she should know." Sue attended a special summer program in an attempt to improve her reading skills.

Sue has normal vision and hearing and no apparent physical problems. Peer relationships are as expected for her age.

PARENT CONFERENCE

Sue's parents reported that Sue is a well-adjusted child who enjoys playing outside, listening to music, and playing on the computer. Her parents believe that Sue's academic difficulties began to surface over a year ago. They stated that they thought Sue would be able to catch up with her peers in reading; however, she still doesn't seem to "get it." Her parents have hired a tutor in the neighborhood to help Sue with her homework. They said that Sue seems to enjoy working with this high school student because she enjoys having another girl to talk to rather than her brothers. Her parents said Sue doesn't appear to get as frustrated as when she works with her parents.

CLASSROOM OBSERVATIONS

Sue was observed on three separate occasions before the testing sessions. She seemed to stay on task and attempted all assigned work. Her teacher reported that more than half of Sue's assignments were incomplete. It appeared that the pace of the class might be too rapid, especially in reading and language arts. Sue did not exhibit many inappropriate behaviors for her age and seemed to have friends within the classroom. Sue's teacher used peer tutors for some of the reading and language arts assignments, which she reports helped Sue to finish some of her work.

TEST RESULTS

Wechsler Intelligence Scale for Children—IV

Block Design	7
Similarities	7
Digit Span	4
Picture Concepts	10
Coding	5
Vocabulary	7
Letter-Number Sequencing	5
Matrix Reasoning	7
Comprehension	7
Symbol Search	5

	Standard Score	95 % Confidence Interval	Percentile Rank
Verbal Comprehension	83	(77–91)	13
Receptual Reasoning	88	(81–97)	21
Working Memory	68	(63–78)	2
Processing Speed	73	(67–85)	4
Full Scale	73	(69–79)	4

Woodcock–Johnson III Tests of Achievement: Standard and Extended Batteries

Cluster/Test	PR	SS	(90% BAND)	GE
Oral Language (Ext)	5	76	(69–82)	2.0
Oral Expression	12	83	(74–92)	2.1
Listening Comprehension	9	80	(73–86)	1.9
Total Achievement	.3	59	(56–62)	1.9
Broad Reading	.2	57	(54–60)	1.5
Broad Math	23	89	(85–93)	3.5
Broad Written Language	0.4	60	(54–66)	1.6
Basic Reading Skills	0.3	59	(55–63)	1.3
Reading Comprehension	1	67	(62–72)	1.7
Math Calculation Skills	39	96	(90–101)	4.4
Math Reasoning	30	92	(87–97)	3.8
Basic Writing Skills	2	68	(63–73)	1.7
Written Expression	4	74	(66–81)	2.3
Academic Skills	1	66	(63–69)	1.7
Academic Fluency	3	72	(69–76)	2.2
Academic Applications	4	75	(70–79)	1.9
Academic Knowledge	35	94	(87–101)	4.3
Phoneme/Grapheme Knowledge	0.2	56	(49–63)	1.0

The following achievement tests of Form A were administered:

Letter-Word Identification	<0.1	48	(43–52)	1.1
Reading Fluency	5	76	(72–79)	2.2
Story Recall	2	68	(50–86)	K.3
Understanding Directions	<0.1	50	(43–57)	K.0
Calculation	76	110	(101–120)	6.2
Math Fluency	1	62	(56–67)	1.5
Spelling	<0.1	52	(45–60)	K.9
Writing Fluency	5	75	(66–83)	2.5
Passage Comprehension	2	68	(61–74)	1.5
Applied Problems	12	82	(76–89)	2.6
Writing Samples	8	79	(68–90)	1.9
Word Attack	5	75	(68–82)	1.6
Picture Vocabulary	29	92	(84–100)	3.1
Oral Comprehension	47	99	(91–107)	4.5
Editing	14	84	(77–91)	2.9
Reading Vocabulary	7	78	(73–83)	1.9
Quantitative Concepts	70	108	(98–117)	5.9
Academic Knowledge	35	94	(87–101)	4.3
Spelling of Sounds	<0.1	26	(11–41)	<K.0
Sound Awareness	11	82	(76–88)	1.9
Punctuation & Capitals	<0.1	49	(35–62)	K.9
Handwriting	38	96	(85–106)	3.9

Test of Auditory-Perceptual Skills

	Scaled Score	Percentile Rank
Auditory Number Memory		
Forward	6	9
Reversed	5	5
Auditory Sentence Memory	8	25
Auditory Word Memory	5	5
Auditory Interpretation of Directions		
Total Correct Sentences	7	16
Auditory Word Discrimination	3	1
Auditory Processing (thinking and reasoning)	7	16
Auditory Quotient	70	

TEST INTERPRETATIONS

On measures of intellectual ability, Sue performed within the low-average/borderline range. This indicates that on this assessment, Sue is considered to have a range of abilities that are consistent with the low end of average and bordering in the below-average range. Discrepancies exist between her higher-end scores of verbal comprehension and perceptual reasoning skills and her lower scores of working memory and processing speed. Sue performed with relative strength on tasks requiring verbal skills and concepts and on tasks requiring abstract visual-perceptual reasoning skills. Sue seems to have more difficulty with tasks requiring her to sustain attention to encode and sequence information using auditory memory skills. She worked at a somewhat slow and deliberate pace on some tasks, which may have influenced her processing speed score.

On overall achievement measures of the Woodcock–Johnson III Tests of Achievement, Sue performed as expected for her age on items of math calculation and math reasoning. Sue's general academic knowledge was in the range expected for her age when she completed tasks of science, social studies, and humanities. Sue also demonstrated age-appropriate skills in the ability to comprehend orally and in handwriting ability. She performed within the low-average to slightly below the average range in areas of oral expression, oral language, and listening comprehension.

Sue's difficulties in academics were demonstrated through formal assessment in the areas of written language, including reading, spelling, sound awareness, and phoneme/grapheme knowledge. The weaknesses result in the inability to decode new words, spell sounds, and comprehend content that is read. An error analysis of word attack skills revealed weaknesses in decoding single consonants, digraphs, consonant blends, vowels, and multisyllabic words.

Sue demonstrated weakness in most areas assessed by the Test of Auditory-Perceptual Skills. She seems to have relative weaknesses on subtests that measure memory for isolated words and numbers. She appears to have slightly higher ability to remember meaningful auditory stimuli, such as sentences or directions. However, she had difficulty on similar items of the WJ III, indicating inconsistent skill mastery or inconsistent abilities.

On items requiring oral language responses, Sue was somewhat shy and tended to limit her responses to one-word answers. This may have affected some of her scores on tests assessing the language areas. These scores may underestimate her true ability.

Responses provided by Sue's teacher on the Teacher Report Form of the Child Behavior Checklist indicated that Sue is unable to complete most of her schoolwork as expected of students her age. The teacher endorsed items that indicate Sue may be having some emerging problems with anxiety. Items were also endorsed that are consistent with difficulties with concentration and attention. These may be related to her current performance in school. None of the scores were within a clinical range for behavior problems.

Work sample analysis indicated that Sue has a relative strength in the ability to compute simple math operations and to understand math concepts and math reasoning. Her samples for spelling, writing, and reading comprehension were within the failure range. The work samples indicated difficulty with her ability to associate written letters with sounds consistently, which is consistent with her performance on standardized achievement measures.

Three separate classroom observations indicated that Sue was cooperative and remained quiet during all of the observation periods. She attempted to begin her work when instructed to do so but was unable to complete language arts assignments as instructed. She also appeared to increase the amount of time that she was off task during language arts classes compared with her ability to concentrate during math class.

SUMMARY AND CONCLUSIONS

Sue is currently functioning in the low-average range of intellectual ability, with significant weaknesses in phoneme/grapheme awareness and short-term auditory memory. These weaknesses influence Sue's ability to decode words, spell, and comprehend new material. The weakness may also decrease the efficiency with which Sue can obtain new information through a standard teaching (lecture) format. Sue's performance on standardized and informal

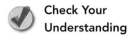

Check Your Understanding

To check your understanding of this case, complete Activity 11.3 below.

Activity 11.3

Answer the following questions about the case study.

1. Why was Sue referred for testing? _____

2. How is Sue functioning intellectually? _____

3. What are the discrepancies in Sue's functioning according to the test results? _____

4. What are Sue's strengths as indicated through the assessment process? _____

5. What are Sue's weaknesses, and how do these weaknesses appear to influence Sue's academic functioning? _____

6. What additional assessment was recommended for Sue? _____

7. According to these results, what are Sue's specific academic skill deficits? _____

8. What types of educational interventions and strategies were recommended? _____

Apply Your Knowledge

Write any additional concerns you may have about Sue after reading this report. _____

_____

_____

---

assessment instruments resulted in a profile consistent with that of a student with specific learning disabilities in the areas of reading and written language skills. This may be the result of her difficulties with processing information presented auditorily and an inability to form sound-symbol relationships.

RECOMMENDATIONS

1. Sue may benefit from additional educational support in the areas of reading and language arts. (Reasons: Student has difficulty with sound awareness, phoneme/grapheme awareness, auditory memory, verbal skills, and attention; this would support the decision that she may benefit from additional educational interventions.)

2. New material should be presented through both visual and auditory formats. (Reasons: Weakness appears to be auditory memory; pairing all auditory material with visual cues may help student to focus attention.)

3. Sue will benefit from direct instruction techniques that require her to actively respond to new material. (Reasons: Student may increase academic engaged time; active responding may help student to focus attention and receive positive feedback from teacher.)

4. Sue may benefit from phonemic awareness training activities. (Assessment results are consistently low in these areas; additional instruction may decrease her difficulties with reading).

5. Sue may benefit from advanced organizers in content areas, introduction of new vocabulary terms before reading them in new chapters, outlines of class lectures or presentations, and note-taking training. (Reasons: Student may increase ability to focus on relevant material, increase attention to task.)

Hazel Competent, M. Ed.

Educational Diagnostician

WRITING EDUCATIONAL OBJECTIVES

At the eligibility meeting, team members discuss the results and recommendations of the psychoeducational reports with the parents. If the student is eligible for special education services, the team writes the specific educational objectives that the student's IEP will comprise. If the student does not meet eligibility criteria, the student may be considered to need accommodations under Section 504. The team may also decide that the student does not need additional services under 504 or IDEA, but additional referrals, programs, or interventions may be suggested within the general curriculum. Let's continue with the example of Sue Smith to see how the team would use its results to write Sue's educational objectives.

IEP TEAM MEETING RESULTS

The following results were presented in the IEP team meeting along with additional information from Sue's parents, school psychologist, and classroom teachers. At that time, the team agreed that Sue would receive reading and language arts instruction in a resource room setting. This decision was made so that Sue could receive intensive training in phonemic awareness, reading decoding, reading comprehension, reading fluency, and spelling in a one-on-one and small-group environment. Additional assessments would be completed to further pinpoint the specific weaknesses in phoneme/grapheme awareness and other areas of language arts.

The resource room teacher plans to use curriculum-based measurement to monitor progress.

SUE'S IEP

During the IEP meeting, the IEP was developed. Portions of the IEP are presented here.

Student's Present Level of Educational Performance

Cognitive Abilities. Current assessment data indicate that Sue is functioning in the low-average range of intelligence. Sue's strengths are in the areas of performance or nonverbal skills.

Reading

- *Basic Reading Skills.* Formal assessment, curriculum-based assessments, and informal measures indicate that Sue is performing below the range expected for her age on tasks of reading decoding—specifically, word attack and phoneme/ grapheme awareness. Her performance in curriculum-based measures are at the first- to second-grade level.
- *Comprehension.* Comprehension skills were at the first- to second-grade level on all measures.
- *Fluency.* Reading fluency was assessed to be at the first- to second-grade level.

Spelling. Sue's spelling skills were measured to be at the first-grade level. Sue has difficulty with the spelling of basic cvc (consonant-vowel-consonant) words.

Written Language. Sue's written language skills were measured to be at the first- to second-grade level on both formal and informal classroom measures.

Mathematics. Sue is performing at the level expected for her age in areas of math calculation and math reasoning.

Science. Sue's standardized achievement scores and classroom measures indicate that Sue is comprehending science at the level expected for her age.

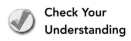 **Check Your Understanding**

To check your understanding of writing objectives, complete Activity 11.4 below.

Activity 11.4

Additional classroom assessment indicated that Sue has difficulty with the following sound/letter associations when asked to decode words. She also had difficulty with spelling of first-grade-level words. Using the following information, write behaviorally stated short-term objectives for these skills.

> Reading Decoding Errors; Letter/Sound Association Errors: /cr/, /pl/, /dr/, /st/, /sh/, /ch/
>
> Spelling Errors: tree, church, play, drop, drip, drank, drink, meat, meet, hand, sand, band, milk, silk, some, come, home
>
> 1. When presented with _____, Sue will be able to _____ with % accuracy by _____.
> 2. _____
> 3. _____
> 4. _____
>
> *Apply Your Knowledge*
>
> Using the information provided for this case, write a long-term annual goal for written expression. _____
> _____
> _____

Social Studies. Sue's standardized achievement scores and classroom measures indicate that Sue is performing at the level expected for her age.

Listening. Assessment results of Sue's listening comprehension were inconsistent with comprehension measured to be within the low-average range, consistent with her measured cognitive abilities. Other areas were assessed to be below the level expected for her age. Auditory discrimination and memory were below the level expected for her age.

Sample IEP Annual Goal for Basic Reading Skills   Sue will master the decoding skills required in the reading series, Spinners, at the mid-second-grade level by the end of the school year.

Sample IEP Short-term Objective   When given a list of 20 random words from the highest-level first-grade reader (1.E Level) from the series Spinners, Sue will be able to decode the list with 85% accuracy at the end of the 6-week reporting period.

Methods and Evaluation

Methods/Material Used	Method of Monitoring/Assessment
Spinners Reader Level 1.E	Curriculum-based measurement

Following is the general format for writing an educational behaviorally stated short-term objective:

When presented with _____, Sue will be able to _____ with _____% accuracy by _____.

REEVALUATIONS

The 1997 IDEA Amendments changed the focus of the reevaluation process. In the past, students were assessed in the same areas they were assessed for their initial evaluations (cognitive, academic, speech/language, adaptive functioning, and so on). The regulations now state that data is collected only in the areas that the team members feel they need additional information in order to make a decision regarding continued eligibility and interventions. For example, a student with a specific learning disability in math may need only additional data and/or assessment in the area of math. Rather than requiring total comprehensive evaluations every 3 years, reevaluations now consist of only the additional assessment determined to be needed in order to thoroughly review the case.

Case Study 2: Travis

Name: Travis Shores
Date of Birth: 8-9-84
Date of Evaluation: 10-28-02
Age: 18-2
Examiner: Mark House
Instruments: Wechsler Adult Intelligence Scale–Third Edition
            Conners' Continuous Performance Test
            Woodcock Language Proficiency Battery–Revised
            Clinical interview

BACKGROUND AND REFERRAL INFORMATION

Travis is currently enrolled as a freshman in Anywhere Community College and reported having difficulty with study habits, time management, spelling skills, writing skills, reading comprehension, and grammar. He also expressed concern about his ability to master a foreign language at the college level. Travis said that he has difficulty with attention span, finishing tasks, test taking, and listening in class. He reported that he gets distracted easily in lecture classes.

Travis reported that he has no history of testing for learning or attention difficulties. He stated that he had a difficult time in high school during his sophomore year but then felt that things were better for him during his junior and senior years. Travis attempted to take Spanish this semester and decided to drop the course because of his inability to make the progress he expected. He is taking economics and believes he is doing well in that class.

TEST RESULTS

Wechsler Adult Intelligence Scale–Third Edition

Verbal Tests		Performance Tests	
Vocabulary	9	Picture Completion	12
Similarities	11	Digit Symbol-Coding	10
Arithmetic	8	Block Design	14
Digit Span	8	Matrix Reasoning	13
Information	8	Picture Arrangement	9
Comprehension	12		

Verbal IQ	95
Performance IQ	110
Full-Scale IQ	96

Conners' Continuous Performance Test

Measure	Percentile	Range of Performance
Number of Hits	99.59	Markedly atypical
Number of Omissions	94.86	Markedly atypical
Number of Commissions	50.90	Within average range
Hit Rate	21.46	Within average range
Hit Rate Standard Error	93.44	Markedly atypical
Variability of SES	77.87	Within average range
Attentiveness	84.42	Mildly atypical
Risk Taking	99.00	Markedly atypical
Hit RT Block Change	95.96	Markedly atypical
Hit SE Block Change	82.60	Within average range
Hit RT ISI Change	80.90	Within average range
Hit SE ISI Change	76.78	Within average range

Travis performed with some inconsistency on the Conners Continuous Performance Test. He performed like students his age with attention problems on several indices. He was within the average range on other indices. His performance indicates that he may have difficulty sustaining attention on some tasks but not others. His performance showed some evidence of an impulsive responding pattern.

Woodcock Language Proficiency Battery—Revised

Subtest	Standard Score	Percentile Rank	Grade Equivalent
Memory for Sentences	95	38	10.2
Picture Vocabulary	85	15	9.3
Oral Vocabulary	86	17	9.6
Listening Comprehension	103	57	14.2
Verbal Analogies	81	10	6.2

	Standard Score	Percentile Rank	Grade Equivalent
Letter-Word Identification	96	39	11.9
Passage Comprehension	90	25	10.0
Word Attack	103	57	14.4
Dictation	90	25	9.8
Writing Samples	136	99	16.9
Proofing	70	2	5.0
Writing Fluency	88	22	9.5
Punctuation	71	3	5.7
Spelling	92	29	10.5
Usage	86	18	8.8
Cluster Scores			
Oral Language	88	22	9.6
Broad Reading	93	31	10.9
Basic Reading Skills	99	47	12.5
Broad Written Language	107	67	16.0
Basic Writing Skills	77	6	7.2
Written Expression	110	74	16.1

Travis is currently functioning within the average range of intellectual ability. A significant discrepancy exists between his verbal IQ score of 95 and his performance IQ score of 110. This indicates that Travis is able to use nonverbal strategies rather than verbal strategies for most problem solving. This discrepancy also indicates that Travis's full scale IQ score may not be representative of his true ability. Travis's performance IQ score may better represent his true cognitive potential. Analysis of individual subtests and factors also indicates strengths and weaknesses in processing. Travis demonstrated significant strength in the ability to comprehend common verbal concepts. He also demonstrated significant strength in visual perceptual organization of nonverbal stimuli. His performance on this instrument indicates relative weakness in short-term auditory memory and in the ability to remain free from distraction. Travis appears to have relative weakness in long-term retention of factual information.

Travis was administered the Conners Continuous Performance Test to determine whether he has significant difficulty maintaining sustained, focused attention. On this instrument, the more measures found to be within the atypical range, the greater the likelihood that attention problems exist. On this test, Travis gave slower responses at the end than at the beginning of the test, indicating an ability to sustain attention. He made a larger number of omission errors, indicating poor attention to the task. He was highly inconsistent in responding, indicating inattentiveness as measured by standard error. Numerous indices strongly suggest that Travis has attention problems according to his performance on this test.

SUMMARY

Write your summary for the assessment data in the space provided.

_____

_____

_____

_____

_____

RECOMMENDATIONS

Write recommendations: discuss appropriate interventions in class and for studying outside of class. Include accommodations for the college environment based on data provided. Should Travis be referred for additional services in any other agencies or with other professionals? What considerations should be discussed with Travis regarding his future plans and course of study at the college level? What issues regarding his functioning as an adult should be considered?

Recommendations:

1. _____
   _____

2. _____
   _____

3. _____
   _____

4. _____
   _____

Case Study 3: Burt

Name: Burt Down

Date of Birth: 5-10-1989

Date of Evaluation: 11-27-2003

Age: 14-7

Current Grade Placement: 9.3

Examiner: Phil Mood

Instruments: Selected subtests of the Woodcock–Johnson III

Math Work Samples

Behavior Assessment System for Children: Self-Report (ages 12–18)

Behavioral Observation Data

Functional Behavioral Assessment

BACKGROUND AND REFERRAL INFORMATION

Burt was referred for a reevaluation due to recent behavioral difficulties. Burt has been receiving special education support for specific learning disabilities since he was in the fourth grade. He receives his English instruction in the resource room setting. He has previously been found to have attention deficit hyperactivity disorder and has been prescribed medication as part of his treatment for this disorder. His parents and teachers agree that his behavior improves when he complies with his medication treatment. His parents also acknowledge that things have been rough at home lately. They told the team that they have not been able to manage Burt's behavior within the home and attribute this to "just his age." They report that Burt has been staying out later than he is supposed to and that he argues with them about school and homework. They said that Burt tells them he is old enough to make up his own mind about curfews and selecting his friends. Mr. and Mrs. Down said they do not approve of Burt's friends.

Burt was assessed last year for his regular triennial evaluation. His cognitive ability has been assessed to be within the average range (full scale IQ 108). Due to recent difficulties in mathematics and his behavioral difficulties, another reevaluation was requested. The team members, including Burt's parents, met to discuss possible data needed to analyze the current areas of difficulty. All members agreed that a behavioral analysis and other measures of behavior would be collected. In addition, selected subtests of the WJ III and math work samples would be analyzed.

TEST RESULTS

Woodcock–Johnson III Tests of Achievement

Clusters	PR	SS (90% BAND)	GE
Broad Math	6	77 (73–81)	4.7
Math Calculation Skills	7	78 (72–84)	5.2
Math Reasoning	16	85 (80–90)	5.3
Subtest			
Calculation	15	84 (76–93)	5.7
Math Fluency	3	71 (67–75)	4.2
Applied Problems	8	79 (74–84)	4.1
Quantitative Concepts	40	96 (89–104)	7.5

Math Work Samples

An analysis of Burt's math class work indicates that he attempted to answer 80% of the problems he was assigned in class; however, he successfully completed 35% of the problems he was given to complete in class. His errors included miscalculations, errors of alignment, errors of wrong applications in story problems (adding when he should subtract), and skipping steps needed in multiple-step problems. Burt was not able to complete an entire math assignment, working only about 75% to 85% of the problems before he either quit or ran out of time.

Burt's homework assignments did not show much evidence of his understanding the tasks presented. He turned in only 6 of 15 assignments since the beginning of the school year, and he successfully completed 38% of the problems assigned. His errors on homework assignments were consistent with the errors made on his classwork assignments.

Behavioral Assessments
Behavioral Assessment System for Children: Self-Report (ages 12–18)

Rank*	T-Score*	Percentile
Clinical Profile		
Attitude to School	68	95
Attitude to Teachers	68	94
Sensation Seeking	67	95
School Maladjustment Composite	72	99
Atypicality	52	65
Locus of Control	74	98
Somatization	50	62
Social Stress	64	94
Anxiety	49	51
Clinical Maladjustment Composite	60	81
Depression	85	99
Sense of Inadequacy	83	99

*On the clinical scales, a T-score greater than 70 is considered to be the area of caution for the student's current behaviors. For percentile ranks on clinical scales, the higher the score, the more significant. A percentile rank of 50 is average.

Rank*	T-Score*	Percentile
Adaptive Profile		
Relations with Parents	12	1
Interpersonal Relations	43	18
Self-Esteem	26	4
Self-Reliance	39	15
Personal Adjustment Composite	23	2

*High scores on the adaptive scales indicate high levels of adaptive skills.

On the BASC, Burt endorsed critical items indicating that he feels he has trouble controlling his behavior, he feels he does not do anything right, he thinks no one understands him, he doesn't care anymore, he feels that nothing goes his way and that no one listens to him.

Figure 11.1 illustrates the behavioral observations for Burt during math class for "off-task" behavior across three observation periods.

Figure 11.1   Frequency of off-task behavior in Math class (Burt).

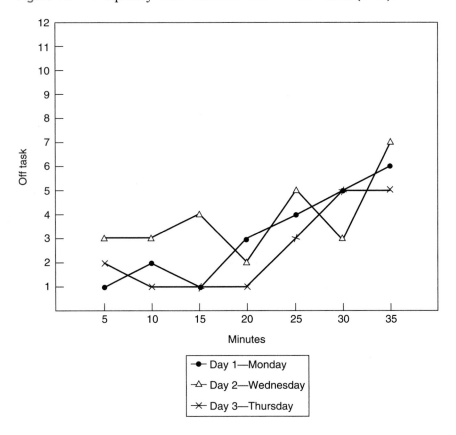

To compare Burt's behavior in additional settings, he was observed in his resource room, where he receives English instruction (Figure 11.2), and in his art class (Figure 11.3).

Functional Behavioral Interview
Following the observations sessions, Burt was interviewed by the school psychologist to determine Burt's perspective on his recent behavioral difficulties and to determine the function of these behaviors. Burt told the psychologist he knows that he is not doing well in math and that he just can't seem to keep up. He stated that he was able to do math last year and felt his teacher was "nicer to me." He stated that his teacher last year offered to stay after school and help him so he could complete his homework assignments. Burt reported that he feels lost in math so he gets bored and wants to do something else. He figures there is no use in trying to do the work, because "I just get Fs anyway."

When Burt is in his other classes, he says he can get along just fine. He says he has lots of friends in his other classes who help him with things he doesn't understand.

Figure 11.2 Frequency of off-task behavior in English class (Burt).

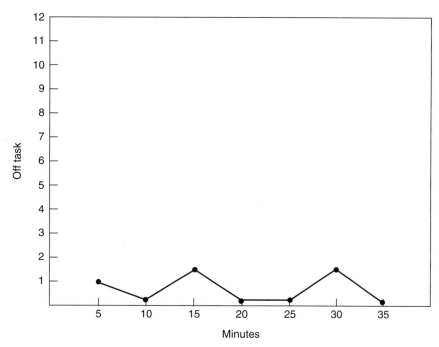

Figure 11.3 Frequency of off-task behavior in art class (Burt).

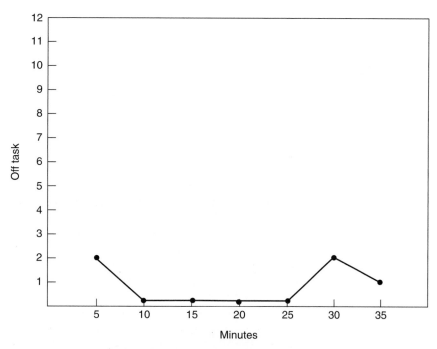

Source: From D. J. Tharinger and N. M. Lambert (1990). "The Contributions of Developmental Psychology to School Psychology," in T. Gutkin and C. R. Reynolds (Eds.), *The Handbook of School Psychology* (2nd ed.). New York: Wiley, pp. 74–103. (© John Wiley & Sons, Inc. Reprinted by permission of the publisher.)

Burt reported that his parents have been yelling at him about his grades in math. He said his parents try to help him, but he still doesn't get it and so they get even more upset. He stated that he has been avoiding going home, because "I know they will yell at me some more."

When asked about his medication, Burt said that he hasn't been taking it as prescribed. He said he doesn't like the way he feels when he takes it even though he agreed that he can pay attention better in school when he takes his medicine. He reported that some of his friends found out that he has to take medicine and that they began calling him names like "hyper" and "dummy." He said that he doesn't feel as good about himself or his relationships with his peers as he did last year.

SUMMARY

Write your summary in the space provided.

_____

_____

_____

_____

_____

_____

_____

RECOMMENDATIONS

Write recommendations, discussing appropriate interventions in class, including determining any changes in setting or any needed additional assessment information based on data provided.

Recommendations:

1. _____

_____

2. _____

_____

3. _____

_____

4. _____

_____

TEAM MEETING

Write the team's discussion and deliberations in the space provided. What are the decisions for Burt? What types of services are needed? Where will these services take place? Who will provide services?

_____

_____

_____

_____

_____

Write the present levels of performance for Burt:

_____

_____

_____

Write behavioral objectives for Burt that will be the basis of the behavioral intervention plan for him:

_____

_____

_____

_____

_____

_____

Write the short-term objectives for Burt relating to the areas assessed in the reevaluation:

_____

_____

_____

_____

_____

_____

_____

Case Study 4: Alicia

Name: Alicia Young
Date of Birth: 2-7-98
Date of Evaluation: 4-7-01
Age: 3-2
Current Grade Placement: None
Examiner: Beth Child
Stanford–Binet V
Vineland Adaptive Behavior Scales
Evaluation Methods: AGS Early Screening Profiles

Play evaluation

Home visit

Parent interview

BACKGROUND AND REFERRAL INFORMATION

Alicia was referred by her maternal grandmother, who is her legal guardian. Sociological information indicates that Alicia's grandmother does not know her daughter's residence at this time. Health information provided by the grandmother on the Health History Survey indicates that Alicia was born prematurely and that Alicia's mother has a long history of substance abuse. At the time of Alicia's birth, Alicia's mother was 17 years of age. Alicia has one older sibling, a 6-year-old brother who is currently receiving special education support services. Alicia's grandmother believes that Alicia is not developing at the expected pace and requested a screening evaluation to determine whether Alicia might be considered for the early childhood at-risk program.

TEST RESULTS

K-ABC-II

Age 3: Global Scale Index
Mental Processing Composite

	Scaled Scores
Atlantis	6
Conceptual Thinking	7
Face Recognition	6
Triangles	6
Word Order	6
Mental Processing Composite Standard Score	66
95% Confidence Interval	59–77

Vineland Adaptive Behavior Scales: Interview Edition (Expanded Form)

Communication	
Receptive	Moderately low
Expressive	Low
Written	Low

Daily Living Skills	
Personal	Moderately low
Domestic	Low
Community	Low

Socialization	
Interpersonal Relationships	Low
Play and Leisure Time	Moderately low
Coping Skills	Low

AGS Early Screening Profile

	Standard Score	Percentile Rank	Age Equivalent
Cognitive/Language	60	1	2-0
Motor	75	5	2-1
Self-Help/Parent	68	2	2-0

Survey Scores

Articulation	Below average/poor
Home Behavior	Average
Cognitive/Language	Below average
Motor	Below average

Play Evaluation and Home Visit

Alicia sat quietly on the carpet during the play evaluation. Alicia's grandmother was present during the first part of the evaluation. When her grandmother left the room to complete a survey, Alicia sat motionless and did not exhibit any change in her behavior following the separation. Alicia did not initiate any spontaneous use of language or communication, such as gesturing. She did not interact with the examiner when encouraged to do so and played with only one object, a stuffed toy. Her play can be best described as mechanistic and without any noticeable motive or affect exhibited. Alicia did not react to her grandmother when she returned, but joined her grandmother on the sofa when requested.

A home visit was made 2 days following the evaluation. The home environment was clean, and several educational toys and materials were available. All interactions between the grandmother and Alicia were initiated by the grandmother. Alicia displayed very flat affect during both the home visit and the evaluation. Alicia's grandmother stated that the only reaction she sees from Alicia is when it is time to eat. She described Alicia's appetite as fair because Alicia likes only a few types of food. When she is given something new to taste, she usually spits it out after she tries it.

Parent Interview

When Alicia's grandmother was asked to list her priorities and concerns for Alicia, she expressed the need for some support to help her toilet train Alicia, improve Alicia's speech development, and improve Alicia's self-help skills, such as dressing and washing her face. Alicia's grandmother believes that Alicia's motor skills are different from her grandson's. She believes that Alicia is somewhat clumsy and too dependent on her for routine activities that other 3-year-olds are learning to do, such as self-feed with a spoon.

Alicia's grandmother reported that she has been able to access monetary assistance using public resources including Medicaid for

Alicia's medical needs and transportation to and from the community agencies for Alicia's care. She reported that Alicia's needs are primarily being met within the home environment but expressed desire for additional assistance in training Alicia within the home environment and in managing her behavior.

SUMMARY

Write your summary for Alicia's assessment data in the space provided.

_____

_____

_____

_____

_____

_____

_____

RECOMMENDATIONS

Write recommendations, discussing appropriate interventions including interventions within the home and between the home and school environment. For this case, you must first determine how children of Alicia's age are served in your state and local community. Following the discussion, complete the "Team Meeting" section with members in your class.

Recommendations:

1. _____

_____

2. _____

_____

3. _____

_____

4. _____

_____

TEAM MEETING

Write the team's discussion and deliberations in the space provided. What are the decisions for Alicia? What types of services are needed? Where will these services take place? Who will provide services? Include statements about Alicia's inclusion activities with children who do not have disabilities. After discussing the results with members in your class, complete the IEP.

_____

_____

_____

_____

_____

_____

_____

IEP

Write the present levels of development for Alicia in the following areas: physical development, cognitive development, social/emotional development, and adaptive development.

_____

_____

_____

_____

Write annual goals for Alicia:

_____

_____

_____

_____

_____

_____

_____

Write the short-term objectives or benchmarks for Alicia:

_____

_____

_____

_____

_____

_____

_____

_____

_____

_____

THINK AHEAD

EXERCISES

Part I

Match the following terms with the correct definitions.

a. educational planning
b. eligibility decision
c. behaviorally stated objective
d. Section 504
e. benchmarks
f. interindividual interpretation
g. intra-individual interpretation
h. projective tests
i. reevaluations

_____ 1. This level of test interpretation compares the student with the age or grade expectations according to the norm-group statistics.

_____ 2. These are based on specific criteria included in state and federal regulations.

_____ 3. Interventions and strategies used to promote educational success.

_____ 4. This is a method of comparing a student's own strengths and weaknesses to determine a pattern of functioning that may be influencing a student's educational performance.

_____ 5. The 1997 and 2004 IDEA Amendments changed this process so that less testing may be necessary for some students.

Answers to these questions can be found in the Appendix of this text or you may also complete these questions and receive immediate feedback on your answers by going to the Think Ahead module in Chapter 11 of the Companion Website.

COURSE PROGRESS MONITORING ASSESSMENT

See how you are doing in the course after the conclusion of Part IV chapters by completing the following assessment. When you are finished, check your answers with your instructor or on the Companion Website at *www.prenhall.com/overton.* Once you know your score, return to Figure 1.9, Student Progress Monitoring Graph in Chapter 1 and plot your progress.

Progress Monitoring Assessment

Select the best answer. Some of these terms may be used more than once.

A. diagnostic tests
B. abnormalities in social reciprocity
C. school neuropsychologist
D. mental retardation
E. FBA

F. CBMs
G. norm-referenced tests
H. standard error of
   measurement
I. interresponse time
J. duration recording

K. criterion referenced tests
L. TBI
M. Ecological Assessment
N. developmental version
O. standardized tests

_____ 1. The core features of an autism spectrum disorder are abnormalities in communication, repetitive patterns of behavior, and ?

_____ 2. The use of a cognitive processing cross battery analysis may be part of an evaluation for ?

_____ 3. This person may conduct cross-battery assessments.

_____ 4. The initial administration of an instrument to a sample population.

_____ 5. These instruments may provide additional information used for specific academic or other weaknesses.

_____ 6. Tests designed to accompany a set of skills.

_____ 7. Assessing the learning environment.

_____ 8. These instruments provide comparisons with students the same age across the United States.

_____ 9. This measurement of error is usually used to calculate confidence intervals.

_____ 10. Measure of time between the presentation of a stimulus and a response.

Fill in the Blanks

11. When writing test reports the analysis of the comprehensive results are included in the _____ section.

12. The purpose of assessment is to _____ .

13. _____ is the type of validity that indicates a measure has items that are representative across the possible items in the domain.

14. _____ validity and _____ validity are differentiated by time.

15. _____ is a behavioral measure that indicates how students in a class view each other.

16. _____ is a computerized assessment of a student's ability to sustain attention across time.

17. Regulatory disturbances might be assessed when the assessment involves _____ .

18. Story starters might be useful in the informal assessment of _____ .

19. Any device that is necessary for a student to function within the educational environment is known as _____.

20. The final result of a comprehensive evaluation is to provide _____.

Appendix

KEY TO END-OF-CHAPTER EXERCISES

CHAPTER 1

Part I
1. overidentification
2. assessment
3. error analysis
4. dynamic assessment
5. eligibility meeting
6. standardized tests
7. prereferral intervention strategies
8. norm-referenced test
9. IFSP (Individual Family Service Plan)
10. CBA (curriculum-based assessment)

Part II
1. Prereferral checklist.
2. High-stakes assessment may be used to make high-stakes decisions, such as funding for school systems.
3. High-stakes assessment provides an accountability measure for all students in schools. This means that all students, including students who are receiving special education support services, should receive the appropriate education that will allow them to achieve as expected.
4. Whole-school approaches and prereferral interventions.
5. Frequent measurement of progress in the general education classroom, early prereferral interventions monitored for integrity, data collected and analyzed by intervention team, additional interventions tried, assessment plan designed, comprehensive assessment completed, team meeting held to determine eligibility, IEP or alternative plan designed and implemented.

CHAPTER 2

Part I

1. o	5. b, e	9. b
2. h	6. bb	10. m
3. w	7. x	11. s
4. d	8. i	

Part II
1. Parents, professionals, litigation.
2. If the student will need accommodations or an alternate test.
3. (a) Upon initial referral for evaluation,
   (b) Upon each notification of an individual education program meeting,

      (c) Upon reevaluation of the child,

      (d) Upon registration of a complaint.

4. (a) Are selected and administered so as not to be discriminatory on a racial or cultural basis,

    (b) Are provided and administered in the child's native language or other mode of communication, unless it is clearly not feasible to do so,

    (c) Measure the extent to which the child has a disability and needs special education, rather than measuring the child's English language skills,

    (d) Have been validated for the specific purpose for which they are used,

    (e) Are administered by trained and knowledgeable personnel in accordance with any instructions provided by the producer of such tests,

    (f) Include those tailored to assess specific areas of educational need and not merely those that are designed to provide a single, general intelligence quotient,

    (g) Are selected and administered so as best to ensure that if a test is administered to a child with impaired sensory, manual, or speaking skills, the test results accurately reflect the child's aptitude or achievement level or whatever other factors the test purports to measure, rather than reflecting the child's impaired sensory, manual, or speaking skills (unless those skills are the factors that the test purports to measure),

    (h) Are technically sound instruments that may assess the relative contribution of cognitive and behavioral factors, in addition to physical or developmental factors.

Part III

1. In the past traditional IEP conference, parents were found to be passive and to attend merely to receive information. Parents are now considered to be equal team members in the IEP process. Additionally, when working with parents from culturally diverse backgrounds, their level of acculturation should be considered.

2. Due process may be discriminatory because its cost may prohibit some families from following this procedure: actual financial costs, emotional and psychic costs, and time spent costs. Therefore, mediation is a free alternative for parents.

3. Evaluation procedures should not be racially or culturally discriminatory. Test bias may have greater implications for students who have linguistic differences and those who may come from culturally different backgrounds or deprived environments. Problems with bias in assessment include inappropriate test content; inappropriate standardization

samples, examiner and language issues, inequitable social consequences, measurement of different constructs, different predictive validity, and qualitatively distinct minority and majority aptitude and achievement. Additionally, there may be problems in biased assessment that also include overinterpretation of test results and problems that may arise in testing students whose dominant language is not English. It has even been recommended that norm-referenced instruments should not be used with bilingual students because norms are usually limited to small samples of minority children, norming procedures routinely exclude students with limited English proficiency, test items tap information that minority children may not be familiar with due to their linguistically and culturally different backgrounds, testing formats do not allow examiners the opportunity to provide feedback or to probe into the children's quality of responses, test scoring systems arbitrarily decide what are the correct responses based on majority culture paradigms, standardized testing procedures assume that the child has appropriate test-taking skills.

CHAPTER 3

Part I

1. s and q
2. t
3. g
4. a
5. p
6. c
7. o
8. e
9. t
10. j

Part II

mean = <u>81.16</u>   median = <u>83</u>   mode = <u>74, 78, 84, 85</u>

range = <u>41</u>   variance = <u>103.086</u>   standard deviation = <u>10.153</u>

Scores that are a significant distance from the mean are <u>58, 60, 63, 70, 72, 95, 96, 97, 99</u>

1. 95.44
2. 50
3. >99
4. between 3 and 4
5. .13% or less than 1%

CHAPTER 4

Part I

1. j
2. i
3. d
4. o
5. g or u
6. r
7. b
8. c
9. m
10. l

Part II

1. error
2. estimated true score
3. standard error of measurement

4. reliable
5. age
6. reliable

7.   mean = 72.92   median = 76   mode = 76
range = 61   variance = 277.91   standard dev. = 16.67
SEM = 6.5

(a) from 43.5 to 56.5
(b) from 68.5 to 81.5
(c) from 24.5 to 37.5
(d) from 70.5 to 83.5
(e) from 58.5 to 71.5
(f) from 74.5 to 87.5
(g) from 83.5 to 96.5
(h) from 85.5 to 98.5
(i) from 69.5 to 82.5
(j) from 67.5 to 80.5
(k) from 81.2 to 94.5
(l) from 81.5 to 94.5

CHAPTER 5

Part I

1. j
2. o
3. n
4. g

5. d
6. l
7. k
8. i

9. b
10. e
11. m

Part II

1. d
2. c
3. a and b
4. d

Part III

Answers will vary but should include the concepts presented in the chapter, such as when students are not able to participate in the assessments, variability across states, purpose of assessment, and what is meant by high stakes.

Part IV

1. Chronological age: 7-10-25
2. Domain scores: 5 1 1 0
3. Raw score: 7

4. Basal item: 4
5. Ceiling item: 8

CHAPTER 6

Part I

1. d	5. k	8. f
2. m	6. e	9. h
3. c	7. a	10. l
4. n		

Part II
1. Curriculum-based assessment, to determine where to place the student in classroom reading texts.
2. Error analysis, to learn where the student seems to have difficulty working with the problems.
3. Error analysis, probes, direct measurement, to assist in determining a pattern of errors.
4. Curriculum-based, direct measurement—these methods are more sensitive and specific than norm-referenced tests.
5. Curriculum-based assessment and the aim line—to monitor progress.

CHAPTER 7

Part I

1. n	5. k	8. d
2. c	6. f	9. j
3. l	7. b	10. g
4. j		

Part II

1. b	5. h	8. f
2. g	6. a	9. d
3. a	7. a, c, f	10. i
4. i		

CHAPTER 8

Part I

1. s	5. m	9. d
2. b	6. k	10. i
3. e	7. l	11. g
4. p	8. c	12. j

Part II
The older brother's aggression is the setting event. The purpose of the student's aggression is to keep others from being aggressive toward him.

CHAPTER 9

Part I

1. g
2. j
3. b
4. e

5. d
6. k
7. c

CHAPTER 10

Part I

1. i
2. f
3. n
4. b

5. a
6. k
7. j

Part II

1. Confusion with the interpretation and implementation of the family assessment component, family's strengths and needs as they relate to the child rather than the parents, equal standing between parents and professionals may not result in a greater degree of cooperation and respect, etc. Answers may vary.
2. Regulatory disturbances, social/environmental disturbances, physiological disturbances, developmental delays.
3. Strengths and needs of the infant or toddler in the areas of physical and cognitive development, communication development, and adaptive development, and the identification of services appropriate to meet such needs, resources, priorities, and concerns of the family, identification of supports and services necessary, etc. Answers may vary.
4. Family involvement component, level of disability necessary for eligibility, assessment instruments, etc. Answers may vary, but should include the considerations presented in this chapter.

Part III

Answers may vary, but should include the concepts presented in this chapter, such as difficulties with implementing self-determination and transferring the rights of majority age.

CHAPTER 11

Part I

1. f
2. b
3. a

4. g
5. i

REFERENCES

Achenbach, T. M. (1986). *Child Behavior Checklist: Direct Observation Form, Revised Edition.* Burlington: University of Vermont Center for Children, Youth, and Families.

Achenbach, T. M. (1991a). *Manual for the Child Behavior Checklist/4–18 and 1991 profile.* Burlington: University of Vermont Department of Psychiatry.

Achenbach, T. M. (1991b). *Manual for the Teacher Report Form and 1991 profile.* Burlington: University of Vermont Department of Psychiatry.

Achenbach, T. M. (1991c). *Manual for the Youth Self-Report and 1991 Profile.* Burlington: University of Vermont Department of Psychiatry.

Achenbach, T. M. (1992). *Manual for the Child Behavior Checklist/2–3 and the 1992 Profile.* Burlington: University of Vermont Department of Psychiatry.

Achenbach, T. M., & McConaughy, S. H. (1989, 1990). *Semistructured Clinical Interview: Observation Form.* Burlington: University of Vermont Center for Children, Youth, and Families.

Achenbach, T. M., & Rescorla, L. A. (2000). *Manual for the ASEBA preschool forms & profiles: An integrated system of multi-informant assessment.* Burlington, VT: Authors.

Achenbach, T. M., & Rescorla, L. A. (2001). *Manual for the ASEBA school-age forms & profiles.* Burlington, VT: University of Vermont, Research Center for Children, Youth, & Families.

Algozzine, B., Christenson, S., & Ysseldyke, J. (1982). Probabilities associated with the referral-to-placement process. *Teacher Education and Special Education, 5,* 19–23.

Algozzine, B., Ysseldyke, J. E., & Christenson, S. (1983). An analysis of the incidence of special class placement: The masses are burgeoning. *The Journal of Special Education, 17,* 141–147.

Allinder, R. N. (1995). An examination of the relationship between teacher efficacy and curriculum-based measurement and student achievement. *Remedial and Special Education, 16,* 247–254.

Allinder, R. N., & Fuchs, L. S. (1992). Screening academic achievement: Review of the Peabody Individual Achievement Test–Revised. *Learning Disabilities Research & Practice, 7*(1), 45–47.

American Educational Research Association (AERA), American Psychological Association (APA) & National Council on Measurement in Education (NCME). (1999). *Standards for educational and psychological testing.* Washington, DC: AERA.

American Psychiatric Association. (1994). *Diagnostic and statistical manual of mental disorders* (4th ed.). Washington, DC: Author.

American Psychiatric Association. (2000). *Diagnostic and statistical manual of mental disorders,* (4th ed. Revised). Arlington, VA: Author.

American Psychological Association. (1985). *Standards for educational and psychological testing.* Washington, DC: Author.

Anastasi, A. (1988). *Psychological testing* (6th ed.). New York: Macmillan.

Anastasi, A., & Urbina, S. (1998). *Psychological testing* (7th ed.). Upper Saddle River, NJ: Prentice Hall.

Andrews, T. J., Wisnieswski, J. J., & Mulick, J. A. (1997). Variables influencing teachers' decisions to refer children for psychological assessment services. *Psychology in the Schools, 34,* 239–244.

Archbald, D. A. (1991). Authentic assessment: Principles, practices, and issues. *School Psychology Quarterly, 6,* 279–293.

Ardoin, S. P., Witt, J. C., Suldo, S. M., Connell, J. M., Koenig, J. L., Resetar, J. L., Slider, N. J., & Williams, K. L. (2004). Examining the incremental benefits of administering maze and three versus one curriculum-based measurement reading probes when conducting universal screening. *School Psychology Review, 33*(2), 218–233.

Bagnato, S. (1980). The efficacy of diagnostic reports as individualized guides to prescriptive goal planning. *Exceptional Children, 46*, 554–557.

Bailey, D. B., & Wolery, M. (1989). *Assessing infants and preschoolers with handicaps.* Upper Saddle River, NJ: Merrill/Prentice Hall.

Baker, S. K., & Good, R. (1995). Curriculum-based measurement of English reading with bilingual Hispanic students: A validation study with second grade students. *School Psychology Review, 24*(4), 561–578.

Barkley, R. A. (1990). *Attention deficit hyperactivity disorder: A handbook for diagnosis and treatment.* New York: Guilford.

Barkley, R. A., DuPaul, G. J., & McMurray, M. B. (1990). Comprehensive evaluation of attention deficit disorder with and without hyperactivity as defined by research criteria. *Journal of Consulting and Clinical Psychology, 58*, 775–789.

Barnes, W. (1986). Informal assessment of reading. *Pointer, 30*, 42–46.

Barnett, D., Zins, J., & Wise, L. (1984). An analysis of parental participation as a means of reducing bias in the education of handicapped children. *Special Services in the Schools, 1*, 71–84.

Barnett, D. W., Bell, S. H., Gilkey, C. M., Lentz, F. E., Graden, J. L., Stone, C. M., Smith, J. J., & Macmann, G. M. (1999). The promise of meaningful eligibility determination: Functional intervention-based multifactored preschool evaluation. *Journal of Special Education, 33*(2), 112–124.

Barnett, D. W., Macmann, G. M., & Carey, K. T. (1992). Early intervention and the assessment of developmental skills: Challenges and directions. *Topics in Early Childhood Special Education, 12*(1), 21–43.

Bayley, N. (1993). *Bayley scales of infant development-II.* San Antonio: Psychological Corporation.

Bellak, L., & Bellak, S. S. (1949). *Children's Apperception Test (animal figures).* Larchmont, NY: C.P.S.

Bellak, L., & Bellak, S. S. (1952). *Manual for the Supplement for the Children's Apperception Test.* Larchmont, NY: C.P.S.

Bellak, L., & Hurvich, M. S. (1965). *Children's Apperception Test (human figures) Manual.* Larchmont, NY: C.P.S.

Bender, W., & Golden, L. (1988). Adaptive behavior of learning disabled and non-learning disabled children. *Learning Disability Quarterly, 11*, 55–61.

Bennett, R. (1981). Professional competence and the assessment of exceptional children. *Journal of Special Education, 15*, 437–446.

Bennett, R. (1982). Cautions for the use of informal measures in the educational assessment of exceptional children. *Journal of Learning Disabilities, 15*, 337–339.

Bennett, R., & Shepherd, M. (1982). Basic measurement proficiency of learning disability specialists. *Learning Disabilities Quarterly, 5*, 177–183.

Bennett, T., Lee, H., & Lueke, B. (1998). Expectations and concerns: What mothers and fathers say about inclusion. *Education and Training in Mental Retardation and Developmental Disabilities, 33*(2), 108–122.

Berninger, V. L. (2006). Research-supported ideas for implementing reauthorized IDEA with intelligent professional psychological services. *Psychology in the Schools, 43*(7), 781–796.

Berninger, V. W. (2001). *Process assessment of the learner: Test battery for reading and writing.* San Antonio, TX: The Psychological Corporation.

Bersoff, D. N. (1981). Testing and the law. *American Psychologist, 36*, 1047–1056.

Bocian, K. M., Beebe, M. E., MacMillan, D., & Gresham, F. M. (1999). Competing paradigms in learning disabilities classification by schools and the variations in the meaning of discrepant achievement. *Learning Disabilities Research, 14*(1), 1–14.

Borg, W., Worthen, B., & Valcarce, R. (1986). Teachers' perceptions of the importance of educational measurement. *Journal of Experimental Education, 5*, 9–14.

Bracken, B. A. & McCallum, R. S. (1998). *Universal Test of Non-verbal Intelligence: Examiner's manual.* Itasca, IL: Riverside Publishing Company.

Brantlinger, E. (1987). Making decisions about special education placement: Do low-income parents have the information they need? *Journal of Learning Disabilities, 20*, 94–101.

Brazelton, T. (1984). *Neonatal Behavioral Assessment Scale-Second Edition.* Philadelphia: Lippincott.

Brigance, A. H. (1981). *Brigance diagnostic inventory of essential skills.* N. Billerica, MA: Curriculum Associates.

Brigance, A. H. (1997). *K & 1 screen.* North Billerica, MA: Curriculum Associates.

Brigance, A. H. (1998a). *Early preschool screen.* North Billerica, MA: Curriculum Associates.

Brigance, A. H. (1998b). *Preschool screen.* North Billerica, MA: Curriculum Associates.

Brigance, A. H. (1999). *Brigance Diagnostic Comprehensive Inventory of Basic Skills.* N. Billerica, MA: Curriculum Associates.

Brigance, A. H. (2004). *Brigance Diagnostic Inventory of Early Development-Second Edition.* N. Billerica, MA: Curriculum Associates.

Brigham, F. J., Tochterman, S., & Brigham, M. S. P. (2000). Students with emotional and behavioral disorders and their teachers in test-linked systems of accountability. *Assessment for Effective Intervention, 26*(1), 19–27.

Brotherson, M. J., & Berdine, W. H. (1993). Transition to adult services: Support for ongoing parent participation. *Remedial & Special Education, 14*(4), 44–52.

Brown, L., & Hammill, D. (1990). *Behavior Rating Profile* (2nd ed.). Austin, TX: Pro-Ed.

Brown, L., & Leigh, J. E. (1986). *Adaptive Behavior Inventory.* Austin, TX: Pro-Ed.

Brown, L., Sherbenou, R. J., & Johnsen, S. K. (1997). *Test of Nonverbal Intelligence, 3rd Edition.* Austin, TX: Pro-Ed.

Brown, T., Reynolds, C. R., & Whitaker, J. S. (1999). Bias in mental testing since Bias in Mental Testing. *School Psychology Quarterly, 14*(3), 208–238.

Brown, V. L., Cronin, M. E., & McEntire, E. (1994). *Test of mathematical abilities* (2nd ed.). Austin, TX: Pro-Ed.

Brown, V. L., Hammill, D. D., & Wiederholt, J. L. (1995). *The test of reading comprehension* (3rd ed.). Austin, TX: Pro-Ed.

Bruininks, R., Thurlow, M., & Gilman, C. (1987). Adaptive behavior and mental retardation. *Journal of Special Education, 21*, 69–88.

Bryant, B. R. (1998). Assistive technology: An introduction. *Journal of Learning Disabilities, 31*(1), 2–3.

Budoff, M., & Orenstein, A. (1981). Special education appeals hearings: Are they fair and are they helping? *Exceptional Education Quarterly, 2*, 37–48.

Burger, S. E., & Burger, D. L. (1994). Determining the validity of performance-based assessment. *Educational Measurement: Issues and Practices, 13*, 9–15.

Burnette, J. (1998, March). Reducing the disproportionate representation of minority students in special education. ERIC/OSEP Digest E566.

Burns, P. C., & Roe, B. D. (1989). *Informal Reading Inventory* (3rd ed.). Boston: Houghton Mifflin.

Cahan, S. (1989). Don't throw the baby out with the bath water: The case for using estimated true scores in normative comparisons. *Journal of Special Education, 22*, 503–506.

Campbell, E., Schellinger, T., & Beer, J. (1991). Relationship among the ready or not parental checklist for school readiness, the Brigance kindergarten and first grade screen, and SRA scores. *Perceptual and Motor Skills, 73*, 859–862.

Canivez, G. L. (1995). Validity of the Kaufman Brief Intelligence Test: Comparisons with the Wechsler Intelligence Scale for Children-Third Edition. *Psychological Assessment Resources, Inc. 2*(2), 101–111.

Canivez, G. L. (1996). Validity and diagnostic efficiency of the Kaufman Brief Intelligence Test in reevaluating students with learning disability. *Journal of Psychoeducational Assessment, 14*, 4–19.

Canter, A. (1991). Effective psychological services for all students: A data-based model of service delivery. In G. Stoner, M. R. Shinn, & H. M. Walker (Eds.), *Interventions for achievement and behavioral problems* (pp. 49–78). Silver Spring, MD: National Association of School Psychologists.

Canter, A. S. (1997). The future of intelligence testing in the schools. *School Psychology Review, 26*(2), 255–261.

Carroll, J. B. (1997). Commentary on Keith and Witta's hierarchical and cross-age confirmatory factor analysis of the WISC-III. *School Psychology Quarterly, 12*(2), 108–109.

Carroll, J. B. (2005). The three stratum theory of cognitive abilities. In D. P. Flanagan & P.L. Harrison (Eds.), *Contemporary intellectual assessment: Theories, tests, and issues* (pp. 69–76). New York: The Guilford Press.

Carter, J., & Sugai, G. (1989). Survey on pre-referral practices: Responses from state departments of education. *Exceptional Children, 55*, 298–308.

Cascella, P. W. (2006). Standardised speech-language tests and students with intellectual disability: A review of normative data. *Journal of Intellectual & Developmental Disability, 3*(2), 120–124.

Centers for Disease Control and Prevention (2007). Autism Information Center, ADDM, 2007. Available from the Centers for Disease Control and Prevention Web site, *http://www.cdc.gov/ncbddd/autism/overview.htm*

Chalfant, J. C., & Psyh, M. (1989). Teachers assistance teams: Five descriptive studies on 96 teams. *Remedial and Special Education, 10*(6), 49–58.

Clarizio, H. F., & Higgins, M. M. (1989). Assessment of severe emotional impairment: Practices and problems. *Psychology in the Schools, 26*, 154–162.

Clark, G. M. (1996). Transition planning assessment for secondary-level students with learning disabilities. *Journal of Learning Disabilities, 29*(1), 79–93.

Clark, G., & Patton, J. (1997). *Transition Planning Inventory.* Austin, TX: Pro-Ed.

Clark, G. M., & Patton, J. R. (2006). *Transition planning inventory: Update version.* Austin, TX: Pro-Ed.

Clark, G. M., Patton, J. R., & Moulton, L. R. (2000). *Informal assessments for transition planning.* Austin, TX: Pro-Ed.

Clarke, B., & Shinn, M. R. (2004). A preliminary investigation into the identification and development of early mathematics curriculum-based measurement. *School Psychology Review, 33*(2), 234–248.

Cohen, L. G., & Spenciner, L. J. (1994). *Assessment of young children.* New York: Longman.

Cole, J., D'Alonzo, B., Gallegos, A., Giordano, G., & Stile, S. (1992). Test biases that hamper learners with disabilities. *Diagnostique, 17*, 209–225.

Cole, J. C., Muenz, T. A., Ouchi, B. Y., Kaufman, N. L., & Kaufman, A. S. (1997). The impact of pictorial stimulis on written expression output of adolescents and adults. *Pyschology in the Schools, 34*, 1–9.

Cole, N. (1981). Bias in testing. *American Psychologist, 36*, 1067–1075.

Connelly, J. (1985). Published tests: Which ones do special education teachers perceive as useful? *Journal of Special Education, 19*, 149–155.

Conners, C. K. (1993). *Conners' Continuous Performance Test.* North Tonawanda, NY: Multi-Health Systems.

Conners, C. K. (1997). *Conners' Rating Scales–Revised: Technical Manual.* North Tonawanda, NY: Multi-Health Systems.

Connolly, A. J. (1988). *KeyMath-Revised: A Diagnostic Inventory of Essential Mathematics, manual. Forms A and B.* Circle Pines, MN: American Guidance Service.

Connolly, A. J. (2007). *KeyMath 3: Diagnostic battery.* Minneapolis, MN: NCS Pearson, Inc.

Conroy, M. A., Clark, D., Gable, R. A., & Fox, J. (1999). Building competence in the use of functional behavioral assessment. *Preventing School Failure, 43*(4), 140–144.

Council for Exceptional Children (1993). CEC policies for delivery of services: Ethnic and multicultural groups. *CEC Policy Manual,* section 3, part 1 (pp. 6, 20–21). Reston, VA: Author.

Council for Exceptional Children (1997–1999). *Standards for professional practice.* Reston, VA: Author.

Cronis, T. G., & Ellis, D. N. (2000, Summer). Issues facing special educators in the new millennium. *Education, 120*(4), 639–648.

Daly, E. J., Witt, J. C., Martens, B. K., & Dool, E. J. (1997). A model for conducting a functional analysis of academic performance problems. *School Psychology Review, 26*, 554–574.

Davis, L. B., Fuchs, L. S., Fuchs, D., & Whinnery, K. (1995). "Will CBM help me learn?" Students' perception of the benefits of curriculum-based measurement. *Education and Treatment of Children, 18,* 19–32.

Davis, W., & Shepard, L. (1983). Specialists' use of tests and clinical judgments in the diagnosis of learning disabilities. *Learning Disabilities Quarterly, 6,* 128–137.

deGruijter, D. N. M. (1997). On information of percentile ranks. *Journal of Educational Measurement, 34,* 177–178.

Del'Homme, M., Kasari, C., Forness, S. R., & Bagley, R. (1996). Prereferral intervention and students at risk for emotional or behavioral disorders. *Education and Treatment of Children, 19,* 272–285.

Demaray, M. K., & Elliott, S. N. (1998). Teachers' judgment of students' academic functioning: A comparison of actual and predicted performances. *School Psychology Quarterly, 13*(1), 8–24.

Deno, S. L. (1985). Curriculum-based measurement: The emerging alternative. *Exceptional Children, 52*(3), 219–232.

Deno, S. L. (1989). Curriculum-based measurement and alternative special education services: A fundamental and direct relationship. In M. R. Shinn (Ed.), *Curriculum-based measurement: Assessing special children* (pp. 1–17). New York: Gilford Press.

Deno, S. L. (2003). Developments in curriculum-based measurement. *The Journal of Special Education, 37*(3), 184–192.

Deno, S. L., Fuchs, L. S., Marston, D., & Shin, J. (2001). Using curriculum-based measurement to establish growth standards for students with learning disabilities. *School Psychology Review, 30*(4), 507–524.

Deno, S. L., Marston, D., & Mirkin, P. (1982). Valid measurement procedures for continuous evaluation of written expression. *Exceptional Children, 48*(4), 368–371.

Deno, S. L., Marston, D., Shinn, M., & Tindal, G. (1983). Oral reading fluency: A simple datum for scaling reading disability. *Topics in Learning and Learning Disabilities, 2*(4), 53–59.

Detterman, D. K., & Thompson, L. A. (1997). What is so special about special education? *American Psychologist, 52*(10), 1082–1090.

Detterman, D. K., & Thompson, L. A. (1998). They doth protest too much. *American Psychologist, 53*(10), 1162–1163.

Diana v. State Board of Education, Civil Act. No. C-70–37 (N.D. Cal, 1970, further order, 1973).

DiLavore, P., Loard, C., & Rutter, M. (1995). Pre-Linguistic Autism Diagnostic Observation Schedule (PL-ADOS). *Journal of Autism and Pervasive Developmental Disorders, 25,* 355–379.

Doll, E. A. (1935). A genetic scale of social maturity. *American Journal of Orthopsychiatry, 5,* 180–188.

Drasgow, E. & Yell, M. (2001). Functional behavioral assessments: Legal requirements and challenges. *School Psychology Review, 30*(2), 239–251.

Drasgow, E., Yell, M. L., Bradley, R., Shriner, J. G. (1999). The IDEA Amendments of 1997: A school-wide model for conducting functional behavioral assessments and developing behavioral intervention plans. *Education and Treatment of Children, 22*(3), 244–266.

Dunn, L. M., & Dunn, D. M. (1997). *Peabody picture vocabulary yest-III.* Circle Pines, MN: American Guidance Service.

Dunn, L.M., & Dunn, D.M. (2007). *Peabody Picture Vocabulary Test-4.* Wascana Limited Partnership. Minneapolis, MN. NCS Pearson, Inc.

Dunst, C. J., Johanson, C., Trivette, C. M., & Hamby, D. (1991). Family-oriented early intervention policies and practices: Family-centered or not? *Exceptional Children, 58,* 115–126.

Eaves, R. (1985). Educational assessment in the United States [Monograph]. *Diagnostique, 10,* 5–39.

Eckert, T. L., Shapiro, E. S., & Lutz, J. G. (1995). Teachers' ratings of the acceptability of curriculum-based assessment methods. *School Psychology Review, 24,* 497–511.

Education of the Handicapped Act (1975, 1977). PL 94–142, 20 U.S.C. §§ 1400–1485, 34 CFR-300.

Ehri, L. C., Nunes, S. R., Willows, D. M., Schuster, B. V., Yaghoub-Zadeh, Z., & Shanahan, T. (2001). Phonemic awareness instruction helps children learn to read: Evidence from the national reading panel's meta-analysis. *Reading Research Quarterly, 36*(3), 250–287.

Eliason, M. J., & Richman, L. C. (1987). The Continuous Performance Test in learning disabled and nondisabled children. *Journal of Learning Disabilities, 20,* 614–619.

Elliott, S. N., Braden, J. P., & White, J. L. (2001). *Assessing one and all: Educational accountability for students with disabilities.* Arlington, VA: Council for Exceptional Children.

Elliot, S. N., Busse, R. T., & Gresham, F. M. (1993). Behavior rating scales: Issues of use and development. *School Psychology Review, 22,* 313–321.

Elliott, S. N., & Fuchs, L. S. (1997). The utility of curriculum-based measurement and performance assessment as alternatives to traditional intelligence and achievement tests. *School Psychology Review, 26*(3) 224–233.

Elliott, S. N., Kratochwill, T. R., & Schulte, A. G. (1998). The assessment accommodation checklist. *Teaching Exceptional Children,* Nov./Dec., 10–14.

Engiles, A., Fromme, C., LeResche, D., & Moses, P. (1999). *Keys to access: Encouraging the use of mediation by families from diverse backgrounds.* (Document No. EC 307 554). Consortium for Appropriate Dispute Resolution in Special Education. (ERIC Document Reproduction Service No. ED 436 881)

Epstein, M.H., & Cullinan, D. (1998). *Scale for assessing emotional disturbance.* Austin, TX: Pro-Ed.

Ervin, R. A., Radford, P. M., Bertsch, K., Piper, A. L., Ehrhardt, K. E., & Poling, A. (2001). A descriptive analysis and critique of the empirical literature on school-based functional assessment. 193–210.

Etscheidt, S., & Knesting, K. (2007). A qualitative analysis of factors influencing the interpersonal dynamics of a prereferral team. *School Psychology Quarterly, 22*(2), 264–288.

Evans, L., & Bradley-Johnson, S. (1988). A review of recently developed measures of adaptive behavior. *Psychology in the Schools, 25,* 276–287.

Evans, S., & Evans, W. (1986). A perspective on assessment for instruction. *Pointer, 30,* 9–12.

Evans, W. H., Evans, S. S., & Schmid, R. E. (1989). *Behavioral and instructional management: An ecological approach.* Boston: Allyn & Bacon.

Fan, X., Wilson, V. L., & Reynolds, C. R. (1995). Assessing the similarity of the factor structure of the K-ABC for African American and white children. *Journal of Psychoeducational Assessment, 13,* 120–131.

Federal Register (1977, August 23). Washington, DC: U.S. Government Printing Office.

Federal Register. (1992, September 29). Washington, DC: U.S. Government Printing Office.

Federal Register (1993, July 30). Washington, DC: U.S. Government Printing Office.

Federal Register. (1999, March 12). Washington, DC: U.S. Government Printing Office.

Federal Register (2006, August 14). Washington, DC: U.S. Government Printing Office.

Feldt, L., Sabers, D., & Reschly, D. (1988). Comments on the reply by Salvia and Ysseldyke. *Journal of Special Education, 22,* 374–377.

Felton, R. H., & Pepper, P. P. (1995). Early identification and intervention of phonological deficits in kindergarten and early elementary children at risk for reading disability. *School Psychology Review, 24*(3), 405–414.

Fewell, R. R. (1991). Trends in the assessment of infants and toddlers with disabilities. *Exceptional Children, 58,* 166–173.

Field, S. Martin, J., Miller, R., Ward, M., & Wehmeyer, M. (1998). *A practical guide to teaching self-determination.* Reston, VA: Council for Exceptional Children.

Filipek, P. A., Accardo, P. J., Baranek, G. T., Cook, E. H., Jr., Dawson, G., Gordon, B., et al. (1999). The screening and diagnosis of autism spectrum disorders. *Journal of Autism and Developmental Disabilities, 29*(6), 439–484.

Flanagan, D. P., & Harrison, P. L. (Eds.) (2005). *Contemporary intellectual assessment: Theories, tests, and issues.* New York: The Guilford Press.

Flanagan, D. P., & Ortiz, S. (2001). *Essentials of cross-battery assessment.* New York: John Wiley & Sons, Inc.

Flaugher, R. (1978). The many definitions of test bias. *American Psychologist, 33,* 671–679.

Foegen, A., Jiban, C., Deno, S. (2007). Progress monitoring measures in mathematics: A review of the literature. *The Journal of Special Education, 4*(2), 121–139.

Forness, S. R., Swanson, J. M., Cantwell, D. P., Guthrie, D., & Sena, R. (1992). Responses to stimulant medication across six measures of school related performance in children with ADHD and disruptive behavior. *Behavioral Disorders, 18,* 42–53.

Foster-Gaitskell, D., & Pratt, C. (1989). Comparison of parent and teacher ratings of adaptive behavior of children with mental retardation. *American Journal of Mental Retardation, 94,* 177–181.

Fradd, S., & Hallman, C. (1983). Implications of psychological and educational research for assessment and instruction of culturally and linguistically different students. *Learning Disabilities Quarterly, 6,* 468–477.

Fuchs, D. (1991). Mainstream assistance teams: A prereferral intervention system for difficult to teach students. In Stoner, G., Shinn, M. R., & Walker, H. M. (Eds.), *Interventions for achievement and behavior problems* (pp. 241–267). Silver Spring, MD: National Association of School Psychologists.

Fuchs, D., & Fuchs, L. (1989). Effects of examiner familiarity on Black, Caucasian, and Hispanic children: A meta-analysis. *Exceptional Children, 55,* 303–308.

Fuchs, D., Fuchs, L., Benowitz, S., & Barringer, K. (1987). Norm-referenced tests: Are they valid for uses with handicapped students? *Exceptional Children, 54,* 263–271.

Fuchs, D., Zern, D., & Fuchs, L. (1983). A microanalysis of participant behavior in familiar and unfamiliar test conditions. *Exceptional Children, 50,* 75–77.

Fuchs, L. S. (2004). The past, present, and future of curriculum-based measurement research. *School Psychology Review, 33*(2), 188–192.

Fuchs, L., Butterworth, J., & Fuchs, D. (1989). Effects of ongoing curriculum-based measurement on student awareness of goals and progress. *Education and Treatment of Children, 12,* 41–47.

Fuchs, L. S., Deno, S. L., & Mirkin, P. (1984). Effects of frequent curriculum-based measurement and evaluation on pedagogy, student achievement, and student awareness of learning. *American Educational Research Journal, 21,* 449–460.

Fuchs, L. S., & Fuchs, D. (1986). Effects of a systematic formative evaluation: A meta-analysis. *Exceptional Children, 53,* 199–208.

Fuchs, L., & Fuchs, D. (1992). Identifying a measure for monitoring student reading progress. *School Psychology Review, 21,* 45–58.

Fuchs, L. S., & Fuchs, D. (1996). Combining performance assessment and curriculum-based measurement to strengthen instructional planning. *Learning Disabilities Research & Practice, 11,* 183–192.

Fuchs, L. Fuchs, D., & Hamlett, C. (1989). Effects of instrumental use of curriculum-based measurement to enhance instructional programs. *Remedial and Special Education, 10,* 43–52.

Fuchs, L. Fuchs, D., Hamlett, C. L., Phillips, N. B., & Bentz, J. (1994). Classwide curriculum-based measurement: Helping general educators meet the challenge of student diversity. *Exceptional Children, 60,* 518–537.

Fuchs, L. S., Fuchs, D., Hamlett, C. L., Walz, C. L., & Germann, G. (1993). Formative evaluation of academic progress: How much growth can we expect? *School Psychology Review, 22*(1), 27–48.

Fuchs, L. S., Fuchs, D., Hamlett, C. L., & Stecker, P. M. (1991). Effects of curriculum-based measurement and consultation on teacher planning and student achievement in mathematics operations. *American Educational Research Journal, 28,* 617–641.

Fuchs, L., Tindal, G., & Deno, S. (1984). Methodological issues in curriculum-based assessment. *Diagnostique, 9,* 191–207.

Fugate, D. J., Clarizio, H. F., & Phillips, S. E. (1993). Referral-to-placement ratio:

A finding in need of reassessment? *Journal of Learning Disabilities, 26*(6), 413–416.

Fujiura, G. T., & Yamaki, K. (2000). Trends in demography of childhood poverty and disability. *Exceptional Children, 66*(2), 187–199.

Gable, R. A., Hendrickson, J. M., & Smith, C. (1999). Changing discipline policies and practices: Finding a place for functional behavioral assessments in schools. *Preventing School Failure, 43*(4), 167–170.

Gardner, H. (1993). *Multiple intelligences: The theory in practice.* New York: Basic Books.

German, D., Johnson, B., & Schneider, M. (1985). Learning disability vs. reading disability: A survey of practitioners' diagnostic populations and test instruments. *Learning Disability Quarterly, 8*, 141–156.

Gilliam, J.E. (2006). *Gilliam autism rating scale: Examiner's manual.* Austin, TX: Pro-Ed.

Gillis, M., & Olson, M. (1987). Elementary IRIs: Do they reflect what we know about text/type structure and comprehension? *Reading Research and Instruction, 27*, 36–44.

Gindis, B. (1999). Vygotsky's vision: Reshaping the practice of special education for the 21st century. *Remedial and Special Education, 20*, 333–340.

Glascoe, F. P. (1998). *Technical report for the Brigance screens.* North Billerica, MA: Curriculum Associates.

Glascoe, F. P. (1999). *CIBS-R standardization and validation manual.* N. Billerica, MA: Curriculum Associates.

Glascoe, F. P. (2004). *IED-II standardization and validation manual.* N. Billerica, MA: Curriculum Associates.

Glaser, R. (1963). Instructional technology and the measurement of learning outcomes: Some questions. *American Psychologist, 18*(2), 519–521.

Glatthorn, A. A. (1998). *Performance assessment and standards-based curricula: The achievement cycle.* Larchmont, NY: Eye on Education.

Goff, W. H. (2002). *Guidelines for writing objective reports.* Unpublished manuscript.

Goldstein, S., Strickland, B., Turnbull, A., & Curry, L. (1980). An observational analysis of the IEP conference. *Exceptional Children, 46*, 278–286.

Goldstein, S., & Turnbull, A. (1982). Strategies to increase parent participation in IEP conferences. *Exceptional Children, 48*, 360–361.

Good, R., & Salvia, J. (1988). Curriculum bias in published, norm-referenced reading tests: Demonstrable effects. *School Psychology Review, 17*, 51–60.

Goodman, J. F., & Hover, S. A. (1992). The Individual Family Service Plan: Unresolved problems. *Psychology in the Schools, 29*, 140–151.

Gopaul-McNicol, S., & Thomas-Presswood, T. (1998). *Working with linguistically and culturally different children: Innovative clinical and educational approaches.* Boston: Allyn & Bacon.

Gordon, M. (1983). *Gordon Diagnostic System.* DeWitt, NY: Gordon Diagnostic Systems.

Gotham, K., Risi, S., Pickles, A., Lord, C. (2007). The Autism Diagnostic observation schedule: Revised algorithms for improved diagnostic validity. *Journal of Autism and Developmental Disorders, 37*(4), 613–627.

Graden, J., Casey, A., & Bonstrom, O. (1985). Implementing a prereferral intervention system: Part II. The data. *Exceptional Children, 51*, 487–496.

Graden, J., Casey, A., & Christenson, S. (1985). Implementing a prereferral intervention system: Part I. The model. *Exceptional Children, 51*, 377–384.

Graham, M., & Scott, K. (1988). The impact of definitions of high risk on services of infants and toddlers. *Topics in Early Childhood Special Education, 8*(3), 23–28.

Granville, R., Shaver, R. B., & McGrew, K. S. (2003). Interpretation of the Woodcock-Johnson III Tests of Cognitive Abilities: Acting on evidence. In F. A. Schrank & D. P. Flanagan (Eds.), WJ III clinical use and interpretation (pp. 3–39). San Diego, CA: Academic Press.

Greenspan, S. I. (1992). *Infancy and early childhood: The practice of clinical assessment and intervention with emotional and developmental challenges.* Madison, CT: International University Press.

Greenwood, C. R., Tapia, Y., Abott, M., & Walton, C. (2003). A building-based case study of evidence-based literacy practices: Implementation, reading behavior, and growth in reading fluency, K-4. *Journal of Special Education, 37*(2), 95–111.

Gresham, F. M., MacMillan, D. L., & Bocian, K. M. (1998). Agreement between school study team decisions and authoritative definitions in classifications of students at-risk for mild disabilities. *School Psychology Quarterly, 13*(3), 181–191.

Gresham, F. M., Watson, T. S., & Skinner, C. H. (2001). Functional behavioral assessment: Principles, procedures, and future directions. *School Psychology Review, 30*(2), 156–172.

Gridley, B. E., & McIntosh, D. E. (1991). Confirmatory factor analysis of the Stanford–Binet: Fourth Edition for a normal sample. *Journal of School Psychology, 29,* 237–248.

Gronna, S., Jenkins, A., & Chin-Chance, S. (1998). The performance of students with disabilities in a norm-referenced, statewide standardized testing program. *Journal of Learning Disabilities, 31*(5), 482–493.

Guerin, G. R., & Maier, A. S. (1983). *Informal assessment in education.* Palo Alto, CA: Mayfield.

Haager, D, (2007). Promises and cautions regarding using response to intervention with English Language Learners. Learning Disabilities Quarterly, *30*(3), 213–218.

Halgren, D. W., & Clarizio, H. F. (1993). Categorical and programming changes in special education services. *Exceptional Children, 59,* 547–555.

Hammill, D. D. (1998). *Detroit Tests of Learning Aptitude-4.* Austin, TX: Pro-Ed.

Hammill, D. D., & Hresko, W. P. (1994). *Comprehensive Scales of Student Abilities.* Austin, TX: Pro-Ed.

Hammill, D. D., & Larsen, S. C. (1996). *Test of Written Language.* Austin, TX: Pro-Ed.

Hammill, D. D., & Newcomer, P. L. (1997). *Test of Language Development-Intermediate: Third edition.* Austin, TX: Pro-Ed.

Hammill, D. D., Pearson, N. A., & Wiederholt, J. L. (1996). *Comprehensive Test of Nonverbal Intelligence.* Austin, TX: Pro-Ed.

Hammill, D. D., & Larsen, S. C. (1999). *Test of Written Language, Third Edition.* Austin, TX: Pro-Ed.

Harris, D. B. (1963). *Goodenough–Harris drawing test.* New York: Harcourt Brace.

Harris, K., & Graham, S. (1994). Constructivism: Principles, paradigms, and integration. *Journal of Special Education, 28,* 233–247.

Harrison, P. (1987). Research with adaptive behavior scales. *Journal of Special Education, 21,* 37–61.

Harrison, P. L., Kaufman, A. S., Kaufman, N. L., Bruininks, R. H., Rynders, J., Ilmer, S., Sparrow, S. S., & Cicchetti, D. V. (1990). *AGS early screening profiles.* Circle Pines, MN: American Guidance Service.

Harrison, P. L., & Robinson, B. (1995). Best practices in the assessment of adaptive behavior. In A. Thomas & J. Grimes (Eds.), *Best practices in school psychology* (3rd ed.). Washington, DC: National Association of School Psychologists.

Harry, B., & Anderson, M. G. (1995). The disproportionate placement of African American males in special education programs: A critique of the process. *Journal of Negro Education, 63*(4), 602–619.

Hart, K. E., & Scuitto, M. J. (1996). Criterion-referenced measurement of instructional impact on cognitive outcomes. *Journal of Instructional Psychology, 23,* 26–34.

Harvey, V. (1991). Characteristics of children referred to school psychologists: A discriminant analysis. *Psychology in the Schools, 28,* 209–218.

Hasazi, S. B., Johnston, A. P., Liggett, A. M., & Schattman, R. A. (1994). A qualitative policy study of the least restrictive environment provision of the Individuals with Disabilities Education Act. *Exceptional Children, 60,* 491–507.

Heller, K., Holtzman, W., & Messick, S. (Eds.). (1982). *Placing children in special education: A strategy for equity.* Washington, DC: National Academy Press.

Herrnstein, R. J., & Murray, C. (1994). *The bell curve: Intelligence and class structure in American life.* New York: The Free Press.

Heshusius, L. (1991). Curriculum-based assessment and direct instruction: Critical reflections on fundamental assumptions. *Exceptional Children, 57*, 315–328.

Hintze, J. M., & Christ, T. J. (2004). An examination of variability as a function of passage variance in CBM monitoring. *School Psychology Review, 33*(2), 204–217.

Hintze, J. M., Shapiro, E. S., & Lutz, J. G. (1994). The effects of curriculum on the sensitivity of curriculum-based measurement in reading. *Journal of Special Education, 28*, 188–202.

Hobbs, R. (1993). Portfolio use in a learning disabilities resource room. *Reading & Writing Quarterly: Overcoming Learning Difficulties, 9*, 249–261.

Hong, B. S. S., Ivy, W. F., Gonzalez, H. R., & Ehrensberger, W.(2007). Preparing students for post-secondary education. *Teaching Exceptional Children, 40*(1), 32–38.

Hopkins, K. D., Stanley, J. C., & Hopkins, B. R. (1990). *Educational and psychological measurement and evaluation* (7th ed.). Upper Saddle River, NJ: Prentice Hall.

Horn, E., & Fuchs, D. (1987). Using adaptive behavior in assessment and intervention. *Journal of Special Education, 21*, 11–26.

Hosp, M. K., & Hosp, J. L. (2003). Curriculum-based measurement for reading, spelling, and math: How to do it and why. *Preventing School Failure, 48*(1), 10–18.

Howell, K. W., & Morehead, M. K. (1987). *Curriculum-based evaluation for special and remedial education.* Columbus, OH: Merrill.

Hoy, M., & Retish, P. (1984). A comparison of two types of assessment reports. *Exceptional Children, 51*, 225–229.

Huebner, E. (1988). Bias in teachers' special education decisions as a further function of test score reporting format. *Journal of Educational Researcher, 21*, 217–220.

Huebner, E. (1989). Errors in decision making: A comparison of school psychologists' interpretations of grade equivalents, percentiles, and deviation IQs. *School Psychology Review, 18*, 51–55.

Huebner, E. S. (1991). Bias in special education decisions: The contribution of analogue research. *School Psychology Quarterly, 6*(1), 50–65.

Huefner, D. S. (2000). The risks and opportunities of the IEP requirements under the IDEA 1997. *Journal of Special Education, 33*(4), 195–204.

Hultquist, A. M., & Metzke, L. K. (1993). Potential effects of curriculum bias in individual norm-referenced reading and spelling achievement tests. *Journal of Psychoeducational Assessment, 11*, 337–344.

Individuals with Disabilities Education Act Amendments of 1997, PL. 105–17, 105th Congress.

Individuals with Disabilities Education Act (IDEA, 20 U.S.C. § 1400 et seq. (1997).

Individuals with Disabilities Education Improvement Act of 2004, P. L. 108–446, 20 U.S.C. § 1400 et seq.

Individuals with Disabilities Education Act Regulations, 34, CFR. §§ 300 and 303 (1999).

Jackson, G. D. (1975). Another psychological view from the Association of Black Psychologists. *American Psychologist, 30*, 88–93.

Javorsky, J. (1998–1999). Behavior-Rating Profile, Second Edition. *Monograph: Assessment for the New Decade, Diagnostic, 24*(1–4), 33–40.

Jensen, A. R. (1998). *The g factor: The science of mental ability.* Westport, CT: Praeger.

Johnson, S. B. (1999). Test reviews: Normative update for Kaufman Educational Achievement, Peabody Individual Achievement Test–Revised, KeyMath–Revised, and Woodcock Reading Mastery Test–Revised. *Psychology in the Schools, 36*(2),175–176.

Kamphaus, R. (1987). Conceptual and psychometric issues in the assessment of adaptive behavior. *Journal of Special Education, 21*, 27–35.

Kamphaus, R. W., Winsor, A. P., Rowe, E. W., & Kim, S. (2005). A history of intelligence test interpretation. In D. P. Flanagan & P. L. Harrison (Eds.), *Contemporary intellectual assessment: Theories, tests, and issues* (pp. 23–37). New York: The Guilford Press.

Kamps, D., Abbott, M., Greenwood, C., Arregaga-Mayer, C., Wills, H., et al. (2007). Use of evidence-based, small group reading instruction for English language learners in elementary grades: Secondary-tier intervention. *Learning Disability Quarterly, 30*(3), 153–168.

Katsiyannis, A. (1994). Prereferral practices: Under Office of Civil Rights scrutiny.

Journal of Developmental and Physical Disabilities, 6, 73–76.

Katz, K. S. (1989). Strategies for infant assessment: Implications of P.L. 99-457. *Topics in Early Childhood Special Education, 9*(3), 99–109.

Kaufman, A. S. (1979). *Intelligent testing with the WISC–R.* New York: Wiley.

Kaufman, A. S. (1994). *Intelligent Testing With the WISC–III.* New York: Wiley.

Kaufman, A. S., & Horn, J. L. (1996). Age changes on tests of fluid and crystallized ability for women and men on the Kaufman Adolescent and Adult Intelligence Test (KAIT) at ages 17–94 years. *Archives of Clinical Neuropsychology, 11,* 97–121.

Kaufman, A. S., & Kaufman, N. L. (1990). *Kaufman Brief Intelligence Test.* Circle Pines, MN: American Guidance Service.

Kaufman, A. S., & Kaufman, N. L. (1993). *Kaufman Adolescent and Adult Intelligence Test.* Circle Pines, MN: American Guidance Service.

Kaufman, A. S., & Kaufman, N. L. (1993). *K-SEALS: Kaufman survey of early academic and language skills.* Circle Pines, MN: American Guidance Service.

Kaufman, A. S., & Kaufman, N. L. (1994). *Kaufman functional academic skills test.* Circle Pines, MN: American Guidance Service, Inc.

Kaufman, A. S., & Kaufman, N. L. (2004). *Kaufman Test of Educational Achievement* (2nd ed.) Circle Pines, MN: AGS Publishing.

Kaufman, A. S., Litchenberger, E. O., Fletcher-Janzen, E., & Kaufman, N. L. (2005). *Essentials of KABC-II assessment.* New York: John Wiley & Sons, Inc.

Kaufman, A. S., McLean, J. E., & Kaufman, J. C. (1995). The fluid and crystallized abilities of White, Black, and Hispanic adolescents and adults, both with and without an education covariate. *Journal of Clinical Psychology, 51,* 636–647.

Kaufman, A. S., & Wang, J. (1992). Gender, race, and education differences on the K-BIT at ages 4 to 90 years. *Journal of Psychoeducational Assessment, 10,* 219–229.

Kaye, H. S. (1998). Is the status of people with disabilities improving? *Abstract 21: Disability Statistics Center.* San Francisco: University of California.

Keith, T. Z., Fugate, M. H., DeGraff, M., Diamond, C. M., Shadrach, E. A., & Stevens, M. L. (1995). Using multi-sample confirmatory factor analysis to test for construct bias: An example using the K-ABC. *Journal of Psychoeducational Assessment, 13,* 347–364.

Keith, T. Z., & Witta, E. L. (1997). Hierarchical and cross-age confirmatory factor analysis of the WISC-III: What does it measure? *School Psychology Quarterly, 12*(2), 89–107.

Keogh, B. K., Forness, S. R., & MacMillan, D. L. (1998). The real world of special education. *American Psychologist, 53*(10), 1161–1162.

Kerr, M. M., & Nelson, C. M. (2002). *Strategies for addressing behavioral problems in the classroom* (4th ed.). Upper Saddle River, NJ: Merrill/Prentice Hall.

Klinger, J. K., Vaughn, S., Schumm, J. S., Cohen, P., & Forgan, J. W. (1998). Inclusion or pull-out: Which do students prefer? *Journal of Learning Disabilities, 31,* 148–158.

Knoff, H. M. (1998). Review of the Children's Apperception Test (1991 Revision). In J. C. Impara and B. S. Plake (Eds.), *The thirteenth mental measurements yearbook* (pp. 231–233). Lincoln: University of Nebraska Press.

Knoff, H. M., & Prout, H. T. (1985). *Kinetic Family Drawing System for Family and School: A handbook.* Los Angeles: Western Psychological Services.

Koppitz, E. (1968). *Human Figure Drawing Test.* New York: Grune & Stratton.

Kranzler, J. H. (1997). What does the WISC–III measure? Comments on the relationship between intelligence, working memory capacity, and information processing speed and efficiency. *School Psychology Quarterly, 12*(2), 110–116.

Kroon, N., Goudena, P. P., & Rispens, J. (1998). Thematic apperception tests for child and adolescent assessment: A practitioner's consumer guide. *Journal of Psychoeducational Assessment, 16,* 99–117.

Kubicek, F. C. (1994). Special education reform in light of select state and federal court decisions. *Journal of Special Education, 28,* 27–42.

Kubick, R. J., Bard, E. M., & Perry, J. D. (2000). Manifestation determinations: Discipline guidelines for children with disabilities. In Telzrow, C. F., & Tankersley, M. (Eds.), *IDEA: Amendments of 1997: Practice guidelines for school-based teams* (pp. 1–28). Bethesda, MD: National Association of School Psychologists.

Kush, J. C. (1996). Factor structure of the WISC–III for students with learning disabilities. *Journal of Psychoeducational Assessment, 14,* 32–40.

LaGrow, S., & Prochnow-LaGrow, J. (1982). Technical adequacy of the most popular tests selected by responding school psychologists in Illinois. *Psychology in the Schools, 19,* 186–189.

Lambert, N., Nihira, K., & Leland, H. (1993). *AAMR adaptive behavior scale-school, second edition.* Austin, TX: Pro-Ed.

Larry P. v. Riles, 343 F. Supp. 1306, aff'd., 502 F.2d 963, further proceedings, 495 F. Supp. 926, aff'd., 502 F.2d 693 (9th Cir. 1984).

Larsen, S. C., Hammill, D. D., & Moats, L. C. (1999). *Test of Written Spelling–4.* Austin, TX: Pro-Ed.

Lavin, C. (1996). The Wechsler Intelligence Scale for Children–Third Edition and the Stanford–Binet Intelligence Scale, Fourth Edition: A preliminary study of validity. *Psychological Reports, 78,* 491–496.

Lee, S. W., Elliott, J., & Barbour, J. D. (1994). A comparison of cross-informant behavior ratings in school-based diagnosis. *Behavioral Disorders, 192,* 87–97.

Lennon, J. E., & Slesinski, C. (1999). Early intervention in reading: Results of a screening and intervention program for kindergarten students. *School Psychology Review, 28,* 353–365.

Levine, P., & Nourse, S. W. (1998). What follow-up studies say about postschool life for young men and women with learning disabilities: A critical look at the literature. *Journal of Learning Disabilities, 31*(3), 212–233.

Levinson, E. M. (1995). Best practices in transition services. In A. Thomas & J. Grimes (Eds.), *Best practices in school psychology-III*

(pp. 909–915). Washington, DC: The National Association of School Psychologists.

Lidz, C. S. (1997). Dynamic assessment approaches. In D. P. Flanagan, J. L. Genshaft, & P. L. Harrison (Eds.), *Contemporary intellectual assessment: Theories, tests, and issues* (pp. 281–296). New York: Guilford Press.

Linan-Thompson, S., Vaughn, S., Prater, K., & Cirino, P. T. (2006). The response to intervention of English language learners at risk for reading problems. *Journal of Learning Disabilities, 39*(5), 390–398.

Lindsey, P., Wehmeyer, M. L., Guy, B., & Martin, J. (2001). Age of majority and mental retardation: A position statement of the division on mental retardation and developmental disabilities. *Education and Training in Mental Retardation and Developmental Disabilities, 36*(1), 3–15.

Lindstrom, L., Doren, B., Metheny, J., Johnson, P., & Zane, C. (2007). Transition to employment: Role of the family in career development. Exceptional Children, *73*(3), 348–366.

Lipsky, D. K., & Gartner, A. (1997). *Inclusion and school reform: Transforming America's classrooms.* Baltimore, MD: Brookes Publishing.

Litchenberger, E. O., & Smith, D. R. (2005). *Essentials of WIAT-II and KTEA-II assessment.* Hoboken, NJ: John Wiley & Sons, Inc.

Loiser, B. J., McGrath, P. J., & Klein, R. M. (1996). Error patterns on the continuous performance test in nonmedicated and medicated samples of children with and without ADHD: A meta-analytic review. *Journal of Child Psychology and Psychiatry, 37,* 971–987.

Lopez, E. C. (1995). Best practices in working with bilingual children. In Alex Thomas and Jeff Grimes (Eds.), *Best practices in school psychology* (3rd ed., p. 1113). Bethesda, MD: National Association of School Psychologists.

Lopez, R. (1997). The practical impact of current research and issues in intelligence test interpretation and use for multicultural populations. *School Psychology Review, 26*(2), 249–254.

Lora v. New York City Board of Education, 1984: Final order, August 2, 1984, 587F. Supp. 1572 (E.D.N.Y. 1984).

Lord, C., Rutter, M., DiLavore, P. C., & Risi, S. (2002). Autism diagnostic observation schedule. Los Angeles, CA: Western Psychological Services.

Lord, C., Rutter, M., Goode, S., Heemsbergen, J., Jordan, H., Mawhood, L., & Schopler, E. (1989). Autism Diagnostic Observation Schedule: A standardized observation of communicative and social behavior. *Journal of Autism Spectrum Disorders, 19,* 185–212.

Lusting, D. D., & Saura, K. M. (1996, Spring). Use of criterion-based comparisons in determining the appropriateness of vocational evaluation test modifications for criterion-referenced tests. *Vocational Evaluation and Work Adjustment Bulletin.*

MacMillan, D. L., & Forness, S. R. (1998). The role of IQ in special education placement decisions: Primary and determinative or peripheral and inconsequential. *Remedial and Special Education, 19,* 239–253.

MacMillan, D. L., Gresham, F. M., & Bocian, K. (1998). Discrepancy between definitions of learning disabilities and school practices: An empirical investigation. *Journal of Learning Disabilities, 32*(4), 314–326.

Macready, T. (1991). Special education: Some thoughts for policy makers. *Educational Psychology in Practice, 7*(3), 148–152.

Marchand-Martella, N. E., Ruby, S. F., & Martella, R. C. (2007). Intensifying reading instruction for students within a three-tier model: Standard protocol and problem solving approaches within a response-to-intervention (RTI) system. *Teaching Exceptional Children Plus: 3,* 5, Article 2. Retrieved October 1, 2007 from: *http://escholarship.bc.edu/education/tecplus/vol 13/iss5/art2*

Mardell-Czudnowski, C. (1995). Performance of Asian and White children on the K-ABC: Understanding information processing differences. *Psychological Assessment Resources, Inc., 2*(1), 19–29.

Mardell-Czudnowski, C., & Goldenberg, D. (1998). *Developmental indicators for the assessment of learning* (3rd ed.). Circle Pines, MN: American Guidance Service.

Markwardt, F. C. (1989). *Peabody Individual Achievement Test-Revised.* Circle Pines, MN: American Guidance Service.

Marsh, T. Y., & Cornell, D. G. (2001). The contributions of student experiences to understanding ethnic differences in high risk behaviors at school. *Behavior Disorders, 26*(2), 152–163.

Marso, R. N., & Pigge, F. L. (1991). An analysis of teacher-made tests: Item types, cognitive demands, and item construction errors. *Contemporary Educational Psychology, 16,* 279–286.

Marston, D., Fuchs, L., & Deno, S. (1986). Measuring pupil progress: A comparison of standardized achievement tests and curriculum related measures. *Diagnostique, 11,* 77–90.

Marston, D., Mirkin, P. K., & Deno, S. L. (1984). Curriculum-based measurement: An alternative to traditional screening, referral, and identification. *Journal of Special Education, 18,* 109–118.

Marston, D., Muyskens, P., Lau, M., & Canter, A. (2003). Problem-solving model for decision making with high incidence disabilities: The Minneapolis experience. *Learning Disabilities Research & Practice, 18*(3), 187–201.

Marston, D. B. (1989). A curriculum-based measurement approach to assessing academic performance: What it is and why we do it. In M. R. Shinn (Eds.), *Curriculum-based measurement: Assessing special children* (pp. 18–78). New York: Guilford.

Mather, N., Wendling, B. J., & Woodcock, R. W. (2001). *Essentials of WJ III Tests of Achievement assessment.* Hoboken, NJ: John Wiley & Sons, Inc.

Mather, N., & Woodcock, R. W. (2001). *Examiner's manual. Woodcock–Johnson III Tests of Achievement.* Itasca, IL: Riverside Publishing.

Mattison, R. E., Bagnato, S. J., Mayes, S. D., & Felix, B. C. (1990). Reliability and validity of teacher diagnostic ratings for children with behavioral and emotional disorders. *Journal of Psychoeducational Assessment,* 8, 509–517.

Maxam, S., Boyer-Stephens, A., & Alff, M. (1986). *Assessment: A key to appropriate program placement.* (Report No. CE 045 407, pp. 11–13). Columbia: University of Missouri Columbia, Department of Special Education and Department of Practical Arts and Vocational-Technical Education. (ERIC Document Reproduction Service No. ED 275 835)

May, K., & Nicewander, W. A. (1994). Reliability and information functions for percentile ranks. *Journal of Educational Measurement, 31*, 313–325.

May, K. O., & Nicewander, W. A. (1997). Information and reliability for percentile ranks and other monotonic transformations of the number-correct score: Reply to De Gruijter. *Journal of Educational Measurement, 34*, 179–183.

Mayes, L. C. (1991). Infant assessment. In M. Lewis (Ed.), *Child and adolescent psychiatry: A comprehensive textbook* (pp. 437–447). Baltimore: Williams & Wilkins.

McArthur, D. S., & Roberts, G. E. (1982). *Roberts Apperception Test for Children: Manual.* Los Angeles: Western Psychological Services.

McConaughy, S. H., & Achenbach, T. M. (1993). Advances in empirically based assessment of children's behavioral and emotional problems. *School Psychology Review, 22*, 285–307.

McConaughy, S. H., & Achenbach, T. M. (1996). Contributions of a child interview to multimethod assessment of children with EBD and LD. *School Psychology Review, 25*, 24–39.

McGlinchey, M. T., & Hixson, M. D. (2004). Using curriculum-based measurement to predict performance on state assessments in reading. *School Psychology Review, 33*(2), 193–203.

McGrew, K. S., & Flanagan, D. P. (1998). *The intelligence test desk reference (ITDR): Gf-Gc cross-battery assessment.* Boston: Allyn & Bacon.

McGrew, K. S., & Woodcock, R. W. (2001). *Technical manual. Woodcock–Johnson III.* Itasca, IL: Riverside Publishing.

McIntyre, L. (1988). Teacher gender: A predictor of special education referral? *Journal of Learning Disabilities, 21*, 382–384.

McLaughlin, M. J., & Owings, M. F. (1992). Relationship among states' fiscal and demographic data and the implementation of P. L. 94–142. *Exceptional Children, 59*, 247–261.

McLoughlin, J. (1985). Training educational diagnosticians [Monograph]. *Diagnostique, 10*, 176–196.

McLoughlin, J. A., & Lewis, R. B. (1994). *Assessing special students* (4th ed.). Upper Saddle River, NJ: Merrill/Prentice Hall.

McLoughlin, J., & Lewis, R. (2001). *Assessing special students* (5th ed.). Upper Saddle River, NJ: Merrill/Prentice Hall.

McNamara, K., & Hollinger, C. (2003). Intervention-based assessment: Evaluation rates and eligibility findings. *Exceptional Children, 69*(2), 181–193.

McNutt, G., & Mandelbaum, L. (1980). General assessment competencies for special education teachers. *Exceptional Education Quarterly, 1*, 21–29.

Mehrens, W., & Lehmann, I. (1978). *Standardized tests in education.* New York: Holt, Rinehart & Winston.

Meherns, W. A., & Clarizio, H. F. (1993). Curriculum-based measurement: Conceptual and psychometric considerations. *Psychology in the Schools, 30*, 241–254.

Mercer, J. *System of Multicultural Assessment,* NY: The psychological corporation.

Messick, S. (1980). Test validity and the ethics of assessment. *American Psychologist, 35*, 1012–1027.

Messick, S. (1984). Assessment in context: Appraising student performance in relation to instructional quality. *Educational Researcher, 13*, 3–8.

Michael, J. (2000). Implications and refinements of the establishing operation concept. *Journal of Applied Behavior Analysis, 33*, 401–410.

Mick, L. (1985). Assessment procedures as related to enrollment patterns of Hispanic students in special education. *Educational Research Quarterly, 9*, 27–35.

Miller, D. C. (2007). *Essentials of school neuropsychological assessment.* New York: John Wiley & Sons, Inc.

Millman, J. (1994). Criterion-referenced testing 30 years later: Promise broken, promise kept. *Educational Measurement: Issues and Practices, 13*, 19–20, 39.

Minke, K. M., & Scott, M. M. (1993). The development of Individualized Family Service Plans: Roles for parents and staff. *Journal of Special Education, 27*, 82–106.

Missall, K., Reschly, A., Betts, J., McConnell, Heistad, et al. (2007). Examination of the predictive validity of preschool early literacy skills. *School Psychology Review, 36*(3), 433–452.

Morsink, C. V., & Lenk, L. L. (1992). The delivery of special education programs and services. *Remedial and Special Education, 13*(6), 33–43.

Mueller, F., Brozovich, R., & Johnson, C. B. (1998–1999). Conners' Rating Scales— Revised (CRS—R). *Monograph: Assessment for the New Decade, Diagnostic, 24*(1–4), 83–97.

Mullen, E. M. (1995). *Mullen scales of early learning: AGS edition.* Circle Pines, MN: American Guidance Service, Inc.

Naglieri, J. A. (1988). *Draw-a-person: A quantitative scoring system.* New York: Psychological Corporation.

Naglieri, J. A., McNeish, T. J., & Bardos, A. N. (1991). *Draw-a-person: Screening procedure for emotional disturbance.* Austin, TX: Pro-Ed.

National Association of School Psychologists (2000). *National Association of School Psychologists professional conduct manual: Principles for professional ethics; guidelines for the provision of school psychologists.* Bethesda, MD: Author.

NCTM (2000). *Principles and standards for mathematics.* Available from http:// standards.nctm.org.

Nelson, J. R., Smith, D. J., Taylor, L., Dodd, J. M., & Reavis, K. (1992). A statewide survey of special education administrators regarding mandated prereferral interventions. *Remedial and Special Education, 13*(4), 34–39.

Newcomer, P. L., & Hammill, D. D. (1997). *Test of Language Development—Primary: Third Edition.* Austin, TX: Pro-Ed.

Nichols, S. L., & Berliner, D. C. (2007) *Collateral damage: How high stakes testing corrupts America's schools.* Cambridge, MA. Harvard Educational Press.

Nicholson, C. L. (1998–1999). Comprehensive test of nonverbal intelligence (CTONI). *Monograph: Assessment for the New Decade, Diagnostic, 24*(1–4), 57–68.

Nihira, K., Foster, R., Shellhaas, M., & Leland, H. (1974). *AAMD adaptive behavior scale.* Washington, DC: American Association on Mental Deficiency.

No Child Left Behind Act of 2001, PL 107-110, 115 Stat. 1425 (2002).

Norford, B. C., & Barakat, L. P. (1990). The relationship of human figure drawings to aggressive behavior in preschool children. *Psychology in the Schools, 27*, 318–325.

Northup, J., & Gulley, V. (2001). Some contributions of functional analysis to the assessment of behaviors associated with attention deficit hyperactivity disorder and the effects of stimulant medication. *School Psychology Review, 30*(2), 227–238.

Nunnally, J. (1967). *Psychometric theory.* New York: McGraw-Hill.

Oesterheld, J. R., & Haber, J. (1997). Acceptability of the Conners parent rating scale and child behavior checklist to Dakotan/ Lakotan parents. *Journal of the American Academy of Child and Adolescent Psychiatry, 36*, 55–64.

Office of Special Education and Rehabilitative Services (2000). *Questions and answers about provisions in the Individuals with Disabilities Education Act Amendments of 1997 related to students with disabilities and state and district wide assessments.* Washington, DC: Author.

O'Neill, R. E., Horner, R. H., Albin, R. W., Sprague, J. R., Storey, K., & Newton, J. S. (1997). *Functional assessment and program development for problem behavior.* Pacific Grove, CA: Brooks/Cole Publishing Company.

Overton, T. (1987). Analyzing instructional material as a prerequisite for teacher effectiveness. *Techniques: A Journal for Remedial Education and Counseling, 3*, 111–115.

Overton, T. (2003). Promoting academic success through assessment of the academic environment. *Intervention in School and Clinic, 39*(3), 147–153.

Overton, T., Fielding, C., & Garcia de Alba, R. (2007). Differential diagnosis of Hispanic children referred for autism spectrum disorders. *Journal of Autism and Developmental Disorders, 37*(2), 1996–2007.

Overton, T., Fielding, C., & Garcia de Alba, R. (In Press). Application of the ADOS revised algorithm: Exploratory analysis of specificity and predictive value with Hispanic children referred for autism spectrum disorders. *Journal of Autism and Developmental Disabilities.*

Paget, K. D. (1990). Best practices in the assessment of competence in preschool-age children. In A. Thomas & J. Grimes (Eds.), *Best practices in school psychology-II* (pp. 107–119). Washington, DC: National Association of School Psychologists.

Palomares, R. S., Crowley, S. L., Worchel, F. F., Olson, T. K., & Rae, W. A. (1991). The factor analytic structure of the Roberts Apperception Test for Children: A comparison of the standardization sample with a sample of chronically ill children. *Journal of Personality Assessment, 53,* 414–425.

Paratore, J. R. (1995). Assessing literacy: Establishing common standards in portfolio assessment. *Topics in Language Disorders, 16,* 67–82.

Parette, H. P., Peterson-Karlan, G. R., Wojcok, B. W., & Bardi, N. (2007). Monitor that progress: Interpreting data trends for assistive technology decision making. *Teaching Exceptional Children, 40*(1), 22–29.

Parker, L. D. (1993). The Kaufman Brief Intelligence Test: An introduction and review. *Measurement and Evaluation in Counseling and Development, 26,* 152–156.

PASE (Parents in Action in Special Education) v. Hannon, 506 F. Supp. 831 (N.D. Ill. 1980).

Patton, J. M. (1998). The disproportionate representation of African Americans in special education: Looking behind the curtains for understanding and solutions. *Journal of Special Education, 32*(1), 25–31.

Perner, D. E. (2007). No Child Left Behind: Issues of assessing students with the most significant cognitive disabilities. *Education and Training in Developmental Disabilities, 42*(3), 243–251.

Phillips, N. B., Hamlett, C. L., Fuchs, L. S., & Fuchs, D. (1993). Combining classwide curriculum-based measurement and peer tutoring to help general educators provide adaptive education. *Learning Disabilities Research & Practice, 8,* 148–156.

Poon-McBrayer, F., & Garcia, S. B. (2000). Profiles of Asian American students with learning disabilities at initial referral, assessment, and placement in special education. *Journal of Learning Disabilities, 33*(1), 61–71.

Portes, P. R. (1996). Ethnicity and culture in educational psychology. In D. C. Berliner & R. C. Calfee (Eds.), *Handbook of Educational Psychology* (pp. 331–357). New York: Simon Schuster McMillan.

Prewett, P. N. (1992). The relationship between the Kaufman Brief Intelligence Test (K-BIT) and the WISC–R with referred students. *Psychology in the Schools, 29,* 25–27.

Prewett, P. N., & McCaffery, L. K. (1993). A comparison of the Kaufman Brief Intelligence Test (K-BIT) with the Stanford–Binet, a two-subtest short form, and the Kaufman Test of Educational Achievement (K-TEA) Brief Form. *Psychology in the Schools, 30,* 299–304.

Prifitera, A., Saklofske, D. H., & Weiss, L. G. (2005). *WISC-IV: Clinical use and interpretation.* Burlington, MA: Elsevier Academic Press.

Psychological Corporation. (1997). *WAIS-III WMS-III Technical Manual.* San Antonio: Author.

Psychological Corporation. (2001). *Wechsler Individual Achievement Test, Second Edition.* San Antonio, TX: Author.

Reid, R. (1995). Assessment of ADHD with culturally different groups: The use of behavioral rating scales. *School Psychology Review, 24,* 537–560.

Reid, R., DuPaul, G. J., Power, T. J., Anastopoulos, A. D., Rogers–Adkinson, D., Nell, M., & Ricco, C. (1998). Assessing culturally different students for attention deficit hyperactivity disorder using behavior rating scales. *Journal of Abnormal Child Psychology, 26,* 187–198.

Reinehr, R. C. (1998). Review of the Children's Apperception Test (1991 Revision). In J. C.

Impara and B. S. Plake (Eds.), *The thirteenth mental measurements yearbook* (pp. 233–234). Lincoln: University of Nebraska Press.

Reschly, D. (1981). Psychological testing in educational classification and placement. *American Psychologist, 36,* 1094–1102.

Reschly, D. (1982). Assessing mild mental retardation: The influence of adaptive behavior, sociocultural status, and prospects for nonbiased assessment. In C. R. Reynolds & T. B. Gutkin (Eds.), *The handbook of school psychology* (pp. 209–242). New York: Wiley.

Reschly, D. (1986). Functional psychoeducational assessment: Trends and issues. *Special Services in the Schools, 2,* 57–69.

Reschly, D. (1988). Assessment issues, placement litigation, and the future of mild mental retardation classification and programming. *Education and Training in Mental Retardation, 23,* 285–301.

Reschly, D. (1988). Special education reform. *School Psychology Review, 17,* 459–475.

Reschly, D. J., & Grimes, J. P. (1995). Best practices in intellectual assessment. In A. Thomas & J. Grimes (Eds.), *Best practices in school psychology-II.* Washington, DC: National Association of School Psychologists.

Reynolds, C. R. (1982). The problem of bias in psychological assessment. In C. R. Reynolds & T. B. Gutkin (Eds.), *The handbook of school psychology,* (pp. 178–208). New York: Wiley.

Reynolds, C. R., & Kamphaus, R. W. (1998). *Behavior assessment system for children.* Circle Pines, MN: American Guidance Service.

Reynolds, C. R., & Kamphaus, R.W. (2004). *Behavior assessment system for children, second edition.* Circle Pines, MN: American Guidance Service.

Reynolds, C. R., Lowe, P. A., & Saenz, A. L. (1999). The problems of bias in psychological assessment. In C. R. Reynolds & T. Gutkin (Eds.), *The handbook of school psychology* (3rd ed., pp. 556–557). New York: Wiley.

Ricco, C. A., Cohen, M. J., Hall, J., & Ross, C. M. (1997). The third and fourth factors of the WISC-III: What they don't measure. *Journal of Psychoeducational Assessment, 15,* 27–39.

Roberts, G. E. (1982). *Roberts apperception test for children: Test pictures.* Los Angeles: Western Psychological Services.

Roberts, G. E., & Gruber, C. (2005). *Roberts-2.* Los Angeles: Western Psychological Services.

Roberts, M. L., Marshall, J., Nelson, J. R., & Albers, C. A. (2001). Curriculum-based assessment procedures embedded within functional behavioral assessments: Identifying escape-motivated behaviors in a general education classroom. *School Psychology Review, 30*(2), 264–277.

Roid, G. H. (2003a). *Stanford–Binet intelligence scales* (5th ed.) Itasca, IL: Riverside Publishing.

Roid, G. H. (2003b). *Stanford–Binet intelligence scales* (5th ed.). *Examiner's manual.* Itasca, IL: Riverside Publishing.

Roid, G. H. (2003c). *Stanford–Binet intelligence scales* (5th ed.). *Technical manual.* Itasca, IL: Riverside Publishing.

Roid, G. H., & Pomplin, M. (2005). Interpreting the Stanford-Binet Intelligence Scales, Fifth Edition. In D. P. Flanagan & P. L. Harrison (Eds.), *Contemporary intellectual assessment: Theories, tests, and issues* (pp. 325–343). New York: The Guilford Press.

Rorschach, H. (1921, 1942). *Psycho-Diagnostics: A diagnostic test based on perception* (P. Lemkau & B. Kroenburg, Trans.). Berne: Heber. (First German Edition, 1921. Distributed in the United States by Grune & Stratton.)

Rosenfield, S., & Kurait, S. K. (1990). Best practices in curriculum-based assessment. In A. Thomas & J. Grimes (Eds.), *Best practices in school psychology-II* (pp. 275–286). Washington, DC: National Association of School Psychology.

Rotter, J., & Rafferty, J. (1950). *The Rotter incomplete sentence test.* New York: Psychological Corporation.

Ruddell, M. R. (1995). Literacy assessment in middle level grades: Alternatives to traditional practices. *Reading & Writing Quarterly: Overcoming Learning Difficulties, 11,* 187–200.

Rueda, R., & Garcia, E. (1997). Do portfolios make a difference for diverse students?

The influence of type of data on making instructional decisions. *Learning Disabilities Research & Practice, 12*(2), 114–122.

Ruehl, M. E. (1998). Educating the child with severe behavioral problems: Entitlement, empiricism, and ethics. *Behavioral Disorders, 23,* 184–192.

Rutter, M., LeCouteur, A., & Lord, C. (2002). *Autism diagnostic interview, revised.* Los Angeles, CA: Western Psychological Services.

Rutter, M., LeCouteur, A., & Lord, C. (2003). *Autism Diagnostic Interview–Revised.* Los Angeles, CA: Western Psychological Services.

Sabers, D., Feldt, L., & Reschly, D. (1988). Appropriate and inappropriate use of estimated true scores for normative comparisons. *Journal of Special Education, 22,* 358–366.

Salend, S. J., & Taylor, L. (1993). Working with families: A cross-cultural perspective. *Remedial and Special Education, 14*(5), 25–32, 39.

Salvia, J., & Hughes, C. (1990). *Curriculum-based assessment: Testing what is taught.* New York: Macmillan.

Salvia, J., & Ysseldyke, J. (1988a). *Assessment in remedial and special education* (4th ed.). Dallas: Houghton Mifflin.

Salvia, J., & Ysseldyke, J. (1988b). Using estimated true scores for normative comparisons. *Journal of Special Education, 22,* 367–373.

Salvia, J., & Ysseldyke, J. E. (1988). *Assessment in special and remedial education* (4th ed.). Boston: Houghton Mifflin.

Sandall, S., Hemmeter, M. L., Smith, B. J., McLean, M. E. (2005). DEC recommended practices: A comprehensive guide for practical approaches in early intervention/early childhood. Copyright 2005 by the Division of Early Childhood (DEC) of the Council for Exceptional Children (CEC). Longmont, CO: Sopris West.

Sapp, G., Chissom, B., & Horton, W. (1984). An investigation of the ability of selected instruments to discriminate areas of exceptional class designation. *Psychology in the Schools, 5,* 258–262.

Schaughency, E. A., & Rothlind, J. (1991). Assessment and classification of attention deficit hyperactive disorders. *School Psychology Review, 20,* 187–202.

Schopler, E., Reichler, R. J., Renner, B. R. (1998). Childhood autism rating scale. Los Angeles, CA: Western Psychological Services.

Schrank, F. A., & Flanagan, D. P. (Eds.) (2003*). WJ III clinical use and interpretation.* San Diego, CA: Academic Press.

Schrank, F. A., Flanagan, D. P., Woodcock, R. W., & Mascolo, J. T. (2002). *Essentials of WJ III cognitive abilities assessment.* New York: John Wiley & Sons.

Scott, V. G., & Weishaar, M. K. (2003). Curriculum-based measurement for reading progress. *Intervention in School and Clinic, 38*(3), 153–159.

Scruggs, T. E., & Mastropieri, M. A. (1996). Teacher perceptions of mainstreaming/inclusion, 1958–1995: A research synthesis. *Exceptional Children, 63,* 59–74.

Section 504 of the Rehabilitation Act of 1973, 29 U.S.C. § 794 et seq.

Serna, L. A., Forness, S. R., & Nielsen, M. E. (1998). Intervention versus affirmation: Proposed solutions to the problem of disproportionate minority representation in special education. *Journal of Special Education, 32*(1), 48–51.

Shaklee, B. D., Barbour, N. E., Ambrose, R., & Hansford, S. J. (1997). *Designing and using portfolios.* Boston: Allyn & Bacon.

Shapiro, E. S. (1989). *Academic skills problems: Direct assessment and intervention.* New York: Guilford.

Shapiro, E. S. (1996). *Academic skills problems: Direct assessment and intervention* (2nd ed.). New York: Guilford.

Sheridan, S. M., Cowan, P. J., & Eagle, J. W. (2000). Partnering with parents in educational programming for students with special needs. In C. F. Telzrow & M. Tankersley (Eds.), *IDEA Amendments of 1997: Practice guidelines for school-based teams.* Bethesda, MD: National Association of School Psychologists.

Sherman, A. (1994). *Wasting America's future: The Children's Defense Fund report on the cost of child poverty.* Boston: Beacon Press.

Shinn, M. R. (1989). *Curriculum-based measurement: Assessing special children.* New York: Guilford.

Shinn, M. R. (2002). Best practices in using curriculum-based measurement in a problem-solving model. In A. Thomas & J. Grimes (Eds.), *Best practices in school psychology* (Vol. 4, pp. 671–697). Silver Springs, MD: National Association of School Psychologists.

Shinn, M. R., Habedank, L., Rodden-Nord, K., & Knutson, N. (1993). Using curriculum-based measurement to identify potential candidates for reintegration into general education. *Journal of Special Education, 27,* 202–221.

Shinn, M. R., Nolet, V., & Knutson, N. (1990). Best practices in curriculum-based measurement. In A. Thomas & J. Grimes (Eds.), *Best practices in school psychology.* Washington, DC: National Association of School Psychologists.

Silberglitt, B., & Hintze, J. M. (2007). How much growth can we expect? A conditional analysis of R-CBM growth rates by level of performance. *Exceptional Children, 74*(1), 71–99.

Silver, S. (1987). *Compliance with PL 94-142 mandates: Policy implications.* (ERIC Document Reproduction Service No. ED 284 705)

Sinclair, E., Del'Homme, & M. Gonzalez. (1993). Systematic screening for preschool assessment of behavioral disorders. *Behavioral Disorders, 18,* 177–188.

Slate, J. R. (1996). Interrelations of frequently administered achievement measures in the determination of specific learning disabilities. *Learning Disabilities Research & Practice, 11*(2), 86–89.

Smith, C. R. (1997). Advocacy for students with emotional and behavioral disorders: One call for redirected efforts. *Behavioral Disorders, 22*(2), 96–105.

Smith, D. K. (1998–1999). Kaufman Brief Intelligence Test (K-BIT). *Monograph: Assessment for the New Decade, Diagnostic, 24*(1–4), 125–134.

Snider, V. E. (1995). A primer on phonemic awareness: What it is, why it is important, and how to teach it. *School Psychology Review, 24*(3), 443–455.

Snider, V. E. (1997). The relationship between phonemic awareness and later reading achievement. *Journal of Educational Research, 90*(4), 203–212.

Snyder, P., Bailey, D., & Auer, C. (1994). Preschool eligibility determination for children with known or suspected learning disabilities under IDEA. *Journal of Early Intervention, 18,* 380–390.

Soodak, L. C., & Podell, D. M. (1993). Teacher efficacy and student problem as factors in special education referral. *Journal of Special Education, 27*(1), 66–81.

Sparrow, S. S., Balla, D. A., & Cicchetti, D. V. (1984). *Vineland adaptive behavior scales.* Circle Pines, MN: American Guidance Service.

Sparrow, S.S., Cicchetti, D.V., & Balla, D.A. (2005). *Vineland-II: Vineland Adaptive Behavior Scales, Second Edition.* Circle Pines, MN: AGS Publishing Company.

Spigelman, G., Spigelman, A., & Englesson, I. L. (1992). Analysis of family drawings: A comparison between children from divorce and nondivorce families. *Journal of Divorce & Remarriage, 18,* 31–51.

Stanford, L. D., & Hynd, G. W. (1994). Congruence of behavioral symptomology in children with ADD/H, ADD/WO, and learning disabilities. *Journal of Learning Disabilities, 27,* 243–253.

Stecker, P. M. (2007). Tertiary intervention: Using progress monitoring with intensive services. *Teaching Exceptional Children,* May/June 2007, 50–57.

Stoner, G., Carey, S. P., Ikeda, M. J., & Shinn, M. R. (1994). The utility of curriculum-based measurement for evaluating the effects of methylphenidate on academic performance. *Journal of Applied Behavior Analysis, 27,* 101–113.

Swanson, H. L., & Watson, B. L. (1989). *Educational and psychological assessment of exceptional children* (2nd ed.). Upper Saddle River, NJ: Merrill/Prentice Hall.

Symons, F. J., & Warren, S. F. (1998). Straw men and strange logic issues and pseudo-issues in special education. *American Psychologist, 53*(10), 1160–1161.

Taylor, R. L. (1993). *Assessment of exceptional students: Educational and psychological procedures* (3rd ed.). Boston: Allyn & Bacon.

Taylor, R. L., & Richards, S. B. (1991). Patterns of intellectual differences of black, Hispanic, and white children. *Psychology in the Schools, 28,* 5–9.

Telzrow, C. F., & Tankersley, M. (2000). *IDEA: Amendments of 1997: Practice Guidelines for School-Based Teams.* Bethesda, MD: National Association of School Psychologists.

Tharinger, D. J., & Lambert, N. M. (1990). The contributions of developmental psychology to school psychology. In T. Gutkin & C. R. Reynolds (Eds.), *The handbook of school psychology* (2nd ed.), pp. 74–103. New York: Wiley.

Thoma, C. A., Rogan, P., & Baker, S. R. (2001). Student involvement in transition planning: Unheard voices. *Education and Training in Mental Retardation and Developmental Disabilities, 36*(1), 16–29.

Thomas, A., & Grimes, J. (1990). *Best practices in school psychology-II.* Silver Spring, MD: National Association of School Psychologists.

Thompson, S. J., Morse, A. B., Sharpe, M., & Hall, S. (2005). *Accommodations manual: How to select, administer, and evaluate use of accommodations for instruction and assessment of students with disabilities, 2nd edition.* Washington, DC: Council of Chief State School Officers.

Thompson, S. J., Johnstone, C. J., & Thurlow, M. L. (2002). *Universal design applied to large scale assessments* (Synthesis Report 44). Minneapolis, MN: University of Minnnesota, National Center on Educational Outcomes Retrieved July 7, 2007, from: *http://education.umn.edu? NCeO/ OnlinePubs/Synthesis44. html*

Thurlow, M., Christenson, S., & Ysseldyke, J. (1983). *Referral research: An integrative summary of findings* (Research Report No. 141). Minneapolis: University of Minnesota, Institute for Research on Learning Disabilities.

Thurlow, M. L., Elliott, J. L., & Ysseldyke, J. E. (1998). *Testing students with disabilities: Practical strategies for complying with district and state requirements.* Thousand Oaks, CA: Corwin Press, Inc.

Thurlow, M., & Ysseldyke, J. (1979). Current assessment and decision-making practices in model programs. *Learning Disabilities Quarterly, 2,* 14–24.

Thurlow, M. L., Ysseldyke, J. E., & Anderson, C. L. (1995). *High school graduation requirements: What's happening for students with disabilities?* Minneapolis: National Center on Educational Outcomes.

Tindal, G. (1991). Operationalizing learning portfolios: A good idea in search of a method. *Diagnostique, 2,* 127–133.

Trainor, A. A., Patton, J. R., & Clark, G. M. (2005). Case studies in assessment for transition planning. Austin, TX: Pro-Ed.

Trommer, B. L., Hoeppner, J. B., Lorber, R., & Armstrong, K. (1988). Pitfalls in the use of a Continuous Performance Test as a diagnostic tool deficit disorder. *Developmental and Behavioral Pediatrics, 9,* 339–345.

Truscott, S. D., Cohen, C. E., Sams, D. P., Sanborn, K. J., & Frank, A. J. (2005). The current state(s) of prereferral teams: A report from two national surveys. *Remedial and Special Education, 26*(3), 130–140.

Tucker, J. (1980). Ethnic proportions in classes for the learning disabled: Issues in nonbiased assessment. *Journal of Special Education, 14,* 93–105.

Turnbull, H. R. (1986). *Free and appropriate public education: The law and children with disabilities.* Denver: Love Publishing.

Turnbull, H. R. (1990*). Free and appropriate public education: The law and children with disabilities* (3rd ed.). Denver: Love Publishing.

Turnbull, H. R., Turnbull, A. P., & Strickland, B. (1979). Procedural due process: The two-edged sword that the untrained should not unsheath. *Journal of Education, 161,* 40–59.

Turnbull, R., Turnbull, A., Shank, A., Smith, S., & Leal, D. (2002). *Exceptional lives: Special education in today's schools (3rd ed.).* Upper Saddle River, NJ: Merrill/Prentice Hall.

U.S. Bureau of the Census. (1997). *Statistical abstract of the United States: 1997* (117th ed.). Washington, DC: Author.

U.S. Congress. (1993, March). *Goals 2000: Educate America Act.* PL 103-227, 103rd Congress.

U.S. Department of Education. (1991). *Memorandum to chief state school officers.* Washington, DC: Author.

U.S. Department of Education. (1995). *The Seventeenth annual report to Congress on the implementation of the Individuals with Disabilities Education Act.* Washington, DC: Author.

U.S. Department of Education. (1997). *Nineteenth annual report to Congress on the implementation of the Individuals with Disabilities Education Act.* Washington, DC: Author.

U.S. Department of Education. (1999). *Assistance to states for the education of childern with disabilities and the early intervention Program for infants and toddlers with disabilities: final regulation.* Washington, DC: Author.

U.S. Department of Education. (2000). *The use of tests when making high-stakes decisions for students: A resource guide for educators and policymakers.* Washington, DC: Author.

U.S. Department of Education. (2000). *Twenty-second annual report to Congress on the implementation of the Individuals with Disabilities Education Act.* Washington, DC: Author.

U.S. Department of Education. (2001). *Twenty-third annual report to Congress on the implementation of the Individuals with Disabilities Education Act.* Washington, DC: Author.

U.S. Department of Education. (2002). *Twenty-fourth annual report to Congress on the implementation of the Individuals with Disabilities Education Act.* Washington, DC: Author.

U.S. Department of Education. (2003). *Twenty-fifth annual report to Congress on the implementation of the Individuals with Disabilities Education Act.* Washington, DC: Author.

U.S. Department of Education. (2004). *Twenty-sixth annual report to Congress on the implementation of the Individuals with Disabilities Education Act.* Washington, DC: Author.

U.S. Department of Education. (2006). IDEA regulations: Disproportionality and over identification. Washington, DC: Office of Special Education and Rehabilitative Services. Retrieved from http://www.nichcy.org/reauth/tboverident.pdf

U.S. Office of Technology Assessment. (1992, February). *Testing in American schools: Asking the right questions* (OTA-SET-519). Washington, DC: U.S. Government Printing Office.

Uzgiris, I. C., & Hunt, J. McV. (1975). *Assessment in infancy: Ordinal Scales of Psychological Development.* Urbana: University of Illinois Press.

Valencia, R. R., Rankin, R. J., & Livingston, R. (1995). K-ABC content bias: Comparisons between Mexican American and White children. *Psychology in the Schools, 32,* 153–169.

Valles, E. C. (1998). The disproportionate representation of minority students in special education: Responding to the problem. *Journal of Special Education, 32*(1), 52–54.

VanDerHeyden, A. M., Witt, J. C., Naquin, G. (2003). Development and validation of a process for screening referrals to special education. *School Psychology Review, 32*(2), 204–227.

Vaughn, S., Bos, C., Harrell, J., & Lasky, B. (1988). Parent participation in the initial placement/IEP conference ten years after mandated involvement. *Journal of Learning Disabilities, 21,* 82–89.

Vig, S., & Jedrysek, E. (1996). Stanford–Binet Fourth Edition: Useful for young children with language impairment? *Psychology in the Schools, 33,* 124–131.

Vogel, S. A., Leonard, F., Scales, W., Hayeslip, P., Hermansen, J., & Donnells, L. (1998). The national learning disabilities postsecondary data bank: An overview. *Journal of Learning Disabilities, 31*(3), 234–247.

Vygotsky, L. S. (1993). *The collected works of L. S. Vygotsky: Vol. 2, The fundamentals of defectology (abnormal psychology and learning disabilities* (J. E. Knox & C. B. Stevens, Trans.). New York: Plenum.

Walsh, B., & Betz, N. (1985). *Tests and assessment.* Upper Saddle River, NJ: Prentice Hall.

Ward, S. B., Ward, T. J., & Clark, H. T. (1991). Classification congruence among school psychologists and its relationship to type of referral question and professional experience. *Journal of School Psychology, 29,* 89–108.

Wasserman, J. D., & Tulsky, D. S. (2005). A history of intelligence assessment. In D. P. Flanagan & P.L. Harrison (Eds.), *Contemporary intellectual assessment: Theories, tests, and issues* (pp. 3–22). New York: The Guilford Press.

Weber, J., & Stoneman, Z. (1986). Parental nonparticipation as a means of reducing bias in the education of handicapped children. *Special Services in the Schools, 1,* 71–84.

Wechsler, D. (1974). *Manual for the Wechsler intelligence scale for children–revised.* San Antonio: Psychological Corporation.

Wechsler, D. (1997). *Wechsler adult intelligence scale, 3rd edition: Administration and scoring manual.* San Antonio: Psychological Corporation.

Wechsler, D. (2002). *Wechsler preschool and primary scales of intelligence, third edition.* San Antonio, TX: The Psychological Corporation.

Wechsler, D. (2003). *Wechsler intelligence scale for children* (4th ed.). *Administration and scoring manual.* San Antonio, TX: The Psychological Corporation.

Wechsler, D. (2003). *Wechlser intelligence scale for children* (4th ed.). *Technical and interpretive manual.* San Antonio, TX: The Psychological Corporation.

Weine, A. M., Phillips, J. S., & Achenbach, T. M. (1995). Behavioral and emotional problems among Chinese and American Children: Parent and teacher reports for ages 6 to 13. *Journal of Abnormal Child Psychology, 23,* 619–639.

Weller, C., Strawser, S., & Buchanan, M. (1985). Adaptive behavior: Designator of a continuum of severity of learning disabled individuals. *Journal of Learning Disabilities, 18,* 200–203.

Wendling, B. J., & Mather, N. (2001). *Examiner training workbook Woodcock–Johnson III Tests of Achievement.* Itasca, IL: Riverside Publishing.

Wiederholt, J. L., & Bryant, B. R. (2001). *Gray Oral Reading Tests* (4th ed). Austin, TX: Pro-Ed.

Wiener, J. (1986). Alternatives in the assessment of the learning disabled adolescent: A learning strategies approach. *Learning Disabilities Focus, 1,* 97–107.

Wilkinson, G. S. (1993). *The wide range achievement test: Administration manual.* Wilmington, DE: Jastak, Wide Range.

Williams, R., & Zimmerman, D. (1984). On the virtues and vices of standard error of measurement. *Journal of Experimental Education, 52,* 231–233.

Wilson, C. P., Gutkin, T. B., Hagen, K. M., & Oats, R. G. (1998). General education teachers' knowledge and self-reported use of classroom interventions for working with difficult-to-teach students: Implications for consultation, prereferral intervention and inclusive services. *School Psychology Quarterly, 13*(1), 45–62.

Wilson, V. (1987). Percentile scores. In C. R. Reynolds & L. Mann (Eds.), *Encyclopedia of special education: A reference for the education of the handicapped and other exceptional children and adults* (p. 1656). New York: Wiley.

Witt, J., & Martens, B. (1984). Adaptive behavior: Tests and assessment issues. *School Psychology Review, 13,* 478–484.

Witt, J. C., Daly, E., & Noell, G. H. (2000). *Functional assessments: A step-by-step guide to solving academic and behavior problems.* Longmont, CO: Sopris West.

Wood, F., Johnson, J., & Jenkins, J. (1990). The Lora case: Nonbiased referral, assessment, and placement procedures. *Exceptional Children, 52,* 323–331.

Woodcock, R. W. (1987). *Woodcock Reading Mastery Tests-Revised.* Circle Pines, MN: American Guidance Service.

Woodcock, R. W., McGrew, K. S., & Mather, N. (2001). *Woodcock–Johnson III tests of cognitive abilities.* Itasca, IL: Riverside Publishing.

Woodcock, R. W., McGrew, K. S., & Werder, J. K. (1994). *Woodcock–McGrew–Werder Mini-Battery of Achievement.* Itasca, IL: Riverside Publishing.

Yeh, S. S. (2006). High stakes testing: Can rapid assessment reduce the pressure? *Teachers College Record, 108*(4), 621–661.

Yell, M. L. (1995). Least restrictive environment, inclusion and students with disabilities: A legal analysis. *Journal of Special Education, 28,* 389–404.

Yell, M. L. (1997). *The law and special education.* Upper Saddle River, NJ: Merrill/ Prentice Hall.

Yell, M. L., Drasgow, E., & Ford, L. (2000). The individuals with disabilities education act amendments of 1997: Implications for school-based teams. In Telzrow, C. F., & Tankersley, M. (Eds.), *IDEA: Amendments of 1997: Practice guidelines for school-based teams* (pp. 1–28). Bethesda, MD: National Association of School Psychologists.

Yovanoff, P., & Tindal, G. (2007). Scaling early reading alternate assessments with statewide measures. *Exceptional Children, 73*(2), 184–201.

Ysseldyke, J., & Algozzine, B. (1982). *Critical issues in special and remedial education.* Boston: Houghton Mifflin.

Ysseldyke, J., Algozzine, B., Regan, R., & Potter, M. (1980). Technical adequacy of tests used by professionals in simulated decision making. *Psychology in the Schools, 17,* 202–209.

Ysseldyke, J., Algozzine, B., Richey, L., & Graden, J. (1982). Declaring students eligible for learning disability services: Why bother with the data? *Learning Disabilities Quarterly, 5,* 37–44.

Ysseldyke, J., Christenson, S., Pianta, B., & Algozzine, B. (1983). An analysis of teachers' reasons and desired outcomes for students referred for psychoeducational assessment. *Journal of Psychoeducational Assessment, 1,* 73–83.

Ysseldyke, J. E., Nelson, J. R., & House, A. L. (2000). Statewide and district wide assessments: Current status and guidelines for student accommodations and alternate assessments. In C. F. Telzrow and M. Tankersley (Eds.), *IDEA Amendments of 1997: Practice guidelines for school-based teams.* Bethesda, MD: National Association of School Psychologists.

Ysseldyke, J. E., Thurlow, M. L., Kozleski, E., & Reschly, D. (1998). *Accountability for the results of educating students with disabilities: Assessment conference report on the new assessment provisions of the 1997 Amendments to the Individuals with Disabilities Education Act.* (EC 306929) National Center on Educational Outcomes. (ERIC Document Reproduction Service No. ED 425 588)

Ysseldyke, J. E., Nelson, J. R., & House, A. L. (2000). Statewide and district wide assessments: Current status and guidelines for student accommodations and alternate assessments. In C. F. Telzrow & M. Tankersley (Eds.), *IDEA Amendments of 1997: Practice guidelines for school-based teams.* Bethesda, MD: National Association of School Psychologists.

Ysseldyke, J., & Thurlow, M. (1983). *Identification/classification research: An integrative summary of findings* (Research Report No. 142). Minneapolis: University of Minnesota, Institute for Research on Learning Disabilities.

Zins, J., Graden, J., & Ponti, C. (1989). Prereferral intervention to improve special services delivery. *Special Services in the Schools, 4,* 109–130.

NAME INDEX

Note: *Italicized* page numbers indicate illustrations.

SUBJECT INDEX

Note: *Italicized* page numbers indicate illustrations.